Nissan Micra (K11 series)
Service and Repair Manual

A K Legg LAE MIMI

Models covered

(3254-256-5AH4)

Nissan Micra Hatchback, including automatic transmission (N-CVT) models and special/limited editions
1.0 litre (998 cc) , 1.3 litre (1275 cc) and 1.4 (1348 cc) petrol engines

Does NOT cover new Micra range introduced for 2003 model year

AB

A book in the **Haynes Service and Repair Manual Series**

ISBN **1 84425 155 1**

British Library Cataloguing in Publication Data
A catalogue record for this book is available from the British Library.

Printed in the USA

Haynes Publishing
Sparkford, Yeovil, Somerset BA22 7JJ, England

Haynes North America, Inc
861 Lawrence Drive, Newbury Park, California 91320, USA

Editions Haynes
4, Rue de l'Abreuvoir
92415 COURBEVOIE CEDEX, France

Haynes Publishing Nordiska AB
Box 1504, 751 45 UPPSALA, Sverige

Contents

LIVING WITH YOUR NISSAN MICRA

Roadside Repairs

Weekly Checks

MAINTENANCE

Routine maintenance and servicing

Contents

REPAIRS AND OVERHAUL

Nissan Micra 1.3 Si 3-door - 1998 model

The New Nissan Micra was introduced to the UK in January 1993, and was available with a 16-valve 1.0 or 1.3 litre double-overhead camshaft engine with either a manual or automatic transmission. The previous K10 Micra established itself in the popular small economy car class, and was manufactured from 1983 to the end of 1992.

New Micra L and LX models were originally available with the 1.0 litre engine, and LX, SLX and Super models were available with the 1.3 litre engine. Several special editions have been introduced since 1993 and as from January 1996 all models have front and rear anti-roll bars. A driver's airbag was optional equipment in early 1995 and became standard equipment except on L models later in the same year. The range received a minor facelift in 1996, while the March 1998 facelift models can be identified by the new chrome 'flying wing' radiator grille, larger headlights, and other minor cosmetic changes. Inside, 1998 models gained a revised facia panel, to better incorporate the optional passenger airbag, and an upgraded transponder immobiliser was fitted.

In July 2000 the 1.3 engine was replaced with a 1.4 litre engine and another facelift was carried out, some of the changes made include redesigned body coloured bumpers, clear lens halogen headlamps, chrome door handles and front fog lamps.

The Nissan Micra Team

Haynes manuals are produced by dedicated and enthusiastic people working in close co-operation. The team responsible for the creation of this book included:

Authors	**Andy Legg** **R M Jex**
Sub-editor	**Sophie Yar**
Editor & Page Make-up	**Steve Churchill**
Workshop manager	**Paul Buckland**
Photo Scans	**Paul Tanswell** **John Martin**
Cover illustration & Line Art	**Roger Healing**
Wiring diagrams	**Matthew Marke**

We hope the book will help you to get the maximum enjoyment from your car. By carrying out routine maintenance as described you will ensure your car's reliability and preserve its resale value.

All models covered in this Manual are fitted with 16-valve double-overhead camshaft engines, and have fully independent front suspension and semi-independent rear suspension. Manual or power-assisted steering is fitted according to model.

Provided that regular servicing is carried out in accordance with the manufacturer's recommendations, the Nissan Micra should prove reliable and economical. The engine compartment is particularly well-designed, and most of the items needing frequent attention are easily accessible making the Micra an ideal DIY car.

Your Nissan Micra Manual

The aim of this manual is to help you get the best value from your vehicle. It can do so in several ways. It can help you decide what work must be done (even should you choose to get it done by a garage), provide information on routine maintenance and servicing, and give a logical course of action and diagnosis when random faults occur. However, it is hoped that you will use the manual by tackling the work yourself. On simpler jobs, it may even be quicker than booking the car into a garage and going there twice, to leave and collect it. Perhaps most important, a lot of money can be saved by avoiding the costs a garage must charge to cover its labour and overheads.

The manual has drawings and descriptions to show the function of the various components, so that their layout can be understood. Then the tasks are described and photographed in a clear step-by-step sequence.

References to the 'left' or 'right' are in the sense of a person sitting in the driver's seat facing forwards.

Acknowledgements

Thanks are due to Draper Tools Limited, who provided some of the workshop tools, and to all those people at Sparkford who helped in the production of this manual.

We take great pride in the accuracy of information given in this manual, but vehicle manufacturers make alterations and design changes during the production run of a particular vehicle of which they do not inform us. No liability can be accepted by the authors or publishers for loss, damage or injury caused by any errors in, or omissions from, the information given.

Project vehicles

The main vehicle used in the preparation of this manual, and which appears in many of the photographic sequences, was a 1996 Nissan Micra 1.3 SLX with manual transmission. Also used were a 1996 Nissan Micra 1.0 L and a 1.4 S.

Working on your car can be dangerous. This page shows just some of the potential risks and hazards, with the aim of creating a safety-conscious attitude.

General hazards

Scalding

• Don't remove the radiator or expansion tank cap while the engine is hot.
• Engine oil, automatic transmission fluid or power steering fluid may also be dangerously hot if the engine has recently been running.

Burning

• Beware of burns from the exhaust system and from any part of the engine. Brake discs and drums can also be extremely hot immediately after use.

Crushing

• When working under or near a raised vehicle, always supplement the jack with axle stands, or use drive-on ramps. ***Never venture under a car which is only supported by a jack.***
• Take care if loosening or tightening high-torque nuts when the vehicle is on stands. Initial loosening and final tightening should be done with the wheels on the ground.

Fire

• Fuel is highly flammable; fuel vapour is explosive.
• Don't let fuel spill onto a hot engine.
• Do not smoke or allow naked lights (including pilot lights) anywhere near a vehicle being worked on. Also beware of creating sparks (electrically or by use of tools).
• Fuel vapour is heavier than air, so don't work on the fuel system with the vehicle over an inspection pit.
• Another cause of fire is an electrical overload or short-circuit. Take care when repairing or modifying the vehicle wiring.
• Keep a fire extinguisher handy, of a type suitable for use on fuel and electrical fires.

Electric shock

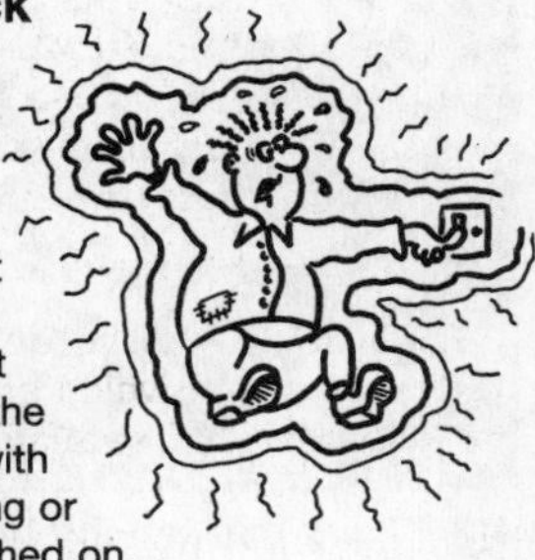

• Ignition HT voltage can be dangerous, especially to people with heart problems or a pacemaker. Don't work on or near the ignition system with the engine running or the ignition switched on.
• Mains voltage is also dangerous. Make sure that any mains-operated equipment is correctly earthed. Mains power points should be protected by a residual current device (RCD) circuit breaker.

Fume or gas intoxication

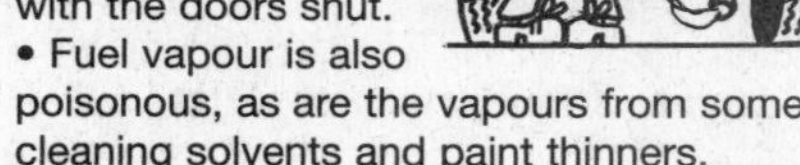

• Exhaust fumes are poisonous; they often contain carbon monoxide, which is rapidly fatal if inhaled. Never run the engine in a confined space such as a garage with the doors shut.
• Fuel vapour is also poisonous, as are the vapours from some cleaning solvents and paint thinners.

Poisonous or irritant substances

• Avoid skin contact with battery acid and with any fuel, fluid or lubricant, especially antifreeze, brake hydraulic fluid and Diesel fuel. Don't syphon them by mouth. If such a substance is swallowed or gets into the eyes, seek medical advice.
• Prolonged contact with used engine oil can cause skin cancer. Wear gloves or use a barrier cream if necessary. Change out of oil-soaked clothes and do not keep oily rags in your pocket.
• Air conditioning refrigerant forms a poisonous gas if exposed to a naked flame (including a cigarette). It can also cause skin burns on contact.

Asbestos

• Asbestos dust can cause cancer if inhaled or swallowed. Asbestos may be found in gaskets and in brake and clutch linings. When dealing with such components it is safest to assume that they contain asbestos.

Special hazards

Hydrofluoric acid

• This extremely corrosive acid is formed when certain types of synthetic rubber, found in some O-rings, oil seals, fuel hoses etc, are exposed to temperatures above 400ºC. The rubber changes into a charred or sticky substance containing the acid. *Once formed, the acid remains dangerous for years. If it gets onto the skin, it may be necessary to amputate the limb concerned.*
• When dealing with a vehicle which has suffered a fire, or with components salvaged from such a vehicle, wear protective gloves and discard them after use.

The battery

• Batteries contain sulphuric acid, which attacks clothing, eyes and skin. Take care when topping-up or carrying the battery.
• The hydrogen gas given off by the battery is highly explosive. Never cause a spark or allow a naked light nearby. Be careful when connecting and disconnecting battery chargers or jump leads.

Air bags

• Air bags can cause injury if they go off accidentally. Take care when removing the steering wheel and/or facia. Special storage instructions may apply.

Diesel injection equipment

• Diesel injection pumps supply fuel at very high pressure. Take care when working on the fuel injectors and fuel pipes.

Warning: Never expose the hands, face or any other part of the body to injector spray; the fuel can penetrate the skin with potentially fatal results.

Remember...

DO

• Do use eye protection when using power tools, and when working under the vehicle.

• Do wear gloves or use barrier cream to protect your hands when necessary.

• Do get someone to check periodically that all is well when working alone on the vehicle.

• Do keep loose clothing and long hair well out of the way of moving mechanical parts.

• Do remove rings, wristwatch etc, before working on the vehicle – especially the electrical system.

• Do ensure that any lifting or jacking equipment has a safe working load rating adequate for the job.

DON'T

• Don't attempt to lift a heavy component which may be beyond your capability – get assistance.

• Don't rush to finish a job, or take unverified short cuts.

• Don't use ill-fitting tools which may slip and cause injury.

• Don't leave tools or parts lying around where someone can trip over them. Mop up oil and fuel spills at once.

• Don't allow children or pets to play in or near a vehicle being worked on.

The following pages are intended to help in dealing with common roadside emergencies and breakdowns. You will find more detailed fault finding information at the back of the manual, and repair information in the main chapters.

If your car won't start and the starter motor doesn't turn

- ☐ If it's a model with automatic transmission, make sure the selector is in 'P' or 'N'.
- ☐ Open the bonnet and make sure that the battery terminals are clean and tight.
- ☐ Switch on the headlights and try to start the engine. If the headlights go very dim when you're trying to start, the battery is probably flat. Get out of trouble by jump starting (see next page) using a friend's car.

If your car won't start even though the starter motor turns as normal

- ☐ Is there fuel in the tank?
- ☐ Is there moisture on electrical components under the bonnet? Switch off the ignition, then wipe off any obvious dampness with a dry cloth. Spray a water-repellent aerosol product (WD-40 or equivalent) on ignition and fuel system electrical connectors like those shown in the photos. Pay special attention to the ignition coil wiring connector and HT leads.

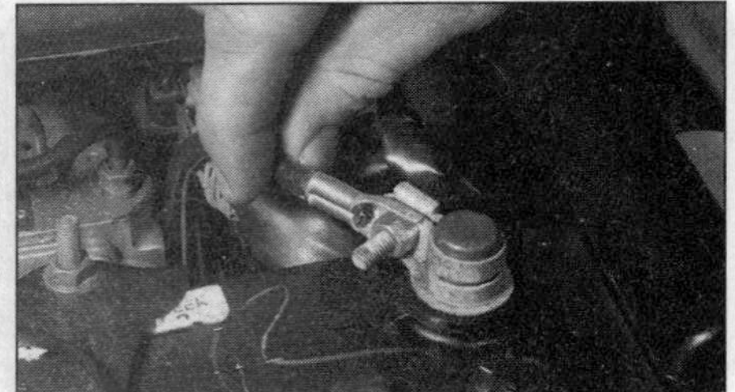

A Check the condition and security of the battery connections

B Check that the HT leads (where applicable) are securely connected by pushing them firmly down onto the spark plugs and the distributor cap

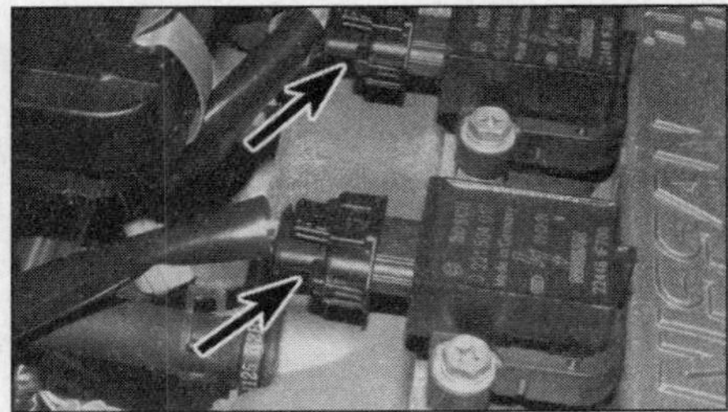

C Also check that the wiring plugs to the coils are securely connected (direct ignition model shown)

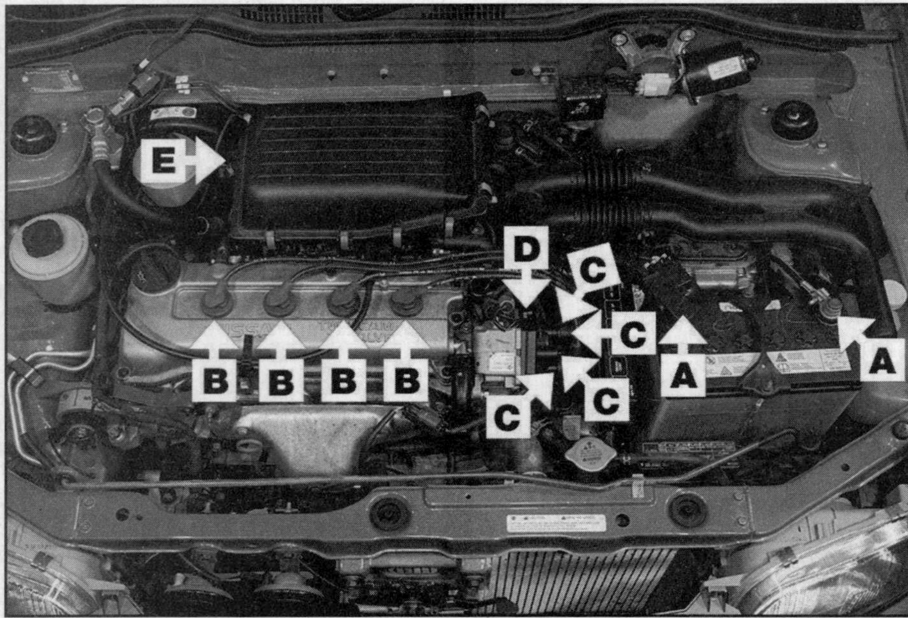

Check that electrical connections are secure (with the ignition switched off) and spray them with a water dispersant spray like WD40 if you suspect a problem due to damp

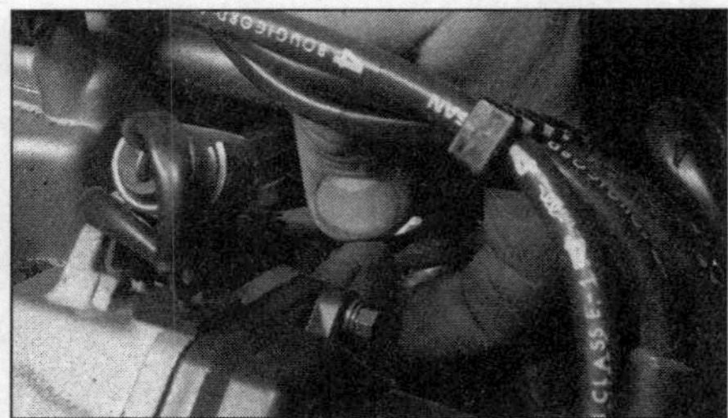

D Check that the two wiring plugs are securely connected to the distributor body (where applicable

E Check that the throttle position switch wiring plug is securely connected

Jump starting

Jump starting will get you out of trouble, but you must correct whatever made the battery go flat in the first place. There are three possibilities:

***1** The battery has been drained by repeated attempts to start, or by leaving the lights on.*

***2** The charging system is not working properly (alternator drivebelt slack or broken, alternator wiring fault or alternator itself faulty).*

***3** The battery itself is at fault (electrolyte low, or battery worn out).*

When jump-starting a car using a booster battery, observe the following precautions:

✔ Before connecting the booster battery, make sure that the ignition is switched off.

✔ Ensure that all electrical equipment (lights, heater, wipers, etc) is switched off.

✔ Take note of any special precautions printed on the battery case.

✔ Make sure that the booster battery is the same voltage as the discharged one in the vehicle.

✔ If the battery is being jump-started from the battery in another vehicle, the two vehicles MUST NOT TOUCH each other.

✔ Make sure that the transmission is in neutral (or PARK, in the case of automatic transmission).

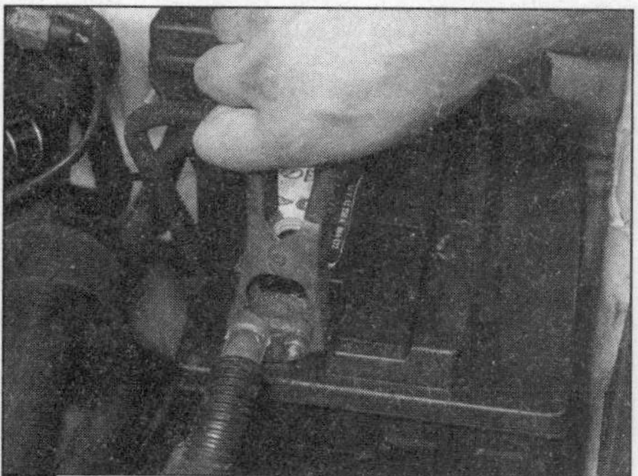

1 Connect one end of the red jump lead to the positive (+) terminal of the flat battery

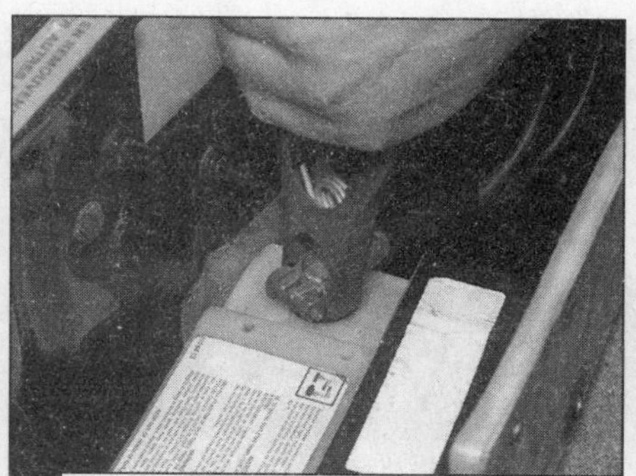

2 Connect the other end of the red lead to the positive (+) terminal of the booster battery.

3 Connect one end of the black jump lead to the negative (-) terminal of the booster battery

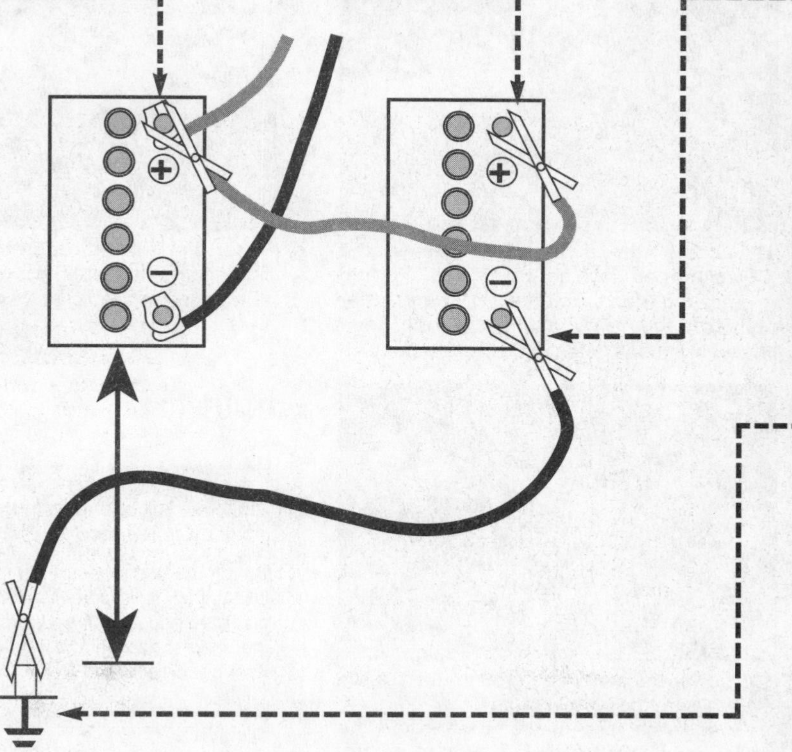

4 Connect the other end of the black jump lead to a bolt or bracket on the engine block, well away from the battery, on the vehicle to be started.

5 Make sure that the jump leads will not come into contact with the fan, drive-belts or other moving parts of the engine.

6 Start the engine using the booster battery and run it at idle speed. Switch on the lights, rear window demister and heater blower motor, then disconnect the jump leads in the reverse order of connection. Turn off the lights etc.

Wheel changing

Some of the details shown here will vary according to model. For instance, the location of the spare wheel and jack is not the same on all cars. However, the basic principles apply to all vehicles.

Warning: Do not change a wheel in a situation where you risk being hit by other traffic. On busy roads, try to stop in a lay-by or a gateway. Be wary of passing traffic while changing the wheel – it is easy to become distracted by the job in hand.

Preparation

- ☐ When a puncture occurs, stop as soon as it is safe to do so.
- ☐ Park on firm level ground, if possible, and well out of the way of other traffic.
- ☐ Use hazard warning lights if necessary.
- ☐ If you have one, use a warning triangle to alert other drivers of your presence.
- ☐ Apply the handbrake and engage first or reverse gear (or Park on models with automatic transmission.
- ☐ Chock the wheel diagonally opposite the one being removed – a couple of large stones will do for this.
- ☐ If the ground is soft, use a flat piece of wood to spread the load under the jack.

Changing the wheel

1 In the boot, lift the parcel shelf and floor covering for access to the spare wheel and tools. The jack is on the rear body panel

2 Unscrew the retaining bolt and lift out the spare wheel

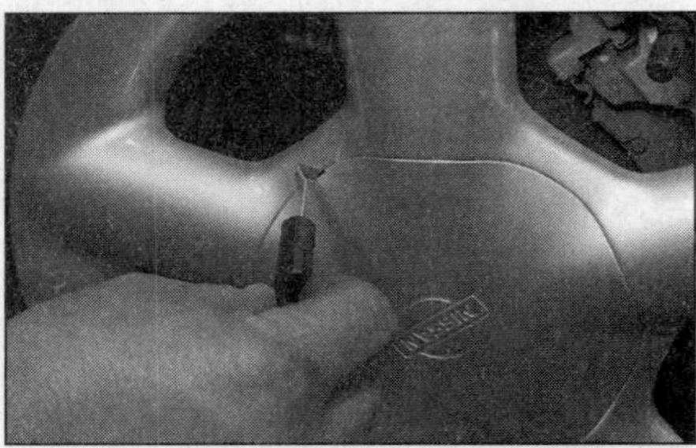

3 Use the tool provided to pull off the wheel trim or to prise it off (according to model)

4 Use the brace provided to loosen each wheel nut by half a turn. **Note:** *One of the wheel nuts is splined for security - locate the special adapter on it before loosening the nut*

5 Locate the jack head below the reinforced jacking point and on firm ground (don't jack the car at any other point on the sill). Ensure the jack head engages with the notch in the jacking point

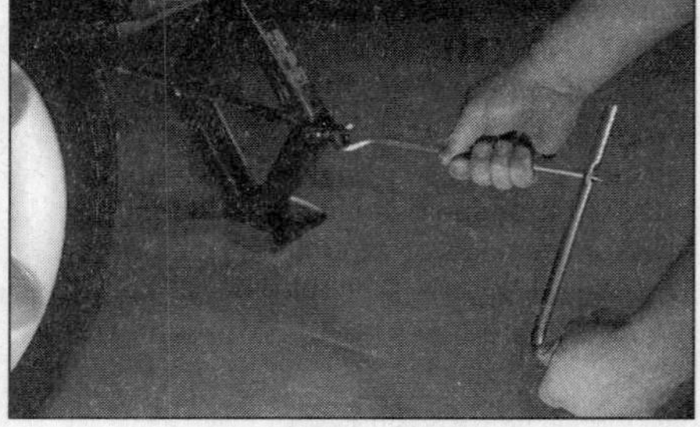

6 Insert the hooked rod in the brace and turn the jack threaded bar clockwise until the wheel is raised clear of the ground

7 Remove the nuts and lift the wheel clear, then fit the spare wheel. Refit the wheel nuts and tighten with the brace

8 Lower the car to the ground, then finally tighten the wheel nuts in a diagonal sequence, and fit the wheel trim. The wheel nuts should be retightened to the specified torque at the earliest opportunity

Finally...

- ☐ Remove the wheel chocks.
- ☐ Stow the jack and tools in the correct locations in the car.
- ☐ Check the tyre pressure on the wheel just fitted. If it is low, or if you don't have a pressure gauge with you, drive slowly to the nearest garage and inflate the tyre to the right pressure.
- ☐ Have the damaged tyre or wheel repaired as soon as possible.

Puddles on the garage floor or drive, or obvious wetness under the bonnet or underneath the car, suggest a leak that needs investigating. It can sometimes be difficult to decide where the leak is coming from, especially if the engine bay is very dirty already. Leaking oil or fluid can also be blown rearwards by the passage of air under the car, giving a false impression of where the problem lies.

Warning: Most automotive oils and fluids are poisonous. Wash them off skin, and change out of contaminated clothing, without delay.

HAYNES HiNT ***The smell of a fluid leaking from the car may provide a clue to what's leaking. Some fluids are distinctively coloured. It may help to clean the car and to park it over some clean paper as an aid to locating the source of the leak. Remember that some leaks may only occur while the engine is running.***

Sump oil

Engine oil may leak from the drain plug...

Oil from filter

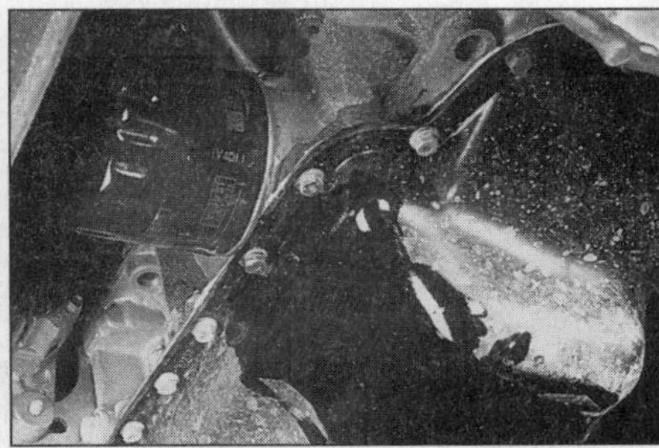

...or from the base of the oil filter.

Gearbox oil

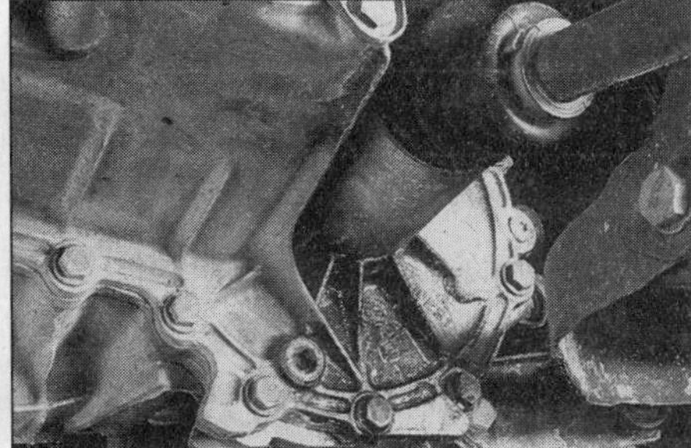

Gearbox oil can leak from the seals at the inboard ends of the driveshafts.

Antifreeze

Leaking antifreeze often leaves a crystalline deposit like this.

Brake fluid

A leak occurring at a wheel is almost certainly brake fluid.

Power steering fluid

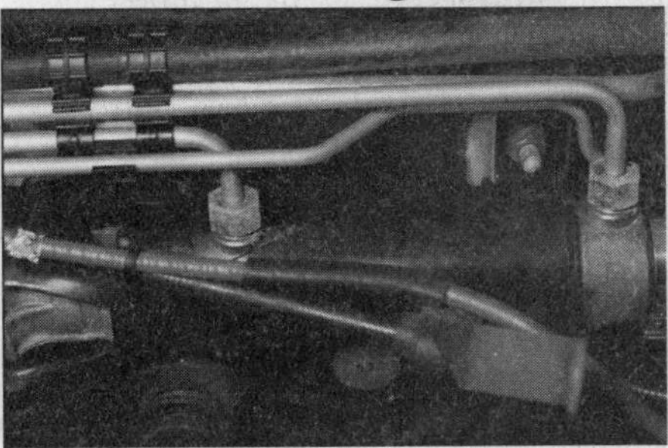

Power steering fluid may leak from the pipe connectors on the steering rack.

Towing

When all else fails, you may find yourself having to get a tow home – or of course you may be helping somebody else. Long-distance recovery should only be done by a garage or breakdown service. For shorter distances, DIY towing using another car is easy enough, but observe the following points:

☐ Use a proper tow-rope – they are not expensive. The vehicle being towed must display an 'ON TOW' sign in its rear window.

☐ Always turn the ignition key to the 'on' position when the vehicle is being towed, so that the steering lock is released, and that the direction indicator and brake lights will work.

☐ Only attach the tow-rope to the towing eyes provided. The front towing eye is located on the right-hand side of the bumper **(see illustration)**. Towing eyes are also located beneath the bumper. The rear towing eye is located below the rear bumper

☐ Before being towed, release the handbrake and select neutral on the transmission.

☐ Note that greater-than-usual pedal pressure will be required to operate the brakes, since the vacuum servo unit is only operational with the engine running.

☐ On models with power steering, greater-than-usual steering effort will also be required.

☐ The driver of the car being towed must keep the tow-rope taut at all times to avoid snatching.

☐ Make sure that both drivers know the route before setting off.

☐ Only drive at moderate speeds and keep the distance towed to a minimum. Drive smoothly and allow plenty of time for slowing down at junctions.

Caution! Do not tow models with automatic transmission, since the internal oil pump will not function with the engine stopped, and serious damage to the transmission will occur.

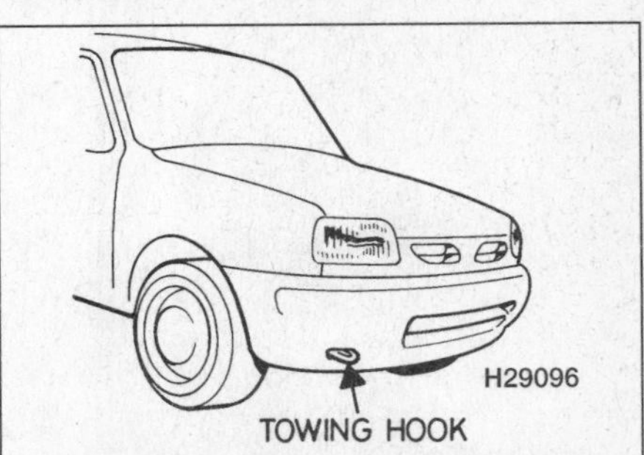

Front towing eye location

Introduction

There are some very simple checks which need only take a few minutes to carry out, but which could save you a lot of inconvenience and expense.

These "Weekly checks" require no great skill or special tools, and the small amount of time they take to perform could prove to be very well spent, for example;

☐ Keeping an eye on tyre condition and pressures, will not only help to stop them wearing out prematurely, but could also save your life.

☐ Many breakdowns are caused by electrical problems. Battery-related faults are particularly common, and a quick check on a regular basis will often prevent the majority of these.

☐ If your car develops a brake fluid leak, the first time you might know about it is when your brakes don't work properly. Checking the level regularly will give advance warning of this kind of problem.

☐ If the oil or coolant levels run low, the cost of repairing any engine damage will be far greater than fixing the leak, for example.

Underbonnet check points

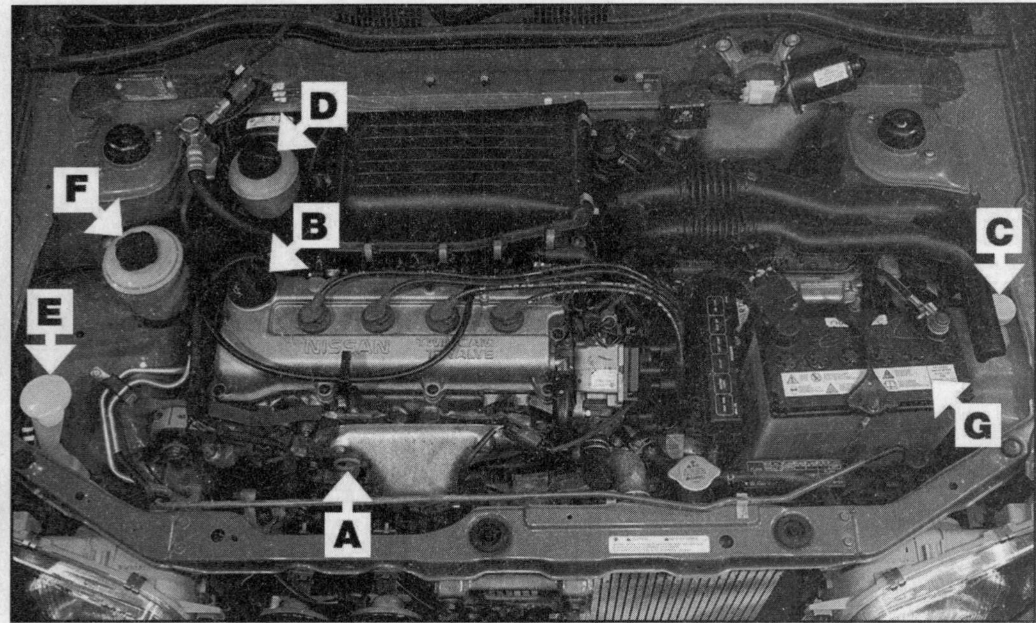

◀ **1.3 litre engine (1.0 and 1.4 litre similar)**

A *Engine oil level dipstick*
B *Engine oil filler cap*
C *Coolant expansion tank (on right-hand side on automatic transmission models)*
D *Brake fluid reservoir*
E *Screen washer fluid reservoir*
F *Power steering fluid reservoir*
G *Battery*

Engine oil level

Before you start

✔ Make sure that your car is on level ground.
✔ Check the oil level before the car is driven, or at least 5 minutes after the engine has been switched off.

If the oil level is checked immediately after driving the vehicle, some of the oil will remain in the upper engine components, resulting in an inaccurate reading on the dipstick!

The correct oil

Modern engines place great demands on their oil. It is very important that the correct oil for your car is used (See "Lubricants, fluids and tyre pressures").

Car care

● If you have to add oil frequently, you should check whether you have any oil leaks. Place some clean paper under the car overnight, and check for stains in the morning. If there are no leaks, the engine may be burning oil.

● Always maintain the level between the upper and lower dipstick marks (see photo 3). If the level is too low severe engine damage may occur. Oil seal failure may result if the engine is overfilled by adding too much oil.

1 The dipstick is located in a tube at the front of the engine (see "Underbonnet check points" on page 0•10 for exact location). Withdraw the dipstick.

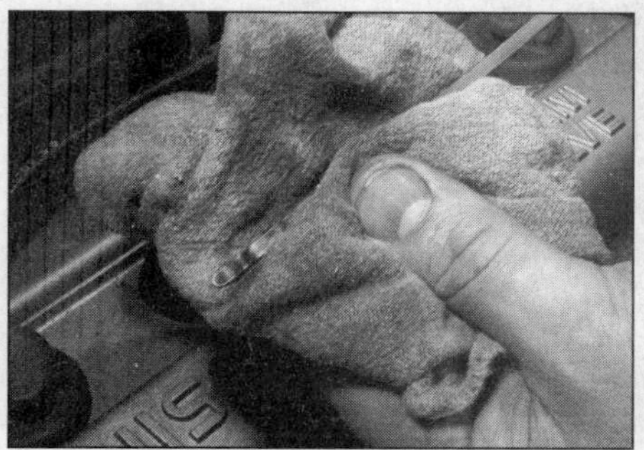

2 Using a clean rag or paper towel, wipe all the oil from the dipstick. Insert the clean dipstick into the tube as far as it will go, then withdraw it again.

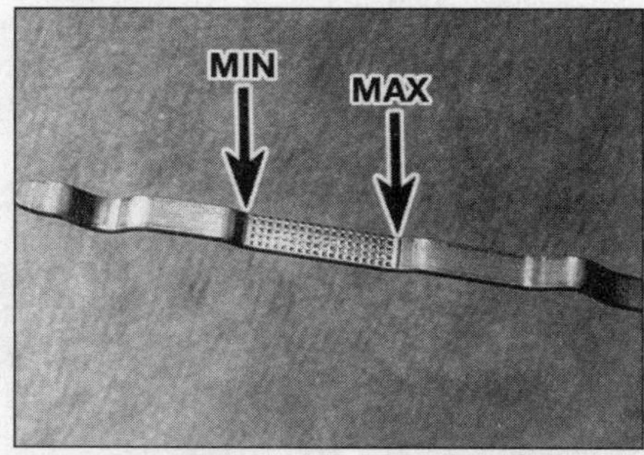

3 Note the oil level on the end of the dipstick, which should be between the upper ("MAX") mark and the lower ("MIN") mark.

4 Oil is added through the filler cap hole. Unscrew the filler cap, then top-up the level. A funnel or some rag may help to reduce spillage. Add the oil slowly, checking the level on the dipstick often. Don't overfill.

Brake fluid level

Warning:
● Brake fluid can harm your eyes and will damage painted surfaces, so use extreme caution when handling and pouring it.
● Do not use fluid that has been standing open for some time, as it absorbs moisture from the air, which can cause a dangerous loss of braking effectiveness.

• Make sure that your car is on level ground.
• The fluid level in the reservoir will drop slightly as the brake pads wear down, but the fluid level must never be allowed to drop below the "MIN" mark.

Safety first!

● If the reservoir requires repeated topping-up this is an indication of a fluid leak somewhere in the system, which should be investigated immediately.
● If a leak is suspected, the car should not be driven until the braking system has been checked. Never take any risks where brakes are concerned.

1 The "MAX" and "MIN" marks are on the side of the reservoir, which is at the rear right-hand side of the engine compartment (rear left on LHD models). The fluid level must be kept between these two marks

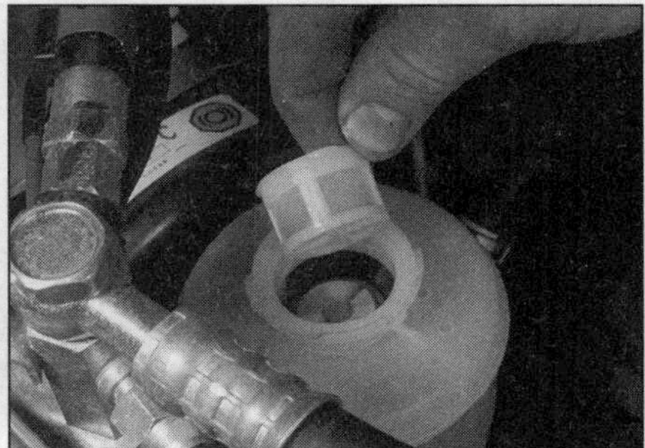

2 Remove the fluid filter, wash clean in methylated spirits, and allow to dry before refitting. If the filter or reservoir is very dirty, the system should be drained and refilled (see Chapter 1 and 9).

3 Carefully add fluid, avoiding spilling it on surrounding paintwork. Use only the specified hydraulic fluid. After filling to the correct level, refit the cap securely and wipe off any spilt fluid.

Coolant level

Warning: DO NOT attempt to remove the radiator pressure cap when the engine is hot, as there is a very great risk of scalding. Do not leave open containers of coolant about, as it is poisonous.

Car care

- Adding coolant should not be necessary on a regular basis. If frequent topping-up is required, it is likely there is a leak. Check the radiator, all hoses and joint faces for signs of staining or wetness, and rectify as necessary.

- It is important that antifreeze is used in the cooling system all year round, not just during the winter months. Don't top-up with water alone, as the antifreeze will become too diluted.

1 The coolant level varies with engine temperature. The level is checked in the expansion tank, which is on the left-hand side of the engine compartment on manual transmission models and on the right-hand side on automatic transmission models. When the engine is cold, the level should be at or near the "MAX" mark.

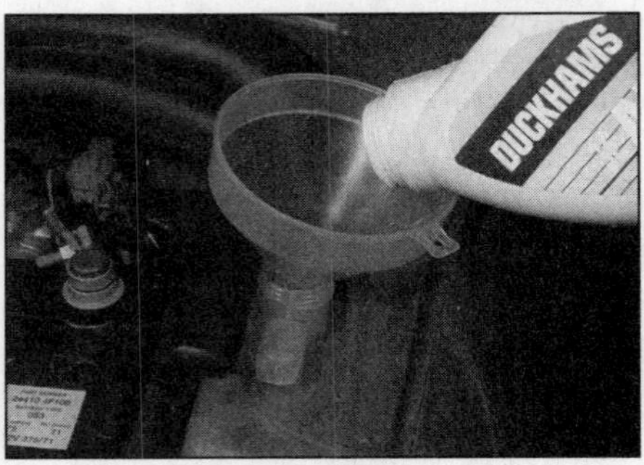

2 If topping up is necessary, wait until the engine is cold, then remove the expansion tank cap and add a mixture of water and antifreeze until the coolant is up to the "MAX" mark.

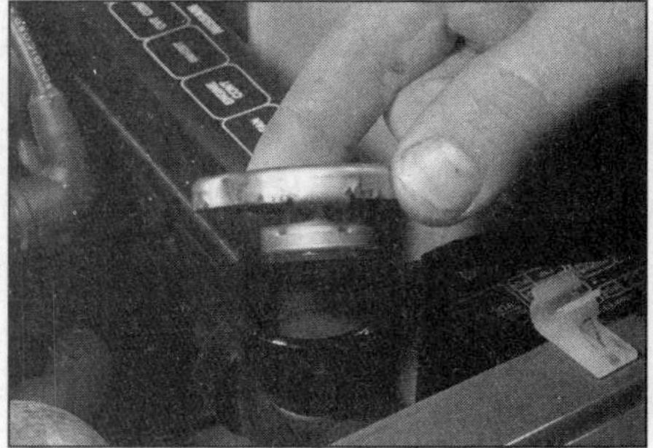

3 If the level in the expansion tank was below the "MIN" mark, also check the level in the radiator. Turn the pressure cap slowly anti-clockwise, and pause until any pressure remaining in the system is released. Remove the cap.

4 Add a mixture of water and antifreeze to the radiator until the level is up to the pressure cap seating. Refit the cap, turning it clockwise as far as it will go until it is secure.

Power steering fluid level

Before you start:

✔ Park the vehicle on level ground.
✔ Set the steering wheel straight-ahead.
✔ The engine should be turned off.

For the check to be accurate, the steering must not be turned once the engine has been stopped.

Safety first!

- The need for frequent topping-up indicates a leak, which should be investigated immediately.

1 The power steering fluid reservoir is on the right-hand side of the engine compartment, just in front of the suspension turret. The fluid level can be checked either cold (vehicle left for at least one hour) or hot (after driving the vehicle). The fluid level should be checked with the engine stopped. The reservoir has "COLDMAX" and "COLDMIN" (and "HOTMAX" and "HOTMIN") markings on the side. The fluid level should be between the two marks. If topping-up is necessary, wipe the surrounding area so that dirt does not enter the reservoir then remove the cap.

2 Top up the fluid level to the appropriate "MAX" mark, using the specified type of fluid (do not overfill the reservoir), then refit and tighten the filler cap.

Automatic transmission fluid level

Before you start:

- ✔ Park the vehicle on level ground.
- ✔ Apply the handbrake.
- ✔ Run the engine and transmission to normal operating temperature, however, DO NOT check the level after the vehicle has been used to tow a trailer, after the engine has been idling in city traffic in hot weather, or after the vehicle has been driven at high speeds. **Note:** *Although a cold level marking is given on the fluid level dipstick, the level must always be re-checked using the HOT marking.*

Safety first!

● The check is made with the engine running - take care to keep loose clothing and long hair out of the way of moving mechanical parts.

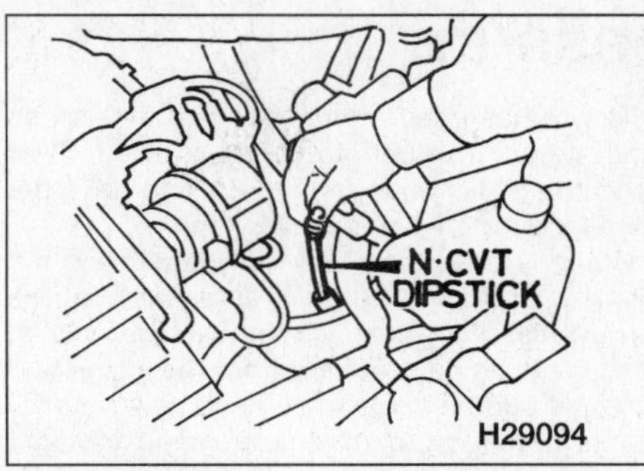

1 The automatic transmission fluid level dipstick is located in a tube on the transmission in the left-hand side of the engine compartment. With the engine idling, move the selector lever through each gear position then finally leave it in the park "P" position.

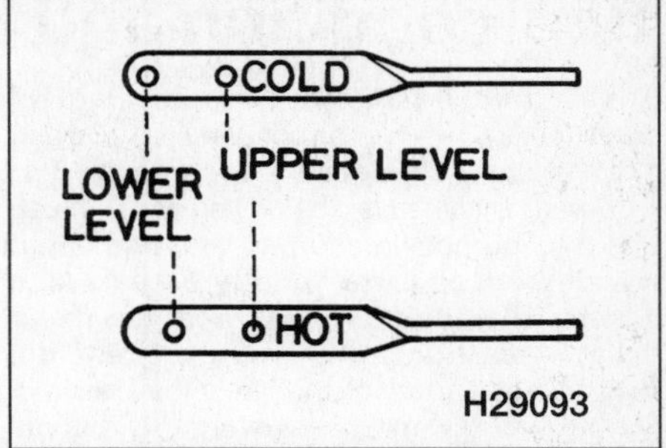

2 Withdraw the dipstick from the tube and wipe it with a clean non-fluffy cloth. Re-insert the dipstick fully into its tube, then withdraw it again and note the fluid level. If necessary, add the specified fluid through the dipstick tube using a suitable funnel until the level is correct. Finally, re-insert the dipstick and switch off the engine.

Screen washer fluid level

Screenwash additives not only keep the winscreen clean during foul weather, they also prevent the washer system freezing in cold weather - which is when you are likely to need it most. Don't top up using plain water as the screenwash will become too diluted, and will freeze during cold weather.

On no account use coolant antifreeze in the washer system - this could discolour or damage paintwork.

1 The windscreen/tailgate/headlight washer fluid reservoir is located in the right-hand corner of the engine compartment. If topping-up is necessary, pull off the cap and add water and screenwash additive in the quantities recommended on the bottle.

Wiper blades

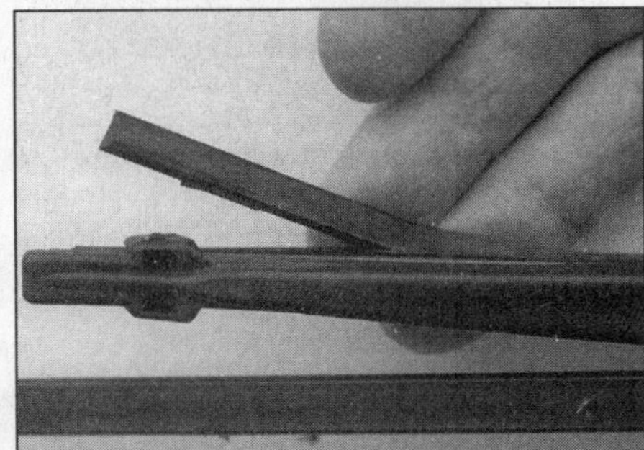

1 Check the condition of the wiper blades; if they are cracked or show any signs of deterioration, or if the glass swept area is smeared, renew them. Wiper blades should be renewed annually.

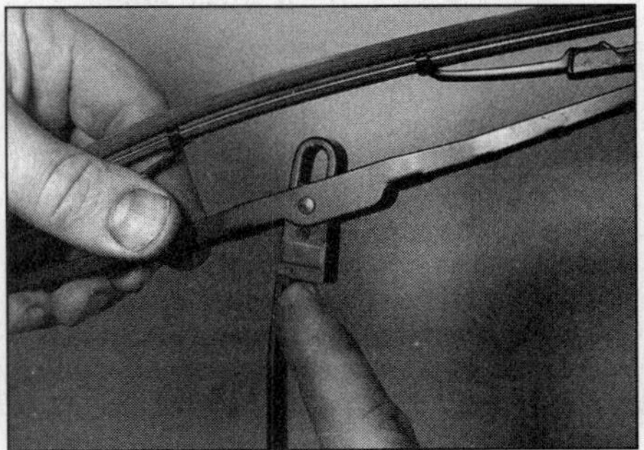

2 To remove a windscreen wiper blade, pull the arm fully away from the screen until it locks. Swivel the blade through 90°, then depress the locking clip at the base of the mounting block.

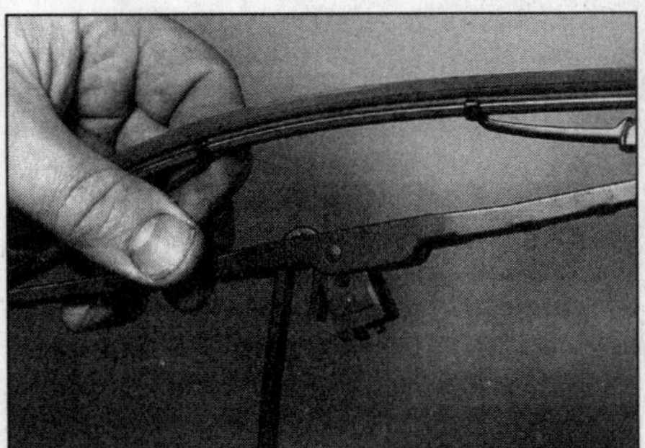

3 Slide the blade downwards from the hooked end of the arm then withdraw it upwards. Make sure the new blade is engaged fully with the hooked end of the arm. Check the tailgate wiper blade as well!

Tyre condition and pressure

It is very important that tyres are in good condition, and at the correct pressure - having a tyre failure at any speed is highly dangerous. Tyre wear is influenced by driving style - harsh braking and acceleration, or fast cornering, will all produce more rapid tyre wear. As a general rule, the front tyres wear out faster than the rears. Interchanging the tyres from front to rear ("rotating" the tyres) may result in more even wear. However, if this is completely effective, you may have the expense of replacing all four tyres at once!

Remove any nails or stones embedded in the tread before they penetrate the tyre to cause deflation. If removal of a nail does reveal that the tyre has been punctured, refit the nail so that its point of penetration is marked. Then immediately change the wheel, and have the tyre repaired by a tyre dealer.

Regularly check the tyres for damage in the form of cuts or bulges, especially in the sidewalls. Periodically remove the wheels, and clean any dirt or mud from the inside and outside surfaces. Examine the wheel rims for signs of rusting, corrosion or other damage. Light alloy wheels are easily damaged by "kerbing" whilst parking; steel wheels may also become dented or buckled. A new wheel is very often the only way to overcome severe damage.

New tyres should be balanced when they are fitted, but it may become necessary to re-balance them as they wear, or if the balance weights fitted to the wheel rim should fall off. Unbalanced tyres will wear more quickly, as will the steering and suspension components. Wheel imbalance is normally signified by vibration, particularly at a certain speed (typically around 50 mph). If this vibration is felt only through the steering, then it is likely that just the front wheels need balancing. If, however, the vibration is felt through the whole car, the rear wheels could be out of balance. Wheel balancing should be carried out by a tyre dealer or garage.

1 ***Tread Depth - visual check***
The original tyres have tread wear safety bands (B), which will appear when the tread depth reaches approximately 1.6 mm. The band positions are indicated by a triangular mark on the tyre sidewall (A).

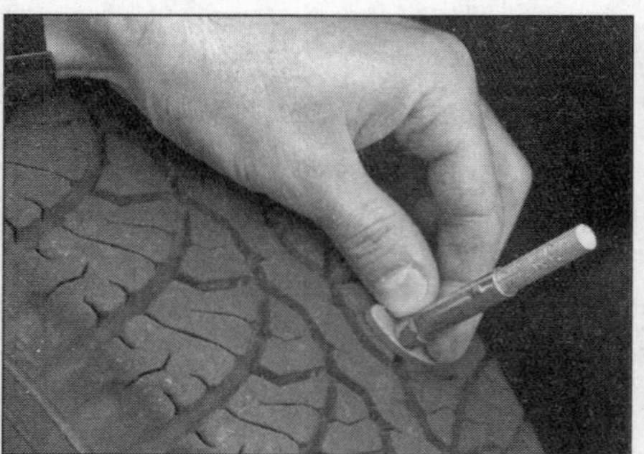

2 ***Tread Depth - manual check***
Alternatively, tread wear can be monitored with a simple, inexpensive device known as a tread depth indicator gauge.

3 ***Tyre Pressure Check***
Check the tyre pressures regularly with the tyres cold. Do not adjust the tyre pressures immediately after the vehicle has been used, or an inaccurate setting will result.

Tyre tread wear patterns

Shoulder Wear

Underinflation (wear on both sides)
Under-inflation will cause overheating of the tyre, because the tyre will flex too much, and the tread will not sit correctly on the road surface. This will cause a loss of grip and excessive wear, not to mention the danger of sudden tyre failure due to heat build-up.
Check and adjust pressures
Incorrect wheel camber (wear on one side)
Repair or renew suspension parts
Hard cornering
Reduce speed!

Centre Wear

Overinflation
Over-inflation will cause rapid wear of the centre part of the tyre tread, coupled with reduced grip, harsher ride, and the danger of shock damage occurring in the tyre casing.
Check and adjust pressures

If you sometimes have to inflate your car's tyres to the higher pressures specified for maximum load or sustained high speed, don't forget to reduce the pressures to normal afterwards.

Uneven Wear

Front tyres may wear unevenly as a result of wheel misalignment. Most tyre dealers and garages can check and adjust the wheel alignment (or "tracking") for a modest charge.
Incorrect camber or castor
Repair or renew suspension parts
Malfunctioning suspension
Repair or renew suspension parts
Unbalanced wheel
Balance tyres
Incorrect toe setting
Adjust front wheel alignment
Note: *The feathered edge of the tread which typifies toe wear is best checked by feel.*

Battery

Caution: *Before carrying out any work on the vehicle battery, read the precautions given in "Safety first" at the start of this manual.*

✔ Make sure that the battery tray is in good condition, and that the clamp is tight. Corrosion on the tray, retaining clamp and the battery itself can be removed with a solution of water and baking soda. Thoroughly rinse all cleaned areas with water. Any metal parts damaged by corrosion should be covered with a zinc-based primer, then painted.

✔ Periodically (approximately every three months), check the charge condition of the battery as described in Chapter 5A.

✔ If the battery is flat, and you need to jump start your vehicle, see ***Roadside Repairs***.

HAYNES HiNT

Battery corrosion can be kept to a minimum by applying a layer of petroleum jelly to the clamps and terminals after they are reconnected.

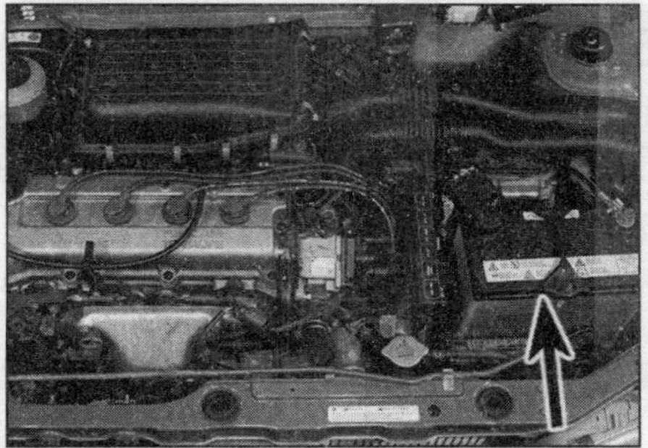

1 The battery is located at the front left-hand corner of the engine compartment. The exterior of the battery should be inspected periodically for damage such as a cracked case or cover.

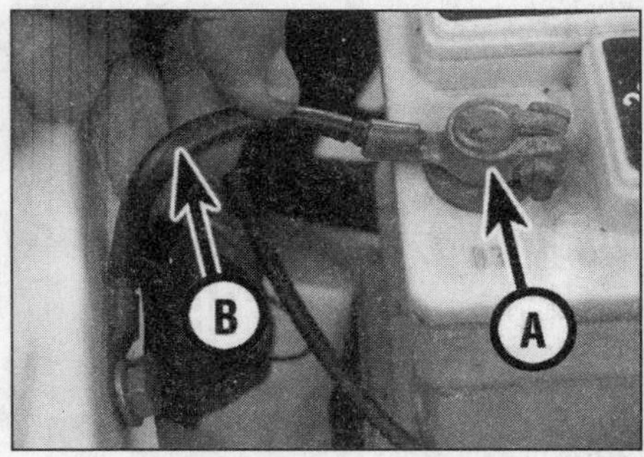

2 Check the tightness of battery clamps (A) to ensure good electrical connections. You should not be able to move them. Also check each cable (B) for cracks and frayed conductors.

3 If corrosion (white, fluffy deposits) is evident, remove the cables from the battery terminals, clean them with a small wire brush, then refit them. Automotive stores sell a tool for cleaning the battery terminals

4 Note that the battery positive lead terminal can be disconnected by lifting the plastic cover and loosening the clamp bolt.

Bulbs and fuses

✔ Check all external lights and the horn. Refer to the appropriate Sections of Chapter 12 for details if any of the circuits are found to be inoperative.

✔ Visually check all accessible wiring connectors, harnesses and retaining clips for security, and for signs of chafing or damage.

If you need to check your brake lights and indicators unaided, back up to a wall or garage door and operate the lights. The reflected light should show if they are working properly.

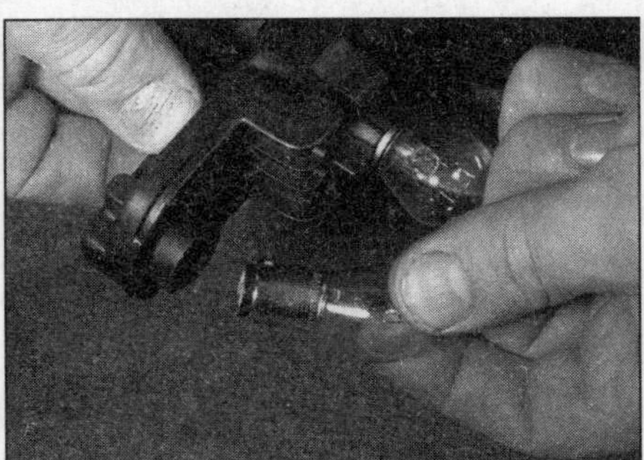

1 If a single indicator light, brake light or headlight has failed, it is likely that a bulb has blown and will need to be replaced. Refer to Chapter 12 for details. If both brake lights have failed, it is possible that the brake light switch operated by the brake pedal has failed. Refer to Chapter 9 for details.

2 If more than one indicator light or headlight has failed, it is likely that either a fuse has blown or that there is a fault in the circuit (see *"Electrical fault finding"* in Chapter 12). The fuses are located behind a plastic cover on the driver's side of the facia. Pull out the top of the cover - the fuse circuits are indicated on the inside of the cover.

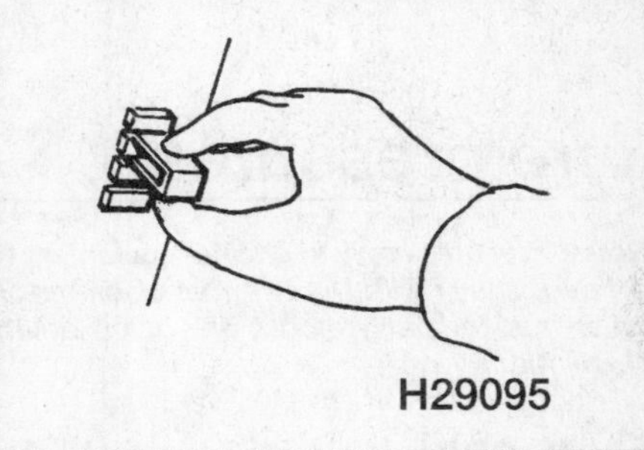

3 To replace a blown fuse, remove it using the tweezers located inside the fusebox. Fit a new fuse of the same rating, available from car accessory shops. It is important that you find the reason for the fuse blowing (see *"Electrical fault finding"* in Chapter 12).

Lubricants and fluids

Engine . . . . Multigrade engine oil, viscosity SAE 15W/40, to API SG, SH or SJ

Cooling system . . . . Ethylene glycol-based antifreeze with corrosion inhibitor, and soft water

Manual transmission . . . . Gear oil, viscosity SAE 80, to API GL4

Automatic transmission . . . . Dexron IIE or Dexron III automatic transmission fluid (ATF)

Brake hydraulic system . . . . Hydraulic fluid to FMVSS 116 DOT 4

Power steering . . . . Dexron type ATF

Choosing your engine oil

Engines need oil, not only to lubricate moving parts and minimise wear, but also to maximise power output and to improve fuel economy.

HOW ENGINE OIL WORKS

• *Beating friction*

Without oil, the moving surfaces inside your engine will rub together, heat up and melt, quickly causing the engine to seize. Engine oil creates a film which separates these moving parts, preventing wear and heat build-up.

• *Cooling hot-spots*

Temperatures inside the engine can exceed 1000° C. The engine oil circulates and acts as a coolant, transferring heat from the hot-spots to the sump.

• *Cleaning the engine internally*

Good quality engine oils clean the inside of your engine, collecting and dispersing combustion deposits and controlling them until they are trapped by the oil filter or flushed out at oil change.

OIL CARE - FOLLOW THE CODE

To handle and dispose of used engine oil safely, always:

- ***Avoid skin contact with used engine oil. Repeated or prolonged contact can be harmful.***
- ***Dispose of used oil and empty packs in a responsible manner in an authorised disposal site. Call 0800 663366 to find the one nearest to you. Never tip oil down drains or onto the ground.***

Tyre pressures

Note: *Pressures apply to original-equipment tyres, and may vary if any other make or type of tyre is fitted; check with the tyre manufacturer or supplier for correct pressures if necessary. The pressures for each model are given on the inside edge of the driver's door pillar* ***(see illustration).***

Tyres cold	**bar/psi**
Front:	
Up to 3 passengers	2.2 / 32
Full load (4 or more passengers)	2.5 / 36
Rear:	
Up to 3 passengers	1.9 / 27
Full load (4 or more passengers)	2.3 / 33

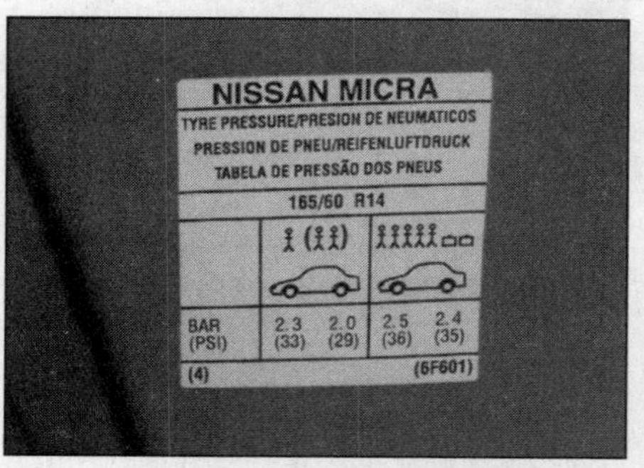

Tyre pressures on the driver's door pillar

Chapter 1
Routine maintenance and servicing

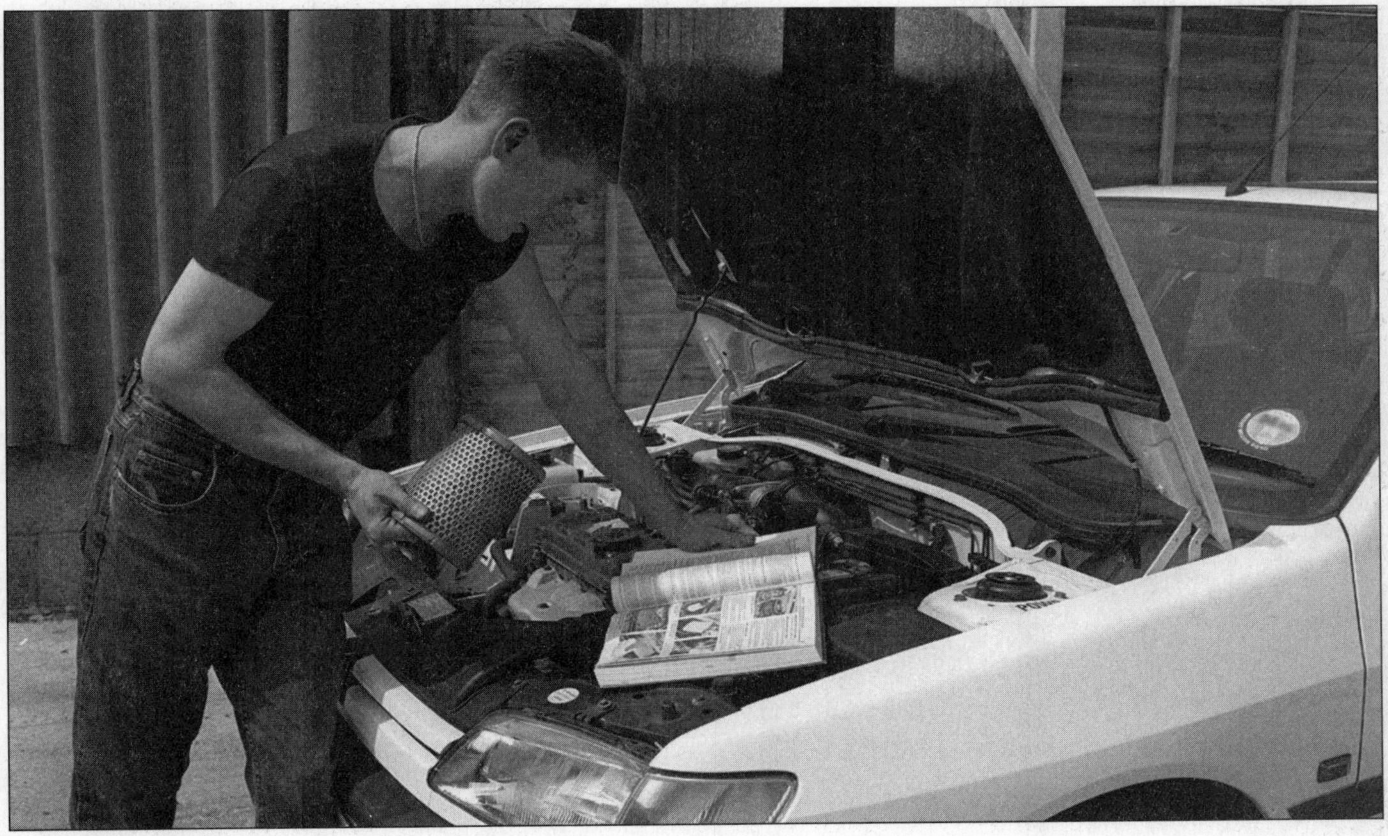

Contents

Degrees of difficulty

Easy, suitable for novice with little experience 

Fairly easy, suitable for beginner with some experience 

Fairly difficult, suitable for competent DIY mechanic 

Difficult, suitable for experienced DIY mechanic 

Very difficult, suitable for expert DIY or professional 

Servicing specifications

Lubricants and fluids

Refer to end of *"Weekly Checks"*

Capacities

Engine oil	
Excluding filter	2.9 litres
Including filter	3.1 litres
Cooling system	
Including expansion tank	4.0 litres
Expansion tank	0.7 litres
Transmission	
Manual transmission	2.8 to 3.0 litres
Automatic transmission	
RE0F05A:	
Including oil cooler	4.2 litres
Excluding oil cooler	3.2 litres
RE0F21A	5.0 litres
Fuel tank	
All models	42 litres

Cooling system

Antifreeze mixture:	
28% antifreeze	Protection down to -15°C
50% antifreeze	Protection down to -30°C

Note: *Refer to antifreeze manufacturer for latest recommendations.*

Ignition system

Ignition timing	Refer to Chapter 5B	
Spark plugs:	**Type**	**Electrode gap**
1.0 and 1.3 litre engines	Bosch FR 7 D+X	1.1 mm
1.4 litre engines	Bosch FR 8 D+X	1.1 mm
Spark plug HT lead resistances (genuine Bougicord leads only)	4.48 to 6.72 k ohms per metre	

Brakes

Brake pad lining minimum thickness	2.0 mm
Brake shoe friction material minimum thickness	1.5 mm
Number of clicks to operate handbrake "on" warning light	1 or less
Number of clicks with handbrake fully on	6 to 8

Wheel alignment and steering angles*

Front wheel camber angle:	
1.0 litre models:	
Up to March 1998	-0°26' to 1°4'
After March 1998	-0°22' to 1°8'
1.3 and 1.4 litre models	-0°22' to 1°8'
Front wheel castor angle:	
1.0 litre models:	
Up to March 1998	1°31' to 3°1'
After March 1998	1°34' to 3°4'
1.3 and 1.4 litre models	1°34' to 3°4'
Kingpin inclination:	
1.0 litre models:	
Up to March 1998	11°52' to 13°22'
After March 1998	11°47' to 13°17'
1.3 and 1.4 litre models	11°47' to 13°17'
Front wheel toe setting (all models)	-0.5 to 1.5 mm (equivalent to -0°5' to 0°16')
Rear wheel camber angle (all models)	-0°35' to 0°5'
Rear wheel toe-setting (all models)	-0°14' to 0°46'

***Note:** *All specifications given are for an unladen vehicle - ie, no driver or passengers, fuel tank full, engine coolant and oil levels normal, and spare wheel, jack and tools fitted in normal locations.*

Auxiliary drivebelt deflection

Alternator drivebelt (without idler)	
New	6.0 mm to 7.0 mm
Used	7.0 mm to 8.0 mm
Alternator drivebelt (with fixed idler or A/C compressor)	
New	5.5 mm to 6.0 mm
Used	6.0 mm to 7.0 mm
Water pump drivebelt (non-power steering models)	
New	3.5 mm to 4.0 mm
Used	3.8 mm to 4.2 mm
Water pump drivebelt (power steering models)	
New	2.8 mm to 3.2 mm
Used	3.0 mm to 3.5 mm

Torque wrench settings

	Nm	lbf ft
Roadwheel nuts	108	80
Spark plugs	25	19
Sump drain plug	34	25
Manual transmission filler/level plug	30	22
Manual transmission oil drain plug		
RS5F41A	15	11
All other types	30	22
Automatic transmission fluid drain plug:		
RE0F05A	25	19
RE0F21A	45	34
Alternator mounting and adjustment lock bolts	44	33
Drivebelt tensioner retaining nut	44	33

Underbonnet view of a Micra SLX 1.3 (RHD model with manual transmission)

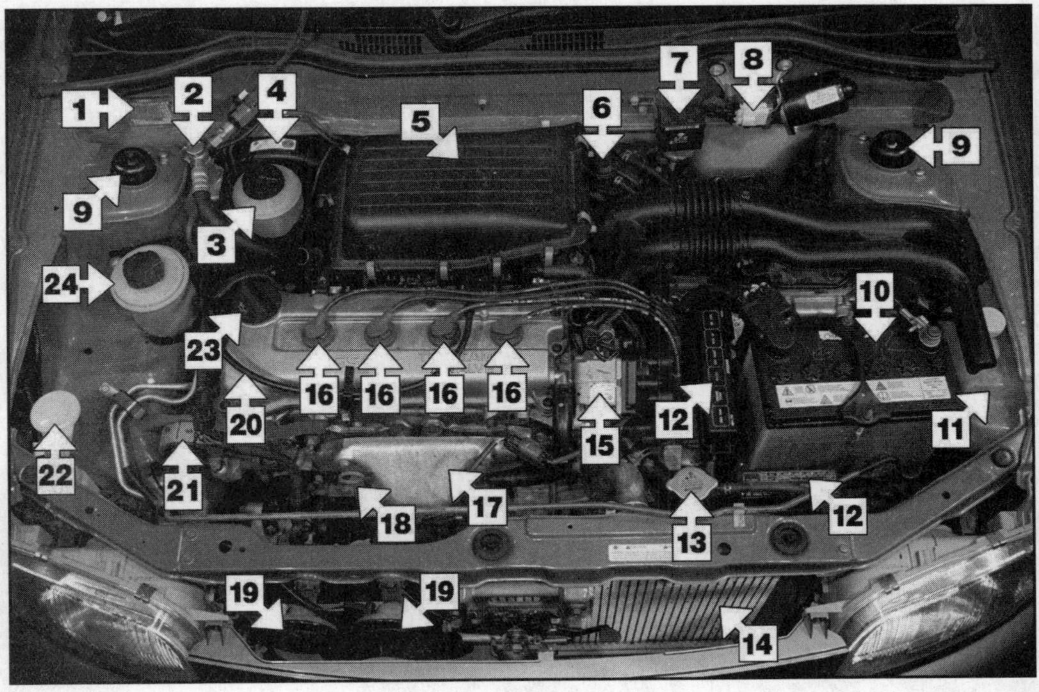

1 Vehicle Identification Number (VIN) Plate
2 Power steering pressure switch
3 Brake hydraulic fluid reservoir
4 Brake vacuum servo unit
5 Air cleaner assembly
6 Evaporative emission carbon canister
7 Wiper amplifier
8 Windscreen wiper motor
9 Front suspension strut upper mountings
10 Battery
11 Cooling system expansion tank (non-pressurised)
12 Relay boxes
13 Radiator pressure cap
14 Radiator
15 Distributor
16 Spark plug HT leads
17 Exhaust manifold and hot air shroud
18 Engine oil level dipstick
19 Horns
20 Accelerator cable
21 Right-hand engine mounting
22 Windscreen washer fluid reservoir
23 Engine oil filler cap
24 Power steering fluid reservoir

Front underbody view of a Micra SLX 1.3 (RHD model with manual transmission)

1 Engine oil sump
2 Alternator
3 Engine oil drain plug
4 Oil filter
5 Exhaust front pipe
6 Engine/transmission centre member
7 Manual transmission
8 Electric cooling fan assembly
9 Manual transmission oil drain plug
10 Radiator
11 Front brake calipers
12 Left-hand driveshaft
13 Front suspension lower arms
14 Front anti-roll bar mounting on lower arms
15 Steering track-rod ends
16 Front anti-roll bar clamp mountings on the underbody
17 Steering gear
18 Gearchange rod
19 Gearchange support rod
20 Right-hand driveshaft

Rear underbody view of a Micra SLX 1.3 (RHD model)

1 Exhaust intermediate section
2 Fuel tank
3 Rear brake pressure regulating valve
4 Rear suspension lower trailing link arms
5 Rear shock absorber lower mountings
6 Fuel tank mountings
7 Rear axle tube
8 Panhard rod
9 Exhaust tailpipe and silencer
10 Rear anti-roll bar

The maintenance intervals in this manual are provided with the assumption that you, not the dealer, will be carrying out the work. These are the minimum maintenance intervals recommended by us for vehicles driven daily. If you wish to keep your vehicle in peak condition at all times, you may wish to perform some of these procedures more often. We encourage frequent maintenance, because it enhances the efficiency, performance and resale value of your vehicle.

When the vehicle is new, it should be serviced by a factory-authorised dealer service department, in order to preserve the factory warranty.

Every 250 miles (400 km) or weekly

- ☐ Refer to *"Weekly checks"*

Every 4500 miles (7500 km) or 6 months - whichever comes first

- ☐ Renew the engine oil and filter (Section 3)

Note: *Nissan recommend oil and filter renewal every 9000 miles (15 000 km) or 12 months. Frequent oil and filter changes are good for the engine. We recommend changing the oil at the interval specified here, or at least twice a year, if the mileage covered is less.*

Every 18 000 miles (30 000 km) or 12 months - whichever comes first

In addition to the items listed above, carry out the following:

- ☐ Renew ventilation system air filter - 1998-on models with air conditioning (Section 4)
- ☐ Check all underbonnet components and hoses for fluid leaks (Section 5)
- ☐ Renew the spark plugs (Section 6)
- ☐ Check clutch cable and pedal (Section 7)
- ☐ Check manual transmission oil level (Section 8)
- ☐ Check the condition of the driveshaft rubber gaiters* (Section 9)
- ☐ Check the wheel alignment, rotate and balance roadwheels (Section 10)
- ☐ Check the front and (where applicable) rear brake pads and discs and renew if necessary* (Section 11)
- ☐ Check (where applicable) the rear brake shoes and drums and renew if necessary* (Section 12)
- ☐ Check the condition, operation and security of all seat belts (Section 13)
- ☐ Check the headlamp beam alignment (Section 14)
- ☐ Check and adjust the handbrake (Section 15)
- ☐ Carry out a road test (Section 16)

**This should be performed more frequently if the vehicle is used in Severe Conditions (ie towing a trailer, repeated short distances, dusty conditions etc).*

Every 12 months (regardless of mileage)

- ☐ Check body for corrosion (Section 17)

Every 27 000 miles (45 000 km) or 2 years - whichever comes first

- ☐ Renew N-CVT automatic transmission fluid (Section 18)
- ☐ Check N-CVT automatic transmission magnetic clutch carbon brushes (Section 19)

Every 36 000 miles (60 000 km) or 2 years - whichever comes first

In addition to the items listed above in the 18 000 miles (30 000 km) service, carry out the following:

- ☐ Check the condition of the auxiliary drivebelt(s), and renew if necessary (Section 20)
- ☐ Renew the air filter* (Section 21)
- ☐ Check the operation of the exhaust gas (Lambda/oxygen) sensor (Section 22)
- ☐ Renew the PCV filter* (Section 23)
- ☐ Check evaporative loss system (Section 24)
- ☐ Renew the brake fluid* (Section 25)
- ☐ Check the brake vacuum servo unit, hose and non-return check-valve (Section 26)
- ☐ Check the steering and suspension components for condition and security* (Section 27)
- ☐ Check the exhaust system (Section 28)
- ☐ Renew the coolant (Section 29)

**This should be performed more frequently if the vehicle is used in Severe Conditions (ie towing a trailer, repeated short distances, dusty conditions etc).*

Every 54 000 miles (90 000 km) or 3 years - whichever comes first

In addition to the items listed above, carry out the following:

- ☐ Renew the fuel filter* (Section 30)
- ☐ Check the ignition system components (Section 31)

**This should be performed more frequently if the vehicle is used in severe conditions (ie towing a trailer, repeated short distances, dusty conditions etc).*

After 10 years, then every 2 years

- ☐ Check the SRS airbag (Section 32)

1 Introduction

General information

This Chapter is designed to help the home mechanic maintain his/her vehicle for safety, economy, long life and peak performance.

The Chapter contains a master maintenance schedule, and Sections dealing specifically with each task in the schedule. Visual checks, adjustments, component renewal and other helpful items are included. Refer to the accompanying illustrations of the engine compartment and the underside of the vehicle for the locations of the various components.

Servicing your vehicle in accordance with the mileage/time maintenance schedule and the following Sections will provide a planned maintenance programme, which should result in a long and reliable service life. This is a comprehensive plan, so maintaining some items but not others at the specified service intervals, will not produce the same results.

As you service your vehicle, you will discover that many of the procedures can - and should - be grouped together, because of the particular procedure being performed, or because of the proximity of two otherwise-unrelated components to one another. For example, if the vehicle is raised for any reason, the exhaust can be inspected at the same time as the suspension and steering components.

The first step in this maintenance programme is to prepare yourself before the actual work begins. Read through all the Sections relevant to the work to be carried out, then make a list and gather all the parts and tools required. If a problem is encountered, seek advice from a parts specialist, or a dealer service department.

2 Intensive maintenance

1 If, from the time the vehicle is new, the routine maintenance schedule is followed closely, and frequent checks are made of fluid levels and high-wear items, as suggested throughout this manual, the engine will be kept in relatively good running condition, and the need for additional work will be minimised.

2 It is possible that there will be times when the engine is running poorly due to the lack of regular maintenance. This is even more likely if a used vehicle, which has not received regular and frequent maintenance checks, is purchased. In such cases, additional work may need to be carried out, outside of the regular maintenance intervals.

3 If engine wear is suspected, a compression test (refer to the relevant Part of Chapter 2) will provide valuable information regarding the overall performance of the main internal components. Such a test can be used as a basis to decide on the extent of the work to be carried out. If, for example, a compression test indicates serious internal engine wear, conventional maintenance as described in this Chapter will not greatly improve the performance of the engine, and may prove a waste of time and money, unless extensive overhaul work is carried out first.

4 The following series of operations are those usually required to improve the performance of a generally poor-running engine:

Primary operations

a) Clean, inspect and test the battery (See "Weekly checks").
b) Check all the engine-related fluids (See "Weekly checks").
c) Check the condition and tension of the auxiliary drivebelts (Section 20).
d) Renew the spark plugs (Section 6).
e) Inspect the ignition HT leads – where applicable (Section 31).
f) Check the condition of the air filter, and renew if necessary (Section 21).
g) Check the fuel filter (Section 30).
h) Check the condition of all hoses, and check for fluid leaks (Section 5).
i) Check the exhaust gas emissions (Chapter 4B).

5 If the above operations do not prove fully effective, carry out the following secondary operations:

Secondary operations

All items listed under "Primary operations", plus the following:

a) Check the charging system (Chapter 5A).
b) Check the ignition system (Chapter 5B).
c) Check the fuel system (see relevant Part of Chapter 4).
d) Renew the ignition HT leads – where applicable (Section 31)

Every 4500 miles or 6 months

3 Engine oil and filter renewal

1 Frequent oil and filter changes are the most important preventative maintenance procedures which can be undertaken by the DIY owner. As engine oil ages, it becomes diluted and contaminated, which leads to premature engine wear.

2 Before starting this procedure, gather together all the necessary tools and materials. Also make sure that you have plenty of clean rags and newspapers handy, to mop up any spills. Ideally, the engine oil should be warm, as it will drain better, and more built-up sludge will be removed with it. Take care, however, not to touch the exhaust or any other hot parts of the engine when working under the vehicle. To avoid any possibility of scalding, and to protect yourself from possible skin irritants and other harmful contaminants in used engine oils, it is advisable to wear gloves when carrying out this work. Access to the underside of the vehicle will be greatly improved if it can be raised on a lift, driven onto ramps, or jacked up and supported on axle stands (see "*Jacking and vehicle support*"). Whichever method is chosen, make sure that the vehicle remains level, or if it is at an angle, that the drain plug is at the lowest point.

3 Remove the oil filler cap from the engine camshaft cover (twist it anti-clockwise and withdraw it).

4 Using a spanner, or preferably a suitable socket and bar, slacken the drain plug about half a turn **(see illustration)**. Position the draining container under the drain plug, then remove the plug completely **(see Haynes Hint)**. Recover the sealing ring from the drain plug.

3.4 Engine oil drain plug

HAYNES HiNT

Keep the drain plug pressed into the sump while unscrewing it by hand the last couple of turns. As the plug releases, move it away sharply so that the stream of oil issuing from the sump runs into the container, not up your sleeve!

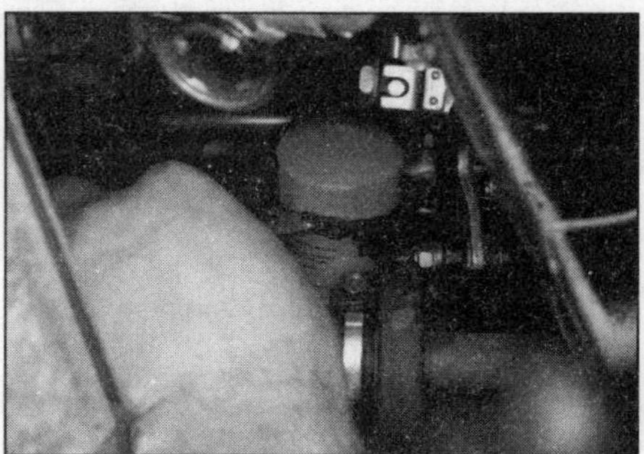
3.9 Using a filter removal tool to unscrew the oil filter

5 Allow some time for the oil to drain, noting that it may be necessary to reposition the container as the oil flow slows to a trickle.
6 After all the oil has drained, wipe the drain plug and the sealing washer with a clean rag. Examine the condition of the sealing washer - renew it if it shows signs of scoring or other damage which may prevent an oil-tight seal. Clean the area around the drain plug opening, and refit the plug complete with the washer. Tighten the plug securely - preferably to the specified torque, using a torque wrench.
7 The oil filter is located at the rear right-hand side of the cylinder block - access is most easily obtained from underneath the vehicle.
8 Move the container into position under the oil filter.
9 Use an oil filter removal tool (if required) to slacken the filter initially, then unscrew it by hand the rest of the way **(see illustration)**.

3.11 Fitting a new oil filter

Empty the oil from the old filter into the container.
10 Use a clean rag to remove all oil, dirt and sludge from the filter sealing area on the engine. Check the old filter to make sure that the rubber sealing ring has not stuck to the engine. If it has, carefully remove it.
11 Apply a light coating of clean engine oil to the sealing ring on the new filter, then screw the filter into position on the engine. Lightly tighten the filter until its sealing ring contacts the block, then tighten it through a further two-thirds of a turn **(see illustration)**.
12 Remove the old oil and all tools from under the vehicle then, if applicable, lower the vehicle to the ground.
13 Fill the engine through the filler in the camshaft cover, using the correct grade and type of oil (refer to *"Weekly Checks"* for details of topping-up). Pour in half the specified

Note: It is antisocial and illegal to dump oil down the drain. To find the location of your local oil recycling bank, call this number free.

quantity of oil first, then wait a few minutes for the oil to drain into the sump. Continue to add oil, a small quantity at a time, until the level is up to the lower mark on the dipstick. Adding a further 1.0 litre will bring the level up to the upper mark on the dipstick.
14 Start the engine and run it for a few minutes, while checking for leaks around the oil filter seal and the sump drain plug. Note that there may be a delay of a few seconds before the low oil pressure warning light goes out when the engine is first started, as the oil circulates through the new oil filter and the engine oil galleries before the pressure builds up. Do not run the engine above idle speed while the warning light is on.
15 Stop the engine, and wait a few minutes for the oil to settle in the sump once more. With the new oil circulated and the filter now completely full, recheck the level on the dipstick, and add more oil as necessary.
16 Dispose of the used engine oil safely, with reference to *"General repair procedures"* in the *Reference* section at the end of this manual.

Every 18 000 miles or 12 months

4 Ventilation system air filter renewal

Note: *This Section only applies to March 1998-on models with air conditioning.*
1 Remove the glovebox as described in Chapter 11, Section 25.
2 If the filter is being renewed for the first time, it will be necessary to cut the facia panel behind the glovebox in order to remove it. Using a sharp knife, cut down the two pre-moulded grooves in the cover panel behind the filter, and remove the section of panel for access to the filter.
3 If the filter has been replaced before, there will be a service replacement panel fitted across the rear of the filter, secured by four screws. Remove the screws for access to the filter.
4 Remove the filter cover retaining screw and remove the cover.
5 Withdraw the filter element, noting the fitted position of its locating tab.
6 Fit the new filter element, ensuring that the locating tab is correctly orientated, then fit the filter cover and tighten the retaining screw.
7 If the filter is being renewed for the first time, obtain the service replacement panel and fixings from your NISSAN dealer.
8 Fit the replacement panel, and secure with the four screws.
9 Refit the glovebox as described in Chapter 11.
10 Check the operation of the ventilation system on completion.

5 Hose and fluid leak check

1 Visually inspect the engine joint faces, gaskets and seals for any signs of water or oil leaks. Pay particular attention to the areas around the camshaft cover, cylinder head, oil filter and sump joint faces. Bear in mind that, over a period of time, some very slight seepage from these areas is to be expected - what you are really looking for is any indication of a serious leak **(see Haynes Hint overleaf)**. Should a leak be found, renew the offending gasket or oil seal by referring to the appropriate Chapters in this manual.
2 Also check the security and condition of all the engine-related pipes and hoses. Ensure that all cable-ties or securing clips are in place and in good condition. Clips which are broken or missing can lead to chafing of the hoses, pipes or wiring, which could cause more serious problems in the future.
3 Carefully check the radiator hoses and heater hoses along their entire length. Renew any hose which is cracked, swollen or deteriorated. Cracks will show up better if the hose is squeezed. Pay close attention to the hose clips that secure the hoses to the cooling system components. Hose clips can pinch and puncture hoses, resulting in cooling system leaks.
4 Inspect all the cooling system components (hoses, joint faces etc.) for leaks. A leak in the cooling system will usually show up as white-

A leak in the cooling system will usually show up as white or rust coloured deposits on the area adjoining the leak

or rust-coloured deposits on the area adjoining the leak. Where any problems of this nature are found on system components, renew the component or gasket with reference to Chapter 3.

5 Where applicable, inspect the automatic transmission fluid cooler hoses for leaks or deterioration.

6 With the vehicle raised, inspect the fuel tank and filler neck for punctures, cracks and other damage. The connection between the filler neck and tank is especially critical. Sometimes a rubber filler neck or connecting hose will leak due to loose retaining clamps or deteriorated rubber.

7 Carefully check all rubber hoses and metal fuel lines leading away from the fuel tank. Check for loose connections, deteriorated hoses, crimped lines, and other damage. Pay particular attention to the vent pipes and hoses, which often loop up around the filler neck and can become blocked or crimped. Follow the lines to the front of the vehicle, carefully inspecting them all the way. Renew damaged sections as necessary.

8 From within the engine compartment, check the security of all fuel hose attachments and pipe unions, and inspect the fuel hoses and vacuum hoses for kinks, chafing and deterioration.

9 Where applicable, check the condition of the power steering fluid hoses and pipes.

10 With the vehicle raised, check all brake hydraulic pipes and hoses for deterioration and damage **(see illustration)**.

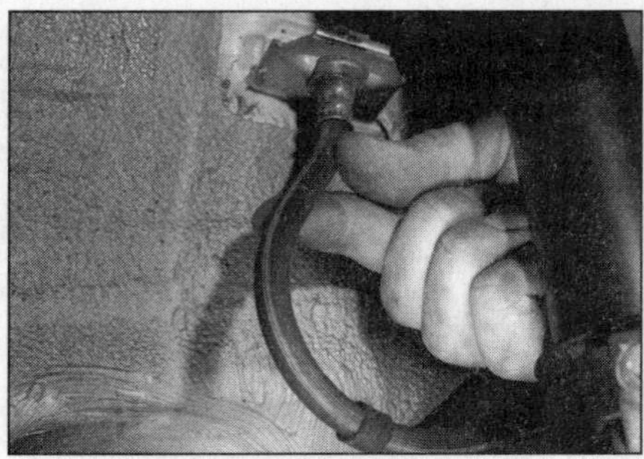

5.10 Checking the flexible brake hydraulic hoses

6 Spark plug renewal

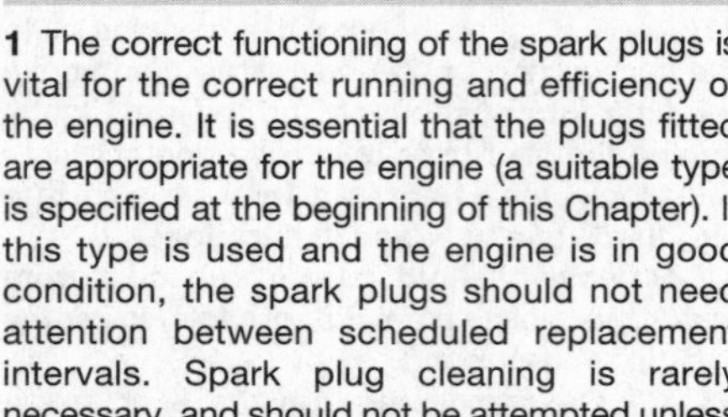

1 The correct functioning of the spark plugs is vital for the correct running and efficiency of the engine. It is essential that the plugs fitted are appropriate for the engine (a suitable type is specified at the beginning of this Chapter). If this type is used and the engine is in good condition, the spark plugs should not need attention between scheduled replacement intervals. Spark plug cleaning is rarely necessary, and should not be attempted unless specialised equipment is available, as damage can easily be caused to the firing ends.

2 On models up to 2000, if the marks on the original-equipment spark plug (HT) leads cannot be seen, mark the leads "1" to "4", to correspond to the cylinder the lead serves (No 1 cylinder is at the timing chain end of the engine). Pull the leads from the plugs by gripping the end fitting, not the lead, otherwise the lead connection may be fractured. Note that, as the spark plugs are deeply recessed, the HT lead end fittings are extended **(see illustration)**.

3 On models from 2000, each spark plug has an individual coil built into the plug cap. Disconnect the wiring plug from the coil, then undo the retaining bolt and remove the coil assembly from the spark plug **(see illustrations)**. For more information see Chapter 5B.

Warning: It is advisable to remove the dirt from the spark plug recesses using a clean brush, vacuum cleaner or compressed air before removing the plugs to prevent dirt dropping into the cylinders.

4 Unscrew the plugs using a spark plug spanner, suitable box spanner or a deep socket and extension bar **(see illustration)**. Keep the socket aligned with the spark plug - if it is forcibly moved to one side, the ceramic insulator may be broken off. As each plug is removed, examine it as follows.

5 Examination of the spark plugs will give a good indication of the condition of the engine. If the insulator nose of the spark plug is clean and white, with no deposits, this is indicative of a weak mixture or too hot a plug (a hot plug transfers heat away from the electrode slowly, a cold plug transfers heat away quickly).

6 If the tip and insulator nose are covered with hard black-looking deposits, then this is

6.2 Disconnecting the HT leads from the spark plugs

6.3a Disconnect the wiring plug . . .

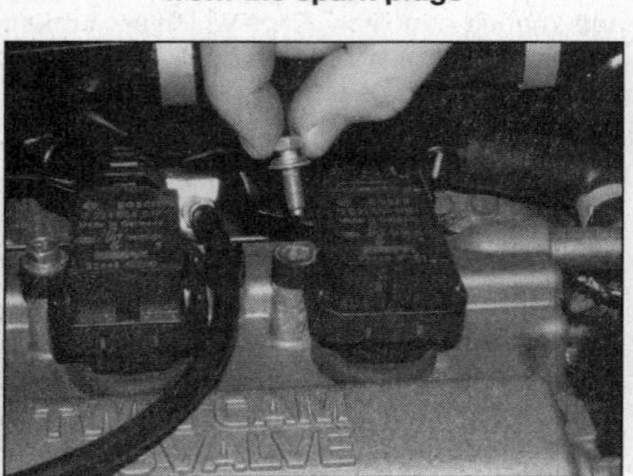

6.3b . . . undo the retaining bolt . . .

6.3c . . . and withdraw the ignition coil/plug cap

6.4 Removing the spark plugs

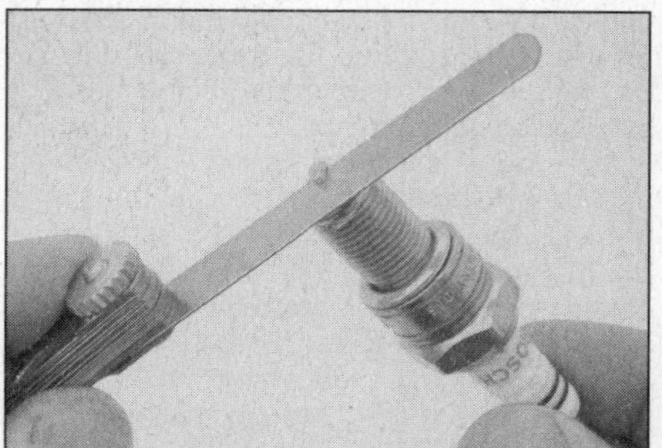

6.9a Measuring the spark plug gap with a feeler blade

6.9b Measuring the spark plug gap with a wire gauge

indicative that the mixture is too rich. Should the plug be black and oily, then it is likely that the engine is fairly worn, as well as the mixture being too rich.

7 If the insulator nose is covered with light tan to greyish-brown deposits, then the mixture is correct and it is likely that the engine is in good condition.

8 The spark plug electrode gap is of considerable importance as, if it is too large or too small, the size of the spark and its efficiency will be seriously impaired. The gap should be set to the value given in the *Specifications* at the beginning of this Chapter.

9 To set the gap, measure it with a feeler blade or wire gauge, and then bend the outer plug electrode until the correct gap is achieved **(see illustrations)**. The centre electrode should never be bent, as this may crack the insulator and cause plug failure, if nothing worse. If using feeler blades, the gap is correct when the appropriate-size blade is a firm sliding fit.

10 Special spark plug electrode gap adjusting tools are available from most motor accessory shops, or from some spark plug manufacturers.

11 Before fitting the spark plugs, check that the threaded connector sleeves are tight, and that the plug exterior surfaces and threads are clean **(see Haynes Hint)**.

12 Tighten the plug to the specified torque using the spark plug socket and a torque wrench. Refit the remaining spark plugs in the same manner **(see illustration)**.

13 On models up to 2000, connect the HT leads in their correct order, making sure they are located in the special support at the left-hand end of the camshaft cover **(see illustration)**.

14 On models from 2000, refit each of the individual coil/plug caps and refit the retaining bolts **(see illustration)**. Reconnect the wiring plug to each of the four coils, making sure the connections are secure. For more information see Chapter 5B.

7 Clutch cable and pedal check

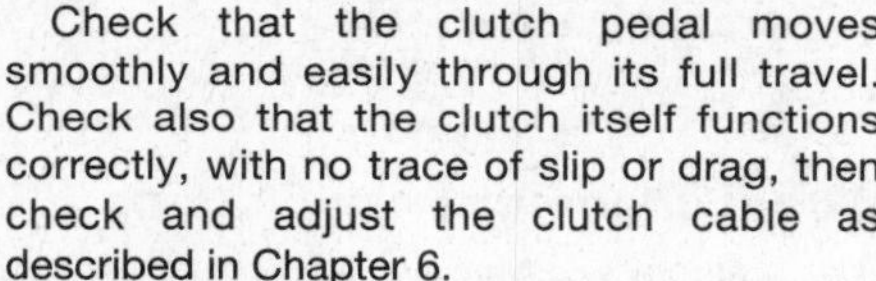

Check that the clutch pedal moves smoothly and easily through its full travel. Check also that the clutch itself functions correctly, with no trace of slip or drag, then check and adjust the clutch cable as described in Chapter 6.

If excessive effort is required to operate the clutch, check first that the cable is correctly routed and undamaged, then remove the pedal to ensure that its pivot is properly greased. Refer to Chapter 6 for further information.

8 Manual transmission oil level check

1 Park the car on a level surface. The oil level must be checked before the car is driven, or at least 5 minutes after the engine has been switched off. If the oil is checked immediately after driving the car, some of the oil will remain distributed around the transmission components, resulting in an inaccurate level reading. To improve access, position the car over an inspection pit, or raise the car off the ground and position it on axle stands (see "*Jacking and vehicle support*"), making sure the vehicle remains level to the ground.

It is very often difficult to insert spark plugs into their holes without cross-threading them. To avoid this possibility, fit a short length of 5/16 inch internal diameter rubber hose over the end of the spark plug. The flexible hose acts as a universal joint to help align the plug with the plug hole. Should the plug begin to cross-thread, the hose will slip on the spark plug, preventing thread damage to the aluminium cylinder head

Early models

2 Remove the speedometer drive and pinion assembly from the transmission as described in Chapter 7A.

3 Using a length of wire or a small steel rule, check the measurement from the drive pinion contact surface on the transmission to the oil surface and compare with the following table.

	RS5F41A	All others
Oil level	28 to 38 mm	45 to 54 mm

4 If necessary add the specified grade of oil to correct the oil level, then refit the speedometer drive and pinion with reference to Chapter 7A.

Later models

5 Wipe clean the area around the filler/level plug, which is on the front face of the

6.12 Tightening the spark plugs with a torque wrench

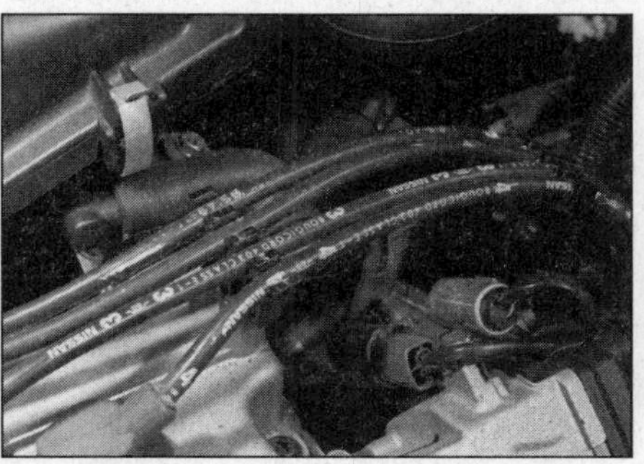

6.13 HT lead support on the left-hand end of the camshaft cover

6.14 Make sure the retaining bolt is secure

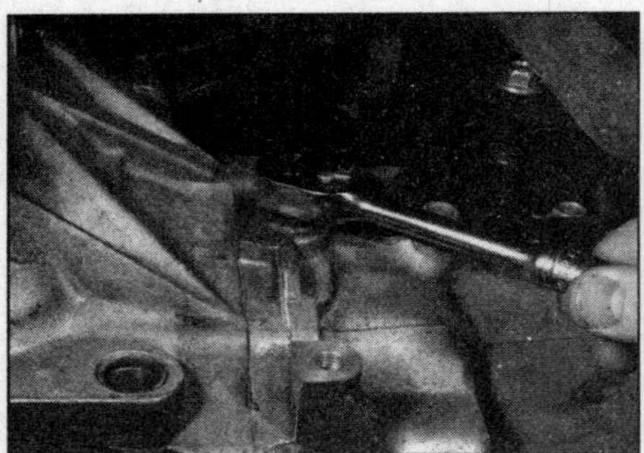

8.5 Unscrewing the manual transmission filler/level plug

transmission. Unscrew the plug and clean it **(see illustration)**.

6 The oil level should reach the lower edge of the filler/level hole. A certain amount of oil will have gathered behind the filler/level plug and will trickle out when it is removed; this does **not** necessarily indicate that the level is correct. To ensure that a true level is established, wait until the initial trickle has stopped, then add oil as necessary until a trickle of new oil can be seen emerging. The level will be correct when the flow ceases; use only good-quality oil of the specified type.

7 On completion refit the filler/level plug and tighten to the specified torque.

9 Driveshaft gaiter check

With the vehicle raised and securely supported on stands, turn the steering onto full lock, then slowly rotate the roadwheel. Inspect the condition of the outer constant velocity (CV) joint rubber gaiters, squeezing the gaiters to open out the folds **(see illustration)**. Check for signs of cracking, splits or deterioration of the rubber, which may allow the grease to escape, and lead to water and grit entry into the joint. Also check the security and condition of the retaining clips. Repeat these checks on the inner CV joints. If any damage or deterioration is found, the gaiters should be renewed (see Chapter 8).

At the same time, check the general condition of the CV joints themselves by first holding the driveshaft and attempting to rotate the wheel. Repeat this check by holding the inner joint and attempting to rotate the driveshaft. Any appreciable movement indicates wear in the joints, wear in the driveshaft splines, or a loose driveshaft retaining nut.

9.1 Checking the condition of a driveshaft gaiter

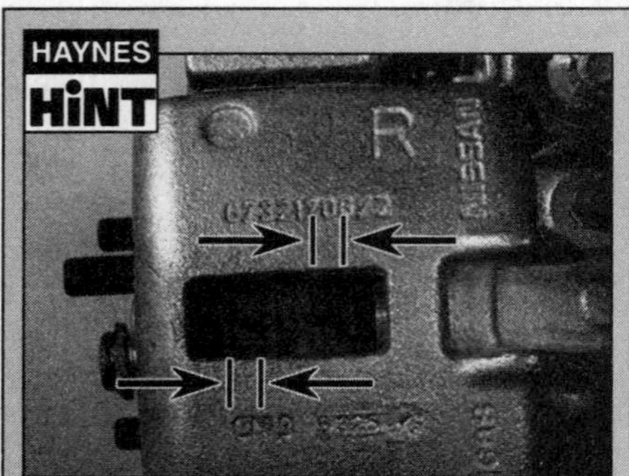

For a quick check, the thickness of the friction material on each brake pad can be measured through the aperture in the caliper body

10 Wheel alignment, rotation and balance check

Wheel alignment - definitions

1 A vehicle's steering and suspension geometry is defined in four basic settings - all angles are expressed in degrees (toe settings are also expressed as a measurement); the steering axis is defined as an imaginary line drawn through the axis of the suspension strut, extended where necessary to contact the ground.

2 Camber is the angle between each roadwheel and a vertical line drawn through its centre and tyre contact patch, when viewed from the front or rear of the car. "Positive" camber is when the roadwheels are tilted outwards from the vertical at the top; "negative" camber is when they are tilted inwards.

3 Camber is not adjustable, and is given for reference only; while it can be checked using a camber checking gauge, if the figure obtained is significantly different from that specified, the vehicle must be taken for careful checking by a professional, as the fault can only be caused by wear or damage to the body or suspension components.

4 Castor is the angle between the steering axis and a vertical line drawn through each roadwheel centre and tyre contact patch, when viewed from the side of the car. "Positive" castor is when the steering axis is tilted so that it contacts the ground ahead of the vertical; "negative" castor is when it contacts the ground behind the vertical.

5 Castor is not adjustable, and is given for reference only; while it can be checked using a castor checking gauge, if the figure obtained is significantly different from that specified, the vehicle must be taken for careful checking by a professional, as the fault can only be caused by wear or damage to the body or suspension components.

6 Steering axis inclination/SAI - also known as **kingpin inclination/KPI** - is the angle between the steering axis and a vertical line drawn through each roadwheel centre and tyre contact patch, when viewed from the front or rear of the car. SAI/KPI is not adjustable.

7 Toe is the difference, viewed from above, between lines drawn through the roadwheel centres and the car's centre-line. "Toe-in" is when the roadwheels point inwards, towards each other at the front, while "toe-out" is when they splay outwards from each other at the front.

8 The front wheel toe setting is adjusted by screwing the track-rod ends in or out of their track-rods, to alter the effective length of the track-rod assemblies.

Wheel alignment - checking

9 Due to the special measuring equipment necessary to check the wheel alignment, and the skill required to use it properly, the checking and adjustment of these settings is best left to a NISSAN dealer or similar expert. Note that most tyre-fitting shops now possess sophisticated checking equipment.

Rotation

10 To ensure even tyre wear, the manufacturer recommends that the tyres are rotated (ie roadwheels removed and refitted to a different hub) periodically. The most sensible option for this is to rotate the tyres from front to rear, as the front tyres will wear faster.

11 Provided that tyre wear is monitored regularly using a depth gauge, this operation is not essential. If it were completely successful, it would result in the owner replacing all four tyres at once, which may not be desirable.

Wheel balance

12 Accurate wheel balancing requires access to specialised test equipment and as such should be entrusted to a suitably equipped NISSAN dealer or a tyre specialist.

11 Brake pad check

Front brake pads

1 Firmly apply the handbrake, then jack up the front of the car and support it securely on axle stands (see "*Jacking and vehicle support*"). Remove the front roadwheels.

2 For a comprehensive check, the brake pads should be removed and cleaned. The operation of the caliper can then also be checked, and the condition of the brake disc itself can be fully examined on both sides. Refer to Chapter 9 for further information **(see Haynes Hint)**.

3 If any pad's friction material is worn to the specified thickness or less, *all four pads must be renewed as a set.*

Rear brake pads (where fitted)

4 Chock the front wheels, then jack up the rear of the vehicle and support it on axle stands (see "*Jacking and vehicle support*"). Remove the rear roadwheels.

5 For a quick check, the thickness of friction material remaining on each brake pad can be measured through the aperture in the top of the caliper body. If any pad's friction material is worn to the specified thickness or less, *all four pads must be renewed as a set.*

6 For a comprehensive check, the brake pads should be removed and cleaned. This will permit the operation of the caliper to be checked, and the condition of the brake disc itself to be fully examined on both sides. Refer to Chapter 9 for further information.

12 Rear brake shoe check

1 Chock the front wheels, then jack up the rear of the vehicle, and support it securely on axle stands (see "*Jacking and vehicle support*").

2 For a quick check, the thickness of friction material remaining on one of the brake shoes can be observed through the hole in the brake backplate which is exposed by prising out the sealing grommet **(see illustration)**. If a rod of the same diameter as the specified minimum friction material thickness is placed against the shoe friction material, the amount of wear can be assessed. A torch or inspection light will probably be required. If the friction material on any shoe is worn down to the specified minimum thickness or less, all four shoes must be renewed as a set.

3 For a comprehensive check, the brake drum should be removed and cleaned. This will allow the wheel cylinders to be checked, and the condition of the brake drum itself to be fully examined (see Chapter 9).

13 Seat belt check

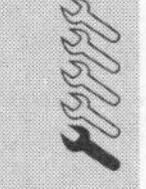

1 All vehicles are fitted with three point, inertia reel front and outer rear seat belts, with a two point lap belt for the centre rear seat.

2 Inspect the belts for signs of fraying or other damage. Also check the operation of the buckles and retractor mechanisms, and ensure that all mounting bolts are securely tightened. Note that the bolts are shouldered so that the belt anchor points are free to rotate **(see illustration)**.

3 If there is any sign of damage, or any doubt about the condition of a belt, it must be renewed. If the vehicle has been involved in a collision, any belts in use at the time should be renewed as a matter of course, and all other belts should be checked carefully.

4 Use only warm water and non-detergent soap when cleaning the belt webbing. Never use chemicals that could attack the belt fabric and reduce its effectiveness. Keep the belts fully extended until they have dried - do not apply heat to accelerate drying.

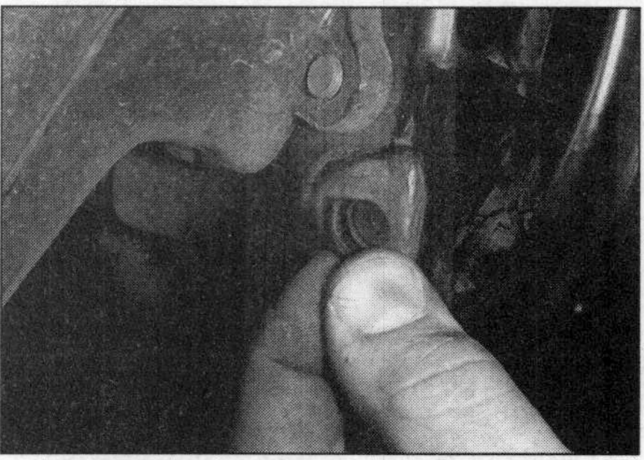

12.2 Removing the rubber grommet from the rear brake backplate

14 Headlight beam adjustment check

1 Accurate adjustment of the headlight beam is only possible using optical beam-setting equipment, and this work should therefore be carried out by a NISSAN dealer or suitably-equipped workshop.

2 For information, the adjustment screws are located on the rear of the headlight units. The outer screw (nearest the vehicle wing) is used to adjust the horizontal alignment, and the inner screw (located on the rear of the aim adjustment motor on models with electric aim adjustment) is used to adjust the vertical alignment. Note that on models with electric aim adjustment, the adjustment switch must be set to position "0" when carrying out beam alignment.

3 Certain models are equipped with a headlight beam adjustment switch, located on the centre console, which allows the aim of the headlights to be adjusted to compensate for the varying loads carried in the vehicle. The switch should be positioned according to the load being carried in the vehicle - eg; position "0" for driver with no passengers or luggage; up to position "3" for maximum load, or towing.

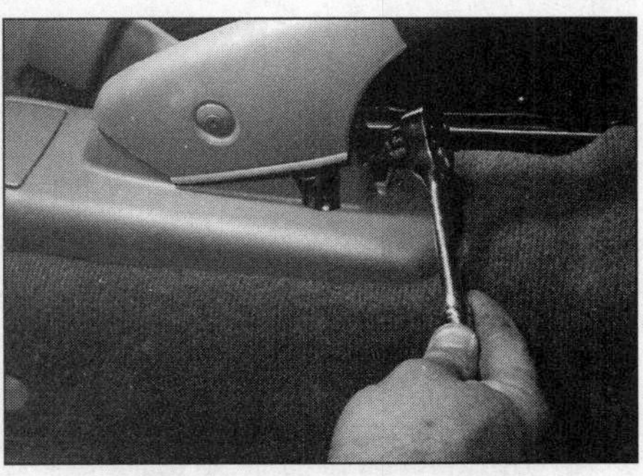

15.6 Adjusting the handbrake cable

13.2 Check the security of the seat belt mountings

15 Handbrake check and adjustment

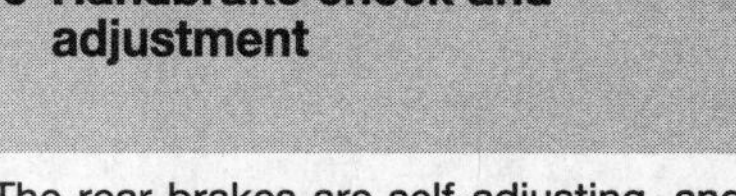

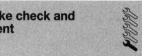

1 The rear brakes are self-adjusting, and the only adjustment required is to the handbrake operating cables.

2 The handbrake should be capable of holding the parked vehicle stationary, even on steep slopes, when applied with moderate force. The mechanism should be firm and positive in feel with no trace of stiffness, and the mechanism should release immediately the handbrake lever is released. If necessary, check the handbrake with reference to Chapter 9.

3 Raise the rear wheels just clear of the ground, using a trolley jack (see *"Jacking and vehicle support"*).

4 Apply normal moderate pressure to operate the handbrake lever, and count the number of clicks necessary to bring the lever to the fully-applied position. The number of clicks should be as given in the *Specifications*. If adjustment is necessary, proceed as follows.

5 Lift the handbrake lever just sufficient to insert a socket and extension bar beneath the lever and onto the adjustment nut. Refer to Chapter 9 if necessary to confirm the position of the adjustment nut. It is located under the lever on the threaded end of the front cable.

6 Turn the adjustment nut as required, then re-check the adjustment as described in paragraph 4 **(see illustration)**.

7 With the handbrake fully released, the rear wheels must rotate freely.

8 On completion lower the vehicle to the ground.

16 Road test

Instruments and electrical equipment

1 Check the operation of all instruments and electrical equipment.

2 Make sure that all instruments read correctly, and switch on all electrical equipment in turn, to check that it functions properly.

Steering and suspension

3 Check for any abnormalities in the steering, suspension, handling or road "feel".
4 Drive the vehicle, and check that there are no unusual vibrations or noises.
5 Check that the steering feels positive, with no excessive "sloppiness", or roughness, and check for any suspension noises when cornering and driving over bumps.

Drivetrain

6 Check the performance of the engine, clutch (where applicable), gearbox/transmission and driveshafts.
7 Listen for any unusual noises from the engine, clutch and gearbox/transmission.
8 Make sure that the engine runs smoothly when idling, and that there is no hesitation when accelerating.
9 Check that, where applicable, the clutch action is smooth and progressive, that the drive is taken up smoothly, and that the pedal travel is not excessive. Also listen for any noises when the clutch pedal is depressed.
10 On manual gearbox models, check that all gears can be engaged smoothly without noise, and that the gear lever action is not abnormally vague or "notchy".
11 On automatic transmission models, make sure that all gearchanges occur smoothly, without snatching, and without an increase in engine speed between changes. Check that all the gear positions can be selected with the vehicle at rest. If any problems are found, they should be referred to a NISSAN dealer.
12 Listen for a metallic clicking sound from the front of the vehicle, as the vehicle is driven slowly in a circle with the steering on full-lock. Carry out this check in both directions. If a clicking noise is heard, this indicates wear in a driveshaft joint, in which case the joint should be renewed.

Braking system

13 Make sure that the vehicle does not pull to one side when braking, and that the wheels do not lock prematurely when braking hard.
14 Check that there is no vibration through the steering when braking.
15 Check that the handbrake operates correctly without excessive movement of the lever, and that it holds the vehicle stationary on a slope.
16 Test the operation of the brake servo unit as follows. With the engine off, depress the footbrake four or five times to exhaust the vacuum. Hold the brake pedal depressed, then start the engine. As the engine starts, there should be a noticeable "give" in the brake pedal as vacuum builds up. Allow the engine to run for at least two minutes, and then switch it off. If the brake pedal is depressed now, it should be possible to detect a hiss from the servo as the pedal is depressed. After about four or five applications, no further hissing should be heard, and the pedal should feel considerably harder.

Every 12 months, regardless of mileage

17 Body corrosion check

1 Jack up the front and rear of the vehicle and support on axle stands (see *"Jacking and vehicle support"*).
2 Working from the front to the rear of the vehicle, check the condition of the entire vehicle structure for signs of corrosion, especially near the load-bearing areas. These include chassis box sections, side sills, cross-members, pillars, and all suspension, steering, braking system and seat belt mountings and anchorages.
3 Check that the anti-corrosion sealing materials on the underbody are intact. Where necessary re-apply the material.
4 In the engine compartment, examine the front suspension upper mountings and inner wing panels, also the lower areas of the front valance for signs of corrosion.
5 Inside the vehicle, lift the carpets where possible and check the floor and inner surfaces of the sills for signs of corrosion.
6 Check the drain holes in the doors for blockages and clear by probing with wire.
7 Where body corrosion is evident, consult a NISSAN dealer to have it repaired.

Every 27 000 miles or 2 years

18 Automatic transmission fluid renewal

1 Run the engine and transmission to normal operating temperature by driving the vehicle for 10 minutes. Switch off the engine.
2 Chock the rear wheels, then jack up the front of the vehicle and support it securely on axle stands (refer to *"Jacking and vehicle support"*).
3 Position a suitable container beneath the transmission, then unscrew the drain plug and allow the fluid to drain for 10 minutes. Note approximately the quantity of fluid drained, and also note how dirty the fluid is.

Caution: The transmission fluid will be hot! Wear protective gloves to prevent personal injury!

4 Clean the drain plug and transmission sump, then refit the plug and tighten to the specified torque.
5 Remove the fluid level dipstick (see *"Weekly Checks"*), then use a funnel in the dipstick tube to fill the transmission with new fluid of the specified type. The quantity poured in should be the same amount as drained in paragraph 3.
6 Run the engine at idle speed for 5 minutes, then select position "D" and accelerate the engine slowly until the speedometer reads 30 mph. Release the accelerator pedal and repeat this procedure two more times.

Caution: Make sure that the vehicle is adequately supported on the axle stands.

7 Stop the engine then check the fluid level (see *"Weekly Checks")*. Top-up if necessary.
8 If the fluid still appears dirty after this procedure, the manufacturers recommend that it is changed again before using the vehicle on the road.

19 Automatic transmission magnetic clutch carbon brushes check

Check and if necessary renew the electromagnetic clutch brushes as described in Chapter 7B, Section 3.

Every 36 000 miles or 2 years

20 Auxiliary drivebelt(s) check and renewal

1 Two auxiliary drivebelts are fitted, one to drive the water pump and (where fitted) the power steering pump, and the other to drive the alternator and (where fitted) the air conditioning compressor. Both drivebelts are driven by the crankshaft pulley, and the alternator drivebelt is the outer one located on the right-hand side of the engine.

Checking the auxiliary drivebelt condition

2 Apply the handbrake, then jack up the front of the car and support it on axle stands (see "*Jacking and vehicle support*"). Remove the right-hand front roadwheel.

3 From underneath the front of the car, undo the retaining screws and remove the plastic wheel arch liners from under the wing to gain access to the crankshaft pulley. If necessary, also undo the retaining screws and remove the engine undershield to improve access.

4 Using a socket and extension bar fitted to the crankshaft pulley bolt, rotate the crankshaft so that the entire length of the drivebelts can be examined. Examine the drivebelts for cracks, splitting, fraying or damage. Check also for signs of glazing (shiny patches) and for separation of the belt plies. Renew the belt if worn or damaged.

5 If the condition of the belt is satisfactory, check the drivebelt tension as described below under the relevant sub-heading.

Alternator drivebelt (without idler) - removal, refitting and tensioning

Removal

6 If not already done, proceed as described in paragraphs 2 and 3.

7 Disconnect the battery negative lead.

8 Slacken both the alternator upper and lower mounting nuts/bolts **(see illustration)**.

9 Back off the adjuster bolt to relieve the tension in the drivebelt, then slip the drivebelt from the pulleys **(see illustrations)**.

Refitting

10 Fit the belt around the pulleys, ensuring that the belt is of the correct type if it is being renewed, and take up the slack in the belt by tightening the adjuster bolt. Tension the drivebelt as follows.

Tensioning

11 If not already done, proceed as described in paragraphs 2 and 3.

12 Correct tensioning of the drivebelt will ensure that it has a long life. Beware, however, of overtightening, as this can cause wear in the alternator bearings.

13 The belt tension is checked at the mid-point between the pulleys on the upper belt run. Apply thumb pressure by pressing down on the drivebelt, and check that it deflects by the amount given in the *Specifications*.

14 To adjust, with the upper mounting nut/bolt just holding the alternator firm, and the lower mounting nut/bolt loosened, turn the adjuster bolt until the correct tension is achieved.

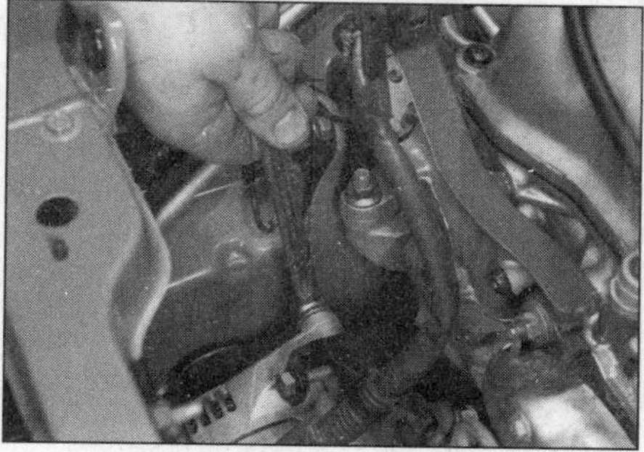

20.8 Loosen the alternator mounting nuts/bolts . . .

Rotate the crankshaft a couple of times, recheck the tension, then securely tighten both the alternator mounting nuts/bolts.

15 Refit the liners and undershield, then refit the roadwheel and lower the car to the ground.

Alternator drivebelt (with fixed idler or A/C compressor)

Removal

16 If not already done, proceed as described in paragraphs 2 and 3.

17 Slacken the nut securing the tensioning pulley assembly to the engine.

18 Turn the adjuster bolt to move the tensioner pulley away from the drivebelt until there is sufficient slack for the drivebelt to be removed from the pulleys.

Refitting

19 Fit the belt around the pulleys, ensuring that the belt is of the correct type if it is being renewed, and take up the slack in the belt by tightening the adjuster bolt.

20 Tension the drivebelt as described in the following paragraphs.

Tensioning

21 If not already done, proceed as described in paragraphs 2 and 3.

22 Correct tensioning of the drivebelt will ensure that it has a long life. Beware, however, of overtightening, as this can cause wear in the water pump bearings.

23 The belt tension is checked at the mid-point between the alternator and crankshaft pulleys at the front of the engine. Apply thumb pressure by pressing on the drivebelt, and check that it deflects by the amount given in the *Specifications*.

24 To adjust the tension, with the tensioner pulley assembly retaining nut slackened, rotate the adjuster bolt until the correct tension is achieved. Once the belt is correctly tensioned, rotate the crankshaft a couple of times and recheck the tension.

25 When the belt is correctly tensioned, tighten the tensioner pulley assembly retaining nut to the specified torque setting.

26 Refit the liners and undershield, then refit the roadwheel and lower the car to the ground.

Water pump drivebelt - removal, refitting and tensioning

Removal

27 Remove the alternator drivebelt as described previously in this Section.

28 Slacken the nut securing the tensioning pulley to the engine **(see illustration)**.

29 Turn the adjuster bolt to move the tensioner pulley away from the drivebelt until there is sufficient slack for the drivebelt to be removed from the pulleys.

Refitting

30 Fit the belt around the pulleys, ensuring that the belt is of the correct type if it is being renewed, and take up the slack in the belt by tightening the adjuster bolt.

31 Tension the drivebelt as described in the following paragraphs.

Tensioning

32 If not already done, proceed as described in paragraphs 2 and 3.

33 Correct tensioning of the drivebelt will ensure that it has a long life. Beware, however, of overtightening, as this can cause wear in the water pump bearings.

34 The belt tension is checked at the mid-point between the water pump and power steering pump pulleys (power steering models) or between the water pump and tensioner pulleys (non-power steering models). Apply thumb pressure by pressing on the drivebelt, and check that it deflects by the amount given in the *Specifications*.

35 To adjust the tension, with the tensioner pulley assembly retaining nut slackened, rotate the adjuster bolt until the correct tension is achieved. Once the belt is correctly

20.9a . . . back off the adjuster bolt . . .

20.9b . . . then slip the belt off the pulleys

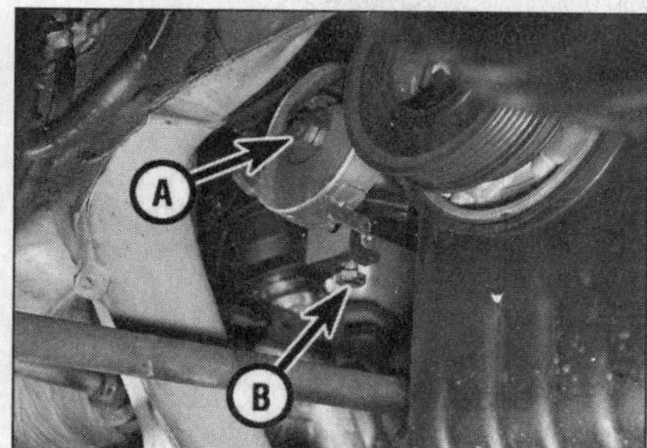

20.28 Drivebelt idler/tensioner securing bolt (A) and adjuster bolt (B)

21.1a Release the clips . . .

21.1b . . . lift off the lid . . .

21.2 . . . and lift out the element

tensioned, rotate the crankshaft a couple of times and recheck the tension.

36 When the belt is correctly tensioned, tighten the tensioner pulley assembly retaining nut to the specified torque setting.

37 Refit the liners and undershield, then refit the roadwheel and lower the car to the ground.

21 Air filter element renewal

1 Release the air cleaner lid retaining clips, then lift off the lid and position it clear of the housing **(see illustrations)**.

2 Note how the element is located in the air cleaner body, then lift it out **(see illustration)**.

3 Wipe the inside of the air cleaner body and lid with a clean cloth to remove all traces of dirt and debris.

4 Install the new filter element, ensuring that it is the right way up and is correctly seated in the housing.

5 Refit the air cleaner lid, and secure it in position with its retaining clips.

22 Lambda/oxygen sensor check

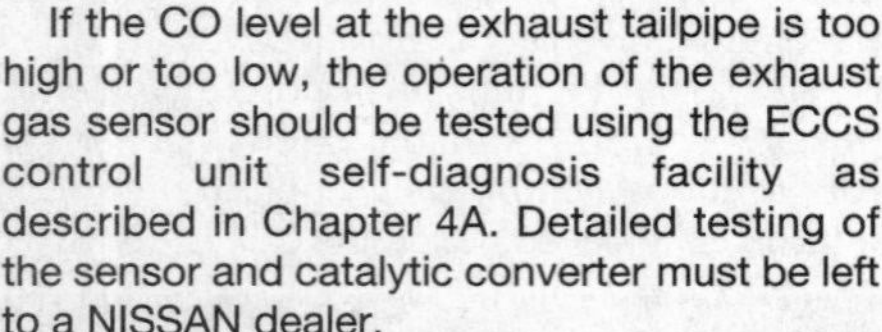

If the CO level at the exhaust tailpipe is too high or too low, the operation of the exhaust gas sensor should be tested using the ECCS control unit self-diagnosis facility as described in Chapter 4A. Detailed testing of the sensor and catalytic converter must be left to a NISSAN dealer.

If the tests indicate a fault in the catalytic converter, the converter should be renewed as described in Chapter 4A.

23 PCV filter renewal

1 Check the crankcase emissions control system and PCV valve as described in Chapter 4B.

2 Release the air cleaner lid retaining clips, then lift off the lid.

3 Lift the filter element from the air cleaner body to gain access to the PCV filter.

4 Remove the filter from the body and wipe clean the surrounding area.

5 Fit a new PCV filter to the housing, and refit the air cleaner filter element **(see illustration)**.

6 Seat the air cleaner lid on the housing, and secure it in position with the retaining clips.

24 Evaporative loss system check

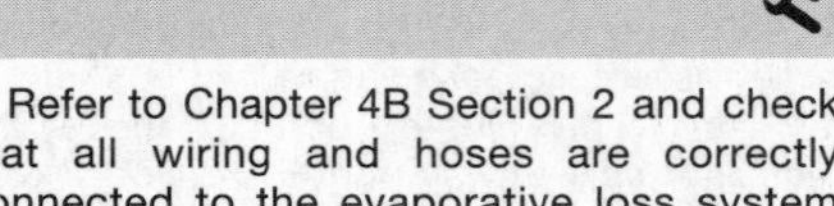

Refer to Chapter 4B Section 2 and check that all wiring and hoses are correctly connected to the evaporative loss system components.

25 Brake fluid renewal

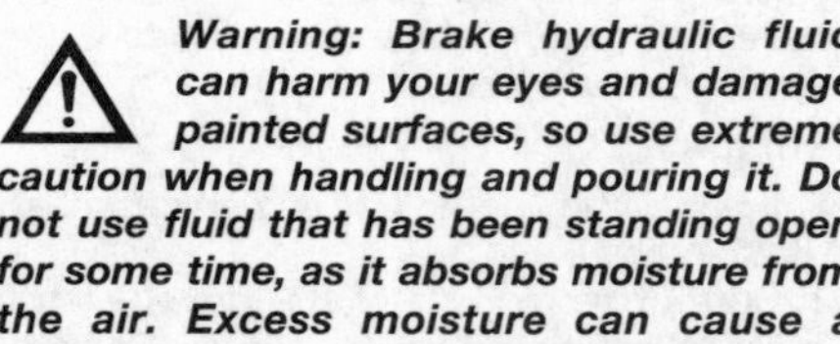

Warning: Brake hydraulic fluid can harm your eyes and damage painted surfaces, so use extreme caution when handling and pouring it. Do not use fluid that has been standing open for some time, as it absorbs moisture from the air. Excess moisture can cause a dangerous loss of braking effectiveness.

1 The procedure is similar to that for the bleeding of the hydraulic system as described in Chapter 9, except that the brake fluid reservoir should be emptied by siphoning, using a clean poultry baster or similar before starting, and allowance should be made for the old fluid to be expelled when bleeding a section of the circuit.

2 Working as described in Chapter 9, open the first bleed screw in the sequence, and pump the brake pedal gently until nearly all the old fluid has been emptied from the master cylinder reservoir.

3 Top-up to the "MAX" level with new fluid, and continue pumping until only the new fluid remains in the reservoir, and new fluid can be seen emerging from the bleed screw. Tighten the screw, and top the reservoir level up to the "MAX" level line.

Old hydraulic fluid is usually much darker in colour than the new, making it easy to distinguish the two.

4 Work through all the remaining bleed screws in the sequence until new fluid can be seen at all of them. Be careful to keep the master cylinder reservoir topped-up to above the "MIN" level at all times, or air may enter the system and greatly increase the length of the task.

5 When the operation is complete, check that all bleed screws are securely tightened, and that their dust caps are refitted. Wash off all traces of spilt fluid, and recheck the master cylinder reservoir fluid level.

6 Check the operation of the brakes before taking the car on the road.

23.5 Remove the PCV filter from the housing

27.4 Check for wear in the hub bearings by grasping the wheel and trying to rock it

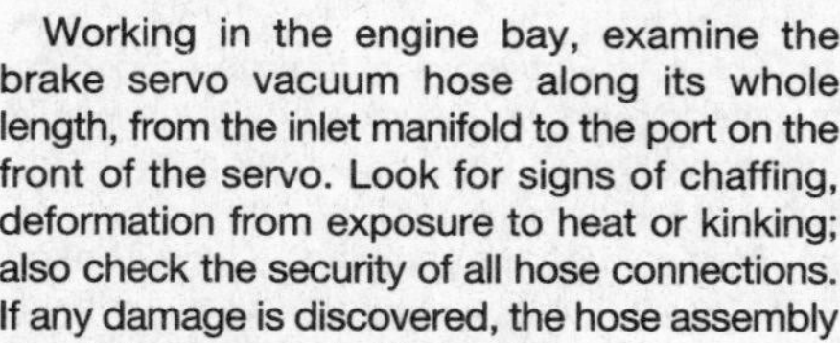

26 Brake vacuum servo unit check

Working in the engine bay, examine the brake servo vacuum hose along its whole length, from the inlet manifold to the port on the front of the servo. Look for signs of chaffing, deformation from exposure to heat or kinking; also check the security of all hose connections. If any damage is discovered, the hose assembly should be renewed without delay.

If required, the non-return valve may be disconnected and checked - refer to Chapter 9 for details.

27 Steering and suspension check

Front suspension and steering check

1 Raise the front of the vehicle, and securely support it on axle stands (see *"Jacking and vehicle support"*).

2 Visually inspect the balljoint dust covers and the steering rack-and-pinion gaiters for splits, chafing or deterioration. Any wear of these components will cause loss of lubricant, together with dirt and water entry, resulting in rapid deterioration of the balljoints or steering gear.

3 On vehicles with power steering, check the fluid hoses for chafing or deterioration, and the pipe and hose unions for fluid leaks. Also check for signs of fluid leakage under pressure from the steering gear rubber gaiters, which would indicate failed fluid seals within the steering gear.

4 Grasp the roadwheel at the 12 o'clock and 6 o'clock positions, and try to rock it **(see illustration)**. Very slight free play may be felt, but if the movement is appreciable, further investigation is necessary to determine the source. Continue rocking the wheel while an assistant depresses the footbrake. If the movement is now eliminated or significantly reduced, it is likely that the hub bearings are at fault. If the free play is still evident with the footbrake depressed, then there is wear in the suspension joints or mountings.

5 Now grasp the wheel at the 9 o'clock and 3 o'clock positions, and try to rock it as before. Any movement felt now may again be caused by wear in the hub bearings or the steering track-rod balljoints. If the inner or outer balljoint is worn, the visual movement will be obvious.

6 Using a large screwdriver or flat bar, check for wear in the suspension mounting bushes by levering between the relevant suspension component and its attachment point. Some movement is to be expected as the mountings are made of rubber, but excessive wear should be obvious. Also check the condition of any visible rubber bushes, looking for splits, cracks or contamination of the rubber.

7 With the car standing on its wheels, have an assistant turn the steering wheel back and forth about an eighth of a turn each way. There should be very little, if any, lost movement between the steering wheel and roadwheels. If this is not the case, closely observe the joints and mountings previously described, but in addition, check the steering column universal joints for wear, and the rack-and-pinion steering gear itself.

Rear suspension check

8 Chock the front wheels, then jack up the rear of the vehicle and support on axle stands (see *"Jacking and vehicle support"*).

9 Working as described previously for the front suspension, check the rear hub bearings, the suspension bushes and the shock absorber mountings for wear.

Suspension strut/ shock absorber check

10 Check for any signs of fluid leakage around the suspension strut/shock absorber body, or from the rubber gaiter around the piston rod. Should any fluid be noticed, the suspension strut/shock absorber is defective internally, and should be renewed. **Note:** *Suspension struts/shock absorbers should always be renewed in pairs on the same axle.*

11 The efficiency of the suspension strut/shock absorber may be checked by bouncing the vehicle at each corner. Generally speaking, the body will return to its normal position and stop after being depressed. If it rises and returns on a rebound, the suspension strut/shock absorber is probably suspect. Examine also the suspension strut/shock absorber upper and lower mountings for any signs of wear.

28 Exhaust system check

1 With the engine cold (at least an hour after the vehicle has been driven), check the complete exhaust system from the engine to the end of the tailpipe. The exhaust system is most easily checked with the vehicle raised on a hoist, or suitably supported on axle stands (see *"Jacking and vehicle support"*), so that the exhaust components are readily visible and accessible.

2 Check the exhaust pipes and connections for evidence of leaks, severe corrosion and damage. Make sure that all brackets and mountings are in good condition, and that all relevant nuts and bolts are tight. Leakage at any of the joints or in other parts of the system will usually show up as a black sooty stain in the vicinity of the leak.

3 Rattles and other noises can often be traced to the exhaust system, especially the brackets and mountings. Try to move the pipes and silencers. If the components are able to come into contact with the body or suspension parts, secure the system with new mountings. Otherwise separate the joints (if possible) and twist the pipes as necessary to provide additional clearance.

29 Coolant renewal

Cooling system draining

Warning: Wait until the engine is cold before starting work. Do not allow antifreeze to come in contact with your skin, or with the painted surfaces of the vehicle. Rinse off spills immediately with plenty of water. Never leave antifreeze lying around in an open container, or in a puddle in the driveway or on the garage floor. Children and pets are attracted by its sweet smell, but antifreeze can be fatal if ingested.

1 With the engine completely cold, cover the radiator filler cap with a wad of rag, and slowly turn the cap anti-clockwise to relieve the pressure in the cooling system (a hissing sound will normally be heard). Wait until any pressure remaining in the system is released, then continue to turn the cap until it can be removed. Also remove the cap from the cooling system expansion tank.

2 Inside the car, turn the heater temperature control knob fully in the hot direction.

3 Where necessary, remove the engine undershield, then position a suitable container beneath the radiator bottom hose connection. Release the retaining clip and ease the hose from the radiator stub. If the hose joint has not been disturbed for some time, it will be necessary to gently manipulate the hose to break the joint. Do not use excessive force, or the radiator stub could be damaged. Allow the coolant to drain into the container.

4 If necessary, remove the expansion tank, drain out the coolant, then refit the tank ensuring that the hose is securely reconnected.

5 If required, re-position the container beneath the cylinder block drain plug. Unscrew the drain plug and allow the coolant to drain, then refit and tighten the plug.

6 If the coolant has been drained for a reason other than renewal, then provided it is clean and less than two years old, it can be re-used.

Cooling system flushing

7 If coolant renewal has been neglected, or if the antifreeze mixture has become diluted, then in time, the cooling system may gradually lose efficiency, as the coolant passages become restricted due to rust, scale deposits, and other sediment. The cooling system efficiency can be restored by flushing the system clean.

8 The radiator should be flushed independently of the engine, to avoid unnecessary contamination.

Radiator flushing

9 To flush the radiator disconnect the top and bottom hoses and expansion tank hose.

10 Insert a garden hose into the radiator top inlet. Direct a flow of clean water through the radiator, and continue flushing until clean water emerges from the radiator bottom outlet.

11 If after a reasonable period, the water still does not run clear, the radiator can be flushed with a good proprietary cooling system cleaning agent. It is important that the manufacturer's instructions are followed carefully. If the contamination is particularly bad, remove the radiator then insert the hose in the radiator bottom outlet, and reverse-flush the radiator.

Engine flushing

12 To flush the engine, remove the thermostat as described in Chapter 3 then temporarily refit the thermostat cover.

13 With the top and bottom hoses disconnected from the radiator, insert a garden hose into the radiator top hose. Direct a clean flow of water through the engine, and continue flushing until clean water emerges from the radiator bottom hose.

14 On completion of flushing, refit the thermostat and reconnect the hoses with reference to Chapter 3.

Cooling system filling

15 Before attempting to fill the cooling system, reconnect all hoses and make sure that all clips are in good condition and tight. Note that an antifreeze mixture must be used all year round, to prevent corrosion of the engine components (see following sub-Section).

16 Fill the system slowly through the radiator filler until the level reaches the bottom of the filler neck. While filling, compress the radiator hoses frequently to purge air locks from the system.

17 Fill the expansion tank with coolant to the "MAX" level mark.

18 Where applicable, make sure that the air conditioning compressor is switched off.

19 With the radiator cap still removed, start the engine and allow it to idle until heat can be felt through the radiator top hose. Accelerate the engine briefly several times, then switch off the ignition and allow the engine to cool (preferably for an hour).

20 Top-up the level in the radiator to the filler neck and refit the radiator cap. Top-up the level in the expansion tank to the "MAX" mark.

21 Start the engine and run it at 3000 rpm for half a minute. Stop the engine then remove the radiator cap and top-up the level if necessary. Refit the cap.

22 Check for leaks, particularly around disturbed components.

Antifreeze mixture

23 The antifreeze should always be renewed at the specified intervals. This is necessary not only to maintain the antifreeze properties, but also to prevent corrosion which would otherwise occur as the corrosion inhibitors become progressively less effective.

24 Always use an ethylene-glycol based antifreeze which is suitable for use in mixed-metal cooling systems. The quantity of antifreeze and levels of protection are indicated in the *Specifications*.

25 Before adding antifreeze, the cooling system should be completely drained, preferably flushed, and all hoses checked for condition and security.

26 After filling with antifreeze, a label should be attached to the expansion tank, stating the type and concentration of antifreeze used, and the date installed. Any subsequent topping-up should be made with the same type and concentration of antifreeze.

27 Do not use engine antifreeze in the windscreen/tailgate/headlamp washer system, as it will cause damage to the vehicle paintwork. A screenwash additive should be added to the washer system in the quantities stated on the bottle.

Every 54 000 miles or 3 years

30 Fuel filter renewal

Warning: Before carrying out the following operation, refer to the precautions given in "Safety first!" at the beginning of this manual, and follow them implicitly.

1 The fuel filter is located in the engine compartment, mounted on the left-hand side of the engine compartment bulkhead **(see illustration)**.

2 Open the bonnet, then refer to Chapter 4A and depressurise the fuel system.

3 Release the fuel filter from its retaining clip noting which way up it is fitted, then loosen the hose clips and disconnect the hoses. Withdraw the fuel filter from the engine compartment. Be prepared for some fuel loss.

30.1 Fuel filter (arrowed) mounted at the rear of the engine compartment

4 Safely dispose of the old filter; it will be highly inflammable, and may explode if thrown onto a fire.

5 Connect the hoses to the new fuel filter, making sure it is fitted the correct way up. The arrow on the filter must point in the direction of fuel flow (ie upwards, towards the fuel rail).

6 Tighten the hose clips, then locate the filter in its retaining clip on the bulkhead.

7 Start the engine and check the filter hose connections for leaks, on completion.

31 Ignition system check

Warning: Voltages produced by an electronic ignition system are considerably higher than those produced by conventional ignition systems. Extreme care must be taken when working on the system with the ignition switched on. Persons with surgically-implanted cardiac pacemaker devices should keep well clear of the ignition circuits, components and test equipment.

1 The ignition system components should be checked for damage or deterioration as follows.

General component check

2 On models from 2000, each spark plug has an individual coil built into the plug cap **(see illustration)**, the only item that can be checked is the wiring plug connections on the coils. For more information see Chapter 5B.

3 On models up to 2000, the spark plug (HT) leads should be checked whenever new spark plugs are fitted. Pull the leads from the plugs by gripping the end fitting, not the lead, otherwise the lead connection may be fractured.

HAYNES HiNT ***Ensure that the leads are numbered before removing them, to avoid confusion when refitting***

31.2 One of the four ignition coils (arrowed) on direct ignition models

4 Check inside the end fitting for signs of corrosion, which will look like a white crusty powder. Push the end fitting back onto the spark plug, ensuring that it is a tight fit on the plug. If not, remove the lead again and use pliers to carefully crimp the metal connector inside the end fitting until it fits securely on the end of the spark plug.

5 Using a clean rag, wipe the entire length of the lead to remove any built-up dirt and grease. Once the lead is clean, check for burns, cracks and other damage. Do not bend the lead excessively, nor pull the lead lengthways - the conductor inside might break.

6 If an ohmmeter is available, check the resistance of the lead by connecting the meter across the ends of the lead. Refit the lead securely on completion.

7 Check the remaining leads one at a time, in the same way.

8 If new spark plug (HT) leads are required, purchase a set for your specific car and engine.

9 Unscrew and remove the distributor cap retaining screws and remove the cap. Wipe the cap clean, and carefully inspect it inside and out for signs of cracks, carbon tracks (tracking) and worn, burned or loose contacts. Check that the cap's carbon brush is unworn and making good contact with the rotor arm. Also check the spring located in the ignition coil for wear and for good contact with the terminal in the distributor cap. Inspect the cap seal for signs of wear or damage, and renew if necessary. Slacken the retaining screw, remove the rotor arm from the distributor shaft, and inspect it. It is a good idea to renew the cap and rotor arm whenever new spark plug (HT) leads are fitted. When fitting a new cap, remove the leads from the old cap one at a time, and fit them to the new cap in the exact same location - do not simultaneously remove all the leads from the old cap, or firing order confusion may occur. On refitting, ensure that the rotor arm is pressed securely onto the distributor shaft, and securely tighten its retaining screw. Ensure that the cap seal is in position, then fit the cap and securely tighten its retaining screws.

10 Even with the ignition system in first-class condition, some engines may still occasionally experience poor starting attributable to damp ignition components. To disperse moisture, apply water-dispersant aerosol.

Ignition timing check/ adjustment

11 See Chapter 5B, Section 5.

After 10 years, then every 2 years

32 Air bag check

This work must be entrusted to a Nissan dealer who will have the necessary specialist equipment and expertise.

Notes

Chapter 2 Part A:
Engine in-car repair procedures

Contents

Degrees of difficulty

Easy, suitable for novice with little experience 

Fairly easy, suitable for beginner with some experience 

Fairly difficult, suitable for competent DIY mechanic 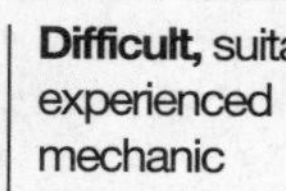

Difficult, suitable for experienced DIY mechanic

Very difficult, suitable for expert DIY or professional

Specifications

General

Engine code:*	
1.0 litre engine	CG10DE
1.3 litre engine	CG13DE
1.4 litre engine	CGA3DE

***Note:** See "Buying Spare Parts and Vehicle Identification" for the location of code marking on the engine.*

Capacity:	
1.0 litre engine	998 cc
1.3 litre engine	1275 cc
1.4 litre engine	1348 cc
Bore:	
998 cc engine	71.0 mm
1275 cc engine	71.0 mm
1348 cc engine	72.0 mm
Stroke:	
998 cc engine	63.0 mm
1275 cc engine	80.5 mm
1348 cc engine	82.8 mm
Direction of crankshaft rotation	Clockwise (viewed from right-hand side of vehicle)
Compression ratio	9.5:1
Cylinder compression pressures:	
Standard	13 bars
Minimum	11 bars
Maximum difference between cylinders	0.98 bars
Firing order	1-3-4-2
No 1 cylinder location	Timing chain (right-hand) end of engine

Camshaft and followers

Drive	Chain
Number of bearings	5
Endfloat:	
Standard	0.070 to 0.143 mm
Service limit	0.24 mm
Camshaft lobe height:	
Inlet:	
998 cc engine	38.005 to 38.195 mm
1275 cc and 1348 cc engines	39.880 to 40.070 mm
Exhaust:	
998 cc engine	38.005 to 38.195 mm
1275 cc and 1348 cc engines	39.880 to 40.070 mm
Wear limit	0.20 mm
Camshaft journal-to-bearing clearance:	
Standard	0.045 to 0.086 mm
Service limit	0.15 mm
Camshaft run-out:	
Standard	Less than 0.02 mm
Service limit	0.1 mm
Camshaft follower-to-cylinder head bore clearance	0.025 to 0.061 mm

Valve clearances

Cold engine*:	
Inlet	0.25 to 0.33 mm
Exhaust	0.32 to 0.40 mm
Hot engine*:	
Inlet	0.32 to 0.40 mm
Exhaust	0.36 to 0.44 mm

**Although Nissan quote valve clearances for "hot" and "cold" engines, the valve clearances should only be checked "cold" prior to starting the engine after an overhaul. Once the engine is at normal temperature they should be checked again to ensure accuracy.*

Lubrication system

Oil pump type	Bi-rotor driven from front of crankshaft
Minimum oil pressure at normal operating temperature:	
At idle	0.8 to 1.2 bars
At 2000 rpm:	
998 cc engine	2.9 to 4.1 bars
1275 cc and 1348 cc engines	2.9 to 3.7 bars
Oil pump clearances:	
Outer rotor-to-cover	0.11 to 0.20 mm
Outer rotor tooth-to-inner rotor recess	0.18 mm maximum
Inner rotor endfloat	0.05 to 0.09 mm
Outer rotor endfloat	0.05 to 0.11 mm
Inner rotor to housing running clearance	0.045 to 0.11 mm
Regulator valve to bore running clearance	0.040 to 0.100 mm

Torque wrench settings

	Nm	lbf ft
Camshaft cover bolts	3	2
Crankshaft pulley bolt	142	105
Timing cover	7	5
Timing chain tensioner bolts (upper and lower)	7	5
Lower timing chain rear guide bolts	7	5
Lower timing chain front tension guide bolts	16	12
Cylinder head camshaft sprocket access cover nuts/bolts	5	4
Timing chain idler sprocket centre bolt	51	38
Camshaft sprocket retaining bolts	113	83
Camshaft bearing cap bolts:		
Stage 1	2	1.5
Stage 2	6	4
Stage 3	11	8
Cylinder head bolts (main):		
Stage 1	39	29
Stage 2	78	58
Fully slacken all the bolts, then tighten to Stage 3	35	26
Stage 4	Angle-tighten 60°	
Cylinder head bolts (6 mm)	7	5
Thermostat housing	7	5
Sump nuts and bolts	7	5

Torque wrench settings (continued)

	Nm	lbf ft
Sump drain plug	34	25
Centre member bolts	69	50
Oil pump:		
Cover retaining screws	4	3
Cover retaining bolts	7	5
Regulator valve plug	49	36
Oil pump pick-up tube to timing cover	7	5
Oil pump pick-up tube support mounting	7	5
Flywheel/driveplate bolts	88	65
Rear oil seal housing nuts and bolts	7	5
Big-end bearing cap nuts:		
Stage 1	15	11
Stage 2	Angle-tighten through 45° to 50°	
Main bearing cap beam bolts:		
Stage 1	28	21
Stage 2	Angle-tighten through 60° to 65°	
Engine-to-transmission bolts:		
998 cc engine:		
20 mm in length	19	14
60 mm in length	35	26
1275 cc and 1348 cc engines:		
16 mm in length	19	14
20 mm in length	19	14
70 mm in length	35	26
Right-hand engine/transmission mounting:		
Mounting lower bracket-to-engine bolts	69	50
Through-bolt	50	37
Mounting upper bracket bolts	40	30
Left-hand engine/transmission mounting:		
Bracket-to-transmission	69	50
Through-bolt:		
Manual transmission	50	37
Automatic transmission	37	27
Front engine/transmission mounting bolts (manual transmission only):		
Mounting bracket-to-engine bolts	69	50
Mounting-to-centre member bolt	49	36
Through-bolt	64	47
Rear engine/transmission mounting:		
Mounting-to-centre member bolts	69	50
Through-bolt	55	41
Mounting bracket retaining bolts	69	50

1 General information

Using this Chapter

Chapter 2 is divided into two Parts; A and B. Repair operations that can be carried out with the engine in the vehicle are described in Part A. Part B covers the removal of the engine/transmission as a unit, and describes the engine dismantling and overhaul procedures.

In Part A the assumption is made that the engine is installed in the vehicle, with all ancillaries connected. If the engine has been removed for overhaul, the preliminary dismantling information which precedes each operation may be ignored.

Engine description

Throughout this Chapter, engines are identified by their capacities. The engines covered, together with their code letters, are given in the *Specifications*.

The 1.0 litre (998 cc), 1.3 litre (1275 cc) and 1.4 litre (1348 cc) engines are of Nissan CG type. They are of sixteen-valve, in-line four-cylinder, double overhead camshaft (DOHC) design, mounted transversely at the front of the car with the transmission attached to the left-hand end.

The crankshaft runs in five main bearings, and the main bearing caps form an integral part of the main bearing cap beam. Thrustwashers are fitted to No 3 main bearing (upper half) to control crankshaft endfloat.

The connecting rods rotate on horizontally-split bearing shells at their big-ends. The pistons are attached to the connecting rods by gudgeon pins, which are an interference fit in the small-end eyes. The aluminium-alloy pistons are fitted with three piston rings - two compression rings and an oil control ring.

The cylinder block is of aluminium and the cylinder bores are an integral part of the block.

The inlet and exhaust valves are each closed by coil springs, and operate in guides pressed into the cylinder head; the valve seat inserts are also pressed into the cylinder head, and can be renewed separately if worn.

The camshafts are driven by a lower and upper timing chain, and an idler sprocket mounted on the cylinder head connects the two chains. The camshafts operate the sixteen valves via bucket-type followers. The followers are situated directly below the camshafts. Valve clearances are adjusted by shims. The camshafts rotate directly in the cylinder head and are retained by five bearing caps.

Lubrication is by means of an oil pump, driven off the right-hand end of the crankshaft and integral with the timing cover. It draws oil through a strainer located in the sump, and then forces it through an externally-mounted filter into galleries in the cylinder block/crankcase. From there, the oil is distributed to the crankshaft (main bearings) and camshafts. The big-end bearings are supplied with oil via internal drillings in the crankshaft, while the camshaft bearings also receive a pressurised supply. The camshaft lobes and valves are lubricated by splash, as are all other engine components.

Repair operations possible with the engine in the car

The following work can be carried out with the engine in the car:

a) Adjustment of the valve clearances.
b) Removal of the timing chains, tensioners, guides and sprockets.
c) Removal of the camshafts and followers
*d) Removal of the cylinder head**
e) Removal of the sump
f) Removal of the oil pump and pick-up tube
g) Renewal of the crankshaft oil seals
h) Removal of the flywheel/driveplate
i) Renewal of the engine mountings

**Cylinder head dismantling procedures are detailed in Chapter 2B.*

Note: *It is possible to remove the pistons and connecting rods (after removing the cylinder head and sump) without removing the engine. However, this is not recommended. Work of this nature is more easily and thoroughly completed with the engine on the bench, as described in Chapter 2B.*

2 Compression test

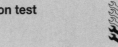

1 When engine performance is down, or if misfiring occurs which cannot be attributed to the ignition or fuel systems, a compression test can provide diagnostic clues as to the engine's condition. If the test is performed regularly, it can give warning of trouble before any other symptoms become apparent.

2 The engine must be fully warmed-up to normal operating temperature, the battery must be fully charged, and all the spark plugs must be removed (Chapter 1). The aid of an assistant will also be required.

3 Depressurise the fuel system (Chapter 4), then disable the ignition system by disconnecting the low tension wiring from the distributor.

4 Fit a compression tester to the No 1 cylinder spark plug hole - the type of tester which screws into the plug thread is to be preferred.

5 Have the assistant hold the throttle wide open, and crank the engine on the starter motor; after one or two revolutions, the compression pressure should build up to a maximum figure, and then stabilise. Record the highest reading obtained.

6 Repeat the test on the remaining cylinders, recording the pressure in each.

7 All cylinders should produce very similar pressures; any difference greater than that specified indicates the existence of a fault. Note that the compression should build up quickly in a healthy engine; low compression on the first stroke, followed by gradually increasing pressure on successive strokes, indicates worn piston rings. A low compression reading on the first stroke, which does not build up during successive strokes, indicates leaking valves or a blown head gasket (a cracked head could also be the cause).

8 If the pressure in any cylinder is reduced to the specified minimum or less, carry out the following test to isolate the cause. Introduce 5ml of clean oil into that cylinder through its spark plug hole and repeat the test.

9 If the addition of oil temporarily improves the compression pressure, this indicates that bore or piston wear is responsible for the pressure loss. No improvement suggests that leaking or burnt valves, or a blown head gasket, may be to blame.

10 A low reading from two adjacent cylinders is almost certainly due to the head gasket having blown between them. Renew the head gasket if this is the case.

11 If one cylinder is about 20 percent lower than the others and the engine has a slightly rough idle, a worn camshaft lobe could be the cause.

12 On completion of the test, refit the spark plugs and reconnect the low tension wiring to the distributor.

3 Top dead centre (TDC) for No 1 piston - locating

1 Disconnect the battery negative lead.

Remove all four spark plugs; this will make the engine easier to turn; refer to Chapter 1 for details.

2 On models up to 2000, trace No 1 spark plug (HT) lead from the plug back to the distributor cap, and use chalk or similar to mark the distributor body or cylinder head nearest to the cap's No 1 terminal. No 1 cylinder is at the timing chain (right-hand) end of the engine. Unscrew the cap retaining screws, remove the cap and recover the seal.

3 Apply the handbrake and ensure that the transmission is in neutral, then jack up the front of the vehicle and support it on axle stands (see "*Jacking and vehicle support*"). Remove the right-hand roadwheel. Undo the retaining screws and remove the wheel arch liners from underneath the wing to gain access to the crankshaft pulley bolt; on some models, the bolt can be accessed via a small hole in the cover.

4 The timing marks are in the form of notches on the crankshaft pulley rim which align with a pointer on the timing chain cover. The notches are spaced at intervals of 5°, and go from 20° before top dead centre (BTDC) to 5° after top dead centre (ATDC). The TDC mark is highlighted with yellow paint to aid identification **(see illustration)**.

5 Using a spanner (or socket and extension bar) applied to the crankshaft pulley bolt, rotate the crankshaft clockwise until the TDC notch on the crankshaft pulley rim is aligned with the pointer on the timing chain cover.

6 With the crankshaft in this position, Nos 1 and 4 cylinders are now at TDC, one of them on the compression stroke. On models up to 2000, if the distributor rotor arm is pointing at (the previously-marked) No 1 terminal, then No 1 cylinder is correctly positioned; if the rotor arm is pointing at No 4 terminal, rotate the crankshaft one full turn (360°) clockwise until the arm points at the marked terminal. No 1 cylinder will then be at TDC on the compression stroke. Viewed from the left-hand end of the engine the rotor arm should point to the 4 o'clock position.

3.4 Timing marks on the crankshaft pulley and timing pointer on the timing cover

7 Once No 1 cylinder has been positioned at TDC on the compression stroke, TDC for any of the other cylinders can then be located by rotating the crankshaft clockwise 180° at a time and following the firing order (see *Specifications*).

4 Camshaft cover - removal and refitting

Removal

1 On models up to 2000, disconnect the spark plug (HT) leads from the plugs, and free them from their retaining clips on the top of the cover. On models from 2000, each spark plug has an individual coil built into the plug cap. Disconnect the wiring plug from the coil, then undo the retaining screws and remove the coil assembly from the spark plug. For more information see spark plug removal in Chapter 1, Section 6.

2 Release the retaining clips and disconnect the breather hoses. There are three hoses, two on the left-hand end of the cover and the PCV hose from the inlet manifold on the rear of the cover. On automatic transmission models also disconnect the kick-down cable from its bracket. Disconnect the accelerator cable from the clip and tie it to one side **(see illustrations)**.

3 Working in the **reverse** of the sequence shown in **illustration 4.11**, slacken and remove the camshaft cover retaining screws and washers **(see illustration)**.

4 Lift off the camshaft cover, and recover the rubber seal from the groove in the cover. Also recover the circular seal from each of the cover spark plug holes **(see illustrations)**.

4.2a Disconnecting the hose from the PCV valve

4.2b Disconnecting the breather hoses from the left-hand end of the timing cover

4.2c Releasing the accelerator cable from the clip

4.3 Unscrewing the camshaft cover retaining screws

4.4a Lifting the camshaft cover from the cylinder head

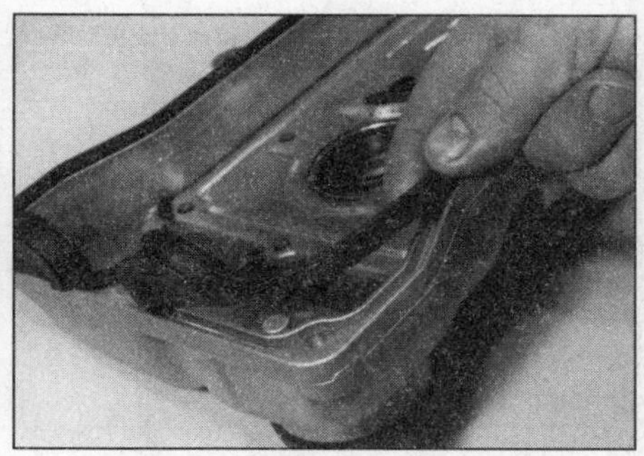

4.4b Removing the rubber seal from the camshaft cover

5 Inspect the cover seals for signs of damage and deterioration, and renew as necessary.

Refitting

6 Carefully clean the camshaft cover mating surfaces, and remove all traces of oil.

7 Apply a bead of sealant to the circular cut-outs on the right-hand end of the cylinder head **(see illustration)**.

8 Fit the rubber seal to the camshaft cover groove, ensuring that it is correctly located along its entire length, and install the four spark plug hole seals, ensuring that they are the correct way round. If necessary, the seals can be held in position using a smear of suitable sealant.

9 Apply a bead of sealant to the cover seal, approximately 1 cm either side of the left-hand exhaust camshaft bearing cap circular cut-out edges.

10 Carefully refit the camshaft cover, taking great care not to displace any of the rubber seals.

11 Make sure the cover is correctly seated, then refit the retaining screws and washers. Working in the sequence shown, tighten all the cover screws to the specified torque **(see illustration)**.

12 Reconnect the breather hoses to the camshaft cover, and secure them in position with the retaining clips. On automatic transmission models reconnect the kick-down cable. Reposition the accelerator cable.

13 Connect the HT lead caps to the correct spark plugs, and clip the leads back into the retaining clips.

5 Valve clearances - checking and adjustment

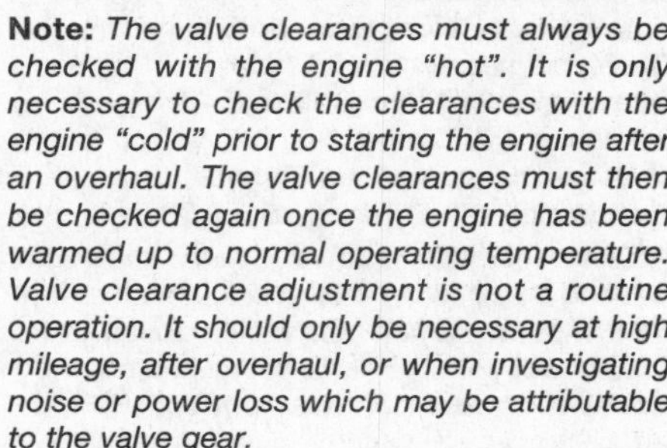

Note: *The valve clearances must always be checked with the engine "hot". It is only necessary to check the clearances with the engine "cold" prior to starting the engine after an overhaul. The valve clearances must then be checked again once the engine has been warmed up to normal operating temperature. Valve clearance adjustment is not a routine operation. It should only be necessary at high mileage, after overhaul, or when investigating noise or power loss which may be attributable to the valve gear.*

1 The importance of having the valve clearances correctly adjusted cannot be overstressed, as they vitally affect the performance of the engine. However, the check should not be regarded as routine maintenance, and should only be carried out when the valve gear has become noisy, after engine overhaul, or when trying to trace the cause of power loss which may be attributable to the valves. The clearances are checked as follows.

2 Draw the outline of the engine on a piece of paper, numbering the cylinders 1 to 4, with No 1 cylinder at the timing chain end of the engine. Show the position of each valve, together with the specified valve clearance. Above each valve, draw two lines for noting the actual clearance and the amount of adjustment required.

3 Warm the engine up to normal operating temperature, then switch off. Remove the camshaft cover as described in Section 4 and the spark plugs as described in Chapter 1.

4 Set No 1 cylinder at TDC on its compression stroke, as described in Section 3.

5 Using feeler blades, measure the clearance

4.7 Apply sealant to the cut-outs in the cylinder head

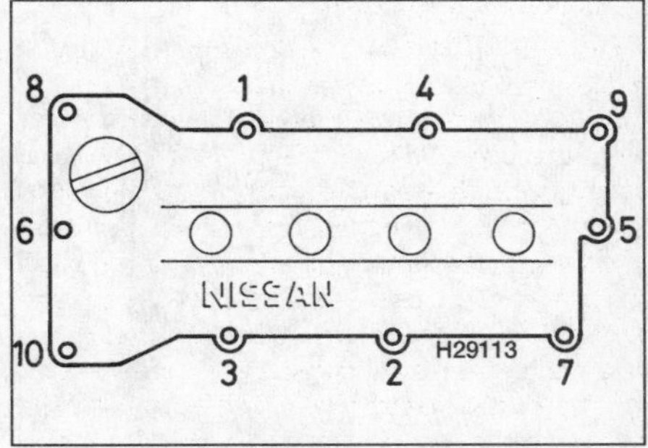

4.11 Camshaft cover bolt tightening sequence

5.5 Checking a valve clearance

between the base of the cam and the follower of the following valves, recording each clearance on the paper **(see illustration)**.

No 1 cylinder inlet and exhaust valves
No 2 cylinder inlet valves
No 3 cylinder exhaust valves

6 Rotate the crankshaft through one complete turn (360°) clockwise until the TDC notch on the crankshaft pulley is realigned with the pointer. No 4 cylinder is now at TDC on its compression stroke.

7 Check the clearances of the following valves, and record them on the paper.

No 2 cylinder exhaust valves
No 3 cylinder inlet valves
No 4 cylinder inlet and exhaust valves

8 Calculate the difference between each measured clearance and the desired value, and record it on the piece of paper. Where a valve clearance differs from the specified value, then the shim for that valve must be replaced with a thinner or thicker shim accordingly.

9 To remove the shim, the follower has to be pressed down against valve spring pressure just far enough to allow the shim to be slid out. To do this, make sure that the cam lobe of the valve on which the shim is to be removed is pointing away from the follower, then rotate the follower so that its notch is at a right-angle to the camshaft centre-line and pointing to the centre-line of the cylinder head.

10 Using a suitable C-spanner or stout screwdriver, carefully lever down between the camshaft and the edge of the follower, until the follower is depressed sufficiently to allow the shim to be slid out of position. With the shim removed, slowly release the follower. If difficulty is experienced in removing the shims, it will be necessary to remove the camshaft(s) as described in Section 9.

11 The shim size is stamped on the bottom face of the shim (eg. 224 indicates the shim is 2.24 mm thick), but it is advisable to use a micrometer to measure the true thickness of any shim removed, as it may have been reduced by wear **(see illustrations)**. **Note:** *Shims are available in thicknesses between 2.00 mm and 2.98 mm, in steps of 0.02 mm.* The size of shim required is calculated as follows.

12 If the measured clearance is less than specified, subtract the measured clearance from the specified clearance, and subtract the result from the thickness of the existing shim. For example:

Sample calculation - inlet valve clearance too small

Clearance measured = 0.26 mm
Clearance = 0.36 mm (0.32 to 0.40 mm)
Difference = 0.10 mm
Shim thickness fitted = 2.50 mm
Shim thickness = 2.50 - 0.10 = 2.40 mm

13 If the measured clearance is greater than specified, subtract the specified clearance from the measured clearance, and add the result to the thickness of the existing shim. For example:

Sample calculation - exhaust valve clearance too big

Clearance measured = 0.51 mm
Clearance = 0.41 mm (0.37 to 0.45 mm)
Difference = 0.10 mm
Shim thickness fitted = 2.76 mm
Shim thickness = 2.76 + 0.10 = 2.86 mm

14 Depress the follower, then slide the required size of shim into position, so that it is fitted with its marked face facing downwards. Ensure that the shim is correctly seated, then repeat the procedure (as required) for the remaining valve(s) which require adjustment.

15 Once all valves have been adjusted, rotate the crankshaft through at least four complete turns in the correct direction of rotation, to settle all disturbed shims in position, then recheck the clearances as described above.

16 With all valve clearances correctly adjusted, refit the camshaft cover as described in Section 4 and the spark plugs as described in Chapter 1, then refit all components removed to gain access to the crankshaft pulley.

5.11a The shim size is stamped on the bottom face of the shim

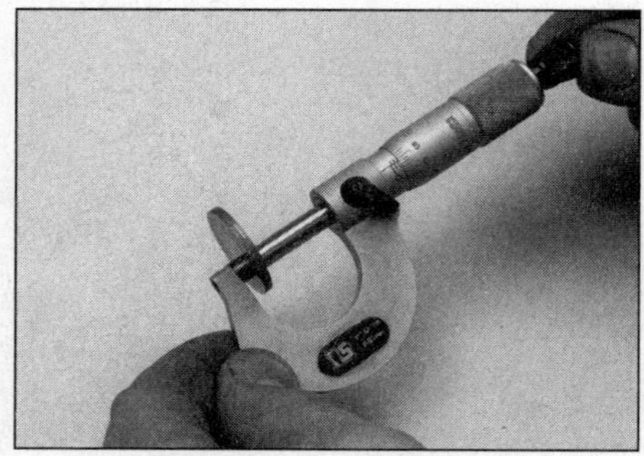

5.11b Measuring the shim with a micrometer

6 Timing chain cover - removal and refitting

Note: *If the timing chain cover is to be removed without disturbing the cylinder head, there is a slight risk of oil leakage from the chain cover-to-cylinder head joint after refitting. Bearing in mind this information, it is up to the individual owner to decide whether or not it is worth renewing the head gasket when the chain cover is removed. Note that the photographic sequences in this Section were taken with the engine removed from the car for clarity.*

Removal

1 Jack up the front of the vehicle and support on axle stands (see "*Jacking and vehicle support*"). Remove the right-hand front wheel.

2 Undo the retaining screws and remove the plastic liner from underneath the wing to gain access to the crankshaft pulley bolt.

3 Refer to Chapter 1 and remove the alternator drivebelt followed by the water pump/power steering pump drivebelt.

4 If necessary position No 1 cylinder at TDC on its compression stroke as described in Section 3.

5 Remove the sump as described in Section 10, then remove the oil pump pick-up/strainer with reference to Section 11.

6 To prevent crankshaft rotation while the pulley bolt is unscrewed, select 4th gear and have an assistant apply the brakes firmly. On automatic transmission models, remove the starter motor and have an assistant engage a wide-bladed screwdriver with the starter ring gear on the driveplate. Alternatively position a block of wood between one of the crankshaft webs and the crankcase wall.

7 Unscrew and remove the pulley bolt and washer, and remove the pulley from the crankshaft. If the pulley Woodruff key is a loose fit, remove it and store it with the pulley for safe-keeping **(see illustrations)**.

8 Support the right-hand end of the engine using a trolley jack and block of wood, then unbolt and remove the right-hand engine mounting and bracket (refer to Section 14 if necessary) **(see illustration)**.

9 Unscrew the nuts and bolts securing the camshaft sprocket access cover to the cylinder head, noting the location of the support bracket on the studs, then remove the cover. On later models, undo the retaining bolt and remove the camshaft position sensor from the cover **(see illustrations)**.

6.7a Remove the bolt and washer . . .

6.7b . . . then slide the pulley from the crankshaft

6.8 Unbolting the right-hand engine mounting from the engine

6.9a Removing the support bracket from the access cover

6.9b Removing the camshaft sprocket access cover

6.9c Undo the retaining bolt (arrowed) to remove the camshaft position sensor

10 Slacken and remove the timing chain cover retaining bolts noting that two of the bolts are located inside the upper timing cover area **(see illustrations)**. Note the correct fitted location of each bolt, as the bolts are of different lengths.

11 Slide the timing chain cover off the end of the crankshaft, and manoeuvre it out of the engine compartment. Recover the special sealing rings from the oil galleries and discard them; new ones must be used on refitting. If the cover locating dowels are a loose fit, remove them and store them with the cover for safe-keeping **(see illustrations)**.

12 If necessary, slide the oil pump drive spacer off the end of the crankshaft **(see illustration)**.

6.10a Two of the bolts are located inside the access cover aperture

6.10b Timing cover, showing retaining bolts

6.11a Removing the timing chain cover

6.11b Removing the special sealing rings from the oil galleries

6.12 Removing the oil pump drive spacer

6.13a Prise the oil seal from the timing chain cover . . .

6.13b . . . then drive a new oil seal using a socket and mallet

6.18a Apply a bead of sealant to the timing cover

6.18b Timing chain cover ready for fitting

6.19 Refitting the timing chain cover

6.21 Apply a bead of sealant to the camshaft sprocket access cover

Refitting

13 Prior to refitting the cover, it is recommended that the crankshaft oil seal be renewed with reference to Section 12 **(see illustrations)**.
14 Ensure that the cover and crankcase mating surfaces are clean and dry.
15 If removed refit the Woodruff key to the groove in the crankshaft. Align the oil pump drive spacer groove with the key, then slide the spacer onto the crankshaft.
16 If removed, refit the cover locating dowels in the cylinder block.
17 Fit the new special sealing rings to the cylinder block oil galleries.
18 Apply a 2.0 to 3.0 mm wide bead of suitable sealant to the timing cover mating surface, making sure it is located around the inner edges of the bolt holes **(see illustrations)**. If the cylinder head is in position, also apply sealant to the upper face of the cover.
19 Offer up the cover, and position the oil pump inner rotor so that it will engage with the drive spacer as the cover is refitted. Slide the cover over the end of the crankshaft, taking great care not to damage the oil seal lip, and seat it on its locating dowels **(see illustration)**.
20 Insert the cover retaining bolts in their original locations and tighten them securely, working in several stages.
21 Apply a 2.0 to 3.0 mm wide bead of suitable sealant to the camshaft sprocket access cover mating surface making sure it is located around the inner edges of the bolt holes, then refit the cover together with the support bracket and tighten the nuts and bolts to the specified torque **(see illustration)**.
22 Refit the camshaft position sensor to the cover then refit the right-hand engine mounting with reference to Section 14. Remove the trolley jack from under the engine.
23 Where removed, refit the Woodruff key to the crankshaft.
24 Align the crankshaft pulley groove with the key, then slide the pulley onto the crankshaft, and refit the retaining bolt and washer.
25 Lock the crankshaft by the method used on removal, and tighten the pulley retaining bolt to the specified torque setting.
26 Refit the oil pump pick-up/strainer and sump with reference to Sections 12 and 10.
27 Refit the wing liner and right-hand front wheel then lower the vehicle to the ground.
28 Check and top-up the engine oil level as described in Chapter 1.

7 Timing chains and sprockets - removal, inspection and refitting

Removal

1 Disconnect the battery negative lead.
2 Jack up the front of the vehicle and support on axle stands (see "*Jacking and vehicle support*"). Remove the right-hand front wheel.
3 Unscrew the retaining screws and remove the wheel arch liners from under the right-hand front wing.
4 Refer to Chapter 1 and remove the alternator drivebelt followed by the water pump/power steering pump drivebelt.
5 Remove the air cleaner assembly as described in Chapter 4A.
6 Remove the camshaft cover as described in Section 4.
7 Where applicable, disconnect the HT leads from the spark plugs, then loosen the screws and remove the distributor cap from the distributor.
8 Remove the spark plugs as described in Chapter 1.
9 Position No 1 cylinder at TDC on its compression stroke, as described in Section 3.
10 Remove the timing chain cover and camshaft sprocket access cover as described in Section 6. Recheck the TDC setting after removing the cover.
11 Unbolt and remove the upper timing chain tensioner taking care to keep the pressure pad inserted in the body **(see illustration)**.
12 Unscrew the camshaft sprocket retaining

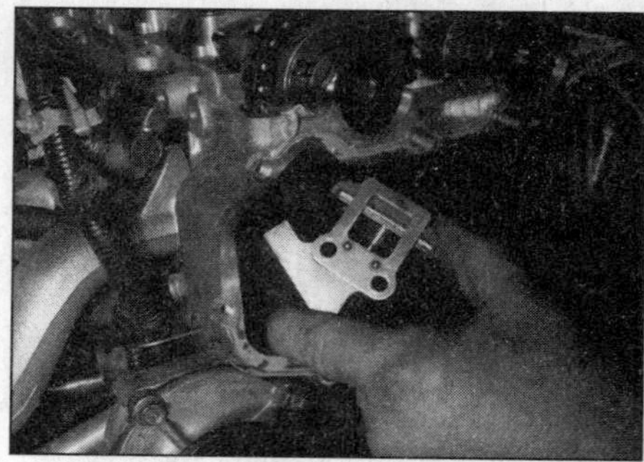
7.11 Removing the timing chain tensioner

7.12a Use a spanner on the special flats to hold the camshafts while loosening the retaining bolts

7.12b Removing the sprocket retaining bolts and washers

7.13 Disengaging the camshaft sprockets from the upper timing chain

7.14a Loosen the idler sprocket bolt . . .

7.14b . . . and remove the bolt and washer

bolts, whilst retaining the camshafts with a large open-ended spanner fitted to the flats on the right-hand end of each shaft. Remove each bolt along with its washer **(see illustrations)**.

13 Disengage each sprocket from the end of its respective camshaft, and manoeuvre them out separately from the upper timing chain **(see illustration)**. If the sprocket locating pins are a loose fit in the camshaft ends, remove them and store them with the sprockets. **Note:** *Identify each sprocket for position as they are identical and have the same part number.*

14 Unscrew and remove the idler sprocket retaining bolt and washer, then use a screwdriver to prise the idler shaft from the roll pin on the cylinder head **(see illustrations)**.

15 Disengage the upper timing chain from the idler sprocket.

7.16c . . . and remove the lower timing chain front tension guide

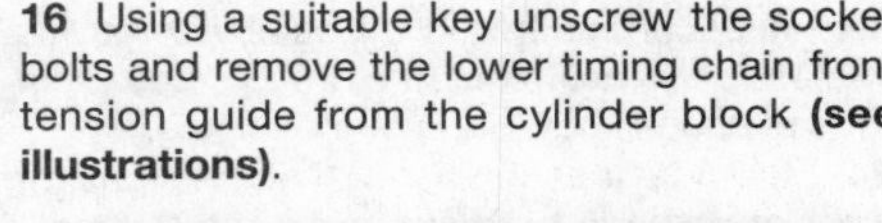

16 Using a suitable key unscrew the socket bolts and remove the lower timing chain front tension guide from the cylinder block **(see illustrations)**.

7.16a Unscrew the upper . . .

7.17a Unscrew the bolts . . .

17 Unbolt the lower timing chain hydraulic tensioner taking care to keep the pressure pad inserted in the body **(see illustrations)**.

18 Lower the idler sprocket and disengage it

7.16b . . . and lower socket bolts . . .

7.17b . . . and remove the lower timing chain hydraulic tensioner

7.18a Lower the idler sprocket through the cylinder head aperture

7.18b Disengaging the lower timing chain from the crankshaft sprocket

from the timing chain, then disengage the timing chain from the crankshaft sprocket **(see illustrations)**. Recover the idler shaft from the rear of the idler sprocket.

19 If not already done remove the oil pump drive spacer from the crankshaft. Slide the crankshaft sprocket from the crankshaft. If the sprocket Woodruff key is a loose fit, remove it and store it with the sprocket for safe-keeping.

20 Unbolt the lower timing chain rear guide from the cylinder block. ***Caution: Do not rotate the crankshaft or camshafts whilst the timing chains are removed.***

Inspection

21 Examine the teeth on the camshaft, idler and crankshaft sprockets for any sign of wear or damage such as chipped or hooked teeth. If there is any sign of wear or damage on either sprocket, *all* sprockets and *both* timing chains should be renewed as a set.

22 Inspect the links of the timing chains for signs of wear or damage on the rollers. The extent of wear can be judged by checking the amount by which the chain can be bent sideways; a new chain will have very little sideways movement. If there is an excessive amount of side play in either timing chain, it must be renewed.

23 Note that it is a sensible precaution to renew the timing chains, regardless of their apparent condition, if the engine has covered a high mileage, or if it has been noted that the chain(s) have sounded noisy with the engine running. Although not strictly necessary, it is always worth renewing the chains and sprockets as a matched set, since it is false economy to run a new chain on worn sprockets and vice-versa. If there is any doubt about the condition of the timing chains and sprockets, seek the advice of a Nissan dealer service department, who will be able to advise you as to the best course of action, based on their previous knowledge of the engine.

24 Examine the chain guides for signs of wear or damage to their chain contact faces, renewing any which are badly marked.

25 Check the upper chain tensioner pad for signs of wear, and check that the plunger is free to slide freely in the tensioner body. The condition of the tensioner spring can only be judged in comparison to a new component. Renew the tensioner if its pad is worn or there is any doubt about the condition of its tensioning spring.

Refitting

26 Check that the crankshaft is still at TDC (the keyway will be in the 12 o'clock position, seen from the right-hand end of the engine) and refit the Woodruff key to the crankshaft groove.

27 Ensure that the crankshaft sprocket is positioned the correct way round, with its timing mark facing away from the crankcase, then align its groove with the key, and slide the sprocket onto the crankshaft **(see illustration)**.

28 Refit the lower timing chain rear guide to the cylinder block and tighten the bolts to the specified torque.

29 Apply a smear of clean engine oil to the idler sprocket shaft, and fit the shaft to the rear of the sprocket so that its flange is positioned between the sprocket and cylinder head **(see illustration)**.

30 Engage the large idler sprocket with the lower timing chain, aligning the timing mark with one of the chain's coloured links. The number of links between the two coloured links is the same for both the right and left sides, so either link can be used for the alignment.

31 Manoeuvre the chain and idler sprocket assembly into position, engaging the chain with the crankshaft sprocket so that its second coloured link is aligned with the timing mark on the crankshaft sprocket; the timing mark is in the form of a small cut-out on the sprocket hub **(see illustration)**.

7.27 Refitting the sprocket on the front of the crankshaft

7.29 Fitting the shaft to the rear of the idler sprocket

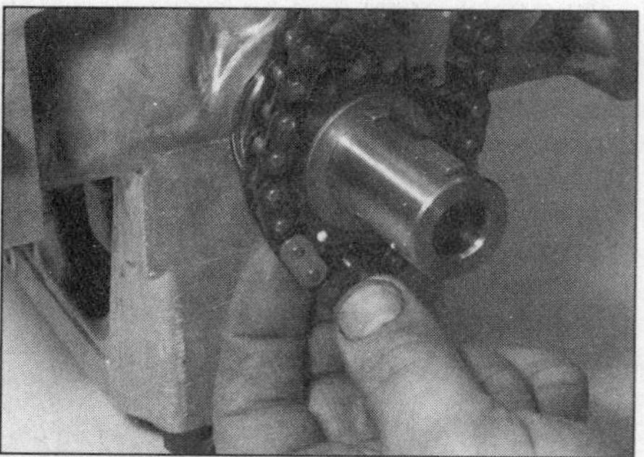

7.31 The chain's second coloured link should be aligned with the timing mark

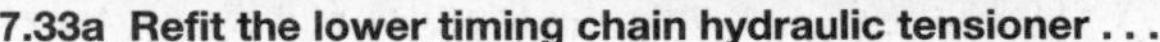

7.33a Refit the lower timing chain hydraulic tensioner . . .

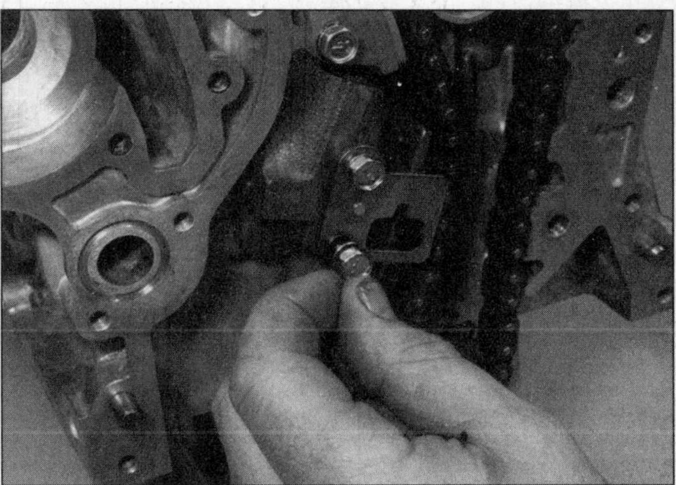

7.33b . . . and insert the bolts

32 Check that the idler sprocket and crankshaft sprocket marks are still correctly aligned with the lower chain coloured links, then locate the idler sprocket shaft on the cylinder head roll pin and temporarily insert the retaining bolt and washer.

33 Refit the lower timing chain hydraulic tensioner while keeping the pressure pad depressed, then insert the bolts and tighten to the specified torque **(see illustrations)**.

34 Refit the lower timing chain front tension guide and tighten the socket bolts to the specified torque.

35 Slide the oil pump drive spacer onto the crankshaft.

36 If removed refit the locating pins to the ends of the camshafts.

37 The upper timing chain has three coloured links, two silver links for the camshaft sprockets and one bronze link for the idler sprocket. Note, however, that the links are not spaced at regular intervals. Unscrew the idler sprocket bolt, then lower the upper chain into position, making sure its coloured links are facing outwards. Engage the chain with the idler sprocket, aligning the bronze link with the sprocket timing mark **(see illustration)**.

38 Refit the idler sprocket bolt and washer and tighten to the specified torque **(see illustrations)**.

39 Manoeuvre both the inlet and exhaust camshaft sprockets into position, ensuring that their timing marks are facing outwards. **Note:** *If the original sprockets are being refitted, locate them in their correct positions as previously noted.* Engage them with the chain, aligning the inlet sprocket timing mark with the first chain silver link and the exhaust timing mark with the second. Check that all the timing marks are correctly aligned with the upper chain links **(see illustration)**.

40 Locate the sprockets on the camshafts, aligning their cut-outs with the locating pins. Check that the chain silver links are correctly aligned with each sprocket's timing mark. If not, disengage the sprocket(s) from the chain, and make the necessary adjustments.

41 With the timing marks correctly positioned, insert the camshaft sprocket retaining bolts and washers, and tighten to the specified torque while holding the camshafts stationary using an open-ended spanner on their flats **(see illustration)**.

42 Before refitting the upper timing chain

7.37 Engaging the timing chain with the idler sprocket

7.38a Refit the idler sprocket bolt and washer . . .

7.38b . . . and tighten to the specified torque

7.39 Engaging the camshaft sprockets with the upper timing chain

7.41 Inserting the sprocket retaining bolts and washers

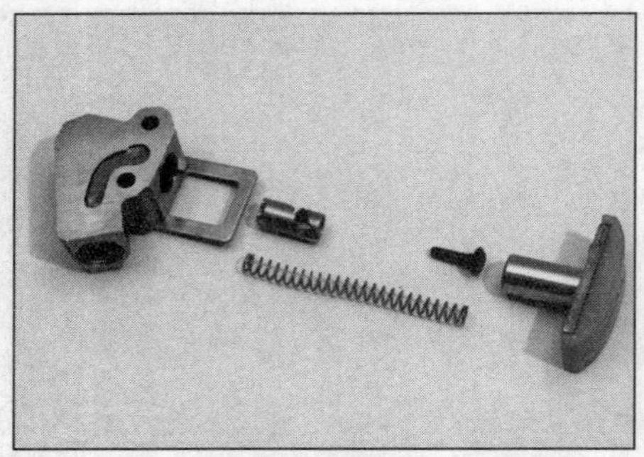
7.42a Upper timing chain tensioner components

7.42b Insert the seat . . .

7.42c . . . spring . . .

7.42d . . . and piston . . .

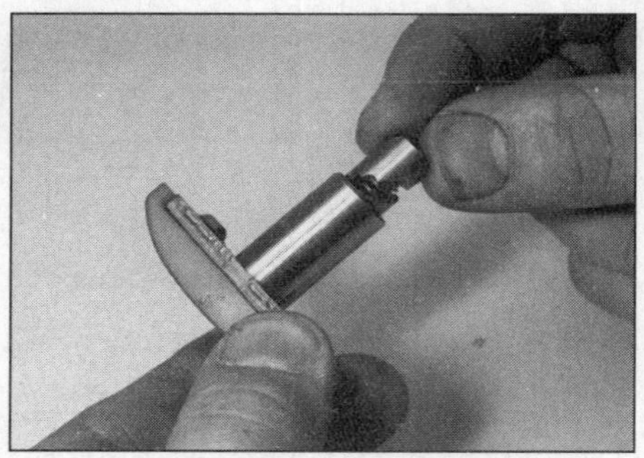
7.42e . . . then push the piston in and turn clockwise to set the ratchet

tensioner it must be reassembled and set to the minimum length. Remove the piston from the body then turn the ratchet fully clockwise while pressing it into the piston against the spring pressure. If now released, it will remain in this position for refitting and will automatically reset itself when the engine is started. Oil the piston and insert it in the tensioner body, then refit the tensioner to the cylinder head and tighten the bolts to the specified torque **(see illustrations)**.

43 Refit the timing chain cover, camshaft sprocket access cover and crankshaft pulley as described in Section 6.

44 Using a spanner on the crankshaft pulley bolt, turn the engine several times to check for clearance between the valves and pistons.

45 Refit the spark plugs as described in Chapter 1 then, where applicable, refit the distributor cap and HT leads.

46 Refit the camshaft cover with reference to Section 4.

47 Refit the air cleaner assembly (Chapter 4A) and drivebelts (Chapter 1).

48 Refit the wheel arch liners and the right-hand front wheel, then lower the vehicle to the ground.

49 Reconnect the battery negative lead.

8 Camshafts and followers - removal, inspection and refitting

Removal

1 Disconnect the battery negative lead.

2 Jack up the front of the vehicle and support on axle stands (see "*Jacking and vehicle support*"). Remove the right-hand front wheel.

3 Unscrew the retaining screws and remove the wheel arch liners from under the right-hand front wing.

4 Remove the air cleaner assembly as described in Chapter 4A.

5 Remove the camshaft cover as described in Section 4.

6 Where applicable, loosen the screws and remove the distributor cap from the distributor.

7 Remove the spark plugs as described in Chapter 1.

8 Set No 1 cylinder at TDC on its compression stroke, as described in Section 3.

9 Mark the position of the distributor body in relation to the cylinder head then unscrew the mounting bolts and remove the distributor.

10 Unscrew the retaining nuts and bolts, and remove the camshaft sprocket access cover from the right-hand end of the cylinder head as described in Section 6.

11 It is now important to mark both camshaft sprockets and the idler sprocket in relation to the upper timing chain. As a further precaution also mark the idler sprocket in relation to the lower timing chain. Wipe the chains and sprockets and use a dab of paint to mark them.

Caution: If the sprockets and chains are not marked as recommended, or if there is any doubt about their positioning on reassembly, it will be necessary to remove the lower timing chain and reassemble it with reference to Section 7. This will involve extra work to remove the crankshaft pulley, sump and timing cover. Note that it will not be possible to use the manufacturer's timing chain link marks for valve timing unless the lower timing chain is removed and refitted first, since the timing marks go out of sync when the engine is running.

12 Unbolt and remove the upper timing chain tensioner taking care to keep the pressure pad inserted in the body.

13 Unscrew the camshaft sprocket retaining bolts, whilst retaining the camshafts with a large open-ended spanner fitted to the flats on the right-hand end of each shaft. Remove each bolt along with its washer.

14 Disengage each sprocket from the end of its respective camshaft, and manoeuvre them out separately from the upper timing chain. If the sprocket locating pins are a loose fit in the camshaft ends, remove them and store them with the sprockets. **Note:** *Identify each sprocket for position as they are identical and have the same part number.*

15 Tie the upper timing chain to one side.

16 The camshaft right- and left-hand end bearing caps are noticeably different to the others, however, the other bearing caps are all similar. They should have identification markings cast into the top of each centre bearing cap; the exhaust camshaft caps are marked "E2" to "E5" and the inlet camshaft caps are marked "I2" to "I5"; the No 2 caps being fitted nearest the timing chain end of the engine. If necessary mark the caps to ensure correct refitting **(see illustration)**.

8.16 The camshaft bearing caps are marked for position

8.17a The inner bolts are identified by having a centre dimple

8.17b Removing the special front camshaft bearing cap

8.17c Removing the exhaust camshaft bearing caps

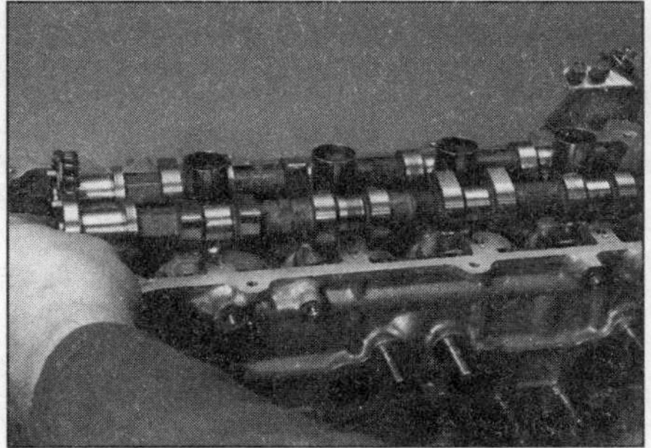
8.18a Removing the exhaust camshaft

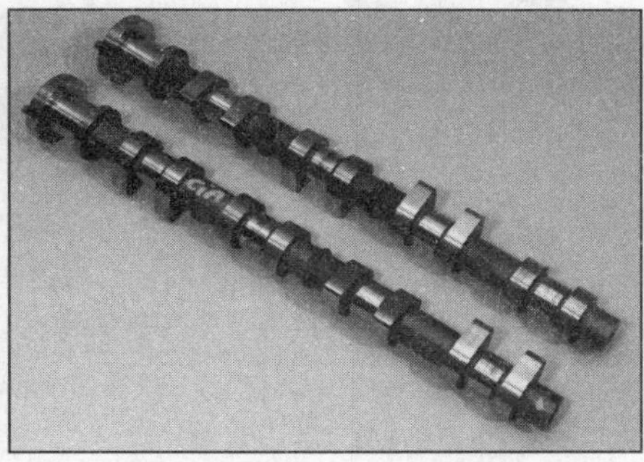
8.18b Inlet and exhaust camshafts removed from the cylinder head

8.18c The exhaust camshaft has a cut-out for engagement of the distributor drive dog

17 Working in the **reverse** of the sequence shown in **illustration 8.35a**, evenly and progressively slacken the camshaft bearing cap retaining bolts by one turn at a time, to relieve the pressure of the valve springs gradually and evenly. Once the valve spring pressure has been relieved, the bolts can be fully unscrewed and removed. Remove the end bearing caps first, then remove the exhaust camshaft caps followed by the inlet camshaft caps. Note that the inner bolts on the front bearing cap are identified by having a centre dimple **(see illustrations)**.

18 Lift the camshafts out of the cylinder head **(see illustrations)**. If necessary, unbolt and remove the distributor mounting cap.

19 Obtain sixteen small, clean plastic containers, and number them 1 to 16. Alternatively, divide a larger container into sixteen compartments. Using a rubber sucker, withdraw each shim and follower in turn, and place it in its respective container. Keep the shims and followers identified for position.

Inspection

20 Inspect the cam bearing surfaces of the head and the bearing caps. Look for score marks and deep scratches. Check the camshaft lobes for score marks, chipped areas or flat spots.

21 Camshaft run-out can be checked by supporting each end of the camshaft on V-blocks, and measuring any run-out at the centre of the shaft using a dial gauge. If the run-out exceeds the specified limit, a new camshaft will be required.

22 Measure the height of each lobe with a micrometer, and compare the results to the figures given in the *Specifications* at the start of this Chapter. If damage is noted or wear is excessive, new camshaft(s) must be fitted.

23 The camshaft bearing oil clearance should now be checked. There are two possible ways of checking this; the first method is by direct measurement and the second by the use of a product called Plastigauge.

24 If the direct measurement method is to be used, fit the bearing caps to the head, using the marks made on removal to ensure that they are correctly positioned. Tighten the retaining bolts to the specified torque in the correct sequence shown in **illustration 8.35a**. Measure each bearing cap inner diameter and the corresponding diameters of the camshaft journals, then calculate the camshaft bearing oil clearance by subtracting journal diameter from the cap diameter. Where the clearance is more than the service limit, the cylinder head and camshafts must be renewed.

25 If the Plastigauge method is to be used, clean the camshafts, the bearing surfaces in the cylinder head and the bearing caps with a clean, lint-free cloth, then lay the camshafts in place in the cylinder head.

26 Cut strips of Plastigauge, and lay one piece on each journal, parallel with the camshaft centreline. Ensuring that the camshafts are not rotated at all, refit the bearing caps and progressively tighten to the specified torque as described later in this Section.

27 Now unscrew the bolts as described in paragraph 4 and carefully lift off the bearing caps, again making sure the camshafts are not rotated.

28 To determine the oil clearance, compare the crushed Plastigauge (at its widest point) on each journal to the scale printed on the Plastigauge container.

29 Compare the results with this Chapter's *Specifications*. Where the clearance is more than the service limit, the cylinder head and camshafts must be renewed.

30 Check the cam follower and cylinder head bearing surfaces for signs of wear or damage. If the necessary measuring equipment is available, the amount of wear can be assessed by direct measurement. Subtract the diameter of each follower from its cylinder head bore and compare with the clearance given in the *Specifications* at the start of this Chapter. Renew worn components as necessary.

Refitting

31 Liberally oil the cylinder head cam follower bores and the followers. Carefully refit the followers to the cylinder head, ensuring that each follower is refitted to its original bore. Some care will be required to enter the followers squarely into their bores. Ensure that all the shims are correctly seated in the top of each follower, then liberally oil the camshaft bearing and lobe contact surfaces **(see illustrations)**.

32 Locate the camshafts in the cylinder head. The exhaust camshaft is easily distinguished by the distributor drive slot on its left-hand

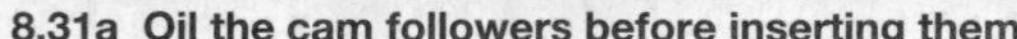

8.31a Oil the cam followers before inserting them

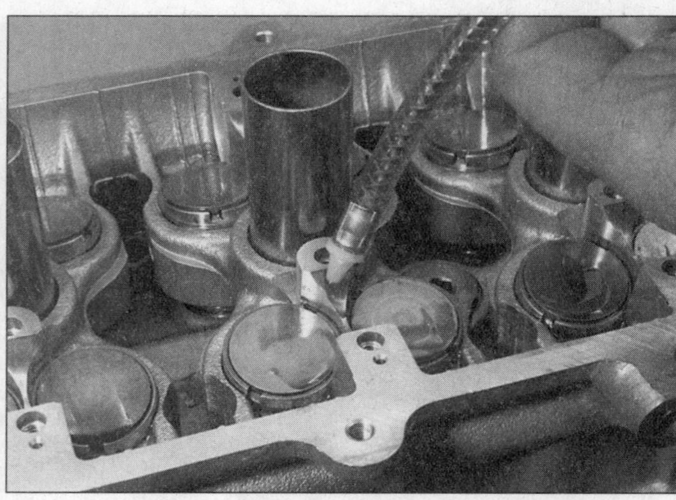

8.31b Oiling the camshaft bearing surfaces

end. The shafts also have identification markings - the inlet camshaft is marked "I" and the exhaust camshaft "E". Check that the crankshaft pulley TDC notch is still aligned with the pointer on the timing chain cover. Position each camshaft so that its No 1 cylinder lobes are pointing away from their valves. With the shafts in this position, the sprocket locating pin in the inlet camshaft's right-hand end will be in the 9 o'clock position when viewed from the right-hand end of the engine, while that of the exhaust camshaft will be in the 12 o'clock position.

33 Ensure that the bearing cap and head mating surfaces are completely clean, unmarked and free from oil. If removed, apply a smear of suitable sealant to the distributor mounting cap mating surface before refitting it and tightening the bolts.

34 Refit the bearing caps, using the identification marks made or noted on removal to ensure that each is installed the correct way round and in its original location.

35 Working in the sequence shown **(see illustration)**, evenly and progressively tighten the camshaft bearing cap bolts by one turn at a time until the caps touch the cylinder head. Then using the same sequence tighten all the bolts to the specified Stage 1 torque setting. Work only as described, to impose the pressure of the valve springs gradually and evenly on the bearing caps **(see illustrations)**.

36 Using the same sequence tighten the bolts to the Stage 2 torque settings, then repeat the procedure and tighten them to the Stage 3 torque settings.

37 If removed refit the locating pins to the ends of the camshafts.

38 Engage the upper timing chain with the idler sprocket making sure that the previously made timing marks are correctly aligned.

39 Manoeuvre both the inlet and exhaust camshaft sprockets into the upper timing chain making sure that the previously made marks are correctly aligned. Locate the sprockets on the camshafts, aligning their cut-outs with the locating pins.

40 With all the timing marks correctly positioned, insert the camshaft sprocket retaining bolts and washers, and tighten them both to the specified torque while holding them stationary using an open-ended spanner on their flats.

41 Before refitting the upper timing chain tensioner it must be set to the minimum length. Remove the piston from the body then turn the ratchet fully clockwise while pressing it into the piston against the spring pressure. If now released, it will remain in this position for refitting and will automatically reset itself when the engine is started.

42 Oil the piston and insert it in the tensioner body, then refit the tensioner to the cylinder head and tighten the bolts to the specified torque.

43 Using a spanner on the crankshaft pulley bolt, turn the engine several times to check for clearance between the valves and pistons. There should be no problems if the original camshafts and followers have been refitted. **Note:** *If the camshafts and followers have been renewed, check and adjust the valve clearances "cold" prior to refitting the camshaft cover.*

44 Refit the sprocket access cover as described in Section 6.

45 Where applicable, refit the distributor with reference to Chapter 5B, and tighten the mounting bolts.

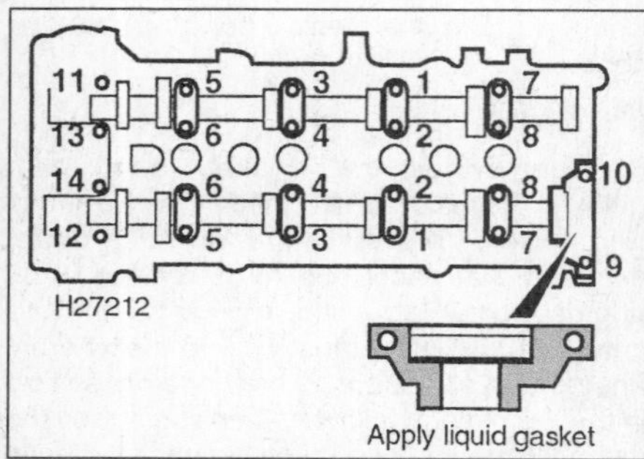

8.35a Camshaft bearing cap bolt tightening sequence. The distributor mounting cap (if removed) must have sealant applied before refitting

8.35b Tightening the camshaft bearing cap bolts

8.35c Camshafts refitted to the cylinder head

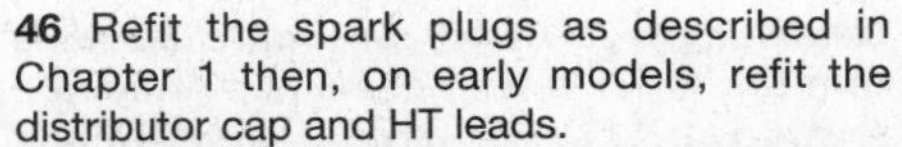
9.2a Earthing cables on the cylinder head bracket

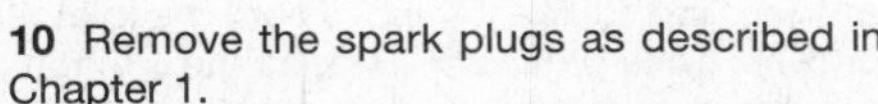
9.2b Releasing the wiring loom from the cylinder head . . .

9.2c . . . and left-hand bracket

46 Refit the spark plugs as described in Chapter 1 then, on early models, refit the distributor cap and HT leads.

47 Refit the camshaft cover with reference to Section 4.

48 Refit the wheel arch liners and the right-hand front wheel, then lower the vehicle to the ground.

49 Refit the air cleaner assembly (Chapter 4A) and drivebelts (Chapter 1).

50 Reconnect the battery negative lead.

51 Start the engine and warm it up to normal operating temperature, then check the valve clearances as described in Section 5.

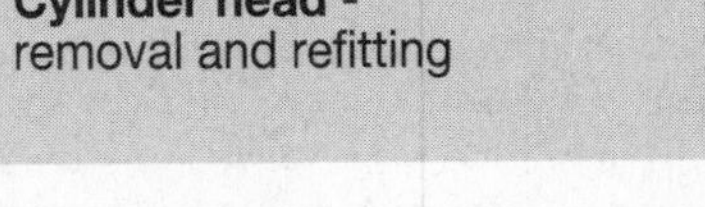

9 Cylinder head - removal and refitting

HAYNES HiNT ***To aid refitting, note the locations of all relevant brackets and the routing of hoses and cables before removal.***

Removal

1 Drain the cooling system as described in Chapter 1.

2 Disconnect the battery negative lead, then disconnect all relevant wiring noting the location points **(see illustrations)**.

3 Jack up the front of the vehicle and support on axle stands (see "*Jacking and vehicle support*"). Remove the right-hand front wheel.

4 Unscrew the retaining screws and remove the wheel arch liners from under the right-hand front wing.

5 Refer to Chapter 1 and remove the alternator drivebelt followed by the water pump/power steering pump drivebelt.

6 Remove the air cleaner assembly as described in Chapter 4A.

7 Remove the exhaust front downpipe section with reference to Chapter 4B.

8 Remove the camshaft cover as described in Section 4.

9 Where applicable, loosen the screws and remove the distributor cap from the distributor.

10 Remove the spark plugs as described in Chapter 1.

11 Set No 1 cylinder at TDC on its compression stroke, as described in Section 3.

12 On earlier models (up to July 2000), mark the position of the distributor body in relation to the cylinder head then unscrew the mounting bolts and remove the distributor.

13 Unscrew the retaining nuts and bolts, and remove the camshaft sprocket access cover from the right-hand end of the cylinder head as described in Section 6.

14 Unscrew the bolts and remove the thermostat housing from the left-hand end of the cylinder head. The coolant hoses can remain attached to the housing.

15 It is now important to mark both camshaft sprockets and the idler sprocket in relation to the upper timing chain. As a further precaution also mark the idler sprocket in relation to the lower timing chain. Wipe the chains and sprockets and use a dab of paint to mark them.

Caution: If the sprockets and chains are not marked as recommended, or if there is any doubt about their positioning on reassembly, it will be necessary to remove the lower timing chain and reassemble it with reference to Section 8. This will involve extra work to remove the crankshaft pulley, sump and timing cover. Note that it will not be possible to use the manufacturer's timing chain link marks for valve timing unless the lower timing chain is removed and refitted first, since the timing marks go out of sync when the engine is running.

16 Unbolt and remove the upper timing chain tensioner taking care to keep the pressure pad inserted in the body.

17 Unscrew the camshaft sprocket retaining bolts, whilst retaining the camshafts with a large open-ended spanner fitted to the flats on the right-hand end of each shaft. Remove each bolt along with its washer.

18 Disengage each sprocket from the end of its respective camshaft, and manoeuvre them out separately from the upper timing chain. If the sprocket locating pins are a loose fit in the camshaft ends, remove them and store them with the sprockets. **Note:** *Identify each sprocket for position as they are identical and have the same part number.*

19 Unscrew and remove the idler sprocket retaining bolt and washer, then use a screwdriver to prise the idler shaft from the roll pin on the cylinder head. This will allow the cylinder head to be lifted up over the idler sprocket. The lower timing chain will remain engaged with the crankshaft sprocket and idler sprocket because the lower guides keep them in position.

20 Disengage the upper timing chain from the idler sprocket.

21 The camshaft right- and left-hand end bearing caps are noticeably different to the others, however, the other bearing caps are all similar. They should have identification markings cast into the top of each centre bearing cap; the exhaust camshaft caps are marked "E2" to "E5" and the inlet camshaft caps are marked "I2" to "I5"; the No 2 caps being fitted nearest the timing chain end of the engine. If necessary mark the caps to ensure correct refitting.

22 Working in the **reverse** of the sequence shown in **illustration 8.35a**, evenly and progressively slacken the camshaft bearing cap retaining bolts by one turn at a time, to relieve the pressure of the valve springs gradually and evenly. Once the valve spring pressure has been relieved, the bolts can be fully unscrewed and removed. Remove the end bearing caps first, then remove the exhaust camshaft caps followed by the inlet camshaft caps.

23 Lift the camshafts out of the cylinder head. If necessary, unbolt and remove the distributor mounting cap.

24 Note that the following procedure assumes that the cylinder head will be removed with both inlet and exhaust manifolds attached; this is easier, but makes it a bulky and heavy assembly to handle. If it is wished to remove the manifolds first, proceed as described in Chapter 4A. If they are to be left in position, disconnect all wiring, hoses and cables with reference to Chapter 4A **(see illustration)**.

25 Slacken and remove the small 6 mm bolts from each end of the cylinder head, including the two bolts located in the camshaft idler sprocket access aperture.

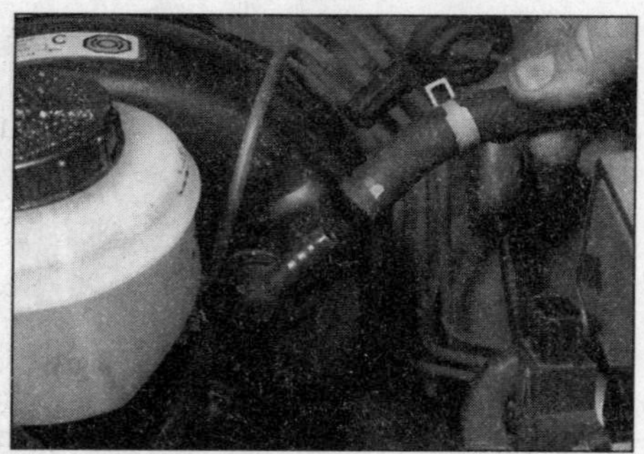

9.24 Disconnecting the hose from the brake vacuum servo unit

26 Working in the **reverse** of the sequence shown in **illustration 9.41a**, progressively slacken the ten main cylinder head bolts by half a turn at a time, until all bolts can be unscrewed by hand.

27 Lift out the cylinder head bolts and recover the washers, noting which way round the washers are fitted.

28 Lift the cylinder head away while guiding the right-hand end over the timing chain idler sprocket; seek assistance if possible, as it is a heavy assembly (especially if complete with manifolds). Remove the gasket from the top of the block noting the two locating dowels. If they are a loose fit in the block, remove them and store them with the head for safe-keeping.

29 If the cylinder head is to be dismantled for overhaul, then refer to Part B of this Chapter.

Preparation for refitting

30 Check the condition of the cylinder head bolts, and particularly their threads, whenever they are removed. Wash the bolts and wipe dry, then check each for any sign of visible wear or damage, renewing any bolt if necessary. Although Nissan do not actually specify that the bolts must be renewed, it is strongly recommended that the bolts should be renewed as a complete set whenever they are disturbed.

31 The mating faces of the cylinder head and cylinder block/crankcase must be perfectly clean before refitting the head. Use a hard plastic or wood scraper to remove all traces of gasket and carbon; also clean the piston crowns. Take particular care, as the surfaces are damaged easily. Also, make sure that the carbon is not allowed to enter the oil and water passages - this is particularly important for the lubrication system, as carbon could block the oil supply to any of the engine's components. Using adhesive tape and paper, seal the water, oil and bolt holes in the cylinder block/crankcase. To prevent carbon entering the gap between the pistons and bores, smear a little grease in the gap. After cleaning each piston, use a small brush to remove all traces of grease and carbon from the gap, then wipe away the remainder with a clean rag. Clean all the pistons in the same way.

32 Check the mating surfaces of the cylinder block/crankcase and the cylinder head for nicks, deep scratches and other damage. If slight, they may be removed carefully with a file, but if excessive, machining may be the only alternative to renewal.

33 If warpage of the cylinder head gasket surface is suspected, use a straight-edge to check it for distortion. Refer to Part B of this Chapter if necessary.

Refitting

34 Wipe clean the mating surfaces of the cylinder head and cylinder block/crankcase. Check that the two locating dowels are in position at each end of the cylinder block/crankcase surface. Check that the crankshaft is still at the TDC position.

Caution: The following procedure assumes that the lower timing chain has remained engaged with the crankshaft sprocket and idler sprocket. If there is any doubt, the lower timing chain should be removed as described in Section 8 then refitted using the special chain links for valve timing.

35 Apply a bead of suitable sealant to the joints at the top of the timing cover where it contacts the cylinder block **(see illustrations)**.

36 Fit a new gasket to the cylinder block/crankcase surface, aligning it with the locating dowels **(see illustrations)**.

37 With the aid of an assistant carefully refit the cylinder head assembly to the block while guiding it over the idler sprocket, and align it with the locating dowels **(see illustration)**.

38 Apply a smear of clean oil to the threads,

9.35a Apply sealant to the timing cover rear joint . . .

9.35b . . . and front joint

9.36a Fitting the new cylinder head gasket on the cylinder block

9.36b Locate the gasket over the special dowels on the cylinder block

9.37 Lowering the cylinder head onto the gasket

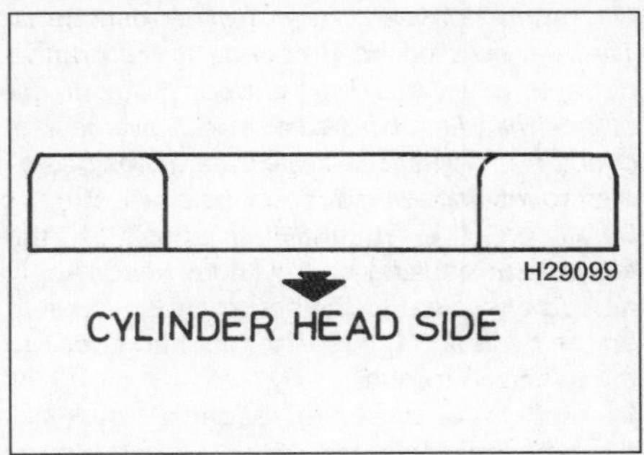

9.39a Correct fitting of the cylinder head bolt washers

9.39b Use a screwdriver to lower the head bolt washers into position

9.40 Inserting the cylinder head bolts

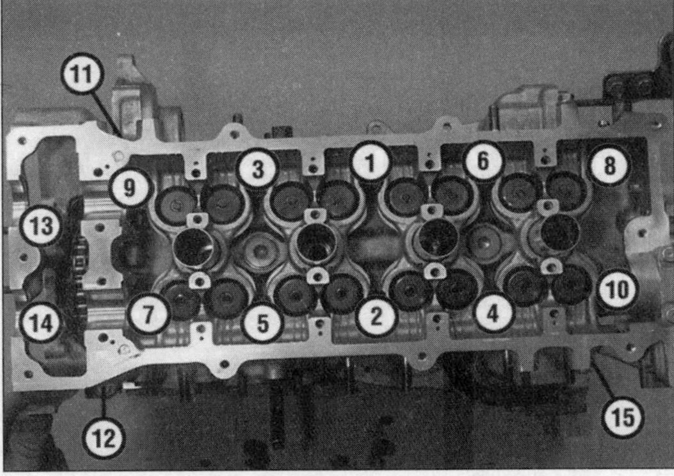

9.41a Cylinder head bolt tightening sequence

9.41b Tightening the cylinder head bolts with a torque wrench

and to the underside of the heads, of the ten main cylinder head bolts.

39 Locate the head bolt washers over the bolt holes in the cylinder head, making sure they are fitted with their tapered edges uppermost. Due to the design of the head it is not possible to fit the washers to the bolts and then fit the bolts to the head, so the washers must be lowered to the centre of the head first, then moved across over the holes. Do this by sliding the washers down a screwdriver then sliding them across **(see illustrations)**.

40 Carefully enter each bolt into the holes (*do not drop them in*) and screw in, by hand only, until finger-tight **(see illustration)**.

41 Working progressively and in the sequence shown, tighten the **ten main** cylinder head bolts to their Stage 1 torque setting, using a torque wrench and suitable socket **(see illustrations)**. **Note:** *Bolts 11 to 15 in the sequence (the 6 mm bolts) should not be tightened now, but only after the ten main bolts have been tightened to Stage 4.*

42 Once the ten main bolts have been tightened to their Stage 1 setting, go around again in the specified sequence and tighten them to the specified Stage 2 torque setting.

43 Leave the bolts a minute then, working in the **reverse** of the specified sequence, progressively slacken the head bolts by half a turn at a time, until all bolts can be unscrewed by hand.

44 Tighten the ten main bolts again by hand, then go around again in the specified sequence and tighten these ten bolts to the specified Stage 3 torque setting.

45 Finally, go around again in the specified sequence and angle-tighten the ten main head bolts through the specified Stage 4 angle. It is recommended that an angle-measuring gauge is used during this stage, to ensure accuracy **(see illustration)**. To ensure each bolt is correctly tightened, draw a plan of them and tick them off individually.

46 With the main cylinder head bolts correctly tightened, fit the five 6 mm bolts (Nos 11 to 15 in the tightening sequence) and tighten them in sequence to their specified torque setting **(see illustrations)**.

47 Locate the camshafts in the cylinder head. The exhaust camshaft is easily distinguished by the distributor drive slot on its left-hand

9.45 Angle-tightening the cylinder head bolts

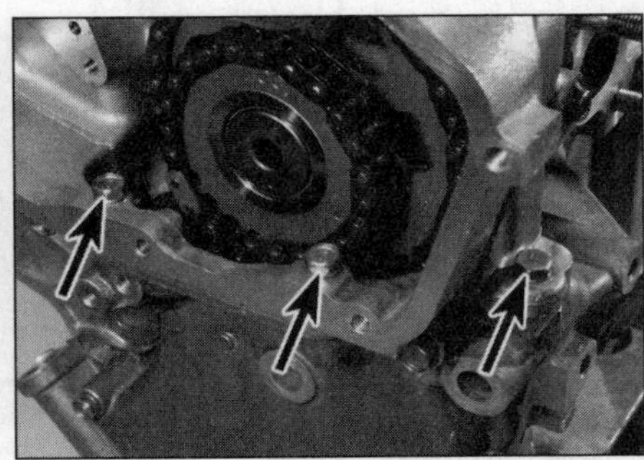
9.46a 6 mm bolts located in the idler sprocket access aperture and on the front of the cylinder head

9.46b 6 mm bolt located on the rear of the cylinder head

9.46c 6 mm bolt located on the left-hand front of the cylinder head

end. The shafts also have identification markings - the inlet camshaft is marked "I" and the exhaust camshaft "E". Check that the crankshaft pulley TDC notch is still aligned with the pointer on the timing chain cover. Position each camshaft so that its No 1 cylinder lobes are pointing away from their valves. With the shafts in this position, the sprocket locating pin in the inlet camshaft's right-hand end will be in the 9 o'clock position when viewed from the right-hand end of the engine, while that of the exhaust camshaft will be in the 12 o'clock position.

48 Ensure that the bearing cap and head mating surfaces are completely clean, unmarked and free from oil. If removed, apply a smear of suitable sealant to the distributor mounting cap mating surface before refitting it and tightening the bolts.

49 Refit the bearing caps, using the identification marks made or noted on removal to ensure that each is installed the correct way round and in its original location.

50 Working in the sequence shown in Section 8, evenly and progressively tighten the camshaft bearing cap bolts by one turn at a time until the caps touch the cylinder head. Then using the same sequence tighten all the bolts to the specified Stage 1 torque setting. Work only as described, to impose the pressure of the valve springs gradually and evenly on the bearing caps.

51 Using the same sequence tighten the bolts to the Stage 2 torque settings, then repeat the procedure and tighten them to the Stage 3 torque settings.

52 If removed refit the locating pins to the ends of the camshafts.

53 Engage the upper timing chain with the idler sprocket making sure that the previously made timing marks are correctly aligned.

54 Locate the idler sprocket shaft on the roll pin then insert the retaining bolt and washer and tighten to the specified torque. **Note:** *Make sure the previously made timing marks are correctly aligned.*

55 Manoeuvre both the inlet and exhaust camshaft sprockets into the upper timing chain making sure that the previously made marks are correctly aligned. Locate the sprockets on the camshafts, aligning their cut-outs with the locating pins.

56 With all the timing marks correctly positioned, insert the camshaft sprocket retaining bolts and washers, and tighten them both to the specified torque while holding them stationary using an open-ended spanner on their flats.

57 Before refitting the upper timing chain tensioner it must be set to the minimum length. Remove the piston from the body then turn the ratchet fully clockwise while pressing it into the piston against the spring pressure. If now released, it will remain in this position for refitting and will automatically reset itself when the engine is started.

58 Oil the piston and insert it in the tensioner body, then refit the tensioner to the cylinder head and tighten the bolts to the specified torque.

59 Using a spanner on the crankshaft pulley bolt, turn the engine several times to check for clearance between the valves and pistons. There should be no problems if the original cylinder head is being refitted. **Note:** *If the cylinder head/camshafts have been overhauled, check and adjust the valve clearances "cold" prior to refitting the cylinder head cover.*

60 Clean the mating surfaces of the thermostat housing and cylinder head. Apply a bead of sealant to the housing then locate it on the head and tighten the mounting bolts to the specified torque.

61 Refit the sprocket access cover as described in Section 6.

62 Where applicable, refit the distributor with reference to Chapter 5B, and tighten the mounting bolts.

63 Refit the spark plugs as described in Chapter 1 then, on early models, refit the distributor cap and HT leads.

64 Refit the camshaft cover (see Section 4).

65 Refit the exhaust front downpipe section with reference to Chapter 4B.

66 Refit the wheel arch liners and the right-hand front wheel, then lower the vehicle to the ground.

67 Refit the air cleaner assembly (see Chapter 4A) and drivebelts (Chapter 1).

68 Reconnect the battery negative lead.

69 Refill the cooling system (Chapter 1).

70 Start the engine and warm it up to normal operating temperature, then check the valve clearances as described in Section 5.

10 Sump - removal and refitting

Removal

1 Firmly apply the handbrake, then jack up the front of the vehicle and support it on axle stands (see "*Jacking and vehicle support*"). Disconnect the battery negative lead.

2 Where applicable, slacken and remove the retaining screws and remove the undershield from beneath the engine.

3 Drain the engine oil, then clean and refit the engine oil drain plug, tightening it to the specified torque. If the engine is nearing its service interval when the oil and filter are due for renewal, it is recommended that the filter is also removed, and a new one fitted. After reassembly, the engine can then be refilled with fresh oil. Refer to Chapter 1 for further information.

4 Unbolt the centre member from under the engine compartment.

5 Remove the exhaust system front downpipe as described in Chapter 4B.

6 Progressively slacken and remove all the sump retaining bolts **(see illustration)**.

7 Break the joint by striking the sump with the palm of your hand, then lower the sump and withdraw it from underneath the vehicle **(see illustration)**.

8 Remove the front and rear sealing strips.

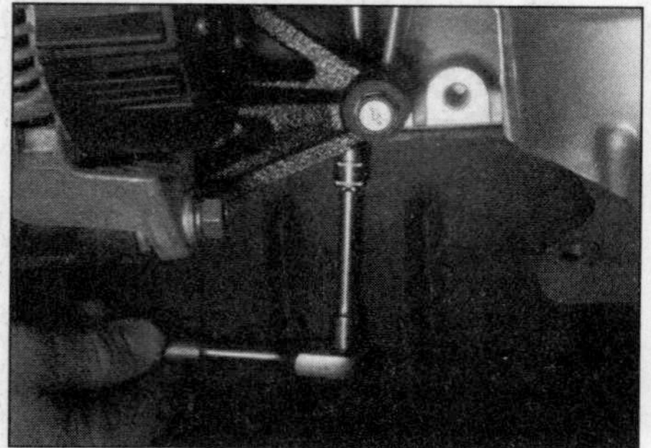
10.6 Unscrew the bolts . . .

10.7 . . . then lower the sump from the cylinder block

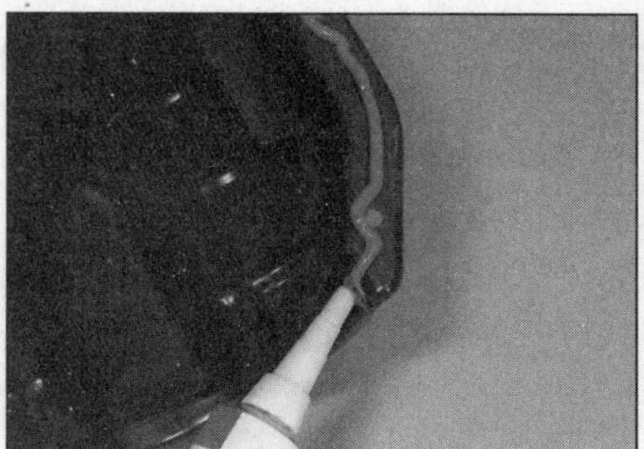

10.10 Apply a bead of sealant to the sump mating surface

10.11 Hold the sealing strips in position with a little sealant

Refitting

9 Clean all traces of sealant from the mating surfaces of the cylinder block/crankcase and sump, then use a clean rag to wipe out the sump and the engine's interior.

10 Ensure that the sump and cylinder block/crankcase mating surfaces are clean and dry. Apply a continuous bead of suitable sealant to the side mating surfaces of the sump making sure that the bead goes around the inner edges of the bolt holes and approximately 20 mm down into the sealing strip curves at each end of the sump **(see illustration)**.

11 Fit the front and rear sealing strips making sure that the 134 mm one is located at the front and the 123 mm one at the rear. The location pips must engage with the central cut-outs provided. Hold the strips in position with a little sealant **(see illustration)**.

12 Offer up the sump and refit its retaining bolts. Tighten them evenly and progressively to the specified torque.

13 Refit the exhaust system front downpipe section as described in Chapter 4B.

14 Refit the centre member and tighten the bolts to the specified torque.

15 Where applicable, refit the undershield and securely tighten the retaining screws.

16 Reconnect the battery and lower the vehicle to the ground.

17 Fill the engine with oil as described in Chapter 1.

11 Oil pump and pick-up tube - removal, inspection and refitting

Removal

1 The oil pump is an integral part of the timing chain cover. First remove the sump as described in Section 10.

2 Unscrew the pick-up tube support mounting bolt, then unscrew the bolts securing the tube to the oil pump on the timing cover. Remove the tube and recover the gasket **(see illustrations)**.

3 Remove the timing chain cover as described in Section 6.

Inspection

4 Unscrew the retaining screws and bolts, and remove the pump cover from the rear of the timing chain cover **(see illustrations)**.

5 Remove both the oil pump rotors from the timing cover.

6 Unscrew the oil pressure regulator valve plug from the oil pump cover, and recover its sealing washer (if fitted). Withdraw the shim (if fitted) followed by the spring and the valve piston, noting which way round the piston is fitted **(see illustration)**.

7 Inspect the pump rotors, regulator valve piston and the cover for obvious signs of wear or damage.

8 Fit the rotors to the timing cover and, using feeler blades of the appropriate thickness,

11.2a Unscrewing the pick-up tube support mounting bolt

11.2b Removing the pick-up tube and gasket from the timing cover

11.4a Oil pump cover and retaining bolts/screws

11.4b Removing the oil pump cover

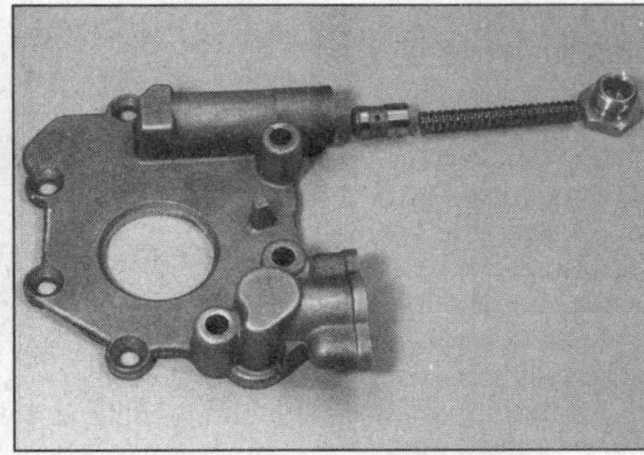

11.6 Oil pressure regulator valve components removed from the timing cover

11.8a Using feeler blades to check the outer rotor-to-cover clearance . . .

11.8b . . . the inner rotor-to-outer rotor clearance . . .

11.9a . . . the inner rotor endfloat . . .

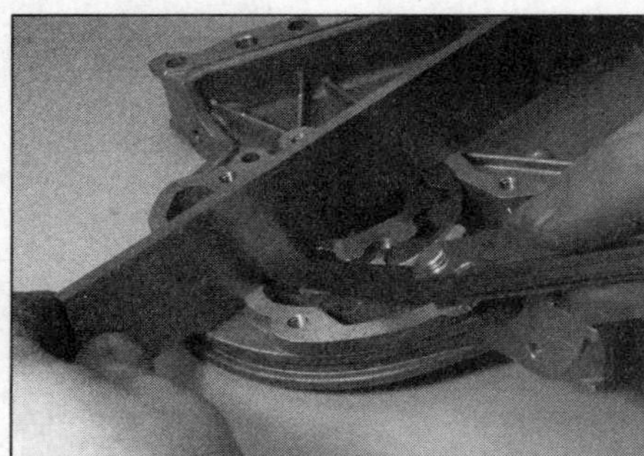
11.9b . . . and the outer rotor endfloat

11.14 Lubricating the rotors with oil

measure the clearance between the outer rotor and cover, and between the tips of outer rotor teeth and inner rotor recesses **(see illustrations)**.

9 Using feeler blades and a straight-edge placed across the top of the cover and the rotors, measure the inner and outer rotor endfloat **(see illustrations)**.

10 If access to the necessary measuring equipment can be gained, measure the diameter of the inner rotor and cover bearing surfaces. Subtract the rotor outer diameter from the cover inner diameter, and calculate the rotor-to-housing clearance.

11 If any measurement is outside the specified limits, or the rotors, valve or cover is damaged, the complete timing chain cover assembly should be renewed.

12 Check the oil pressure regulator valve as follows. Lubricate the piston with engine oil and check that it falls onto its seat by its own weight. If possible measure the diameters of the valve and its bore to determine the running clearance. If not within the specified tolerance renew the cover.

13 Check the oil pressure relief valve as follows. Unscrew the oil filter from the rear of the cylinder block. Inspect the valve ball for signs of wear or damage. Depress the valve ball, and check that it moves smoothly and easily, and returns quickly under spring pressure. If not the valve must be renewed. Pull the valve out from the cylinder block, noting which way round it is fitted. Press the new one into position using a suitable tubular spacer. Fit a new oil filter to the engine (see Chapter 1).

14 Lubricate the rotors with clean engine oil, and refit them to the timing cover **(see illustration)**. Ensure that the inner gear is fitted with its flange towards the timing cover.

15 Ensure that the mating surfaces are clean and dry, and refit the pump cover. Fit the cover retaining bolts and screws, and tighten them to the specified torque settings.

16 Fit the pressure regulator valve piston, ensuring it is the correct way around, followed by the spring and shim. Fit a new sealing washer to the valve plug, and tighten to the specified torque setting.

Refitting

17 Refit the timing chain cover as described in Section 6, but before refitting the sump refit the pick-up tube as follows. Clean the mating surfaces of the pick-up tube and timing cover then offer the tube to the cover together with a new gasket and insert the retaining bolts hand-tight. Insert the support mounting bolt then tighten all the bolts to the specified torque.

12 Crankshaft oil seals - renewal

Right-hand (timing chain cover) oil seal

1 Jack up the front of the vehicle and support on axle stands (see "*Jacking and vehicle support*"). Remove the right-hand front wheel.

2 Undo the retaining screws and remove the plastic liner from underneath the wing to gain access to the crankshaft pulley bolt.

3 To prevent crankshaft rotation while the pulley bolt is unscrewed, select 4th gear and have an assistant apply the brakes firmly. On automatic transmission models, remove the starter motor and have an assistant engage a wide-bladed screwdriver with the starter ring gear on the driveplate.

4 Unscrew and remove the pulley bolt and washer, and remove the pulley from the crankshaft. If the pulley Woodruff key is a loose fit, remove it and store it with the pulley for safe-keeping.

5 Carefully lever the oil seal out of position, using a screwdriver, taking care not to damage the oil pump gears or timing cover **(see illustration)**.

6 Clean the seal housing, and remove any burrs or raised edges.

7 Lubricate the lips of the new seal with a smear of grease and offer up the seal, ensuring its sealing lip is facing inwards. Carefully ease the seal into position, taking care not to

12.5 Levering the crankshaft oil seal from the timing cover with a screwdriver

12.7 Drive the new oil seal into position using a socket and mallet

damage its sealing lip. Drive the seal into position until it seats on its locating shoulder, using a suitable tubular drift, such as a socket, which bears only on the hard outer edge of the seal **(see illustration)**. Take care not to damage the seal lips during fitting. Note that the seal lips should face inwards.

8 Where removed, refit the Woodruff key to the crankshaft.

9 Align the crankshaft pulley groove with the key, then slide the pulley onto the crankshaft, and refit the retaining bolt and washer.

10 Lock the crankshaft by the method used on removal, and tighten the pulley retaining bolt to the specified torque setting.

11 Refit the liner beneath the wing then refit the wheel and lower the vehicle to the ground.

Left-hand (flywheel/driveplate) oil seal

12 Remove the flywheel/driveplate as described in Section 13.

13 Taking care not to mark either the crankshaft or any part of the cylinder block/ crankcase, lever the seal evenly out of its housing using a large flat-bladed screwdriver.

14 Clean the seal housing, and remove any burrs or raised edges.

15 Lubricate the lips of the new seal with grease. Ease the seal over the crankshaft shoulder by hand only, and press the seal evenly into its housing until its outer flange seats evenly on the housing lip. If necessary, a soft-faced mallet can be used to tap the seal gently into place.

16 Refit the flywheel/driveplate as described in Section 13.

13 Flywheel/driveplate - removal, inspection and refitting

Removal

1 Remove the transmission as described in Chapter 7A or 7B.

2 On manual transmission models remove the clutch as described in Chapter 6. On automatic transmission models remove the electro-magnetic clutch housing as described in Chapter 7B.

3 Mark the position of the flywheel/driveplate in relation to the crankshaft using a dab of paint. The flywheel/driveplate must now be held stationary while the bolts are loosened. A home-made locking tool may be fabricated from a piece of scrap metal and used to lock the ring gear **(see illustration)**. Bolt the tool to one of the transmission bellhousing mounting holes.

4 Unscrew the mounting bolts then lift off the flywheel/driveplate. Recover the spacer plate where applicable **(see illustrations)**.

5 Remove the engine rear plate from the location dowels.

Inspection

Manual transmission models

6 If the flywheel's clutch mating surface is deeply scored, cracked or otherwise damaged, the flywheel must be renewed. However, it may be possible to have it surface-ground; seek the advice of a Nissan dealer or engine reconditioning specialist.

7 If the ring gear is badly worn or has missing teeth, it must be renewed. This job is best left to a Nissan dealer or engine reconditioning specialist. The temperature to which the new ring gear must be heated for installation is critical and, if not done accurately, the hardness of the teeth will be destroyed.

Automatic transmission models

8 Check the driveplate for signs of damage and renew it if necessary. If the ring gear is badly worn or has missing teeth, the driveplate must be renewed.

Refitting

9 Clean the mating surfaces of the flywheel/driveplate and crankshaft. Remove any locking compound from the threads of the crankshaft holes, using the correct-size tap, if available.

HAYNES HiNT ***If a tap is not available, cut two slots down the threads of one of the old bolts with a hacksaw, and use the bolt to remove the locking compound.***

10 It is recommended that locking fluid is applied to the threads of the bolts although this is not stipulated by Nissan.

11 Offer up the flywheel/driveplate to the crankshaft (together with the spacer plate where fitted) using the alignment marks made during removal, and fit the new retaining bolts.

12 Lock the flywheel/driveplate using the method employed on dismantling, and tighten the retaining bolts to the specified torque **(see illustration)**.

13.3 Home-made tool for holding the flywheel stationary

13.4a Removing the flywheel mounting bolts . . .

13.4b . . . and spacer plate . . .

13.4c . . . then lift off the flywheel

13.12 Tighten the flywheel mounting bolts

14.7 Right-hand engine mounting

14.24 Front engine mounting

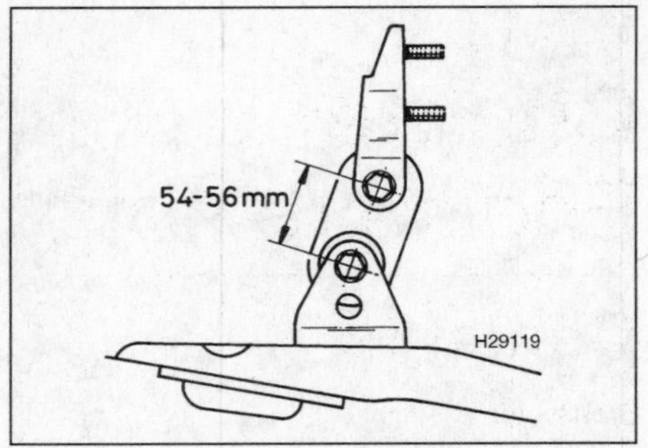

14.28 Front engine mounting fitting dimension

13 Refit the clutch on manual transmission models as described in Chapter 6. On automatic transmission models refit the electro-magnetic clutch housing as described in Chapter 7B.
14 Refit the transmission as described in Chapter 7A or 7B.
15 Refit the engine rear plate to the location dowels on the cylinder block. On automatic transmission models clean away all traces of acrylic tape then apply new tape before refitting the plate.

14 Engine/transmission mountings - inspection and renewal

Inspection

1 Jack up the front of the vehicle and support on axle stands (see *"Jacking and vehicle support"*).
2 Check all the engine/transmission mounting rubbers to see if they are cracked, hardened or separated from the metal at any point; renew the mounting if any such damage or deterioration is evident.
3 Check that all the mounting's fasteners are securely tightened; use a torque wrench to check if possible.
4 Using a large screwdriver or a crowbar, check for wear in the mounting by carefully levering against it to check for free play. Where this is not possible enlist the aid of an assistant to move the engine/transmission back and forth, or from side to side, while you watch the mounting. While some free play is to be expected even from new components, excessive wear should be obvious. If excessive free play is found, check first that the fasteners are correctly secured, then renew any worn components as described below.

Renewal

Right-hand mounting

5 Jack up the front of the vehicle and support on axle stands (see *"Jacking and vehicle support"*). Remove the right-hand front wheel and wheel arch liners.
6 Place a jack beneath the engine, with a block of wood on the jack head. Raise the jack until it is supporting the right-hand end of the engine.
7 Unscrew the through-bolt from the body mounting bracket **(see illustration)**.
8 Unbolt and remove the upper part of the mounting, and recover the rubbers which are fitted to each side of the body mounting bracket. If required, unbolt the lower part of the mounting from the cylinder block.
9 Check the mountings for wear or damage and if necessary renew them.
10 On refitting, fit the lower mounting bracket (where removed) to the engine, and securely tighten its retaining bolts.
11 Fit the rubbers to the body mounting bracket ensuring that their pins are correctly seated in the bracket holes, then fit the upper mounting to the bracket and tighten the bolts.
12 Align the right-hand mounting with the body bracket, then insert the through-bolt and tighten its nut to the specified torque setting. Remove the jack from underneath the engine.
13 Refit the wheel arch liners and front wheel then lower the vehicle to the ground.

Left-hand mounting

14 Remove the battery (refer to Chapter 5A).
15 Place a jack and block of wood beneath the transmission, and raise the jack to take the weight of the transmission.
16 Unscrew and remove the through-bolt, then undo the three bolts and remove the left-hand mounting from the transmission. Recover the rubbers from each side of the mounting bracket and, if necessary, unbolt the mounting bracket from the vehicle body.
17 Check the mountings for wear or damage and if necessary renew them.
18 On refitting, fit the mounting bracket (where removed) and securely tighten its retaining bolts.
19 Refit the rubbers to the mounting bracket, ensuring that their pins are correctly seated in the bracket holes, and manoeuvre the mounting into position. Fit the bolts securing the mounting to the transmission, and tighten them to the specified torque setting.
20 Align the left-hand mounting with its bracket, then insert the through-bolt and tighten its nut to the specified torque setting.
21 Remove the jack from underneath the engine, and refit the battery (see Chapter 5A).

Front mounting - manual transmission models only

22 Jack up the front of the vehicle and support on axle stands (see *"Jacking and vehicle support"*).
23 Place a jack beneath the engine, with a block of wood on the jack head. Raise the jack until it is supporting the weight of the engine.
24 Unscrew and remove the two bolts, then remove the front mounting rubber. If necessary unbolt the mounting bracket from the cylinder block **(see illustration)**.
25 Check for wear or damage and renew if necessary.
26 On refitting, fit the mounting bracket to the engine, and tighten its retaining bolts to the specified torque.
27 Insert the rubber and refit the bolts loosely.
28 Check that the distance between the two bolts is as shown **(see illustration)**. If necessary adjust the engine position until the distance is correct, then fully tighten the bolts.
29 Remove the jack from underneath the engine then lower the vehicle to the ground.

Rear mounting

30 Jack up the front of the vehicle and support on axle stands (see *"Jacking and vehicle support"*).
31 Place a jack beneath the engine, with a block of wood on the jack head. Raise the jack until it is supporting the weight of the engine.
32 Unscrew and remove the through-bolt and recover the large washer.
33 Unbolt the mounting from the engine compartment lower centre member.
34 If necessary unbolt the bracket from the transmission.
35 Check for wear or damage and renew if necessary.
36 On refitting, fit the bracket to the transmission and tighten the bolts.
37 Fit the mounting to the centre member and tighten the bolts.
38 Align the rear mounting with its bracket, then insert the through-bolt and large washer and tighten the nut to the specified torque.
39 Remove the jack from underneath the engine, then lower the vehicle to the ground.

Chapter 2 Part B:
Engine removal and overhaul procedures

Contents

Degrees of difficulty

Easy, suitable for novice with little experience 

Fairly easy, suitable for beginner with some experience 

Fairly difficult, suitable for competent DIY mechanic 

Difficult, suitable for experienced DIY mechanic 

Very difficult, suitable for expert DIY or professional

Specifications

Cylinder head

Maximum gasket face distortion	0.1 mm
Cylinder head height	121.1 to 121.3

Valves

Valve head diameter:	
Inlet	27.40 to 27.60 mm
Exhaust	22.40 to 22.60 mm
Valve stem diameter:	
Inlet	5.465 to 5.480 mm
Exhaust	5.445 to 5.460 mm
Overall length:	
Inlet	95.50 to 96.00 mm
Exhaust	95.57 to 96.07 mm
Valve guide inner diameter:	
Inlet	5.500 to 5.518 mm
Exhaust	5.500 to 5.518 mm
Valve stem-to-guide clearance:	
Inlet	0.020 to 0.053 mm
Exhaust	0.040 to 0.073 mm
Valve spring free length	40 00 mm
Valve spring out-of-square limit	1.74 mm

Cylinder block

Cylinder bore diameter:	
1.0 and 1.3 litre engines:	
Grade 1	71.000 to 71.010 mm
Grade 2	71.010 to 71.020 mm
Grade 3	71.020 to 71.030 mm
Oversizes available	0.2 mm
1.4 litre engines:	
Grade 1	72.000 to 72.010 mm
Grade 2	72.010 to 72.020 mm
Grade 3	72.020 to 72.030 mm
Oversizes available	0.2 mm

Piston and connecting rod

Piston diameter (measured 9.5 mm up from the base of skirt):	
1.0 and 1.3 litre engines:	
Standard piston:	
Grade 1	70.980 to 70.990 mm
Grade 2	70.990 to 71.000 mm
Grade 3	71.000 to 71.010 mm
0.2 mm oversize piston	71.180 to 71.210 mm
1.4 litre engines:	
Standard piston:	
Grade 1	71.980 to 71.990 mm
Grade 2	71.990 to 72.000 mm
Grade 3	72.000 to 72.010 mm
0.2 mm oversize piston	72.180 to 72.210 mm
Piston-to-bore clearance	0.010 to 0.030 mm
Piston gudgeon pin bore diameter	18.004 to 18.010 mm
Gudgeon pin outer diameter	17.994 to 18.000 mm
Piston-to-gudgeon pin clearance	0.004 to 0.016 mm
Connecting rod small-end bush diameter	17.962 to 17.978 mm
Connecting rod small-end bush-to-gudgeon pin clearance	-0.016 to -0.038 mm (ie an interference fit)
Connecting rod big-end bore diameter	43.000 to 43.013 mm
Connecting rod big-end bearing side clearance:	
Standard	0.20 to 0.47 mm
Service limit	0.55 mm

Crankshaft

Endfloat:	
Standard	0.060 to 0.26 mm
Service limit	0.3 mm
Run-out:	
Standard	Less than 0.05 mm
Main bearing journal diameter:	
Grade 0	44.966 to 44.970 mm
Grade 1	44.962 to 44.966 mm
Grade 2	44.958 to 44.962 mm
Grade 3	44.954 to 44.958 mm
Main bearing journal ovality	Less than 0.005 mm
Main bearing journal taper	Less than 0.002 mm
Big-end bearing journal diameter	39.96 to 39.97 mm
Big-end journal ovality	Less than 0.005 mm
Big-end journal taper	Less than 0.002 mm
Main bearing running clearance:	
Standard	0.022 to 0.038 mm
Service limit	0.064 mm
Big-end bearing running clearance:	
Standard	0.010 to 0.044 mm
Service limit	0.064 mm
Main bearing shell thicknesses:	
Standard:	
Black	2.000 to 2.004 mm
Brown/Red	2.002 to 2.006 mm
Green	2.004 to 2.008 mm
Yellow	2.006 to 2.010 mm
Blue	2.008 to 2.012 mm
Pink	2.010 to 2.014 mm
White	2.012 to 2.016 mm
0.25 mm undersize	2.125 to 2.129 mm
Big-end bearing shell thicknesses:	
Standard	1.504 to 1.508 mm
Undersize	1.629 to 1.633 mm

Piston rings

Ring-to-groove clearance:	
Standard:	
Top compression ring	0.50 to 0.73 mm
Second compression ring	0.030 to 0.070 mm
Service limit	0.2 mm

Piston rings (continued)

Ring-to-groove clearance (continued):
End gaps:

Standard:	
Top compression ring	0.20 to 0.30 mm
Second compression ring	0.30 to 0.45 mm
Oil control ring	0.25 to 1.00 mm
Service limit:	
Top compression ring	0.37 mm
Second compression ring	0.54 mm
Oil control ring	1.09 mm

Torque wrench settings

Refer to Chapter 2A Specifications.

1 General information

Included in this Part of Chapter 2 are details of removing the engine from the vehicle, and general overhaul procedures for the cylinder head, cylinder block/crankcase and all other engine internal components.

The information given ranges from advice concerning preparation for an overhaul and the purchase of replacement parts, to detailed step-by-step procedures covering removal, inspection, renovation and refitting of engine internal components.

After Section 6, all instructions are based on the assumption that the engine has been removed from the vehicle. For information concerning in-car engine repair, as well as the removal and refitting of those external components necessary for full overhaul, refer to Part A of this Chapter and to Section 6. Ignore any preliminary dismantling operations described in Part A that are no longer relevant once the engine has been removed from the vehicle.

Apart from torque wrench settings, which are given at the beginning of Part A, all specifications relating to engine overhaul are at the beginning of this Part of Chapter 2.

2 Engine overhaul - general information

It is not always easy to determine when, or if, an engine should be completely overhauled, as a number of factors must be considered.

High mileage is not necessarily an indication that an overhaul is needed, while low mileage does not preclude the need for an overhaul. Frequency of servicing is probably the most important consideration. An engine which has had regular and frequent oil and filter changes, as well as other required maintenance, should give many thousands of miles of reliable service. Conversely, a neglected engine may require an overhaul very early in its life.

Excessive oil consumption is an indication that piston rings, valve seals and/or valve guides are in need of attention. Make sure that oil leaks are not responsible before deciding that the rings and/or guides are worn. Perform a compression test, as described in Part A of this Chapter, to determine the likely cause of the problem.

Check the oil pressure with a gauge fitted in place of the oil pressure switch, and compare it with that specified. If it is extremely low, the main and big-end bearings, and/or the oil pump, are probably worn out.

Loss of power, rough running, knocking or metallic engine noises, excessive valve gear noise, and high fuel consumption may also point to the need for an overhaul, especially if they are all present at the same time. If a complete service does not remedy the situation, major mechanical work is the only solution.

An engine overhaul involves restoring all internal parts to the specification of a new engine. During an overhaul, the pistons and the piston rings are renewed. New main and big-end bearings are generally fitted; if necessary, the crankshaft may be reground, to restore the journals. The valves are also serviced as well, since they are usually in less-than-perfect condition at this point. While the engine is being overhauled, other components, such as the distributor, starter and alternator, can be overhauled as well. The end result should be an as-new engine that will give many trouble-free miles.

Cooling system components such as the hoses, thermostat and water pump should be renewed when an engine is overhauled. The radiator should be checked carefully, to ensure that it is not clogged or leaking. Also, it is a good idea to renew the oil pump whenever the engine is overhauled.

Before beginning the engine overhaul, read through the entire procedure, to familiarise yourself with the scope and requirements of the job. Overhauling an engine is not difficult if you follow carefully all of the instructions, have the necessary tools and equipment, and pay close attention to all specifications. It can, however, be time-consuming. Plan on the car being off the road for a minimum of two weeks, especially if parts must be taken to an engineering works for repair or reconditioning. Check on the availability of parts, and make sure that any necessary special tools and equipment are obtained in advance. Most work can be done with typical hand tools, although a number of precision measuring tools are required for inspecting parts to determine if they must be renewed. Often, the engineering works will handle the inspection of parts, and can offer advice concerning reconditioning and renewal.

Always wait until the engine has been completely dismantled, and until all components (especially the cylinder block/crankcase and the crankshaft) have been inspected, before deciding what service and repair operations must be performed by an engineering works. The condition of these components will be the major factor to consider when determining whether to overhaul the original engine, or to buy a reconditioned unit. Do not, therefore, purchase parts or have overhaul work done on other components until they have been thoroughly inspected. As a general rule, time is the primary cost of an overhaul, so it does not pay to fit worn or sub-standard parts.

As a final note, to ensure maximum life and minimum trouble from a reconditioned engine, everything must be assembled with care, in a spotlessly-clean environment.

3 Engine removal - methods and precautions

If you have decided that the engine must be removed for overhaul or major repair work, several preliminary steps should be taken.

Locating a suitable place to work is extremely important. Adequate work space, along with storage space for the vehicle, will be needed. If a workshop or garage is not available, at the very least, a flat, level, clean work surface is required.

Cleaning the engine compartment and engine/transmission before beginning the removal procedure will help keep tools clean and organised.

An engine hoist or A-frame will also be necessary. Make sure that the equipment is rated in excess of the combined weight of the engine and transmission. Safety is of primary importance, considering the potential hazards involved in removing the engine/transmission from the vehicle.

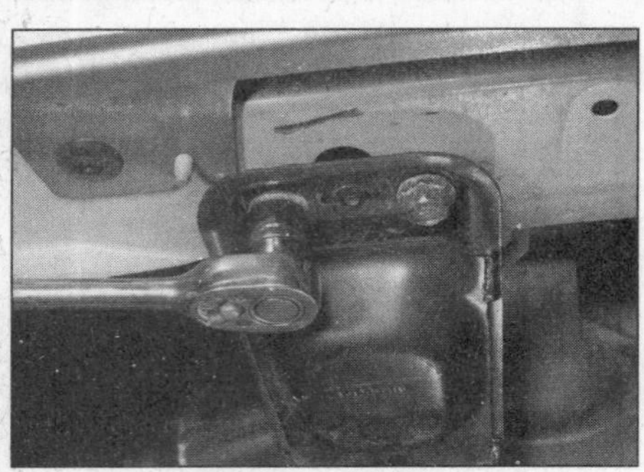

4.39 Unbolting the centre member from under the engine compartment

If this is the first time you have removed an engine, an assistant should ideally be available. Advice and aid from someone more experienced would also be helpful. There are many instances when one person cannot simultaneously perform all of the operations required when lifting the engine out of the vehicle.

Plan the operation ahead of time. Before starting work, arrange for the hire of, or obtain, all of the tools and equipment you will need. Some of the equipment necessary to perform engine/transmission removal and installation safely and with relative ease (in addition to an engine hoist) is as follows: a heavy-duty trolley jack, complete sets of spanners and sockets as described in the front of this manual, wooden blocks, and plenty of rags and cleaning solvent for mopping up spilled oil, coolant and fuel. If the hoist must be hired, make sure that you arrange for it in advance, and perform all of the operations possible without it beforehand. This will save you money and time.

Plan for the vehicle to be out of use for quite a while. An engineering works will be required to perform some of the work which the do-it-yourselfer cannot accomplish without special equipment. These places often have a busy schedule, so it would be a good idea to consult them before removing the engine, in order to accurately estimate the amount of time required to rebuild or repair components that may need work.

Always be extremely careful when removing and refitting the engine/transmission. Serious injury can result from careless actions. Plan ahead and take your time, and a job of this nature, although major, can be accomplished successfully.

The engine and transmission is removed from under the vehicle on all models described in this manual.

TOOL TIP

Drill holes in two flat metal bars and bolt them to the front/left and rear/right of the cylinder head, then attach universal lifting eyes to them

4 Engine and transmission - removal, separation and refitting

Removal

1 Park the vehicle on firm, level ground and apply the handbrake. Jack up the front of the vehicle and support on axle stands (see "*Jacking and vehicle support*"). **Note:** *To allow adequate clearance for removal of the engine/transmission assembly, there should be at least 60 cm between the front bumper and the ground. If a low trolley is being used to move the assembly from under the vehicle, additional height will be required.*

2 Remove both front roadwheels, and where applicable remove the splash guard from under the engine compartment.

3 Remove the bonnet as described in Chapter 11.

4 Depressurise the fuel system as described in Chapter 4A.

5 Remove the battery and mounting bracket as described in Chapter 5A. Also remove the fuse/relay boxes from the engine compartment.

6 Disconnect the radiator bottom hose and drain the cooling system (see Chapter 1), saving the coolant if it is fit for re-use.

7 Drain the transmission oil/fluid with reference to Chapter 7A or 7B (as applicable). Refit and tighten the drain and filler plugs.

8 If the engine is to be dismantled, working as described in Chapter 1, drain the oil and if required remove the oil filter. Clean and refit the drain plug, tightening it to the specified torque.

9 On manual transmission models, working as described in Chapter 7A disconnect the gearchange linkage and support rods and the speedometer cable from the transmission.

10 On automatic transmission models, working as described in Chapter 7B disconnect the selector cable from the transmission.

11 Remove the splash guards from under the right-hand wing.

12 Where necessary, remove the front anti-roll bar as described in Chapter 10.

13 Refer to Chapter 10 and disconnect the front suspension lower arms from the hub carriers.

14 Using a lever, prise each driveshaft inner joint from the transmission while pulling the strut outwards. Tie the struts and driveshafts to one side.

15 Remove the front exhaust section, or if preferred the complete exhaust system as described in Chapter 4B.

16 Remove the cooling system expansion tank with reference to Chapter 3.

17 Remove the air filter assembly as described in Chapter 4A.

18 Disconnect the transmission earth cable.

19 Disconnect the wiring from the exhaust gas sensor (see Chapter 4B).

20 Disconnect the wiring from the distributor (where applicable) and crank angle sensor.

21 Disconnect the wiring as necessary then unbolt and remove the battery tray.

22 On manual transmission models, disconnect the wiring from the gear position switch (998 cc models) or neutral and reverse switches (1275 and 1348 cc models) on the transmission.

23 On manual transmission models, disconnect the clutch cable as described in Chapter 6. Tie the cable to one side.

24 Disconnect and remove the radiator top hose.

25 On automatic transmission models, disconnect the two cooler hoses from the bottom of the radiator. To prevent loss of fluid clamp the hoses and position a container beneath them.

26 Disconnect/unbolt the earth cables from the cylinder head.

27 Disconnect the wiring from the injectors and throttle housing.

28 Disconnect the wiring on the main relay box (near the battery), and the earth cable on the right-hand inner wing.

29 Where applicable, disconnect the wiring from the right-hand front engine mounting.

30 Disconnect the wiring from the engine temperature sensors noting their location for correct reconnection.

31 Detach the earth cable from the body.

32 On models with power steering remove the power steering pump as described in Chapter 10, but without disconnecting the hoses. Tie the pump to the bulkhead.

33 Disconnect the fuel lines and throttle cable as described in Chapter 4A and position them to one side.

34 On automatic transmission models, disconnect the kick-down cable with reference to Chapter 7B.

35 Disconnect the hoses from the EVAP system carbon canister with reference to Chapter 4B.

36 Disconnect the hose from the brake vacuum servo unit.

37 On models fitted with air conditioning, remove the alternator (Chapter 5A) and air conditioning compressor (Chapter 3) however leave the air conditioning system lines connected. Tie the compressor to one side.

38 Unbolt the front (manual transmission only) and rear engine mountings from the centre member located under the engine compartment.

39 Unbolt the centre member from the underbody and remove it from under the vehicle **(see illustration)**.

40 Manoeuvre the engine hoist into position, and attach it to the engine using suitable lifting brackets on the cylinder head. Raise the hoist until it is supporting the weight of the engine/transmission assembly **(see Tool Tip)**.

41 Remove the right-hand and left-hand engine mountings with reference to Chapter 2A.

42 Make a final check that everything has been disconnected. Ensure that components such as the gearchange link rods and driveshafts are secured so that they cannot be damaged on removal.

43 If available, a low trolley should be placed under the engine/transmission assembly. Lower the engine/transmission assembly, making sure that nothing is trapped or damaged. Enlist the help of an assistant during this procedure, as it may be necessary to tilt the assembly slightly to clear the body panels. Great care must be taken to ensure that no components are trapped and damaged during the removal procedure **(see illustration)**.

44 Withdraw the assembly from under the vehicle.

Separation

45 With the engine/transmission assembly removed, support the assembly on suitable blocks of wood, on a workbench or failing that, on a clean area of the workshop floor.

46 On automatic transmission models unbolt the cover from the bottom of the transmission for access to the electromagnetic clutch housing-to-driveplate bolts. Turn the crankshaft as necessary for access, and unscrew the four bolts.

47 Unscrew the retaining bolts, and remove the starter motor from the transmission (refer to Chapter 5A if necessary).

48 Ensure that both engine and transmission are adequately supported, then slacken and remove the bolts securing the transmission to the engine. Note the correct fitted positions of each bolt (and, where fitted, the relevant brackets) as they are removed, to use as a reference on refitting.

49 Carefully withdraw the transmission from the engine. On manual transmission models, ensure that the weight of the transmission is not allowed to hang on the input shaft while it is engaged with the clutch friction disc. On automatic transmission models ensure that the electromagnetic clutch housing remains on the input shaft otherwise the brushes in the brush holder may be damaged.

50 If they are loose, remove the locating dowels from the engine or transmission, and keep them in a safe place.

Refitting

51 If the engine and transmission have been separated, perform the operations described below in paragraphs 52 to 57. If not, proceed as described from paragraph 58 onwards.

52 On manual transmission models, apply a smear of high-melting-point grease to the splines of the transmission input shaft. Do not apply too much, otherwise there is a possibility of the grease contaminating the clutch friction plate. Also ensure that the clutch release bearing is correctly engaged with the fork.

4.43 Lowering engine and transmission assembly from the engine compartment

53 On automatic transmission models make sure that the electromagnetic clutch housing is fully engaged with the input shaft. If it has moved out, remove the brush holder first before pushing the housing onto the input shaft.

54 Ensure that the locating dowels are correctly positioned in the engine or transmission. Carefully offer the transmission to the engine, until the locating dowels are engaged. Ensure that the weight of the transmission is not allowed to hang on the input shaft.

55 Refit the transmission housing-to-engine bolts, ensuring that all the necessary brackets are correctly positioned, and tighten them to the specified torque setting.

56 Refit the starter motor and tighten the retaining bolts.

57 On automatic transmission models align the holes in the driveplate and electromagnetic clutch housing then insert the bolts and tighten them to the specified torque. Refit the cover and tighten the bolts.

58 Position the engine/transmission assembly under the vehicle, then reconnect the hoist and lifting tackle to the engine lifting brackets.

59 With the aid of an assistant, lift the assembly up into the engine compartment, making sure that it clears the surrounding components.

60 Refit the right-hand and left-hand engine mountings with reference to Chapter 2A. Remove the engine hoist.

61 Check that the rubbers are correctly fitted to the centre member **(see illustration)**.

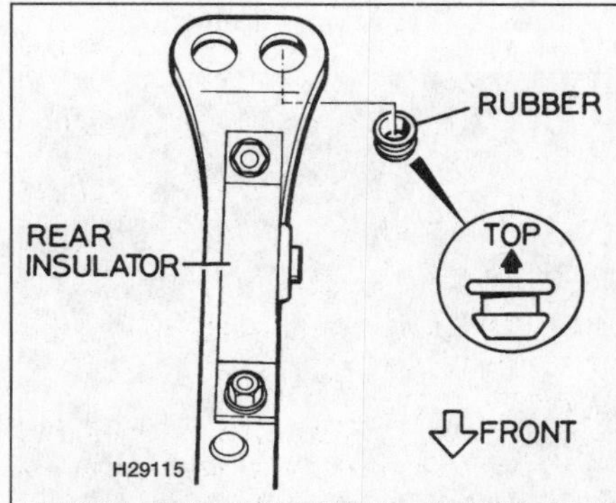

4.61 Make sure the centre member rubbers are fitted as shown

Manoeuvre the centre member into position, aligning it with the engine mountings, and refit its mounting bolts and washers. Tighten the centre member mounting bolts to the specified torque.

62 Refit the bolts to the front (manual transmission only) and rear engine mountings and tighten to the specified torque. Refer to Chapter 2A before tightening the front mounting on manual transmission models.

63 The remainder of the refitting procedure is a direct reversal of the removal sequence, with reference to the relevant Chapters and noting the following points:

a) *Ensure that the wiring harness is correctly routed and retained by all the relevant retaining clips, and all connectors are correctly and securely reconnected.*
b) *Refill the transmission oil/fluid with reference to Chapter 7A or 7B (as applicable).*
c) *Adjust the auxiliary drivebelts as described in Chapter 1.*
d) *On automatic transmission models adjust the kick-down cable with reference to Chapter 7B, and top-up the fluid with reference to Chapter 1.*
e) *Refill the engine with oil with reference to Chapter 1.*
f) *Refill the cooling system as described in Chapter 1.*
g) *On completion, start the engine and check for leaks.*

5 Engine overhaul - dismantling sequence

1 It is much easier to dismantle and work on the engine if it is mounted on a portable engine stand. These stands can often be hired from a tool hire shop. Before the engine is mounted on a stand, the flywheel/driveplate should be removed, so that the stand bolts can be tightened into the end of the cylinder block/crankcase.

2 If a stand is not available, it is possible to dismantle the engine with it blocked up on a sturdy workbench, or on the floor. Be extra-careful not to tip or drop the engine when working without a stand.

3 If you are going to obtain a reconditioned engine, all the external components must be removed first, to be transferred to the replacement engine (just as they will if you are doing a complete engine overhaul yourself). These components include the following:

a) *Alternator, power steering pump and/or air conditioning compressor mounting brackets (as applicable).*
b) *Distributor, HT leads (where applicable) and spark plugs (Chapters 1 and 5).*
c) *Coolant pump and thermostat/coolant outlet housing(s) (Chapter 3).*
d) *The fuel injection system components (see Chapter 4A).*

e) All electrical switches and sensors, and the engine wiring harness.
f) Inlet and exhaust manifolds (Chapter 4A).
g) Engine mountings (Part A of this Chapter).
h) Flywheel/driveplate (Part A of this Chapter).

Note: *When removing the external components from the engine, pay close attention to details that may be helpful or important during refitting. Note the fitted position of gaskets, seals, spacers, pins, washers, bolts, and other small items.*

4 If you are obtaining a "short" engine (which consists of the engine cylinder block/ crankcase, crankshaft, pistons and connecting rods all assembled), then the cylinder head, sump, oil pump, and timing chains will have to be removed also.

5 If you are planning a complete overhaul, the engine can be dismantled, and the internal components removed, in the order given below, referring to Part A of this Chapter unless otherwise stated.

a) Inlet and exhaust manifolds (Chapter 4A).
b) Cylinder head (see Part A).
c) Sump (see Part A).
d) Timing cover, chains and sprockets (see Part A).
e) Piston/connecting rod assemblies (Section 9).
f) Flywheel/driveplate (see Part A).
g) Crankshaft (Section 10).

6 Before beginning the dismantling and overhaul procedures, make sure that you have all of the correct tools necessary. Refer to *"Tools and working facilities"* at the end of this manual for further information.

6 Cylinder head - dismantling

Note: *New and reconditioned cylinder heads can be obtained from the manufacturer and engine overhaul specialists. Be aware that some specialist tools are required for the dismantling and inspection procedures, and new components may not be readily available. It may therefore be more practical and economical for the home mechanic to purchase a reconditioned head, rather than dismantle, inspect and recondition the original head.*

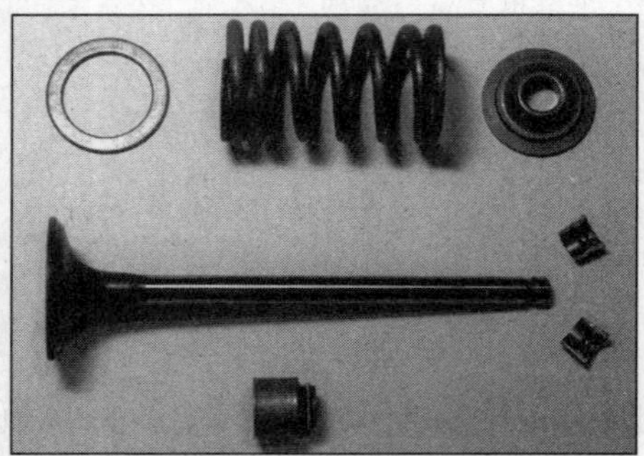

6.4e The valve components

1 Remove the cylinder head as described in Part A of this Chapter.

2 If not already done, remove the inlet and exhaust manifolds, referring to Chapter 4A.

3 Remove the camshafts, followers and shims as described in Part A.

4 Using a valve spring compressor, compress each valve spring in turn until the split collets can be removed. Release the compressor, and lift off the spring retainer, spring and spring seat. Using a pair of pliers, carefully extract the valve stem seal from the top of the guide **(see illustrations)**.

5 If, when the valve spring compressor is screwed down, the spring retainer refuses to free and expose the split collets, gently tap the top of the tool, directly over the retainer, with a light hammer. This will free the retainer.

6 Withdraw the valve through the combustion chamber.

7 It is essential that each valve is stored together with its collets, retainer, spring, and spring seat. The valves should also be kept in their correct sequence, unless they are so badly worn that they are to be renewed. If they are going to be kept and used again, place each valve assembly in a labelled polythene bag or similar small container **(see illustration)**. Note that No 1 valve is nearest to the timing chain end of the engine.

7 Cylinder head and valves - cleaning and inspection

1 Thorough cleaning of the cylinder head and valve components, followed by a detailed inspection, will enable you to decide how much valve service work must be carried out during the engine overhaul. **Note:** *If the engine has been severely overheated, it is best to assume that the cylinder head is warped - check carefully for signs of this.*

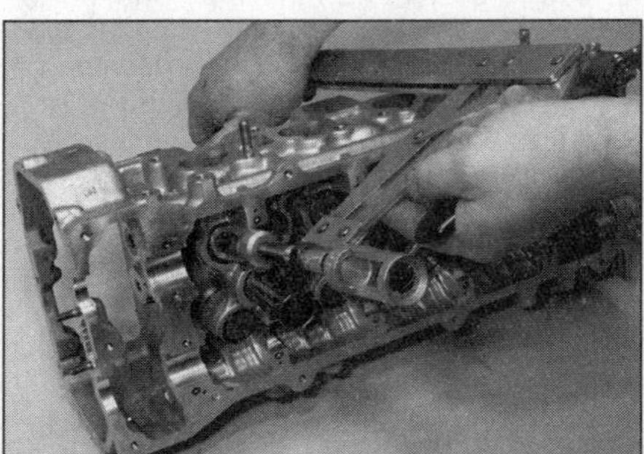

6.4a Use a compressor tool to compress the valve spring and remove the collets . . .

6.4b . . . then remove the spring retainer . . .

6.4c . . . the valve spring . . .

6.4d . . . the spring seat and the valve

6.4f Using pliers to extract the valve stem oil seal

6.7 Place each valve and its associated components in a labelled polythene bag

7.6 Checking cylinder head for distortion with a straight-edge and feeler blade

7.11 Measuring a valve stem diameter

7.14 Grinding-in a valve

Cleaning

2 Scrape away all traces of old gasket material from the cylinder head.
3 Scrape away the carbon from the combustion chambers and ports, then wash the cylinder head thoroughly with paraffin or a suitable solvent.
4 Scrape off any heavy carbon deposits that may have formed on the valves, then use a power-operated wire brush to remove deposits from the valve heads and stems.

Inspection

Note: *Be sure to perform all the following inspection procedures before concluding that the services of a machine shop or engine overhaul specialist are required. Make a list of all items that require attention.*

Cylinder head

5 Inspect the head very carefully for cracks, evidence of coolant leakage, and other damage. If cracks are found, a new cylinder head should be obtained.
6 Use a straight-edge and feeler blade to check that the cylinder head surface is not distorted **(see illustration)**. If it is, it may be possible to have it machined, provided that the cylinder head is not reduced to less than the specified height.
7 Examine the valve seats in each of the combustion chambers. If they are severely pitted, cracked, or burned, they will need to be renewed or re-cut by an engine overhaul specialist. If they are only slightly pitted, this can be removed by grinding-in the valve heads and seats with fine valve-grinding compound, as described below.
8 Check the valve guides for wear by inserting the relevant valve, and checking for side-to-side movement of the valve. A very small amount of movement is acceptable, however, if excessive remove the valve and measure the valve stem diameter (see below) and renew the valve if it is worn. If the valve stem is not worn, the wear must be in the valve guide, and the guide must be renewed. The renewal of valve guides is best carried out by a Nissan dealer or engine overhaul specialist, who will have the necessary tools available.
9 If renewing the valve guides, the valve seats must be re-cut or re-ground only *after* the guides have been fitted.

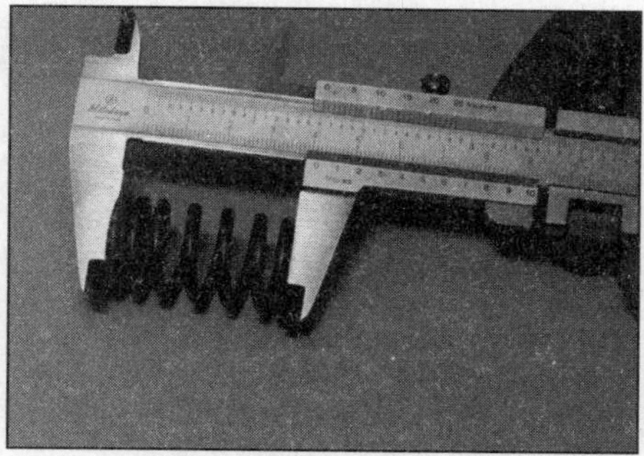
7.17 Measuring a valve spring for free length

7.18 Checking the valve spring with a try square

Valves

10 Examine the head of each valve for pitting, burning, cracks, and general wear. Check the valve stem for scoring and wear ridges. Rotate the valve, and check for any obvious indication that it is bent. Look for pits and excessive wear on the tip of each valve stem. Renew any valve that shows any signs of wear or damage.
11 If the valve appears satisfactory at this stage, measure the valve stem diameter at several points using a micrometer **(see illustration)**. Any significant difference in the readings obtained indicates wear of the valve stem. Should any of these conditions be apparent, the valve(s) must be renewed.
12 If the valves are in satisfactory condition, they should be ground (lapped) into their respective seats, to ensure a smooth, gas-tight seal. If the seat is only lightly pitted, or if it has been re-cut, fine grinding compound *only* should be used to produce the required finish. Coarse valve-grinding compound should *not* be used, unless a seat is badly burned or deeply pitted. If this is the case, the cylinder head and valves should be inspected by an expert, to decide whether seat re-cutting, or even the renewal of the valve or seat insert is required.
13 Valve grinding is carried out as follows. Place the cylinder head upside-down on a bench.
14 Smear a trace of the appropriate grade of valve-grinding compound on the seat face, and press a suction grinding tool onto the valve head. With a semi-rotary action, grind the valve head to its seat, lifting the valve occasionally to redistribute the grinding compound **(see illustration)**. A light spring placed under the valve head will greatly ease this operation.
15 If coarse grinding compound is being used, work only until a dull, matt even surface is produced on both the valve seat and the valve, then wipe off the used compound, and repeat the process with fine compound. When a smooth unbroken ring of light grey matt finish is produced on both the valve and seat, the grinding operation is complete. *Do not* grind-in the valves any further than absolutely necessary.
16 When all the valves have been ground-in, carefully wash off *all* traces of grinding compound using paraffin or a suitable solvent, before reassembling the cylinder head.

Valve components

17 Examine the valve springs for signs of damage and discoloration. The specified Nissan procedure for checking the condition of valve springs involves measuring the force necessary to compress each spring to a specified height. This is not possible without the use of the Nissan special test equipment, and therefore spring checking must be entrusted to a Nissan dealer. A rough idea of the condition of the spring can be gained by measuring the spring free length, and comparing it to the length given in this Chapter's *Specifications* **(see illustration)**.
18 Stand each spring on a flat surface, and position a square alongside the edge of the spring **(see illustration)**. Measure the gap between the upper edge of the spring and the

square, and compare it to the out-of-square limit given in the *Specifications*.

19 If any of the springs are damaged, distorted or have lost their tension, obtain a complete new set of springs. It is normal to renew the valve springs as a matter of course if a major overhaul is being carried out.

20 Renew the valve stem oil seals regardless of their apparent condition.

8 Cylinder head - reassembly

1 Refit the spring seat then, working on the first valve, dip the new valve stem seal in fresh engine oil and locate it onto the guide. Use a suitable socket or metal tube to press the seal firmly onto the guide **(see illustrations)**.

2 Lubricate the stems of the valves, and insert the valves into their original locations taking care not to damage the stem oil seals **(see illustration)**. If new valves are being fitted, insert them into the locations to which they have been ground.

3 Locate the valve spring on top of its seat, then refit the spring retainer.

4 Compress the valve spring, and locate the split collets in the recess in the valve stem **(see Haynes Hint)**. Release the compressor, then repeat the procedure on the remaining valves.

5 With all the valves installed, place the cylinder head flat on the bench and, using a hammer and interposed block of wood, tap the end of each valve stem to settle the components.

6 The cylinder head and associated components may now be refitted as described in Part A of this Chapter.

9 Piston/connecting rod assembly - removal

1 Remove the sump, timing chains and cylinder head as described in Part A of this Chapter.

2 If there is a pronounced wear ridge at the

8.1a Locate the valve stem seal onto the guide . . .

8.1b . . . and use a socket to press it firmly in position

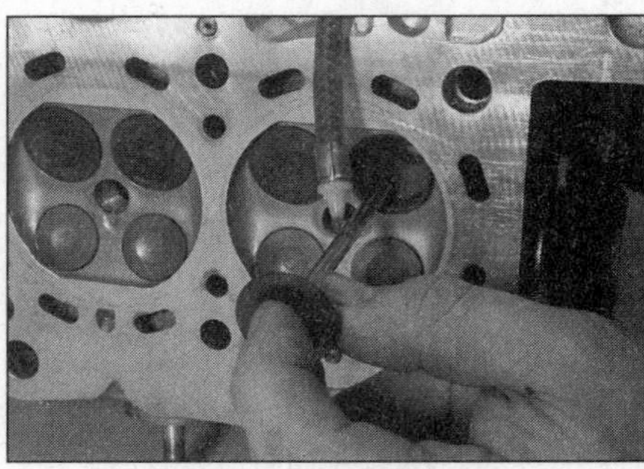

8.2 Lubricate the valves as they are being inserted

Using a dab of grease on a screwdriver and on the collets while locating them on the valve recess

top of any bore, it may be necessary to remove it with a scraper or ridge reamer, to avoid piston damage during removal. Such a ridge indicates excessive wear of the cylinder bore.

3 Each connecting rod and bearing cap should be stamped with its respective cylinder number, No 1 cylinder being at the timing chain end of the engine **(see illustration)**. If no markings are visible, using a hammer and centre-punch, paint or similar, mark each connecting rod and big-end bearing cap with its respective cylinder number on the flat machined surface provided.

4 Turn the crankshaft to bring pistons 1 and 4 near BDC (bottom dead centre). **Note:** *Because of the main bearing cap ladder, the crankshaft must be positioned one side of BDC.*

5 Before removing the pistons and connecting rods, use a feeler blade to measure the big-end bearing side clearances, and compare with the limit given in the *Specifications* **(see illustration)**. Unless the engine has completed a very high mileage, it is unusual to find excessive side wear of the connecting rods.

6 Unscrew the nuts from No 1 piston big-end bearing cap. Take off the cap, and recover the bottom half bearing shell **(see illustration)**. If the bearing shells are to be re-used, tape the cap and the shell together.

7 To prevent the possibility of damage to the crankshaft bearing journals, tape over the connecting rod bolt threads or fit a length of plastic hose to them.

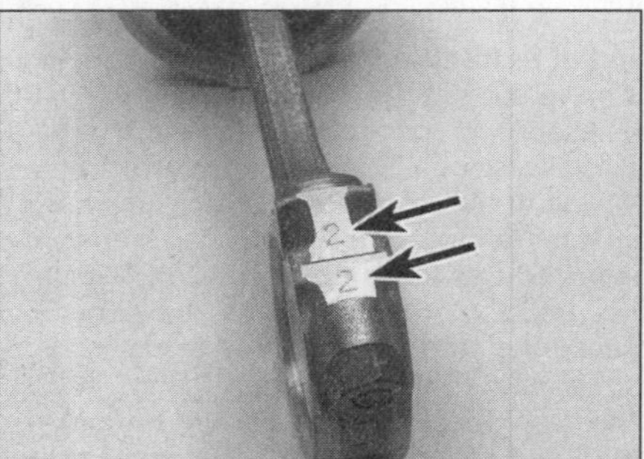

9.3 The connecting rod and bearing cap are both marked with their respective cylinder number

9.5 Checking the big-end bearing side clearances

9.6 Removing a big-end bearing cap

10.1 Removing the engine rear plate

8 Using a hammer handle, push the piston up through the bore, and remove it from the top of the cylinder block. Recover the bearing shell, and tape it to the connecting rod for safe-keeping.

9 Loosely refit the big-end cap to the connecting rod, and secure with the nuts - this will help to keep the components in their correct order.

10 Remove No 4 piston assembly in the same way.

11 Turn the crankshaft through 180° to bring pistons 2 and 3 to near BDC (bottom dead centre), and remove them in the same way.

10 Crankshaft - removal

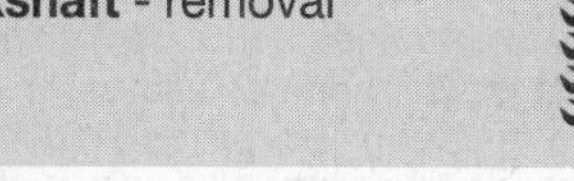

1 Remove the sump, timing chains and flywheel/driveplate (including engine rear plate) as described in Part A of this Chapter **(see illustration)**.

2 Remove the pistons and connecting rods, as described in Section 9. **Note:** *If no work is to be done on the pistons and connecting rods, there is no need to remove the cylinder head, or to push the pistons out of the cylinder bores. The pistons should just be pushed far enough up the bores to position them clear of the crankshaft journals*.

3 Check the crankshaft endfloat as described in Section 13, then proceed as follows.

4 Undo the retaining nuts and bolts, and remove the rear oil seal housing from the left-hand end of the cylinder block. If the locating dowels are a loose fit, remove them and store them with the housing for safe-keeping.

5 Working in the **reverse** of the sequence shown in **illustration 16.25a**, slacken the main bearing cap beam retaining bolts by a turn at a time. Once all bolts are loose, unscrew and remove them from the cylinder block. Note that the arrow on the beam points towards the timing end of the engine **(see illustration)**.

6 Lift the main bearing cap beam from the crankshaft, and recover the lower main bearing shells **(see illustrations)**. Tape each shell to its position on the beam for safe-keeping.

7 Carefully lift out the crankshaft, taking care not to displace the upper main bearing shells **(see illustration)**.

8 Recover the upper bearing shells from the cylinder block, and tape them to their respective positions on the main bearing cap beam. Remove the thrustwasher halves from the side of No 3 main bearing, and store them with the main bearing cap beam.

10.5 Removing the main bearing cap beam bolts

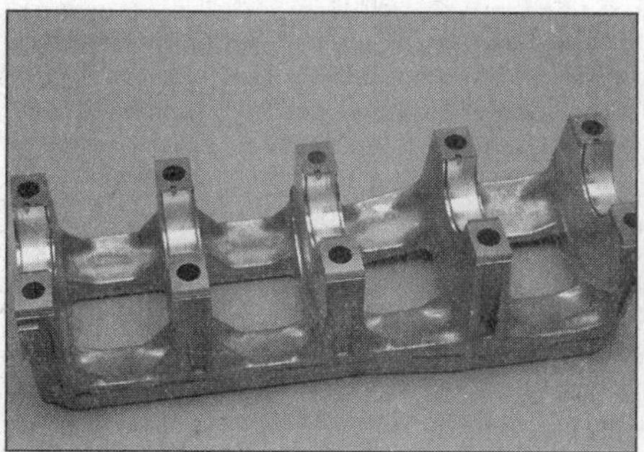

10.6b The lower main bearing shells are located in the beam

10.6a Lifting the main bearing cap beam from the crankshaft

10.7 Lifting the crankshaft from the crankcase

11 Cylinder block/crankcase - cleaning and inspection

Cleaning

1 Remove all external components and electrical switches/sensors from the block, and unbolt the alternator and power steering pump brackets as applicable. Unbolt the crankcase breather bracket from the crankcase and remove the filter mesh **(see illustrations)**.

2 For complete cleaning, the core plugs should ideally be removed **(see illustration)**. Drill a small hole in the plugs, then insert a self-tapping screw into the hole. Pull out the

11.1a Removing the alternator lower mounting bracket

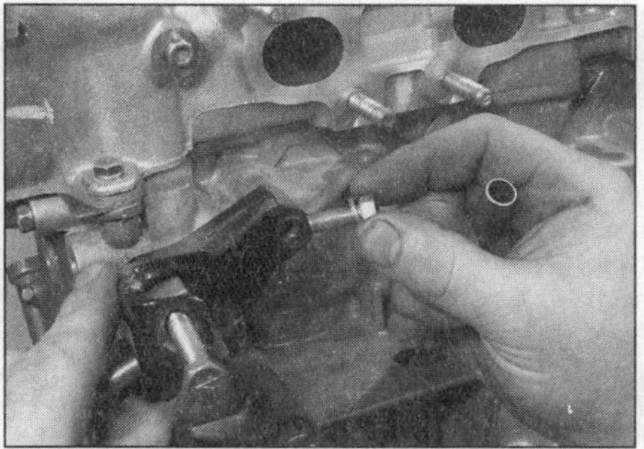

11.1b Removing the alternator upper mounting bracket

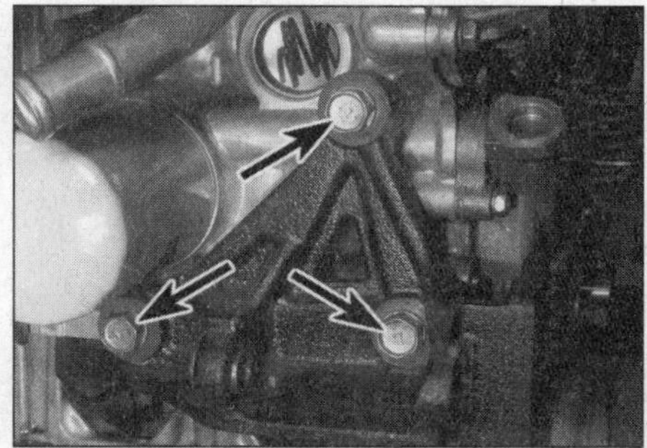

11.1c Unscrew the bolts . . .

11.1d . . . and remove the power steering pump mounting bracket

11.2 A core plug in the cylinder block

plugs by pulling on the screw with a pair of grips, or by using a slide hammer.

3 Scrape all traces of sealant from the cylinder block/crankcase, taking care not to damage the gasket/sealing surfaces.

4 Remove all oil gallery plugs (where fitted). The plugs are usually very tight - they may have to be drilled out, and the holes re-tapped. Use new plugs when the engine is reassembled.

5 If any of the castings are extremely dirty, all should be steam-cleaned.

6 After the castings are returned, clean all oil holes and oil galleries one more time. Flush all internal passages with warm water until the water runs clear. Dry thoroughly, and apply a light film of oil to all mating surfaces and the cylinder bores, to prevent rusting. If you have access to compressed air, use it to speed up the drying process, and to blow out all the oil holes and galleries.

Warning: Wear eye protection when using compressed air!

7 If the castings are not very dirty, you can do an adequate cleaning job with hot (as hot as you can stand!), soapy water and a stiff brush. Take plenty of time, and do a thorough job. Regardless of the cleaning method used, be sure to clean all oil holes and galleries very thoroughly, and to dry all components well. Protect the cylinder bores as described above, to prevent rusting.

8 All threaded holes must be clean, to ensure accurate torque readings during reassembly. To clean the threads, run the correct-size tap

11.1e The crankcase breather bracket and filter mesh are bolted inside the crankcase

11.8 Cleaning a cylinder block threaded hole using a suitable tap

into each of the holes to remove rust, corrosion, thread sealant or sludge, and to restore damaged threads. If possible, use compressed air to clear the holes of debris produced by this operation **(see illustration)**.

Warning: Wear eye protection when cleaning out these holes in this way!

9 Apply suitable sealant to the new oil gallery plugs, and insert them into the holes in the block. Tighten them securely.

10 If the engine is not going to be reassembled right away, cover it with a large plastic bag to keep it clean; protect all mating surfaces and the cylinder bores as described above, to prevent rusting.

Inspection

11 Visually check the casting for cracks and corrosion. Look for stripped threads in the threaded holes. If there has been any history of internal water leakage, it may be worthwhile having an engine overhaul specialist check the cylinder block/crankcase with special equipment. If defects are found, have them repaired if possible, or obtain a new block.

12 Check each cylinder bore for scuffing and scoring. Check for signs of a wear ridge at the top of the cylinder, indicating that the bore is excessively worn.

13 Measure the diameter of each cylinder bore 20 mm from the top of the bore, both parallel to the crankshaft axis and at right-angles to it. Repeat the procedure measuring the bore diameter 60 mm from the top, and then 100 mm from the top, so that a total of six measurements are taken. Using the measurements obtained, calculate the cylinder taper and cylinder out-of-round dimensions. **Note:** *The cylinder bore grade is stamped both on the bottom of the cylinder block and on the piston crown. There are four numbers stamped on the block, one for each cylinder.*

14 Check the pistons and rings as described in Section 12. The piston-to-bore clearance can be calculated by subtracting the piston diameter from the cylinder bore diameter measurement.

15 Compare all results with the Specifications at the beginning of this Chapter. If any measurement exceeds the service limit specified, the cylinders must be rebored, where possible, to the next oversize and new pistons fitted, or the cylinder block must be renewed. Seek the advice of an engine overhaul specialist as to the best course of action. Pistons are available in only one oversize - 0.2 mm.

16 If the cylinder bores and pistons are in reasonably good condition, and not worn to the specified limits, and if the piston-to-bore clearances are not excessive, then it may only be necessary to renew the piston rings.

17 If this is the case, the bores should be honed, to allow the new rings to bed in correctly and provide the best possible seal. The conventional type of hone has spring-loaded stones, and is used with a power drill. You will also need some paraffin or honing oil and rags. The hone should be moved up and down the bore to produce a cross-hatch pattern, and plenty of honing oil should be used. Ideally the cross-hatch lines should intersect at approximately a 60° angle. Do not take off more material than is necessary to produce the required finish. If new pistons are being fitted, the piston manufacturers may specify a finish with a different angle, so their instructions should be followed. Do not withdraw the hone from the bore while it is still being turned - stop it first. After honing a bore, wipe out all traces of the honing oil. If equipment of this type is not available, or if you are not sure whether you are competent to undertake the task yourself, an engine overhaul specialist will carry out the work at moderate cost.

18 After all work has been carried out on the cylinder block/crankcase, clean the crankcase breather filter mesh and refit it together with the breather bracket. Tighten the bolts.

19 Refit all the external components and electrical switches/sensors removed from the block.

12 Piston/connecting rod assembly - inspection

1 Before the inspection process can begin, the piston/connecting rod assemblies must be cleaned, and the original piston rings removed from the pistons.

2 Carefully expand the old rings over the top of the pistons - note that the oil control ring assembly incorporates two rails and an expander. The use of two or three old feeler blades will be helpful in preventing the rings dropping into empty grooves. Be careful not to scratch the piston with the ends of the ring. The rings are brittle, and will snap if they are spread too far. They're also very sharp - protect your hands and fingers. Always remove the rings from the top of the piston. Keep each set of rings with its piston if the old rings are to be re-used **(see illustration)**.

3 Scrape away all traces of carbon from the top of the piston. A hand-held wire brush (or a piece of fine emery cloth) can be used, once the majority of the deposits have been scraped away.

4 Remove the carbon from the ring grooves in the piston, using an old ring. Break the ring in half to do this (be careful not to cut your fingers - piston rings are sharp). Be careful to remove only the carbon deposits - do not remove any metal, and do not nick or scratch the sides of the ring grooves.

5 Once the deposits have been removed, clean the piston/connecting rod assembly with paraffin or a suitable solvent, and dry thoroughly. Make sure that the oil return holes in the ring grooves are clear.

6 Using a micrometer, measure the piston diameter at right-angles to the gudgeon pin axis (at the specified distance up from the bottom of the skirt), and compare the results with the *Specifications* at the beginning of this Chapter. The piston size grade is stamped onto the piston crown. Renew any piston which has worn beyond its specified limits.

7 Check the ring-to-groove clearance by inserting each ring from the outside, together with a feeler blade between the ring's top surface and the piston land. If the ring-to-groove clearance is excessive, renew the rings and recheck the clearance. If the clearance is still excessive, even with new piston rings, then the piston must be renewed.

8 Check the ring end gaps by inserting each ring into the cylinder bore and pushing it in with the piston crown to ensure that it is square in the bore. Push the ring down into the bore until the piston skirt is level with the block mating surface, then withdraw the piston. Using feeler blades, measure the piston ring end gap. If the ring end gap is excessive, renew the rings and repeat the checking procedure. If the clearance is still excessive, even with new piston rings, then the cylinder bores must be rebored/renewed (see Section 11).

9 Carefully inspect each piston for cracks around the skirt, around the gudgeon pin holes, and at the piston ring "lands" (between the ring grooves).

10 Look for scoring and scuffing on the piston skirt, holes in the piston crown, or burned areas at the edge of the crown. If the skirt is scored or scuffed, the engine may have been suffering from overheating, and/or abnormal combustion which caused excessively-high operating temperatures. The cooling and lubrication systems should be checked thoroughly. Scorch marks on the sides of the pistons show that blow-by has occurred. A hole in the piston crown, or burned areas at the edge of the piston crown, indicates that abnormal combustion (pre-ignition, knocking, or detonation) has been occurring. If any of the above problems exist, the causes must be investigated and corrected, or the damage will occur again. The causes may include incorrect ignition timing or inlet air leaks.

11 Corrosion of the piston, in the form of pitting, indicates that coolant has been leaking into the combustion chamber and/or the crankcase. Again, the cause must be corrected, or the problem may persist in the rebuilt engine.

12 Examine each connecting rod carefully for signs of damage, such as cracks around the big-end and small-end bearings. Check that the rod is not bent or distorted. Damage is highly unlikely, unless the engine has been seized or badly overheated. Detailed checking of the connecting rod assembly can only be carried out by a Nissan dealer or engine repair specialist with the necessary equipment.

13 The pistons and connecting rods can be separated by a Nissan dealer or engine repair specialist with suitable equipment to press the gudgeon pins from the connecting rods, but the pistons cannot be re-used afterwards. The connecting rod small ends must be heated to 200°C when the gudgeon pins are refitted. If the pistons are being renewed, have the new pistons fitted by the specialist.

14 The connecting rods themselves should not need renewal, unless seizure or some other major mechanical failure has occurred. Check the alignment of the connecting rods visually, and if the rods are not straight, take them to an engine overhaul specialist for a more detailed check.

13 Crankshaft - inspection

Checking crankshaft endfloat

1 If the crankshaft endfloat is to be checked, this must be done when the crankshaft is still installed in the cylinder block/crankcase, but is free to move (see Section 10).

2 Check the endfloat using a dial gauge in contact with the end of the crankshaft. Push the crankshaft fully one way, and then zero the gauge. Push the crankshaft fully the other way, and check the endfloat. The result can be compared with the specified amount, and will give an indication as to whether new thrustwashers are required **(see illustration)**.

12.2 Use an old feeler blade to remove the piston rings from their grooves

13.2 Using a dial gauge to check the crankshaft endfloat

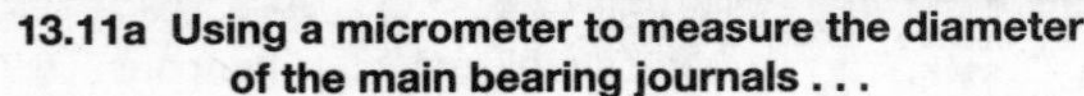

13.11a Using a micrometer to measure the diameter of the main bearing journals . . .

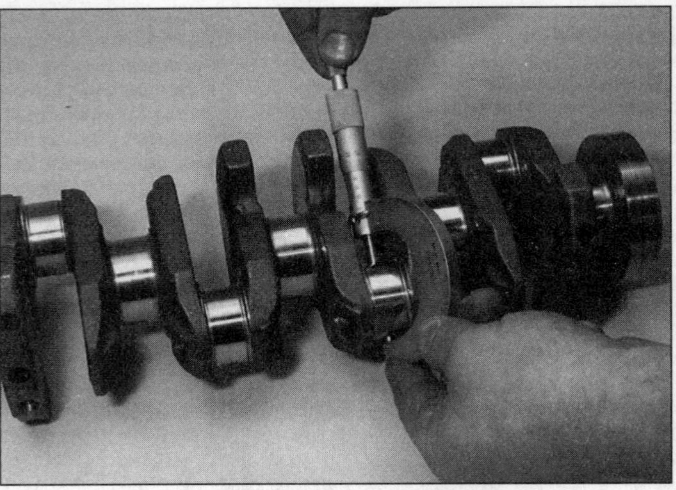

13.11b . . . and big-end bearing journals

3 If a dial gauge is not available, feeler blades can be used. First push the crankshaft fully towards the flywheel end of the engine, then use feeler blades to measure the gap between the No 3 crankpin web and No 3 main bearing thrustwasher.

Inspection

4 Clean the crankshaft using paraffin or a suitable solvent, and dry it, preferably with compressed air if available.

Warning: Wear eye protection when using compressed air!

5 Check the main and big-end bearing journals for uneven wear, scoring, pitting and cracking.

6 Big-end bearing wear is accompanied by distinct metallic knocking when the engine is running (particularly noticeable when the engine is pulling from low speed) and some loss of oil pressure.

7 Main bearing wear is accompanied by severe engine vibration and rumble - getting progressively worse as engine speed increases - and again by loss of oil pressure.

8 Check the bearing journal for roughness by running a finger lightly over the bearing surface. Any roughness (which will be accompanied by obvious bearing wear) indicates that the crankshaft requires regrinding (where possible) or renewal.

9 Crankshaft run-out can be checked by supporting each end of the crankshaft on V-blocks, and measuring any run-out at the centre of the shaft using a dial gauge. If the run-out exceeds the specified limit, a new crankshaft will be required.

10 If the crankshaft has been reground, check for burrs around the crankshaft oil holes (the holes are usually chamfered, so burrs should not be a problem unless regrinding has been carried out carelessly). Remove any burrs with a fine file or scraper, and thoroughly clean the oil holes as described previously.

11 Using a micrometer, measure the diameter of the main and big-end bearing journals, and compare the results with the *Specifications* **(see illustrations)**. By measuring the diameter at a number of points around each journal's circumference, you will be able to determine whether or not the journal is out-of-round. Take the measurement at each end of the journal, near the webs, to determine if the journal is tapered. Compare the results obtained with those given in the *Specifications*.

12 Check the oil seal contact surfaces at each end of the crankshaft for wear and damage. If the seal has worn a deep groove in the surface of the crankshaft, consult an engine overhaul specialist. Repair may be possible, but otherwise a new crankshaft will be required.

13 Nissan produce undersize bearing shells for both the main bearings and big-end bearings as given in the *Specifications*. Refer to your Nissan dealer for further information on parts availability. If undersize bearing shells are available, and the crankshaft has worn beyond the specified limits, providing that the crankshaft journals have not already been reground, it may be possible to have the crankshaft reconditioned, and to fit the undersize shells. Seek the advice of your Nissan dealer or engine specialist on the best course of action.

14 Main and big-end bearings - inspection

1 Even though the main and big-end bearings should be renewed during the engine overhaul, the old bearings should be retained for close examination, as they may reveal valuable information about the condition of the engine. The bearing shells are graded by thickness, the grade of each shell being indicated by the colour code marked on it.

2 Bearing failure can occur due to lack of lubrication, the presence of dirt or other foreign particles, overloading the engine, or corrosion. Regardless of the cause of bearing failure, the cause must be corrected (where applicable) before the engine is reassembled, to prevent it from happening again **(see illustration)**.

3 When examining the bearing shells, remove them from the cylinder block/crankcase, the main bearing cap beam, the connecting rods and the connecting rod big-end bearing caps. Lay them out on a clean surface in the same general position as their location in the engine. This will enable you to match any bearing problems with the corresponding crankshaft journal. *Do not* touch any shell's

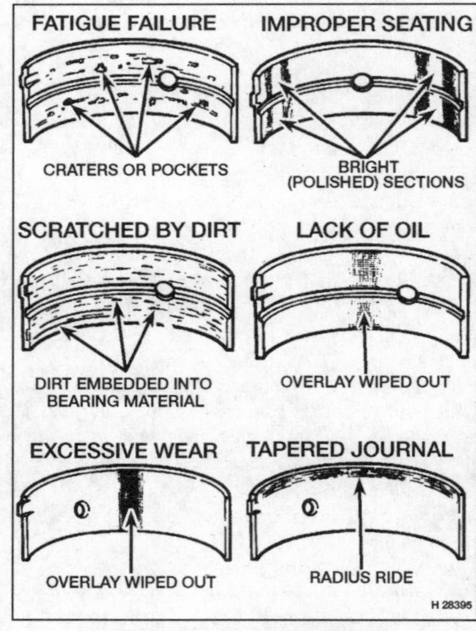

14.2 Typical bearing failures

bearing surface with your fingers while checking it, or the delicate surface may be scratched.

4 Dirt and other foreign matter gets into the engine in a variety of ways. It may be left in the engine during assembly, or it may pass through filters or the crankcase ventilation system. It may get into the oil, and from there into the bearings. Metal chips from machining operations and normal engine wear are often present. Abrasives are sometimes left in engine components after reconditioning, especially when parts are not thoroughly cleaned using the proper cleaning methods. Whatever the source, these foreign objects often end up embedded in the soft bearing material, and are easily recognised. Large particles will not embed in the bearing, and will score or gouge the bearing and journal. The best prevention for this cause of bearing failure is to clean all parts thoroughly, and keep everything spotlessly-clean during engine assembly. Frequent and regular engine oil and filter changes are also recommended.

5 Lack of lubrication (or lubrication breakdown) has a number of interrelated causes. Excessive heat (which thins the oil), overloading (which squeezes the oil from the bearing face) and oil leakage (from excessive bearing clearances, worn oil pump or high engine speeds) all contribute to lubrication breakdown. Blocked oil passages, which usually are the result of misaligned oil holes in a bearing shell, will also oil-starve a bearing, and destroy it. When lack of lubrication is the cause of bearing failure, the bearing material is wiped or extruded from the steel backing of the bearing. Temperatures may increase to the point where the steel backing turns blue from overheating.

6 Driving habits can have a definite effect on bearing life. Full-throttle, low-speed operation (labouring the engine) puts very high loads on bearings, tending to squeeze out the oil film. These loads cause the bearings to flex, which produces fine cracks in the bearing face (fatigue failure). Eventually, the bearing material will loosen in pieces, and tear away from the steel backing.

7 Short-distance driving leads to corrosion of bearings, because insufficient engine heat is produced to drive off the condensed water and corrosive gases. These products collect in the engine oil, forming acid and sludge. As the oil is carried to the engine bearings, the acid attacks and corrodes the bearing material.

8 Incorrect bearing installation during engine assembly will lead to bearing failure as well. Tight-fitting bearings leave insufficient bearing running clearance, and will result in oil starvation. Dirt or foreign particles trapped behind a bearing shell result in high spots on the bearing, which lead to failure.

9 *Do not* touch any shell's bearing surface with your fingers during reassembly; there is a risk of scratching the delicate surface, or of depositing particles of dirt on it.

10 As mentioned at the beginning of this Section, the bearing shells should be renewed as a matter of course during engine overhaul; to do otherwise is false economy. Refer to Section 16 for details of bearing shell selection.

15 Engine overhaul - reassembly sequence

1 Before reassembly begins, ensure that all new parts have been obtained, and that all necessary tools are available. Read through the entire procedure, to familiarise yourself with the work involved, and to ensure that all items necessary for reassembly of the engine are at hand. In addition to all normal tools and materials, thread-locking compound will be needed. A suitable tube of liquid sealant will also be required for the joint faces that are fitted without gaskets; it is recommended that Nissan's Genuine Liquid Gasket (available from your Nissan dealer) is used.

2 In order to save time and avoid problems, engine reassembly can be carried out in the following order:

a) Crankshaft (Section 16).
b) Piston/connecting rod assemblies (Sections 17 and 18).
c) Timing chains, sprockets and cover (see Part A).
d) Sump (see Part A).
e) Cylinder head (see Part A).
f) Inlet and exhaust manifolds (Chapter 4A or 4B).
g) Flywheel/driveplate (see Part A).
h) Engine external components.

3 At this stage, all engine components should be absolutely clean and dry, with all faults repaired. The components should be laid out (or in individual containers) on a completely clean work surface.

16 Crankshaft - refitting and main bearing running clearance check

Selection of new bearing shells

Note: *This information applies only to standard size bearing shells. Undersize shells are not graded.*

1 New bearing shells are selected using the identification marks on the crankshaft and cylinder block.

2 The crankshaft markings are stamped on the side of No 1 cylinder crankweb (at the timing chain end of the crankshaft). The five-digit code refers to the main bearing journal diameters - the first number in the sequence is for No 1 bearing journal, and the last for No 5 journal.

3 The cylinder block markings are stamped on the flywheel end of the cylinder block base. There are two sets of codes; the five-digit code is for the main bearing bores - the first number in the sequence is for No 1 main bearing journal, and the last for No 5 journal. The four-digit code is for the cylinder bore size grades.

4 Obtain the identification number of both the relevant crankshaft journal and the cylinder block bearing bore, and select the correct grade of main bearing shell required for each journal, using the following table. The grade of each shell is indicated by a dab of paint on the side of the shell.

Crankshaft code	Block code	Bearing shell grade
0	0	Black
0	1	Brown
0	2	Green
0	3	Yellow
1	0	Brown
1	1	Green
1	2	Yellow
1	3	Blue
2	0	Green
2	1	Yellow
2	2	Blue
2	3	Pink
3	0	Yellow
3	1	Blue
3	2	Pink
3	3	White

Main bearing running clearance check

5 Clean the backs of the bearing shells, and the bearing locations in both the cylinder block and the main bearing cap beam.

6 Press the bearing shells into their locations, ensuring that the tab on each shell engages in the notch in the cylinder block/crankcase or main bearing cap beam location **(see illustration)**. Take care not to touch any shell's bearing surface with your fingers. Note that all the upper bearing shells are grooved, and have oil holes in them; the lower shells are plain. If the original bearing shells are being used for the check, ensure that they are refitted in their original locations. The clearance can be checked in either of two ways.

7 One method (which will be difficult to achieve without a range of internal micrometers or internal/external expanding calipers) is to refit the main bearing cap beam to the cylinder block, with the bearing shells in

16.6 Fitting the main bearing upper shells

place. With the retaining bolts correctly tightened, measure the internal diameter of each assembled pair of bearing shells. If the diameter of each corresponding crankshaft journal is measured and then subtracted from the bearing internal diameter, the result will be the main bearing running clearance.

8 The second (and more accurate) method is to use a product called Plastigauge. This consists of a fine thread of perfectly-round plastic, which is compressed between the bearing shell and the journal. When the shell is removed, the plastic is deformed, and can be measured with a special card gauge supplied with the kit. The running clearance is determined from this gauge. Plastigauge should be available from your Nissan dealer; otherwise, enquiries at one of the larger specialist motor factors should produce the name of a stockist in your area. The procedure for using Plastigauge is as follows.

9 With the main bearing upper shells in place, carefully lay the crankshaft in position. Do not use any lubricant; the crankshaft journals and bearing shells must be perfectly clean and dry.

10 Cut several lengths of the appropriate-size Plastigauge (they should be slightly shorter than the width of the main bearings), and place one length on each crankshaft journal axis **(see illustration)**.

11 With the main bearing lower shells in position, refit the main bearing cap beam making sure that the arrow is pointing towards the timing chain end of the engine **(see illustration)**. Refit the main bearing cap beam bolts and, working in the sequence shown in **illustration 16.25a**, tighten them evenly and progressively to the specified Stage 1 torque setting. Take care not to disturb the Plastigage, and *do not* rotate the crankshaft at any time during this operation.

12 Using an angle gauge, tighten each bolt in the same tightening sequence through the specified Stage 2 angle. Take care not to disturb the Plastigauge, and *do not* rotate the crankshaft at any time during this operation.

13 Working in **reverse** to the tightening sequence, progressively slacken the bearing cap beam retaining bolts by one turn at a time. Once all bolts are loose, unscrew them and remove them from the cylinder block.

14 Remove the main bearing cap beam, again taking great care not to disturb the Plastigauge, nor to rotate the crankshaft.

15 Compare the width of the crushed Plastigauge on each journal to the scale printed on the Plastigauge envelope, to obtain the main bearing running clearance. Compare the clearance measured with that given in the *Specifications* at the start of this Chapter **(see illustration)**.

16 If the clearance is not as specified, the bearing shells may be the wrong size (or excessively worn, if the original shells are being re-used). Before deciding that different-size shells are required, make sure that no dirt or oil was trapped between the bearing shells and the main bearing cap beam or block when the clearance was measured. If the Plastigauge was wider at one end than at the other, the crankshaft journal may be tapered.

17 If the clearance is not as specified with the original bearing shells, repeat the checking procedure using new bearing shells. If the clearance is not as specified even with new bearing shells, then seek the advice of a Nissan dealer or suitable engine overhaul specialist. They will be able to advise you on the best course of action, and whether or not it will be necessary to have the crankshaft journals reground and fit undersize shells.

18 Where necessary, obtain the required grades of bearing shell, and repeat the running clearance checking procedure as described above.

19 On completion, carefully scrape away all traces of the Plastigauge material from the crankshaft and bearing shells. Use your fingernail, or a wooden or plastic scraper which is unlikely to score the bearing surfaces.

Final crankshaft refitting

20 Carefully lift the crankshaft out of the cylinder block once more.

21 Place the bearing shells in their locations as described in paragraph 5 and 6. If new shells are being fitted, ensure that all traces of protective grease are cleaned off using paraffin. Wipe dry the shells and connecting rods with a lint-free cloth. Liberally lubricate each bearing shell in the cylinder block/crankcase with clean engine oil **(see illustration)**.

22 Using a little grease, stick the upper thrustwashers to each side of the No 3 main bearing upper location; ensure that the oilway grooves on each thrustwasher face outwards (away from the No 3 main bearing shell) **(see illustration)**.

16.10 Length of Plastigauge on the crankshaft journal

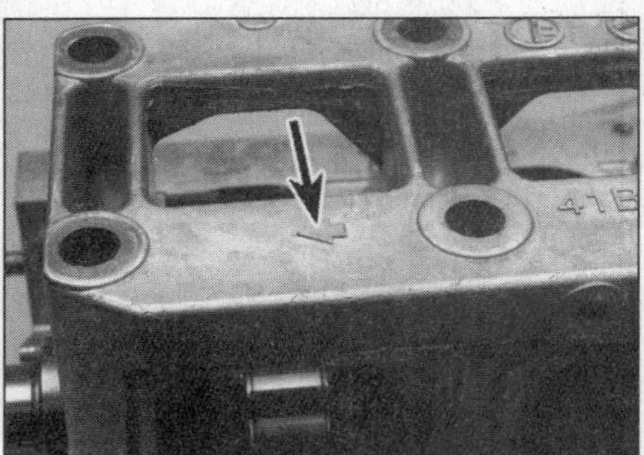

16.11 Arrow on main bearing cap beam must face timing chain end of the engine

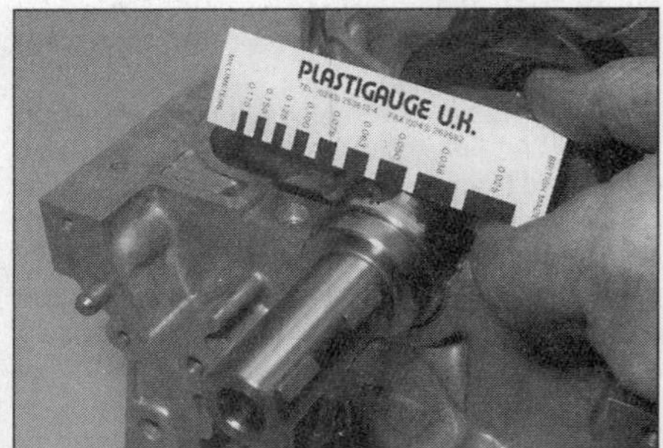

16.15 Using the card scale to determine the main bearing running clearance

16.21 Lubricating the main bearing shells

16.22 Use grease to stick the crankshaft thrustwashers in place

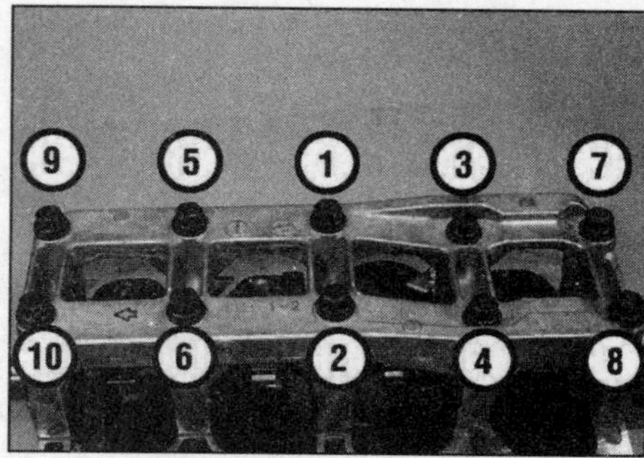

16.25a Main bearing cap beam bolt tightening sequence

16.25b Tightening the main bearing cap beam bolts

16.26 Angle-tightening the main bearing cap beam bolts

23 Lower the crankshaft into position, and check the crankshaft endfloat as described in Section 13.

24 Lubricate the lower bearing shells in the main bearing cap beam with clean engine oil. Make sure that the locating lugs on the shells engage with the corresponding recesses in the beam.

25 Fit the main bearing cap beam, making sure that the arrow is pointing towards the timing chain end of the engine. Insert the main bearing cap beam bolts and, working in the sequence shown **(see illustrations)** tighten them evenly and progressively to the specified Stage 1 torque setting.

26 Working again in the specified sequence, tighten each bolt through the specified Stage 2 angle **(see illustration)**.

27 Check that the crankshaft rotates freely, then fit the piston/connecting rod assemblies as described in Sections 17 and 18.

28 Ensure that the mating surfaces of the rear oil seal housing and cylinder block are clean and dry. Note the fitted depth of the oil seal then, using a large flat-bladed screwdriver, lever the seal out of the housing **(see illustration)**.

29 Fit a new seal to the housing, making sure that its sealing lip is facing inwards. Tap the seal squarely into the housing until it is flush using a block of wood **(see illustration)**.

30 Apply a bead of suitable sealant to the oil seal housing mating surface, and make sure that the locating dowels are in position. Slide the housing over the end of the crankshaft, and into position on the cylinder block. Tighten the housing retaining nuts and bolts to the specified torque setting **(see illustrations)**.

31 Refit the flywheel/driveplate (including engine rear plate), timing chains and sump as described in Part A of this Chapter.

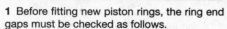

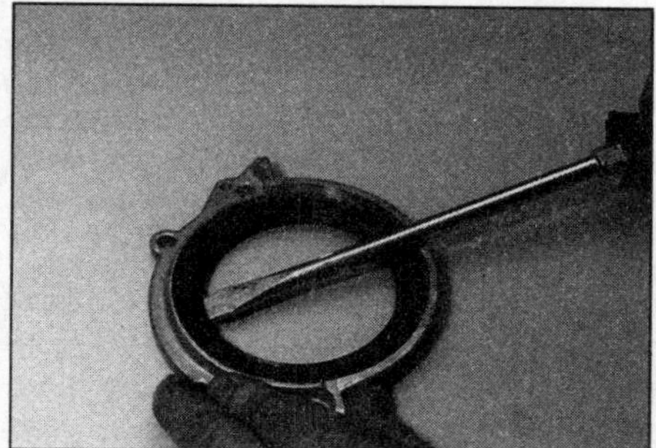

16.28 Levering out the crankshaft rear oil seal

16.29 Use a block of wood to tap the rear oil seal into its housing

16.30a Apply a bead of sealant to the oil seal housing mating surface

16.30b Tightening the rear oil seal housing nuts and bolts

17 Piston rings - refitting

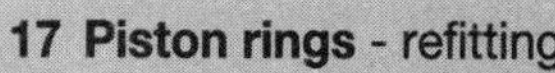

1 Before fitting new piston rings, the ring end gaps must be checked as follows.

2 Lay out the piston/connecting rod assemblies and the new piston ring sets, so that the ring sets will be matched with the same piston and cylinder during the end gap measurement and subsequent engine reassembly.

3 Insert the top ring into the first cylinder, and push it down the bore using the top of the piston. This will ensure that the ring remains square with the cylinder walls. Push the ring down into the bore until the piston skirt is level with the block mating surface, then withdraw the piston.

4 Measure the end gap using feeler blades, and compare the measurements with the figures given in the *Specifications* **(see illustration)**.

5 If the gap is too small (unlikely if genuine Nissan parts are used), it must be enlarged, or the ring ends may contact each other during engine operation, causing serious damage. Ideally, new piston rings providing the correct end gap should be fitted. As a last resort, the end gap can be increased by filing the ring ends very carefully with a fine file. Mount the file in a vice with soft jaws, slip the ring over the file with the ends contacting the file face, and slowly move the ring to remove material from the ends. Take care, as piston rings are sharp, and are easily broken.

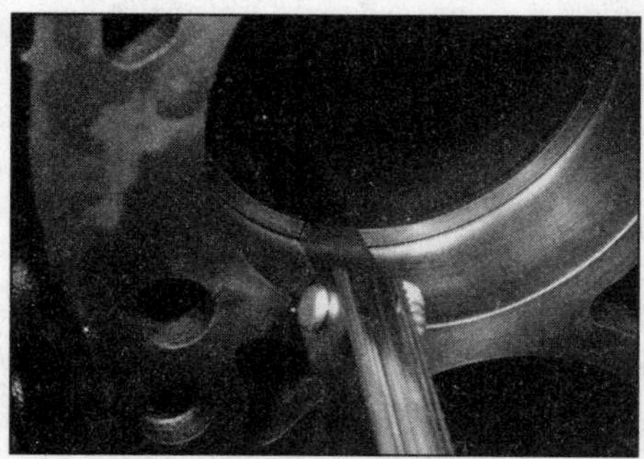

17.4 Measuring a piston ring end gap

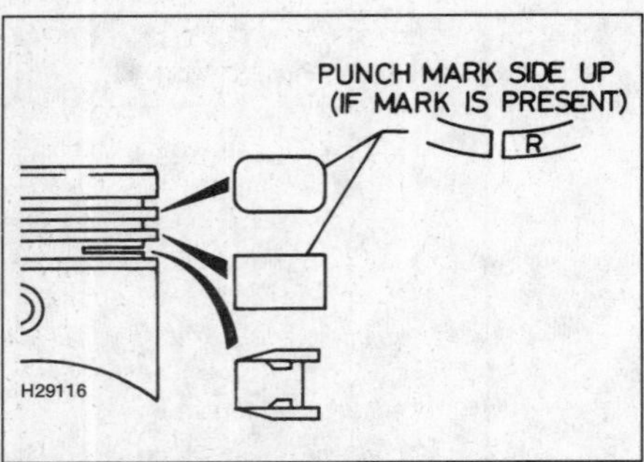

17.10 Piston ring identification

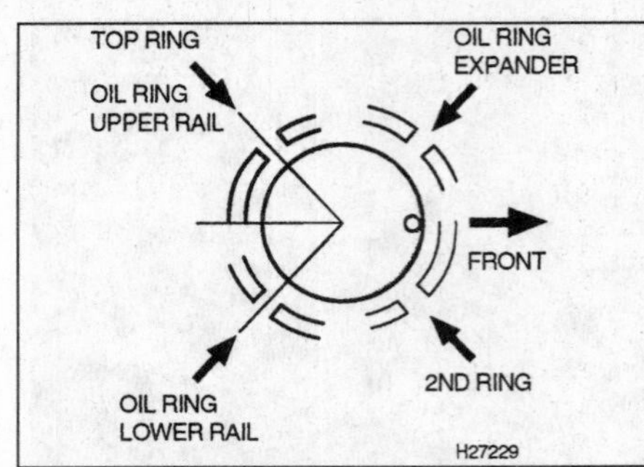

17.12 Position the piston ring end gaps as shown

6 With new piston rings, it is unlikely that the end gap will be too large. If the gaps are too large, check that you have the correct rings for your engine and for the particular cylinder bore size.

7 Repeat the checking procedure for each ring in the first cylinder, and then for the rings in the remaining cylinders. Remember to keep rings, pistons and cylinders matched up.

8 Once the ring end gaps have been checked and if necessary corrected, the rings can be fitted to the pistons. **Note:** *Always follow any instructions supplied with the new piston ring sets - different manufacturers may specify different procedures. Do not mix up the top and second compression rings, as they have different cross-sections.*

9 The oil control ring (lowest on the piston) is installed first. It is composed of three separate components. Slip the expander into the groove, then install the upper side rail into the groove between the expander and the ring land, then install the lower side rail in the same manner.

10 Install the second ring next taking care not to expand the ring any more than is necessary. **Note:** *The second ring and top ring are different, and can be identified by their cross-sections (the bottom ring has a larger, squarer section).* Making sure the ring is the correct way up with any markings facing upwards, fit the ring into the middle groove on the piston, taking care not to expand the ring any more than is necessary **(see illustration)**.

11 Install the top ring in the same way, making sure the ring is the correct way up with its identification marking facing upwards.

12 With all the rings in position on the piston, space the ring end gaps as shown **(see illustration)**.

13 Repeat the above procedure for the remaining pistons and rings.

18 Piston/connecting rod assembly - refitting and big-end bearing running clearance check

Selection of new bearing shells

1 There are two sizes of big-end bearing shell produced by Nissan; a standard size for use with the standard crankshaft, and an undersize for use once the crankshaft journals have been reground.

2 Consult your Nissan dealer for the latest information on parts availability. If possible quote the diameter of the crankshaft big-end crankpins when ordering bearing shells.

3 Prior to refitting the piston/connecting rod assemblies, it is recommended that the big-end bearing running clearance is checked as follows.

Big-end bearing running clearance check

4 Clean the backs of the bearing shells, and the bearing locations in both the connecting rod and bearing cap.

5 Press the bearing shells into their locations, ensuring that the tab on each shell engages in the recess in the connecting rod and cap **(see illustration)**. Take care not to touch any shell's bearing surface with your fingers, and ensure that the shells are correctly installed. If the original bearing shells are being used for the check, ensure that they are refitted in their original locations. The clearance can be checked in either of two ways.

6 One method is to refit the big-end bearing cap to the connecting rod, ensuring that they are fitted the correct way round, with the bearing shells in place. With the cap retaining nuts correctly tightened, use an internal micrometer or vernier caliper to measure the internal diameter of each assembled pair of bearing shells. If the diameter of each corresponding crankshaft journal is measured and then subtracted from the bearing internal diameter, the result will be the big-end bearing running clearance.

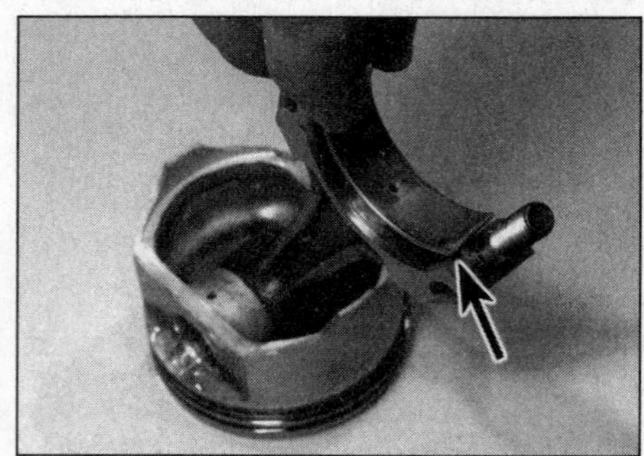

18.5 Fit each bearing shell to its connecting rod, aligning its tab with the rod cut-out (arrowed)

7 The second, and more accurate, method is to use Plastigauge (see Section 16).

8 Ensure that the bearing shells are correctly fitted. Place a strand of Plastigauge on each (cleaned) crankpin journal.

9 Refit the (clean) piston/connecting rod assemblies to the crankshaft, and refit the big-end bearing caps, using the marks made or noted on removal to ensure that they are fitted the correct way round.

10 Tighten the bearing cap nuts in the specified two Stages as described below. Take care not to disturb the Plastigauge, nor to rotate the connecting rod during the tightening sequence.

11 Dismantle the assemblies without rotating the connecting rods. Use the scale printed on the Plastigauge envelope to obtain the big-end bearing running clearance.

12 If the clearance is not as specified, the bearing shells may be the wrong size (or excessively worn, if the original shells are being re-used). Make sure that no dirt or oil was trapped between the bearing shells and the caps or connecting rods when the clearance was measured. If the Plastigauge was wider at one end than at the other, the crankpins may be tapered.

13 If the clearance is not as specified with the original bearing shells, repeat the checking procedure using new bearing shells. If the clearance is not as specified even with new bearing shells, then seek the advice of a Nissan dealer or engine overhaul specialist. They will be able to advise you on the best course of action, and whether or not it will be necessary to have the crankpin journals reground and fit undersize shells.

14 Where necessary, obtain the required grades of bearing shell, and repeat the running clearance checking procedure as described above.

15 On completion, carefully scrape away all traces of the Plastigauge material from the crankshaft and bearing shells. Use your fingernail, or a wooden or plastic scraper which is unlikely to score the bearing surfaces.

Final piston/ connecting rod refitting

16 Note that the following procedure assumes that the crankshaft and main bearing cap beam are in place (see Section 16).

17 Ensure that the bearing shells are correctly fitted as described in paragraphs 4 and 5. If new shells are being fitted, ensure that all traces of the protective grease are cleaned off using paraffin. Wipe dry the shells and connecting rods with a lint-free cloth.

18 Lubricate the cylinder bores, the pistons, and piston rings, then lay out each piston/connecting rod assembly in its respective position.

19 Start with assembly No 1. Make sure that the piston rings are still spaced as described in

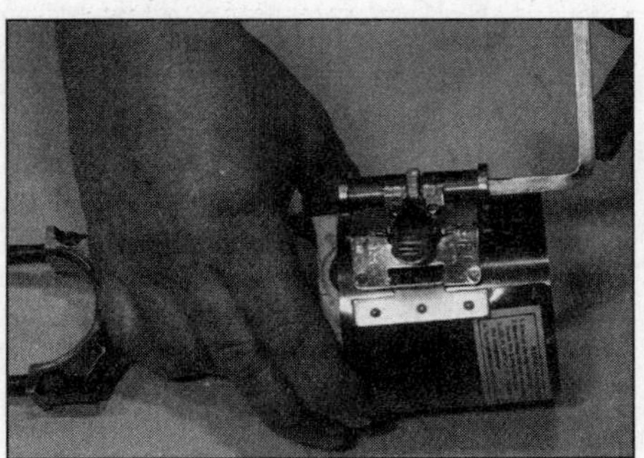

18.19 With the ring end gaps positioned correctly, clamp them with a piston ring compressor

Section 17, then clamp them in position with a piston ring compressor **(see illustration)**.

20 Insert the piston/connecting rod assembly into the top of cylinder No 1. Ensure that the piston front marking (in the form of either an arrow or a dot) on the piston crown is on the timing chain side of the bore. Using a block of wood or hammer handle against the piston crown, tap the assembly into the cylinder until the piston crown is flush with the top of the cylinder **(see illustrations)**.

21 Ensure that the bearing shell is still correctly installed. Liberally lubricate the crankpin and both bearing shells. Taking care not to mark the cylinder bores, tap the piston/connecting rod assembly down the bore and onto the crankpin. Refit the big-end bearing cap, tightening its retaining nuts finger-tight at first. Note that the faces with the identification marks must match (which means that the bearing shell locating tabs abut each other).

22 Tighten the bearing cap retaining nuts to their Stage 1 torque setting, using a torque wrench and suitable socket, then tighten them through the specified Stage 2 angle setting **(see illustrations)**.

23 Rotate the crankshaft and check that it turns freely; some stiffness is to be expected if new components have been fitted, but there should be no signs of binding or tight spots.

24 Refit the remaining three piston/connecting rod assemblies in the same way.

25 Refit the cylinder head, timing chains and sump as described in Part A of this Chapter **(see illustration)**.

19 Engine - initial start-up after overhaul

1 With the engine refitted in the vehicle, double-check the engine oil and coolant levels. Make a final check that everything has been reconnected, and that there are no tools or rags left in the engine compartment.

2 Remove the spark plugs, and disable the ignition system by disconnecting the low tension wiring from the coil(s).

3 Turn the engine on the starter until the oil pressure warning light goes out. Refit the spark plugs, and reconnect the low tension wiring.

4 Start the engine, noting that this may take a little longer than usual, due to the fuel system components having been disturbed.

5 While the engine is idling, check for fuel, water and oil leaks. Don't be alarmed if there are some odd smells and smoke from parts getting hot and burning off oil deposits.

6 Assuming all is well, keep the engine idling until hot water is felt circulating through the radiator top hose, then switch off the engine.

7 After a few minutes, recheck the oil and coolant levels as described in Chapter 1, and top-up as necessary.

8 If new pistons, rings or crankshaft bearings have been fitted, the engine must be treated as new, and run-in for the first 500 miles (800 km). *Do not* operate the engine at full-throttle, or allow it to labour at low engine speeds in any gear. It is recommended that the oil and filter be changed at the end of this period.

18.20a Arrow on the piston crown must face the timing chain end of the engine

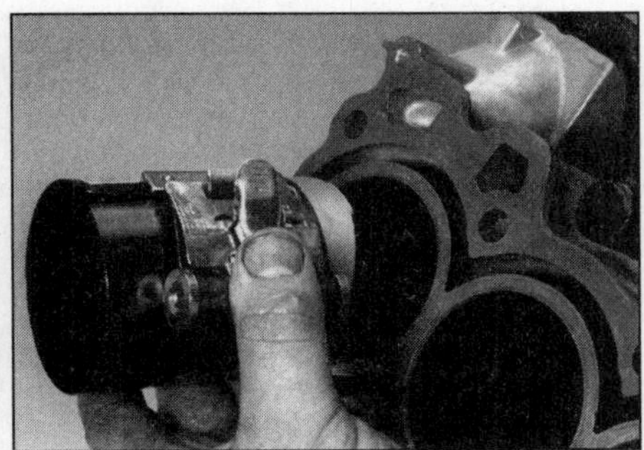

18.20b Insert the piston/connecting rod assembly into the cylinder . . .

18.20c . . . and carefully tap it down the bore using a hammer handle

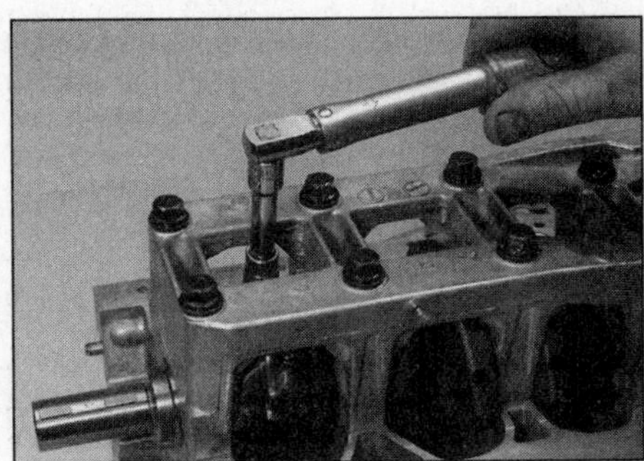

18.22a Torque tightening the main bearing cap beam bolts

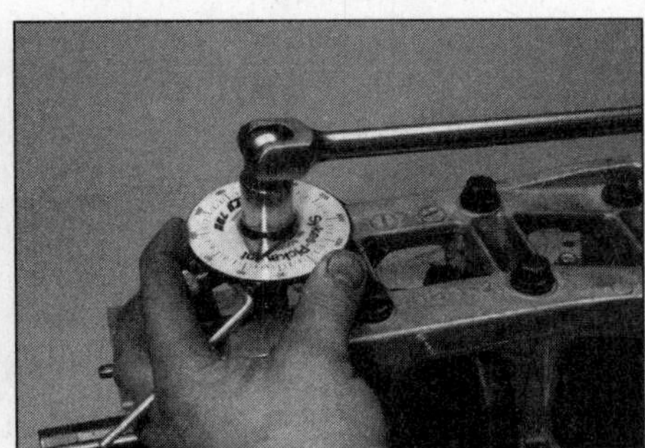

18.22b Angle-tightening the main bearing cap beam bolts

18.25 Refitting the lower timing chain during the engine re-build procedure

Notes

Chapter 3
Cooling, heating and ventilation systems

Contents

Degrees of difficulty

Easy, suitable for novice with little experience 	**Fairly easy,** suitable for beginner with some experience 	**Fairly difficult,** suitable for competent DIY mechanic 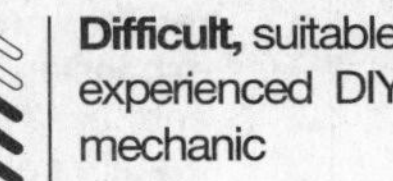	**Difficult,** suitable for experienced DIY mechanic 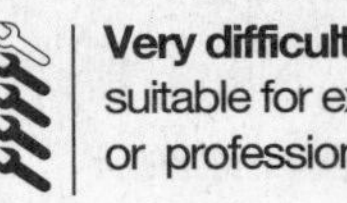	**Very difficult,** suitable for expert DIY or professional

Specifications

General

Radiator cap opening pressure	0.78 to 0.98 bars (11.0 to 14.0 psi)

Thermostat

Opening temperature:	
Starts to open	82°C
Fully open	95°C
Maximum valve lift (approximate)	8.0 mm

Engine temperature sensor

Resistance:	
20°C	2.5 k ohms (approx)
50°C	0.85 k ohms (approx)
90°C	0.25 k ohms (approx)

Engine temperature gauge sensor

Resistance:	
52.5°C	2100 ohms
65°C	1175 to 1420 ohms
91°C	470 to 570 ohms
119°C	210 to 235 ohms

Torque wrench settings	Nm	lbf ft
Coolant pump pulley securing bolts	7	5
Coolant pump securing bolts	7	5
Thermostat cover securing bolts	7	5
Thermostat housing securing bolts	7	5

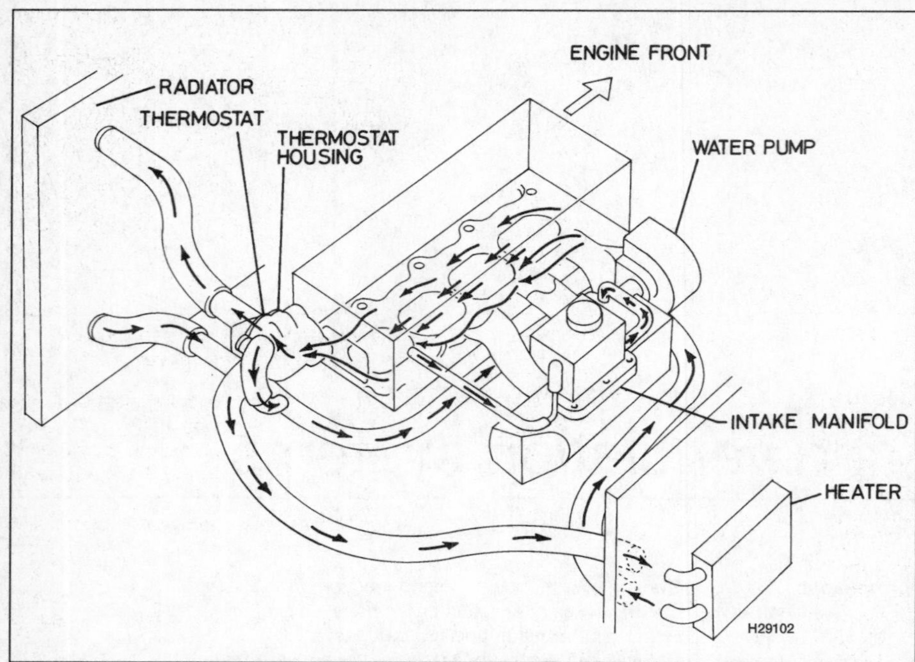

1.1 Diagrammatic view of the cooling system

1 General information and precautions

General information

The cooling system is of pressurised type, comprising a coolant pump driven by a V-belt from the crankshaft pulley, a crossflow radiator, a coolant expansion tank, an electric cooling fan, a thermostat, heater matrix, and all associated hoses and switches **(see illustration)**. On manual transmission models the expansion tank is mounted by the battery on the left-hand side of the engine compartment, however on automatic transmission models it is mounted on the right-hand side.

The system functions as follows. The coolant pump pumps cold water around the cylinder block and head passages, and through the inlet manifold, throttle body and heater matrix.

When the engine is cold, the coolant is returned from the thermostat housing to the coolant pump. When the coolant reaches a predetermined temperature, the thermostat opens, and the coolant passes through the top hose to the radiator. As the coolant circulates through the radiator, it is cooled by the inrush of air when the car is in forward motion. The airflow is supplemented by the action of the electric cooling fan when necessary. Upon reaching the bottom of the radiator, the coolant has now cooled, and the cycle is repeated.

When the engine is at normal operating temperature, the coolant expands, and some of it is released through the valve in the radiator pressure cap, and displaced into the expansion tank. Coolant collects in the tank, and is returned to the radiator when the system cools.

The electric cooling fan is mounted on the rear of the radiator. At a predetermined coolant temperature, the sensor actuates the fan via the ECU.

Precautions

Warning: Do not attempt to remove the radiator pressure cap, or to disturb any part of the cooling system, while the engine is hot, as there is a high risk of scalding. If the radiator pressure cap must be removed before the engine and radiator have fully cooled (even though this is not recommended), the pressure in the cooling system must first be relieved. Cover the cap with a thick layer of cloth, to avoid scalding, and slowly unscrew the pressure cap until a hissing sound is heard. When the hissing has stopped, indicating that the pressure has reduced, slowly unscrew the pressure cap until it can be removed; if more hissing sounds are heard, wait until they have stopped before unscrewing the cap completely. At all times, keep your face well away from the pressure cap opening, and protect your hands.

Do not allow antifreeze to come into contact with your skin, or with the painted surfaces of the vehicle. Rinse off spills immediately, with plenty of water. Never leave antifreeze lying around in an open container, or in a puddle in the driveway or on the garage floor. Children and pets are attracted by its sweet smell, but antifreeze can be fatal if ingested.

If the engine is hot, the electric cooling fan may start rotating even if the engine is not running. Be careful to keep your hands, hair, and any loose clothing well clear when working in the engine compartment.

Refer to Section 10 for precautions to be observed when working on models equipped with air conditioning.

2 Cooling system hoses - disconnection and renewal

Note: *Refer to the warnings given in Section 1 of this Chapter before proceeding. Hoses should only be disconnected once the engine has cooled sufficiently to avoid scalding.*

1 If the checks described in Chapter 1 reveal a faulty hose, it must be renewed as follows.

2 First drain the cooling system (see Chapter 1). If the coolant is not due for renewal, it may be re-used if it is collected in a clean container. Squirt a little penetrating oil onto the hose clips if they are corroded.

3 To disconnect a hose, release its retaining clips, then move them along the hose, clear of the stubs. Carefully work the hose free. **Do not** attempt to disconnect any part of the system while it is still hot.

4 Note that the radiator stubs are fragile; do not use excessive force when attempting to remove the hoses. If a hose proves difficult to remove, try to release it by twisting it.

If all else fails, cut the hose with a sharp knife, then slit it so that it can be peeled off in two pieces. Although this may prove expensive if the hose is otherwise undamaged, it is preferable to buying a new radiator.

5 When fitting a hose, first slide the clips onto the centre of the hose, then work the hose into position. If clamp type clips were originally fitted, it is a good idea to replace them with screw type clips when refitting the hose. If the hose is stiff, use a little soapy water as a lubricant.

6 Work the hose into position, checking that it is correctly routed, then slide each clip along the hose until it passes over the flared end of the relevant outlet, before securing it in position with the retaining clip.

7 Refill the cooling system with reference to Chapter 1.

8 Check thoroughly for leaks as soon as possible after disturbing any part of the cooling system.

3.3a Disconnecting the expansion tank hose from the top of the radiator

3.3b Removing the radiator top hose

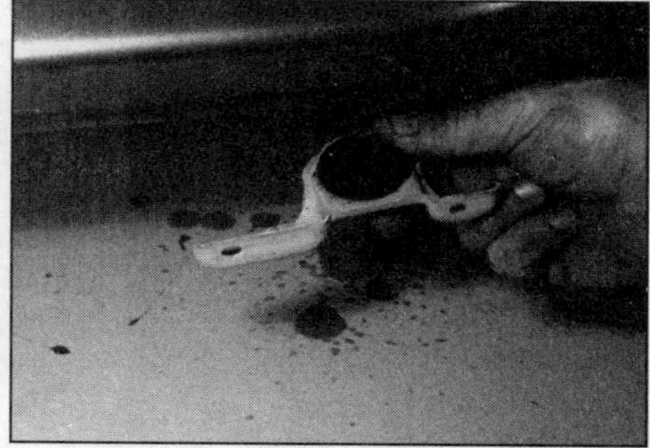

3.6 Removing the radiator bottom mounting bracket

3.7a One of the radiator upper mounting rubbers

3.7b Lifting the radiator from the engine compartment

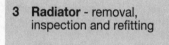

3 Radiator - removal, inspection and refitting

Removal

Note: *If leakage is the reason for removing the radiator, bear in mind that minor leaks can often be cured using a radiator sealant with the radiator in situ.*

1 Disconnect the battery negative lead.

2 Drain the cooling system by disconnecting the radiator bottom hose as described in Chapter 1.

3 Disconnect the remaining coolant hoses from the radiator, and also disconnect the top hose from the thermostat housing **(see illustrations)**. On models with automatic transmission, clamp and disconnect the fluid cooler hoses from the bottom of the radiator.

4 For improved access, remove the cooling fan and shroud assembly, as described in Section 5.

5 Jack up the front of the vehicle and support on axle stands (see "*Jacking and vehicle support*").

6 Working beneath the engine compartment, while supporting the radiator unscrew the bolts securing the radiator mounting brackets to the front valance **(see illustration)**.

7 Lower the radiator from the upper mounting rubbers then lift it upwards from the engine compartment **(see illustrations)**.

8 Recover the rubbers from the lower mounting brackets.

9 Recover the upper mounting rubbers from the engine compartment crossmember.

Inspection

10 If the radiator has been removed due to suspected blockage, reverse-flush it as described in Chapter 1. Clean dirt and debris from the radiator fins, using an air line (in which case, wear eye protection) or a soft brush. Be careful, as the fins are sharp, and easily damaged.

11 If necessary, a radiator specialist can perform a "flow test" on the radiator, to establish whether an internal blockage exists.

12 A leaking radiator must be referred to a specialist for permanent repair. Do not attempt to weld or solder a leaking radiator, as damage to the plastic components may result.

13 In an emergency, minor leaks from the radiator can be cured by using a suitable radiator sealant, in accordance with its manufacturer's instructions, with the radiator *in situ*.

14 If the radiator is to be sent for repair, or is to be renewed, remove all hoses, and the cooling fan switch.

15 Inspect the condition of the radiator mounting rubbers, and renew them if necessary.

Refitting

16 Refitting is a reversal of removal, but on completion, refill and bleed the cooling system as described in Chapter 1.

4 Thermostat - removal, testing and refitting

Removal

Note: *Suitable sealant (liquid gasket) will be required when refitting the thermostat cover.*

1 The thermostat is located in a housing bolted to the transmission end of the cylinder head.

2 Drain the cooling system as described in Chapter 1.

3 Disconnect the coolant hose from the thermostat cover **(see illustrations)**.

4 Unscrew the securing bolts, and remove the thermostat cover from the housing. If the

4.3a Loosen the clip . . .

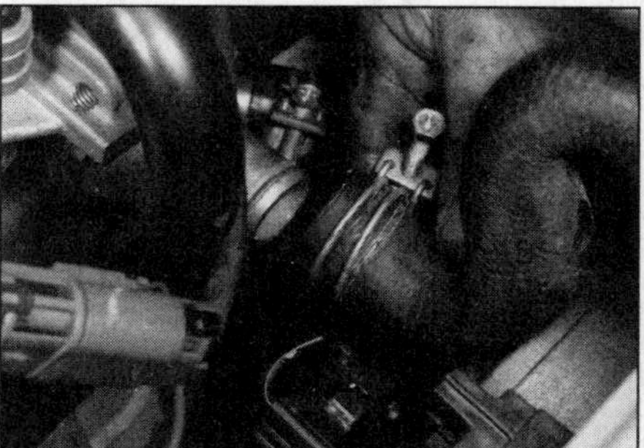

4.3b . . . and disconnect the top hose from the thermostat housing cover

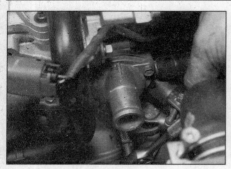

4.4a Unscrew the thermostat cover securing bolts . . .

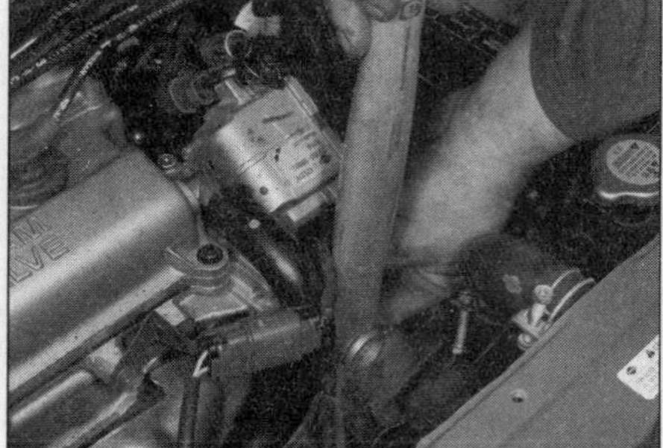
4.4b . . . then tap the cover with the handle of a hammer to free it . . .

4.4c . . . and withdraw the cover with the thermostat

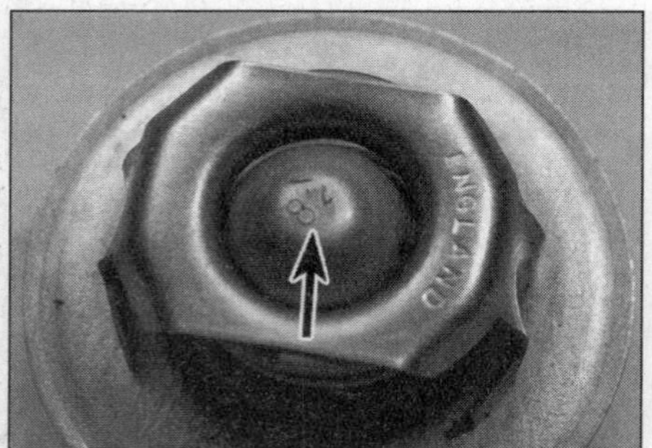
4.7 Opening temperature marked on the thermostat

4.10 "TOP" markings on the thermostat

cover is stuck to the housing, tap it gently with the handle of a hammer, or rock it back and forth to free it - **do not** lever between the mating faces **(see illustrations)**.

5 The thermostat will probably come away with the cover, and it should be prised away from it with a screwdriver. If it remains in the housing, prise it out noting that the bleed valve is located at the top.

Testing

6 A rough test of the thermostat may be made by suspending it with a piece of string in a container full of water. Heat the water to bring it to the boil - the thermostat must open by the time the water boils. If not, renew it.

7 If a thermometer is available, the precise opening and fully open temperatures of the thermostat may be determined; compare with the figures given in the *Specifications*. The opening temperature is also marked on the thermostat **(see illustration)**.

8 If the thermostat fails to close as the water cools, it must be renewed.

Refitting

9 Commence refitting by thoroughly cleaning the mating faces of the cover and the housing.

10 Refit the thermostat to the housing with the bleed valve uppermost. An arrow and "TOP" marking also indicates the correct location **(see illustration)**

11 Apply a continuous bead of sealant (liquid gasket) to the housing mating face of the thermostat cover, taking care not to apply excess sealant, which may enter the cooling system.

12 Fit the cover to the thermostat housing, then refit the securing bolts, and tighten to the specified torque.

13 Reconnect the coolant hose to the thermostat cover.

14 Refill the cooling system as described in Chapter 1.

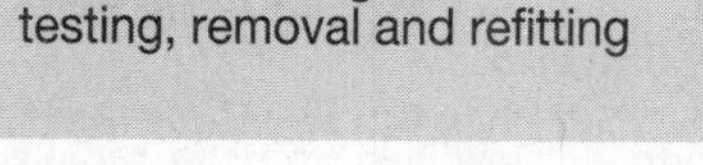

5 Electric cooling fan - testing, removal and refitting

Testing

1 Current supply to the cooling fan is via the radiator fan relay which is triggered by the engine temperature sensor, via the engine management electronic control unit. The ECU uses signals from the vehicle speed sensor, engine temperature sensor and air conditioner switch to control the cooling fan. The engine temperature sensor is located behind the thermostat housing on the left-hand end of the cylinder head.

2 Detailed fault diagnosis can be carried out by a Nissan dealer using suitable test equipment, but basic diagnosis can be carried out as follows.

3 If the fan does not appear to work, run the engine until normal operating temperature is reached, then allow it to idle. The fan should cut in within a few minutes (before the temperature gauge needle enters the red section). If not, switch off the ignition and disconnect the cooling fan motor wiring connector.

4 The motor can be tested by disconnecting it from the wiring loom, and connecting a 12-volt supply directly to it (connect the supply to the Blue and Black wire). The motor should operate - if not, the motor or wiring is faulty.

5 If the motor operates when tested as described in paragraph 4, the fault must lie in the engine wiring harness, the relay, the engine management electronic control unit, or the temperature sensor. The temperature sensor can be tested as described in Section 6. Any further fault diagnosis should be referred to a suitably-equipped Nissan dealer - **do not** attempt to test the electronic control unit.

Removal

6 Disconnect the battery negative lead. Unclip and remove the relay box located behind the radiator and in front of the battery **(see illustrations)**.

5.6a Release the clip . . .

5.6b . . . and remove the relay box

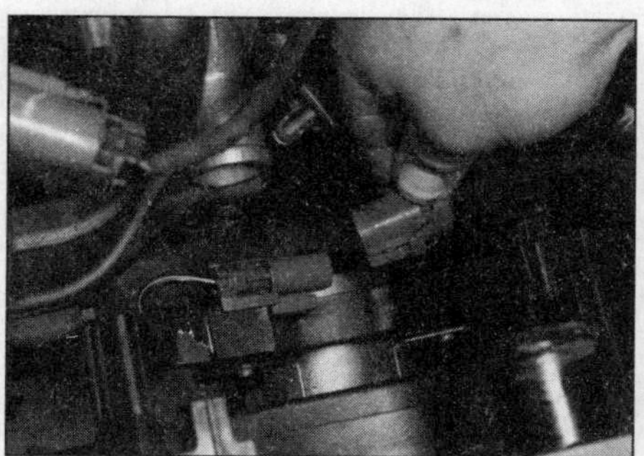

5.7 Disconnecting the wiring from the cooling fan

5.8a Unscrew the left-hand mounting screw . . .

5.8b . . . and right-hand mounting screw . . .

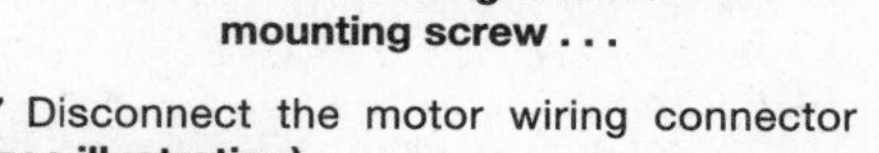

5.8c . . . then lift out the cooling fan assembly

7 Disconnect the motor wiring connector **(see illustration)**.

8 Unscrew the two securing screws from the top of the shroud, then lift out the assembly to release the lower clips **(see illustrations)**.

Refitting

9 Refitting is a reversal of removal.

6 Cooling system electrical sensors - testing, removal and refitting

Engine temperature sensor

General

1 The engine temperature sensor provides information to the engine management electronic control unit to control the fuel and ignition systems, and the radiator cooling fan.

Testing

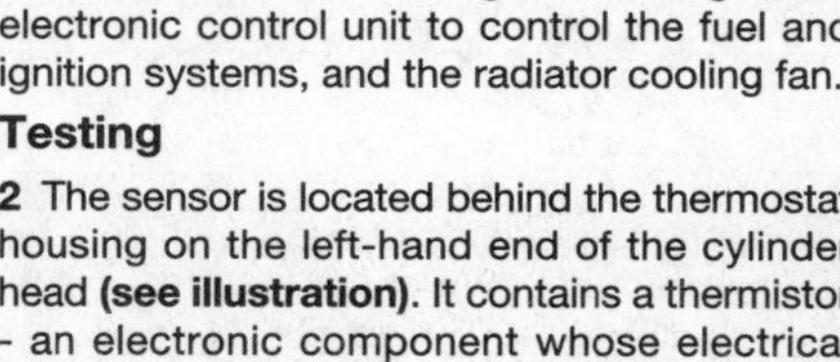

2 The sensor is located behind the thermostat housing on the left-hand end of the cylinder head **(see illustration)**. It contains a thermistor - an electronic component whose electrical resistance decreases at a predetermined rate as its temperature rises.

3 The fuel injection/engine management ECU supplies the sensor with a set voltage and then, by measuring the current flowing in the sensor circuit, it determines the engine temperature. This information is then used, in conjunction with other inputs, to control the fuel injection/engine management system, and the engine cooling fan.

4 If the sensor circuit should fail to provide adequate information, the ECU back-up facility will override the sensor signal. In this event, the ECU assumes a predetermined setting which will allow the fuel injection/engine management system to run, albeit at reduced efficiency. When this occurs, the engine warning light on the instrument panel will come on, and the advice of a Nissan dealer should be sought. The sensor itself can be tested by removing it, and checking the resistances at various temperatures using an ohmmeter (heat the sensor in a container of water, and monitor the temperature with a thermometer). The resistance values are given in the *Specifications*. **Do not** attempt to test the circuit with the sensor fitted to the engine, and the wiring connector fitted, as there is a high risk of damaging the ECU.

5 Refer to Chapter 4A for further details of the fuel injection/engine management system.

6.2 The engine temperature sensor is located behind the thermostat housing

Removal

6 Disconnect the battery negative lead.

7 Partially drain the cooling system to just below the level of the sensor (as described in Chapter 1). Alternatively, have ready a suitable bung to plug the aperture when the sensor is removed.

8 Disconnect the wiring plug from the sensor.

9 Unscrew the sensor from the cylinder head. If the system has not been drained, plug the sensor aperture to prevent further coolant loss.

Refitting

10 Refitting is a reversal of removal, but tighten the sensor to the specified torque and refill (or top-up) the cooling system as described in Chapter 1. On completion start the engine and run it until it reaches normal operating temperature, then continue to run the engine until the cooling fan cuts in and out correctly.

Coolant temperature gauge sender

Testing

11 The sender is located in the left-hand end of the cylinder head. The sender is the smaller of the two senders.

12 The temperature gauge is fed with a stabilised voltage from the instrument panel feed (via the ignition switch and a fuse). The gauge earth is controlled by the sender. The sender contains a thermistor - an electronic component whose electrical resistance decreases at a predetermined rate as its temperature rises. When the coolant is cold, the sender resistance is high, current flow through the gauge is reduced, and the gauge needle points towards the blue (cold) end of the scale. As the coolant temperature rises and the sender resistance falls, current flow increases, and the gauge needle moves towards the upper end of the scale. If the sender is faulty, it must be renewed.

13 If the gauge develops a fault, first check the other instruments; if they do not work at all, check the instrument panel electrical feed. If the readings are erratic, there may be a fault in the voltage stabiliser, which will necessitate renewal of the stabiliser (the stabiliser is integral with the instrument panel printed circuit board - see Chapter 12). If the fault lies in the temperature gauge alone, check it as follows.

14 If the gauge needle remains at the "cold" end of the scale when the engine is hot, disconnect the sender wiring plug, and earth the relevant wire to the cylinder head. If the needle then deflects when the ignition is switched on, the sender unit is proved faulty, and should be renewed. If the needle still does not move, remove the instrument panel (Chapter 12) and check the continuity of the wire between the sender unit and the gauge, and the feed to the gauge unit. If continuity is shown, and the fault still exists, then the

7.1 For improved access to the coolant pump, unclip the power steering reservoir and move it to one side

7.4 Removing the coolant pump pulley

gauge is faulty, and the gauge should be renewed.

15 If the gauge needle remains at the "hot" end of the scale when the engine is cold, disconnect the sender wire. If the needle then returns to the "cold" end of the scale when the ignition is switched on, the sender unit is proved faulty, and should be renewed. If the needle still does not move, check the remainder of the circuit as described previously.

Removal and refitting

16 The procedure is similar to that described previously in this Section for the engine temperature sensor.

Air conditioning system temperature sensor

Testing

17 The sensor is integral with the air conditioning temperature control unit, located on the side of the heater/air conditioning unit behind the facia. Testing should be entrusted to a Nissan dealer.

Removal and refitting

18 Removal and refitting should be entrusted to a Nissan dealer suitably equipped to test the unit.

7 Coolant pump - removal, inspection and refitting

Removal

1 Disconnect the battery negative lead. For improved access unclip the power steering fluid reservoir and move it to one side **(see illustration)**.

2 Drain the cooling system as described in Chapter 1.

3 Remove the auxiliary drivebelts as described in Chapter 1.

4 Unscrew the securing bolts, and remove the coolant pump pulley **(see illustration)**. It will be necessary to counterhold the pulley in order to unscrew the bolts, and this is most easily achieved with a strap wrench or by wrapping an old drivebelt tightly around the pulley to act in a similar manner to a strap wrench.

5 Unscrew the securing bolts, and withdraw the coolant pump from the cylinder block **(see illustration)**. If the pump is stuck, tap it gently using a soft-faced mallet - **do not** lever between the pump and cylinder block mating faces.

Inspection

6 Check the pump body and impeller for signs of excessive corrosion. Turn the impeller, and check for stiffness due to corrosion, or roughness due to excessive end play.

7 No spare parts are available for the pump, and if faulty, worn or corroded, a new pump should be fitted.

Refitting

8 Commence refitting by thoroughly cleaning all traces of sealant from the mating faces of the pump and cylinder block.

9 Apply a continuous bead of sealant (liquid gasket) to the mating face of the pump, taking care not to apply excessive sealant, which may enter the pump itself. The bead must be on the *inner* side of the mounting bolt holes.

7.5 Removing the coolant pump

10 Place the pump in position in the cylinder block, then refit and tighten the bolts to the specified torque.

11 Refit the pump pulley and tighten the securing bolts to the specified torque.

12 Refit and tension the auxiliary drivebelts as described in Chapter 1.

13 Refill the cooling system (see Chapter 1).

14 Reconnect the battery negative lead and clip the power steering fluid reservoir into position.

8 Heating and ventilation system - general information

1 The heater/ventilation system consists of a blower motor (housed behind the facia), face level vents in the centre and at each end of the facia, and air ducts to the front footwells.

2 The control unit is located in the facia, and the controls operate flap valves to deflect and mix the air flowing through the various parts of the heating/ventilation system. The flap valves are contained in the air distribution housing, which acts as a central distribution unit, passing air to the various ducts and vents.

3 Cold air enters the system through the grille at the rear of the engine compartment. If required, the airflow is boosted by the blower fan, and then flows through the various ducts, according to the settings of the controls. Stale air is expelled through ducts at the rear of the vehicle. If warm air is required, the cold air is passed over the heater matrix, which is heated by the engine coolant.

4 On models fitted with air conditioning, a recirculation switch enables the outside air supply to be closed off, while the air inside the vehicle is recirculated. This can be useful to prevent unpleasant odours entering from outside the vehicle, but should only be used briefly, as the recirculated air inside the vehicle will soon become stale.

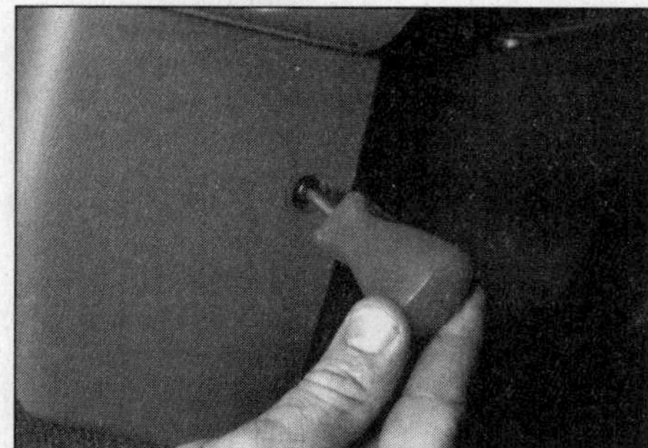
9.3a Unscrew the side screws . . .

9.3b . . . and remove the facia lower panel

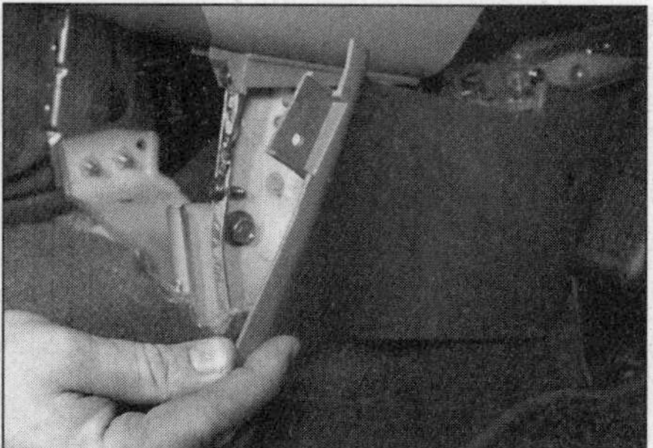
9.3c Removing the footwell panels

9.5a Centre surround panel lower mounting screw . . .

9.5b . . . upper mounting screws . . .

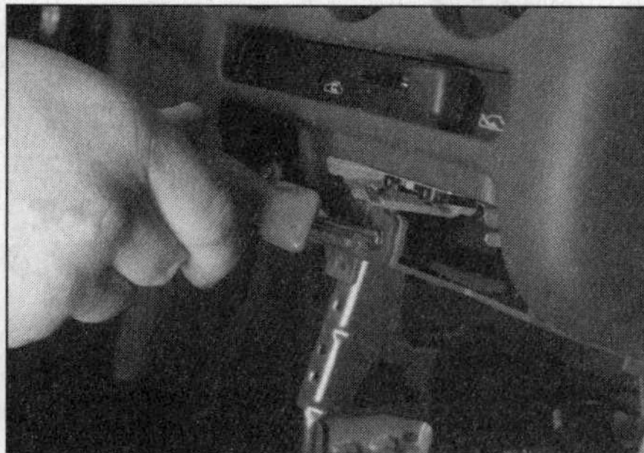
9.5c . . . and mounting screw on ashtray location

9.6a Prise out the centre surround panel with a plastic lever

9.6b Withdrawing the centre surround panel from the facia

9 Heating and ventilation system components - removal and refitting

Heater/ventilation control panel

Removal

Note: *Models from March 1998 onwards have a revised heater control panel, with the rotary dials uppermost. The illustrations accompanying this Section are of a 1996 model, but the procedure described is equally valid for later models.*

1 Disconnect the battery negative lead.

2 Remove the centre console (Chapter 11).

3 Unscrew the side screws and remove the panel from below the centre of the facia. If necessary also remove the remaining panels from the footwells **(see illustrations)**.

4 Remove the ashtray.

5 Unscrew the mounting screws securing the centre surround panel to the facia **(see illustrations)**.

6 Using a plastic lever, prise out the top of the surround panel and withdraw it from the facia **(see illustrations)**.

7 Note the location of the wiring and disconnect it from the various components **(see illustration)**.

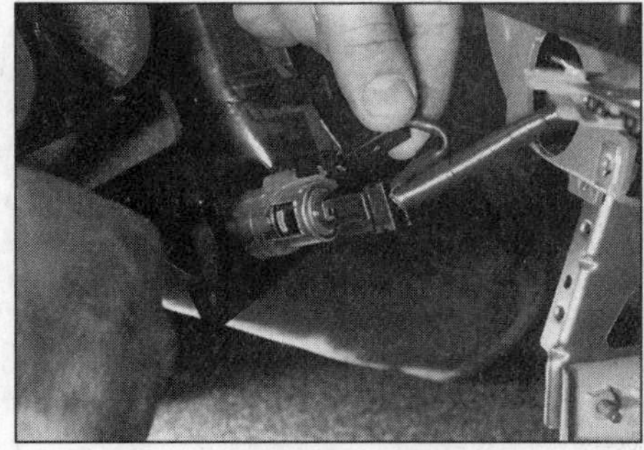
9.7 Disconnecting the wiring from the cigar lighter

9.8 Heater control panel mounting screws

9.9a Control cable connection on the right-hand side of the heater assembly

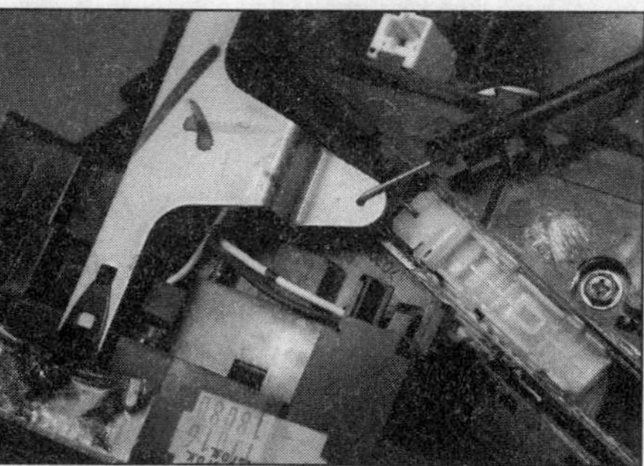

9.9b Cable connection on the top of the control panel

9.9c Cable connection on the bottom of the control panel

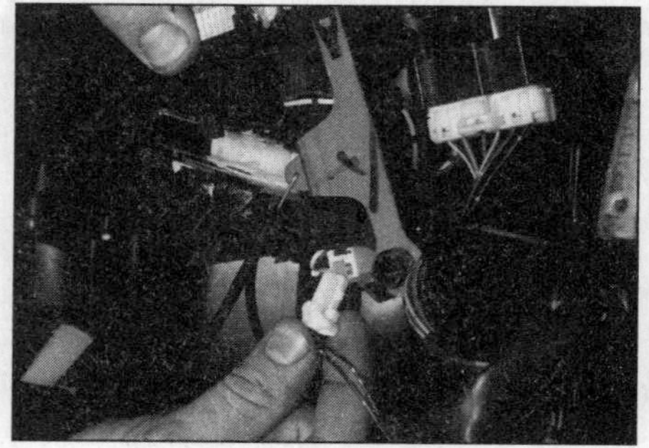

9.9d Disconnecting the small wiring plug . . .

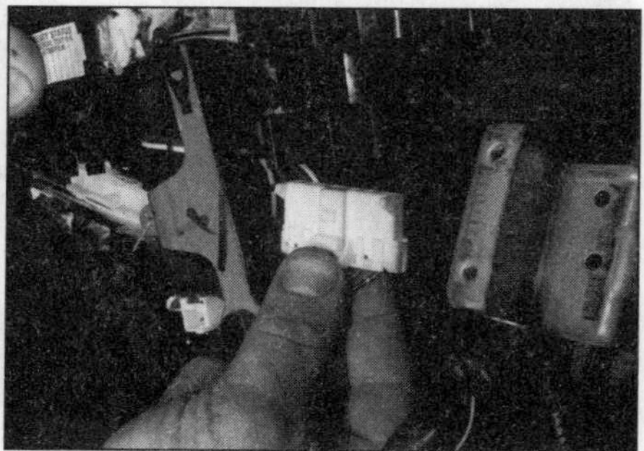

9.9e . . . and large wiring plug from the control panel

8 Unscrew the mounting screws and withdraw the control panel from the facia **(see illustration)**.

9 Disconnect the wiring and control cables from the heater unit/blower housing and/or the control panel, noting their locations for correct refitting **(see illustrations)**.

Refitting

10 Refitting is a reversal of removal, but reconnect and adjust the temperature control cable as follows:

a) Move the temperature control lever on the control panel to the fully hot position.

b) Move the air mix door lever on the heater unit to the fully hot position.

c) Reconnect the end of the cable to the lever on the heater unit, then push the securing clip over the cable.

Heater assembly

Warning: On models fitted with air conditioning, do not attempt to remove the cooling unit, which is located between the heater blower motor casing and the main heater assembly. Removal of the cooling unit entails disconnection of refrigerant lines - refer to Section 10 for precautions to be observed. If in any doubt as to the procedure to follow on models with air conditioning, consult a Nissan dealer for advice.

Removal

11 Disconnect the battery negative lead.

12 Drain the cooling system (see Chapter 1).

13 Remove the heater/ventilation control panel as described previously in this Section.

14 Remove the facia (refer to Chapter 11).

15 Working inside the engine compartment, loosen the clips and disconnect the heater hoses from the heater matrix stubs on the left-hand side of the bulkhead **(see illustration)**.

16 Note the location of the wiring plugs then disconnect them from the heater assembly.

17 Unscrew the mounting bolts securing the heater assembly to the bulkhead **(see illustrations)**.

9.15 Disconnecting heater hoses from the matrix stubs in the engine compartment

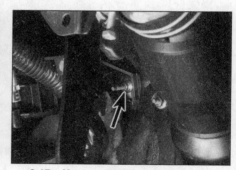

9.17a Heater mounting nut near the steering column

9.17b Upper right heater mounting nut

9.17c Upper left heater mounting nut

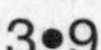

9.18 Removing the heater assembly

9.19a Upper right blower housing mounting bolt

9.19b Left blower housing mounting nut

9.19c Disconnecting the control cable from the blower housing

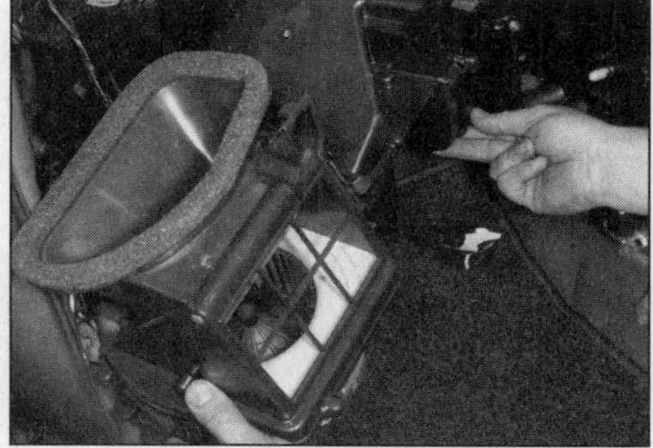
9.19d Removing the blower housing

9.23a Unscrew the heater housing screws . . .

18 Withdraw the assembly from the bulkhead and remove from the vehicle. Be prepared for some loss of coolant from the heater matrix stubs **(see illustration)**.

19 If necessary, the heater blower motor and housing can be unbolted from the bulkhead at this time after disconnecting the wiring and control cable **(see illustrations)**.

Refitting

20 Refitting is a reversal of removal, but note the following:

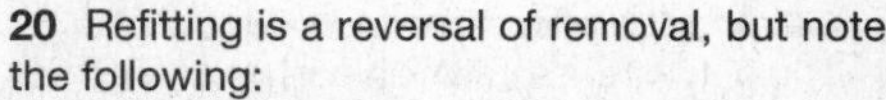
a) Make sure that all wiring and cables are routed as noted during dismantling.

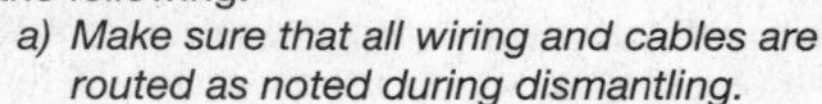
b) Make sure that all air ducts are securely reconnected.

c) Refit the facia components with reference to Chapter 11.

d) On completion, refill and bleed the cooling system as described in Chapter 1.

9.23b . . . and lift out the heater matrix

9.26a Heater blower motor wiring plug

Heater matrix

Removal

21 Remove the complete heater assembly as described previously in paragraphs 11 to 17.

22 Unhook the actuating rod spring from the water valve lever on the heater matrix, and withdraw the actuating rod.

23 Unscrew the screws and separate the heater housing halves, then lift out the heater matrix **(see illustrations)**. Take care not to damage the matrix fins.

Refitting

24 Refitting is a reversal of removal, but refit the heater assembly as described previously in this Section.

9.26b Disconnecting the large wiring plug . . .

9.26c . . . and small wiring plug from the heater blower motor

Heater blower motor

Removal

25 Disconnect the battery negative lead.

26 Working under the left-hand side of the facia, disconnect the wiring plugs **(see illustrations)**.

27 Disconnect the cooling air hose from the bottom of the motor casing.

28 Unscrew the mounting screws, noting the

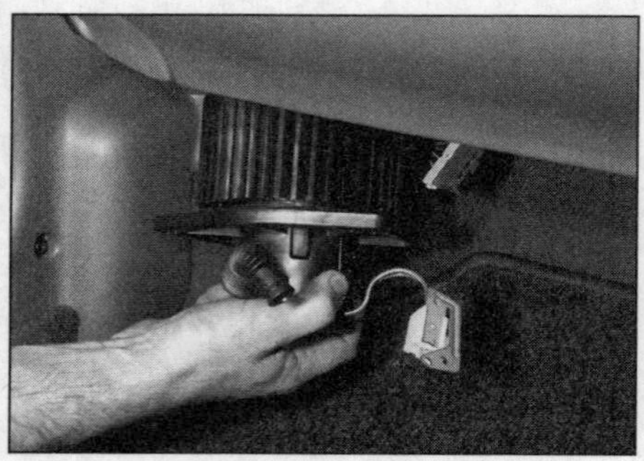

9.28 Removing the heater blower motor

9.32a Resistor mounting bolts

9.32b Removing the heater blower motor resistor

locations of the wiring support bracket, then withdraw the motor assembly downwards from the housing **(see illustration)**.

Refitting

29 Refitting is a reversal of removal, but ensure that any brackets are positioned as noted before removal, and make sure that the cooling air hose is reconnected.

Heater blower motor resistor

Removal

30 The resistor is located at the bottom of the heater casing.

31 Disconnect the wiring plug from the resistor.

32 Remove the two securing screws, and withdraw the resistor from the heater unit **(see illustrations)**.

Refitting

33 Refitting is a reversal of removal.

10 Air conditioning system - general information and precautions

General information

1 An air conditioning system is available on certain models. It enables the temperature of incoming air to be lowered, and also dehumidifies the air, which makes for rapid demisting and increased comfort.

2 The cooling side of the system works in the same way as a refrigerator. Refrigerant gas is drawn into a belt-driven compressor, and passes into a condenser mounted on the front of the radiator, where it loses heat and becomes liquid. The liquid passes through an expansion valve to an evaporator, where it changes from liquid under high pressure to gas under low pressure. This change is accompanied by a drop in temperature, which cools the evaporator. The refrigerant returns to the compressor, and the cycle begins again.

3 Air blown through the evaporator passes to the air distribution unit, where it is mixed with hot air blown through the heater matrix to achieve the desired temperature in the passenger compartment. On models from March 1998 onwards, the air entering the passenger compartment is filtered by a renewable paper element (see Chapter 1, Section 4).

4 The heating side of the system works in the same way as on models without air conditioning (see Section 8).

5 The system is electronically-controlled. Any problems with the system should be referred to a Nissan dealer.

Precautions

6 With an air conditioning system, it is necessary to observe special precautions whenever dealing with any part of the system, or its associated components. If for any reason the system must be disconnected, entrust this task to your Nissan dealer or a refrigeration engineer.

Warning: The refrigeration circuit contains a liquid refrigerant (Freon). The refrigerant is potentially dangerous, and should only be handled by qualified persons. If it is splashed onto the skin, it can cause frostbite. It is not itself poisonous, but in the presence of a naked flame (including a cigarette), it forms a poisonous gas. Uncontrolled discharging of the refrigerant is dangerous, and potentially damaging to the environment. For all these reasons, it is dangerous to disconnect any part of the system without specialised knowledge and equipment.

7 Do not operate the air conditioning system if it is known to be short of refrigerant, as this may damage the compressor.

11 Air conditioning system components - removal and refitting

Warning: Do not attempt to open the refrigerant circuit. Refer to the precautions in Section 10.

The only operation which can be carried out easily without discharging the refrigerant is renewal of the compressor drivebelt as described in Chapter 1. All other operations must be referred to a Nissan dealer or an air conditioning specialist.

If necessary for access to other components, the compressor can be unbolted and moved aside, *without disconnecting its flexible hoses*, after removing the drivebelt.

Chapter 4 Part A:
Fuel and exhaust systems

Contents

Degrees of difficulty

Easy, suitable for novice with little experience 	**Fairly easy,** suitable for beginner with some experience 	**Fairly difficult,** suitable for competent DIY mechanic	**Difficult,** suitable for experienced DIY mechanic	**Very difficult,** suitable for expert DIY or professional

Specifications

General

System type	Nissan Electronic Concentrated Control System (ECCS) multi-point injection
Engine codes:	
998 cc	CG10DE
1275 cc	CG13DE
1348 cc	CGA3DE

Fuel system data

Fuel pump type	Electric, immersed in tank
Fuel pump regulated constant pressure (approximate)	2.5 bars

Idle speed and mixture settings

Idle speed:	
Manual transmission models:	
With throttle potentiometer disconnected	600 ± 50 rpm
With throttle potentiometer connected	650 ± 50 rpm
Automatic transmission models:	
With throttle potentiometer disconnected	700 ± 50 rpm
With throttle potentiometer connected	775 ± 50 rpm
Mixture	Less than 0.1%

Fuel system component test data

Throttle potentiometer resistances:	
Throttle valve closed	0.5 kilohm (approx)
Throttle valve partially open	0.5 to 4.2 kilohms
Throttle valve fully open	4.2 kilohms (approx)
Idle Air Control Valves and Auxiliary Air Control (AAC) valve resistance (at 20°C):	
Up to 2000 MY (across terminals 2 and 3, or 3 and 4)	50 to 100 ohms
From 2000 MY (across terminals 1 and 2, or 2 and 3)	20 to 24 ohms
Airflow meter voltage (models up to 2000):	
Between terminals 2 and 3 (engine stopped, ignition on)	0.5 volts (approx)
Between terminals 2 and 3 (engine idling)	2.0 volts (approx)
Fast idle thermowax element adjustment	0.68 to 1.08 mm
Mass Air Flow Sensor voltage (models from 2000):	
At terminal 2	Battery Voltage
At terminal 4	5 volts (approx)

Fuel system component test data (continued)

Intake Air Temperature Sensor voltage (models from 2000):	
At terminal 1	5 volts (approx)
Intake Air Temperature sensor resistance (at 25°C) models from 2000:	
Across terminals 1 and 3	0.09 to 43 ohms
Fuel pump resistance	0.5 ohms (approx)
Fuel injector resistance:	
Up to 2000 MY	10 ohms (approx)
From 2000 MY	15.5 ohms (approx)
Fast idle control device (FICD) solenoid valve:	
Apply 12 volts across solenoid terminals	Solenoid should click, indicating correct operation
Power steering pressure switch:	
Steering wheel being turned	Continuity between switch terminals
Steering wheel stationary	Open-circuit between switch terminals
Coolant temperature sensor resistances:	
20°C	2.5 kilohms (approx)
50°C	0.85 kilohms (approx)
90°C	0.25 kilohms (approx)

Inlet manifold (maximum distortion) 0.1 mm

Exhaust manifold (maximum distortion) 0.3 mm

Recommended fuel (all models) 95 RON unleaded. Leaded fuel (eg UK "4-star") must **not** be used

Torque wrench settings

	Nm	lbf ft
Fuel tank access cover ring	33	24
Fuel tank mounting bolts	31	23
Filler neck mounting	9	7
Throttle body/housing	24	18
Fuel rail retaining bolts:		
Stage 1	8	6
Stage 2	19	14
Injector retaining plate	3	2
AAC valve	6	4
Thermo element	3.5	3
Accelerator cable support bracket	3.5	3
Pressure regulator	3.5	3
Inlet manifold nuts and bolts	19	14
Inlet manifold support bracket	19	14
Wiring support bracket to inlet manifold	7	5
Exhaust manifold to head	20	15
Primary catalytic converter to exhaust manifold	32	24
Heatshield to primary catalytic converter	11	8
Heatshield to exhaust manifold	4	3
Exhaust front pipe to catalytic converter	49	36
Exhaust front pipe heat shield	6	4
Secondary catalytic converter flange nuts	49	36
Exhaust intermediate pipe to tailpipe	35	26

1 General information and precautions

The fuel system consists of a fuel tank mounted under the rear of the vehicle with an electric fuel pump immersed in it, a fuel filter, fuel feed and return lines. The fuel pump supplies fuel to the fuel rail which acts as a reservoir for the four fuel injectors which inject fuel into the inlet tracts. A fuel filter is incorporated in the feed line from the pump to the fuel rail to ensure that the fuel supplied to the injectors is clean.

Refer to Section 6 for information on the fuel injection system, and Section 17 for information on the exhaust system.

Warning: Many of the procedures in this Chapter require the removal of fuel lines and connections which may result in some fuel spillage. Before carrying out any operation on the fuel system refer to the precautions given in Safety first! at the beginning of this Manual and follow them implicitly. Petrol is a highly dangerous and volatile liquid and the precautions necessary when handling it cannot be overstressed.

Note: *Residual pressure will remain in the fuel lines long after the vehicle was last used. When disconnecting any fuel line, depressurise the fuel system as described in Section 7.*

2 Air cleaner and inlet duct - removal and refitting

Removal

Inlet duct

1 Unscrew the mounting screw(s) on the left-hand side of the bulkhead **(see illustration)**. There are two screws on manual transmission models and four screws on automatic transmission models.

2 Disconnect the inlet duct from the left-hand end of the air cleaner and release the breather hose from the clip **(see illustrations)**.

3 Beneath the coolant expansion tank, pull

2.1 Air inlet duct mounting screw on the bulkhead

2.2a Disconnect the air inlet duct from the air cleaner body . . .

2.2b . . . and release the breather hose from the clip

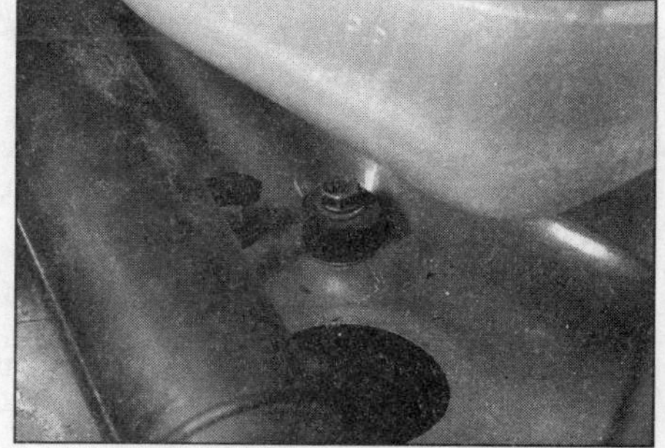

2.3 Pull inlet duct from rubber mounting beneath the coolant expansion tank

2.4 Removing the air inlet duct from the engine compartment

2.6a Loosening the air cleaner body to throttle housing clip

the inlet duct from the rubber mounting **(see illustration)**. For improved access remove the battery as described in Chapter 5A.

4 Withdraw the duct while turning it to clear the expansion tank **(see illustration)**.

Air cleaner

5 If necessary remove the air cleaner element at this stage with reference to Chapter 1.

6 Unscrew the air cleaner body retaining bolt and clip, then free it from the top of the throttle housing. Disconnect the PCV valve and breather hoses from the base of the body, noting their correct fitted positions. Remove the sealing ring from the top of the throttle housing **(see illustrations)**.

Refitting

7 Refitting is a reversal of removal, ensuring that all hoses are properly reconnected, and that all ducts are correctly seated and securely held. Tighten the mounting bolts to the specified torque. When refitting the sealing ring to the top of the throttle housing, smear its inner surface with a little water to help it onto the housing.

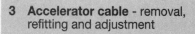

3 Accelerator cable - removal, refitting and adjustment

Removal

1 Remove the air cleaner assembly as described in Section 2 to improve access to the throttle body end of the cable.

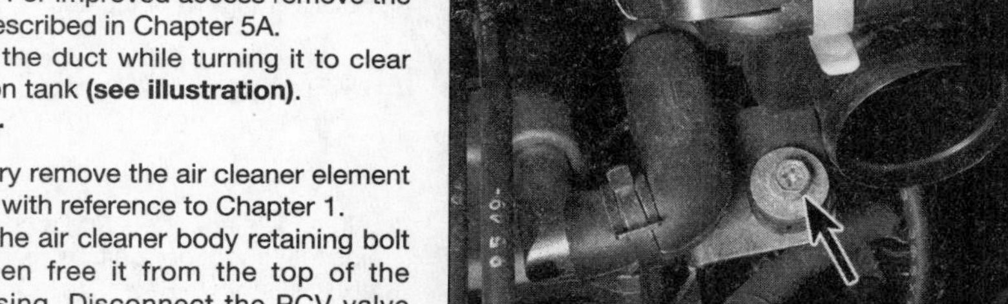

2.6b Air cleaner body retaining bolt

2.6c Withdraw the air cleaner body from the throttle housing . . .

2.6d . . . then disconnect the breather hose . . .

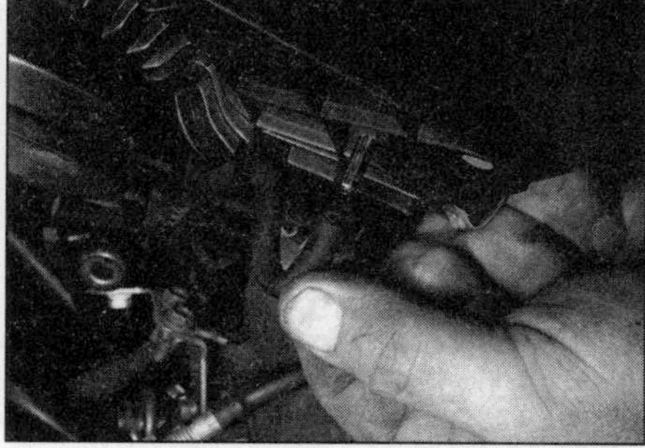

2.6e . . . and where applicable PCV valve hose

2 Hold the throttle cam open by hand, then disconnect the end of the inner cable from the cam **(see illustration)**.

3 Note the position of the adjustment locknuts on the outer cable ferrule, then slacken one of them and free the outer cable from its mounting bracket **(see illustration)**.

4 Release the cable from the support on the camshaft cover, and note the correct routing of the cable.

3.2 Disconnecting the accelerator cable from the throttle cam

3.3 Accelerator cable and adjustment nuts on the mounting bracket

3.5a Unscrew the screws . . .

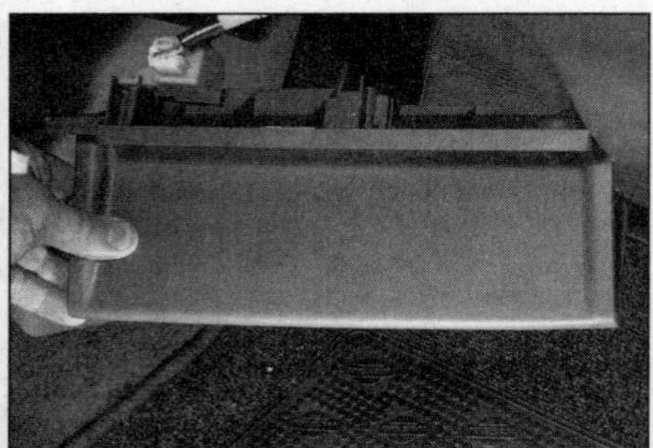
3.5b . . . and remove the small shelf from below the steering column

3.6 Accelerator cable attachment to the top of the accelerator pedal, showing the end fitting mounting nuts

5 Working inside the vehicle, unscrew the screws and remove the small shelf from below the steering column **(see illustrations)**.
6 Reach up behind the facia, and detach the inner cable from the top of the accelerator pedal **(see illustration)**.
7 Undo the nuts securing the cable end fitting to the bulkhead, and withdraw the cable through the bulkhead into the engine compartment **(see illustration 3.6)**.

Refitting

8 From inside the vehicle, feed the cable through the hole in the bulkhead. Secure the cable end fitting to the bulkhead and tighten the nuts. Clip the inner cable into position on the top of the accelerator pedal.
9 From inside the engine compartment, route the cable as previously noted. Attach the cable to the support on the camshaft cover.
10 Locate the outer cable in the mounting bracket, and reconnect the inner cable to the throttle cam. Adjust the cable as described below.
11 Make sure the cable is securely retained, then refit the shelf below the steering column.

Adjustment

12 With both adjusting nuts loose check that the inner cable is slack. Unscrew the nut nearest the cam several turns.
13 Tighten the nut furthest from the cam until the cam just starts to move, then back off the nut 1.5 to 2.0 turns to provide the correct amount of play. Tighten the locknut to retain the ferrule in this position.
14 Have an assistant depress the accelerator pedal, and check that the throttle cam opens fully and returns smoothly to its stop.
15 Refit the air cleaner assembly as described in Section 2.

4 Accelerator pedal - removal and refitting

Removal

1 Unscrew the screws and remove the small shelf from below the steering column.
2 Reach up behind the facia, and detach the inner cable from the top of the accelerator pedal.
3 Undo the two mounting bolts securing the pedal mounting bracket to the bulkhead, and remove the pedal assembly from underneath the facia **(see illustration)**.
4 If necessary, remove the retaining clip from the end of the accelerator pedal pivot shaft, then slide the pedal out of position and recover the return spring from the mounting bracket.
5 Examine the mounting bracket and pedal pivot points for signs of wear, and renew as necessary.

Refitting

6 Refitting is a reversal of the removal procedure, applying a little multi-purpose grease to the pedal pivot shaft. On completion, adjust the accelerator cable as described in Section 3.

5 Unleaded petrol - general information and usage

1 The fuel recommended by Nissan is given in the *Specifications* of this Chapter.
2 All Nissan Micra models covered by this manual are designed to run on unleaded fuel with a minimum octane rating of 95 (RON). All models have a catalytic converter and must be run on unleaded fuel **only**. Under no circumstances should leaded fuel (UK "4-star") be used, as this may damage the catalytic converter.
3 Super unleaded petrol (98 octane) can also be used in all models if wished, though there is no advantage in doing so.

6 Fuel injection system - general information

1 All models are fitted with a combined multi-point fuel injection/ignition (engine management) system. Refer to Chapter 5 for information on the ignition side of the system, the fuel injection side of the system operates as follows.
2 The fuel pump, immersed in the fuel tank, supplies fuel from the fuel tank to the fuel rail, via a filter mounted on the engine compartment bulkhead. Fuel supply pressure is controlled by the pressure regulator, on the end of the fuel rail, which lifts to allow excess

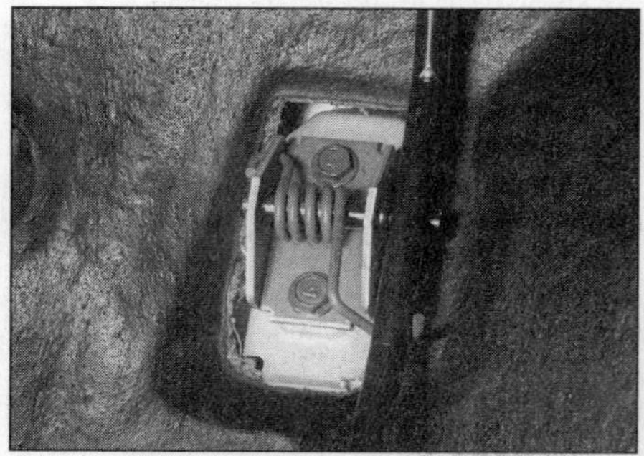
4.3 Accelerator pedal return spring and mounting bolts

fuel to return to the tank when the optimum operating pressure of the fuel system is exceeded.

3 The electrical control system consists of the control unit, along with the following sensors:

a) *Throttle potentiometer - informs the control unit of the throttle valve position, and the rate of throttle opening/closing.*
b) *Coolant temperature sensor - informs the control unit of engine temperature.*
c) *On models up to July 2000, airflow meter (integral with the top of the throttle housing) - informs the control unit of the mass of the air passing through the inlet duct.*
d) *On models from July 2000, Mass air flow/air temperature sensor (integral with the top of the throttle housing) - informs the control unit of the mass of the air and the temperature of the air passing through the inlet duct.*
e) *On models up to July 2000, crank angle sensor (housed in the distributor) - informs the ECCS control unit of the engine speed and crankshaft position (see Chapter 5 for further information).*
f) *On models from July 2000, camshaft position sensor (housed in the timing chain sprocket cover) - informs the ECCS control unit of the engine speed and camshaft position (see Chapter 5 for further information).*
g) *Vehicle speed sensor (built into the speedometer on models up to March 1998, attached to the transmission speedometer drive pinion on later models) - informs the control unit of the vehicle speed.*
h) *Power steering and air conditioning system switches (where fitted) - informs the control unit if the system(s) are in operation, to allow it to adjust the idle speed to compensate for the extra load on the engine.*
i) *Exhaust gas sensor - informs the control unit of the oxygen content of the exhaust gases (see Part B of this Chapter for further information).*
j) *Manual transmission neutral or position switch (attached to the transmission housing) - informs the control unit when the transmission is in neutral (see Chapter 7A for more information).*

4 All the above signals are analysed by the control unit. Based on this information, the control unit selects the response appropriate to those values, and controls the fuel injectors (varying their pulse width - the length of time each injector is held open - to provide a richer or weaker mixture, as appropriate). The mixture and idle speed are constantly varied by the control unit to provide the best settings for cranking, starting (with either a hot or cold engine) and engine warm-up, idle, cruising, and acceleration.

5 The control unit also has full control over the engine idle speed via the auxiliary air control (AAC) valve. The valve, which is fitted to the throttle housing, controls the opening of an air passage which bypasses the throttle valve. When the throttle valve is closed, the control unit controls the opening of the valve, which regulates the amount of air which flows through the valve, and so controls the idle speed. This compensates for the additional load on the engine when the power steering and/or air conditioning is operating.

6 On models with air conditioning, idle speed is also controlled by a fast idle control device (FICD) solenoid valve located near the AAC valve on the throttle housing. This unit compensates for power drain when the air conditioning compressor switches on.

7 The control unit also controls the exhaust and evaporative emission control systems, which are described in detail in Chapter 4B.

8 If there is an abnormality in any of the readings obtained from the sensors, the control unit switches to its back-up mode. If this happens, it ignores the abnormal sensor signal, and assumes a pre-programmed value which will allow the engine to continue running, albeit at reduced efficiency. If the control unit enters its back-up mode, the "CHECK" warning light on the instrument panel will come on, and the relevant fault code will be stored in the control unit memory.

9 If the warning light comes on, the vehicle should be taken to a Nissan dealer at the earliest opportunity. Once there, a complete test of the engine management system can be carried out, using an electronic diagnostic test unit which is simply plugged into the system's diagnostic connector. **Note:** *On models up to July 2000, the ECCS control unit also has a self-diagnostic mode which can be accessed by the DIY mechanic. See Section 12 for further information.*

7 Fuel injection system - depressurisation

Warning: Refer to the warning in Section 1 before proceeding. The following procedure will merely relieve the pressure in the fuel system - remember that fuel will still be present in the system components, and take precautions accordingly before disconnecting any of them.

1 The fuel system referred to in this Section is defined as the tank-mounted fuel pump, the fuel filter, the fuel rail and injectors, the pressure regulator, and the metal pipes and flexible hoses of the fuel lines between these components. All these contain fuel which will be under pressure while the engine is running and/or while the ignition is switched on. The pressure will remain for some time after the ignition has been switched off, and must be relieved before any of these components are disturbed for servicing work.

2 Identify and remove the fuel pump fuse from the vehicle fusebox - if necessary refer to the wiring diagrams at the end of this manual.

3 Start the engine, and allow it to run until it stalls.

4 Try to start the engine at least twice more, to ensure that all residual pressure has been relieved then switch off the ignition.

5 Refit the fuel pump fuse. **Do not** switch on the ignition until completion of work.

8 Fuel gauge sender unit - removal and refitting

Warning: Refer to the warning in Section 1 before proceeding. Since a fuel tank drain plug is not provided, it is preferable to carry out this work when the tank is nearly empty.

Removal

1 Depressurise the fuel system as described in Section 7.

2 Disconnect the battery negative lead.

3 To gain access to the top of the fuel tank, remove the rear seat cushion as described in Chapter 11.

4 Undo the retaining screws, and lift up the fuel tank access plate **(see illustrations)**.

5 Disconnect the wiring connectors for the fuel gauge sender unit and fuel pump, and tape them to the vehicle body **(see illustration)**.

6 Slacken the feed and return hose retaining clips, then disconnect both hoses from the

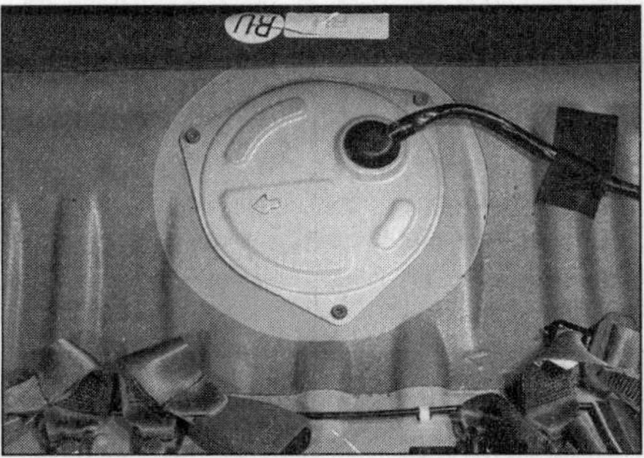

8.4a The fuel tank access plate is located beneath the rear seat squab

8.4b Removing the fuel tank access plate

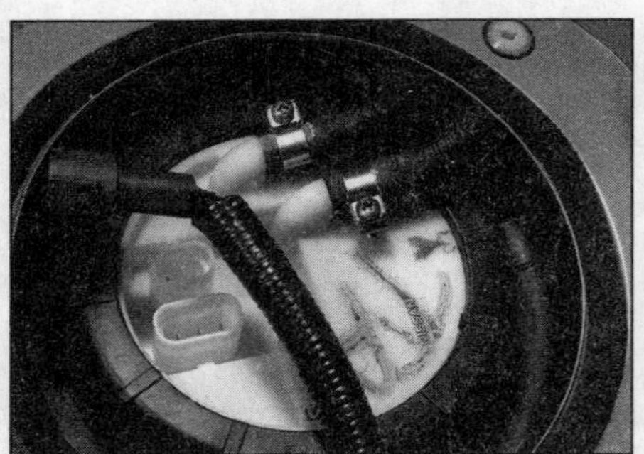

8.5 **Disconnecting the wiring from the fuel gauge sender unit, showing fuel outlet and return hoses**

8.7 **Removing the locking ring from the top of the fuel tank**

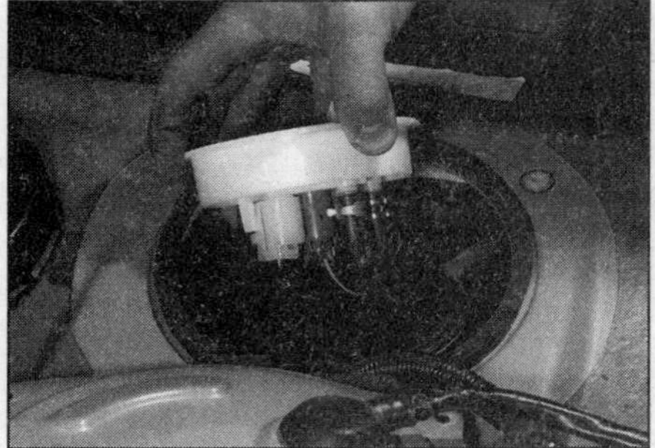

8.8 **Lifting the access cover assembly from the fuel tank**

top of the access cover, and plug the hose ends. Note that the hoses are colour-coded - the yellow hose locates on the feed port and the white hose locates on the return port.

7 Note the position of the alignment mark on the access cover, and mark the position of the locking ring before loosening it. Unscrew the locking ring and remove it from the tank **(see illustration)**. This is best accomplished by using a screwdriver on the raised ribs of the locking ring. Carefully tap the screwdriver to turn the ring anti-clockwise until it can be unscrewed by hand.

8 Carefully lift the access cover assembly from the top of the fuel tank **(see illustration)**. As the cover is being removed, disconnect the pump wiring and hoses from its base noting the location of the hoses.

9 Reach into the tank, and pull up the retaining clip to release the sender unit from the fuel pump support bracket. Carefully withdraw the sender unit from the fuel tank aperture taking care not to bend the float level arm. Note that the low-fuel warning light switch is located on the fuel gauge sender unit.

10 Recover the rubber sealing ring from the top of the fuel tank and discard it; a new one must be used on refitting.

Refitting

11 Refitting is a reversal of the removal procedure, noting the following points:

a) Fit a new rubber sealing ring to the fuel tank.

b) Make sure the sender unit is correctly located on the fuel pump support bracket and retaining clip.

c) Check that the hoses are correctly connected to the access cover - the arrows on the ports indicate the fuel flow.

d) Before tightening the locking ring, align the arrow on the access cover with the arrow on the top of the fuel tank. The locking ring should be tightened to the specified torque, however this will be difficult unless the special tool is available so tighten it until the previously made marks are aligned with each other.

e) Prior to refitting the access plate, reconnect the battery, then start the engine and check the fuel hoses for signs of leaks.

9 Fuel pump - removal and refitting

Warning: Refer to the warning in Section 1 before proceeding. Since a fuel tank drain plug is not provided, it is preferable to carry out this work when the tank is nearly empty.

Removal

1 Remove the fuel gauge sender unit as described in Section 8.

2 Reach into the tank, release the clips and withdraw the fuel pump and its housing through the aperture.

3 Disconnect the hoses from the fuel pump, then unclip the housing cover and remove the pump.

4 Wash the fuel pump, housing and strainer in clean fuel.

Refitting

5 Refitting is a reversal of removal. Refit the fuel gauge sender unit with reference to Section 8.

10 Fuel tank - removal and refitting

Warning: Refer to the warning in Section 1 before proceeding. Since a fuel tank drain plug is not provided, it is preferable to carry out this work when the tank is nearly empty.

Removal

1 Depressurise the fuel system as described in Section 7.

2 Disconnect the battery negative lead.

3 To gain access to the top of the fuel tank and disconnect the wiring, remove the rear seat cushion as described in Chapter 11. Alternatively the wiring can be disconnected underneath the vehicle **(see illustration)**. If this last option is taken, continue at paragraph 6.

4 Undo the retaining screws, and lift up the fuel tank access plate.

5 Disconnect the wiring connectors for the fuel gauge sender unit and fuel pump, and tape them to the vehicle body. Leave the fuel feed and return hoses connected as these are disconnected at the fuel lines under the vehicle.

6 If the tank is not empty at this stage, remove the access cover from the top of the tank with reference to Section 8 and syphon or hand-pump the remaining fuel into a suitable container. Refit the cover to prevent entry of dust and dirt.

7 Chock the front wheels, then jack up the rear of the vehicle and support on axle stands (see "*Jacking and vehicle support*").

8 Identify the location of the fuel feed and return hoses and breather hose on the fuel lines running to the engine compartment. Disconnect the hoses and plug their ends to prevent entry of dust and dirt.

9 Working under the left-hand rear wheelarch, disconnect the fuel filler and ventilation hoses from the fuel tank **(see illustrations)**. Pull the ventilation hose through the inner wing panel. Plug or cover the ends of the hoses.

10 Unbolt and remove the exhaust heat shields from the fuel tank.

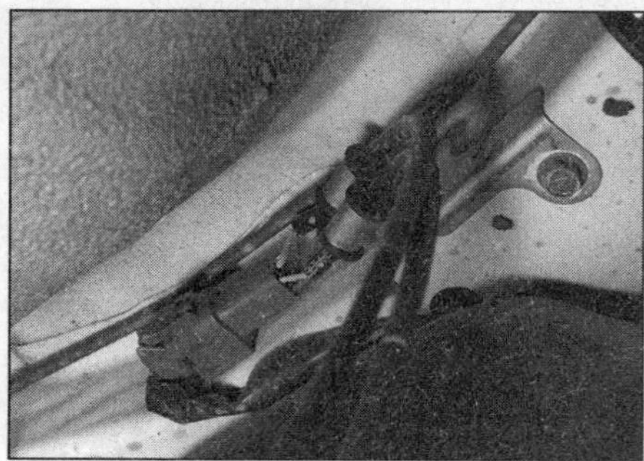

10.3 Fuel tank wiring underneath the vehicle

10.9a Fuel filler cover and retaining clips located beneath left-hand rear wheel arch

10.12a Fuel tank retaining strap rear bolt

11 Place a trolley jack with an interposed block of wood beneath the tank, then raise the jack until it is supporting the weight of the tank.

12 Unscrew and remove the retaining strap rear bolts, then pivot each strap away from the tank **(see illustrations)**.

13 Slowly lower the fuel tank to the ground, and remove it from underneath the vehicle.

14 If necessary, remove the sender unit and fuel pump with reference to Sections 8 and 9. Disconnect the breather hose noting the location of the fuel check valve.

15 Swill out the tank with clean fuel. The tank is injection-moulded from a synthetic material, and if damaged, it should be renewed. However, in certain cases, it may be possible to have small leaks or minor damage repaired. Seek the advice of a specialist before attempting to repair the fuel tank.

10.9b Fuel filler hose connection to the fuel tank

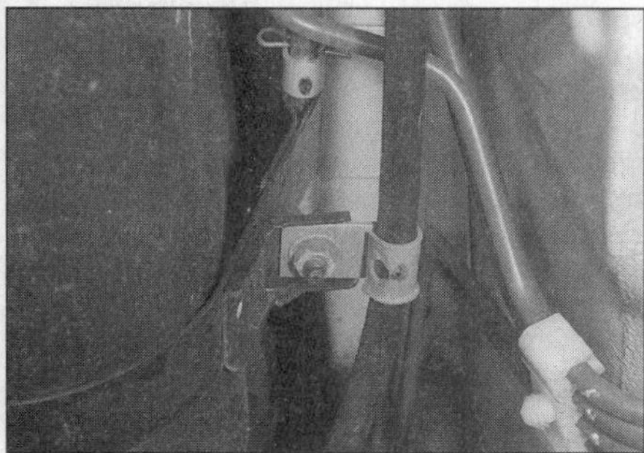

10.12b The handbrake cables are attached to the fuel tank straps

Refitting

16 Refitting is a reversal of the removal procedure, noting the following points:

a) *Make sure the fuel check valve is fitted correctly in the breather hose.*

b) *When lifting the tank back into position, take care to ensure that none of the hoses become trapped between the tank and vehicle body. Tighten the fuel tank mounting bolts to the specified torque setting.*

c) *Ensure that all pipes and hoses are correctly routed,. and securely held in position with their retaining clips.*

d) *On completion refill the tank with fuel, run the engine, and check for signs of leakage prior to taking the vehicle out on the road.*

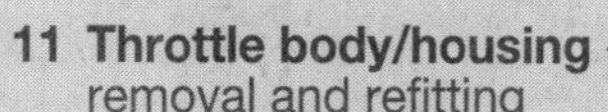

11 Throttle body/housing - removal and refitting

Warning: Refer to the warning in Section 1 before proceeding.

1 Remove the air cleaner assembly as described in Section 2.

2 Disconnect the wiring connectors from the throttle potentiometer, the auxiliary air control valve, the airflow meter and the fast idle control device (FICD) solenoid valve **(see illustrations)**.

3 Release the accelerator inner cable from the throttle cam, then loosen the outer cable locknut and adjuster nut, and free the outer cable from its mounting bracket.

4 Make a note of the correct fitted positions of all the relevant vacuum pipes and breather hoses, to ensure that they are correctly positioned on refitting, then release the retaining clips (where fitted) and disconnect them from the throttle body/housing.

5 Release any pressure in the cooling system (cold) by unscrewing the radiator cap slowly (refer to Chapter 3 if necessary). Refit the cap and have ready some plugs to plug the ends of the coolant hoses. Release the retaining clips, disconnect the coolant hoses from each side of the throttle body/housing, and plug the hose ends. Work quickly, to minimise coolant loss.

6 Unscrew and remove the bolts securing the throttle body/housing assembly to the inlet manifold, and remove it from the engine compartment. Remove the gasket and discard it; a new one must be used on refitting. Plug the inlet manifold with a wad of clean cloth, to prevent the possible entry of foreign matter **(see illustrations)**.

Refitting

7 Refitting is a reversal of the removal procedure, but note the following:

a) *Ensure that the mating surfaces of the manifold and throttle body/housing are clean and dry, and fit a new gasket to the manifold making sure it is the correct way round. Fit the throttle body/housing then, working in a diagonal sequence,*

11.2a Disconnecting the throttle potentiometer wiring from the throttle housing (models up to 2000)

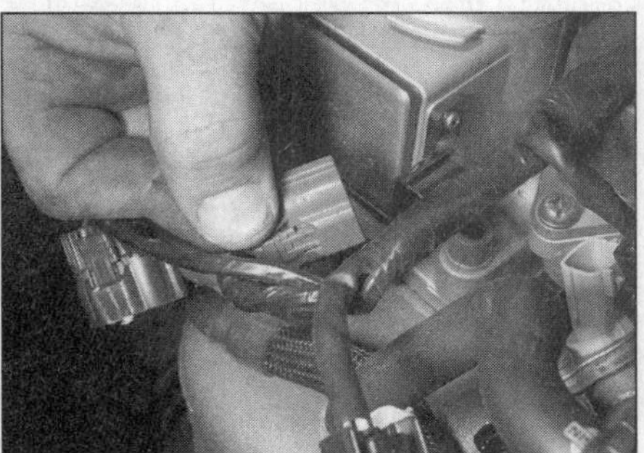

11.2b Disconnecting the airflow meter wiring from the throttle housing (models up to 2000)

11.2c Disconnecting auxiliary air control valve and fast idle control device solenoid valve wiring from the throttle housing (models up to 2000)

11.6a Unscrew the bolts . . .

11.6b . . . and remove the throttle body/ housing from the inlet manifold

11.6c Removing the throttle body/ housing gasket

progressively tighten the retaining bolts to the specified torque setting.

b) Ensure that all hoses are correctly and securely reconnected.

c) Adjust the accelerator cable as described in Section 3. On automatic transmission models, also check the kickdown cable adjustment as described in Chapter 7B.

d) If necessary, top-up the cooling system with reference to Chapter 1.

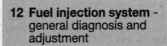

12 Fuel injection system - general diagnosis and adjustment

Note: *The following procedures can only be carried out on vehicles up to July 2000. On later models, there is a Diagnostic connector inside the vehicle **(see illustration)**, which can only be accessed using special test equipment to read the fault codes. If any fault occurs, take your vehicle to your local Nissan dealer so they can diagnose the fault.*

General diagnosis

General information

1 If a fault appears in the fuel injection/ignition system, first ensure that all the system wiring connectors are securely connected and free of corrosion. Then ensure the fault is not due to poor maintenance - ie, check that the air cleaner filter element is clean, the spark plugs are in good condition and correctly gapped, the valve clearances are correctly adjusted, the cylinder compression pressures are correct, and the emission control systems are operating correctly, referring to Chapters 1, 2A, 4B and 5B for more information.

2 If these checks fail to reveal the cause of the problem, a quick check of the fuel injection/ignition circuits can be performed by setting the ECCS control unit to its self-diagnostic mode "2". In mode "2", the ECCS control unit will reveal any fault codes stored in its memory, using the engine check light in the instrument panel and the red LED on the right-hand side of the control unit.

3 Faults detected by the ECCS control unit are stored in its memory, until the starter motor has been operated 50 times. If the fault is not detected again within this period, it will automatically be erased from the memory. Fault codes can also be erased from the memory by setting the control unit to self-diagnostic mode "2" and then switching it back to mode "1", as described below, or by leaving the battery disconnected for more than 24 hours.

Setting the self-diagnostic modes

4 Remove the cover from the right-hand side of the centre console, to gain access to the red LED on the ECCS control unit.

5 Remove the fusebox cover, to gain access to the diagnostic connector which is clipped to the base of the fusebox. Turn the ignition switch to the "ON" position, but do not start the engine. The ECCS control unit is now in self-diagnostic mode "1".

6 Using a spare piece of wire, connect the "IGN" terminal of the diagnostic connector to the "CHK" terminal **(see illustration)**. Keep the terminals connected for at least two seconds, then disconnect the wire. The ECCS control unit is now in self-diagnostic mode "2".

7 In mode "2", the control unit will reveal any fault codes stored in its memory.

8 The code is revealed using a series of long (0.6 second) and short (0.3 second) flashes of the instrument panel engine check light and the red LED on the right-hand side of the control unit. The long flashes, which indicate the first digit of the fault code, will be given out first, then after a gap of approximately 0.9 seconds, the short flashes, which indicate the second digit of the fault code, will follow. There will be a gap of 2.1 seconds before any other codes are revealed. Once all codes have been revealed, the ECU will continuously run through the code(s) stored in its memory, revealing each one in turn with a gap of 2.1 seconds between each code. The fault codes are as follows.

Code number	Faulty circuit
11	Crank angle sensor circuit
12	Airflow meter circuit
13	Coolant temperature sensor circuit
21	Ignition signal circuit
43	Throttle potentiometer circuit
55	All circuits operating correctly

Note: *If both codes 11 and 21 are displayed, check the crank angle sensor circuit before checking the rest of the ignition circuit. If code 28 is displayed it should be ignored.*

9 If the engine is started with the control unit in mode "2", it will automatically enter its exhaust gas sensor check mode. In this mode, the light and LED indicates the condition of the exhaust gases. When the light and LED are illuminated, the exhaust gas mixture is lean, and when they are off, the mixture is rich. To check the sensor, with the control unit in self-diagnostic mode "2", start the engine and warm it up to normal operating temperature. Once it is warm, raise the engine speed to approximately 2000 rpm, and hold it there for approximately 2 minutes whilst observing the instrument panel light or control unit LED. If the exhaust gas sensor is functioning correctly, the light/LED should flash on and off at least 5 times every 10 seconds.

10 When all the checks are complete, exit the self-diagnostic mode "2". If the engine has not

12.0 Diagnostic connector (arrowed) under facia to the right of the steering column

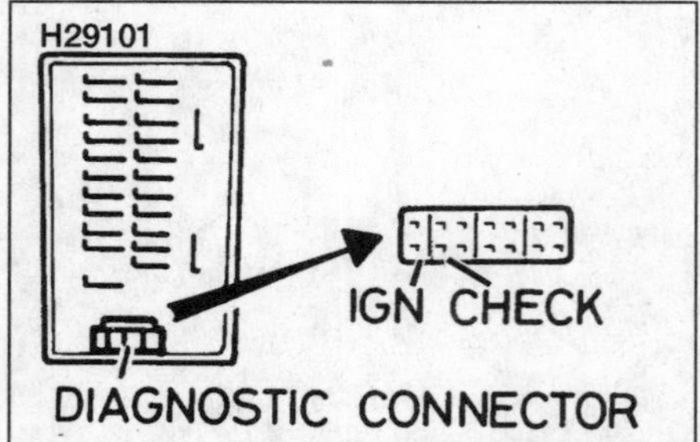

12.6 Connect "IGN" terminal of diagnostic connector to "CHK" terminal to turn on the self-diagnosis mode "1"

been started, this can be achieved by reconnecting the "IGN" and "CHK" terminals of the diagnostic connector again for at least two seconds. If the engine has been started, switch off the ignition to exit the modes.

11 If a more detailed check of the fuel injection/ignition system is required, take the vehicle to a Nissan dealer. They will have access to the special electronic diagnostic test unit which is plugged into the system's diagnostic connector, and can carry out a full check of the system components.

Adjustment

12 On all models covered by this manual, only the base idle speed is adjustable although it is possible to *check* the idle mixture and ignition timing. Refer to Section 13 and Chapter 5B.

13 Idle speed and mixture - check and adjustment

Note: *The following procedures can only be carried out on vehicles up to July 2000. On later models, there is a Diagnostic connector inside the vehicle* ***(see illustration 12.0)****, which can only be accessed using special test equipment to read the fault codes. If any fault occurs, take your vehicle to your local Nissan dealer so they can diagnose the fault.*

1 Before checking the idle speed and mixture setting, always check first the following.

a) Check that the ignition timing is accurate (Chapter 5B).
b) Check that the spark plugs are in good condition and correctly gapped (Chapter 1).
c) Check that the accelerator cable is correctly adjusted (Section 3).
d) Check that the crankcase breather hoses are secure, with no leaks or kinks (Chapter 4B).
e) Check that the air cleaner filter element is clean (Chapter 1).
f) Check that the exhaust system is in good condition (Chapter 1).
g) If the engine is running very roughly, check the compression pressures as described in Chapter 2A.

2 Turn off all electrical components including the air conditioning system (where fitted). On models fitted with power steering keep the front wheels pointing straight ahead during the checking and adjustment procedure.

Idle speed

3 Connect a tachometer to the engine in accordance with its manufacturer's instructions.

4 Run the engine to normal operating temperature. **Note:** *Checking and adjustment should be completed without stopping the engine. If the radiator electric cooling fan operates, wait for the cooling fan to stop. Clear any excess fuel from the inlet manifold by racing the engine two or three times to between 2000 and 3000 rpm, then allow it to idle again.*

5 Stop the engine and disconnect the wiring connector from the throttle potentiometer, which is mounted on the side of the throttle body/housing.

6 Start the engine, clear excess fuel from the inlet manifold by racing the engine two or three times to between 2000 and 3000 rpm, then allow it to idle again. Check that the idle speed is within the limits given in the *Specifications*. If adjustment is necessary, the idle speed adjusting screw is situated next to the throttle potentiometer on the throttle housing. Screw it in or out as necessary to obtain the specified speed. When the idle speed is correctly set, switch off the engine and reconnect the throttle potentiometer wiring connector. Disconnect the tachometer.

Mixture

7 Experienced home mechanics with a considerable amount of skill and equipment (including a tachometer and exhaust gas analyser) will be able to *check* the exhaust CO level. However, if it is found to be in need of *adjustment,* there must be a fault in the ECCS control system; no adjustment of the mixture is possible.

8 If the exhaust gas CO content is incorrect, check the operation of the exhaust gas sensor and fuel injection system components using the ECCS control unit self-diagnostic function. If this fails to show the problem, the vehicle must be taken to a Nissan dealer for testing.

14 Fuel injection system components - removal and refitting

Warning: Refer to the warning in Section 1 before proceeding.

Note: *Some test procedures are included in this Section.*

Fuel rail and injectors

Note: *If a faulty injector is suspected, before condemning the injector, it is worth trying the effect of one of the proprietary injector-cleaning treatments.*

1 Depressurise the fuel system as described in Section 7.

2 Disconnect the battery negative terminal. To improve access to the fuel rail, remove the air cleaner assembly (refer to Section 2).

3 Slacken the retaining clips and disconnect the fuel feed and return hoses from the left-hand end of the fuel rail. Label the hoses if wished, to avoid confusion on refitting. Also disconnect the vacuum pipe from the fuel pressure regulator **(see illustrations)**.

4 Depress the retaining tangs, and disconnect the wiring connectors from the four injectors **(see illustration)**.

5 Unscrew the fuel rail retaining bolts, then carefully ease the fuel rail and injector assembly out from the inlet manifold, and remove it from the vehicle. Recover the spacers fitted between the rail and manifold, and remove each injector seal from the manifold **(see illustrations)**.

6 Undo the two retaining screws, and remove the retaining plate from the relevant injector.

14.3a Fuel feed and return hoses on the fuel rail

14.3b Disconnecting the vacuum pipe from the pressure regulator

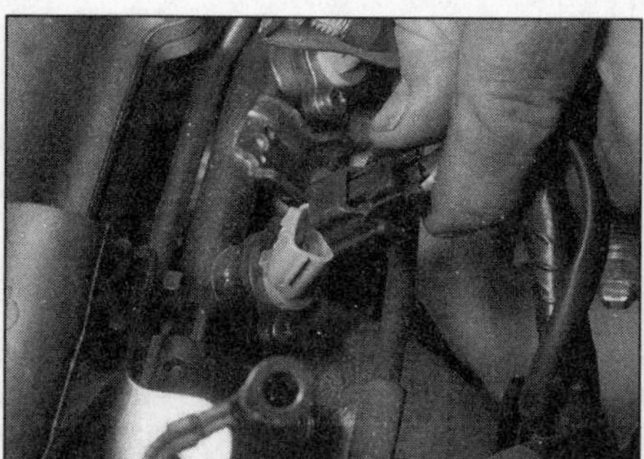

14.4 Disconnecting the injector wiring

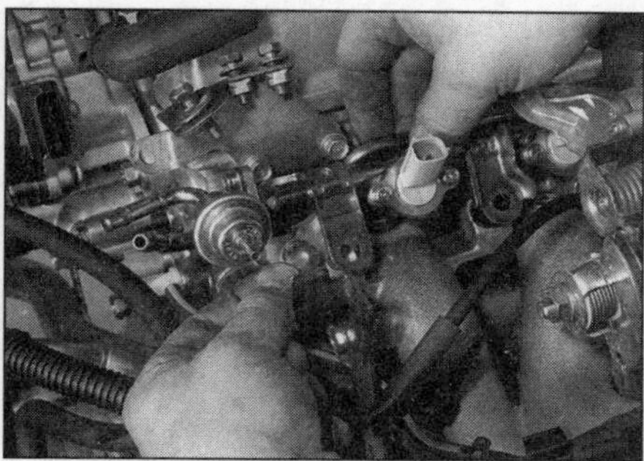

14.5a Removing the spacers from the fuel rail

14.5b Removing the injector seals from the inlet manifold

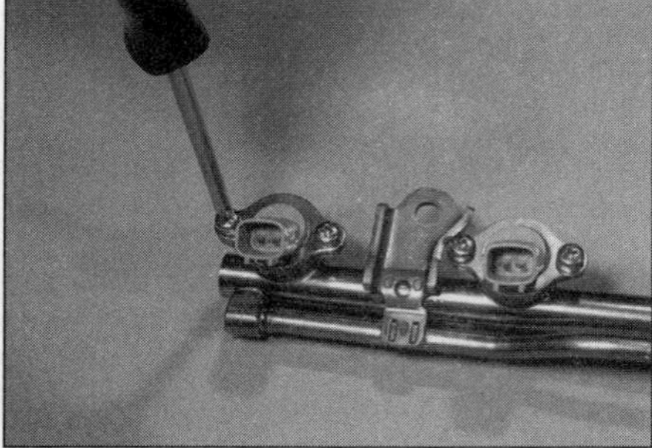
14.6a Unscrew the screws . . .

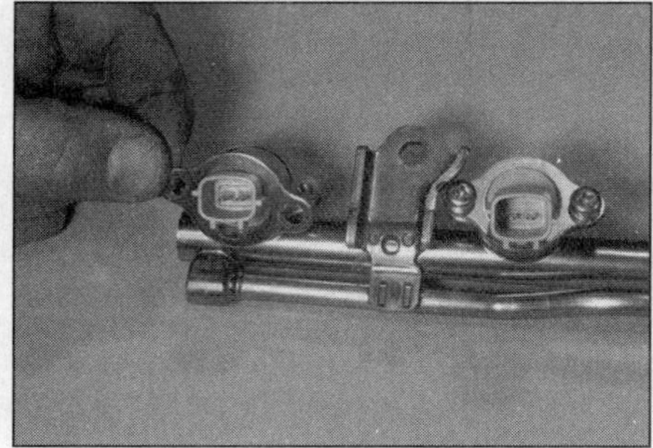
14.6b . . . and remove the retaining plate . . .

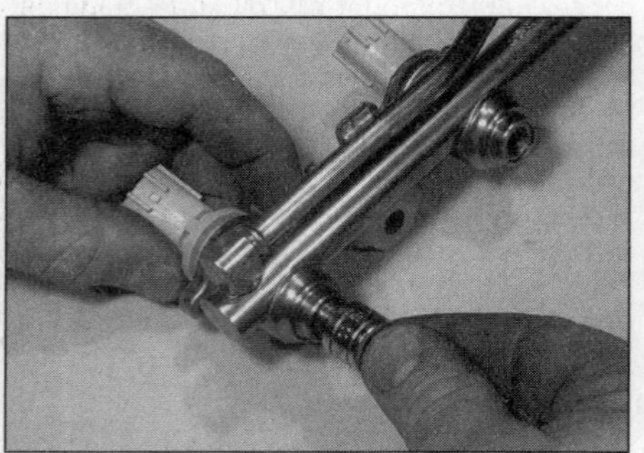
14.6c . . . then use a socket (or similar tool) to press out the injector . . .

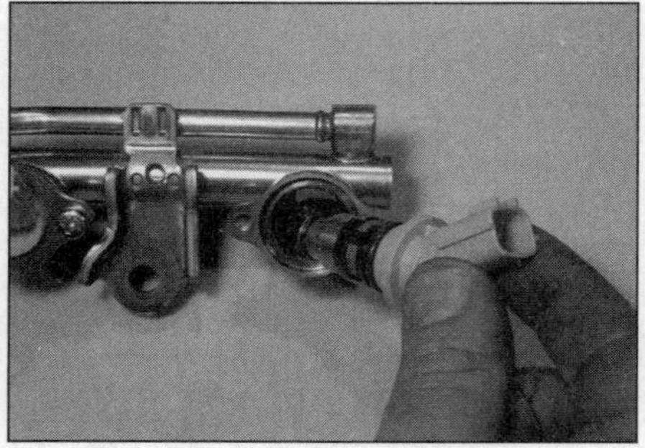
14.6d . . . and withdraw the injector

14.7 Injector and seals

Push the injector out of position, and recover the sealing rings **(see illustrations)**. Repeat the procedure as required to remove any other injectors.

7 Remove and discard the seals; new ones must be used on refitting **(see illustration)**.

8 Refitting is a reversal of the removal procedure, noting the following points:

a) Fit new O-rings to all disturbed injectors, and fit new injector seals to the manifold.

b) Apply a smear of engine oil to the O-rings to aid installation, then ease the injectors into the fuel rail and refit the retaining plates.

c) Fit a new seal to each injector, and ease the fuel rail assembly into position in the manifold. Fit the spacers between the rail and manifold then, working in a diagonal sequence from the centre outwards, tighten the bolts to their specified Stage 1 torque setting. Go around again in sequence, and tighten them to the specified Stage 2 torque.

d) On completion, start the engine and check for fuel leaks.

Fuel pressure regulator

9 Depressurise the fuel system as described in Section 7

10 Disconnect the battery negative terminal, then disconnect the vacuum hose from the fuel pressure regulator, which is mounted on the left-hand end of the fuel rail.

11 Slacken the retaining clips and disconnect the fuel hose from the base of the regulator.

12 On models up to 2000, undo the two retaining bolts, and remove the regulator from the end of the fuel rail. On models from 2000, withdraw the retaining clip and remove the regulator from the end of the fuel rail. Recover the sealing ring fitted to the regulator and discard it; a new one must be used on refitting.

13 Refitting is the reverse of removal, using a new sealing ring. On completion, start the engine and check for fuel leaks.

Throttle potentiometer

14 The throttle potentiometer is mounted onto the right-hand side of the throttle housing. Prior to removal, disconnect the battery negative terminal.

15 Disconnect the wiring connector from the throttle potentiometer.

16 Using a dab of white paint or a suitable marker pen, make alignment marks between the potentiometer and the throttle housing.

17 Undo the two retaining screws, and remove the potentiometer **(see illustration)**.

18 On refitting, offer up the potentiometer, making sure its lever is correctly engaged with the throttle valve spindle lever.

19 Align the marks made prior to removal, and lightly tighten the retaining screws. Adjust the potentiometer as follows.

20 Using an ohmmeter connected to the rear and middle terminals on the potentiometer, check that the resistance readings are as given in the *Specifications*. If necessary, slacken the retaining screws and reposition the potentiometer until its resistances are as specified.

21 When the potentiometer is correctly positioned, securely tighten its retaining screws and reconnect the wiring connector.

22 Reconnect the battery negative terminal.

Auxiliary air control (AAC) valve

23 On models up to 2000, the auxiliary air control (AAC) valve is mounted onto the front

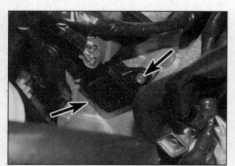

14.17 Undo the screws arrowed to remove the potentiometer

14.23 Auxiliary air control valve (arrowed) fitted to the rear of the throttle body

of the throttle body and is integral with the fast idle control device (FICD) solenoid valve. On models from 2000, it is on the rear of the throttle body **(see illustration)** and is integral with the Idle Air Control Valve (IACV). Prior to removal, disconnect the battery negative terminal.

24 Disconnect the wiring connector from the control valve.

25 On models up to 2000, connect an ohmmeter between terminals 2 and 3 (viewed from the front of the engine), then 3 and 4 and check that the resistance is as given in the *Specifications*. On models from 2000, connect an ohmmeter between terminals 2 and 1, then 2 and 3, check that the resistance is as given in the *Specifications*.

26 Undo the retaining screws, then remove the valve from the throttle body and recover the gasket.

27 Check that the valve plunger is free to move easily, and returns quickly under spring pressure. If not, the valve assembly must be renewed.

28 Refitting is the reversal of the removal procedure, using a new gasket.

Fast idle control device (FICD) solenoid valve

29 The fast idle control device (FICD) solenoid valve (early models) and the Idle Air Control Valve (IACV) later models, is integral with the AAC valve and its removal is described in paragraphs 23 to 28.

30 Refitting is the reversal of the removal procedure, using a new gasket.

Airflow meter (models up to 2000)

31 The airflow meter consists of a hot wire located in the top of the throttle body/housing. It is not possible to renew the airflow meter without the throttle body/housing, however it can be checked as follows.

32 Run the engine to normal operating temperature, then using a voltmeter with back-probes check the voltage between terminals 2 and 3 on the airflow meter wiring connector. Compare the result with the *Specifications* then stop the engine and repeat the check with the ignition switched on.

33 If the results are not correct remove the air cleaner assembly, then look through the protection grid and check the hot wire grid for damage and dust. The complete unit will require renewing if the readings are not correct.

Fast idle thermowax element (models up to 2000)

34 The fast idle thermowax element is fitted to the rear of the throttle body. It uses the coolant temperature to control the fast idle speed during engine warm-up. To check the element first remove the throttle body/housing as described in Section 11 leaving the element in position.

35 Drain any remaining coolant from the housing then allow the assembly to stabilise to room temperature for at least 3 hours. Do not allow any heat source (such as the rays of the sun) to affect the temperature of the assembly.

36 Using vernier calipers measure the movement of the element plunger L1 **(see illustration)** and compare with the graph shown. If the movement is within limits the element is in good condition, but if not the element must be renewed. Undo the screw and remove the retaining plate then lift the element out of the throttle body/housing. Recover the O-ring seal.

37 Fit the new element with a new O-ring seal and secure with the retaining screw. Adjust the element as follows.

38 Loosen the locknut and adjust the screw located above the element until the cam hole is aligned with the hole in the housing. Use a suitable pin to lock the cam in this position.

39 The clearance between the fast idle cam and the throttle cam (A) must now be adjusted to the dimensions in the *Specifications*. The adjustment screw (S2) is located *beneath* the fast idle cam **(see illustration)**.

40 After making the adjustment remove the pin, then adjust the screw located *over* the element (S1) so that the bottom part of it (ie the part on the opposite side to the locknut) measures 4.3 mm **(see illustration 14.39)**.

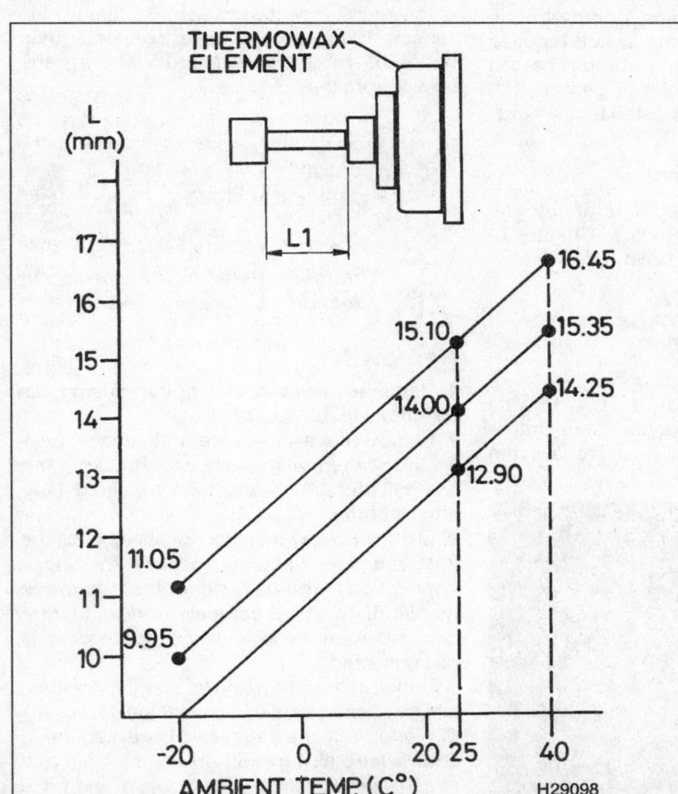

14.36 Graph showing movement of the fast idle thermowax element plunger

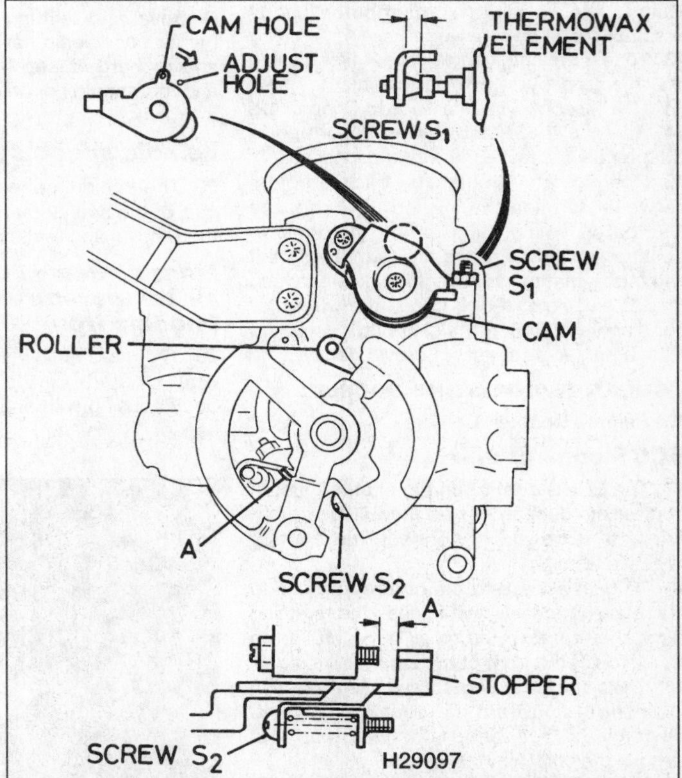

14.39 Adjustment of the thermowax element plunger

14.47 ECCS control unit (shown with the facia removed for clarity)

From this base setting the screw must be adjusted clockwise or anticlockwise to compensate for ambient temperature, then locked. To determine the number of turns use the following formula.

No of turns = (Actual clearance (mm) - Desired clearance (mm)) x 2

If the result is positive turn the screw anti-clockwise, and if negative turn the screw clockwise. Tighten the locknut on completion.

41 Refit the throttle body/housing as described in Section 11.

Crank angle sensor and power transistor (models up to 2000)

42 The crank angle sensor and power transistor are integral parts of the distributor, and cannot be renewed separately. If either is faulty, the complete distributor body assembly must be renewed.

43 To test the crank angle sensor first disable the injectors by removing the injector fuse from the fusebox with reference to Chapter 12.

44 Remove the distributor as described in Chapter 5B but leave the wiring connected.

45 Connect a voltmeter (by back-probing) between terminals 1(-) and 3(+) on the distributor wiring plug. With the ignition switched on slowly rotate the distributor shaft and check that the voltage fluctuates between 5 volts and zero. If not, check the wiring for good contact. Renew the distributor complete if the crank angle sensor is proved faulty.

Coolant temperature sensor

46 Refer to Chapter 3.

ECCS control unit

47 The ECCS control unit is situated just in front of the centre console **(see illustration)**. Prior to removal, disconnect the battery negative terminal.

48 To gain access to the control unit, undo the retaining screws and release the retaining clips, then remove the small trim panel from each side of the front of the centre console.

49 Undo the retaining screws, and release the control unit from its mounting bracket. Disconnect the wiring connector(s), and remove the unit from the vehicle.

50 Refitting is the reverse of removal, ensuring that the wiring connector is securely reconnected.

Neutral switch - manual transmission models

51 Refer to Chapter 7A.

Starter inhibitor/ reversing light switch - automatic transmission models

52 Refer to Chapter 7B.

ECCS control unit and fuel pump relays

53 Refer to Chapter 12.

Power steering idle-up switch

54 The power steering idle-up switch is screwed into the power steering feed pipe, in the right-hand rear corner of the engine compartment. Prior to removal, set the front wheels in the straight-ahead position, then disconnect the battery negative terminal.

55 Locate the switch and disconnect its wiring connector.

56 Unscrew the switch, recover its sealing washer, and plug the opening in the pipe. Work quickly, to minimise fluid loss and to prevent dirt entering the hydraulic system.

57 Refitting is the reverse of removal, using a new sealing washer.

Air conditioning system idle-up switch

58 The air conditioning switch is screwed into the air conditioning pipe, in the left-hand front corner of the engine compartment. Removal and refitting of the switch requires the air conditioning system to be discharged and recharged (see Chapter 3, Section 10), and this should not be attempted by the home mechanic.

Vehicle speed sensor

59 The vehicle speed sensor is an integral part of the speedometer. Refer to Chapter 12 for removal and refitting details.

Mass airflow sensor/ air temperature sensor (models from 2000)

60 The mass airflow sensor consists of a hot wire located in the top of the throttle body/housing with an integral air temperature sensor. It is not possible to renew the sensor(s) without the throttle body/housing, however it can be checked as follows.

14.64 Undo the retaining bolt (arrowed) to remove the camshaft position sensor

61 To check the mass airflow sensor, disconnect the wiring connector to the sensor, then switch the ignition on and check the voltage at terminals 2 and 4 on the wiring connector. Compare the result with the mass airflow sensor readings in the *Specifications* at the beginning of the Chapter. Switch the ignition OFF, then reconnect the wiring connector to the sensor.

62 To check the air temperature sensor, disconnect the wiring connector to the sensor, then switch the ignition on and check the voltage at terminal 1 on the wiring connector. The sensor can also be checked by connecting an ohm meter across terminals 1 and 3 of the sensor and comparing the result with the readings in the *Specifications* at the beginning of the Chapter. Switch the ignition OFF, then reconnect the wiring connector to the sensor.

63 If the results are not correct remove the air cleaner assembly, then look through the protection grid and check the hot wire grid for damage and dust. The complete unit will require renewing if the readings are not correct.

Camshaft position sensor (models from 2000)

64 The camshaft position sensor is fitted in the timing chain cover on the right-hand side of the engine **(see illustration)**. To remove the sensor, disconnect the wiring connector then undo the retaining bolt and withdraw the sensor from the cover.

15 Inlet manifold - removal and refitting

Warning: Refer to the warning in Section 1 before proceeding.

Removal

1 Remove the throttle body/housing as described in Section 11.

2 Remove the fuel rail (refer to Section 14).

3 Unbolt the manifold support bracket from the cylinder block and inlet manifold **(see illustrations)**.

4 Make a note of the fitted locations of all the inlet manifold vacuum and breather hose connections, and disconnect them from the manifold. To avoid confusion on refitting, it may be wise to label each hose as it is disconnected.

5 Unbolt the wiring support bracket from the left-hand end of the inlet manifold.

6 Working in the **reverse** of the sequence shown **(see illustration 15.9a)**, slacken and remove the manifold retaining nuts and bolts **(see illustration)**.

7 Remove the manifold from the cylinder head, and out of the engine compartment.

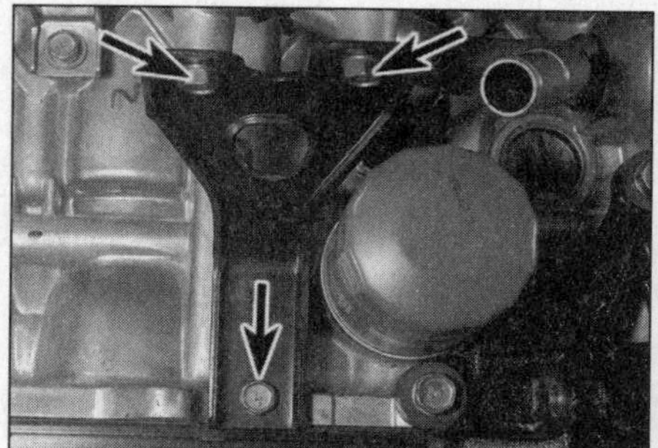

15.3a Unscrew the bolts . . .

15.3b . . . and remove the inlet manifold support bracket

15.6 Right-hand end of the inlet manifold showing mounting bolt

15.7a Removing the inlet manifold . . .

15.7b . . . and gasket

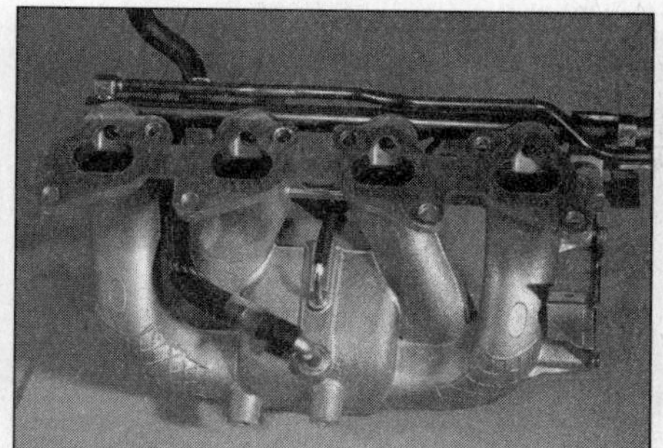

15.7c Inlet manifold removed from the cylinder head

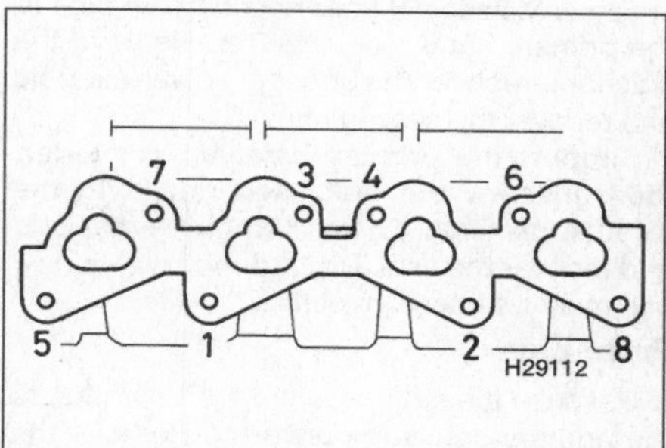

15.9a Inlet manifold mounting nuts/bolts tightening sequence

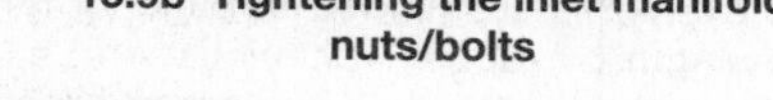

15.9b Tightening the inlet manifold nuts/bolts

Remove the gasket and discard it **(see illustrations)**.

8 Clean the surfaces of the inlet manifold and cylinder head and check the inlet manifold for distortion using a straight-edge and feeler blade. If the distortion exceeds the specified maximum, renew the manifold.

Refitting

9 Refitting is a reversal of the removal procedure with reference to Sections 14 and 11 and noting the following points **(see illustrations)**:

a) The manifold and cylinder head mating surfaces must be clean and dry. Fit the new gasket to the head studs. Install the manifold, and tighten its nuts and bolts to the specified torque in the order shown.

b) Ensure that all relevant hoses are reconnected to their original positions, and are securely held by their retaining clips.

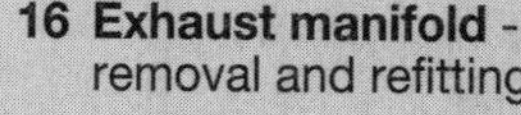

16 Exhaust manifold - removal and refitting

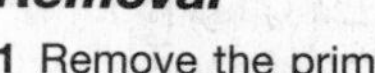

Removal

1 Remove the primary catalytic converter as described in Chapter 4B.

2 Remove the exhaust gas sensor as described in Chapter 4B. Also unbolt and remove the hot air shroud, noting the location of the support bracket **(see illustrations)**.

3 Working in the **reverse** of the sequence shown **(see illustration 16.6a)**, slacken and remove the manifold nuts **(see illustrations)**.

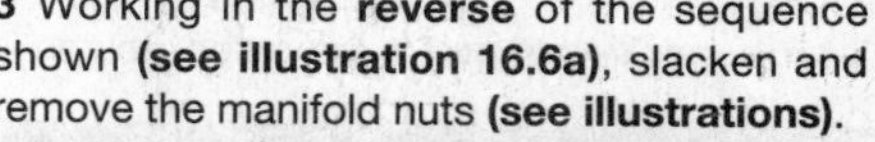

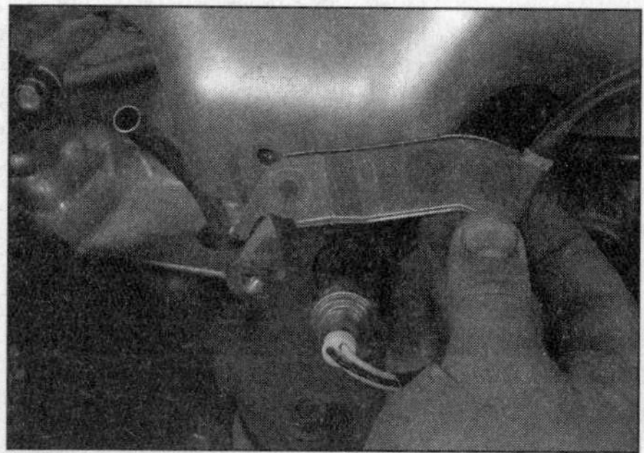

16.2a Removing the support bracket . . .

16.2b . . . and the hot air shroud

16.3a Unscrew the manifold nuts . . .

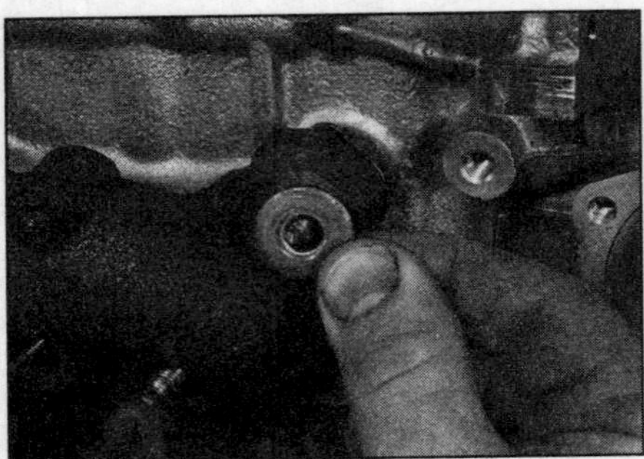
16.3b . . . and remove the washers

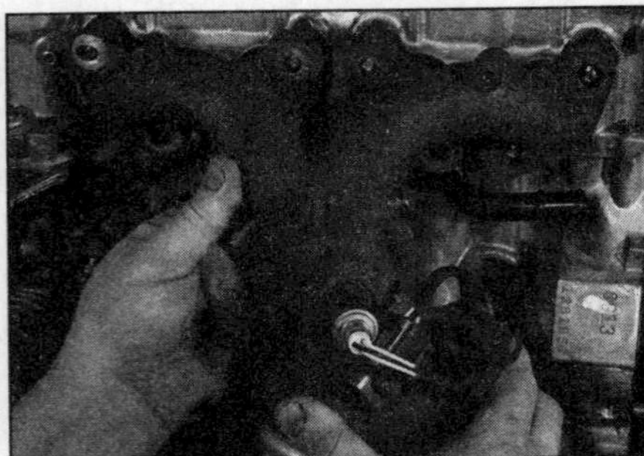
16.4a Removing the exhaust manifold . . .

16.4b . . . and gaskets

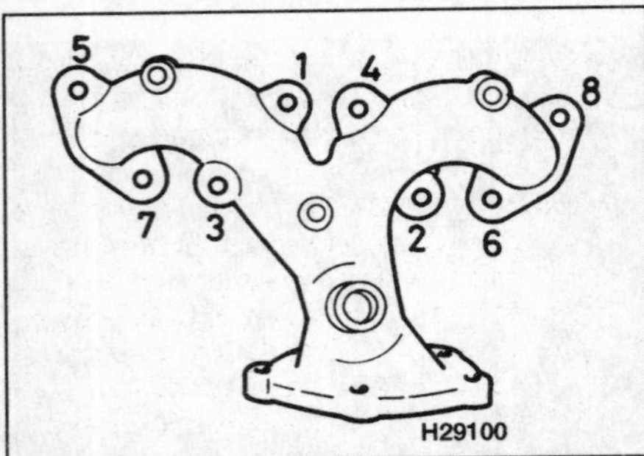

16.6a Exhaust manifold mounting nuts tightening sequence

16.6b Tightening the exhaust manifold mounting nuts

4 Remove the manifold from the cylinder head, and out of the engine compartment. Remove the gaskets from the studs and discard them **(see illustrations)**.

5 Clean the surfaces of the exhaust manifold and cylinder head and check the exhaust manifold for distortion using a straight-edge and feeler blade. If the distortion exceeds the specified maximum, renew the manifold.

Refitting

6 Refitting is a reversal of the removal procedure with reference to Chapter 4B and noting the following points **(see illustrations)**:

a) *Examine all the manifold studs for damage or corrosion; remove all traces of corrosion, and repair or renew any damaged studs.*
b) *The manifold and cylinder head mating surfaces must be clean and dry. Fit the new manifold gaskets to the head studs. Install the manifold, and tighten its nuts to the specified torque in the order shown.*

17 Exhaust system - general information, removal and refitting

General information

1 The exhaust system consists of five sections, the primary catalytic converter, the front pipe, the secondary catalytic converter, the intermediate pipe (including a silencer box on 1275 cc models), and the tailpipe and main silencer box.

2 The system is suspended throughout its entire length by rubber mountings, and all exhaust sections are joined by flanged joints which are secured together by studs and nuts on the main exhaust sections. The primary catalytic converter is secured to the exhaust manifold by bolts and a circular seal, and to the exhaust front pipe by two special bolts and springs and a sealing ring.

Removal

3 Each exhaust section can be removed individually or, alternatively, the main part of the system excluding the primary catalytic converter and tailpipe can be removed as a unit.

4 First jack up the car, and support it on axle stands (see "*Jacking and vehicle support*"). Alternatively, position the car over an inspection pit, or on car ramps.

Primary catalytic converter

5 Unbolt the heatshield from the primary catalytic converter.

6 Support the exhaust front pipe then unscrew the special bolts securing the pipe to the primary catalytic converter. Remove the bolts and recover the springs. Lower the pipe and recover the sealing ring.

7 Support the primary catalytic converter, then unscrew the bolts securing it to the exhaust manifold. Lower it from the manifold and recover the seal. Discard the seal - a new one must be fitted on refitting.

Front pipe

8 Unscrew the nuts securing the front pipe to the primary catalytic converter. Remove the bolts and recover the springs. Lower the pipe and recover the sealing ring.

9 Support the secondary catalytic converter, then unscrew the two nuts securing the front pipe flange joint to the secondary catalytic converter noting the location of the support bracket. Withdraw the front pipe from underneath the vehicle, and recover the gasket from the joint. Note that it may be necessary to release the heat shield and mounting rubbers from the support bracket to allow the front pipe to be withdrawn **(see illustrations)**.

10 With the front pipe removed, unbolt the heat shields from it.

Secondary catalytic converter

11 Support the intermediate and front pipes, then unscrew the two nuts securing the front pipe flange joint to the secondary catalytic converter noting the location of the support bracket. Similarly unscrew the two nuts securing the intermediate pipe flange to the secondary catalytic converter.

12 Separate the intermediate pipe from the catalytic converter and recover the gasket,

17.9a Exhaust front pipe to secondary catalytic converter joint and mounting

17.9b Unbolting the heat shield from the secondary catalytic converter

then separate the converter from the front pipe and recover the gasket. Withdraw the converter from under the vehicle.

13 With the catalytic converter removed, unbolt the heat shield from it.

Intermediate pipe

14 Unscrew the nuts securing the intermediate pipe to the secondary catalytic converter and tailpipe.

15 Separate the joints and recover the gaskets, then withdraw the pipe from under the vehicle.

Tailpipe and silencer

16 Support the intermediate pipe, then unscrew the two nuts securing the intermediate pipe to the tailpipe **(see illustration)**.

17 Separate the joint and recover the gasket.

18 Release the tailpipe from the mounting rubbers and withdraw it from under the vehicle **(see illustration)**.

System (excluding the primary catalytic converter and tailpipe)

19 Unscrew the special nuts securing the front pipe to the primary catalytic converter. Remove the bolts and recover the springs. Lower the pipe and recover the sealing ring.

20 Unscrew the two nuts securing the intermediate pipe to the tailpipe, then separate the joint and recover the joint.

17.16 Exhaust intermediate pipe-to-tailpipe joint

17.18 Exhaust tailpipe mounting

21 With the aid of an assistant, free the system from all its mounting rubbers, and withdraw it from underneath the vehicle.

Heat shields

22 Heat shields are bolted to the underbody and may be removed with the exhaust system in position.

Refitting

23 Each section is refitted by a reversal of the removal sequence, noting the following points:

a) *Ensure that all traces of corrosion have been removed from the flanges, and renew the gasket(s).*

b) *Inspect the rubber mountings for damage or deterioration, and renew as necessary.*

c) *Prior to tightening the exhaust system fasteners to the specified torque, ensure that all rubber mountings are correctly located, and that there is adequate clearance between the exhaust system and vehicle underbody/suspension components, etc.*

Chapter 4 Part B: Emissions control systems

Contents

Degrees of difficulty

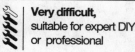

Easy, suitable for novice with little experience 	**Fairly easy,** suitable for beginner with some experience 	**Fairly difficult,** suitable for competent DIY mechanic 	**Difficult,** suitable for experienced DIY mechanic 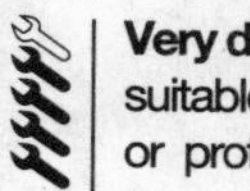	**Very difficult,** suitable for expert DIY or professional

Specifications

Torque wrench settings

	Nm	lbf ft
Exhaust gas sensor	50	37
Exhaust gas sensor adapter to exhaust manifold	78	58

1 General information

All Nissan Micra models covered in this manual are fitted with the following emission control systems.

a) Crankcase emission control
b) Catalytic converter
c) Evaporative emission control

The systems operate as follows.

Crankcase emissions control

To reduce the emission of unburned hydrocarbons from the crankcase into the atmosphere, the engine is sealed, and the blow-by gases and oil vapour are drawn from inside the crankcase, through the PCV valve, into the inlet manifold, to be burned by the engine during normal combustion.

Under conditions of high manifold vacuum, the gases will be sucked positively out of the crankcase. Under conditions of low manifold vacuum, the gases are forced out of the crankcase by the (relatively) higher crankcase pressure; if the engine is worn, the raised crankcase pressure (due to increased blow-by) will cause some of the flow to return under all manifold conditions.

Catalytic converter

To minimise the amount of pollutants which escape into the atmosphere, two catalytic converters (primary and secondary) are fitted in the exhaust system. The primary "cat" is bolted to the exhaust manifold and the secondary "cat" is located between the exhaust front pipe and intermediate pipe. The system is of "closed-loop" type, in which an exhaust gas sensor provides the fuel system control unit constant feedback, enabling the unit to adjust the mixture to provide the best possible conditions for the converter to operate.

The exhaust gas sensor's tip is sensitive to oxygen, and sends the control unit a varying voltage depending on the amount of oxygen in the exhaust gases; if the inlet air/fuel mixture is too rich, the sensor sends a high-voltage signal. The voltage falls as the mixture weakens. Peak conversion efficiency of all major pollutants occurs if the inlet air/fuel mixture is maintained at the chemically-correct ratio for the complete combustion of petrol - 14.7 parts (by weight) of air to 1 part of fuel (the "stoichiometric" ratio). The sensor output voltage alters in a large step at this point, the control unit using the signal change as a reference point, and correcting the inlet air/fuel mixture accordingly by altering the fuel injector pulse width (injector opening time). The sensor has a built-in heating element (controlled by the control unit), to quickly bring the sensor's tip to an efficient operating temperature.

Evaporative emissions control system

An evaporative emissions control system is fitted in order to minimise the escape of unburned hydrocarbons into the atmosphere. The fuel tank filler cap is sealed, and a carbon canister collects the petrol vapours generated in the tank when the car is parked. It stores them until the vapours can be cleared into the inlet manifold when the engine is running. To ensure that the engine runs correctly when it is cold and/or idling, and to protect the catalytic converter from the effects of an over-rich mixture, the system is designed to operate only when the engine has warmed up and is under load.

The system is controlled by a thermal vacuum valve (TVV) located on the left-hand end of the cylinder head. At coolant temperatures below 50°C the valve is open to atmospheric pressure and the system is disabled, however at temperatures above 50°C the valve is closed and the system is enabled.

2 Emissions control systems - testing and component renewal

Crankcase emissions control

1 Disconnect the crankcase ventilation hoses and check that they are clear and undamaged then refit them.

2 With the engine idling, disconnect the PCV valve from the rubber seal on the rear of the camshaft cover. A hissing noise should be heard and vacuum should be felt when a finger is placed over the valve inlet. Switch off the engine after making the check and refit the valve to the seal in the camshaft cover.

3 Renew the PCV valve filter **(see illustration)** at the specified intervals as described in Chapter 1.

2.3 Remove the PCV filter from the housing

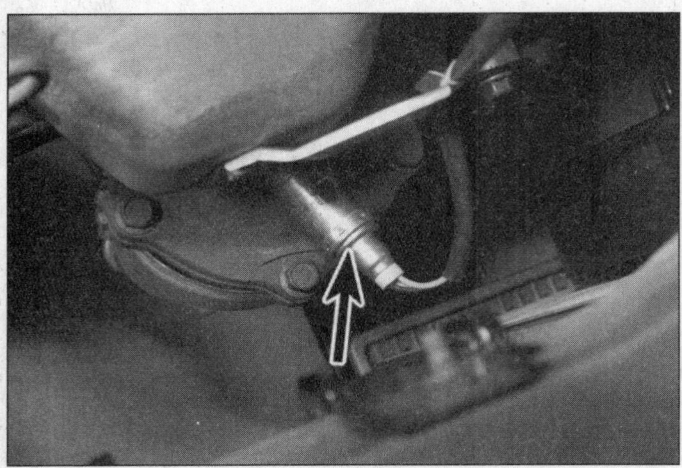

2.6 The exhaust gas sensor is screwed into the exhaust manifold

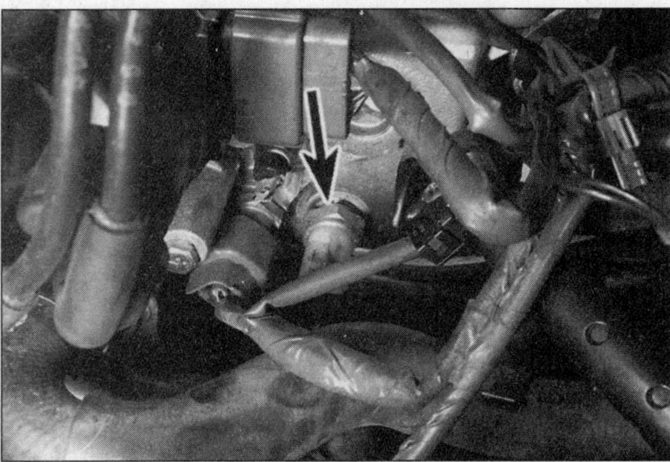

2.13 Thermal vacuum valve

Exhaust emissions control system

Testing

4 If the CO level at the tailpipe is too high, the operation of the exhaust gas sensor should be tested using the ECCS control unit self-diagnosis facility as described in Chapter 4A. Detailed testing of the sensor and catalytic converter must be left to a Nissan dealer.

Catalytic converter - renewal

5 Refer to Chapter 4A.

Exhaust gas sensor - renewal

Note: *The exhaust gas sensor is delicate, and it will not work if it is dropped or knocked, if its power supply is disrupted, or if any cleaning materials are used on it.*

6 Trace the wiring back from the exhaust gas sensor, which is screwed into the exhaust manifold **(see illustration)**. Disconnect the wiring connector, and free the wiring from any relevant retaining clips or ties.

7 Unscrew and remove the sensor. If necessary also unscrew the adapter from the manifold.

8 Refitting is a reversal of the removal procedure, but prior to installing the sensor, apply a smear of high-temperature grease to the sensor threads. Tighten the sensor to the specified torque. Check that the wiring is correctly routed, and in no danger of contacting either the exhaust system or the engine.

Evaporative emissions control system

Testing

9 To test the system, disconnect the hoses between the carbon canister, thermal vacuum valve and throttle housing, and check that they are clear by blowing through them.

10 The purge control valve may be tested using a vacuum pump. Connect the pump to the purge valve outlet on the side of the canister and apply a vacuum of 15.75 inHg. The vacuum should hold, proving that the internal valve is functioning correctly. Now apply the vacuum to the inlet manifold control inlet on top of the canister, and check that the vacuum held is slightly reduced proving that the internal spring is applying pressure to the valve.

11 To check the thermal vacuum valve (TVV) located on the left-hand end of the cylinder head, remove it as described later in this Section. Connect suitable hoses to the inlet and outlet ports, then immerse the valve in water and blow through one of the hoses. With the water temperature below 50°C the valve should be open and it should be possible to blow through the hoses, however with the temperature above 50°C the valve should be closed. On completion refit the valve and refill the cooling system with reference to Chapter 1.

Thermal vacuum valve - renewal

12 Partially drain the cooling system as described in Chapter 1 until the coolant level is just below the valve, or alternatively have a suitable plug which can be used to plug the valve aperture in the cylinder head.

13 Disconnect the hoses then unscrew and remove the valve **(see illustration)**.

14 Refitting is a reversal of the removal procedure. Refill the cooling system with reference to Chapter 1.

Carbon canister - renewal

15 The canister is located on the bulkhead behind the left-hand side of the engine.

16 Make a note of the correct fitted location of each hose on the canister **(see illustration)**.

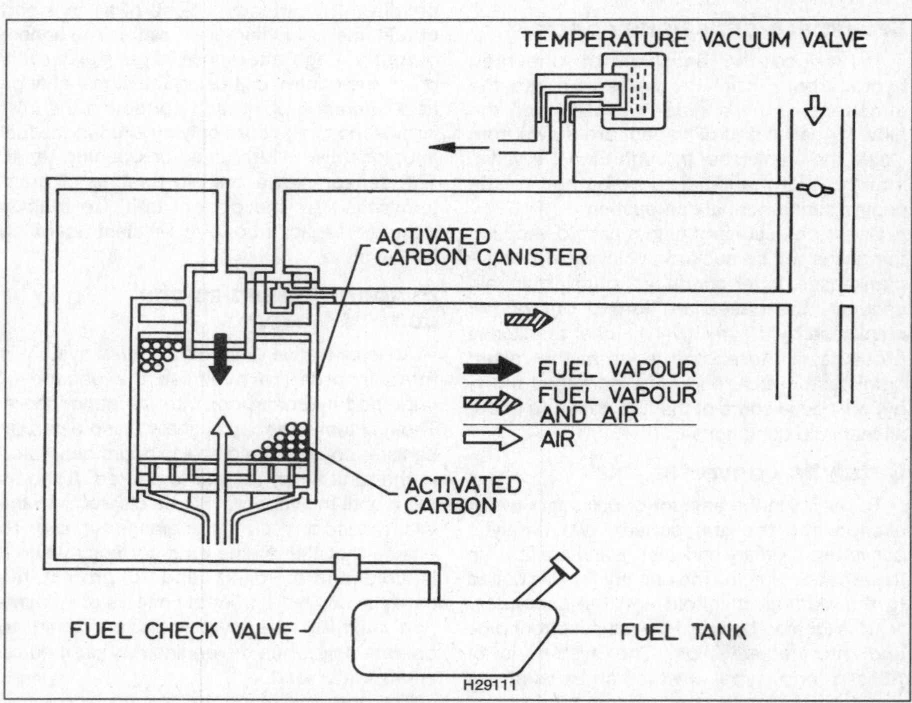

2.16 Evaporative loss carbon canister and hose connections

2.17 Disconnecting the hoses from the top of the carbon canister

17 Release the retaining clips (where fitted) and disconnect the hoses from the top of the canister **(see illustration)**.

18 Free the canister from its mounting bracket, and remove it from the engine compartment.

19 Refitting is a reverse of the removal procedure, ensuring that the hoses are correctly reconnected.

3 Catalytic converters - general information and precautions

The catalytic converters are reliable and simple devices which need no maintenance in itself, but there are some facts an owner should be aware of to ensure the converters function properly for their full service life.

a) *DO NOT use leaded petrol in a vehicle with a catalytic converter - the lead will coat the precious metals, reducing their converting efficiency, and will eventually destroy the converter.*

b) *Always keep the ignition and fuel systems well-maintained in accordance with the manufacturer's schedule.*

c) *If the engine develops a misfire, do not drive the car at all (or at least as little as possible) until the fault is cured.*

d) *DO NOT push- or tow-start the car - this will soak the catalytic converter in unburned fuel, causing it to overheat when the engine does start.*

e) *DO NOT switch off the ignition at high engine speeds - ie do not "blip" the throttle before switching off the engine.*

f) *DO NOT use fuel or engine oil additives - these may contain substances harmful to the catalytic converter.*

g) *DO NOT continue to use the car if the engine burns oil to the extent of leaving a visible trail of blue smoke.*

h) *Remember that the catalytic converter operates at very high temperatures. DO NOT, therefore, park the car in dry undergrowth, over long grass, or over piles of dead leaves, after a long run.*

i) *Remember that the catalytic converter is FRAGILE - do not strike it with tools during servicing work.*

Notes

Chapter 5 Part A:
Starting and charging systems

Contents

Degrees of difficulty

Easy, suitable for novice with little experience	**Fairly easy,** suitable for beginner with some experience	**Fairly difficult,** suitable for competent DIY mechanic	**Difficult,** suitable for experienced DIY mechanic	**Very difficult,** suitable for expert DIY or professional

Specifications

General

System type	12 volt, negative earth

Battery

Type	Low-maintenance or maintenance-free
Capacity	36 Ah
Charge condition:	
Poor	12.5 volts
Normal	12.6 volts
Good	12.7 volts

Alternator

Type:	
Up to 2000 MY	Bosch
From 2000 MY	Hitachi
Rating	65 amp
Minimum brush length:	
Up to 2000 MY	10.0 mm
From 2000 MY	6.0 mm

Starter motor

Type	Bosch
Output:	
Standard	0.9 kW
Certain non-UK market	1.1 kW
Minimum brush length:	
Up to 2000 MY	5.0 mm
From 2000 MY	3.0 mm

Torque wrench settings

Torque wrench settings	Nm	lbf ft
Alternator mounting and adjustment lock bolts	44	33
Alternator upper mounting brackets	18	13
Starter motor mounting bolts	37	27

1 General information and precautions

General information

This Part of Chapter 5 includes the charging and starting systems. Because of their engine-related functions, these components are covered separately from the body electrical devices such as the lights, instruments, etc (which are covered in Chapter 12). Refer to Part B of this Chapter for information on the ignition system.

The electrical system is of 12-volt negative earth type.

The battery is of low-maintenance or "maintenance-free" (sealed for life) type, and is charged by the alternator, which is belt-driven from the crankshaft pulley.

The starter motor is of pre-engaged type incorporating an integral solenoid. On starting, the solenoid moves the drive pinion into engagement with the flywheel/driveplate ring gear before the starter motor is energised. Once the engine has started, a one-way clutch prevents the motor armature being driven by the engine until the pinion disengages.

Precautions

Further details of the various systems are given in the relevant Sections of this Chapter. While some repair procedures are given, the usual course of action is to renew the component concerned. The owner whose interest extends beyond mere component renewal should obtain a copy of the *"Automobile Electrical & Electronic Systems Manual"*, available from the publishers of this manual.

It is necessary to take extra care when working on the electrical system to avoid damage to semi-conductor devices (diodes and transistors), and to avoid the risk of personal injury. In addition to the precautions given in *"Safety first!"* at the beginning of this manual, observe the following when working on the system:

Always remove rings, watches, etc before working on the electrical system. Even with the battery disconnected, capacitive discharge could occur if a component's live terminal is earthed through a metal object. This could cause a shock or nasty burn.

Do not reverse the battery connections. Components such as the alternator, electronic control units, or any other components having semi-conductor circuitry could be irreparably damaged.

If the engine is being started using jump leads and a slave battery, connect the batteries positive-to-positive and negative-to-negative (see "Jump starting"). This also applies when connecting a battery charger but in this case both of the battery terminals should first be disconnected.

Never disconnect the battery terminals, the alternator, any electrical wiring or any test instruments when the engine is running.

Do not allow the engine to turn the alternator when the alternator is not connected.

Never "test" for alternator output by "flashing" the output lead to earth.

Never use an ohmmeter of the type incorporating a hand-cranked generator for circuit or continuity testing.

Always ensure that the battery negative lead is disconnected when working on the electrical system.

Before using electric-arc welding equipment on the car, disconnect the battery, alternator and components such as the fuel injection/ignition electronic control unit to protect them from the risk of damage.

The radio/cassette unit fitted as standard is equipped with a built-in security code to deter thieves. If the power source to the unit is cut, the anti-theft system will activate. Even if the power source is immediately reconnected, the radio/cassette unit will not function until the correct security code has been entered. Therefore, if you do not know the correct security code for the radio/cassette unit do not disconnect the battery negative terminal of the battery or remove the radio/cassette unit from the vehicle. Refer to your dealer for further information on whether the unit fitted to your car has a security code.

2 Battery - testing and charging

Standard and low maintenance battery - testing

1 If the vehicle covers a small annual mileage, it is worthwhile checking the specific gravity of the electrolyte every three months to determine the state of charge of the battery. Use a hydrometer to make the check and compare the results with the following table. The temperatures quoted in the table are ambient (air) temperatures. Note that the specific gravity readings assume an electrolyte temperature of 15°C (60°F); for every 10°C (50°F) below 15°C (60°F) subtract 0.007. For every 10°C (50°F) above 15°C (60°F) add 0.007.

	Above 25°C(77°F)	Below 25°C(77°F)
Fully-charged	*1.210 to 1.230*	*1.270 to 1.290*
70% charged	*1.170 to 1.190*	*1.230 to 1.250*
Discharged	*1.050 to 1.070*	*1.110to 1.130*

2 If the battery condition is suspect, first check the specific gravity of electrolyte in each cell. A variation of 0.040 or more between any cells indicates loss of electrolyte or deterioration of the internal plates.

3 If the specific gravity variation is 0.040 or more, the battery should be renewed. If the cell variation is satisfactory but the battery is discharged, it should be charged as described later in this Section.

Maintenance-free battery - testing

4 In cases where a "sealed for life" maintenance-free battery is fitted, topping-up and testing of the electrolyte in each cell is not possible. The condition of the battery can therefore only be tested using a battery condition indicator or a voltmeter.

5 Some models may be fitted with a maintenance-free battery with a built-in charge condition indicator. The indicator is located in the top of the battery casing, and indicates the condition of the battery from its colour. If the indicator shows green, then the battery is in a good state of charge. If the indicator turns darker, eventually to black, then the battery requires charging, as described later in this Section. If the indicator shows clear/yellow, then the electrolyte level in the battery is too low to allow further use, and the battery should be renewed. **Do not** attempt to charge, load or jump start a battery when the indicator shows clear/yellow.

6 If testing the battery using a voltmeter, connect the voltmeter across the battery and compare the result with those given in the *Specifications* under "charge condition". The test is only accurate if the battery has not been subjected to any kind of charge for the previous six hours. If this is not the case, switch on the headlights for 30 seconds, then wait four to five minutes before testing the battery after switching off the headlights. All other electrical circuits must be switched off, so check that the doors and tailgate are fully shut when making the test.

7 If the voltage reading is less than 12.2 volts, then the battery is discharged, whilst a reading of 12.2 to 12.4 volts indicates a partially discharged condition.

8 If the battery is to be charged, remove it from the vehicle (Section 3) and charge it as described later in this Section.

Standard and low maintenance battery - charging

Note: *The following is intended as a guide only. Always refer to the manufacturer's recommendations (often printed on a label attached to the battery) before charging a battery.*

9 Charge the battery at a rate of 3.5 to 4 amps and continue to charge the battery at this rate until no further rise in specific gravity is noted over a four hour period.

10 Alternatively, a trickle charger charging at the rate of 1.5 amps can safely be used overnight.

11 Specially rapid "boost" charges which are claimed to restore the power of the battery in 1 to 2 hours are not recommended, as they can cause serious damage to the battery plates through overheating.

12 While charging the battery, note that the temperature of the electrolyte should never exceed 38°C.

Maintenance-free battery - charging

Note: *The following is intended as a guide only. Always refer to the manufacturer's recommendations (often printed on a label attached to the battery) before charging a battery.*

13 This battery type takes considerably longer to fully recharge than the standard type, the time taken being dependent on the extent of discharge, but it can take anything up to three days.

14 A constant voltage type charger is required, to be set, when connected, to 13.9 to 14.9 volts with a charger current below 25 amps. Using this method, the battery should be usable within three hours, giving a voltage reading of 12.5 volts, but this is for a partially discharged battery and, as mentioned, full charging can take considerably longer.

15 If the battery is to be charged from a fully discharged state (condition reading less than 12.2 volts), have it recharged by your local automotive electrician, as the charge rate is higher and constant supervision during charging is necessary.

3 Battery - removal and refitting

Note: *If the vehicle has a security coded radio, check that you have a copy of the code number before disconnecting the battery cable.*

Removal

1 The battery is located in the left-hand front corner of the engine compartment.

2 Loosen the clampbolt, and disconnect the clamp from the battery negative terminal **(see illustration)**.

3 Remove the insulation cover (where fitted) and disconnect the positive clamp in the same way.

4 Unscrew the nuts, and remove the battery retaining clamp from the tops of the metal rods. Unhook and remove the metal rods **(see illustrations)**.

5 Lift the battery out of the engine compartment. If necessary, the battery mounting bracket can also be unbolted and removed from the engine compartment after removing the relay boxes **(see illustrations)**.

Refitting

6 Refitting is a reversal of removal, but smear petroleum jelly on the terminals when reconnecting the leads, and always reconnect the positive lead first followed by the negative lead.

4 Charging system - testing

Note: *Refer to the warnings given in "Safety first!" and in Section 1 of this Chapter before starting work.*

1 If the ignition warning light fails to illuminate when the ignition is switched on, first check the alternator wiring connections for security. If satisfactory, check that the warning light bulb has not blown, and that the bulbholder is secure in its location in the instrument panel. If the light still fails to illuminate, check the continuity of the warning light feed wire from the alternator to the bulbholder. If all is satisfactory, the alternator is at fault and should be renewed or taken to an auto-electrician for testing and repair.

2 If the ignition warning light illuminates when the engine is running, stop the engine and check that the drivebelt is correctly tensioned (see Chapter 1) and that the alternator connections are secure. If all is so far satisfactory, have the alternator checked by an auto-electrician.

3 If the alternator output is suspect even though the warning light functions correctly, the regulated voltage may be checked as follows.

4 Connect a voltmeter across the battery terminals and start the engine.

5 Increase the engine speed to 1500 rpm and check that the reading is between 13 and 15 volts and no more.

3.2 Disconnecting the clamp from the battery negative terminal

3.4a Loosen the battery retaining clamp nuts . . .

3.4b . . . then unhook the metal rods and lift the clamp assembly from the battery

3.5a Relay box mounting bolt

3.5b Unscrew the mounting bolts . . .

3.5c . . . and remove the battery mounting bracket

5.2 Removing the splash guard from the right-hand side of the engine compartment

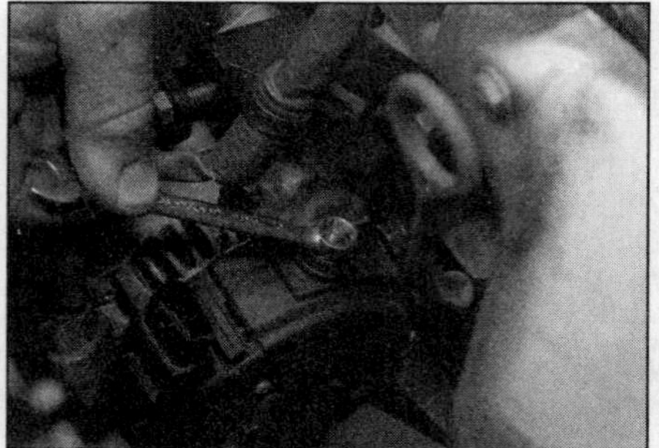

5.3a Disconnecting the main terminal from the alternator

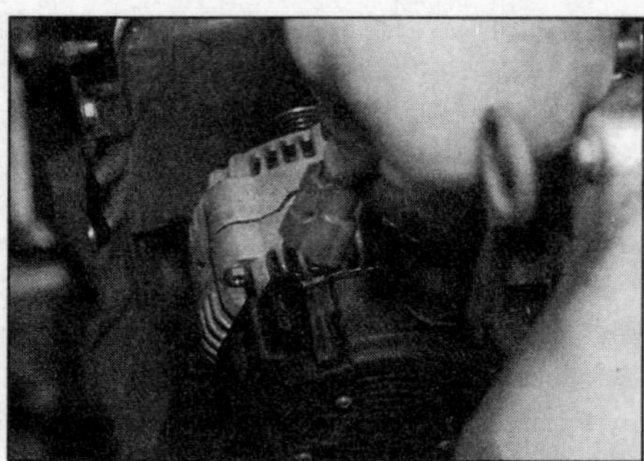

5.3b Disconnecting the wiring connector from the alternator

6 Switch on as many electrical accessories (eg, the headlights, heated rear window and heater blower) as possible, and check that the alternator maintains the regulated voltage at around 13 to 15 volts.

7 If the regulated voltage is not as stated, the fault may be due to worn brushes, weak brush springs, a faulty voltage regulator, a faulty diode, a severed phase winding or worn or damaged slip rings. The alternator should be renewed or taken to an auto-electrician for testing and repair.

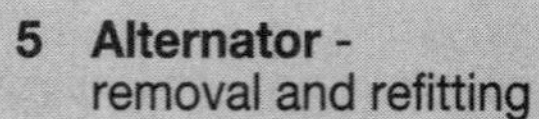

5 Alternator - removal and refitting

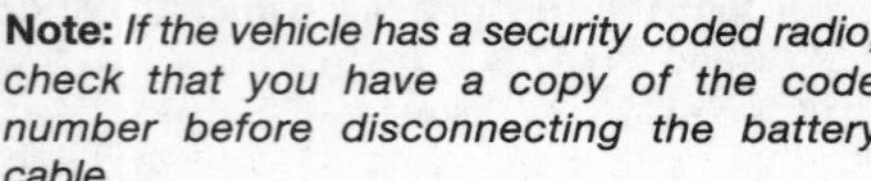

Note: *If the vehicle has a security coded radio, check that you have a copy of the code number before disconnecting the battery cable.*

Removal

1 Disconnect the battery negative lead.

2 Loosen the auxiliary drivebelt tension with reference to Chapter 1, and disengage it from the alternator pulley. To improve access remove the splash guard from the right-hand side of the engine compartment **(see illustration)**.

3 Remove the rubber cover from the alternator main terminal, then unscrew the retaining nut and disconnect the cable. Disconnect the wiring connector from the alternator **(see illustrations)**.

5.4a Unscrewing the alternator mounting bolts

5.4b Removing the alternator from the engine compartment

4 Unscrew and remove the upper adjustment locknut from the upper bracket and recover the spacer fitted between the alternator and adjuster strap, then unscrew and remove the alternator lower mounting bolts. Manoeuvre the alternator away from its mounting brackets and out of the engine compartment **(see illustrations)**.

Refitting

5 Refitting is a reversal of removal, tensioning the auxiliary drivebelt as described in Chapter 1, and ensuring that the alternator mounting and adjustment bolts are securely tightened.

6 Alternator - brush holder/regulator renewal

1 Remove the alternator (see Section 5).

2 Remove the screws and special clips and withdraw the plastic cover from the rear of the alternator **(see illustrations)**.

3 Remove the screws and carefully withdraw the brush holder/regulator from the alternator housing **(see illustrations)**. Take care not to damage the brushes as they are brittle.

4 Using a steel rule check the length of the brushes. If less than 10.0 mm the complete brush holder assembly should be renewed. **Note:** *It may be possible to obtain the brushes separately, in which case the*

6.2a Remove the screws . . .

6.2b . . . then prise back the special clips . . .

6.2c . . . and withdraw the plastic cover from the alternator

6.3a Remove the screws . . .

6.3b . . . and withdraw the brush holder/regulator

brush leads should be unsoldered from the terminals and the new brush leads soldered onto the terminals.

5 Check the slip rings for excessive wear and clean them with a rag soaked in fuel.

6 Fit the new holder using a reversal of the removal procedure but make sure that each brush moves freely first. Check that the bushes are correctly located in the lower mounting lugs on the alternator.

7 Starting system - testing

Note: *Refer to the precautions given in "Safety first!" and in Section 1 of this Chapter before starting work.*

1 If the starter motor fails to operate when the ignition key is turned to the appropriate position, the following possible causes may be to blame.

a) *The battery is faulty.*
b) *The electrical connections between the switch, solenoid, battery and starter motor are somewhere failing to pass the necessary current from the battery through the starter to earth.*
c) *The solenoid is faulty.*
d) *The starter motor is mechanically or electrically defective.*

2 To check the battery, switch on the headlights. If they dim after a few seconds, this indicates that the battery is discharged - recharge (see Section 2) or renew the battery. If the headlights glow brightly, operate the starter motor on the ignition switch and observe the lights. If they dim, then this indicates that current is reaching the starter motor, therefore the fault must lie in the starter motor. If the lights continue to glow brightly (and no clicking sound can be heard from the starter motor solenoid), this indicates that there is a fault in the circuit or solenoid - see following paragraphs. If the starter motor turns slowly when operated, but the battery is in good condition, then this indicates that either the starter motor is faulty, or there is considerable resistance somewhere in the circuit.

3 If a fault in the circuit is suspected, disconnect the battery leads (including the earth connection to the body), the starter/solenoid wiring and the engine/transmission earth strap. Thoroughly clean the connections, and reconnect the leads and wiring, then use a voltmeter or test lamp to check that full battery voltage is available at the battery positive lead connection to the solenoid, and that the earth is sound. Smear petroleum jelly around the battery terminals to prevent corrosion - corroded connections are amongst the most frequent causes of electrical system faults.

4 If the battery and all connections are in good condition, check the circuit by disconnecting the wire from the solenoid blade terminal. Connect a voltmeter or test lamp between the wire end and a good earth (such as the battery negative terminal), and check that the wire is live when the ignition switch is turned to the "start" position. If it is, then the circuit is sound - if not, the circuit wiring can be checked as described in Chapter 12.

5 The solenoid contacts can be checked by connecting a voltmeter or test lamp across the solenoid. When the ignition switch is turned to the "start" position, there should be a reading or lighted bulb, as applicable. If there is no reading or lighted bulb, the solenoid is faulty and should be renewed.

6 If the circuit and solenoid are proved sound, the fault must lie in the starter motor. In this event, it may be possible to have the starter motor overhauled by a specialist, but check on the cost of spares before proceeding, as it may prove more economical to obtain a new or exchange motor.

8 Starter motor - removal and refitting

Note: *If the vehicle has a security coded radio, check that you have a copy of the code number before disconnecting the battery cable.*

Removal

1 Disconnect the battery negative lead, then remove the air inlet duct and air cleaner with reference to Chapter 4A.

2 So that access to the motor can be gained both from above and below, firmly apply the handbrake, then jack up the front of the vehicle and support it on axle stands (see "*Jacking and vehicle support*"). On manual transmission models the starter motor is located on the rear of the engine, whereas on automatic transmission models it is located on the front of the engine.

Manual transmission models

3 Unscrew and remove the terminal nut, and disconnect the main battery cable from the starter motor solenoid. Also disconnect the wiring connector from the solenoid **(see illustration)**.

4 Unscrew the starter motor mounting bolts, supporting the motor as the bolts are withdrawn, and manoeuvre the starter motor out from the engine **(see illustration)**.

Automatic transmission models

5 Unscrew and remove the starter motor upper mounting bolt which is inserted from the left-hand side of the transmission housing.

6 Working under the vehicle, unbolt and remove the inlet manifold support bracket from the rear of the cylinder block.

7 Unscrew and remove the terminal nut, and disconnect the main battery cable from the

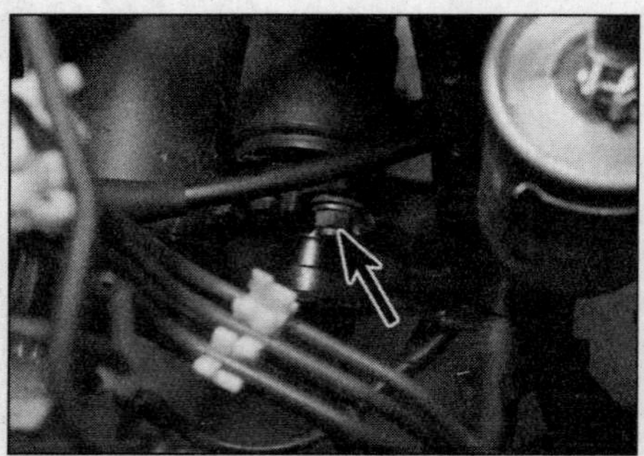

8.3 Starter motor main battery cable terminal

8.4 Removing the starter motor from the engine compartment

starter motor solenoid. Also disconnect the wiring connector from the solenoid.

8 Unscrew and remove the starter motor lower mounting bolt, supporting the motor as the bolt is withdrawn, then manoeuvre the starter motor out from beneath the engine.

Refitting

9 Refitting is a reversal of removal but tighten the bolts to the specified torque.

9 Starter motor - testing and overhaul

If the starter motor is thought to be suspect, it should be removed from the vehicle and taken to an auto-electrician for testing. Most auto-electricians will be able to supply and fit brushes at a reasonable cost. However, check on the cost of repairs before proceeding as it may prove more economical to obtain a new or exchange motor.

Chapter 5 Part B:
Ignition system

Contents

Degrees of difficulty

Easy, suitable for novice with little experience 	**Fairly easy,** suitable for beginner with some experience 	**Fairly difficult,** suitable for competent DIY mechanic	**Difficult,** suitable for experienced DIY mechanic	**Very difficult,** suitable for expert DIY or professional 

Specifications

General

Ignition system type:	
Up to 2000	Breakerless electronic ignition controlled by ECCS control unit
From 2000	Distributorless ignition system controlled by engine management ECU
Firing order	1-3-4-2 (No 1 cylinder at timing chain end)

Ignition system data

Ignition timing (base at idle speed - see Chapter 4A)	15° ± 2° BTDC
Ignition HT coil resistances (at 20°C) 1.0 and 1.3 litre engines (up to 2000):	
Primary windings	0.8 ohms
Secondary windings	1.0 k ohms
Ignition HT coil resistances (at 25°C) 1.0 and 1.4 litre engines (from 2000):	
Terminals 3-2	infinity
Terminals 1-3	Except 0
Terminals 1-2	infinity

1 Ignition system - general information and precautions

The ignition system is integrated with the fuel system, to form a combined fuel/ignition system which is controlled by the ECCS/ECM control unit (see Chapter 4A for further information).

On models up to 2000 model year, the distributor contains a crank angle sensor, which informs the ECU of engine speed and crankshaft position. On models from 2000 model year, the camshaft position sensor informs the ECU of the engine speed. Based on this information, and the information received from its other sensors, the ECU then calculates the correct ignition timing setting, and switches the power transistor unit on and off accordingly. This causes a high voltage to be induced in the coil secondary (HT) windings, which is then transferred to the relevant spark plug.

On models up to 2000 model year, the crank angle sensor, ignition coil and power transistor are all located inside the distributor body, and the distributor cap performs its normal function of transferring the HT current to the rotor arm. On models from 2000 model year, each spark plug has its own coil, built into each individual spark plug cap.

2 Ignition system - testing

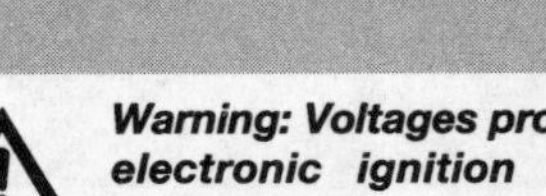

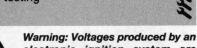

Warning: Voltages produced by an electronic ignition system are considerably higher than those produced by conventional ignition systems. Extreme care must be taken when working on the system with the ignition switched on. Persons with surgically-implanted cardiac pacemaker devices should keep well clear of the ignition circuits, components and test equipment

1 If a fault appears in the ignition system (eg misfiring), first ensure that the fault is not due to a poor electrical connection or poor maintenance; check that the air cleaner filter element is clean, that the spark plugs are in good condition and correctly gapped, that the engine breather hoses are clear and undamaged, referring to Chapter 1 for further information. If the engine is running very roughly, check the compression pressures and the valve clearances, as described in the relevant Part of Chapter 2.

2 On models up to 2000 model year, refer to Chapter 4A and carry out a self-diagnosis check on the ECCS system - crank angle sensor and ignition signal fault codes will show up if there are faults in these circuits. For more information refer also to the removal and refitting procedures for these components in Chapter 4A.

3 Check the ignition coil(s) with reference to Section 3 of this Chapter.

4 On models up to 2000 model year, check the distributor cap with reference to Chapter 1.

5 If these checks fail to reveal the cause of the problem, the vehicle should be taken to a Nissan dealer for testing. A wiring block connector is incorporated in the engine management circuit (near the fusebox) into which a special electronic diagnostic tester can be plugged. The tester will locate the fault quickly and simply alleviating the need to test all the system components individually which is a time consuming operation that carries a high risk of damaging the ECU.

6 If necessary, the system wiring and wiring connectors can be checked with reference to Chapter 12 ensuring that the ECU wiring connectors have first been disconnected.

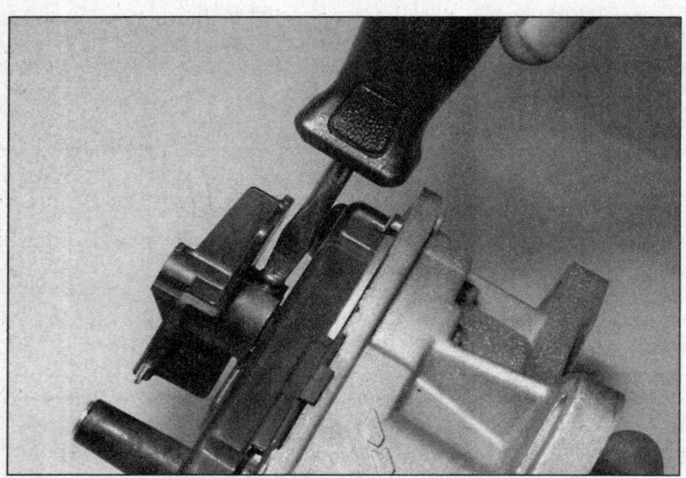

3.2 Removing the rotor arm grub screw

3.3a Cover retaining screws

3 Ignition HT coil - testing

Models up to 2000

1 Remove the distributor as described in Section 4.

2 With the distributor cap removed, undo the grub screw and remove the rotor arm from the end of the driveshaft **(see illustration)**.

3 Remove the screws and lift off the cover **(see illustrations)**.

3.3b Lifting the cover over the distributor shaft

3.9a Slacken and remove the retaining bolt . . .

4 Identify the wires for position then disconnect them from the coil.

5 Remove the spring from the coil tower and check it for condition.

6 The primary and secondary coil windings can be checked for continuity and resistance using an ohmmeter. The primary (LT) windings are checked by connecting the ohmmeter to the two LT wires. Connect the ohmmeter between the positive terminal and high tension (HT) terminal to check the secondary windings. Compare the results obtained to those given in the *Specifications*. Note the resistance of the coil windings varies slightly according to the coil temperature; the results in the *Specifications* are approximate values for the coil at 20°C.

3.8 Disconnecting one of the wiring plugs from the one of the ignition coils

3.9b . . . then withdraw the ignition coil/plug cap

7 At the time or writing it appears that Nissan do not supply the ignition coil as a separate item, therefore if the coil is proved faulty it will be necessary to renew the distributor as a complete assembly or obtain a second-hand unit.

Models from 2000

8 Disconnect the wiring connectors from the ignition coils **(see illustration)**.

9 Undo the retaining bolts and withdraw the coils from the sparkplugs **(see illustrations)**.

10 The coil windings can be checked for continuity and resistance using an ohmmeter. Connect the ohmmeter between the terminals and compare the results obtained to those given in the *Specifications* at the beginning of this Chapter. Note the resistance of the coil windings varies slightly according to the coil temperature; the results in the *Specifications* are approximate values for the coil at 25°C.

11 If any of the coils are proved faulty it will be necessary to renew it or obtain a second-hand unit.

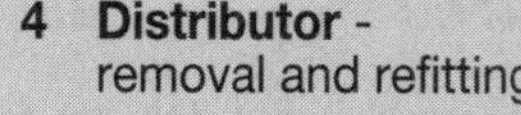

4 Distributor - removal and refitting

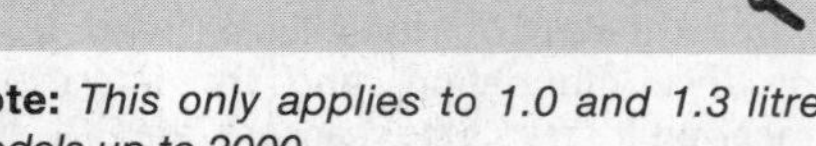

Note: *This only applies to 1.0 and 1.3 litre models up to 2000.*

Removal

1 Unscrew and remove the distributor cap retaining screws. Remove the cap, position it clear of the distributor body, and recover the cap seal **(see illustrations)**. Also recover the spring from the ignition coil tower inside the distributor body.

2 Disconnect the wiring connectors from the distributor **(see illustrations)**.

3 Check the cylinder head and distributor

4.1a Remove the retaining screws . . .

4.1b . . . and withdraw the cap

flange for alignment marks. If no marks are visible, use a scriber or suitable marker pen to mark the distributor body in relation to the cylinder head.

4 Unscrew the two mounting bolts, and withdraw the distributor from the cylinder head. Remove the O-ring from the end of the distributor body and discard it; a new one must be used on refitting **(see illustrations)**.

Refitting

5 Lubricate the new O-ring with a smear of engine oil, and fit it to the groove in the distributor body. Examine the distributor cap seal for wear or damage, and renew if necessary.

6 Align the distributor rotor shaft drive coupling key with the slots in the camshaft end, noting that the slots are offset to ensure that the distributor can only be fitted in one position. Carefully insert the distributor into the cylinder head, whilst rotating the rotor arm slightly to ensure that the coupling is correctly engaged.

7 Align the marks noted or made on removal, then insert the distributor retaining bolts and tighten them securely.

8 Ensure that the seal is correctly located in

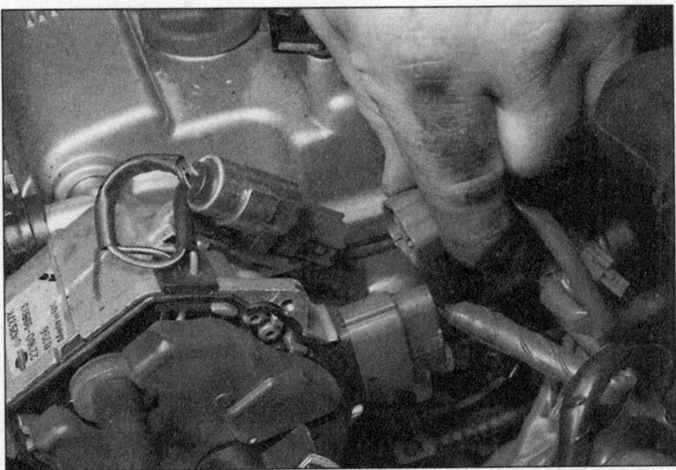

4.2a Disconnecting the ignition coil wiring from the distributor

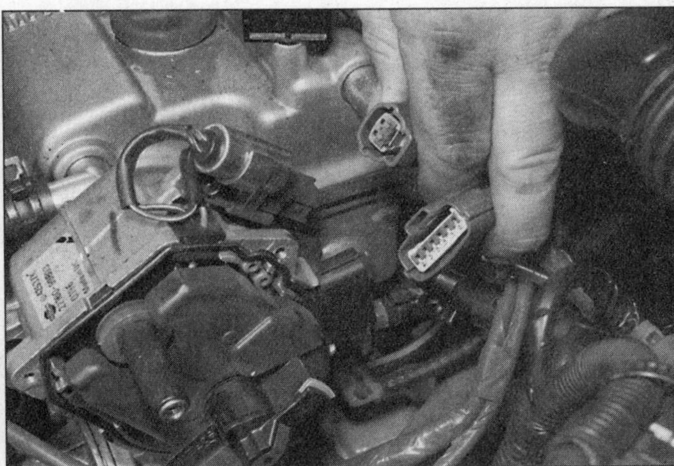

4.2b Disconnecting the engine management wiring from the distributor

4.4a Loosen . . .

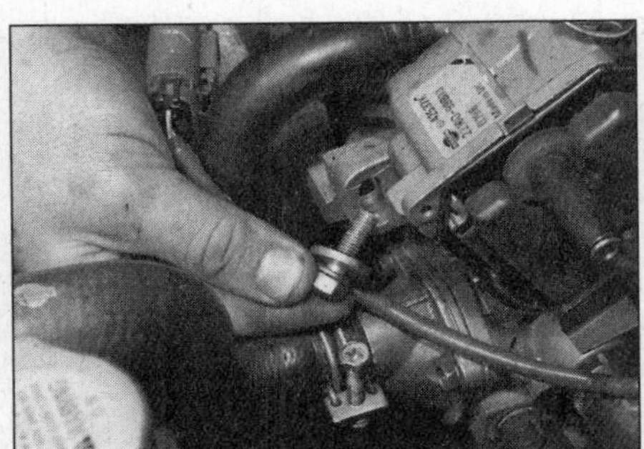

4.4b . . . and remove the mounting bolts . . .

4.4c . . . and withdraw the distributor from the cylinder head

its groove, then refit the cap assembly to the distributor and tighten its retaining screws securely. Reconnect the wiring plug.

9 Check and, if necessary, adjust the ignition timing as described in Section 5.

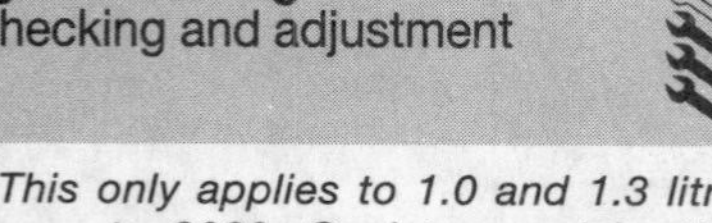

5 Ignition timing - checking and adjustment

Note: *This only applies to 1.0 and 1.3 litre models up to 2000. On later models, the ignition timing is not adjustable and is controlled by the engine management ECU.*

1 To check the ignition timing, a stroboscopic timing light will be required, preferably the type which clips over the No 1 HT lead. If this type is not available, an adapter must be fitted between No 1 spark plug and the HT lead so that the timing light trigger wire can be connected to it.

2 The timing marks are in the form of notches on the crankshaft pulley rim, which align with a pointer on the timing chain cover. The notches are spaced at intervals of 5°, and go from 20° before top dead centre (BTDC) to 5° after top dead centre (ATDC). The TDC mark is highlighted with paint to aid identification.

3 Start the engine and warm it up to normal operating temperature, then check the idle speed as described in Chapter 4A. Leave the wiring disconnected from the throttle potentiometer at this stage.

4 Connect the timing light to No 1 cylinder plug lead (nearest the timing chain) as described in the timing light manufacturer's instructions.

5 Start the engine, allowing it to idle at the specified speed, and point the timing light at the crankshaft pulley. The specified timing mark should be aligned with the pointer on the timing chain cover.

6 If adjustment is necessary, slacken the two distributor mounting bolts, then slowly rotate the distributor body as required until the crankshaft pulley marks are correctly positioned. Tighten the bolts and switch off the engine.

Warning: At all times, avoid touching the HT leads, and keep loose clothing, long hair, etc, well away from the moving parts of the engine.

7 Disconnect the timing light and reconnect the throttle potentiometer wiring.

Chapter 6
Clutch

Contents

Degrees of difficulty

Easy, suitable for novice with little experience 

Fairly easy, suitable for beginner with some experience 

Fairly difficult, suitable for competent DIY mechanic 

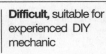

Difficult, suitable for experienced DIY mechanic 

Very difficult, suitable for expert DIY or professional

Specifications

Type	Single dry plate with diaphragm spring. Cable-operated release mechanism

Adjustment data

Clutch pedal height:	
Right-hand drive models:	
Up to March 1998	187 to 197 mm
March 1998 onwards	176 mm
Left-hand drive models:	
Up to March 1998	183 to 193 mm
March 1998 onwards	180 mm
Clutch pedal free play (measured at pedal pad)	11.0 to 15.5 mm

Friction plate

Diameter:	
998 cc engine	160 mm
1275 and 1348 cc engines	180 mm
Friction material thickness (total, new)	6.7 to 7.3 mm
Minimum friction material-to-rivet head depth	0.3 mm
Maximum friction plate run-out:	
998 cc engine (measured 75 mm from plate centre)	1.0 mm
1275 and 1348 cc engines (measured 85 mm from plate centre)	1.0 mm

Torque wrench settings

Torque wrench settings	Nm	lbf ft
Clutch pedal height adjustment bolt locknut	19	14
Clutch pedal pivot bolt	19	14
Clutch pedal bracket	10	7
Pressure plate retaining bolts	26	19

1 General information

The clutch consists of a friction plate, a pressure plate assembly, a release bearing and the release mechanism. All of these components are contained in the transmission bellhousing, attached to the left-hand end of the engine. The release mechanism is mechanical, being operated by a cable.

The friction plate is fitted between the engine flywheel and the clutch pressure plate, and is allowed to slide on the transmission input shaft splines.

The pressure plate assembly is bolted to the engine flywheel, and is located by two dowel pins. When the engine is running, drive is transmitted from the crankshaft via the flywheel to the friction plate, and from the friction plate to the transmission input shaft.

To interrupt the drive, the spring pressure must be relaxed. This is achieved by a sealed release bearing fitted concentrically around the transmission input shaft. When the driver depresses the clutch pedal, the release bearing is pressed against the fingers at the centre of the diaphragm spring. Since the spring is held by rivets between two annular fulcrum rings, the pressure at its centre causes it to deform, so that it flattens and thus releases the clamping force it exerts, at its periphery, on the pressure plate.

Depressing the clutch pedal pulls the control cable inner wire, and this in turn rotates the release fork by acting on the lever at the fork's upper end, above the bellhousing. The fork itself is clipped to the release bearing.

As the friction plate facings wear, the pressure plate moves towards the flywheel; this causes the diaphragm spring fingers to push against the release bearing, thus reducing the clearance which must be present in the mechanism. To ensure correct operation, the clutch cable must be regularly adjusted.

2 Clutch - adjustment

1 The clutch adjustment is checked by first by setting the clutch pedal height, and then by adjusting the pedal free play.

2 Pull back the carpet from underneath the clutch pedal, and ensure that there are no obstructions between the pedal and floor panel. Measure the distance from the centre of the clutch pedal pad to the floor **(see illustration)**. **Note:** *This measurement can be taken with the carpet in position, so long as the thickness of the carpet is added onto the pedal height measurement.* The pedal height should be within the range given in the *Specifications*.

3 If height adjustment is necessary, loosen the pedal height adjusting bolt locknut located on the pedal bracket. If necessary, unscrew the screws and remove the small shelf from below the steering column to improve access to the bolt. Position the bolt as required, so that the pedal height is correctly set, then tighten the locknut to the specified torque.

4 With the pedal height correctly set, check the pedal free play as follows.

5 Slowly depress the clutch pedal, and measure the distance that the clutch pedal pad travels from the at-rest position to the point where resistance is felt. This is the pedal free play, and should be within the range given in the *Specifications*.

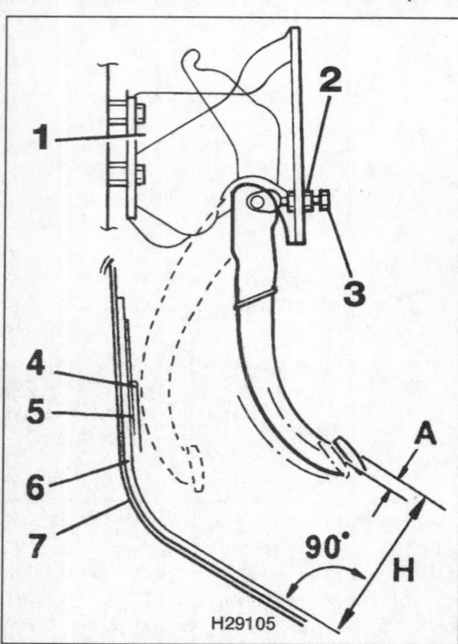

2.2 Clutch pedal height adjustment details

Dimension "H" pedal height measurement
Dimension "A" pedal free play measurement
1 Pedal mounting bracket
2 Locknut
3 Pedal height adjustment bolt
4 Carpet
5 Insulator sheet
6 Insulator sheet
7 Floor panel

6 If free play adjustment is necessary, working within the engine compartment, locate the clutch release lever, which is on top of the transmission. Slacken the clutch cable locknut, and push the release lever rearwards until resistance is felt. Holding the lever in this position, fully tighten the starwheel adjuster, ensuring that the threaded rod does not turn. Now slacken the adjuster by approximately 3 turns, and hold it there while the locknut is retightened. Re-check the free play as described in paragraph 5.

7 With the pedal height and free play correctly adjusted, refit all components removed for access.

3 Clutch cable - removal and refitting

Removal

1 For improved access, remove the battery and battery mounting bracket as described in Chapter 5A. Also remove the air cleaner inlet duct with reference to Chapter 4A.

2 Locate the clutch release lever which is situated on the top of the transmission, then slacken the locknut and knurled adjuster nut situated on the cable end fitting **(see illustrations)**.

3.2a Clutch cable connection to the release lever on top of the transmission

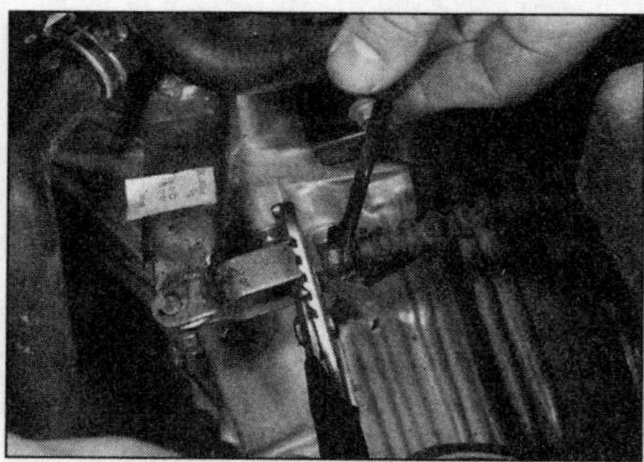

3.2b Loosening the adjustment locknut on the clutch cable

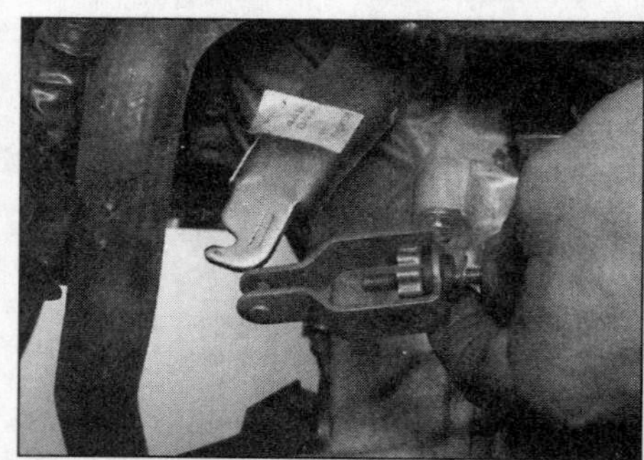

3.3a Releasing the inner cable end fitting from the release lever

3.3b Disconnecting the outer cable fitting from the mounting bracket

3 Release the inner cable end fitting from the release lever, and the outer cable fitting from its mounting bracket on the transmission **(see illustrations)**.

4 Working inside the vehicle, unscrew the screws and remove the small shelf from below the steering column. Unhook the clutch inner cable from the top of the clutch pedal. Note that access to the top of the pedal is very poor, but can only be significantly improved by removing the complete facia.

5 Return to the engine compartment, and withdraw the cable from the engine compartment bulkhead. If necessary, undo the two nuts securing the cable retainer to the bulkhead, and remove the retainer along with the cable **(see illustration)**.

6 Work back along the cable, releasing it from any relevant retaining clips and guides, and noting its correct routing, and remove it from the vehicle.

7 Examine the cable, looking for worn end fittings or a damaged outer casing, and for signs of fraying of the inner wire. Check the cable's operation; the inner wire should move smoothly and easily through the outer casing. Remember that a cable that appears serviceable when tested off the car may well be much heavier in operation, when compressed into its working position. Renew the cable if it shows any signs of excessive wear or damage.

Refitting

8 Apply a little multi-purpose grease to the cable end fittings, then pass the cable through the engine compartment bulkhead. Locate the

3.5 Clutch cable retainer on the bulkhead in the engine compartment

cable retainer on its studs (where removed), and tighten its retaining nuts securely.

9 From inside the vehicle, hook the inner cable onto the clutch pedal, and check that it is securely retained.

10 Work along the cable, ensuring that it is correctly routed, and retained by all the relevant retaining clips and guides. Clip the outer cable into its mounting bracket on the transmission.

11 Hook the inner cable end fitting over the end of the clutch release lever, and adjust the clutch pedal settings as described in Section 2.

4 Clutch pedal - removal and refitting

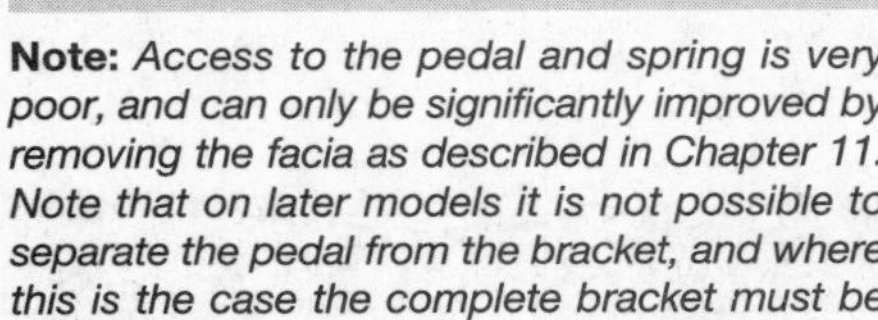

Note: *Access to the pedal and spring is very poor, and can only be significantly improved by removing the facia as described in Chapter 11. Note that on later models it is not possible to separate the pedal from the bracket, and where this is the case the complete bracket must be renewed if the pedal is worn or damaged.*

Removal

1 Working in the engine compartment, loosen the clutch cable locknut and knurled adjuster nut to obtain maximum free play in the cable.

2 Working inside the vehicle, unscrew the screws and remove the small shelf from below the steering column, then unhook the clutch inner cable from the top of the clutch pedal.

3 On 998 cc models, unhook the return spring from the mounting bracket. On 1275 and 1348 cc models note the location of the return spring on the pivot bolt.

4 Unscrew the nut and withdraw the pivot bolt, then lower the clutch pedal from the bracket. On 1275 and 1348 cc models recover the return spring.

5 If necessary, unbolt the clutch pedal bracket from the bulkhead.

6 Clean all components, and renew any that are worn or damaged. Check the bearing surfaces of the pivot bushes and bolt and renew them as necessary.

Refitting

7 If removed, refit the clutch pedal bracket and tighten the mounting nuts/bolts to the specified torque.

8 Press the pivot bushes into the pedal bore, then apply a little multi-purpose grease to the bearing surfaces.

9 Refit the pedal to the bracket and insert the pivot bolt. On 1275 and 1348 cc models make sure the return spring is correctly located. Tighten the nut to the specified torque.

10 On 998 cc models hook the return spring on the pedal and bracket.

11 Reconnect the clutch cable to the pedal, then adjust the clutch pedal settings as described in Section 2.

5 Clutch assembly - removal, inspection and refitting

Warning: Dust created by clutch wear and deposited on the clutch components may contain asbestos, which is a health hazard. DO NOT blow it out with compressed air, or inhale any of it. DO NOT use petrol or petroleum-based solvents to clean off the dust. Brake system cleaner or methylated spirit should be used to flush the dust into a suitable receptacle. After the clutch components are wiped clean with rags, dispose of the contaminated rags and cleaner in a sealed, marked container.

Note: *Although some friction materials may no longer contain asbestos, it is safest to assume that they DO, and to take precautions accordingly*

Removal

1 Unless the complete engine/transmission is to be removed from the car, and separated for major overhaul (see Chapter 2B), the clutch can be reached by removing the transmission as described in Chapter 7A.

2 Before disturbing the clutch, use paint or a marker pen to mark the relationship of the pressure plate assembly to the flywheel **(see illustration)**.

3 Working in a diagonal sequence, slacken the pressure plate bolts by half a turn at a time, until the spring pressure is released and the bolts can be unscrewed by hand.

4 Prise the pressure plate assembly off its locating dowels, and collect the friction plate, noting which way round the friction plate is fitted **(see illustration)**.

Inspection

Note: *Due to the amount of work necessary to remove and refit clutch components, it is usually considered good practice to renew the clutch friction plate, pressure plate assembly and release bearing as a matched set, even if only one of these is actually worn enough to require renewal.*

5 When cleaning clutch components, first read the warning at the beginning of this Section. Remove the dust only as described -

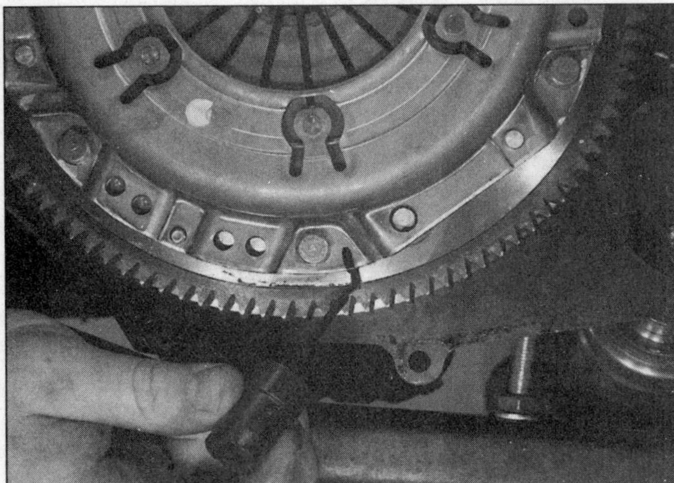

5.2 Using paint to mark the relationship of the pressure plate assembly to the flywheel

5.4 Removing the clutch pressure plate and friction plate

5.16a Checking the centralisation of the friction plate with a steel rule

5.16b Using a clutch-aligning tool to centralise the friction plate

working with dampened cloths will help to keep dust levels to a minimum. Wherever possible, work in a well-ventilated area.

6 Check the friction plate facings for signs of wear, damage or oil contamination. If the friction material is cracked, burnt, scored or damaged, or if it is contaminated with oil or grease (shown by shiny black patches), the friction plate must be renewed. Measure the depth of the rivets below the friction material surface. If the depth of any rivet is equal to, or less than, the service limit given in the *Specifications*, then the friction plate must be renewed.

7 If the friction material is still serviceable, check that the centre boss splines are unworn, that the torsion springs are in good condition and securely fastened, and that all the rivets are tightly fastened. If excessive wear or damage is found, the friction plate must be renewed.

8 If the friction material is fouled with oil, this must be due to an oil leak from the crankshaft left-hand oil seal, from the sump-to-crankcase joint, or from the transmission input shaft seal. Renew the seal or repair the joint, as appropriate, as described in Chapter 2A or 7A before installing the new friction plate.

9 Check the pressure plate assembly for obvious signs of wear or damage; shake it to check for loose rivets, or worn or damaged fulcrum rings. Check that the drive straps securing the pressure plate to the cover do not show signs (such as a deep yellow or blue discoloration) of overheating. If the diaphragm spring is worn or damaged, or if its pressure is in any way suspect, the pressure plate assembly should be renewed.

10 Examine the machined bearing surfaces of the pressure plate and of the flywheel; they should be clean, completely flat, and free from scratches or scoring. If either is discoloured from excessive heat, or shows signs of cracks, it should be renewed; however, minor damage can sometimes be polished away using emery paper.

11 Check that the release bearing rotates smoothly and easily, with no sign of noise or roughness, and that the contact surface itself is smooth and unworn, with no signs of cracks, pitting or scoring. If there is any doubt about its condition, the bearing must be renewed

Refitting

12 On reassembly, ensure that the bearing surfaces of the flywheel and pressure plate are completely clean, smooth, and free from oil or grease. Use solvent to remove any protective grease from new components.

13 Fit the friction plate so that its spring hub assembly faces away from the flywheel; there may also be a marking showing which way round the plate is to be refitted.

14 Refit the pressure plate assembly, aligning the marks made on dismantling if the original pressure plate is re-used, and locating the pressure plate on its locating dowels. Fit the pressure plate bolts, but tighten them only finger-tight so that the friction plate can still be moved.

15 The friction plate must now be centralised, so that when the transmission is refitted, its input shaft will pass through the splines at the centre of the friction plate.

16 Centralisation can be achieved by passing a screwdriver or other long bar through the friction plate, and into the hole in the crankshaft. The friction plate can then be moved around until it is centred on the crankshaft hole - check that the plate is centred by measuring from the diaphragm spring fingers to the centre hub with a steel rule. Alternatively, a clutch-aligning tool can be used to eliminate the guesswork. These can be obtained from most accessory shops, or can be made up from a length of metal rod or wooden dowel which fits closely inside the crankshaft hole, and has insulating tape wound around it to match the diameter of the friction plate splined hole **(see illustrations)**.

17 When the friction plate is centralised, tighten the pressure plate bolts evenly and in a diagonal sequence to the specified torque.

18 Apply a thin smear of high-melting point grease to the splines of the friction plate and the transmission input shaft, also to the release bearing bore and release fork shaft.

19 Refit the transmission as described in Chapter 7A.

6 Clutch release mechanism - removal, inspection and refitting

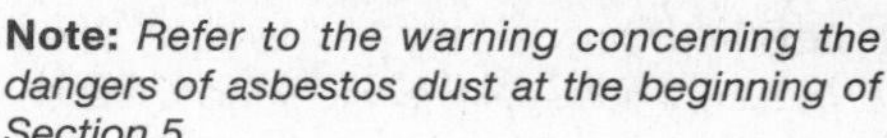

Note: *Refer to the warning concerning the dangers of asbestos dust at the beginning of Section 5*

Removal

1 Unless the complete engine/transmission is to be removed from the car, and separated for major overhaul (see Chapter 2B), the clutch release mechanism can be reached by removing the transmission (see Chapter 7A).

2 Lift the retaining clips, then disengage the release bearing from the fork and **off** the guide tube, and remove it from the transmission. Note the correct fitted direction of each clip on the bearing.

3 Rotate the release fork then, using a hammer and suitable punch, drive out the roll pins securing the release fork to the shaft (drive out the small inner pins first, then remove the outer pins). Discard the roll pins and obtain new ones **(see illustration)**.

4 Note the correct fitted position of the return spring, then withdraw the release lever from the top of the transmission. Recover the release fork and spring from the transmission housing.

6.3 The release fork is secured to the release lever shaft by two dual-roll pins

Inspection

5 Check the release mechanism, renewing any component which is worn or damaged. Carefully check all bearing surfaces and points of contact.

6 Inspect the bush and dust seal fitted to the transmission housing for signs of damage and deterioration, and renew if necessary. The old bush can be tapped out of position, and the new one installed using a hammer and suitable tubular socket.

7 When checking the release bearing itself, it is usually considered worthwhile to renew it as a matter of course, given the amount of work required to gain access to it. Check that the contact surface rotates smoothly and easily, with no sign of noise or roughness. Also check that the surface itself is smooth and unworn, with no signs of cracks, pitting or scoring. If there is any doubt about its condition, the bearing must be renewed.

Refitting

8 Apply a smear of high-melting point grease to the shaft pivot points and the contact surfaces of the release fork.

9 Slide the release lever partially into position in the transmission.

10 Offer up the release fork and spring, aligning them with the lever shaft, and push the release lever fully into position.

11 Align the release fork holes with the holes in the lever shaft, and drive the two new roll pins into position.

12 Fit the retaining clips (where removed) to the release bearing, making sure that they are fitted the correct way round. Apply a smear of high-melting point grease to the contact surfaces of the bearing and input shaft, then slide the bearing along the shaft and clip it onto the release fork **(see illustrations)**.

13 Check the operation of the release mechanism, ensuring that it moves smoothly, and returns easily under the pressure of the return spring, then refit the transmission as described in Chapter 7A.

6.12a Ensure that the retaining clips are correctly fitted to the release bearing . . .

6.12b . . . then fit the bearing to the guide tube, ensuring that the clips engage with the release fork ends

Chapter 7 Part A:
Manual transmission

Contents

Degrees of difficulty

Easy, suitable for novice with little experience 

Fairly easy, suitable for beginner with some experience 

Fairly difficult, suitable for competent DIY mechanic 

Difficult, suitable for experienced DIY mechanic 

Very difficult, suitable for expert DIY or professional

Specifications

General

Type	Manual, five forward speeds and reverse. Synchromesh on all forward speeds
Designation:	
998 cc models	RS5F41A, RS5F30A
1275 and 1348 cc models	RS5F31V, RS5F30A

Gear ratios (typical)

998 cc models:	up to 1998	1998 to 2000	from 2000
1st	3.412 : 1	3.062 : 1	3.333 : 1
2nd	1.958 : 1	1.826 : 1	1.782 : 1
3rd	1.323 : 1	1.207 : 1	1.207 : 1
4th	1.028 : 1	0.927 : 1	0.902 : 1
5th	0.850 : 1	0.756 : 1	0.756 : 1
Reverse	3.385 : 1	3.417 : 1	3.417 : 1
Final drive	4.050 : 1	4.471 : 1	4.471 : 1
1275 cc models:			
1st	3.333 : 1		
2nd	1.955 : 1		
3rd	1.286 : 1		
4th	0.927 : 1		
5th	0.756 : 1		
Reverse	3.417 : 1		
Final drive	3.895 : 1		
1348 cc models:			
1st	3.333 : 1		
2nd	1.782 : 1		
3rd	1.207 : 1		
4th	0.902 : 1		
5th	0.733 : 1		
Reverse	3.417 : 1		
Final drive	3.895 : 1		

Torque wrench settings

	Nm	lbf ft
Gearchange linkage components:		
Selector rod front pivot bolt	16	12
Selector rod rear pivot bolt	21	16
Support rod-to-transmission bolt	41	31
Support rod-to-gear lever retaining plate bolts	11	8
Support rod rear mounting bracket nuts	14	10
Support rod-to-rear mounting bracket nut	26	19
Gaiter retaining plate nuts	5	4
Filler/level plug (where applicable)	30	22
Oil drain plug:		
RS5F41A	15	11
All other types	30	22
Position switch mounting bolt (998 cc models)	3	2
Neutral switch	25	19
Reversing light switch	25	19
Speedometer drive assembly	5	4
Engine-to-transmission bolts:		
998 cc models:		
20 mm in length	19	14
60 mm in length	35	26
1275 and 1348 cc models:		
16 mm in length	19	14
20 mm in length	19	14
70 mm in length	35	26
Left-hand engine/transmission mounting:		
Bracket-to-transmission	69	50
Through-bolt	50	37
Front engine/transmission mounting bolts:		
Mounting bracket-to-engine bolts	69	50
Mounting-to-centre member bolt	49	36
Through-bolt	64	47
Rear engine/transmission mounting:		
Mounting-to-centre member bolts	69	50
Through-bolt	55	41
Mounting bracket retaining bolts	69	50

1 General information

The transmission is contained in a cast-aluminium alloy casing bolted to the engine's left-hand end, and consists of the gearbox and final drive differential, often called a transaxle.

Drive is transmitted from the crankshaft via the clutch to the input shaft, which has a splined extension to accept the clutch friction plate, and rotates in sealed ball-bearings. From the input shaft, drive is transmitted to the output shaft, which rotates in a roller bearing at its right-hand end, and a sealed ball-bearing at its left-hand end. From the output shaft, the drive is transmitted to the differential crownwheel, which rotates with the differential case and planetary gears, thus driving the sun gears and driveshafts. The rotation of the planetary gears on their shaft allows the inner roadwheel to rotate at a slower speed than the outer roadwheel when the car is cornering.

The input and output shafts are arranged side by side, parallel to the crankshaft and driveshafts, so that their gear pinion teeth are in constant mesh. In the neutral position, the output shaft gear pinions rotate freely, so that drive cannot be transmitted to the crownwheel.

Gear selection is via a floor-mounted lever and selector rod mechanism. The selector rod causes the appropriate selector fork to move its respective synchro-sleeve along the shaft, to lock the gear pinion to the synchro-hub. Since the synchro-hubs are splined to the output shaft, this locks the pinion to the shaft so that drive can be transmitted. To ensure that gearchanging can be made quickly and quietly, a synchromesh system is fitted to all forward gears, consisting of baulk rings and spring-loaded fingers, as well as the gear pinions and synchro-hubs; the synchromesh cones are formed on the mating faces of the baulk rings and gear pinions.

2 Gearchange linkage - general information

If a stiff, sloppy or imprecise gearchange leads you to suspect that a fault exists within the linkage, first remove and dismantle it completely. Check it for wear or damage as described in Section 3, then reassemble it, applying a smear of multi-purpose grease to all bearing surfaces.

If this does not cure the fault, the car should be examined by an expert, as the fault must lie within the transmission itself. No adjustment of the linkage is possible.

3 Gearchange linkage - removal and refitting

Removal

1 Remove the centre console as described in Chapter 11.

2 Firmly apply the handbrake, then jack up the front of the vehicle and support it on axle stands (see "*Jacking and vehicle support*").

3 For improved access to the bottom of the gear lever, either remove the complete exhaust system or just the central section of the exhaust with reference to Chapter 4B.

4 Unbolt the front heat shield from the underbody for access to the gearchange linkage **(see illustrations)**.

5 Using pliers, unhook the spring securing the rear of the selector rod to the support rod.

6 Unscrew the nuts, and withdraw the pivot bolts securing the selector rod to the gear lever and transmission. Withdraw the selector rod from under the vehicle.

7 Unscrew the nut and washer securing the support rod to the rear engine mounting, but leave the mounting bolt in position. Unscrew the nuts securing the rear of the support rod and the support rod bracket to the underside of the vehicle, and manoeuvre the rod and bracket assembly out of position. If

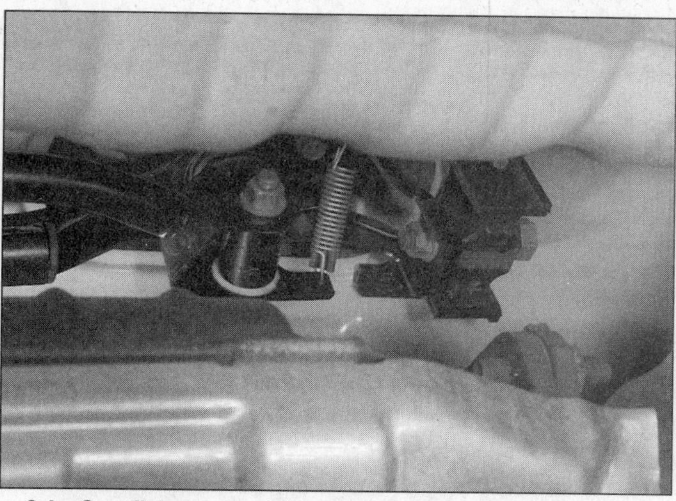
3.4a Gear linkage attachment to the bottom of the gear lever (left-hand side)

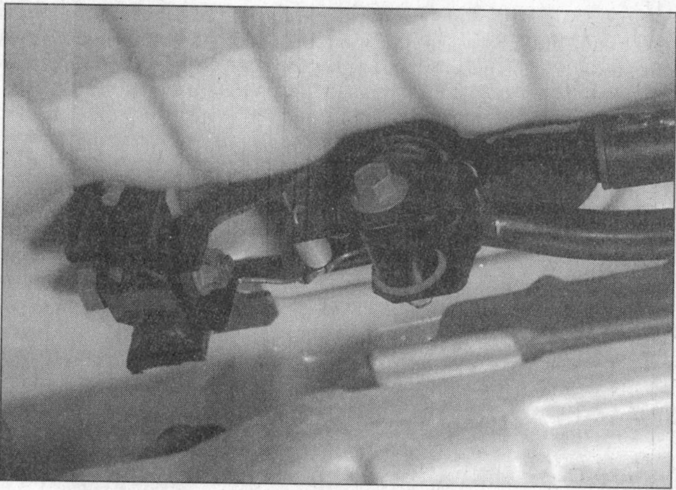
3.4b Gear linkage attachment to the bottom of the gear lever (right-hand side)

necessary, undo the retaining nut, and separate the support rod and mounting bracket.

8 From inside the vehicle, lift out the gear lever and retaining plate, and recover the small rubber gaiter from the base of the lever.

9 If necessary, unscrew the retaining nuts, then lift off the retaining plate and remove the main gear lever gaiter from the vehicle.

10 Inspect all the linkage components for signs of wear or damage, paying particular attention to the pivot bushes and selector rod universal joint, and renew worn components as necessary. Renew the rubber gaiters if they are split or badly perished.

Refitting

11 Refitting is a reversal of the removal procedure, applying a smear of multi-purpose grease to the gear lever pivot ball and bushes, and to the selector rod rear pivot bolt. Tighten all the linkage nuts and bolts to their specified torque settings.

4 Oil seals - renewal

Driveshaft oil seal

1 Chock the rear wheels of the car, firmly apply the handbrake, then jack up the front of the car and support it on axle stands (see "*Jacking and vehicle support*"). Remove the appropriate front wheel.

2 Position a suitable container beneath the drain plug located on the bottom of the transmission. Unscrew the plug and allow the oil to drain. On completion, clean and refit the plug and tighten it to the specified torque (the manufacturers recommend applying sealant to the threads of the plug before inserting it).

3 Refer to Chapter 8 and disconnect the inner end of the driveshaft from the transmission. There is no need to unscrew the driveshaft retaining nut as the driveshaft can be left secured to the hub. Support the driveshaft, to avoid placing any strain on the joints or gaiters.

4 Carefully prise the oil seal out of the transmission using a large flat-bladed screwdriver **(see illustration)**.

5 Remove all traces of dirt from the area around the oil seal aperture, then apply a smear of grease to the outer lip of the new oil seal, and locate it in its aperture. Drive the seal squarely into position until it seats against its locating shoulder, using a suitable tubular drift (such as a socket) which bears only on the hard outer edge of the seal.

6 Refit the driveshaft with reference to Chapter 8, then refit the wheel and lower the vehicle to the ground.

7 Fill the transmission with the specified type and amount of oil with reference to Chapter 1.

Input shaft oil seal

8 To renew the input shaft seal, the transmission must be dismantled. This task should therefore be entrusted to a Nissan dealer.

Selector shaft oil seal

9 Chock the rear wheels of the car, firmly apply the handbrake, then jack up the front of the car and support it on axle stands (see "*Jacking and vehicle support*"). Drain the transmission oil as described in paragraph 2 of this Section, or be prepared for some oil loss as the seal is removed.

10 Slide back the transmission selector rod rubber gaiter, to reveal the roll pin **(see illustration)**.

11 Using a hammer and suitable punch, tap out the roll pin (tap out the small inner pin first, followed by the larger outer pin) then free the selector rod from the transmission. Discard the roll pin; a new one should be used on refitting.

12 Remove the rubber gaiter, then carefully lever the selector shaft oil seal out of position and slide it off the shaft.

13 Before fitting a new seal, check the selector shaft's seal rubbing surface for signs of burrs, scratches or other damage which may have caused the seal to fail in the first place. It may be possible to polish away minor faults of this sort using fine abrasive paper, but more serious defects will require the renewal of the selector shaft.

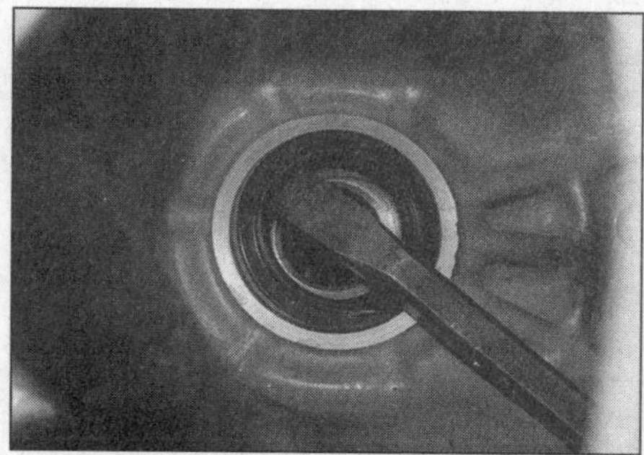
4.4 Using a large flat-bladed screwdriver to lever out the driveshaft oil seal

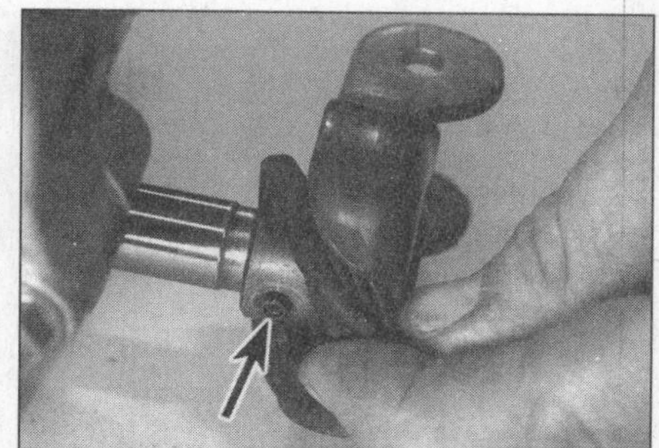
4.10 The selector shaft end fitting is retained by a dual-roll pin

14 Apply a smear of grease to the new seal's outer edge and sealing lip, then carefully slide the seal along the selector rod. Press the seal fully into position in the transmission housing.
15 Refit the rubber gaiter, making sure that it is correctly seated on the seal.
16 Engage the selector rod with the shaft. Align the pin holes, and tap the new roll pins into position.
17 Lower the vehicle to the ground, and top-up/refill (as applicable) the transmission oil as described in Chapter 1.

5 Position switch - testing, removal and refitting

Testing

1 A position switch is fitted to the rear of the transmission on 998 cc models up to March 1998. The switch forms part of the engine management system (see Chapter 4A) and serves the purpose of both a neutral switch and reversing light switch.
2 To test the switch, trace the wiring back from the switch to its connector, which is on top of the transmission. Disconnect the wiring connector and note the terminal positions **(see illustration)**.
3 Connect an ohmmeter between terminals 1 and 2 and switch on the ignition. Check that there is continuity between the terminals only when the transmission is in neutral.
4 Connect the ohmmeter between terminals 3 and 4 and check that there is continuity only when the transmission is in reverse.
5 If the switch does not function correctly, and there are no obvious breaks or other damage to the wires, the switch is faulty and must be renewed.

Removal

6 Chock the rear wheels of the car, firmly apply the handbrake, then jack up the front of the car and support it on axle stands (see "*Jacking and vehicle support*"). Drain the transmission oil as described in Section 4, paragraph 2.
7 Trace the switch wiring back to its connector, and disconnect it from the main harness.

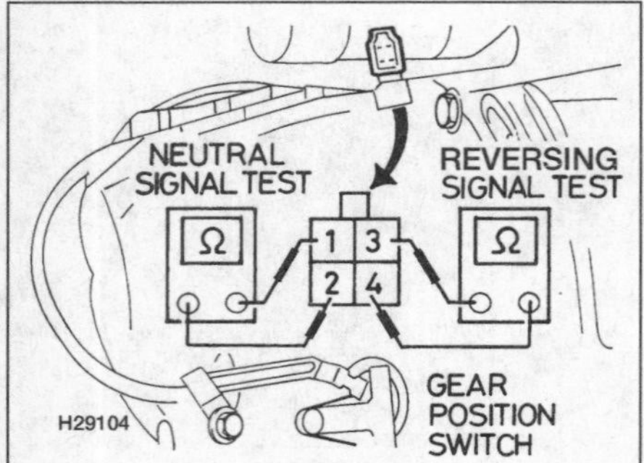

5.2 Position switch and terminal locations

8 Unscrew the mounting bolt and remove the retaining plate, then withdraw the position switch from the transmission and recover the O-ring seal.
9 Unscrew the wiring support bolts and withdraw the switch. Cover the transmission housing aperture to prevent dust and dirt entry.

Refitting

10 Clean the mating surfaces of the switch and housing, then refit the switch together with a new O-ring seal.
11 Refit the retaining plate, then apply sealant to the threads of the mounting bolt, insert it, and tighten to the specified torque.
12 Reposition the wiring supports and tighten the bolts.
13 Reconnect the wiring, then lower the vehicle to the ground.
14 Refill the transmission with oil with reference to Chapter 1.

6 Neutral switch - testing, removal and refitting

Testing

1 A neutral switch is fitted to the rear of the transmission (except on 998 cc models up to March 1998). The switch forms part of the engine management system (see Chapter 4A).
2 To test the switch, trace the wiring back from the switch to its connector, which is on top of the transmission. Disconnect the wiring connector, and use an ohmmeter or a battery-and-bulb test circuit to check that there is continuity between the switch terminals only when the transmission is in neutral. If this is not the case, and there are no obvious breaks or other damage to the wires, the switch is faulty and must be renewed.

Removal

3 Chock the rear wheels of the car, firmly apply the handbrake, then jack up the front of the car and support it on axle stands (see "*Jacking and vehicle support*").
4 Drain the transmission oil as described in Section 4, paragraph 2, or be prepared for some oil loss as the switch is removed.
5 Trace the switch wiring back to its connector, and disconnect it from the main harness.
6 Unscrew the switch from the transmission, and remove it. Plug the transmission housing aperture to prevent dust and dirt entry.

Refitting

7 Clean the threads of the switch, and apply a little sealant to them.
8 Insert the switch and tighten to the specified torque.
9 Reconnect the wiring, then lower the vehicle to the ground.
10 Top-up/refill the transmission oil (as applicable) with reference to Chapter 1.

7 Reversing light switch - testing, removal and refitting

Testing

1 A reversing light switch is fitted to the left-hand end of the transmission (except on 998 cc models up to March 1998).
2 To test the switch, trace the wiring back from the switch to its connector, which is on top of the transmission. Disconnect the wiring connector, and use an ohmmeter or a battery-and-bulb test circuit to check that there is continuity between the switch terminals only when reverse gear is selected. If this is not the case, and there are no obvious breaks or other damage to the wires, the switch is faulty and must be renewed.

Removal

3 Chock the rear wheels of the car, firmly apply the handbrake, then jack up the front of the car and support it on axle stands (see "*Jacking and vehicle support*").
4 Drain the transmission oil as described in Section 4, paragraph 2, or be prepared for some oil loss as the switch is removed.
5 Trace the switch wiring back to its connector, and disconnect it from the main harness.
6 Unscrew the switch from the transmission, and remove it. Plug the transmission housing aperture to minimise oil loss, and to prevent dirt entry.

Refitting

7 Remove all traces of sealant from the threads of the switch, and apply a little sealant to them.
8 Remove the plug from the switch aperture in the transmission, and screw the switch into position.
9 Tighten the switch to the specified torque, then reconnect the wiring connector and check the operation of the circuit.
10 Lower the vehicle to the ground, and top-up/refill the transmission oil (as applicable) with reference to Chapter 1.

8 Speedometer drive - removal and refitting

Removal

1 Chock the rear wheels, apply the handbrake, then jack up the front of the car and support it on axle stands (see '*Jacking and vehicle support*'). The speedometer drive is at the rear of the transmission housing, next to the right-hand driveshaft.
2 On models up to March 1998, unscrew the knurled retaining ring, and disconnect the speedometer cable from the speedometer drive. On models from March 1998 onwards, disconnect the wiring plug from the speedometer drive.

8.3a Unscrew the retaining bolt . . .

8.3b . . . and withdraw the speedometer drive

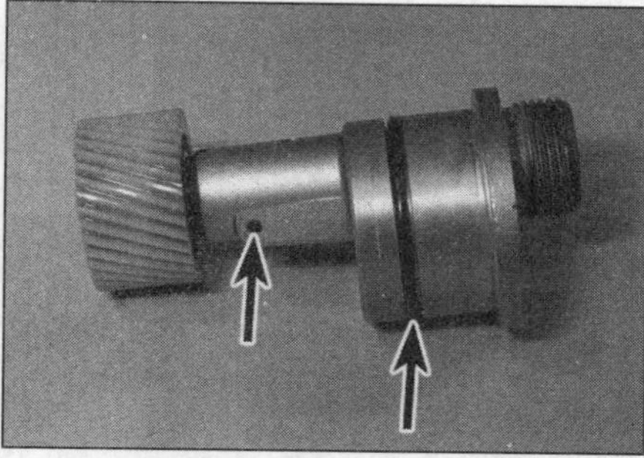
8.4 Pinion retaining roll pin and housing O-ring - pre-1998 model

3 Unscrew the retaining bolt, and withdraw the speedometer drive and pinion assembly from the transmission housing, along with its O-ring **(see illustrations)**.

4 On models up to March 1998, if necessary, tap out the roll pin, then slide the pinion out of the housing and recover the thrustwasher and oil seal **(see illustration)**. The speedometer drive fitted to models from March 1998 onwards cannot be dismantled.

5 Examine all components for signs of damage, and renew if necessary. Renew the housing O-ring as a matter of course. Note that the thrustwasher on early models is available in various thicknesses - measure the thickness of the original, and quote this when ordering a new one.

6 If the pinion is worn or damaged, also examine the drive gear in the transmission housing for signs of wear or damage. To renew the drive pinion, the transmission must be dismantled and the differential gear removed. This task should therefore be entrusted to a Nissan dealer.

Refitting

7 If the drive was dismantled, press the new oil seal into the housing. Apply a smear of multi-purpose grease to the driven pinion shaft, and slide on the thrustwasher. Insert the driven pinion into the housing, and secure it in position with the roll pin.

8 Fit a new O-ring to the speedometer drive, then refit it to the transmission and tighten the retaining bolt.

9 Reconnect the speedometer cable and tighten the knurled retaining ring, or reconnect the wiring plug, as applicable. Lower the vehicle to the ground.

9 Manual transmission - removal and refitting

Removal

1 Chock the rear wheels then apply the handbrake, jack up the front of the vehicle and support on axle stands (see "*Jacking and vehicle support*"). Remove both front wheels. For additional working room remove the bonnet as described in Chapter 11.

2 Position a suitable container beneath the drain plug located on the bottom of the transmission **(see illustration)**. Unscrew the plug and allow the oil to drain. On completion, clean and refit the plug and tighten it to the specified torque (Nissan recommend applying suitable sealant to the threads of the plug before fitting it).

3 Remove the battery and mounting bracket as described in Chapter 5A. This procedure will include removal of the relay boxes located on the left-hand side of the cylinder head.

4 Remove the air cleaner air duct as described in Chapter 4A **(see illustrations)**. It is not necessary to remove the air cleaner from the throttle housing.

5 Loosen the clutch cable locknut and knurled adjuster nut, then free the cable end fitting from the release lever, and the outer cable fitting from its mounting bracket. Place the cable to one side.

6 Unscrew the knurled retaining ring, and disconnect the speedometer cable from the transmission **(see illustration)**. On models from March 1998 onwards, disconnect the speedometer drive wiring plug.

7 Remove the starter motor as described in Chapter 5A.

8 Disconnect the wiring from the position switch or the reversing light switch and neutral switch **(see illustration)**.

9 Disconnect the earth lead from the terminal

9.2 Transmission oil drain plug (arrowed)

9.4a Air inlet duct front mounting screw

9.4b Removing the air inlet duct

9.6 Speedometer cable knurled retaining ring

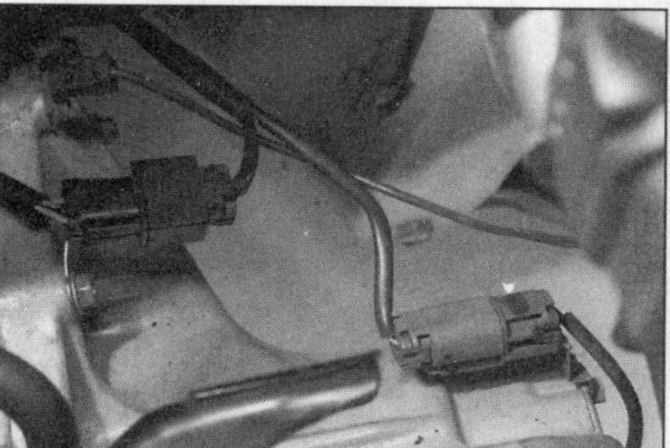
9.8 Wiring connectors for reversing light switch and neutral switch

9.10a Gearchange linkage attachment to the transmission

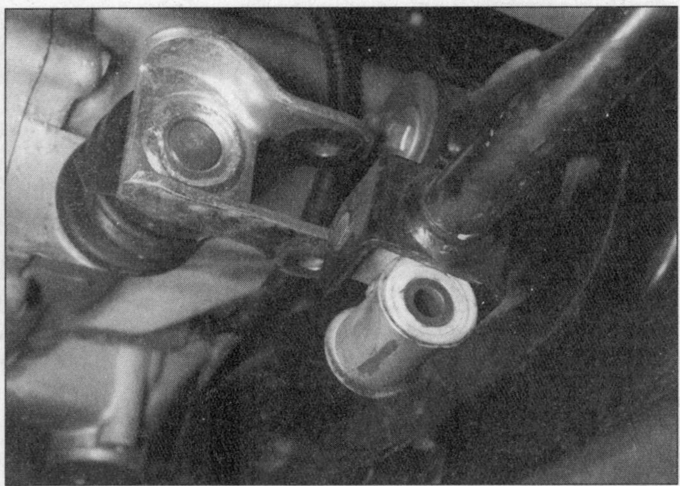
9.10b Gearchange linkage disconnected from the transmission

9.12a Unbolting the exhaust front pipe from the exhaust manifold

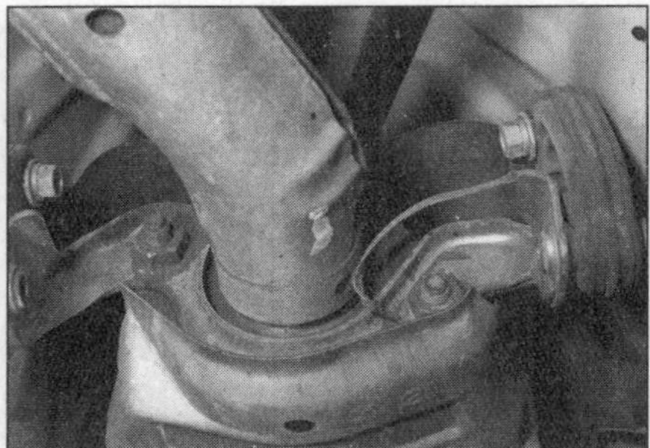
9.12b Exhaust front pipe to intermediate section joint

9.12c Temporarily re-attach the exhaust intermediate section to the mounting to support it

on top of the transmission housing. Free the wiring from any relevant retaining clips, and position it clear of the transmission.

10 Unscrew the nut and pivot bolt securing the gearchange linkage selector rod to the transmission, and position the rod to one side **(see illustrations)**.

11 Unscrew the nut and washer securing the support rod to the rear engine mounting. Remove the support rod from the mounting.

12 Remove the exhaust front pipe as described in Chapter 4A. Support the rear exhaust system on an axle stand or temporarily re-attach it to the front mounting **(see illustrations)**.

13 Remove the splash guard from under the left-hand wheel arch for access to the transmission **(see illustration)**.

14 Remove the left-hand driveshaft and hub carrier as described in Chapters 8 and 10.

15 Remove the right-hand brake caliper and mounting bracket as described in Chapter 9, but leave the hydraulic brake hose connected. Tie the caliper to the suspension coil spring. Also detach the steering track rod from the hub carrier with reference to Chapter 10.

16 Unscrew the bolts securing the right-hand strut to the hub carrier noting that the bolt heads face to the rear. Lever the right-hand driveshaft from the transmission while pulling the hub carrier outwards. Take care not to strain the hydraulic brake hoses.

17 The engine must now be supported before removal of the rear engine mounting and bracket. Use a trolley jack and block of wood to do this, or alternatively make up a length of threaded rod with a nut which can be inserted through the lower centre member to support the rear of the engine **(see illustration)**. Use a small metal plate on the base of the crankcase to prevent damage to it.

18 Place a jack and block of wood beneath the transmission, and raise the jack to take the weight of the transmission.

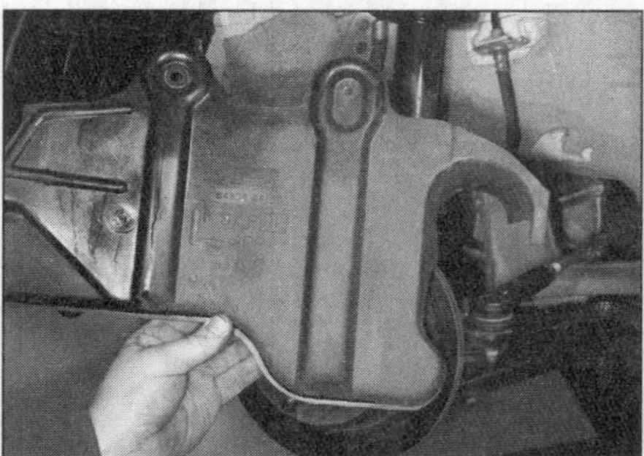
9.13 Removing the splash guard

9.17 Home-made support bar for the engine while the transmission is being removed

9.19 Removing the rear engine mounting bracket

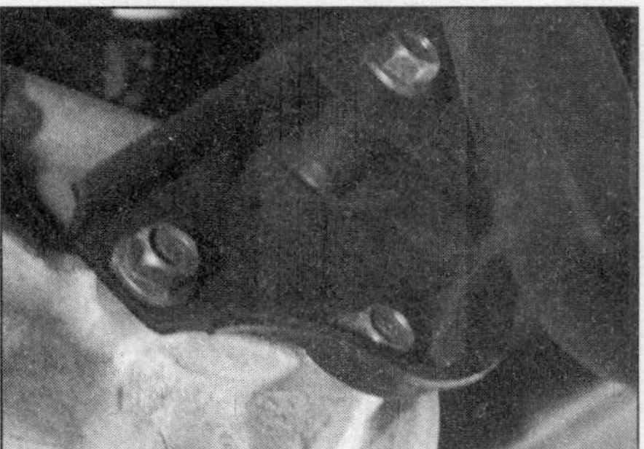
9.20 Transmission left-hand mounting bracket

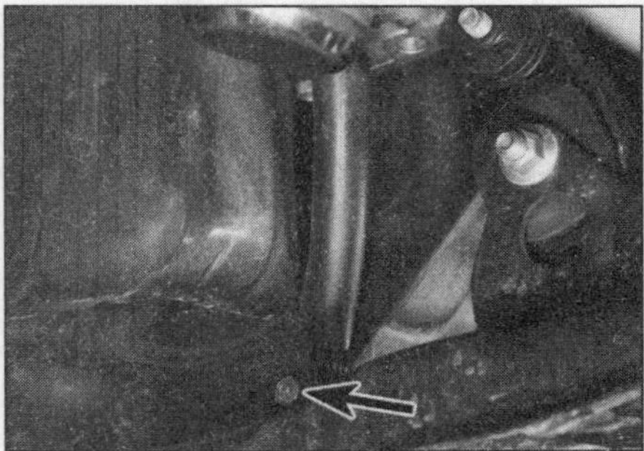
9.21a Transmission stay bar lower mounting bolt . . .

9.21b . . . and upper mounting bolt

9.24 Lowering the transmission from the engine

19 Unbolt and remove the rear engine mounting bracket with reference to Chapter 2A **(see illustration)**.

20 Unscrew and remove the through-bolt, then undo the three bolts and remove the left-hand mounting from the transmission **(see illustration)**. Recover the rubbers from each side of the mounting bracket and, if necessary, unbolt the mounting bracket from the vehicle body.

21 Unscrew and remove the bolts securing the transmission to the engine. Note the correct fitted positions of each bolt (and the relevant brackets) as they are removed, to use as a reference on refitting. Also unscrew the bolts securing the two stay bars and engine rear cover to the transmission lower bellhousing. If necessary the stay bars can be unbolted from the crankcase **(see illustrations)**.

22 Make a final check that all necessary components have been disconnected, and are positioned clear of the transmission so that they will not hinder the removal procedure.

23 Move the trolley jack and transmission to the left to free it from its locating dowels. Keep the transmission fully supported until the input shaft is free of the engine.

24 Once the transmission is free, lower the jack and manoeuvre the unit out from under the car **(see illustration)**.

Refitting

25 The transmission is refitted by a reversal of the removal procedure, bearing in mind the following points:

a) Apply a little high-melting point grease to the splines of the transmission input shaft. Do not apply too much, otherwise there is a possibility of the grease contaminating the clutch friction plate.

b) Ensure that the locating dowels are correctly positioned in the rear of the engine.

c) Insert the transmission-to-engine bolts into their original locations, as noted on removal. Tighten all nuts and bolts to the specified torque.

d) Renew the driveshaft oil seals as described in Section 4.

e) On completion, refill the transmission with the specified type and quantity of lubricant with reference to Chapter 1.

10 Manual transmission overhaul - general information

Overhauling a manual transmission is a difficult and involved job for the DIY home mechanic. In addition to dismantling and reassembling many small parts, clearances must be precisely measured and, if necessary, changed by selecting shims and spacers. Internal transmission components are also often difficult to obtain, and in many instances, extremely expensive. Because of this, if the transmission develops a fault or becomes noisy, the best course of action is to have the unit overhauled by a specialist repairer, or to obtain an exchange reconditioned unit.

Nevertheless, it is not impossible for the more experienced mechanic to overhaul the transmission, if the special tools are available, and the job is done in a deliberate step-by-step manner so that nothing is overlooked.

The tools necessary for an overhaul include internal and external circlip pliers, bearing pullers, a slide hammer, a set of pin punches, a dial test indicator, and possibly a hydraulic press. In addition, a large, sturdy workbench and a vice will be required.

During dismantling of the transmission, make careful notes of how each component is fitted, to make reassembly easier and accurate.

Before dismantling the transmission, it will help if you have some idea which area is malfunctioning. Certain problems can be closely related to specific areas in the transmission, which can make component examination and replacement easier. Refer to the *"Fault finding"* Section at the rear of this manual for more information.

Chapter 7 Part B: Automatic transmission

Contents

Degrees of difficulty

Easy, suitable for novice with little experience	**Fairly easy,** suitable for beginner with some experience	**Fairly difficult,** suitable for competent DIY mechanic	**Difficult,** suitable for experienced DIY mechanic	**Very difficult,** suitable for expert DIY or professional

Specifications

General

Type	NCVT (Nissan Continuously Variable Transmission)
Designation:	
Up to 2000	RE0F05A
From 2000	RE0F21A
Ratios (at transmission):	
Lowest	2.504
Highest	0.498
Reverse:	
RE0F05A	2.476
RE0F21A	1.931:1
Final drive:	
RE0F05A:	
998 cc models	6.140:1
1275 cc models	5.247:1
RE0F21A:	
998 cc models	6.305:1
1348 cc models	5.246:1
Kickdown cable stroke	49.2 mm to 53.2 mm

Lubrication

Lubricant type	See *Lubricants and fluids* on page 0•16
Lubricant capacity:	
RE0F05A:	
Including oil cooler	4.2 litres
Excluding oil cooler	3.2 litres
RE0F21A	5.0 litres

Torque wrench settings	Nm	lbf ft
Electromagnetic clutch to driveplate	34	25
Electromagnetic clutch brush holder	7	5
Engine-to-transmission bolts (measured in length):		
20 mm	19	14
25 mm	19	14
50 and 70 mm	35	26
Fluid sump	6	4
Kickdown cable to transmission	5	4
Selector cable to rod adjustment nuts	14	10
Oil pump	10	7
Inhibitor switch	39	29
Drain plug:		
RE0F05A	25	19
RE0F21A	45	34

1 General information

General description

The automatic transmission fitted is electronic and is designated NCVT (Nissan Continuously Variable Transmission). The main components of the transmission are an electromagnetic clutch, a variable-ratio coupling, a final drive/differential unit, and the associated control mechanisms **(see illustration)**.

The variable-ratio coupling consists of two pulleys and a flexible metal drivebelt. The effective diameter of the two pulleys can be varied to provide different transmission ratios between them.

During normal driving, the transmission automatically selects the ratio giving the best compromise between economy and speed. When the driver depresses the accelerator pedal to the floor, a 'kickdown' effect is provided, and the transmission selects a lower ratio for improved acceleration.

The gear selector control resembles that fitted to conventional automatic transmissions. The control positions are as follows:

P (Parking) *The transmission is mechanically locked by the engagement of a pawl with a toothed segment on the driven pulley. Always use this position together with the handbrake.*
R (Reverse) *Reverse gear is engaged.*
N (Neutral) *The transmission is in neutral.*
D (Drive) *Normal driving position. Transmission ratio is varied automatically to suit prevailing speed and load.*
Ds (Low) *Prevents the transmission moving into high ratios. Provides maximum acceleration and maximum engine braking.*

The engine can only be started in positions 'P' and 'N'.

The electromagnetic clutch consists of a driving element bolted to the engine driveplate, and a driven element splined to the transmission input shaft. The degree of coupling between the two elements is determined by the intensity of a magnetic field generated by a current passing through windings in the driven element. The magnetic field acts on a layer of metallic powder between the driving and driven elements. When no magnetic field is present, the powder is loose and the two elements are effectively disconnected. As the magnetic field increases, the powder sticks together, and the coupling between the elements becomes increasingly rigid.

Selection of reverse, neutral and forward gears is by the movement of a sliding sleeve on a hub keyed to the drive pulley shaft. In forward gear, the sleeve engages with the gear on the end of the input shaft, which is then locked to the drive pulley shaft. When reverse is selected, the sleeve engages with reverse driven gear, which is in constant mesh with an idler gear driven by transfer gears from the input shaft gear. In neutral, the sleeve is in an intermediate position, and the two shafts are not connected.

The drive pulley and driven pulley both consist of fixed and moving halves. The movement of the drive pulley halves is controlled hydraulically, while the driven pulley halves move under the influence of a spring and the tension exerted by the drivebelt. As the drive pulley opens, the driven pulley closes, and vice-versa. In this way, the transmission ratio between the two pulleys can be varied. The ratios are continuously variable between preset limits; the difference between the lowest and highest ratios available is approximately 5:1.

Hydraulic pressure is generated by a gear-type pump inside the transmission. The pump driveshaft runs inside the input and drive pulley shafts, and is splined to the centre of the engine driveplate. This means that hydraulic pressure is only generated when the engine is running, which is why a car with this type of transmission cannot be push- or tow-started.

Application of hydraulic pressure to the pulley halves is via a control unit, which receives information on accelerator pedal position, transmission selector lever position, transmission ratio currently in use, and drive pulley speed. From this information, the control unit determines whether, and in which direction, to change the pulley ratios.

When reverse gear is selected, the control unit keeps the transmission in low ratio. If this were not the case, it would, in theory, be possible to drive as fast in reverse as in forward gear.

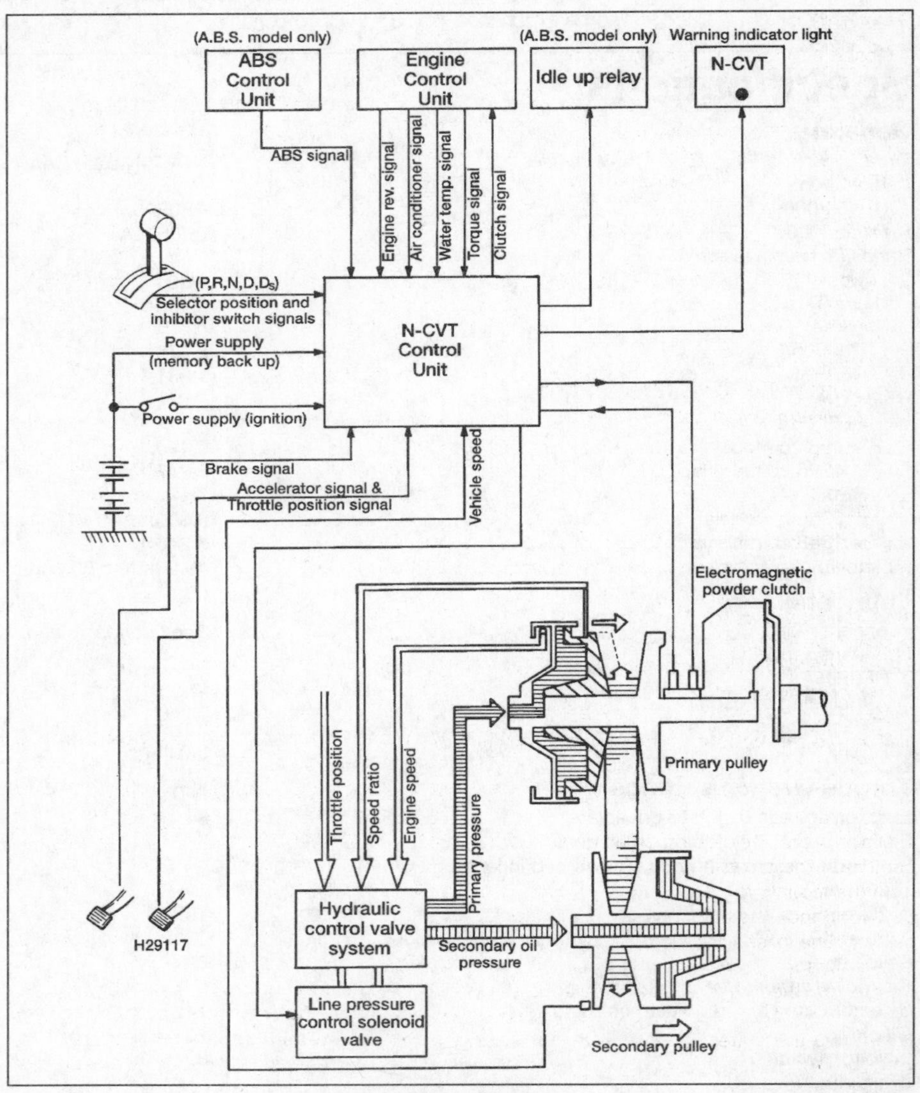

1.1 NCVT control system

An electronic control unit supplies the current to energise the clutch. The control unit receives signals concerning engine speed, road speed, accelerator pedal position, and gear selector position. Sensors include the following.

a) Engine rpm sensor (from the injection/ignition control unit)
b) Accelerator pedal switch
c) Brake pedal sensor
d) Throttle valve position sensor
e) Selector lever position sensor
f) Vehicle speed sensor
g) Coolant temperature sensor
h) Air conditioning sensor
i) ABS sensor

The final drive/differential unit is conventional. Drive from the driven pulley is transmitted to the differential by an intermediate reduction gear.

The NCVT incorporates a warning light which illuminates when a fault occurs.

Precautions

Observe the following precautions to avoid damage to the automatic transmission:

a) Do not attempt to start the engine by pushing or towing the car.
b) Never tow the car with the front wheels on the ground. The automatic transmission oil pump is driven by the engine and serious internal damage could occur.
c) Only engage 'P' or 'R' when the vehicle is stationary.

2 Automatic transmission - removal and refitting

Removal

1 Select a solid, level surface to park the vehicle on. Give yourself enough space to move around it easily. Apply the handbrake then jack up the front of the vehicle and support on axle stands (see *"Jacking and vehicle support"*). Remove both front wheels.

2 Remove the air cleaner assembly and air inlet duct as described in Chapter 4A.

3 Remove the battery and mounting tray as described in Chapter 5. Also unbolt and remove the fuse/relay box from the engine compartment.

4 Disconnect the kickdown cable at the sector on the throttle housing and detach it from the mounting.

5 Disconnect the wiring from the inhibitor switch, line pressure solenoid and vehicle speed sensor.

6 Unscrew the knurled collar and disconnect the speedometer cable from the transmission.

7 Remove the cotter pin and disconnect the inner selector cable from the lever on top of the transmission. Recover the washers and bush.

8 Pull out the retaining plate and remove the outer selector cable from the bracket. Position the cable to one side.

9 Drain the automatic transmission fluid as described in Chapter 1.

10 If necessary remove the front anti-roll bar as described in Chapter 10.

11 Refer to Chapter 10 and disconnect the front suspension lower arms from the struts.

12 Using a lever, prise each driveshaft inner joint from the transmission while pulling the strut outwards. Tie the struts and driveshafts to one side.

13 Place a jack with interposed block of wood beneath the engine, to take the weight of the engine. Alternatively, attach a hoist or support bar to the engine.

14 Unbolt the centre member from the underbody and from the front and rear engine mountings, and remove it from under the vehicle.

15 Place a jack and block of wood beneath the transmission, and raise the jack to take the weight of the transmission.

16 Loosen the clips and disconnect the fluid cooler hoses from the bottom of the radiator. Be prepared for some loss of fluid by placing a suitable container beneath the radiator.

17 Unscrew and remove the through-bolt, then undo the three bolts and remove the left-hand mounting from the transmission. Recover the rubbers from each side of the mounting bracket and, if necessary, unbolt the mounting bracket from the vehicle body.

18 Remove the electromagnetic clutch brush holder as described in Section 3.

19 Unbolt and remove the lower driveplate cover from the transmission.

20 Hold the driveplate stationary using a wide-blade screwdriver engaged with the starter ring gear, then unscrew the bolts securing the electromagnetic clutch housing to the driveplate. There are 4 bolts and it will be necessary to turn the engine to position the bolts in the access aperture.

21 Unbolt and remove the starter motor with reference to Chapter 5A.

22 Unscrew and remove the bolts securing the automatic transmission to the engine, noting the location of the fluid cooler brackets. Note the location of each bolt as they are of different lengths.

23 Move the transmission away from the engine making sure that the electromagnetic clutch housing remains in the transmission bellhousing and the oil pump driveshaft is disconnected from the rear of the crankshaft. Lower the transmission and remove it from under the vehicle.

Warning: Keep the transmission supported adequately on the jack head until the transmission is safely on the ground. Do not allow the electromagnetic clutch housing to slide off the input shaft, otherwise the carbon brushes in the brush holder may be damaged.

Refitting

24 Refitting is a reversal of the removal procedure, but note the following points.

a) Check that the electromagnetic clutch housing and oil pump shaft are fully engaged (refer to Section 3).
b) Tighten all nuts and bolts to the specified torque.
c) Fill the transmission with fluid with reference to Chapter 1.
d) If necessary, adjust the selector cable as described in Section 8.

3 Electromagnetic clutch brush holder - removal, inspection and refitting

Removal

1 Remove the battery and battery tray as described in Chapter 5A.

2 Disconnect the wiring connector for the brushes.

3 Unscrew the mounting bolts and withdraw the brush holder from the transmission. Take care not to break the carbon brushes.

Inspection

4 Inspect the brushes. If they are worn down to the limit lines, or if they do not move smoothly in their holders, renew the brush holder assembly **(see illustration)**. **Note:** *Be careful not to damage the brush supply leads when checking the brushes for free movement.* It is not possible to renew the brushes separately.

Refitting

5 Refitting is a reversal of removal, but clean the mounting contact surfaces and tighten the mounting bolts as follows. First hand-tighten both bolts, then tighten the lower bolt to the specified torque followed by the upper bolt.

4 Electromagnetic clutch housing - removal, inspection and refitting

Removal

1 Remove the transmission as described in Section 2.

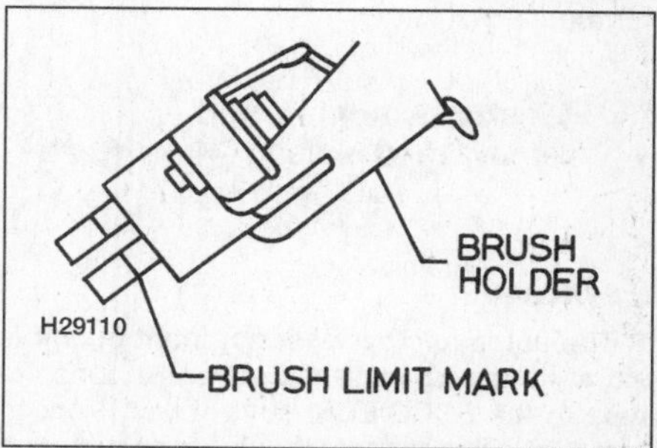

3.4 Electromagnetic clutch brush holder

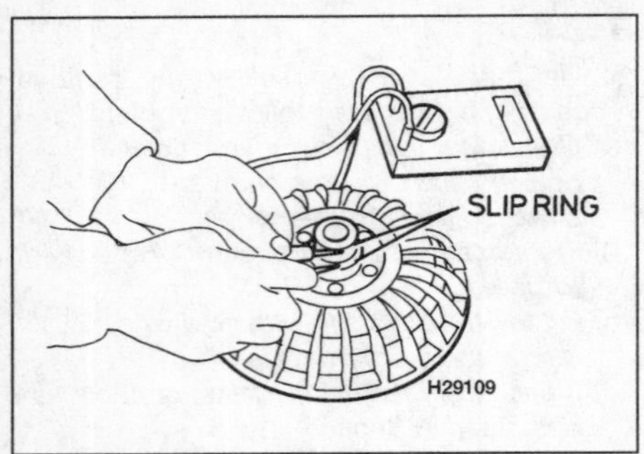

4.5 Checking the electromagnetic clutch windings with an ohmmeter

2 Slide the electromagnetic clutch housing from the transmission input shaft splines. **Note:** *The housing should be stored with the domed side facing upwards to prevent damage to the slip rings.*

Inspection

3 Turn the driven element by means of the slip rings, and check that the bearing is not noisy or rough.

4 Inspect the slip rings for wear or other damage. Clean them if necessary using fuel and a clean rag.

5 Check the resistance of the clutch windings, using an ohmmeter connected across the slip rings. The resistance at 20°C should be 2 to 4 ohms **(see illustration)**.

6 Check the insulation of the windings, using an ohmmeter connected between either slip ring and the body of the clutch. Resistance should be infinity.

7 If the clutch fails any of the checks, renew it. Apart from the brush holder, individual spares are not available.

Refitting

8 Refitting is a reversal of removal but check first that the oil pump driveshaft is correctly engaged with the oil pump. **Do not** apply grease to the input and oil pump shaft splines. Rotate the housing as necessary until it fully engages with the splines on the input and oil pump shafts, but do not force the housing otherwise the slip rings may be damaged. Check that the housing is fully engaged by measuring the distance from the surface of the bellhousing to the electromagnetic clutch housing. This should be between 16 mm and 20 mm. Tighten all bolts to the specified torque.

5 Electronic control unit - removal and refitting

Removal

1 The automatic transmission control unit is situated just in front of the centre console, next to the ECCS/ECM control unit. Prior to removal, disconnect the battery negative terminal.

2 To gain access to the control unit, undo the retaining screws and release the retaining clips, then remove the small trim panel from each side of the front of the centre console.

3 Undo the retaining screws, and release the control unit from its mounting bracket. Disconnect the wiring connectors, and remove the unit from the vehicle.

Refitting

4 Refitting is the reverse of removal, ensuring that the wiring connectors are securely reconnected.

6 Kickdown cable - removal and refitting

Removal

1 Apply the handbrake then jack up the front of the vehicle and support on axle stands (see "*Jacking and vehicle support*").

2 Drain the hydraulic fluid as described in Chapter 1, then clean the drain plug and washer, and tighten the plug to the specified torque.

3 Unscrew the bolts securing the oil pan to the transmission, and lower the oil pan. Remove the gasket.

4 Disconnect the end of the kickdown inner cable from the control valve segment.

5 Unscrew the bolt securing the cable to the transmission and pull out the cable. Remove the O-ring from the end of the outer cable.

6 Working in the engine compartment, disconnect the end of the kick-down cable at the throttle housing lever and withdraw the cable (refer to Chapter 4A if necessary).

Refitting

7 Fit a new O-ring to the groove in the end of the outer cable, then insert the cable in the transmission. Insert and tighten the retaining bolt to the specified torque.

8 Connect the end of the inner cable to the control valve segment. Check that it is correctly fitted by pulling the cable from the engine side - it should move smoothly and must not contact the casing.

9 Connect the inner cable to the throttle housing lever (refer to Chapter 4A if necessary).

10 Adjust the kickdown cable as described in Section 7.

11 Wipe clean the contact surfaces of the oil pan and transmission, then refit the oil pan using a new gasket and tighten the bolts to the specified torque.

12 Lower the vehicle to the ground and fill the transmission with new fluid with reference to Chapter 1.

7 Kickdown cable - adjustment

1 Remove the air cleaner assembly and air inlet duct as described in Chapter 4A. The accelerator cable is located on top of the throttle housing sector and the kickdown cable is located on the bottom of the sector.

2 Mark the inner cable near the outer cable end, then use vernier calipers to check the stroke of the cable from the idle position to the wide open position. The stroke should be as given in the *Specifications*.

3 To adjust the cable, check that the ignition is switched off then depress the lock plate and move the adjustment tube away from the throttle housing to just eliminate play. Release the lock plate to lock the cable in this position.

4 Check and if necessary adjust the accelerator cable as described in Chapter 4A.

5 Fully depress the accelerator pedal and check that the kickdown cable is also fully open.

6 Refit the air cleaner assembly and air inlet duct with reference to Chapter 4A.

7 Road test the vehicle and check for correct operation.

8 Gear selector cable - removal and refitting

Removal

1 Apply the handbrake, then jack up the front of the vehicle and support on axle stands (see "*Jacking and vehicle support*").

2 Working beneath the vehicle, unscrew the end nut securing the inner cable end fitting to the control rod.

3 Unscrew the support bracket bolt securing the cable to the underbody.

4 Pull out the retaining plate and disconnect the cable from the bracket on the underbody.

5 Working in the engine compartment, remove the battery and battery tray as described in Chapter 5A. Also remove the fuse and relay box.

6 Remove the cotter pin and disconnect the inner selector cable from the lever on top of the transmission. Recover the washers and bush.

7 Pull out the retaining plate and remove the outer selector cable from the bracket. Withdraw the selector cable from the vehicle.

Refitting

8 Refitting is a reversal of removal, but adjust the cable as described in Section 9.

9 Check that it is only possible to start the engine in positions 'P' and 'N'.

10 Road test the vehicle, and check for correct operation in all selector lever positions.

9 Gear selector cable - adjustment

1 Apply the handbrake, then jack up the front of the vehicle and support on axle stands (see "*Jacking and vehicle support*").

2 Working beneath the vehicle, loosen the two adjustment nuts securing the inner cable end fitting to the control rod.

3 Inside the vehicle move the selector lever to the "P" (Park) position.

4 Beneath the car check that the transmission lever is in the "P" position with the transmission locked.

5 Hold the inner cable and control rod end fitting at right-angles to each other, then run the adjustment nuts up to each side of the control rod fitting without moving the cable or rod.

6 Tighten the adjustment nuts and lower the car to the ground.

7 Road test the vehicle, and check for correct operation in all selector lever positions.

10 Transmission oil pump - removal and refitting

Removal

1 Apply the handbrake, then jack up the front of the vehicle and support on axle stands (see "*Jacking and vehicle support*"). Remove the left-hand wheel.

2 Unscrew the screws and remove the wheel arch liner.

3 Working through the left-hand wheel arch, remove the three bolts which secure the oil pump.

4 Attach a slide hammer to the oil pump, using the two tapped holes provided. Withdraw the pump using the slide hammer. Be prepared for some oil spillage. Recover the gasket and O-ring **(see illustration)**.

5 If the pump is defective, it must be renewed; no spares are available.

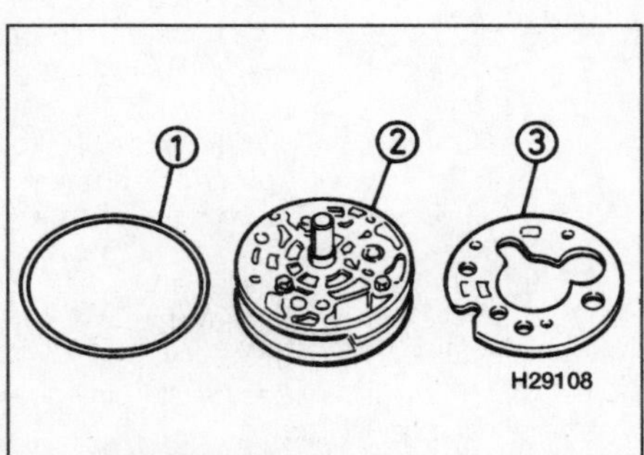

10.4 Automatic transmission oil pump O-ring (1), housing (2) and gasket (3)

Refitting

6 Before refitting the oil pump, clean the mating surfaces of the transmission and pump.

7 Fit the oil pump, using a new gasket and a new O-ring. Secure the pump with the three bolts and tighten to the specified torque.

8 Refit the wheel arch liner, then refit the wheel and lower the vehicle to the ground.

9 Check the transmission fluid level as described earlier in Chapter 1, and top-up if necessary.

11 Accelerator and throttle position micro-switches - checking

1 The accelerator pedal micro switch informs the NCVT control unit when the throttle is initially opened so that the electromagnetic clutch can be energised. The throttle position switch informs the control unit when the throttle is part opened so that the clutch current can be adjusted. Correct adjustment of the micro-switches is essential for correct operation of the electromagnetic clutch. A quick check can be made by listening for the switches clicking as the accelerator pedal is depressed. For an accurate check, proceed as follows.

2 Disconnect the accelerator pedal micro switch wiring connector inside the vehicle noting that the accelerator pedal switch is the upper one and the relevant terminals are Nos 1 and 2. Connect an ohmmeter across the terminals and slowly depress the pedal. With the pedal released, the switch must be closed (zero resistance), but the switch must open (infinite resistance) when the pedal is depressed 3.0 mm **(see illustration)**.

3 To check the throttle position switch, disconnect the wiring connector and connect an ohmmeter across terminals 3 and 4. The switch must operate when the top of the pedal has moved 17.5 mm from its released position.

4 If either switch is permanently open or permanently closed, renew it.

5 Reconnect the wiring on completion.

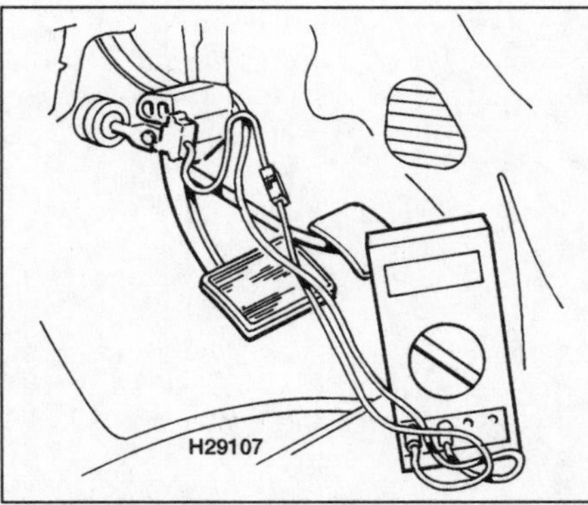

11.2 Checking the accelerator pedal micro-switch with an ohmmeter

12 Inhibitor switch - checking and adjustment

1 The inhibitor switch is located on the top of the automatic transmission and is connected to the selector lever.

2 If necessary, remove the air inlet duct as described in Chapter 4A.

3 Extract the cotter pin and remove the washer, then disconnect the selector cable from the lever on the transmission.

4 Move the lever to the "N" position on the transmission (ie the middle position).

5 Check that it is possible to insert a 4.0 mm diameter drill or dowel rod through the inhibitor switch plate into the hole in the switch body. If not, loosen the switch mounting bolts and reposition the switch until the alignment is correct. Tighten the bolts on completion.

6 Reconnect the selector cable and refit the washer and cotter pin.

7 If removed refit the air inlet duct with reference to Chapter 4A.

13 Oil seals - renewal

Driveshaft oil seal

1 Chock the rear wheels of the car, firmly apply the handbrake, then jack up the front of the car and support it on axle stands (see "*Jacking and vehicle support*"). Remove the appropriate front wheel.

2 Position a suitable container beneath the drain plug located on the bottom of the transmission. Unscrew the plug and allow the fluid to drain. On completion, clean and refit the plug and tighten it to the specified torque.

3 Refer to Chapter 8 and disconnect the inner end of the driveshaft from the transmission. There is no need to unscrew the driveshaft retaining nut as the driveshaft can be left secured to the hub. Support the driveshaft, to avoid placing any strain on the joints or gaiters.

4 Carefully prise the oil seal out of the transmission using a large flat-bladed screwdriver.

5 Remove all traces of dirt from the area around the oil seal aperture, then apply a smear of grease to the outer lip of the new oil seal, and locate it in its aperture. Drive the seal squarely into position until it is flush with the outer face of the transmission housing or a maximum of 0.5 mm recessed. Use a suitable tubular drift (such as a socket) which bears only on the hard outer edge of the seal.

6 Refit the driveshaft with reference to Chapter 8, then refit the wheel and lower the vehicle to the ground.

7 Fill the transmission with the specified type and amount of fluid with reference to Chapter 1.

Input shaft oil seal

8 To renew the input shaft seal, the transmission must be dismantled. This task should therefore be entrusted to a Nissan dealer.

14 Automatic transmission - overhaul

Apart from the operations described earlier in this Section, transmission overhaul should be entrusted to a Nissan dealer or automatic transmission specialist.

Chapter 8
Driveshafts

Contents

Degrees of difficulty

Easy, suitable for novice with little experience		**Fairly easy,** suitable for beginner with some experience		**Fairly difficult,** suitable for competent DIY mechanic		**Difficult,** suitable for experienced DIY mechanic	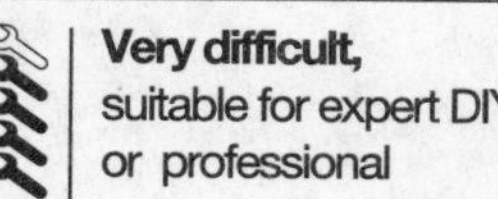	**Very difficult,** suitable for expert DIY or professional	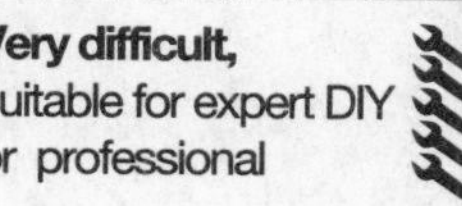

Specifications

General

Type	Unequal-length, solid steel shafts, splined to inner and outer constant velocity joints. Inner joint of ball-and-cage type, outer joint of tripod type.

Lubrication

Lubricant type	Nissan grease supplied with gaiter repair kit

Torque wrench settings

	Nm	lbf ft
Driveshaft nut	177	131
Roadwheel nuts	108	80
Track-rod end-to-steering arm nut	34	25

1 General information

Drive is transmitted from the differential to the front wheels by means of two solid-steel driveshafts of unequal length.

Both driveshafts are splined at their outer ends, to accept the wheel hubs, and are threaded so that each hub can be fastened to the driveshaft by a large nut. The inner end of each driveshaft is splined, to accept the differential sun gear.

Constant velocity (CV) joints are fitted to each end of the driveshafts, to ensure that the smooth and efficient transmission of power at all suspension and steering angles. The outer constant velocity joints are of the ball-and-cage type, and the inner joints of tripod type.

The joints are protected by rubber gaiters and are packed with grease to provide permanent lubrication. Refer to Chapter 1 for details of checking the joints and gaiters.

2 Driveshafts - removal and refitting

Note: *A balljoint separator tool will be required for this operation. A new driveshaft nut split-pin must be used on refitting, and renewal of the driveshaft-to-sun gear inner retaining clip is also recommended.*

Removal

1 Before jacking up the vehicle, loosen the driveshaft nut as follows. Remove the wheel trim, then extract the split-pin from the outer end of the driveshaft **(see illustration)**. Discard the split-pin - a new one must be used on refitting.

2 Firmly apply the handbrake and have an assistant apply the footbrake. Using a socket and extension bar, loosen the driveshaft nut half a turn **(see illustration)**.

⚠ ***Warning: The nut is very tight!***

3 Chock the rear wheels, then jack up the front of the vehicle and support on axle stands (see *"Jacking and vehicle support"*). Remove

2.1 Removing the split pin from the outer end of the driveshaft

2.2 Loosening the driveshaft nut

2.3a Unscrew the driveshaft nut . . .

2.3b . . . and remove the thrustwasher . . .

2.5a Removing the brake disc

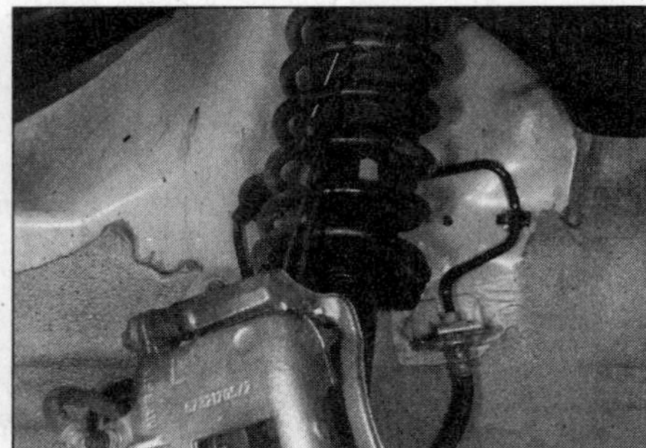
2.5b Suspend the brake caliper from the front coil spring

the appropriate wheel, then unscrew the driveshaft nut and remove the thrustwasher **(see illustrations)**.

4 To reduce spillage when the inner end of the driveshaft is withdrawn from the transmission, drain the transmission oil/fluid with reference to Chapter 7A or 7B (as applicable) and Chapter 1.

5 Unscrew the guide pin bolts, and withdraw the brake caliper from the hub carrier as described in Chapter 9. If necessary remove the brake disc. Note that there is no need to disconnect the brake fluid hose. Suspend the caliper from the front coil spring using wire or string. **Do not** depress the brake pedal whilst the caliper is removed, as this will cause the piston to be ejected **(see illustrations)**.

6 Remove the split-pin, then partially unscrew the castellated nut securing the track-rod end to the steering arm. Using a balljoint separator tool, separate the track-rod end from the steering arm. Remove the nut. Discard the split-pin - a new one must be used on refitting.

7 Unscrew and remove the bolts securing the hub carrier to the bottom of the front suspension strut. Note which way round the bolts are fitted to ensure correct refitting.

8 Pull the top of the hub carrier outwards while pushing the driveshaft through the hub. If the driveshaft is tight on the hub splines, temporarily refit the driveshaft nut to the end of the driveshaft to prevent damage to the driveshaft threads, then using a soft-faced mallet, carefully tap the driveshaft from the hub carrier while pulling the carrier outwards. Alternatively a suitable puller can be used to force the end of the shaft from the hub. Support the end of the driveshaft - do not allow the end of the driveshaft to hang down.

9 Separate the driveshaft from the transmission, using a suitable lever inserted between the casing of the inner constant velocity joint and the transmission casing. Prise out the driveshaft until the retaining clip compresses into its groove, and is released from the differential sun gear **(see illustration)**.

10 Withdraw the driveshaft assembly **(see illustration)**.

Refitting

11 Before installing the driveshaft, examine the driveshaft oil seal in the transmission for signs of damage or deterioration and, if necessary, renew it, referring to Chapter 7A or 7B for further information. Fit a new inner retaining clip to the end of the driveshaft.

12 Thoroughly clean the driveshaft splines, and the apertures in the transmission and hub assembly. Apply a thin film of grease to the oil seal lips, and to the driveshaft splines and shoulders. Check that all driveshaft gaiter clips are securely fastened.

13 When refitting the driveshaft, great care must be taken to prevent damage to the driveshaft oil seal. Nissan specify the use of a special tool which guides the shaft through the seal lips on refitting. Provided that the seal lips and the shaft ends are lightly greased, and that care is taken on refitting, these tools should not be necessary.

14 Insert the inner end of the driveshaft into the transmission, taking care not to damage the oil seal. Engage the driveshaft splines with those of the differential sun gear, and press the driveshaft into place until the retaining clip fully

2.9 Use a lever to prise the driveshaft out of the transmission

2.10 Withdrawing the driveshaft from the vehicle

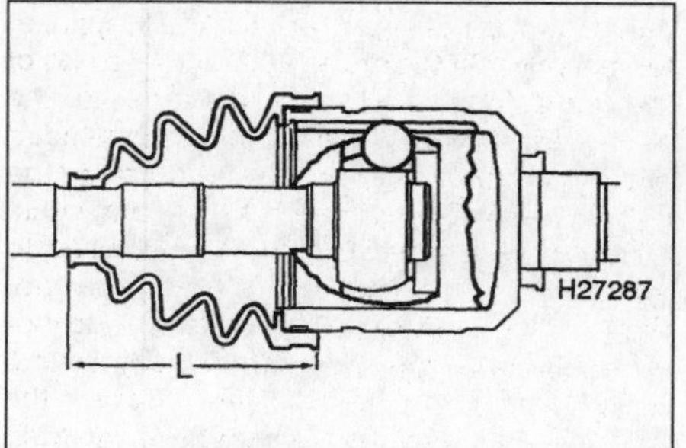

3.2 Measure the length (L) of the gaiter before removing it

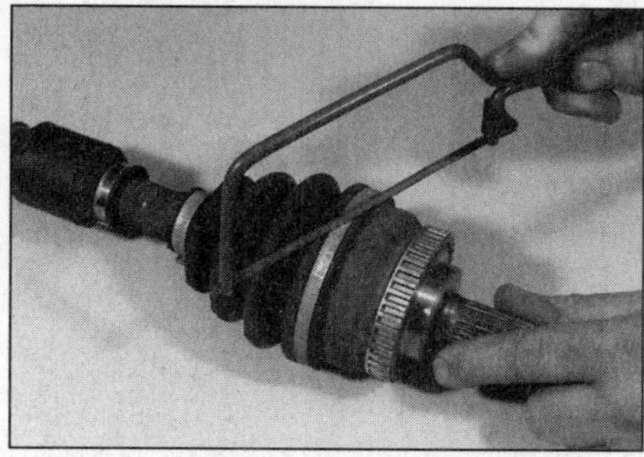

3.3a Cutting the gaiter large clip free

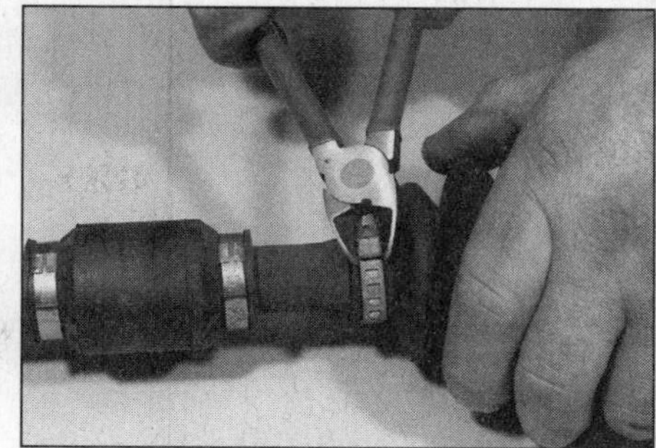

3.3b Cutting the gaiter small clip free

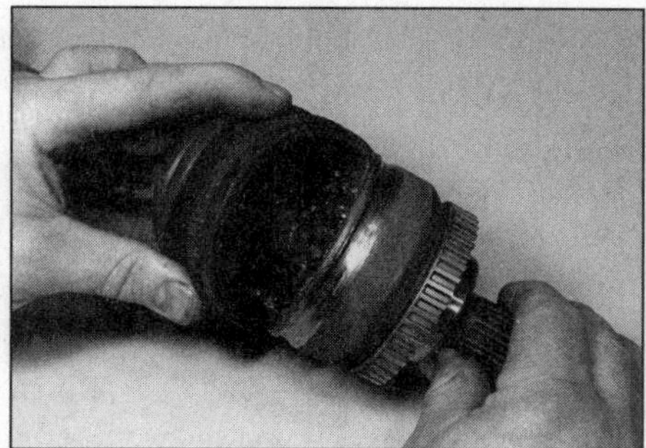

3.3c Sliding the gaiter from the outer joint

3.4 Make alignment marks between the joint and the driveshaft

engages the groove in the sun gear. Grasp the inner joint body firmly, and check that the clip is correctly engaged by attempting to pull the driveshaft from the transmission.

15 Engage the outer end of the driveshaft with the hub ensuring that the splines engage correctly, and push the top of the hub carrier in towards the strut.

16 Locate the top of the hub carrier with the strut and insert the bolts making sure the bolt heads are facing the correct way. Tighten the bolts to the specified torque.

17 Refit the washer and nut to the driveshaft, and tighten the nut moderately at this stage. Leave final tightening of the nut until the car is lowered to the ground.

18 Reconnect the track-rod end to the steering arm, then refit the castellated nut, and tighten to the specified torque. Align the holes and fit a new split pin.

19 Refit the brake caliper with reference to Chapter 9 and tighten the guide pin bolts.

20 Refit the wheel, and lower the vehicle to the ground.

21 Fully tighten the driveshaft nut to the specified torque.

22 Fit the spacer and the castellated locking ring. Make sure that the ring is fitted so that two serrations are aligned with the split pin hole in the driveshaft - it will be necessary to offer the ring up in several positions before the correct alignment occurs. Insert a new split pin and spread the ends around the shaft. Refit the wheel trim.

23 Refill the transmission with oil/fluid with reference to Chapter 7A or 7B (as applicable) and Chapter 1.

3 Driveshaft rubber gaiters - renewal

Outer joint

Note: *New gaiter securing clips and a new joint retaining clip are required for this procedure.*

1 Remove the driveshaft as described in Section 2.

2 Measure the length of the gaiter, so that the new gaiter can be set to the same length before securing it in position **(see illustration)**.

3 Loosen the gaiter securing clips, then slide the gaiter away from the joint towards the centre of the driveshaft. Where crimped clips are fitted, carefully cut them free using a small hacksaw **(see illustrations)**.

4 If the original joint is to be re-used, make alignment marks between the joint and the driveshaft **(see illustration)**.

5 The joint must now be pulled from the end of the driveshaft. Clamp the driveshaft in a vice.

6 To remove the joint, tap the driveshaft joint inner race outwards using a mallet and soft metal drift. This will force the retaining clip to contract into its groove, and enable the joint to be removed from the shaft **(see illustrations)**.

7 Slide the gaiter from the end of the shaft and if necessary remove the circlips from the end of the driveshaft. The square-section clip is particularly difficult to expand and it will be

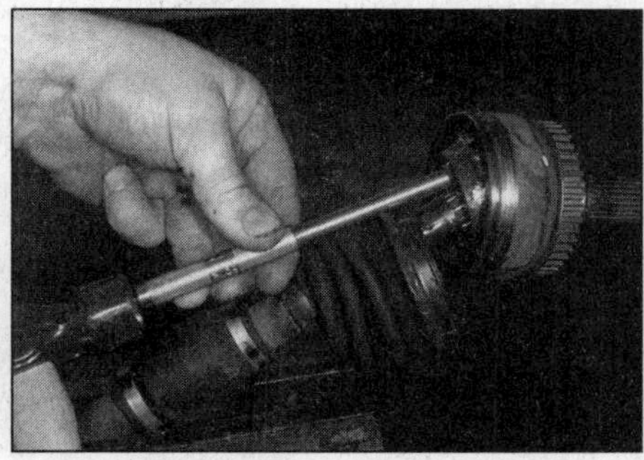

3.6a Using a soft metal drift to free the outer joint from the driveshaft

3.6b Removing the outer driveshaft joint

3.7a Slide the gaiter from the end of the driveshaft . . .

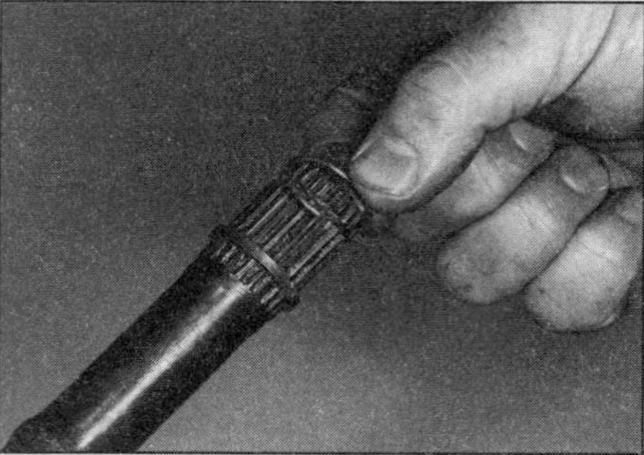

3.7b . . . then remove the round-section circlip . . .

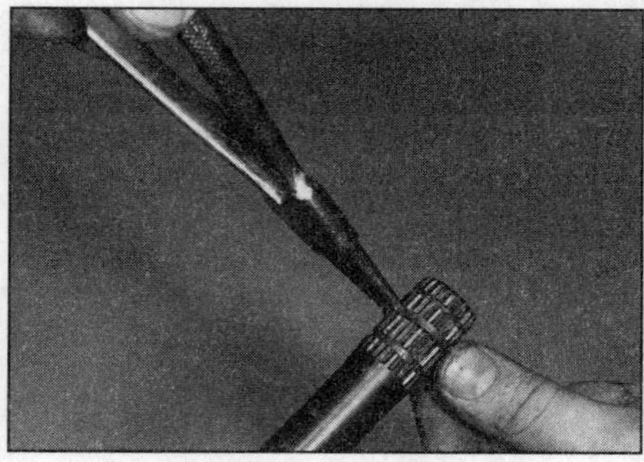

3.7c . . . and square-section circlip

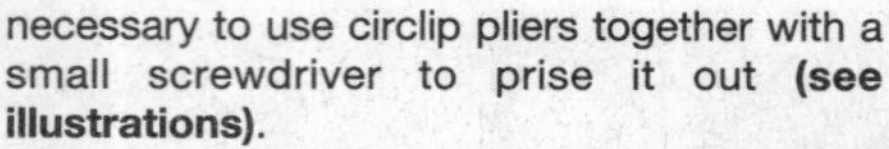

necessary to use circlip pliers together with a small screwdriver to prise it out **(see illustrations)**.

8 Scoop out the grease from the outer constant velocity joint, then wipe clean the joint and end of the driveshaft.

9 Commence refitting by winding a thin layer of tape around the end of the shaft, to protect the gaiter from the shaft splines.

10 Slide the smaller gaiter securing clip onto the shaft, followed by the gaiter and larger clip **(see illustrations)**.

11 Remove the tape from the end of the shaft, then fit new circlips to the grooves in the end of the shaft **(see illustrations)**.

12 Fit the outer joint to the shaft, and engage it with the shaft splines **(see illustration)**. If the original joint is re-used, align the previously made marks.

13 Temporarily refit the driveshaft nut to protect the joint threaded end, then clamp the driveshaft in a vice, and use a mallet to tap the joint onto the shaft until the retaining clip engages correctly.

14 Pack the joint with the correct amount of the specified grease (supplied with the gaiter kit). Pack any surplus grease into the gaiter itself **(see illustration)**.

15 Slide the gaiter onto the outer joint, then fit and tighten the new outer gaiter securing clip.

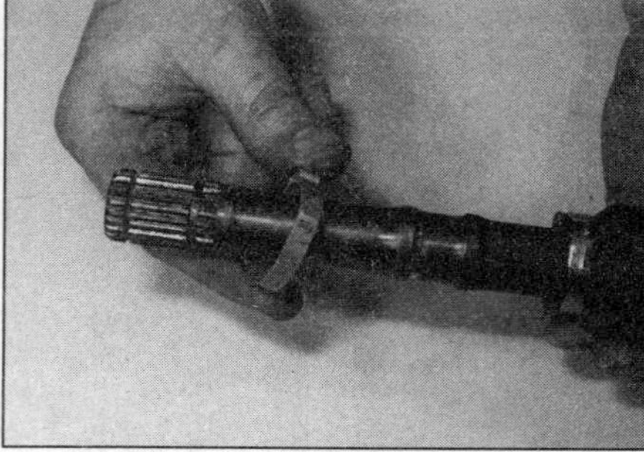

3.10a Slide the small gaiter onto the driveshaft . . .

3.10b . . . followed by the gaiter

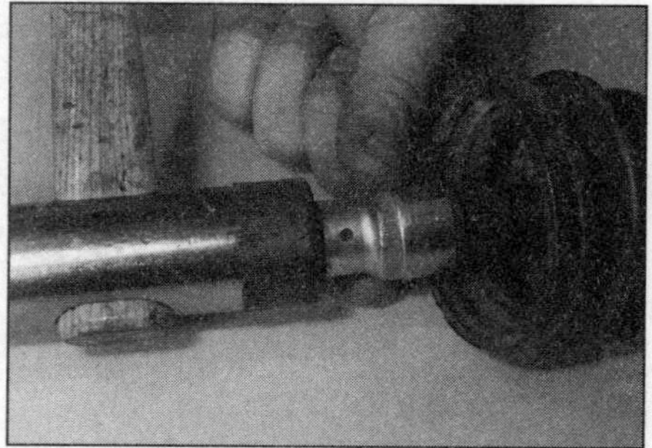

3.11a Using a socket to fit square-section circlip to the groove in the driveshaft

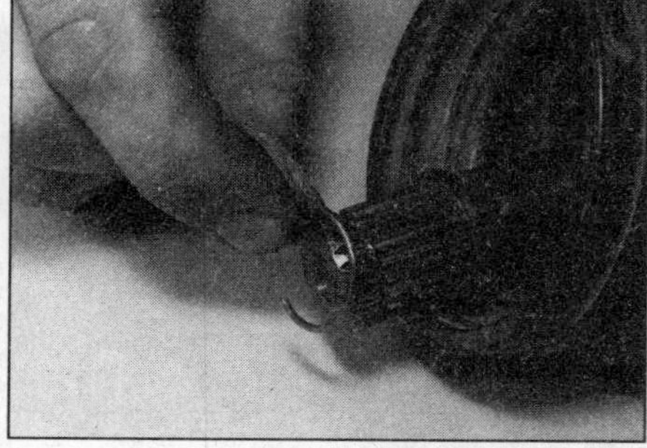

3.11b Fitting a new round-section circlip to the groove in the driveshaft

3.12 Refitting the outer joint

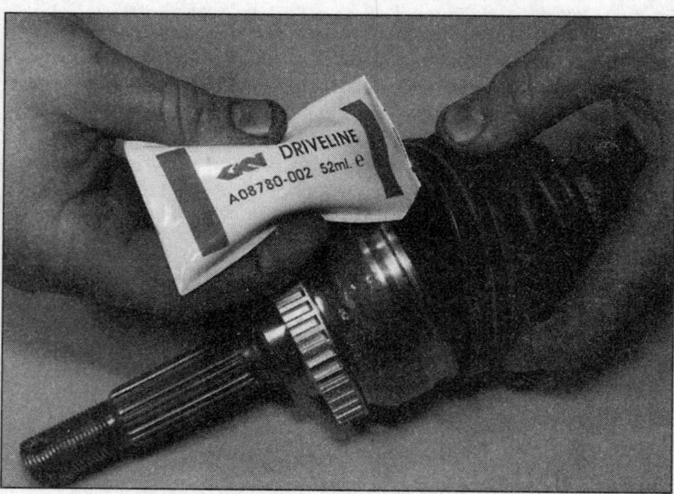

3.14 Packing the outer joint with grease

3.17 Tightening the small clip onto the gaiter

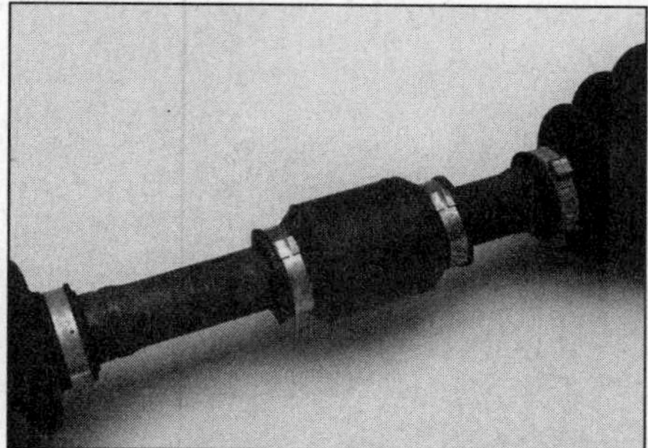
3.20a Vibration damper on the left-hand driveshaft

3.20b Remove the clips . . .

3.20c . . . and remove the vibration damper

3.22a Cut free the inner joint large clip . . .

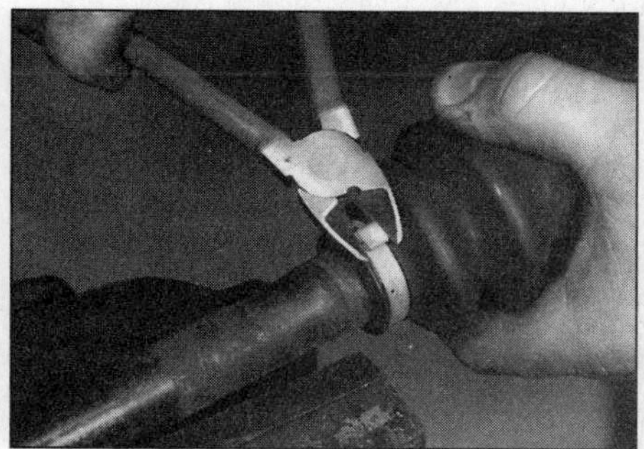
3.22b . . . and small clip . . .

16 Set the gaiter so that the length is as previously measured (see paragraph 2), then check that the smaller end of the gaiter is located in the driveshaft groove.

17 Slide the smaller securing clip onto the gaiter, and tighten **(see illustration)**.

18 Refit the driveshaft as described in Section 2.

Inner joint

Note: *New gaiter securing clips are required for this procedure. It is not possible to separate the inner joint from the driveshaft - access to the inner gaiter is gained by first removing the outer joint and outer gaiter.*

19 Remove the outer joint as previously described in this Section.

20 Mark or measure the position of the vibration damper on the driveshaft, then remove the clips and slide the damper from the outer end of the driveshaft **(see illustrations)**. **Note:** *The dampers are different for each driveshaft and it is important the correct one is fitted.*

21 Measure the length of the inner gaiter, so that the new gaiter can be set to the same length before securing it in position.

22 Loosen or cut the gaiter securing clips, and slide the gaiter off the outer end of the driveshaft. Recover the securing clips **(see illustrations)**.

23 Scoop out the grease from the inner constant velocity joint, then wipe clean the joint and the driveshaft.

24 Commence refitting by winding a thin layer of tape around the splines on the outer end of the shaft, to protect the gaiters from the shaft splines.

3.22c . . . then slide off the inner joint gaiter

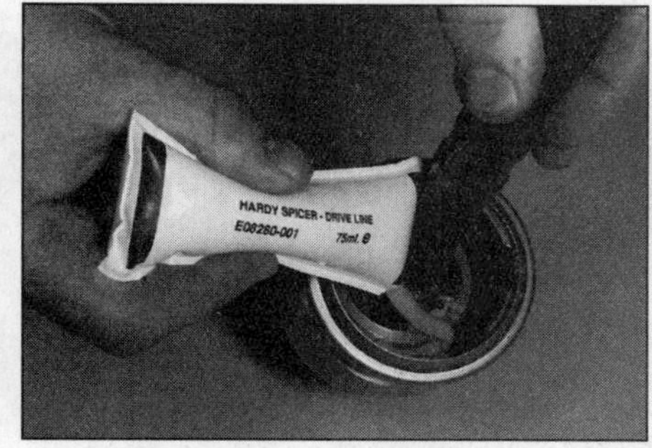

3.25 Packing the inner joint with grease

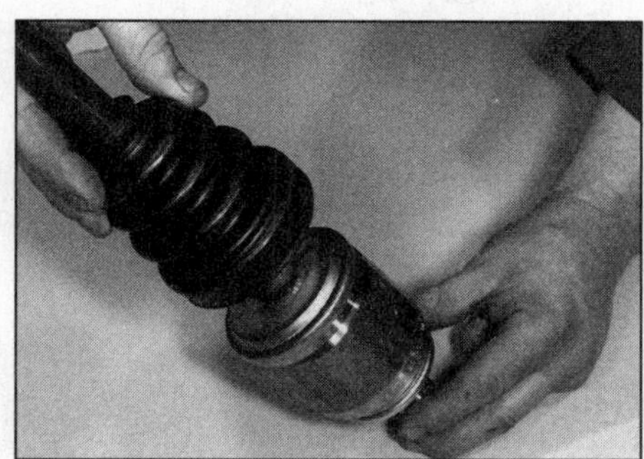
3.26 Slide the gaiter into position . . .

3.28 . . . and tighten the clips

25 Pack the correct amount of the specified grease (supplied with the gaiter kit), around the spider rollers and into the inner joint body **(see illustration)**.

26 Slide the gaiter onto the inner joint, then fit and tighten the large clip **(see illustration)**.

27 Set the gaiter so that the length is as previously measured (see paragraph 21), then check that the smaller end of the gaiter is located in the driveshaft groove.

28 Locate the smaller gaiter clip on the gaiter, and tighten **(see illustration)**.

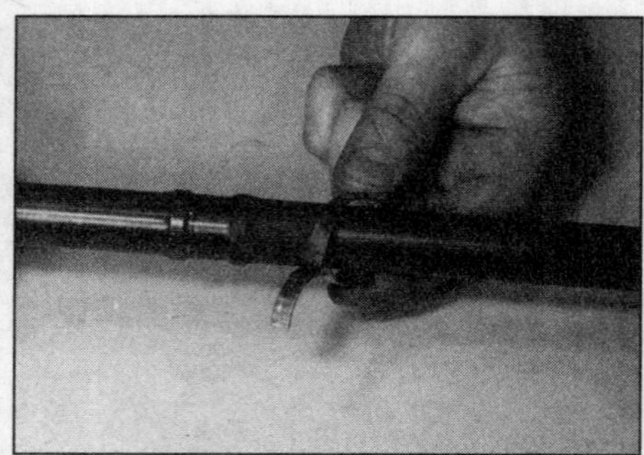

3.29a Locate the inner clip on the driveshaft . . .

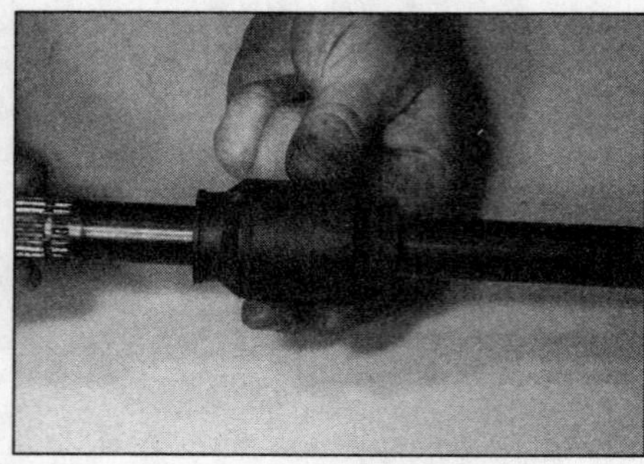

3.29b . . . followed by the vibration damper and outer clip . . .

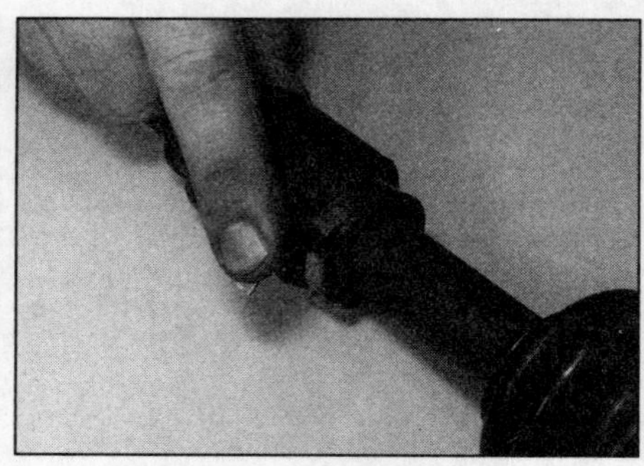

3.29c . . . and tighten the clips

29 Refit the vibration damper in its previously noted position and tighten the clips **(see illustrations)**.
30 Refit the outer joint as previously described in this Section.

4 Driveshaft overhaul - general information

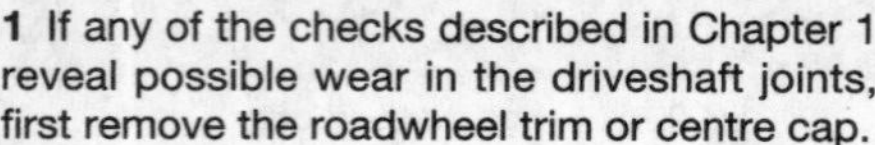

1 If any of the checks described in Chapter 1 reveal possible wear in the driveshaft joints, first remove the roadwheel trim or centre cap.
2 Check that the driveshaft nut is correctly tightened; if in doubt, remove the split pin and the castellated locking ring and spacer. Check that the nut is tightened to the specified torque, then refit the spacer, the locking ring, and a new split-pin. Refit the roadwheel trim or centre cap, and repeat the check on the remaining driveshaft nut.
3 Road test the vehicle, and listen for a metallic clicking from the front as the vehicle is driven slowly in a circle on full-lock. If a clicking noise is heard, this indicates wear in the outer constant velocity joint.
4 If vibration, consistent with road speed, is felt through the car when accelerating, there is a possibility of wear in the inner constant velocity joints.
5 To check the joints for wear, remove the driveshafts, then remove the gaiters as described in Section 3. If any wear or free play is found, the outer joint may be renewed separately, however if the inner joint is worn it must be renewed together with the shaft.

Chapter 9
Braking system

Contents

Degrees of difficulty

Easy, suitable for novice with little experience 

Fairly easy, suitable for beginner with some experience 

Fairly difficult, suitable for competent DIY mechanic

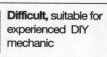

Difficult, suitable for experienced DIY mechanic 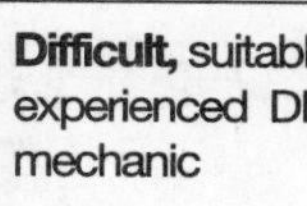

Very difficult, suitable for expert DIY or professional

Specifications

General

System type	Dual hydraulic circuit. Anti-lock braking system optional. Rear drum brakes on models without ABS, and models with ABS after March 1998. Rear disc brakes on models with ABS up to March 1998. Vacuum servo-assistance on all models. Cable-operated handbrake acting on rear wheels

Front brakes

Type	Vented or solid discs (depending on model), with single-piston sliding caliper
Solid disc:	
Diameter :	
Up to 1999	237.0 mm
From 1999	234.0 mm
Thickness	12.0 mm
Minimum thickness (0.02 mm maximum variation between sides)	10.0 mm
Vented disc:	
Diameter	238.0 mm
Thickness	18.0 mm
Minimum thickness (0.02 mm maximum variation between sides)	16.0 mm
Maximum disc run-out	0.07 mm
Minimum pad friction material thickness	2.0 mm

Rear disc brakes

Type	Solid disc, with single-piston sliding caliper
Disc diameter	240.0 mm
Disc thickness:	
New	7.0 mm
Minimum thickness (0.02 mm maximum variation between sides)	6.0 mm
Maximum disc run-out	0.07 mm
Minimum pad friction material thickness	2.0 mm

Rear drum brakes

Type	Leading and trailing shoes operated by twin-piston wheel cylinder
Drum inner diameter:	
New	180 mm
Maximum diameter after machining	181.5 mm
Maximum out-of-round	0.03 mm
Minimum shoe lining thickness	1.5 mm

Brake pedal

Free height:	**Right-hand-drive models**	**Left-hand-drive models**
Manual transmission	170.0 to 179.0 mm	164.0 to 173.0 mm
Automatic transmission	177.0 to 186.0 mm	171.0 to 180.0 mm
Pedal free-play	1.0 to 3.0 mm	
Stop-lamp switch clearance (between threaded end of switch and pedal stop)	0.75 to 2.0 mm	

Vacuum servo

Diaphragm diameter:	
Models without ABS	177.8 mm
Models with ABS	203.2 mm
Pushrod protrusion (models with ABS only)	22.2 to 22.6 mm
Clevis setting dimension (models without ABS only)	138.0 mm (approx)

Handbrake

Number of clicks to operate handbrake "on" warning light	1 or less
Number of clicks with handbrake fully on	6 to 8

Torque wrench settings

	Nm	lbf ft
ABS modulator mounting nuts:		
Models up to March 1998	19	14
March 1998 and later models	13	10
ABS wheel sensor mounting bolt:		
Models up to March 1998	13	10
March 1998 and later models	22	16
Brake fluid hose union banjo bolts	20	15
Brake fluid pipe union nuts	17	13
Brake hydraulic system bleed screws	8	6
Brake pedal bracket securing nuts	10	7
Front brake caliper guide pin bolts	27	20
Front brake caliper mounting bracket bolts	59	44
Handbrake cable mounting	4	3
Handbrake lever mounting bolts	10	7
Hydraulic hose to front caliper union	31	23
Hydraulic hose to rear caliper union	19	14
Master cylinder securing nuts	14	10
Rear brake backplate bolts (drum brake models)	45	33
Rear brake caliper guide pin bolts	27	20
Rear brake caliper handbrake lever stop-bolt	11	8
Rear brake caliper mounting bracket bolts	45	33
Rear brake pressure-regulating valve adjustment nut	10	7
Rear wheel cylinder mounting bolts	9	7
Vacuum servo unit mounting	15	11
Vacuum servo unit pushrod locknut	19	14

1 General information

The braking system is of servo-assisted, dual-circuit hydraulic type. The arrangement of the hydraulic system is such that each circuit operates one front and one rear brake from a tandem master cylinder. Under normal circumstances, both circuits operate in unison. However, in the event of hydraulic failure in one circuit, full braking force will still be available at two diagonally-opposite wheels. An anti-lock braking system (ABS) is available as on option on certain models.

All models are fitted with front disc brakes. Rear disc brakes were fitted to pre-1998 models with ABS; 1998-on models with ABS have rear drum brakes, as do all models without ABS.

The front disc brakes are actuated by single-piston sliding type calipers, which ensure that equal pressure is applied to each disc pad.

The rear drum brakes incorporate leading and trailing shoes, which are actuated by twin-piston wheel cylinders. A self-adjust mechanism is incorporated, to automatically compensate for brake shoe wear. As the brake shoe linings wear, the footbrake operation automatically operates the adjuster mechanism, which effectively lengthens the shoe strut and repositions the brake shoes, to adjust the lining-to-drum clearance. The mechanical handbrake linkage operates the brake shoes via a lever attached to the trailing brake shoe.

The rear disc brakes are actuated by single-piston sliding type calipers, and incorporate a mechanical handbrake mechanism.

A load-sensitive pressure-regulating valve is fitted (on models without ABS) in the rear brake lines, to prevent the possibility of the rear wheels locking before the front wheels under heavy braking.

Note: *When servicing any part of the system, work carefully and methodically; also observe scrupulous cleanliness when overhauling any part of the hydraulic system. Always renew components (in axle sets, where applicable) if in doubt about their condition, and use only genuine Nissan replacement parts, or at least those of known good quality. Note the warnings given in "Safety first" and at relevant points in this Chapter concerning the dangers of asbestos dust and hydraulic fluid.*

2 Hydraulic system - bleeding

Warning: Hydraulic fluid is poisonous; wash off immediately and thoroughly in the case of skin contact, and seek immediate medical advice if any fluid is swallowed, or gets into the eyes. Certain types of hydraulic fluid are inflammable, and may ignite when allowed into contact with hot components. When servicing any hydraulic system, it is safest to assume that the fluid IS inflammable, and to take precautions against the risk of fire as though it is fuel that is being handled. Hydraulic fluid is also an effective paint stripper, and will attack plastics; if any is spilt, it should be washed off immediately, using copious quantities of fresh water. Finally, it is hygroscopic (it absorbs moisture from the air) - old fluid may be contam-inated and unfit for further use. When topping-up or renewing the fluid, always use the recommended type, and ensure that it comes from a freshly-opened sealed container.

General

1 The correct operation of any hydraulic system is only possible after removing all air from the components and circuit; and this is achieved by bleeding the system.

2 During the bleeding procedure, add only clean, unused hydraulic fluid of the recommended type; never re-use fluid that has already been bled from the system. Ensure that sufficient fluid is available before starting work.

3 If there is any possibility of incorrect fluid being already in the system, the brake components and circuit must be flushed completely with uncontaminated, correct fluid, and new seals should be fitted throughout the system.

4 If hydraulic fluid has been lost from the system, or air has entered because of a leak, ensure that the fault is cured before proceeding further.

5 Park the vehicle on level ground, switch off the engine and select first or reverse gear (or "P"), then chock the wheels and release the handbrake.

6 Check that all pipes and hoses are secure, unions tight and bleed screws closed. Remove the dust caps (where applicable), and clean any dirt from around the bleed screws.

7 Unscrew the master cylinder reservoir cap, and top the master cylinder reservoir up to the "MAX" level line; refit the cap loosely. Remember to maintain the fluid level at least above the "MIN" level line throughout the procedure, otherwise there is a risk of further air entering the system.

8 There are a number of one-man, do-it-yourself brake bleeding kits currently available from motor accessory shops. It is recommended that one of these kits is used whenever possible, as they greatly simplify the bleeding operation, and also reduce the risk of expelled air and fluid being drawn back into the system. If such a kit is not available, the basic (two-man) method must be used, which is described in detail below.

9 If a kit is to be used, prepare the vehicle as described previously, and follow the kit manufacturer's instructions, as the procedure may vary slightly according to the type being used; generally, they are as outlined below in the relevant sub-section.

10 Whichever method is used, the same sequence must be followed to ensure the removal of all air from the system.

Bleeding sequence

11 If the system has been only partially disconnected, and suitable precautions were taken to minimise fluid loss, it should be necessary to bleed only that part of the system (ie the primary or secondary circuit).

12 If the complete system is to be bled, then it should be done working in the following sequence:

a) Left-hand rear wheel.
b) Right-hand front wheel.
c) Right-hand rear wheel.
d) Left-hand front wheel.

Bleeding - basic (two-man) method

13 Collect a clean glass jar, a suitable length of plastic or rubber tubing which is a tight fit over the bleed screw, and a ring spanner to fit the screw. The help of an assistant will also be required.

14 With the dust cap removed from the first screw in the sequence, fit a suitable spanner and tube to the screw and place the other end of the tube in the jar. Pour in sufficient fluid to cover the end of the tube.

15 Ensure that the master cylinder reservoir fluid level is maintained at least above the "MIN" level line throughout the procedure.

16 Have the assistant fully depress the brake pedal several times to build up pressure, then maintain it on the final downstroke.

17 While pedal pressure is maintained, unscrew the bleed screw (approximately one turn) and allow the compressed fluid and air to flow into the jar. The assistant should maintain pedal pressure, following the pedal down to the floor, and should not release the pedal until instructed to do so. When the flow stops, tighten the bleed screw again, have the assistant release the pedal slowly, and recheck the reservoir fluid level.

2.22 Using a one-man brake bleeding kit

18 Repeat the steps given in paragraphs 16 and 17 until the fluid emerging from the bleed screw is free from air bubbles. If the master cylinder has been drained and refilled, and air is being bled from the first screw in the sequence, allow approximately five seconds between cycles for the master cylinder passages to refill.

19 When no more air bubbles appear, tighten the bleed screw securely, remove the tube and spanner, and refit the dust cap. Do not overtighten the bleed screw.

20 Repeat the procedure on the remaining screws in the sequence, until all air is removed from the system, and the brake pedal feels firm again.

Bleeding - using a one-way valve kit

21 As their name implies, these kits consist of a length of tubing with a one-way valve fitted, to prevent expelled air and fluid being drawn back into the system; some kits include a translucent container, which can be positioned so that the air bubbles can be more easily seen flowing from the end of the tube.

22 The kit is connected to the bleed screw, which is then opened **(see illustration)**. The user returns to the driver's seat, depresses the brake pedal with a smooth, steady stroke, and slowly releases it; this is repeated until the expelled fluid is clear of air bubbles.

23 Note that these kits simplify work so much that it is easy to forget the master cylinder reservoir fluid level; ensure that this is maintained at least above the "MIN" level line at all times.

Bleeding - using a pressure-bleeding kit

24 These kits are usually operated by the reservoir of pressurised air contained in the spare tyre. However, note that it will probably be necessary to reduce the pressure to a lower level than normal; refer to the instructions supplied with the kit.

25 By connecting a pressurised, fluid-filled container to the master cylinder reservoir, bleeding can be carried out simply by opening each screw in turn (in the specified sequence), and allowing the fluid to flow out until no more air bubbles can be seen in the expelled fluid.

26 This method has the advantage that the large reservoir of fluid provides an additional

3.2a Hydraulic flexible brake hose mounting under the front wheel arch

3.2b Pulling out the brake hose securing spring clip

3.2c Removing the brake hose support bracket bolt

safeguard against air being drawn into the system during bleeding.

27 Pressure-bleeding is particularly effective when bleeding "difficult" systems, or when bleeding the complete system at the time of routine fluid renewal.

All methods

28 When bleeding is complete, and firm pedal feel is restored, wash off any spilt fluid, tighten the bleed screws securely, and refit their dust caps.

29 Check the hydraulic fluid level in the master cylinder reservoir, and top-up if necessary ("*Weekly checks*").

30 Discard any hydraulic fluid that has been bled from the system; it will not be fit for re-use.

31 Check the feel of the brake pedal. If it feels at all spongy, air must still be present in the system, and further bleeding is required. Failure to bleed satisfactorily after a reasonable repetition of the bleeding procedure may be due to worn master cylinder seals.

3 Hydraulic pipes and hoses - inspection and renewal

Note: *Before starting work, refer to the note at the beginning of Section 2 concerning the dangers of hydraulic fluid.*

1 If any pipe or hose is to be renewed, minimise fluid loss by first removing the master cylinder reservoir cap, then tighten the cap down onto a piece of polythene to obtain an airtight seal. Alternatively, flexible hoses can be sealed, if required, using a proprietary brake hose clamp; metal brake pipe unions can be plugged (if care is taken not to allow dirt into the system) or capped immediately they are disconnected. Place a wad of rag under any union that is to be disconnected, to catch any spilt fluid.

2 If a flexible hose is to be disconnected unscrew the brake pipe union nut before removing the spring clip which secures the hose to its mounting bracket. Unscrew any support bracket bolts before removing the hose **(see illustrations)**.

3 To unscrew the union nuts, it is preferable to obtain a brake pipe spanner of the correct size; these are available from most large motor accessory shops. Failing this, a close-fitting open-ended spanner will be required, though if the nuts are tight or corroded, their flats may be rounded-off if the spanner slips. In such a case, a self-locking wrench is often the only way to unscrew a stubborn union, but it follows that the pipe and the damaged nuts must be renewed on reassembly. Always clean a union and surrounding area before disconnecting it. If disconnecting a component with more than one union, make a careful note of the connections before disturbing any of them.

4 If a brake pipe is to be renewed, it can be obtained, cut to length and with the union nuts and end flares in place, from Nissan dealers. All that is then necessary is to bend it to shape, following the line of the original, before fitting it to the vehicle. Alternatively, most motor accessory shops can make up brake pipes from kits, but this requires very careful measurement of the original, to ensure that the replacement is of the correct length. The safest answer is usually to take the original to the shop as a pattern.

5 On refitting, do not overtighten the union nuts. It is not necessary to exercise brute force to obtain a sound joint.

6 Ensure that the pipes and hoses are correctly routed, with no kinks, and that they are secured in the clips or brackets provided. After fitting, remove the polythene from the reservoir, and bleed the hydraulic system as described in Section 2. Wash off any spilt fluid, and check carefully for fluid leaks.

4.3a Loosen the brake caliper mounting bolts . . .

4.3b . . . and remove them

4 Front brake pads - renewal

Warning: Renew BOTH sets of front brake pads at the same time - NEVER renew the pads on only one wheel, as uneven braking may result.

Dust created by wear of the pads may contain asbestos, which is a health hazard. Never blow it out with compressed air, and don't inhale any of it. An approved filtering mask should be worn when working on the brakes. DO NOT use petroleum-based solvents to clean brake parts. Use brake cleaner or methylated spirit only.

1 Chock the rear wheels, apply the handbrake, then jack up the front of the vehicle and support it on axle stands (see "*Jacking and vehicle support*"). Remove the front roadwheels.

2 Working on one side of the vehicle, push the caliper piston into its bore by pulling the caliper outwards.

3 Unscrew the upper and lower caliper guide pin bolts (if necessary, use an open-ended spanner to counterhold the head of the guide pin), then lift the caliper from the hub/disc assembly **(see illustrations)**. **Do not** depress the brake pedal until the caliper is refitted.

4 Ensure that the caliper is adequately supported - use wire to hang the caliper on the front suspension coil spring. Note the location of the shims and anti-rattle springs.

4.5a Removing the front brake inner pad . . .

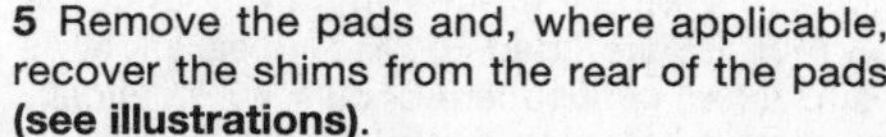

4.5b . . . and outer pad

4.8 Removing the anti-rattle clips

5 Remove the pads and, where applicable, recover the shims from the rear of the pads **(see illustrations)**.

6 Measure the thickness of each brake pad's friction material. If either pad is worn at any point to the specified minimum thickness or less, all four front brake pads must be renewed. Also, the pads should be renewed if any are fouled with oil or grease; there is no satisfactory way of degreasing friction material, once contaminated. If any of the brake pads are worn unevenly, or are fouled with oil or grease, trace and rectify the cause before reassembly. New brake pads and shim/clip kits are available from Nissan dealers.

7 If the brake pads are still serviceable, clean them using a clean, fine wire brush or similar, paying particular attention to the sides and back of the metal backing.

8 Remove the anti-rattle clips from the caliper bracket, and clean the surfaces of the bracket, clips, and the pad locations in the caliper body/mounting bracket **(see illustration)**.

9 Prior to fitting the pads, check that the guide pins are free to slide easily in the caliper body/mounting bracket, and check that the rubber guide pin gaiters are undamaged. Brush the dust and dirt from the caliper and piston, but *do not* inhale it, as it is a health hazard. Inspect the dust seal around the piston for damage, and the piston for evidence of fluid leaks, corrosion or damage. If attention to any of these components is necessary, refer to Section 9.

10 If new brake pads are to be fitted, the caliper piston must be pushed back into the cylinder, to make room for them. Either use a G-clamp or similar tool, or use suitable pieces of wood as levers. Provided that the master cylinder reservoir has not been overfilled with hydraulic fluid, there should be no spillage, but keep a careful watch on the fluid level while retracting the piston. If the fluid level rises above the "MAX" level line at any time, the surplus should be siphoned off or ejected via a plastic tube connected to the bleed screw (see Section 2). **Note:** *Do not syphon the fluid by mouth, as it is poisonous; use a syringe or an old poultry baster.*

11 Apply a little anti-squeal brake grease to the contact surfaces of the pad backing plates and the shims (where applicable), but take great care not to allow any grease onto the pad friction linings. Similarly, apply brake grease to the contact surfaces of the anti-rattle clips - again take care not to apply excess grease, which may contaminate the pads.

12 Refit the anti-rattle clips to the caliper mounting bracket, then refit the pads and shims (where applicable), in the positions noted before removal, ensuring that the pad friction material is against the disc.

13 Slide the caliper into position on the mounting bracket, then refit the bolts. Tighten the bolts to the specified torque wrench setting.

14 Check that the caliper body slides smoothly on the guide pins.

15 Repeat the procedure on the remaining front caliper.

16 With both sets of front brake pads refitted, depress the brake pedal repeatedly until the pads are pressed into firm contact with the brake disc, and normal pedal pressure is restored.

17 Refit the roadwheels, and lower the vehicle to the ground.

18 Finally, check the hydraulic fluid level as described in Chapter 1.

5 Rear brake pads - renewal

Warning: Renew BOTH sets of rear brake pads at the same time - NEVER renew the pads on only one wheel, as uneven braking may result.

Before starting work, refer to the warning given at the beginning of Section 4, concerning the dangers of asbestos dust.

1 Chock the front wheels, then jack up the rear of the vehicle, and support on axle stands (see *"Jacking and vehicle support"*). Remove the rear roadwheels, and release the handbrake fully.

2 Push the caliper piston into its bore by pulling the caliper outwards.

3 Unscrew the caliper guide pin bolts. If necessary, use a slim open-ended spanner to counterhold the head of the guide pins **(see illustration)**.

4 Withdraw the caliper body upwards to expose the brake pads, and support the caliper to one side **(see illustration)**. **Do not** depress the brake pedal until the caliper is refitted. Take care not to strain the brake fluid

5.3 Unscrew the rear caliper mounting bolts . . .

5.4 . . . and withdraw the caliper body upwards

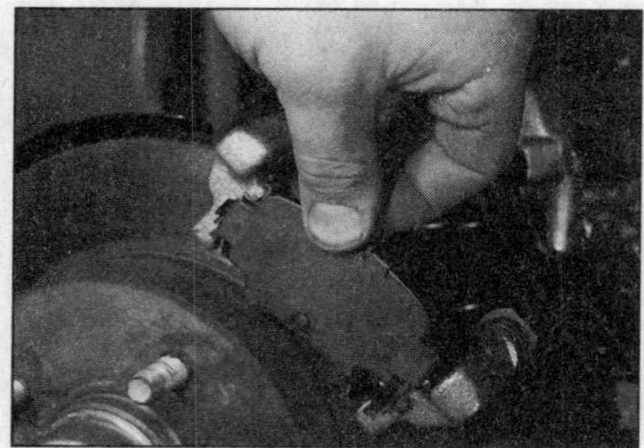

5.5a Removing the rear outer pad . . .

5.5b . . . inner pad . . .

5.5c . . . and anti-rattle springs

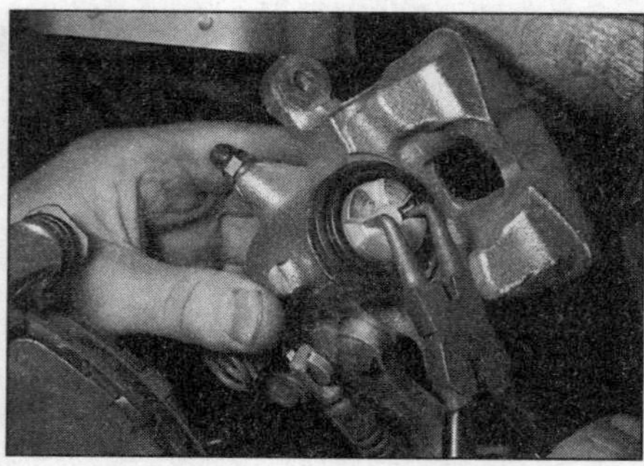

5.9 Using circlip pliers to retract the rear caliper piston

hose. Where applicable, note the locations and orientation of the shims fitted to the rear of each pad and the anti-rattle shims fitted to the top and bottom of the pads.

5 Withdraw the pads and shims (where fitted), and remove the anti-rattle springs **(see illustrations)**.

6 Measure the thickness of each brake pad's friction material. If either pad is worn at any point to the specified minimum thickness or less, all four rear pads must be renewed. Also, the pads should be renewed if any are fouled with oil or grease; there is no satisfactory way of degreasing friction material, once contaminated. If any of the brake pads are worn unevenly, or are fouled with oil or grease, trace and rectify the cause before reassembly. New brake pads and shim/spring kits are available from Nissan dealers.

7 If the brake pads are still serviceable, clean them using a clean, fine wire brush or similar, paying particular attention to the sides and back of the metal backing. Clean the pad locations in the caliper body/mounting bracket.

8 Prior to fitting the pads, check that the guide pins are free to slide easily in the caliper body/mounting bracket, and check that the rubber guide pin gaiters are undamaged. Brush the dust and dirt from the caliper and piston, but *do not* inhale it, as it is a health hazard. Inspect the dust seal around the piston for damage, and the piston for evidence of fluid leaks, corrosion or damage. If attention to any of these components is necessary, refer to Section 10.

9 If new brake pads are to be fitted, the caliper piston must be moved back into the cylinder, to make room for them. To retract the piston, engage a suitable pair of circlip pliers with the notches in the piston, and turn the piston clockwise (viewed from the outboard end of the caliper) **(see illustration)**. Take care not to damage the surface of the piston, or twist the dust seal. Provided that the master cylinder reservoir has not been overfilled with hydraulic fluid, there should be no spillage, but keep a careful watch on the fluid level while retracting the piston. If the fluid level rises above the "MAX" level line at any time, the surplus should be siphoned off or ejected via a plastic tube connected to the bleed screw (see Section 2). **Note:** *Do not syphon the fluid by mouth, as it is poisonous; use a syringe or an old poultry baster.*

10 Apply a little anti-squeal brake grease to the contact surfaces of the pad backing plates and the shims (where applicable), but take great care not to allow any grease onto the pad friction linings. Similarly, where applicable, apply brake grease to the contact surfaces of the anti-rattle springs - again take care not to apply excess grease, which may contaminate the pads. Note that new pads may be supplied with an anti-squeal coating on their contact faces, in which case there is no need to apply brake grease.

11 Where applicable, refit the anti-rattle springs to the caliper mounting bracket, then refit the pads and the shims (where applicable), in the positions noted before removal. Ensure that the pad friction material is against the disc.

12 Locate the caliper body downwards over the brake pads. Ensure that the peg on the back of the inboard pad engages with the nearest notch in the piston. It may be necessary to rotate the piston to align the nearest notch with the peg.

13 Insert the caliper guide pin bolts and tighten to the specified torque.

14 Check that the caliper body slides smoothly on the guide pins.

15 Repeat the procedure on the remaining rear caliper.

16 With both sets of rear brake pads refitted, operate the handbrake repeatedly until the correct brake pad-to-disc clearance is established (adjustment occurs automatically when the handbrake is operated).

17 Depress the brake pedal repeatedly to ensure that normal pedal pressure is restored.

18 Refit the roadwheels, and lower the vehicle to the ground.

19 Finally check the hydraulic fluid level as described in "*Weekly checks*".

6 Rear brake shoes - inspection and renewal

Warning: Renew BOTH sets of rear brake shoes at the same time - NEVER renew the shoes on only one wheel, as uneven braking may result.

Before starting work, refer to the warning given at the beginning of Section 4, concerning the dangers of asbestos dust.

1 Remove the rear brake drums, as described in Section 8.

2 Working on one side of the vehicle, brush the dirt and dust from the brake backplate and drum. **Do not** inhale the dust, as it may be a health hazard.

3 Note the position of each shoe, and the location of the return and steady springs. Also make a note of the adjuster component locations, in case the components are disturbed during the removal procedure **(see illustration)**.

6.3 Note the location of the rear brake shoe components before removing them

6.4a Use pliers to turn the hold-down spring outer seat through 90°

6.4b Removing the hold-down spring outer seat

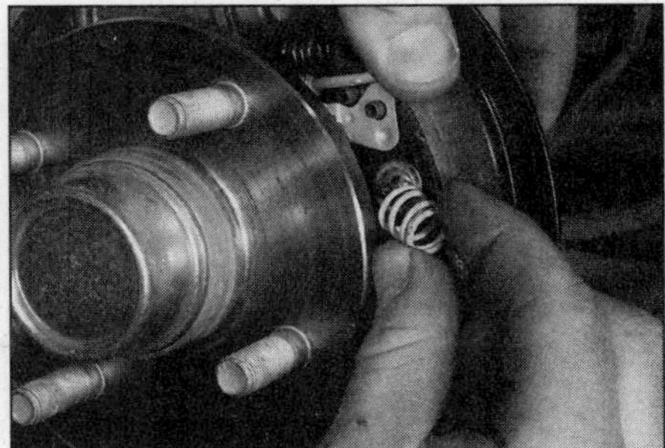
6.5a Remove the leading shoe hold-down spring . . .

6.5b . . . lower seat . . .

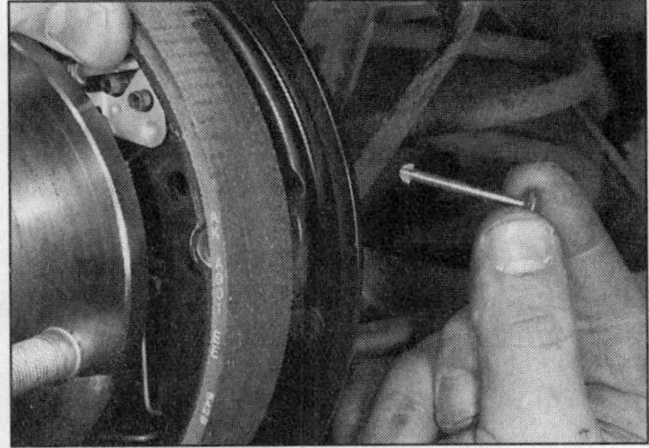
6.5c . . . and retainer pin . . .

6.5d . . . then turn the trailing spring hold-down spring outer seat through 90° . . .

6.5e . . . remove the seat . . .

6.5f . . . followed by the spring . . .

6.5g . . . and special seat

4 Remove the shoe hold-down springs. Use pliers to depress the outer spring cups, and turn them through 90° **(see illustrations)**.

5 Recover the springs and outer cups, and remove the spring retainer pins from the backplate. On the trailing shoe also remove the spring seat which acts as a stop for the handbrake operating lever **(see illustrations)**.

6.6a Disengage the bottom of the trailing brake shoe . . .

6.6b . . . and unhook the lower return spring

6 Disengage the bottom of the trailing brake shoe from the backplate anchor, and using a pair of pliers, unhook and remove the lower return spring from both shoes **(see illustrations)**.

7 Disengage the upper return spring from the shoes, then remove the strut **(see illustrations)**. Unhook the adjuster spring.

8 If necessary, position a rubber band or a cable-tie over the wheel cylinder, to prevent the pistons from being ejected **(see illustration)**. If there is any evidence of fluid leakage from the wheel cylinder, renew it or overhaul it as described in Section 11.

9 Unhook the handbrake cable from the lever on the trailing brake shoe **(see illustration)**.

10 Working on the trailing brake shoe, prise off the retaining clip, then remove the pivot pin and withdraw the handbrake operating lever.

6.7a Unhook the upper return spring from the trailing shoe . . .

6.7b . . . and from the leading shoe . . .

6.7c . . . and remove the strut

6.8 Rubber band over rear wheel cylinder to prevent the pistons being ejected

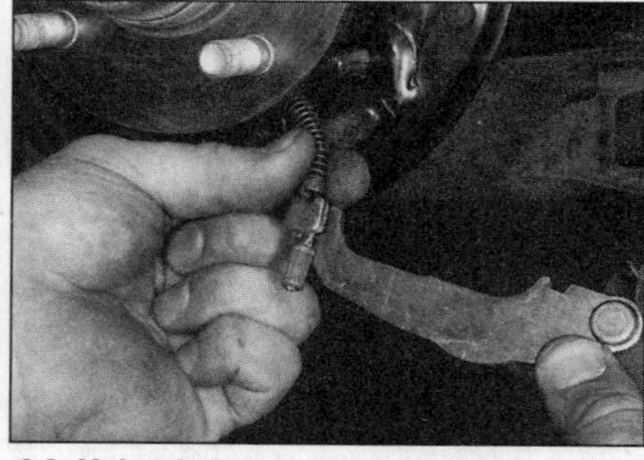

6.9 Unhook the handbrake cable from the lever on the trailing brake shoe

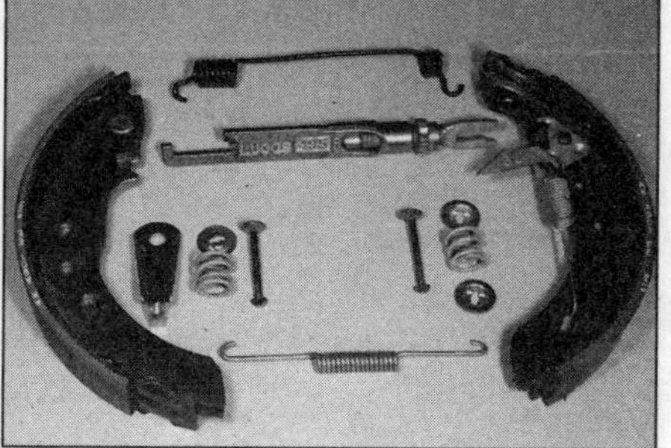

6.14 Rear brake shoe components ready for refitting

11 Transfer the handbrake operating lever to the new trailing shoe as required, and secure with a new retaining clip. Note that the lever and adjuster strut components are different on each side of the vehicle - take care not to mix up the components.

12 Shorten the adjuster strut to its minimum length by turning the toothed wheel, and apply a small amount of brake grease to the contact faces of the adjuster strut and handbrake operating lever.

13 Apply brake grease sparingly to the shoe contact surfaces of the brake backplate. On later models with ABS, take care not to get any grease on the sensor tip or rotor.

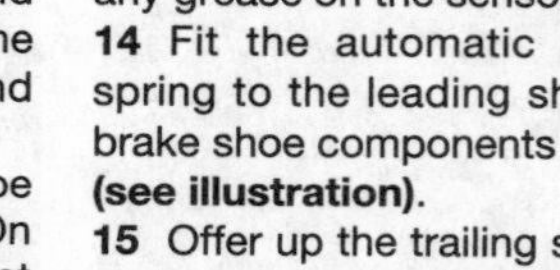

14 Fit the automatic adjusting lever and spring to the leading shoe, then lay out the brake shoe components ready for reassembly **(see illustration)**.

15 Offer up the trailing shoe to the backplate and engage the handbrake cable with the operating lever on the shoe. Manipulate the shoe into position, and secure with the hold-down pin, spring seat/stop plate, spring and cup **(see illustrations)**.

16 Engage the adjuster strut with the relevant cut-out in the trailing shoe and refit the upper return spring. Ensure that the adjuster strut is fitted the correct way round.

17 Engage the upper return spring with the leading shoe and locate the shoe on the wheel cylinder.

18 Refit the lower return spring and pull the lower ends of the shoes onto the lower anchor.

19 Refit the hold-down pin, spring and cup to secure the leading shoe.

6.15a Offer up the trailing brake shoe and strut to the backplate . . .

6.15b . . . locate the spring seat . . .

6.15c . . . insert the pin . . .

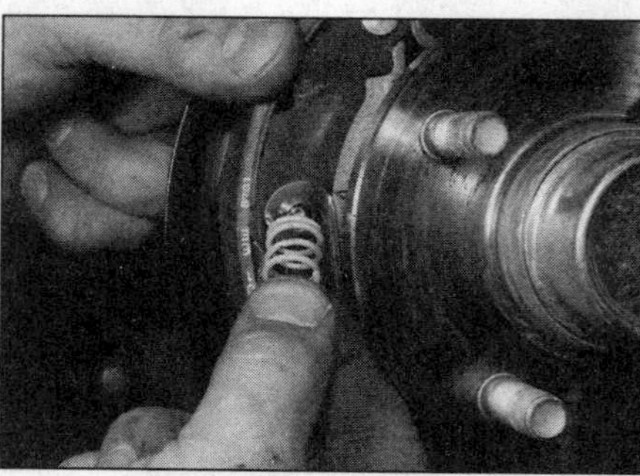

6.15d . . . fit the spring . . .

6.15e . . . and outer seat

20 Check that all components have been correctly refitted, and check that the adjuster mechanism operates correctly.
21 If necessary, turn the adjuster wheel to ensure that the diameter of the shoes is less than that of the drum.
22 Repeat the procedure on the remaining side of the vehicle, then refit the brake drums as described in Section 8.

7 Brake disc - inspection, removal and refitting

Warning: Before starting work, refer to the warning in Section 4 concerning the dangers of asbestos dust.

Front disc

Inspection

Note: *If either disc requires renewal, BOTH should be renewed at the same time, to ensure even and consistent braking. New brake pads should also be fitted.*
1 Chock the rear wheels, apply the handbrake, then jack up the front of the vehicle and support it on axle stands (see *"Jacking and vehicle support"*). Remove the appropriate front roadwheel.
2 Slowly rotate the brake disc so that the full area of both sides can be checked. Light scoring is normal in the area swept by the brake pads, but if heavy scoring or cracks are found, the disc must be renewed.
3 It is normal to find a lip of rust and brake dust around the disc's perimeter; this can be scraped off if required. If, however, a lip has formed due to excessive wear of the brake pad swept area, then the disc's thickness must be measured using a micrometer. Take measurements at several places around the disc, at the inside and outside of the pad swept area; if the disc has worn at any point to the specified minimum thickness or less, the disc must be renewed **(see illustrations)**.
4 If the disc is thought to be warped, it can be checked for run-out. Either use a dial gauge mounted on any convenient fixed point, while the disc is slowly rotated, or use feeler blades to measure (at several points all around the disc) the clearance between the disc and a fixed point, such as the caliper mounting bracket. **Note:** *As the disc is held in position by the roadwheel it will be necessary to use suitable washers and two of the wheel nuts to secure the disc during the check.* If the measurements obtained exceed the specified maximum amount, the disc is excessively warped and must be renewed; however, it is worth checking first that the hub bearing is in good condition (Chapters 1 and/or 10). Also try the effect of removing the disc and turning it through 180°, to reposition it on the hub; if the run-out is still excessive, the disc must be renewed.
5 Check the disc for cracks, especially around the wheel stud holes, and any other wear or damage, and renew if necessary.

Removal

6 Remove the front brake pads (Section 4).
7 Unscrew the two bolts securing the caliper mounting bracket to the hub carrier and withdraw the carrier **(see illustration)**.
8 If the original disc is to be refitted, mark the relationship between the disc and the hub, then pull the disc from the roadwheel studs **(see illustration)**.
9 If the disc is stuck, it can be pushed off by screwing two M8 bolts into the holes provided in the disc, and evenly tightening the bolts to push the disc from the hub.

Refitting

10 Ensure that the mating faces of the disc and the hub are clean and flat. If necessary, wipe the mating surfaces clean.
11 Refit the disc on the wheel studs. If the original disc is being refitted, align the marks made on the disc and hub before removal. If a new disc is being fitted, use a suitable solvent to wipe any preservative coating from the disc.
12 Refit the caliper mounting bracket and tighten the bracket securing bolts to the specified torque **(see illustration)**. **Note:** *Use thread locking compound on the mounting bolts when they are refitted.*
13 Refit the front brake pads as described in Section 4.

Rear disc

Inspection

Note: *If either disc requires renewal, BOTH should be renewed at the same time, to ensure even and consistent braking. New brake pads should also be fitted.*

7.3a Using a micrometer to check the thickness of the front brake disc

7.3b The minimum thickness is stamped on the outer perimeter of the disc

7.7 Unbolting the front brake mounting bracket

7.8 Removing the front brake disc

7.12 Tightening the front brake caliper mounting bracket bolts

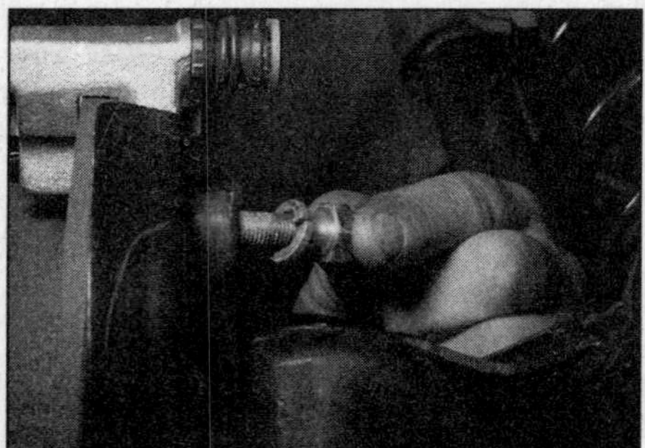

7.18a Remove the bolts . . .

7.18b . . . and remove the rear brake caliper mounting bracket . . .

7.18c . . . then remove the rear brake disc

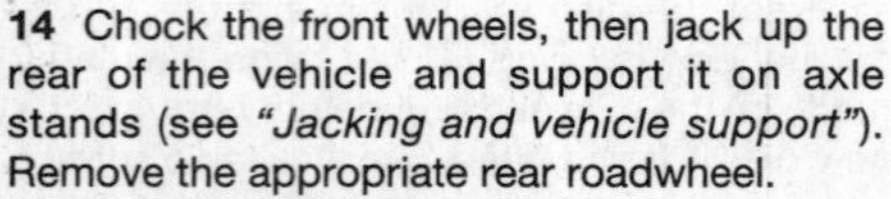

14 Chock the front wheels, then jack up the rear of the vehicle and support it on axle stands (see *"Jacking and vehicle support"*). Remove the appropriate rear roadwheel.

15 Fully release the handbrake.

16 Proceed as described for the front disc in paragraphs 2 to 5.

Removal

17 Remove the rear brake pads as described in Section 5.

18 Proceed as described for the front brake disc in paragraphs 7 to 9 **(see illustrations)**.

Refitting

19 Proceed as described for the front brake disc in paragraphs 10 to 12.

20 Refit the rear brake pads as described in Section 5.

8 Rear brake drum - removal, inspection and refitting

Warning: Before starting work, refer to the warning in Section 4 concerning the dangers of asbestos dust.

Removal

1 Chock the front wheels, then jack up the rear of the vehicle and support it on axle stands (see *"Jacking and vehicle support"*). Remove the appropriate rear roadwheel.

2 Fully release the handbrake.

3 If the drum cannot easily be pulled from the wheel studs, retract the brake shoes as follows.

4 Remove the blanking plug from the rear of the brake backplate. Insert a suitable tool through the hole in the backplate and through the hole in the shoe, until the tool contacts the handbrake operating lever stop plate. Press lightly on the tool in order to push out the stop plate and allow the lever to fully retract **(see illustrations)**. Remove the tool.

5 If the original drum is to be refitted, mark the relationship between the drum and the hub, then pull the drum from the roadwheel studs **(see illustration)**.

Inspection

6 If either drum requires renewal, BOTH should be renewed at the same time, to ensure even and consistent braking. New brake shoes should also be fitted.

7 Remove all traces of brake dust from the drum, but *avoid inhaling the dust, as it is a health hazard.*

8 Clean the outside of the drum, and check it for obvious signs of wear or damage, such as cracks around the roadwheel stud holes; renew the drum if necessary.

9 Carefully examine the inside of the drum. Light scoring of the friction surface is normal, but if heavy scoring is found, the drum must be renewed.

10 It is usual to find a lip on the drum's inboard edge which consists of a mixture of rust and brake dust which should be scraped away to leave a smooth surface. If, however, the lip is due to the friction surface being recessed by excessive wear, then the drum must be renewed.

11 If the drum is thought to be excessively worn, or oval, its internal diameter must be measured at several points using an internal micrometer. Take measurements in pairs, the second at right-angles to the first, and compare the two to check for signs of ovality. Provided that it does not enlarge the drum to beyond the specified maximum diameter, it may be possible to have the drum refinished by skimming or grinding; if this is not possible, the drums on both sides must be renewed **(see illustration)**. Note that if the drum is to be skimmed, BOTH drums must be refinished, to maintain a consistent internal diameter on both sides.

8.4a Removing the blanking plug from the rear brake backplate

8.4b Using a screwdriver to push out the handbrake operating lever stop plate

8.5 Removing a rear brake drum

8.11 The maximum diameter of the rear brake drum inner surface is stamped on the outside of the drum

Refitting

12 If a new brake drum is to be installed, use a suitable solvent to remove any preservative coating that may have been applied to its internal friction surfaces. Note that it may also be necessary to shorten the adjuster strut length, by rotating the strut wheel, to allow the drum to pass over the brake shoes.

13 If the original drum is being refitted, align the marks made on the drum and hub before removal, then fit the drum over the wheel studs and refit the roadwheel. If the handbrake operating lever was retracted as in paragraph 4, make sure that it is repositioned before refitting the drum.

14 Depress the footbrake repeatedly to expand the brake shoes against the drum, and ensure that normal pedal pressure is restored.

15 Check and if necessary adjust the handbrake cable as described in Chapter 1.

16 Lower the vehicle to the ground.

9 Front brake caliper - removal, overhaul and refitting

Warning: Before starting work, refer to the note at the beginning of Section 2 concerning the dangers of hydraulic fluid, and to the warning at the beginning of Section 4 concerning the dangers of asbestos dust.

Removal

1 Chock the rear wheels, apply the handbrake, then jack up the front of the vehicle and support it on axle stands (see *"Jacking and vehicle support"*). Remove the appropriate front roadwheel.

2 To minimise fluid loss during the following operations, remove the master cylinder reservoir cap, then tighten it down onto a piece of polythene, to obtain an airtight seal. Alternatively, use a brake hose clamp, a G-clamp or a similar tool to clamp the flexible hose running to the caliper.

3 Clean the area around the fluid hose union on the caliper, then unscrew the union bolt. Recover the two sealing washers. Cover the open ends of the joint and the caliper, to prevent dirt ingress.

4 Remove the brake pads as described in Section 4, and withdraw the caliper from the vehicle. **Do not** depress the brake pedal until the caliper is refitted.

5 Unbolt the caliper mounting bracket from the hub carrier.

Overhaul

6 With the caliper on the bench, wipe away all traces of dust and dirt, but *avoid inhaling the dust, as it is a health hazard.*

7 Extract the caliper guide pins, if necessary by screwing the bolts into the pins, and pulling on the bolts to withdraw the pins. Remove the rubber dust cover from each guide pin.

8 Place a small block of wood between the caliper body and the piston. Remove the piston, including the dust seal, by applying a jet of low-pressure compressed air, such as that from a tyre pump, to the fluid inlet port.

9 Remove the dust seal from the piston, and use a blunt instrument, such as a knitting needle, to extract the piston seal from the caliper cylinder bore.

10 Thoroughly clean all components, using only methylated spirit or clean hydraulic fluid. Never use mineral-based solvents such as petrol or paraffin, which will attack the hydraulic system rubber components.

11 The caliper piston seal and the dust seal, the guide pin dust covers, and the bleed nipple dust cap, are only available as part of a seal kit. Since the manufacturers recommend that the piston seal and dust seal are renewed whenever they are disturbed, all of these components should be discarded, and new ones fitted on reassembly as a matter of course.

12 Carefully examine all parts of the caliper assembly, looking for signs of wear or damage. In particular, the cylinder bore and piston must be free from any signs of scratches, corrosion or wear. If there is any doubt about the condition of any part of the caliper, the relevant part should be renewed; note that if the caliper body or the mounting bracket are to be renewed, they are available only as part of the complete assembly.

13 The manufacturers recommend that minor scratches, rust, etc, may be polished away from the cylinder bore using fine emery paper, but the piston must be renewed if it has such defects. The piston surface is plated, and **must not** be polished with emery or similar abrasives.

14 Check that both guide pins are undamaged, and (when cleaned) a reasonably tight sliding fit in the mounting bracket bores.

15 Use compressed air to blow clear the fluid passages.

Warning: Wear eye protection when using compressed air.

16 Before commencing reassembly, ensure that all components are spotlessly clean and dry.

17 Soak the new piston seal in clean hydraulic fluid, and fit it to the groove in the cylinder bore, using your fingers only (no tools) to manipulate it into place.

18 Fit the new dust seal to the piston groove, smear clean hydraulic fluid over the piston and caliper cylinder bore, and refit the piston. Press the piston fully into the caliper body, then fit the dust seal to the groove in the caliper body.

19 Fit a new rubber dust cover to each guide pin, and apply a smear of brake grease to the guide pins before refitting them to their bores.

Refitting

20 Refit the caliper mounting bracket to the hub carrier, and tighten the mounting bolts to the specified torque. **Note:** *Use thread locking compound on the mounting bolts when they are refitted.*

21 Refit the brake pads and caliper with reference to Section 4, however **do not** depress the brake pedal at this stage.

22 Check that the brake fluid hose is correctly routed, without being twisted, then reconnect the union to the caliper, using two new sealing washers. Refit the union bolt, and tighten to the specified torque.

23 Remove the polythene from the master cylinder reservoir cap, or remove the clamp from the fluid hose, as applicable.

24 Bleed the hydraulic fluid circuit as described in Section 2. Note that if no other part of the system has been disturbed, it should only be necessary to bleed the relevant front circuit.

25 Depress the brake pedal repeatedly to bring the pads into contact with the brake disc, and ensure that normal pedal pressure is restored.

26 Refit the roadwheel, and lower the vehicle to the ground.

10 Rear brake caliper - removal, overhaul and refitting

Warning: Before starting work, refer to the note at the beginning of Section 2 concerning the dangers of hydraulic fluid, and to the warning at the beginning of Section 4 concerning the dangers of asbestos dust.

Removal

1 Chock the front wheels, then jack up the rear of the vehicle and support securely on axle stands (see *"Jacking and vehicle support"*). Remove the appropriate rear roadwheel.

2 Working inside the car use a socket to back off the handbrake cable adjustment nut located beneath the handbrake lever. This is necessary in order to provide enough free play to disconnect the rear end of the cable from the lever on the rear caliper.

3 Using pliers, pull out the spring clip securing the handbrake cable to the mounting bracket, then disconnect the end of the cable from the lever on the caliper and withdraw the cable **(see illustrations)**.

4 To minimise fluid loss during the following operations, remove the master cylinder reservoir cap, then tighten it down onto a piece of polythene, to obtain an airtight seal. Alternatively, use a brake hose clamp, a G-clamp or a similar tool to clamp the flexible hose running to the caliper **(see illustration)**.

5 Clean the area around the fluid hose union on the caliper, then unscrew the union bolt. Recover the two sealing washers. Cover the

10.3a Pull out the spring clip . . .

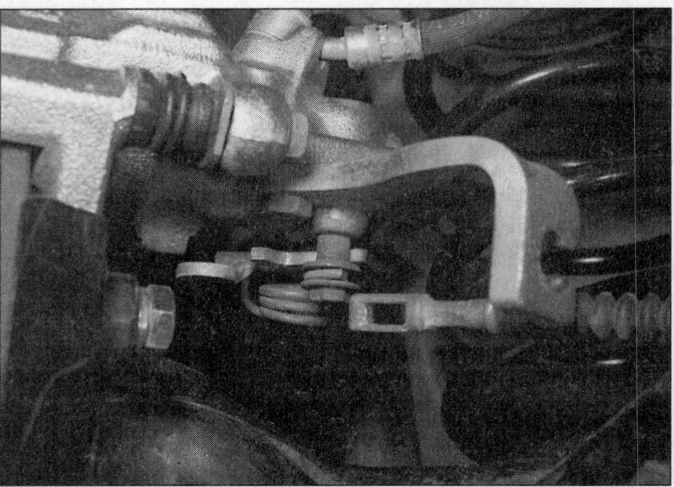
10.3b . . . and disconnect the end of the cable from the lever on the caliper

10.4 Brake hose clamp fitted to the rear brake hose

open ends of the banjo and the caliper, to prevent dirt ingress.

6 Remove the brake pads as described in Section 5, and withdraw the caliper from the vehicle. **Do not** depress the brake pedal until the caliper is refitted.

7 Unbolt the caliper mounting bracket from the rear axle.

Overhaul

8 With the caliper on the bench, wipe away all traces of dust and dirt, but *avoid inhaling the dust, as it is a health hazard.*

9 Extract the caliper guide pins, if necessary by screwing the bolts into the pins, and pulling on the bolts to withdraw the pins. Remove the rubber dust cover from each guide pin.

10 Engage a suitable pair of long-nosed pliers with the notches in the piston, then turn the piston anti-clockwise (viewed from the outboard end of the caliper), to unscrew it from the caliper. Withdraw the piston from the caliper body, and remove the dust seal from the groove.

11 Working inside the rear of the piston, use circlip pliers to extract the circlip, then remove the first spacer, the wave washer, the second spacer, the ball bearing, and the adjusting nut. Prise the cup seal off the adjusting nut.

12 Working inside the caliper cylinder bore, use circlip pliers to extract the circlip, whilst using a suitable length of tubing to compress the spring cap against the spring pressure.

13 With the circlip removed from its groove, allow the spring to push out the components until pressure is relaxed, then withdraw the circlip, the spring cap, the spring and the spring seat.

14 Use circlip pliers to extract the remaining circlip, then withdraw the key plate, the pushrod and the plunger. Prise the sealing O-ring off the pushrod.

15 Using a blunt instrument such as a knitting needle, extract the piston seal from the caliper cylinder bore.

16 Unhook the return spring from the stop-bolt then unscrew and remove the stop-bolt. Recover the spring.

17 Withdraw the lever assembly from the caliper body.

18 Thoroughly clean all components, using only methylated spirit or clean hydraulic fluid. Never use mineral-based solvents such as petrol or paraffin, which will attack the hydraulic system rubber components.

19 Discard all seals, cups, dust covers and other rubber components. These are available as part of a caliper seal kit, and should be renewed as a matter of course whenever they are disturbed.

20 Carefully examine all parts of the caliper assembly, looking for signs of wear or damage. In particular, the cylinder bore and piston must be free from any signs of scratches, corrosion or wear. If there is any doubt about the condition of any part of the caliper, the relevant part should be renewed. Note that if the caliper body or the mounting bracket are to be renewed, they are available only as part of the complete assembly.

21 The manufacturers recommend that minor scratches, rust, etc, may be polished away from the cylinder bore using fine emery paper, but the piston must be renewed if it has such defects. The piston surface is plated, and **must not** be polished with emery or similar abrasives.

22 Check that both guide pins are undamaged, and (when cleaned) a reasonably tight sliding fit in the mounting bracket bores.

23 Use compressed air to blow clear the fluid passages.

Warning: Wear eye protection when using compressed air.

24 Before commencing reassembly, ensure that all components are spotlessly clean and dry.

25 Slide the handbrake lever into the caliper body, ensuring that the lever cam cut-out aligns with the pushrod aperture. Refit and tighten the stop-bolt, then refit the return spring, hooking it onto the lever and stop-bolt.

26 Soak the new piston seal in clean hydraulic fluid, and fit it to the groove in the cylinder bore, using your fingers only to manipulate it into position.

27 Fit a new O-ring to the pushrod, and apply a smear of rubber grease to the plunger and the pushrod. Assemble the plunger and pushrod, and fit them to the caliper body.

28 Refit the key plate so that its cut-out fits over the squared section of the pushrod, and its convex locating pip matches the concave depression in the caliper body. Secure the assembly by refitting the circlip.

29 Refit the spring seat, the spring and the spring cap, then compress the spring cap (using a suitable length of tubing as during removal) while refitting the securing circlip. Check that the circlip is correctly seated in its groove.

30 Fit the new cup seal to the adjusting nut, using only your fingers to manipulate it into position. Ensure that the seal is correctly fitted.

31 Smear rubber grease over the cup seal lips, and fit the adjusting nut into the piston.

10.40 Refitting the handbrake cable securing spring clip

32 Pack the ball bearing with brake grease and refit it, followed by the spacer, the wave washer, and the remaining spacer. Secure the components with the remaining circlip.
33 Apply a smear of rubber grease to the inner and outer lips of the new dust seal, then fit it to the groove in the piston.
34 Smear clean hydraulic fluid over the piston and the caliper cylinder bore, then refit the piston assembly, and screw it in clockwise (using a retractor tool or long-nosed pliers) until it seats.
35 Engage the dust seal with the caliper body.
36 Fit a new rubber dust cover to each guide pin. Apply a smear of brake grease to the guide pins before refitting them to their bores.

Refitting

37 Refit the caliper mounting bracket to the rear axle, and tighten the mounting bolts to the specified torque. **Note:** *Use thread locking compound on the mounting bolts when they are refitted.*
38 Refit the brake pads as described in Section 5, however **do not** depress the brake pedal at this stage.
39 Check that the brake fluid hose is correctly routed, without being twisted, then reconnect the union to the caliper, using two new sealing washers. Refit the union bolt, and tighten to the specified torque.
40 Insert the handbrake cable and reconnect it to the lever. Refit the spring clip securing the cable to the mounting bracket **(see illustration)**.
41 Remove the polythene from the master cylinder reservoir cap, or remove the clamp from the fluid hose, as applicable.
42 Bleed the hydraulic fluid circuit as described in Section 2. Note that if no other part of the system has been disturbed, it should only be necessary to bleed the relevant rear circuit.
43 Depress the brake pedal repeatedly to bring the pads into contact with the brake disc, and ensure that normal pedal pressure is restored.
44 Refit the roadwheel, and lower the vehicle to the ground.

11 Rear wheel cylinder - removal, overhaul and refitting

Warning: Before starting work, refer to the note at the beginning of Section 2 concerning the dangers of hydraulic fluid, and to the warning at the beginning of Section 4 concerning the dangers of asbestos dust.

Removal

1 Remove the brake drum as described in Section 8.
2 Remove the brake shoes as described in Section 6.
3 To minimise fluid loss during the following operations, remove the master cylinder reservoir cap, then tighten it down onto a piece of polythene, to obtain an airtight seal.
4 Clean the brake backplate around the wheel cylinder mounting bolts and the hydraulic pipe union, then unscrew the union nut and disconnect the hydraulic pipe. Cover the open ends of the pipe and the wheel cylinder to prevent dirt ingress.
5 Unscrew the mounting bolts and withdraw the wheel cylinder from the backplate.

Overhaul

6 Clean the assembly thoroughly, using only methylated spirit or clean brake fluid.
7 Pull the rubber dust covers from the grooves in the wheel cylinder, then use paint or similar to mark one of the pistons so that the pistons are not interchanged on reassembly.
8 Withdraw both pistons and the spring.
9 Discard the rubber piston seals and the dust covers. These components should be renewed as a matter of course, and are available as part of an overhaul kit, which also includes the bleed nipple dust cap.
10 Check the condition of the cylinder bore and the piston - the surfaces must be perfect and free from scratches, scoring and corrosion. It is advisable to renew the complete wheel cylinder if there is any doubt as to the condition of the cylinder bore or piston.
11 Ensure that all components are clean and dry. The pistons, spring and seals should be fitted wet, using hydraulic fluid as a lubricant - dip them in clean fluid before installation.
12 Fit the seals to the grooves in the pistons, ensuring that they are the correct way round. Use only your fingers to manipulate the seals into position.
13 Fit the first piston to the cylinder, taking care not to distort the seal. If the original pistons are being re-used, the marks made on dismantling should be used to ensure that the pistons are refitted to their original bores.
14 Refit the spring and the second piston.
15 Apply a smear of rubber grease to the exposed end of each piston and to the dust cover sealing lips, then fit the dust covers.

Refitting

16 Refitting is a reversal of removal, bearing in mind the following points:

a) Tighten the mounting bolts to the specified torque.
b) Refit the brake shoes as described in Section 6, and refit the brake drum as described in Section 8.
c) Before refitting the roadwheel and lowering the vehicle to the ground, remove the polythene from the fluid reservoir, and bleed the hydraulic system as described in Section 2. Note that if no other part of the system has been disturbed, it should only be necessary to bleed the relevant rear circuit.

12 Master cylinder - removal, overhaul and refitting

Warning: Before starting work, refer to the note in Section 2 concerning the dangers of hydraulic fluid.

Removal

1 Remove the air cleaner assembly as described in Chapter 4A. Additionally, on left-hand drive models, also remove the air ducting. Position a cloth rag over the throttle housing as a precaution.
2 Disconnect the wiring from the low fluid warning switch on the side of the fluid reservoir.
3 Remove the master cylinder fluid reservoir cap, and syphon the hydraulic fluid from the reservoir. **Note:** *Do not syphon the fluid by mouth, as it is poisonous; use a syringe or an old poultry baster.* Alternatively, open any convenient bleed screw in the system, and pump the brake pedal to expel the fluid through a tube connected to the screw (see Section 2).
4 Wipe clean the area around the brake pipe unions on the side of the master cylinder, and place absorbent rags beneath the pipe unions to catch any surplus fluid. Make a note of the correct fitted positions of the unions, then unscrew the union nuts and carefully withdraw the pipes. Plug or tape over the pipe ends and master cylinder orifices, to minimise the loss of brake fluid, and to prevent the entry of dirt into the system. Wash off any spilt fluid immediately with cold water.
5 Unscrew and remove the nuts securing the master cylinder to the vacuum servo unit, then withdraw the unit from the engine compartment. On left-hand drive models it will be necessary to remove the fuel filter from its mounting clip before removing the master cylinder.
6 Recover the seal from the rear of the master cylinder. Examine the seal for deterioration, and if necessary obtain a new one.

Overhaul

7 Press out the retaining pin (where fitted) from the base of the reservoir, then pull the

fluid reservoir from the top of the master cylinder. Prise the reservoir seals from the master cylinder.

8 Where fitted, use a suitable screwdriver to bend back the tangs securing the master cylinder end cap, then withdraw the end cap.

9 Push on the end of the primary piston to compress the primary and secondary piston assemblies, then use long-nosed pliers to remove the secondary piston stop-pin. On models without ABS, the pin is located in the secondary port on top of the cylinder, however on models with ABS it is located on the bottom of the cylinder and accessed by unscrewing a plug.

10 Noting the order of removal, and the direction of fitting of each component, withdraw the piston assemblies with their springs and seals, tapping the body onto a clean wooden surface to dislodge them. If necessary, clamp the master cylinder body in a vice (fitted with soft jaw covers) and use compressed air (applied through the secondary circuit fluid port) to assist the removal of the secondary piston assembly.

Warning: Wear eye protection when working with compressed air.

11 Thoroughly clean all components using only methylated spirit or clean hydraulic fluid. Never use mineral-based solvents such as petrol or paraffin, as they will attack the hydraulic system rubber components. Dry the components immediately, using compressed air or a clean, lint-free cloth.

12 Check all components, and renew any that are worn or damaged (note that individual seal components are not available - the overhaul kit will contain complete primary and secondary piston assemblies, complete with all seals, washers, etc). Check particularly the cylinder bores and pistons; the complete assembly should be renewed if these are scratched, worn or corroded. If there is any doubt about the condition of the assembly or of any of its components, renew it. Check that the cylinder body fluid passages are clear.

13 Before reassembly, soak the pistons and the new seals in clean hydraulic fluid. Smear clean fluid on the cylinder bore.

14 Insert the piston assemblies into the cylinder bore making sure that the assemblies are inserted squarely. Use a twisting motion to avoid trapping the seal lips. Ensure that all components are refitted in the correct order and the right way round. Where applicable, follow the assembly instructions supplied with the repair kit. On models with ABS, ensure that the slot in the secondary piston assembly aligns with the hole in the bottom of the master cylinder.

15 Compress the piston assemblies into the cylinder bore, then refit the stop-pin. On non-ABS models keep the cylinder upright. On ABS models refit and tighten the plug.

16 Press the piston assemblies fully into the bore, and secure them in position with the new end cap (supplied in the overhaul kit). Bend the tangs into position to secure the end cap.

17 Examine the fluid reservoir seals, and if necessary renew them. Fit the reservoir seals to the master cylinder body, then refit the reservoir.

Refitting

18 Remove all traces of dirt from the master cylinder and servo unit mating surfaces, and fit the seal between the master cylinder body and the servo.

19 Fit the master cylinder to the servo unit, locating the servo unit pushrod in the primary piston. Refit the mounting nuts, and tighten them to the specified torque.

20 Wipe clean the brake pipe unions, then refit them to the correct master cylinder ports, as noted before removal, and tighten the union nuts securely.

21 Reconnect the wiring to the low fluid warning switch on the side of the reservoir.

22 Refill the master cylinder reservoir with new fluid, and bleed the complete hydraulic system as described in Section 2.

23 Refit the air cleaner assembly (and air ducting where applicable) with reference to Chapter 4A.

13 Brake pedal - adjustment, removal and refitting

Adjustment

1 The pedal free height should be measured from the upper face of the pedal to the floor protection sheet. To take the measurement, first pull back the carpet.

2 Check that the measured height is as given in the *Specifications*. If the height of the pedal requires adjustment, proceed as follows.

3 Loosen the locknut on the servo pushrod, and turn the pushrod as required until the specified height is achieved. Retighten the locknut on completion.

4 Check the free play of the pedal by pressing the pedal slowly until resistance is felt. The free play should be as specified.

5 Check that the stop-lights go out when the pedal is released (see Section 19 for switch adjustment).

6 On completion, refit the carpet.

Removal

7 Working in the driver's footwell, unscrew the screws and remove the small shelf from below the steering column.

8 Remove the clip from the end of the servo pushrod clevis pin, then withdraw the clevis pin. On later models, depress the integral tangs in the end of the clevis pin before withdrawing it **(see illustration)**.

9 Remove the stop-light switch as described in Section 19.

10 Unscrew the four nuts securing the pedal bracket to the bulkhead (note that these nuts also secure the vacuum servo).

11 Unscrew the pedal bracket upper securing bolt, then withdraw the pedal/bracket assembly from the footwell.

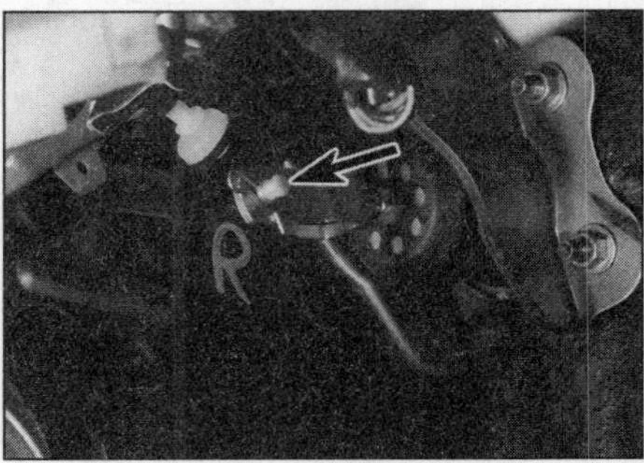

13.8 Clevis pin securing the servo pushrod to the brake pedal

12 The brake pedal is integral with the bracket assembly, and cannot be renewed individually.

Refitting

13 Refitting is a reversal of removal but, on completion, check the pedal height adjustment as described earlier in this Section.

14 Vacuum servo unit - removal and refitting

Removal

1 Remove the master cylinder (Section 12).

2 Release the brake lines from the clip on the bulkhead and tie them to one side without bending them excessively. Move them sufficiently to provide room for the removal of the servo unit.

3 Unbolt the power steering hose/switch bracket from the bulkhead and tie the bracket to one side.

4 Disconnect the vacuum hose from the servo.

5 Inside the vehicle, remove the clip from the end of the servo pushrod clevis pin, then withdraw the clevis pin to disconnect the brake pedal from the pushrod. On later models, depress the integral tangs in the end of the clevis pin before withdrawing it **(see illustration)**.

6 Unscrew the four nuts securing the pedal bracket to the bulkhead (note that these nuts also secure the vacuum servo).

7 On left-hand drive models with ABS, unscrew the ABS actuator unit mounting nuts in the left-

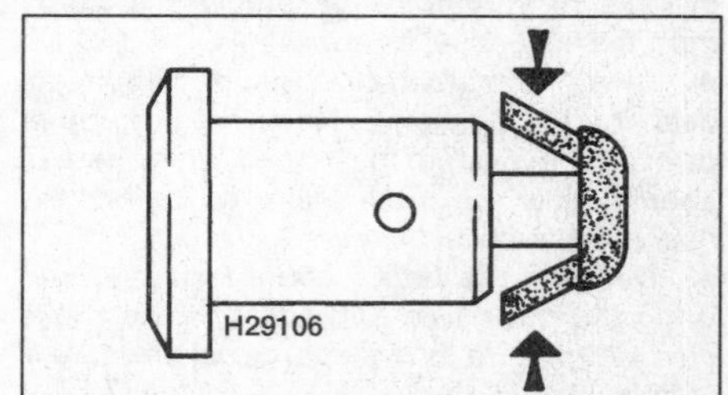

14.5 Later type servo pushrod clevis pin with integral tangs

hand side of the engine compartment, and position the unit slightly to one side.

8 In the engine compartment, tilt the servo unit upwards and withdraw it from the bulkhead. Recover the gasket.

Caution: Working room is restricted, and care must be taken to prevent damage to the mounting stud threads on the servo unit as it is withdrawn from the bulkhead.

Refitting

9 On models with ABS, use vernier calipers to check that the protrusion of the pushrod from the front face of the servo unit is as given in the *Specifications*. If necessary, loosen the locknut and adjust the pushrod then tighten the locknut to secure.

10 On models without ABS, if a new servo unit is being fitted, use vernier calipers to temporarily set the dimension from the rear mounting face to the clevis pin hole in the clevis to the dimension given in the *Specifications*. This will give a starting point for adjustment of the brake pedal height (see Section 13).

11 Locate a new gasket on the servo unit studs, then fit the unit to the bulkhead taking care not to damage the stud threads.

12 Locate the pedal bracket on the servo unit studs and refit the mounting nuts. Tighten the nuts to the specified torque.

13 On left-hand drive models with ABS, refit the ABS actuator unit and tighten the mounting nuts.

14 Align the pushrod clevis with the hole in the brake pedal, then insert the clevis pin. Refit the clip where applicable.

15 Reconnect the vacuum hose to the servo.

16 Refit the power steering hose/switch bracket to the bulkhead and tighten the bolts.

17 Adjust the brake pedal height as described in Section 13.

18 Refit the master cylinder (see Section 12).

19 Position the brake lines in the bulkhead clip and secure the clip.

15 Vacuum servo unit check valve - removal, testing and refitting

Removal

1 The valve is a push-fit in the front of the servo.

2 Release the securing clip, and disconnect the vacuum hose from the valve.

3 Withdraw the valve from its rubber sealing grommet, using a pulling and twisting motion. Remove the grommet from the servo.

Testing

4 Examine the check valve for signs of damage, and renew if necessary. The valve may be tested by blowing through it in both directions. Air should flow through the valve in one direction only - when blown through from the servo unit end of the valve. Renew the valve if this is not the case.

5 Examine the rubber sealing grommet and vacuum hose for signs of damage or deterioration, and renew as necessary.

Refitting

6 Press the sealing grommet into position in the servo unit.

7 Carefully ease the check valve into position, taking care not to displace or damage the grommet. Reconnect the vacuum hose to the valve and tighten the clip.

8 Check the hose for direction arrow, if the hose is marked then arrow should point towards the engine.

9 On completion, check the servo unit as described in Chapter 1.

16 Handbrake lever - removal and refitting

Removal

1 Chock the wheels, and fully release the handbrake.

2 Remove the screws/clips and remove the plastic cover from the top of the handbrake lever **(see illustrations)**.

3 Prise the cover from the rear of the handbrake lever surround, then unscrew the mounting screws and withdraw the surround over the handbrake lever **(see illustrations)**.

4 Count the number of exposed threads on the cable adjustment fitting, then unscrew and

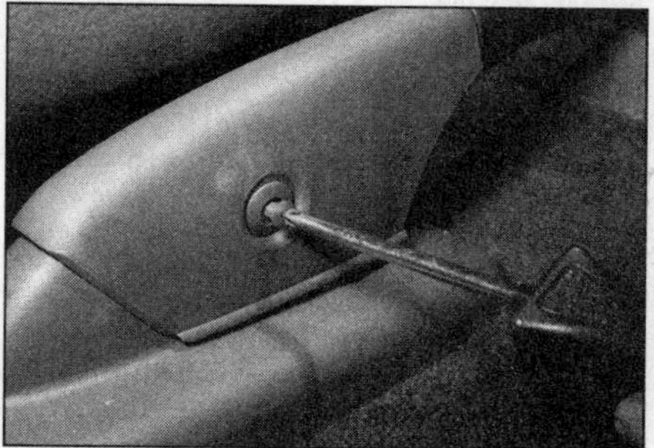

16.2a Unscrew the screws . . .

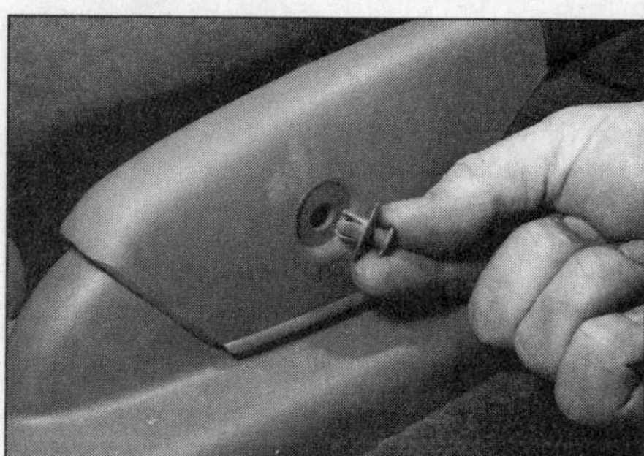

16.2b . . . and remove the clips . . .

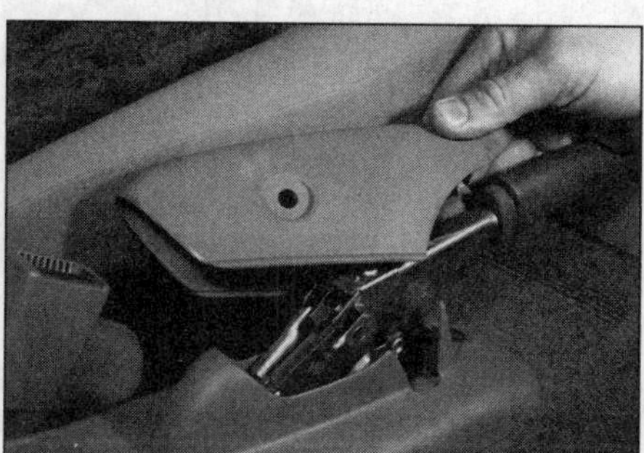

16.2c . . . then remove the handbrake cover

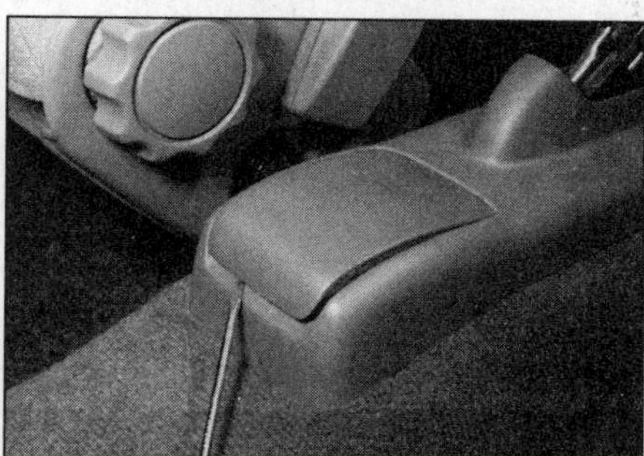

16.3a Prise out the cover . . .

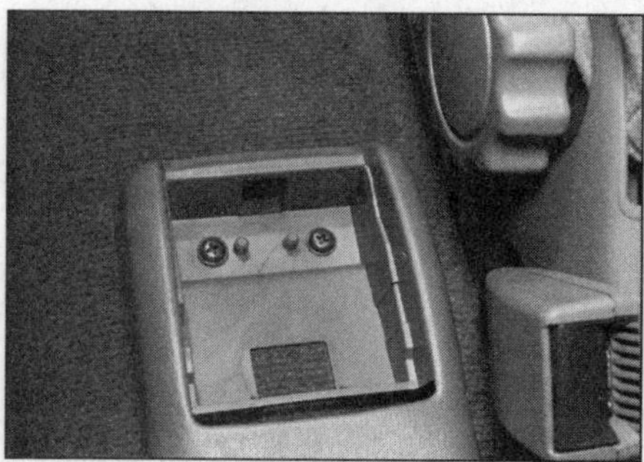

16.3b . . . remove the rear screws . . .

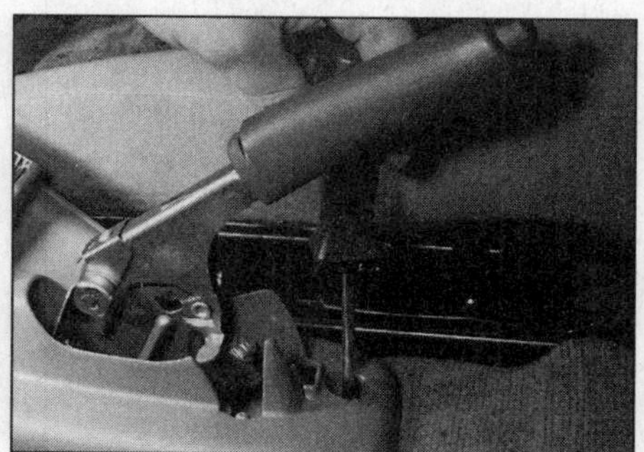

16.3c . . . and front screw . . .

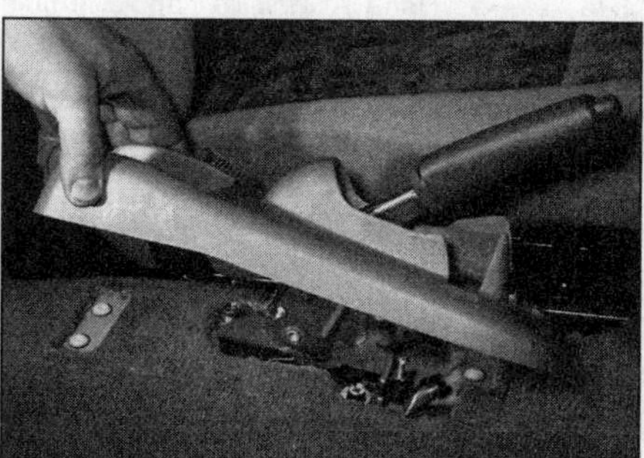

16.3d . . . then withdraw the surround

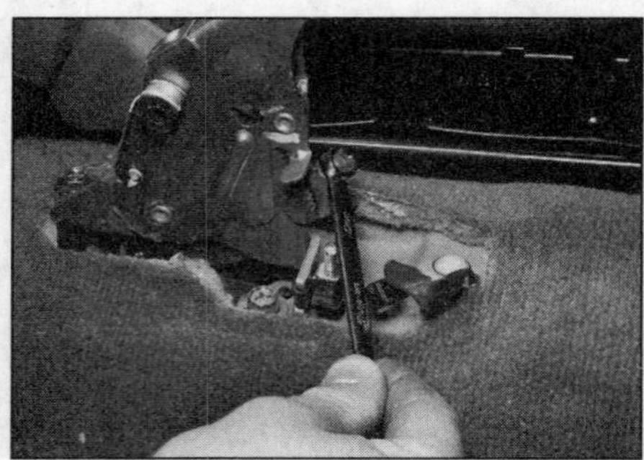

16.4 Loosening the handbrake cable adjustment nut

remove the adjustment nut and release the primary cable from the lever assembly **(see illustration)**.

5 Disconnect the wiring from the handbrake "on" warning light switch.

6 Unscrew the two mounting bolts and withdraw the handbrake lever assembly **(see illustration)**.

Refitting

7 Refitting is a reversal of removal, but note the following points:

a) Screw the adjuster nut onto the cable adjuster rod to give the number of exposed threads noted before removal, then check the handbrake operation, and adjust if necessary, as described in Chapter 1.

b) Before refitting the handbrake lever surround and plastic cover, check the operation of the handbrake "on" warning light. The plastic cover screws are pushed into position without using a screwdriver.

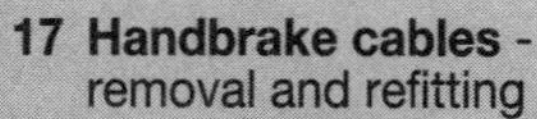

17 Handbrake cables - removal and refitting

Rear cable

Removal

1 There are two rear handbrake cables, one on each side of the vehicle. To renew either rear cable, proceed as follows.

2 Chock the front wheels, then jack up the rear of the vehicle and support securely on axle stands (see *"Jacking and vehicle support"*). Release the handbrake fully.

3 Lift the handbrake lever slightly, then unscrew the adjustment nut on the front of the handbrake lever to provide slack in the rear handbrake cables.

4 On models with rear drum brakes, remove the brake shoes, and disconnect the end of the handbrake cable from the lever on the trailing shoe, as described in Section 6. Pull the cable from the backplate while using pliers to depress the retaining tabs **(see illustration)**.

5 On models with rear disc brakes, pull out the spring clip securing the cable to the mounting bracket at the rear caliper, then

16.6 Handbrake lever mounting screws

disconnect the end of the cable from the lever on the caliper and detach the cable from the bracket.

6 Unbolt the heat shields from the underbody for access to the front of the cable.

7 Unscrew the nuts and bolts securing the handbrake cable brackets to the underbody and suspension **(see illustrations)**.

8 Disconnect the front of the cable from the cable equaliser, then withdraw the cable from under the vehicle.

Refitting

9 Refitting is a reversal of removal, with reference to Section 6 where necessary. On completion check and adjust the handbrake as described in Chapter 1.

Front cable

Removal

10 A single front brake cable and equaliser is fitted between the handbrake lever and the rear brake cables. First remove the handbrake lever as described in Section 16.

11 Chock the front wheels, then jack up the rear of the vehicle and support securely on axle stands (see *"Jacking and vehicle support"*).

12 Unbolt the heat shields from the underbody for access to the front cable.

13 Disconnect the rear handbrake cables from the equaliser, then lower the front cable assembly down through the floor panel and withdraw from under the vehicle.

Refitting

14 Refitting is a reversal of removal, but refer to Section 16 when refitting the handbrake lever and finally adjust the handbrake as described in Chapter 1.

18 Rear brake pressure-regulating valve - adjustment, removal and refitting

Adjustment

1 A load-sensitive valve is fitted between the rear suspension upper link and the underbody **(see illustration)**. A 2.0 mm thick spacer should be fabricated out of metal in order to check the adjustment. Cut the piece of metal 20 mm by 30 mm, then cut a slot in it 7.0 mm wide to locate under the valve top screw.

2 To check the adjustment of the valve, the following conditions must be met. Ideally the vehicle should be positioned over an inspection

17.4 Releasing the end of the handbrake cable from the rear brake backplate

17.7a Handbrake cable front mountings

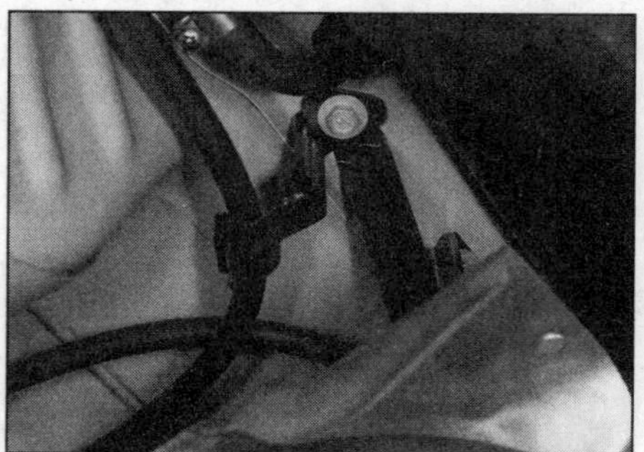

17.7b Handbrake cable rear mountings

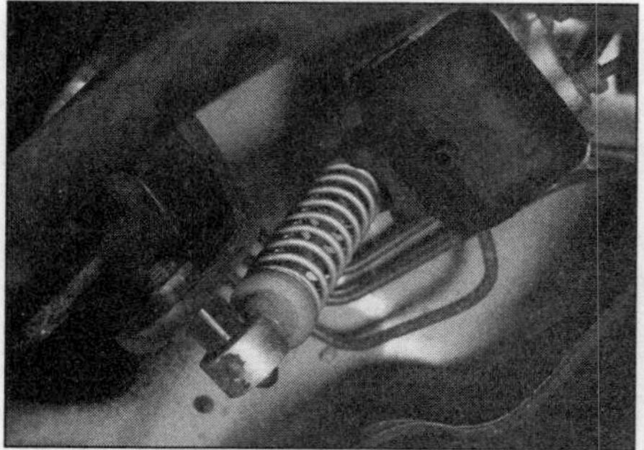

18.1 Rear brake pressure-regulating valve

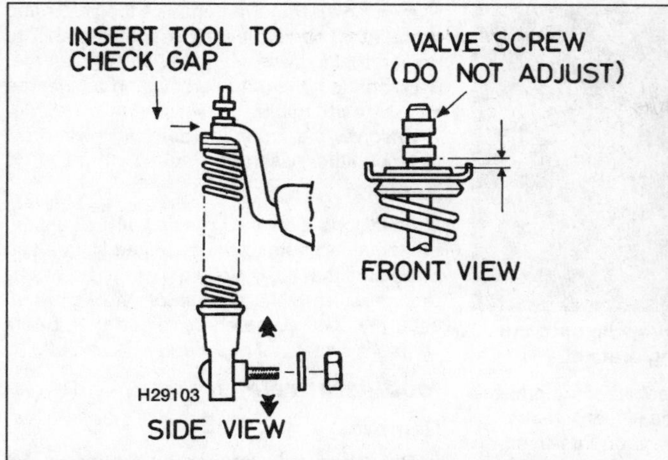

18.3 Rear brake pressure-regulating valve adjustment

18.7 Hydraulic fluid pipe connections to the rear brake pressure-regulating valve

pit to improve access to the valve with the weight of the vehicle on its suspension.:

a) A half-full tank of fuel.

b) Engine oil and coolant levels normal.

c) Spare wheel, jack and tools fitted in correct positions.

d) Suspension settled by rolling the vehicle backwards and forwards.

3 Using the special tool, check that the gap between the top of the valve bracket and the valve top screw is 1.9 mm to 2.2 mm **(see illustration)**. If not, loosen the valve lower adjustment nut and reposition the rod until the dimension is correct, then tighten the nut.

Removal

4 Chock the front wheels then jack up the rear of the vehicle and support on axle stands (see *"Jacking, and vehicle support"*).

5 Mark the position of the valve adjustment rod on the rear suspension upper link, then unscrew and remove the nut.

6 Before proceeding, place a suitable container under the valve, to collect the brake fluid which will escape as the fluid pipes are disconnected.

7 Unscrew the fluid pipe unions from the valve body, and disconnect the pipes from the valve, taking care not to strain them **(see illustration)**. Note the locations of the pipes, to ensure correct refitting. Plug or cover the open ends of the pipes and valve, to reduce fluid spillage and to prevent dirt ingress. **Do not** depress the brake pedal whilst the valve is removed.

8 Unscrew the bolts securing the valve to its mounting bracket, and withdraw the valve.

9 Note that the valve spring cannot be renewed independently of the valve - the components are only available as an assembly.

Refitting

10 Refitting is a reversal of removal, but bleed the hydraulic system as described in Section 2, and adjust the valve as described earlier in this Section.

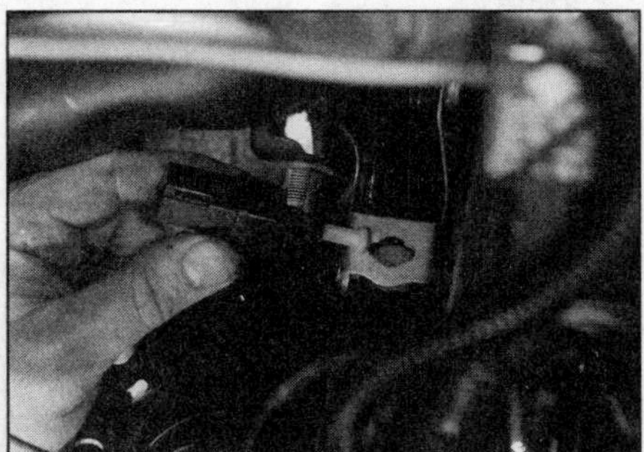

19.7 Removing the stop-light switch

19 Stop-light switch - adjustment, removal and refitting

Note: *There are two types of stop-light switches fitted:*

a) Bayonet fit which has an automatic adjuster, if faulty it must be renewed.

b) Threaded switch with locknut which can be adjusted in the pedal bracket.

Adjustment

Threaded type

1 Disconnect the wiring connector from the stop-light switch, then slacken the locknut on the stop-light switch.

2 Rotate the switch until the threads at the lower part of the switch, are the correct distance away from the pedal stop (see *Specifications*).

Bayonet type

3 The switch plunger operates on a ratchet.

4 If adjustment is required, pull the plunger fully out - the switch is then self-adjusting.

Removal

5 For improved access, remove the driver's side lower facia shelf (2 screws).

6 Disconnect the wiring plug from the switch.

7 Bayonet fit, twist the switch anti-clockwise, and withdraw the switch from the pedal bracket **(see illustration)**.

8 On threaded type switch, slacken the locknut and rotate the switch until it is free of the pedal bracket.

Refitting

9 Refitting is a reversal of removal, but on bayonet type switch, pull the plunger fully out before refitting (see paragraph 4).

20 Handbrake "on" warning light switch - removal and refitting

Removal

1 Remove the screws and remove the plastic cover from the top of the handbrake lever.

2 Prise the cover from the rear of the handbrake lever surround, then unscrew the mounting screws and withdraw the surround over the handbrake lever.

3 Disconnect the wiring plug from the switch **(see illustration)**.

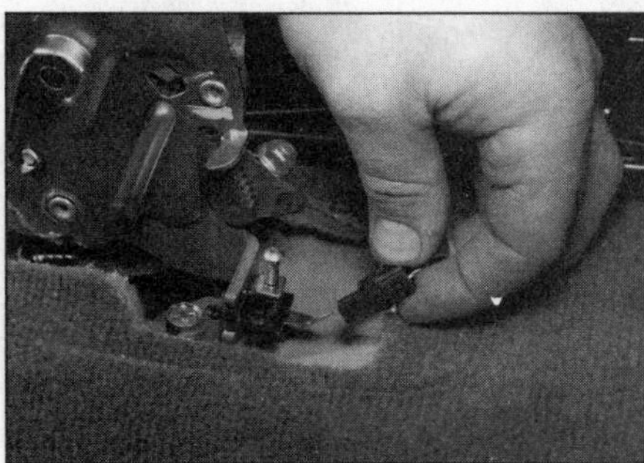

20.3 Disconnect the wiring plug . . .

20.4 . . . and remove the handbrake "on" warning light switch

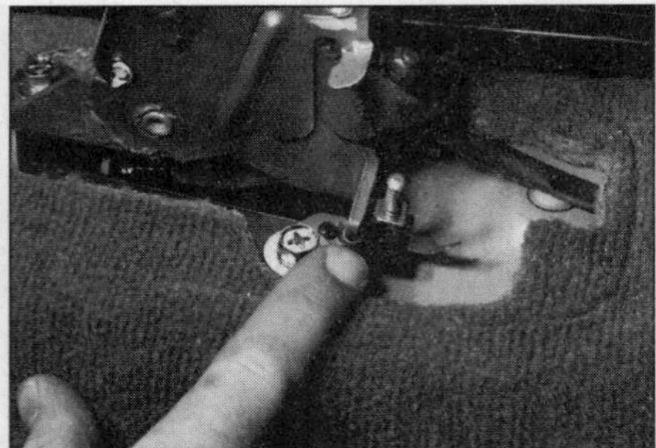

20.5 Pressing the spring clip onto the switch mounting bracket

4 Remove the screw or prise apart the spring clip, and withdraw the switch **(see illustration)**.

Refitting

5 Refitting is a reversal of removal, but before refitting the surround, check that the warning light comes on before the first ratchet on the handbrake **(see illustration)**. If necessary, bend the switch bracket to give the correct adjustment.

21 Anti-lock braking system (ABS) - general information

ABS is available as an option on certain models. The system is fail-safe, and is fitted in addition to the conventional braking system, so that the vehicle retains conventional braking in the event of an ABS failure. The system has self-test capabilities and does not work at speeds less than 6 mph (10 km/h).

To prevent wheel locking, the system provides a means of modulating (varying) the hydraulic pressure in the braking circuits, to control the amount of braking effort at each wheel. To achieve this, sensors mounted at all four wheels monitor the rotational speeds of the wheels, and are thus able to detect when there is a risk of wheel locking (low rotational speed, relative to vehicle speed). Solenoid valves are positioned in the brake circuits to each wheel, and the solenoid valves are incorporated in a modulator assembly, which is controlled by an electronic control unit. The electronic control unit controls the braking effort applied to each wheel, according to the information supplied by the wheel sensors.

The braking system components used on models fitted with ABS are similar to those used on models with a conventional braking system. Rear disc brakes are fitted to all models with ABS.

Should a fault develop in the system, the system can be tested using specialist diagnostic equipment available to a Nissan dealer.

22 Anti-lock braking system (ABS) components - removal and refitting

Modulator assembly

Note: *Before starting work, refer to the warning at the beginning of Section 2 concerning the dangers of hydraulic fluid.*

Removal

1 Remove the battery as described in Chapter 5A.

2 Remove the air cleaner and air ducting as described in Chapter 4A.

3 Drain the brake fluid from the hydraulic system by opening any convenient bleed screw in the system, and gently pumping the brake pedal to expel the fluid through a tube connected to the screw (see Section 2).

4 Remove the ABS relay box and bracket.

5 Identify each fluid pipe connected to the modulator assembly, to ensure correct refitting. Unscrew the union nuts, and disconnect the fluid pipes from the modulator. Plug or cover the open ends of the pipes and modulator, to reduce fluid spillage and to prevent dirt ingress.

6 Disconnect the modulator wiring connector, and the earth cable.

7 Unscrew the mounting nuts, and withdraw the modulator assembly .

Refitting

8 Refitting is a reversal of removal, but tighten the mounting nuts to the specified torque and make sure that the hydraulic pipes are correctly reconnected to the modulator and tightened securely. On completion, bleed the brake hydraulic system as described in Section 2.

Modulator relays

Removal

9 The relays are mounted on the modulator assembly.

10 Disconnect the battery negative lead.

11 Remove the air cleaner and air ducting as described in Chapter 4A.

12 Remove the securing screw, and withdraw the cover to expose the relays.

13 Disconnect the wiring connector, then pull the relevant relay from its location. Note that the black relay controls the modulator motor, and the white relay controls the solenoid valves.

Refitting

14 Refitting is a reversal of removal.

Electronic control unit

Removal

15 The ABS electronic control unit is situated beneath the ECCS control unit in front of the centre console on RHD models, or on the driver's side door pillar on LHD models. Remove the trim (as applicable) with reference to Chapter 11. Prior to removal, disconnect the battery negative terminal.

16 Unscrew the retaining screws and release the retaining clips, then remove the small trim panel from each side of the front of the centre console.

17 Undo the retaining screws, and release the control unit from its mounting bracket. Disconnect the wiring connector, and remove the unit from the vehicle.

Refitting

18 Refitting is the reverse of removal, ensuring that the wiring connector is securely reconnected.

Front wheel sensor

Removal

19 Apply the handbrake, then jack up the front of the vehicle and support securely on axle stands (see *"Jacking and vehicle support"*). Remove the relevant roadwheel.

20 Trace the wiring back from the sensor, and remove the screws securing the wiring brackets to the suspension and body **(see illustrations)**.

22.20a Removing the front ABS sensor wiring from the front suspension strut

22.20b Front ABS sensor wiring support bracket under the front wheel arch

21 Locate the wiring connector, and separate the two halves of the connector (where applicable, feed the wiring through the grommet in the wheel arch, noting its routing).
22 Unscrew the bolt securing the sensor to the hub carrier, and withdraw the sensor complete with the wiring and brackets.

Refitting

23 Refitting is a reversal of removal, but ensure that the faces of the sensor and hub carrier are clean, and tighten the securing bolt to the specified torque.

Rear wheel sensor

Removal

24 Chock the front wheels, then jack up the rear of the vehicle and support it securely on axle stands (refer to *"Jacking and vehicle support"*).
25 Trace the wiring back from the sensor, and remove the screws securing the wiring brackets to the suspension and underbody.

22.27 Rear ABS sensor location on backplate (arrowed) - rear disc brake model shown

26 Locate the wiring connector, and separate the two halves of the connector.
27 Unscrew the bolt securing the sensor to the backplate, and withdraw the sensor complete with the wiring and brackets **(see illustration)**.

Refitting

28 Refitting is a reversal of removal, but ensure that the faces of the sensor and backplate are clean, and tighten the securing bolt to the specified torque.

Sensor rotors

Removal

29 Remove the driveshaft or rear hub as applicable with reference to Chapter 8 or 10.
30 Use a puller or suitable drift to remove the rotor.

Refitting

31 Clean the contact surfaces of the rotor and driveshaft/hub.
32 Using a suitable metal tube, drive or press the rotor onto the driveshaft or hub. Alternatively use a block of wood and a hammer to fit the front rotor taking care to keep the rotor square. When fitting the rear rotor on models with rear disc brakes, its final position must be between 12.5 mm and 13.5 mm from the inner end of the hub.

Chapter 10
Suspension and steering

Contents

Degrees of difficulty

Easy, suitable for novice with little experience		**Fairly easy,** suitable for beginner with some experience		**Fairly difficult,** suitable for competent DIY mechanic		**Difficult,** suitable for experienced DIY mechanic		**Very difficult,** suitable for expert DIY or professional	

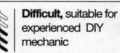

Specifications

Front suspension

Type	Independent by MacPherson struts, with coil springs and integral shock absorbers, and lower arms. Anti-roll bar fitted to all models.

Rear suspension

Type	Semi-independent by trailing upper and lower links and axle beam, and located by Panhard rod. Coil springs and telescopic shock absorbers. Anti-roll bar on some models (see text)

Wheel bearings

Endfloat at hub (front and rear)	Zero

Steering

Type	Rack-and-pinion, manual or power-assisted, depending on model.
Maximum steering wheel free play	35.0 mm
Steering column length (see Section 13):	
RHD	555.9 to 558.1 mm
LHD	545.9 to 548.1 mm

Roadwheels

Type	Pressed-steel or aluminium alloy (depending on model)
Size	5J x 13 or 5J x 14

Tyres

Size:	
998 cc models	155/70 R13 or 165/60 R 14
1275 cc models	155/70 R13, 175/60 R13 or 165/60 R 14
1348 cc models	165/60 R 14

Pressures - See end of "*Weekly checks*"

Torque wrench settings

	Nm	lbf ft
Front suspension		
Front anti-roll bar drop link-bolt	19	14
Front anti-roll bar mounting clamp bolts	61	45
Driveshaft to front hub nut	177	131
Hub carrier-to-suspension strut nuts and bolts	118	87
Lower arm balljoint-to-hub carrier nut	59	44
Lower arm front mounting nut	98	72
Lower arm rear mounting clamp bolts	61	45
Suspension strut damper rod top nut	37	27
Suspension strut upper mounting nuts	28	20
Rear suspension		
Panhard rod nut	88	65
Rear anti-roll bar drop link nut	44	33
Rear anti-roll bar mounting clamp bolt	44	33
Rear brake backplate	45	33
Rear disc splash guard	12	9
Rear hub bearing nut	221	163
Shock absorber lower mounting nut	88	65
Shock absorber upper mounting nut	22	16
Upper/lower trailing link arm mounting bolts	88	65
Steering		
Air bag module special side Torx bolts	20	15
Air bag slip ring	1.5	1.1
Fluid high pressure line-to-steering gear union	20	15
Fluid low pressure clip-to-steering gear	4	3
Power steering fluid pipe union banjo-to-pump bolt	59	44
Power steering pump-to-bracket lower bolts	37	27
Power steering pump-to-bracket upper bolts	19	14
Steering column lower gaiter securing nuts	5	4
Steering column securing nuts and bolts	17	13
Steering column universal joint clamp bolts	27	20
Steering gear mounting clamp bolts	85	63
Steering wheel securing nut	34	25
Track-rod end locknut	42	31
Track-rod end-to-steering arm balljoint nut	34	25
Roadwheels		
Roadwheel nuts	108	80

1 General information

The independent front suspension is of MacPherson strut type, incorporating coil springs and integral telescopic shock absorbers. The upper ends of the MacPherson struts are attached to the bodyshell turrets; the lower ends are bolted to the hub carriers, which carry the wheel bearings, brake calipers and hub/disc assemblies. The hub carriers are located at their lower ends by transverse lower arms. A front anti-roll bar is fitted to all models.

The rear suspension is of semi-independent type, with upper and lower links, a rigid axle beam and a Panhard rod. Separate coil springs and telescopic shock absorbers are fitted between the axle beam and the vehicle body. The rear of the axle beam is located transversely by a Panhard rod connected between the axle beam and body. A rear anti-roll bar was originally only fitted to 1.3 litre engine models, but was fitted across the range from 1996 onwards.

The one-piece steering column has a universal joint fitted at its lower end which is clamped to the column and steering gear pinion.

The steering gear is mounted on the engine compartment bulkhead, and incorporates track rods with outer balljoints attached to the steering arms on the hub carriers.

Power steering is fitted to some models. The hydraulic system is powered by a belt-driven pump, which is driven from the crankshaft pulley. The hydraulic fluid is cooled by passing it through a single bore cooling tube located in front of the radiator. The hydraulic system incorporates a pressure switch (for the engine management system) located on the right-hand front suspension turret **(see illustration)**.

1.5 Power steering hydraulic pressure switch

2 Front hub carrier - removal and refitting

Removal

1 Before jacking up the vehicle, loosen the driveshaft nut as follows. Remove the wheel trim, then extract the split-pin from the outer end of the driveshaft and withdraw the castellated locking ring and the spacer. Discard the split-pin - a new one must be used on refitting.

2 Firmly apply the handbrake and have an assistant apply the footbrake. Using a socket and extension bar, loosen the driveshaft nut half a turn.

Warning: The nut is very tight!

3 Chock the rear wheels, then jack up the front of the vehicle and support on axle stands (see *"Jacking and vehicle support"*). Remove the wheel, then unscrew the driveshaft nut and remove the thrustwasher.
4 Remove the brake disc as described in Chapter 9. This procedure includes removal of the brake caliper, brake pads and caliper mounting bracket.
5 On models with ABS unbolt the sensor from the hub carrier.
6 Remove the split pin from the castellated nut securing the track-rod end to the steering arm, then partially unscrew nut. Using a balljoint separator tool, separate the track-rod end from the steering arm. Remove the nut. Discard the split pin - a new one must be used on refitting.
7 Remove the two nuts from the bolts securing the lower end of the strut to the hub carrier, noting that the nuts fit on the front of the strut. Withdraw the bolts, and support the hub carrier.
8 Pull the top of the hub carrier outwards while pushing the driveshaft through the hub. Support the driveshaft to one side. If the driveshaft is tight in the hub, refer to Chapter 8.
9 Remove the split pin from the castellated nut securing the suspension lower arm balljoint to the hub carrier, then partially unscrew the nut. Using a balljoint separator tool, separate the balljoint then unscrew the nut and withdraw the hub carrier.

Refitting

10 Locate the hub carrier on the lower arm balljoint and refit the nut. Tighten the nut moderately at this stage.
11 Engage the outer end of the driveshaft with the hub ensuring that the splines engage correctly, and push the top of the hub carrier in towards the strut.
12 Locate the top of the hub carrier with the strut and insert the bolts making sure the bolt heads are facing the rear of the vehicle. Tighten the bolts to the specified torque.
13 Refit the washer and nut to the driveshaft, and tighten the nut moderately at this stage. Leave final tightening of the nut until the car is lowered to the ground.
14 Reconnect the track-rod end to the steering arm, then refit the castellated nut, and tighten to the specified torque. Align the holes and fit a new split pin.
15 Fully tighten the lower arm balljoint nut, then align the holes and fit a new split pin.
16 On models with ABS refit the sensor and tighten the mounting bolt.
17 Refit the brake disc with reference to Chapter 9.
18 Refit the wheel, and lower the vehicle to the ground.
19 Fully tighten the driveshaft nut to the specified torque.
20 Fit the spacer and the castellated locking ring. Make sure that the ring is fitted so that two serrations are aligned with the split pin hole in the driveshaft - it will be necessary to offer the ring up in several positions before the correct alignment occurs. Insert a new split pin and spread the ends around the shaft. Refit the wheel trim.

3 Front hub bearings - checking and renewal

Checking

1 Remove the brake disc as described in Chapter 9.
2 Wear in the front hub bearings can be checked by measuring the amount of side play present. To do this, a dial gauge should be fixed so that its probe is in contact with the disc contact face of the hub. Attempt to move the hub in and out, and check that no play is evident. Any play indicates wear in the bearings, and in this case they must be renewed.

Renewal

Note: *Removal of the bearing renders it unserviceable for further use.*
3 Remove the front hub carrier as described in Section 2.
4 Unscrew the brake disc shield retaining bolts and remove the shield from the hub carrier.
5 Support the outer face of the hub carrier on blocks of wood, ensuring that the hub is free. Using a soft-metal drift, press or drive the hub from the wheel bearing. Note that one half of the inner bearing race will remain on the hub
6 Support the inner bearing race which is still attached to the hub, then press or drive the hub from the race. Alternatively, pull the bearing race from the hub using a suitable puller. Recover the outer oil seal from the hub.
7 Prise the inner oil seal from the hub carrier.
8 Using a screwdriver, extract the inner bearing retaining circlip from the hub carrier. Recover the remaining inner bearing race if it is loose.
9 Support the inner face of the hub carrier, then using a suitable metal tube which bears only on the outer bearing race, press or drive the bearing from the hub carrier.
10 Before installing the new bearing, thoroughly clean the bearing location in the hub carrier and wipe dry.
11 Press or drive the bearing into position until it contacts the inner shoulder, applying pressure only to the bearing outer race. This can be achieved using a long threaded bar and end plates.
12 Fit the outer bearing retaining circlip to its groove in the hub carrier.
13 Pack the lips of the new outer oil seal with grease then, using a tube of suitable diameter, carefully press or tap the seal into position in the outer face of the hub carrier.
14 Pack the lips of the new inner oil seal with grease then, using a tube of suitable diameter, carefully press or tap the seal into position in the inner face of the hub carrier.
15 Support the bearing using a suitable diameter metal bar or tube, which will just pass through the inner oil seal to support the wheel bearing inner race. Press or draw the hub into the bearing, noting that the bearing inner race **must** be supported during this operation. This can be achieved using a suitable socket, threaded rod, washers and a length of bar as shown.
16 Check that the hub rotates freely in the hub carrier.
17 Refit the brake disc shield and tighten the retaining bolts to the specified torque.
18 Refit the front hub carrier as described in Section 2.

4 Front suspension strut - removal, overhaul and refitting

Removal

1 Chock the rear wheels, apply the handbrake, then jack up the front of the vehicle and support securely on axle stands (see *"Jacking and vehicle support"*). Remove the relevant roadwheel.
2 Pull out the clip and release the hydraulic brake fluid hose from the bracket on the strut **(see illustration)**.
3 Remove the two nuts from the bolts securing the lower end of the strut to the hub carrier, noting that the nuts fit on the front of the strut. Withdraw the bolts and separate the strut from the hub carrier. Support the hub carrier **(see illustrations)**.
4 Have an assistant support the strut from underneath the wheel arch then, working in the engine compartment, unscrew the nuts securing the top of the strut to the suspension turret and withdraw the strut from under the front wing **(see illustrations)**.

Warning: Do not unscrew the centre damper rod nut. Release the lower end of the strut from the hub carrier, then withdraw the assembly from under the wheel arch.

4.2 Hydraulic brake fluid hose retaining clip on the front suspension strut

4.3a Unscrew the nuts . . .

4.3b . . . and remove the bolts . . .

4.3c . . . then separate the strut from the hub carrier

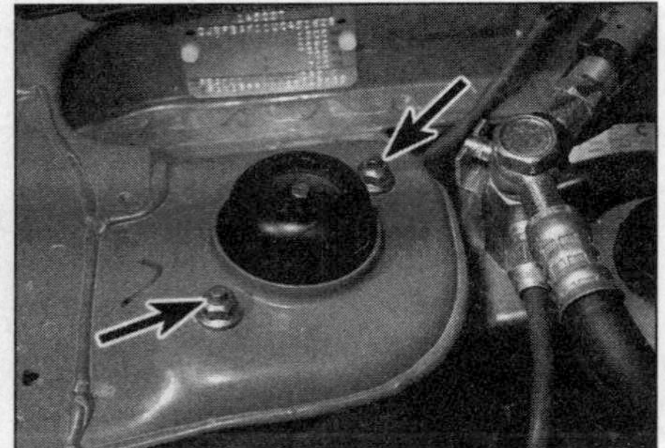

4.4a Unscrew the top mounting nuts . . .

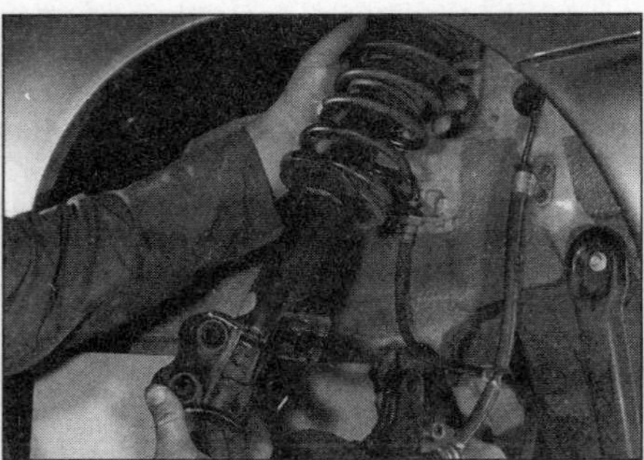

4.4b . . . then withdraw the strut from under the front wing

Overhaul

Note: *Suitable coil spring compressor tools will be required for this operation.*

5 Clamp the lower end of the strut in a vice fitted with jaw protectors.

6 The damper rod top nut must now be loosened. This is a difficult task because the nut is deeply recessed in the upper mounting, and ideally a purpose-made tool should be obtained from your Nissan dealer. Alternatively, use a short box spanner together with an adjustable spanner to hold

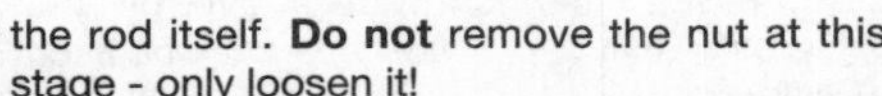

the rod itself. **Do not** remove the nut at this stage - only loosen it!

7 Fit spring compressors to the spring, and compress the spring until there is no pressure on the upper mounting.

8 Fully unscrew and remove the damper rod top nut and withdraw the upper mounting **(see illustrations)**.

9 Withdraw the thrust seat and spring seat **(see illustrations)**.

10 Withdraw the bump stop and spring seat rubber **(see illustrations)**.

11 Withdraw the spring, complete with the compressors **(see illustration)**.

12 With the strut assembly now dismantled, examine all the components for wear and damage **(see illustration)**. Check the rubber components for deterioration. Renew the components as necessary.

13 Examine the damper for signs of fluid leakage. Check the damper rod for signs of pitting along its entire length, and check the

4.8a Unscrew the damper rod top nut . . .

4.8b . . . and withdraw the upper mounting

4.9a Withdraw the thrust seat . . .

4.9b . . . and spring seat

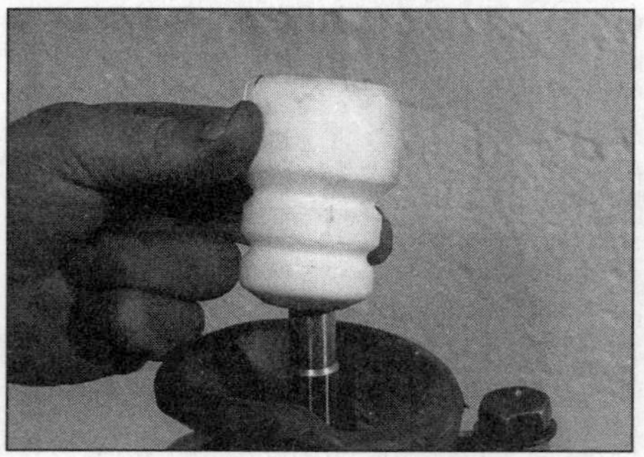

4.10a Withdraw the bump stop . . .

4.10b . . . and spring seat rubber

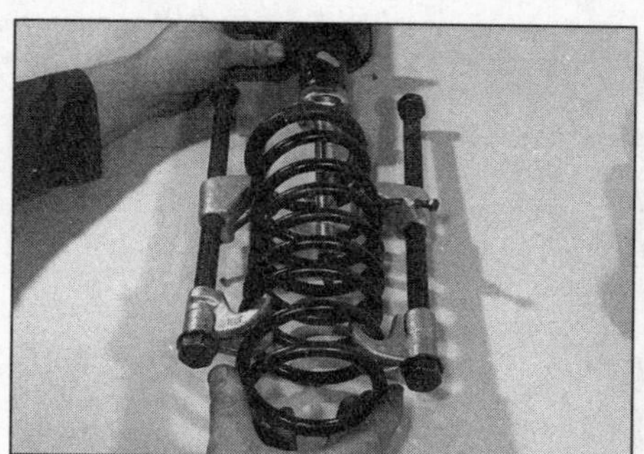
4.11 Removing the coil spring with compressors

4.12 Front strut components

4.23 Tightening the bolts securing the strut to the hub carrier

strut body for signs of damage. While holding it in an upright position, test the operation of the strut by moving the damper rod through a full stroke, and then through short strokes of 50 to 100 mm. In both cases, the resistance felt should be smooth and continuous. If the resistance is jerky, or uneven, or if there is any visible sign of wear or damage to the strut, renewal is necessary. Note that the damper cannot be renewed independently, and if leakage or damage is evident, the complete strut/damper assembly must be renewed.

14 Renew the coil spring if it is damaged or distorted.

15 Clamp the strut body in the vice.

16 Ensure that the coil spring is compressed sufficiently to enable the upper mounting components to be fitted, then fit the spring over the damper rod, ensuring that the lower end of the spring is correctly located on the lower spring seat on the strut.

17 Refit the spring seat rubber, again making sure that it is located correctly on the upper end of the coil spring.

18 Refit the bump stop over the top of the damper rod and push it down below the upper mounting location.

19 Refit the spring seat and thrust seat.

20 Refit the upper mounting, then refit the damper rod top nut and tighten to the specified torque.

21 Release the spring compressors making sure that the upper and lower ends of the coil spring are correctly located.

Refitting

22 Manoeuvre the strut assembly into position under the wheel arch, passing the mounting studs through the holes in the body turret. Refit the upper mounting nuts, and tighten them to the specified torque.

23 Engage the lower end of the strut with the hub carrier, then fit the securing bolts and nuts, noting that the nuts fit on the front of the strut, and tighten to the specified torque **(see illustration)**.

24 Refit the brake fluid line to the bracket on the hub carrier, and secure with the clip.

25 Refit the roadwheel, and lower the vehicle to the ground.

5 Front suspension lower arm - removal, overhaul and refitting

Removal

Note: *A balljoint separator tool may be required for this operation. The lower arm balljoint split pin must be renewed on refitting.*

1 Chock the rear wheels, apply the handbrake, then jack up the front of the vehicle and support securely on axle stands (see *"Jacking and vehicle support"*). Remove the relevant roadwheel.

2 Unscrew the nut securing the anti-roll bar drop link to the lower arm, and recover the washer and bush. Note that it may be necessary to counterhold the drop link in order to unscrew the nut.

3 Unscrew the two bolts securing the lower arm rear mounting clamp to the vehicle floor, and remove the clamp.

4 Unscrew the lower arm front mounting nut and remove the bolt noting that the head of the bolt faces the front of the vehicle **(see illustration)**.

5 Remove the split pin, then unscrew the nut securing the lower end of the hub carrier to the lower arm balljoint. Discard the split pin - a new one must be used on refitting **(see illustrations)**.

6 Separate the hub carrier from the lower arm. If necessary use a balljoint separator tool, however there is limited access to the top of the balljoint because of the driveshaft outer joint. If the balljoint is particularly tight in the hub carrier and there is insufficient room to use the balljoint separator tool, remove the outer end of the driveshaft from the hub with reference to Chapter 8 **(see illustration)**.

7 Withdraw the lower arm forwards over the

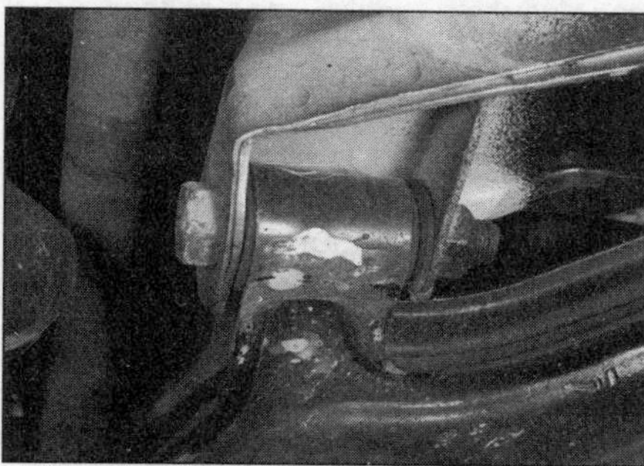
5.4 Front suspension lower arm front mounting

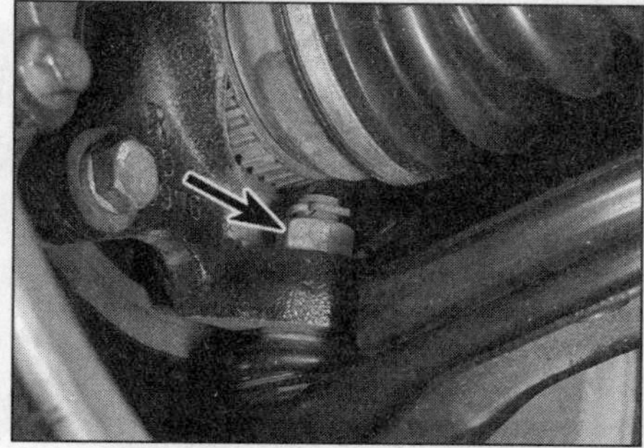
5.5a Lower arm balljoint nut

5.5b Removing the split pin from the lower arm balljoint shaft

5.6 Using a separator tool to disconnect the lower arm balljoint from the hub carrier

anti-roll bar and withdraw from under the vehicle. Recover the remaining bush and washer from the anti-roll bar drop link.

Overhaul

8 With the lower arm removed, examine the lower arm itself, and the mounting bushes, for wear, cracks or damage. Check the balljoint for wear, excessive play, or stiffness. Also check the balljoint dust boot for cracks or damage.

9 The mounting bushes and balljoint assembly are integral with the lower arm, and cannot be renewed independently. If either the bushes or the balljoint are worn or damaged, the complete lower arm assembly must be renewed.

Refitting

10 Locate the upper washer and bush on the anti-roll bar drop link making sure that the concave side of the washer contacts the bush. Engage the lower arm with the anti-roll bar drop link and refit the bush, washer and nut on the drop link. Tighten the nut to the specified torque while counterholding the drop link.

11 Locate the rear of the lower arm over the anti-roll bar and the front in the mounting bracket. Insert the front mounting bolt from the front and screw on the nut. Do not fully tighten the nut at this stage.

12 Refit the lower arm rear mounting clamp, and refit the securing bolts. Do not fully tighten the bolts at this stage.

13 Engage the lower arm balljoint with the hub carrier, then refit the balljoint nut and tighten to the specified torque. Align the next serration on the nut with the hole in the balljoint stud and insert a new split pin. Bend the pin legs to secure.

14 Refit the roadwheel, and lower the vehicle to the ground.

15 Make sure that the vehicle is parked on level ground, then release the handbrake. Roll the vehicle backwards and forwards, and bounce the front of the vehicle to settle the suspension components. Fully tighten the lower arm front and rear mounting bolts to the specified torque.

16 On completion the front wheel alignment should be checked, with reference to Chapter 1.

6 Front suspension anti-roll bar and drop links - removal and refitting

Anti-roll bar

Removal

1 Apply the handbrake, then jack up the front of the vehicle and support on axle stands (see *"Jacking and vehicle support"*). Remove the front roadwheels.

2 Working at one side of the anti-roll bar, where necessary hold the drop link, then unscrew the nut securing the end of the anti-roll bar to the drop link. Recover the washer and nut **(see illustration)**.

6.2 Front anti-roll bar connection to the drop link

3 Repeat the procedure in paragraph 2 on the remaining side of the anti-roll bar.

4 Unscrew the bolts, and withdraw the clamps securing the anti-roll bar to the vehicle floor **(see illustration)**.

6.4 Front anti-roll bar mounting clamp on the vehicle floor

5 Withdraw the anti-roll bar from under the vehicle.

6 Inspect the mounting clamp rubbers for cracks or deterioration. If renewal is necessary, slide the old rubbers from the bar, and fit the new rubbers. Note that the rubbers should be positioned with the paint marks on the bar against their inner edges.

Refitting

7 Refitting is a reversal of removal, but make sure that the clamps are positioned with the paint marks on the anti-roll bar against their inner edges and the cut-outs facing the rear of the vehicle **(see illustration)**. Delay fully tightening the mounting clamp bolts until the vehicle is resting on its roadwheels.

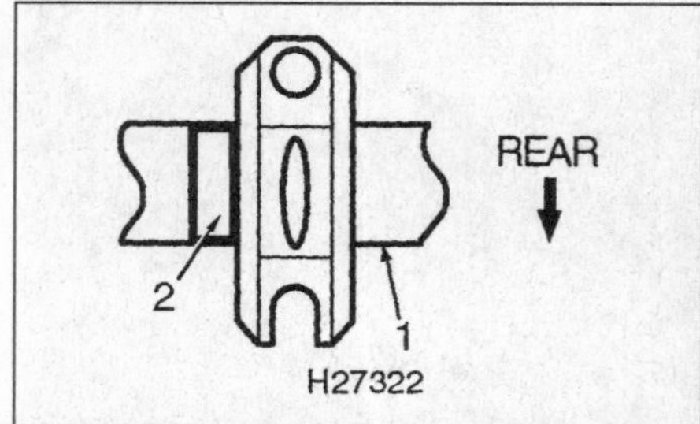

6.7 Correct position of the front anti-roll bar clamp

1 Anti-roll bar *2 Paint mark*

Drop link

Removal

8 Apply the handbrake, then jack up the front of the vehicle and support securely on axle stands (see *"Jacking and vehicle support "*). Remove the relevant front roadwheel.

9 Hold the drop link, then unscrew the nut securing the anti-roll bar to the drop link. Recover the washer and bush.

10 Hold the drop link and unscrew the nut securing it to the lower arm **(see illustration)**. Recover the washer and bush.

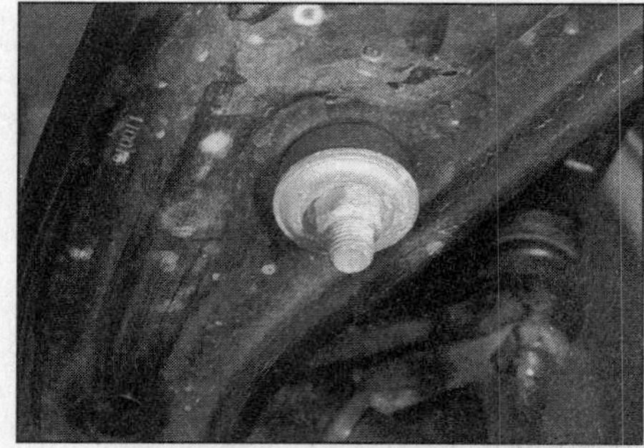

6.10 Front anti-roll bar drop link attachment to the front suspension lower arm

11 Lift out the drop link, and recover the remaining bushes and washers.

12 Check the condition of the bushes, and renew if necessary.

Refitting

13 Refitting is a reversal of removal, but make sure that the concave sides of the washers are positioned against the bushes, and tighten the nuts to the specified torque.

7 Rear hub and bearings - checking, removal and refitting

Checking

1 Remove the rear brake drum or rear brake disc as described in Chapter 9.

2 Wear in the rear hub bearings can be checked by measuring the amount of side play present. To do this, a dial gauge should be fixed so that its probe is in contact with the outer face of the hub. Attempt to move the hub in and out, and check that no play is evident. Any play indicates wear in the bearings, and in this case the complete hub must be renewed. It is not possible to renew the bearings separately as the outer races are formed on the hub itself.

Removal

3 If not already done, remove the rear brake drum or rear brake disc as described in Chapter 9.

4 Remove the dust cap from the hub using a

7.4a Using a cold chisel to remove the dust cap . . .

7.4b . . . from the rear hub

7.4c Extracting the split pin

7.5a Unscrew . . .

7.5b . . . and remove the hub nut . . .

7.5c . . . then remove the thrustwasher

7.6 Removing the hub assembly

7.8 Tightening the rear hub nut

cold chisel or screwdriver, then remove the split pin from the end of the stub axle. Discard the split pin - a new one should be used on refitting **(see illustrations)**.

5 Unscrew the hub nut, using a suitable socket and extension bar and remove the thrustwasher **(see illustrations)**.

Warning: Take care, the nut is very tight!

6 Withdraw the hub assembly from the stub axle **(see illustration)**.

Refitting

7 Thoroughly clean the stub axle, then slide the hub assembly into position.

8 Fit the thrustwasher, then refit the hub nut and tighten to the specified torque **(see illustration)**.

9 Check that the hub spins freely, then fit a new split pin and tap the dust cap into position.

10 Refit the rear brake drum or brake disc (as applicable) with reference to Chapter 9, then refit the roadwheel and lower the vehicle to the ground.

8 Rear suspension components - removal, checking and refitting

Shock absorber

Removal

1 Chock the front wheels, then jack up the rear of the vehicle and support securely on axle stands (see *"Jacking and vehicle support"*). Remove the relevant rear roadwheel.

2 Place a trolley jack beneath the outer end of the axle tube, then raise the axle slightly to tension the coil spring.

3 Working inside the rear of the vehicle, prise the cap from the shock absorber upper mounting then unscrew the nut securing the piston rod to the body while holding the rod with an adjustable spanner **(see illustrations)**. Recover the washer and upper bush noting their order of removal.

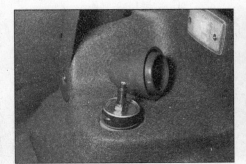

8.3a Prise the cap from the shock absorber upper mounting . . .

8.3b . . . then unscrew the nut while holding the piston rod

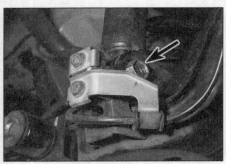

8.4 Rear shock absorber lower mounting bolt

4 Unscrew the nut and remove the bolt securing the shock absorber to the axle assembly, then withdraw the shock absorber from under the vehicle **(see illustration)**.

5 Recover the bush, bump stop cover, dust cover and remaining bump stops from the top of the piston rod. Note the order of removal for correct reassembly.

Checking

6 Examine the shock absorber for signs of fluid leakage. Check the shock absorber piston rod for pitting, and check the shock absorber body for damage. While holding it in an upright position, test the operation of the shock absorber by moving the rod through a full stroke, and then through short strokes of 50 to 100 mm. In both cases, the resistance felt should be smooth and continuous. If the resistance is jerky, or uneven, or if there is any visible sign of wear or damage to the shock absorber, renewal is necessary.

7 Inspect the mounting bushes for signs of cracking or wear and obtain new ones where necessary.

Refitting

8 Locate the bump stops, dust cover, bump stop cover and bush over the top of the shock absorber piston rod.

9 Offer the shock absorber into position and insert the top of the piston rod through the mounting hole.

10 Position the lower end of the shock absorber in the mounting bracket on the axle assembly, then refit the bolt (with its head facing outwards) and fit the nut finger-tight. Do not fully tighten the nut at this stage.

11 Working inside the vehicle, refit the upper bush, washer and nut. Tighten the nut to the specified torque and refit the cap.

12 Withdraw the trolley jack from under the axle, then refit the roadwheel and lower the vehicle to the ground.

13 With the vehicle parked on level ground, release the handbrake and roll the vehicle backwards and forwards, then bounce the rear of the vehicle to settle the suspension components. Re-apply the handbrake.

14 Fully tighten the shock absorber lower mounting nut to the specified torque **(see illustration)**.

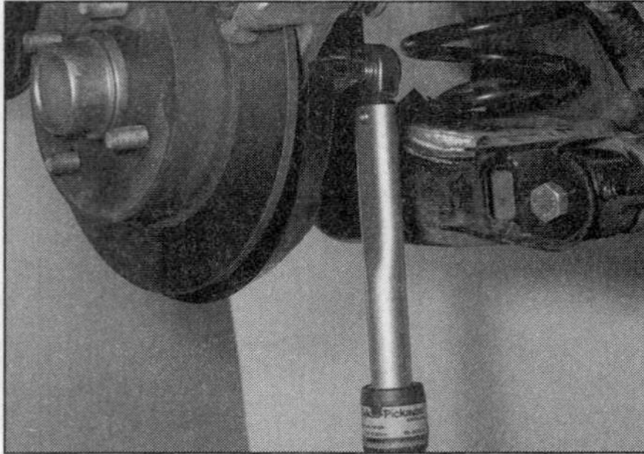

8.14 Tightening the rear shock absorber lower mounting bolt

Coil spring

Removal

15 Chock the front wheels, then jack up the rear of the vehicle and support securely on axle stands (see *"Jacking and vehicle support"*). Remove both rear roadwheels.

16 Place a trolley jack and interposed block of wood beneath the centre of the axle tube, then raise the axle slightly to tension the coil springs.

17 Unscrew the nuts and remove the bolts securing the shock absorbers to the axle tube.

18 Unscrew and remove the nut and bolt securing the Panhard rod to the axle tube.

19 Where fitted disconnect the ABS wiring or remove the sensors with reference to Chapter 9.

20 Disconnect the rear brake pressure-regulating valve with reference to Chapter 9.

21 Lower the jack sufficiently to relieve the tension in the coil springs, then withdraw the coil springs together with their upper and lower seats.

22 Check the springs for damage and renew if necessary.

Refitting

23 Clean the spring locations in the axle and underbody, then locate the lower seats on the axle followed by the coil springs and upper seats. Note that the coil springs must be positioned with the paint identification marks towards the axle.

24 Raise the axle making sure that the upper seats locate correctly on the underbody.

25 Re-connect the brake pressure-regulating valve and ABS wiring/sensors as applicable.

8.32 Panhard rod mounting nut on the axle tube

26 Locate the lower end of the Panhard rod on the axle tube and insert the bolt. Do not fully tighten the bolt at this stage.

27 Position the lower ends of the shock absorbers in the mounting brackets on the axle tube, then refit the bolts from the outer side. Do not fully tighten the nuts at this stage.

28 Refit the roadwheels, and lower the vehicle to the ground.

29 Make sure that the vehicle is parked on level ground, then release the handbrake, roll the vehicle backwards and forwards, and bounce the rear of the vehicle to settle the suspension components. Re-apply the handbrake.

30 Tighten the shock absorber and Panhard rod mounting bolts to the specified torque.

Panhard rod

Removal

31 Chock the front wheels, then jack up the rear of the vehicle and support securely on axle stands (see *"Jacking and vehicle support"*).

32 Unscrew the nut securing the lower end of the Panhard rod to the axle tube and recover the washer **(see illustration)**.

33 Unscrew the nut securing the top end of the Panhard rod to the underbody, then withdraw the bolt and remove the Panhard rod **(see illustration)**.

Checking

34 Examine the Panhard rod for cracks or signs of damage. Similarly, examine the mounting bushes. If the bushes are worn or damaged, the complete Panhard rod must be renewed.

Refitting

35 Locate the Panhard rod in the underbody bracket, insert the bolt and tighten the nut finger-tight at this stage.

36 Locate the lower end of the Panhard rod on the axle tube and fit the washer and nut.

37 Lower the vehicle to the ground.

38 Make sure that the vehicle is parked on level ground, then roll the vehicle backwards and forwards, and bounce the rear of the vehicle to settle the suspension components. Apply the handbrake.

39 Tighten the mounting nuts to the specified torque.

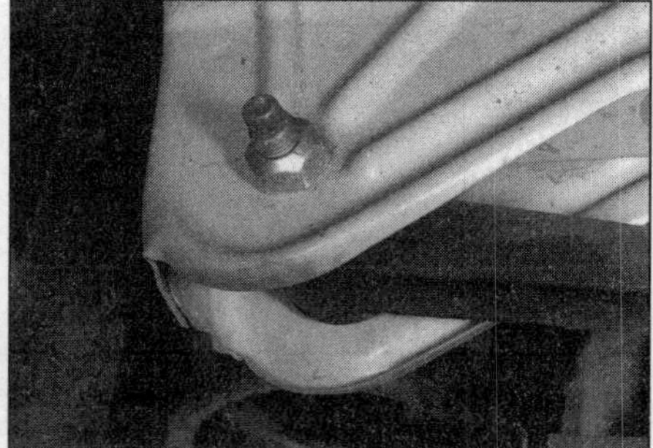

8.33 Panhard rod mounting on the underbody

8.42a Upper trailing link arm mounting on the underbody

8.42b Lower trailing link arm mounting on the axle tube

8.49 Rear anti-roll bar drop link mounting on the underbody bracket

8.50 Rear anti-roll bar mounting on the axle tube

Upper/lower trailing link arm

Removal

40 Chock the front wheels, then jack up the rear of the vehicle and support securely on axle stands (see *"Jacking and vehicle support"*). Remove the relevant roadwheel.

41 Place a trolley jack and interposed block of wood beneath the end of the axle tube, then raise the axle slightly to tension the coil spring.

42 Unscrew and remove the bolts securing the trailing link arm to the axle tube and underbody, and withdraw the arm. Note that the bolt head at the axle end is facing outwards, but the bolt at the underbody is facing inwards **(see illustrations)**.

Checking

43 Examine the link arm and bushes for damage and wear. If the bushes are worn or damaged, the complete link arm must be renewed.

Refitting

44 Locate the arm on the axle and underbody and refit the bolts the correct way round. Hand-tighten the bolts at this stage.

45 Refit the wheel and lower the vehicle to the ground.

46 Make sure that the vehicle is parked on level ground, then roll the vehicle backwards and forwards, and bounce the rear of the vehicle to settle the suspension components. Apply the handbrake.

47 Tighten the link arm mounting nuts to the specified torque.

Rear anti-roll bar

Removal

48 Chock the front wheels, then jack up the rear of the vehicle and support securely on axle stands (see *"Jacking and vehicle support"*). Remove both rear roadwheels.

49 Unscrew the nut securing the drop link to the underbody bracket on both sides and lower the front ends of the anti-roll bar **(see illustration)**.

50 Unscrew the mounting bolts securing the anti-roll bar to the axle tube, release the clamps and lower the anti-roll bar **(see illustration)**.

51 Unscrew the nuts and remove the drop links from the anti-roll bar, then remove the rubber bushes after noting their fitted position.

Checking

52 Examine the anti-roll bar, drop links and bushes for damage and wear and renew as necessary.

Refitting

53 Slide the rubber bushes onto the anti-roll bar and position them as previously noted.

54 Locate the drop links on the anti-roll bar and hand-tighten the mounting nuts.

55 Offer the anti-roll bar onto the axle tube and loosely fit the mounting clamps. Raise the drop links and attach to the underbody brackets. Loosely fit the mounting nuts.

56 Refit the roadwheels and lower the vehicle to the ground.

57 Make sure that the vehicle is parked on level ground, then roll the vehicle backwards and forwards, and bounce the rear of the vehicle to settle the suspension components. Apply the handbrake.

58 Tighten the anti-roll bar and drop link mountings to the specified torque. Before tightening the drop link nuts make sure that the sockets are positioned centrally.

Rear axle assembly

Removal

59 Chock the front wheels, then jack up the rear of the vehicle and support securely on axle stands (see *"Jacking and vehicle support"*). Remove the rear roadwheels.

60 Remove the rear brake shoes and rear wheel cylinders, or rear brake calipers and discs as described in Chapter 9.

61 Remove the rear hubs as described in Section 7, and unbolt the backplates from the axle tube. On models with ABS, also remove the rear wheel sensors as described in Chapter 9, Section 22.

62 Remove the handbrake cables from the axle tube with reference to Chapter 9.

63 On models with rear brake shoes disconnect the hydraulic lines from the axle tube with reference to Chapter 9.

64 Remove the rear coil springs as described earlier in this Section.

65 Unbolt the upper and lower trailing link arms from the axle tube, then lower the rear axle assembly to the ground and withdraw from under the vehicle.

Checking

66 Examine the rear axle for damage and if necessary renew it.

Refitting

67 Refitting is a reversal of removal. Do not fully tighten the upper and lower trailing link arm mounting bolts until the weight of the car is on the rear suspension. Bleed the brake hydraulic system as described in Chapter 9. Check the handbrake adjustment as described in Chapter 1. Check the adjustment of the rear brake pressure-regulating valve as described in Chapter 9.

9 Steering wheel - removal and refitting

Warning: Later models are equipped with an air bag system. The air bag is mounted in the steering wheel centre pad. Make sure the safety recommendations given in Chapter 12 are followed, to prevent personal injury.

Models without air bag

Removal

1 Disconnect the battery negative lead.

2 Set the front wheels in the straight-ahead position, then release the steering lock by inserting the ignition key.

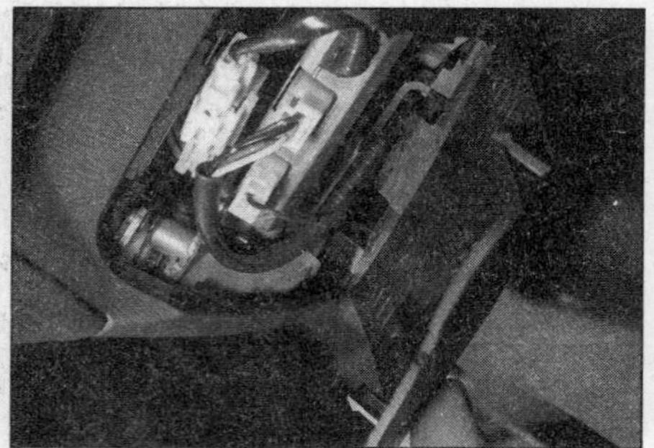
9.11a Prise the lower cover from the bottom of the steering wheel . . .

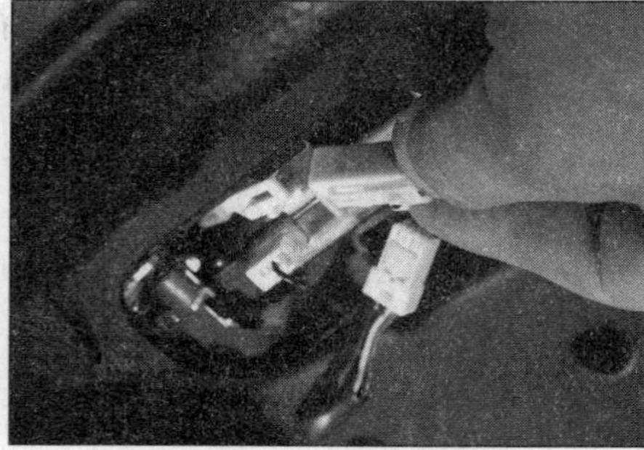
9.11b . . . and disconnect the air bag wiring connector

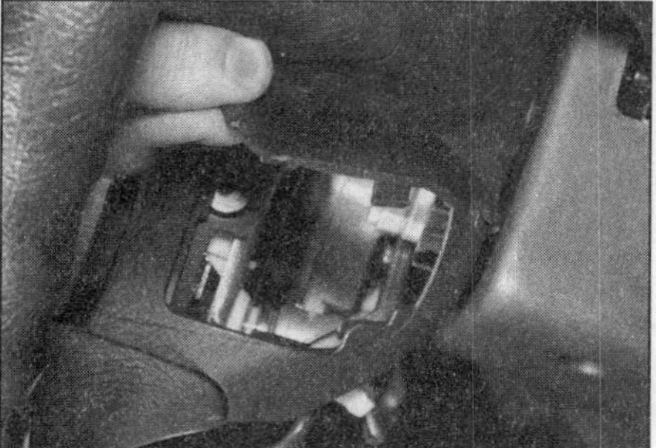
9.12a Prise the side covers from the steering wheel . . .

9.12b . . . to expose the special air bag securing bolts

9.12c Special Torx bolt and bit

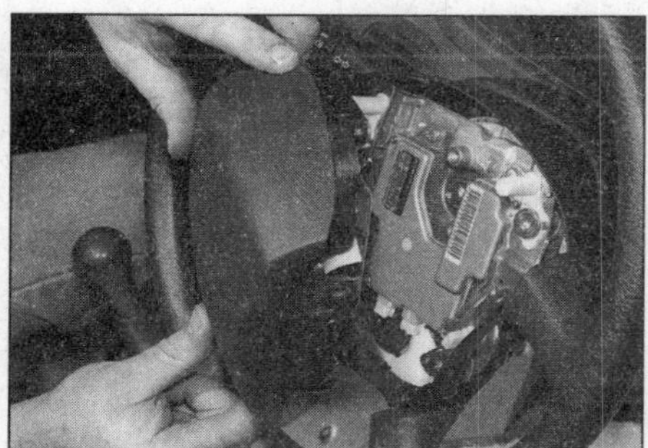
9.13a Removing the air bag unit

3 Prise out the bottom of the horn pad from the steering wheel and disconnect the locating pegs. Withdraw the pad and disconnect the horn wiring.

4 Disconnect the earth terminal from the steering wheel.

5 Make alignment marks between the steering wheel and the end of the steering column shaft.

6 Slacken and remove the steering wheel securing nut.

7 Ease the steering wheel off the column splines by rocking it back and forth. If it is tight, it will be necessary to use a puller to remove it.

Refitting

8 Before commencing refitting, lightly coat the surfaces of the direction indicator cancelling mechanism components and the horn contact slip ring components with grease.

9 Refitting is a reversal of removal, but note the following:

a) *Ensure that the direction indicator switch is in the central (cancelled/off) position, otherwise the switch may be damaged as the wheel is refitted.*

b) *Align the marks made on the wheel and the steering column shaft before removal.*

c) *Tighten the securing nut to the specified torque.*

d) *If necessary, the position of the steering wheel on the column shaft splines can be altered in order to centralise it (ensure that the front roadwheels are pointing in the straight-ahead position).*

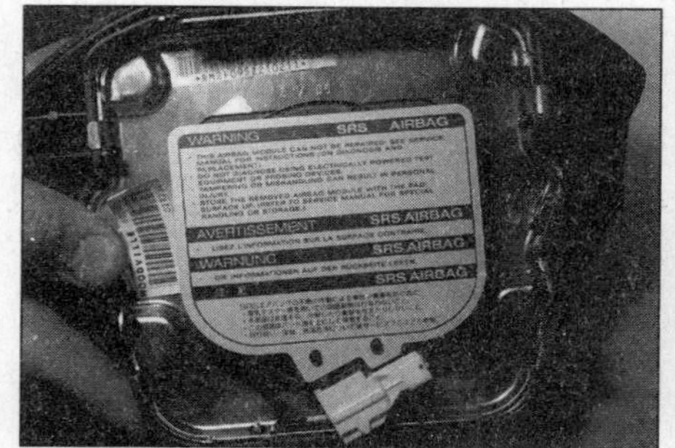

9.13b Warning instructions on the underside of the air bag unit

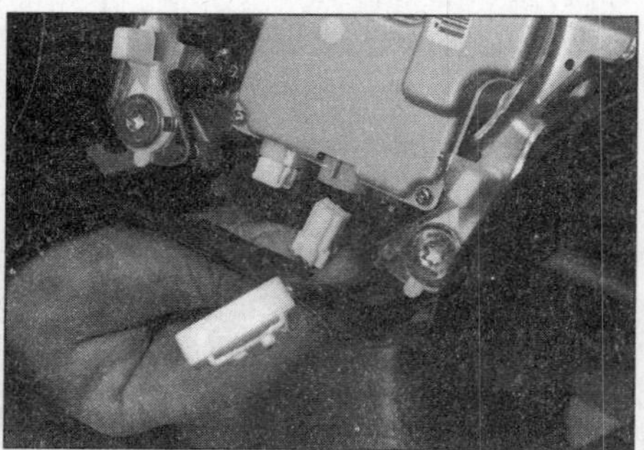
9.15 Disconnecting the horn wiring connector

Models with air bag

Warning: Refer to the precautions given in Chapter 12 before proceeding. Take great care not to drop the steering wheel centre pad, or to allow objects to impact the steering wheel centre pad, during this procedure.

Removal

10 Ensure that the ignition is switched off and the front wheel in the straight-ahead position, then disconnect the battery negative lead. *Wait for at least ten minutes before carrying out any further work.*

11 Carefully prise the lower cover from the bottom of the steering wheel and disconnect the air bag wiring connector **(see illustrations)**.

12 Prise the side covers from the steering wheel to expose the air bag bolts. These are special security Torx bolts with a centre pin, requiring a special Torx bit **(see illustrations)**.

13 Using the Torx bit, remove the two air bag unit securing bolts (one each side), then carefully lift the unit from the steering wheel. ***Caution: Take care not to drop the air bag unit, and do not attempt to dismantle it.*** Discard the bolts, new ones must be used on refitting. Always store the air bag unit with the pad side (visible side) facing upwards - observe the warning instructions on the underside of the air bag unit **(see illustrations)**.

14 Set the front wheels in the straight-ahead position, then release the steering lock by inserting the ignition key.

15 Disconnect the horn wiring connector **(see illustration)**.

16 Make alignment marks between the steering wheel and the end of the steering column shaft.

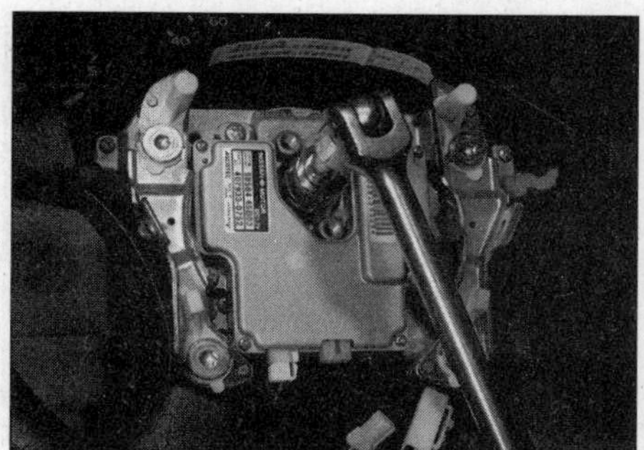
9.17 Loosening the steering wheel securing nut

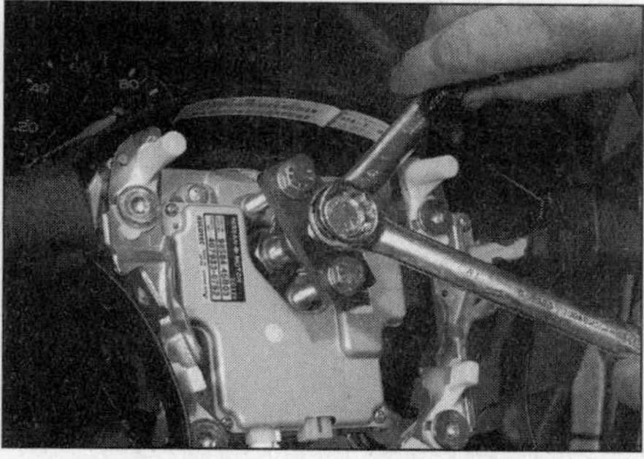
9.18a Using a puller to release the steering wheel from the steering column splines

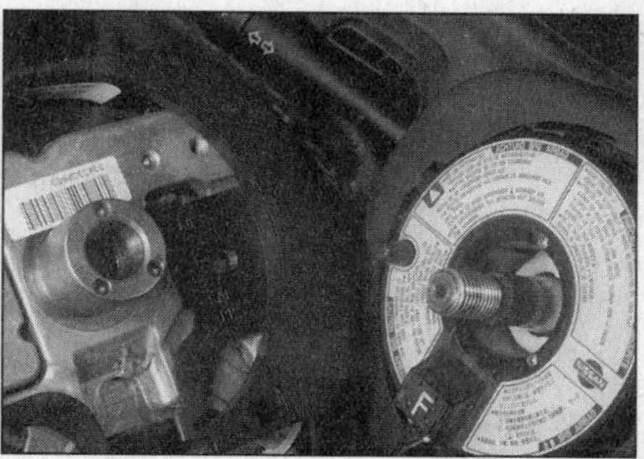
9.18b Removing the steering wheel

17 Slacken and remove the steering wheel securing nut **(see illustration)**.

18 Ease the steering wheel off the column splines by rocking it back and forth. If it is tight, it will be necessary to use a puller to remove it **(see illustrations). Do not** move the air bag slip ring with the steering wheel removed otherwise it could be damaged internally after refitting the steering wheel. If necessary, follow the instructions on the unit itself to centralise it.

Refitting

19 Refitting is a reversal of removal, but note the following:

a) Ensure that the direction indicator switch is in the central (cancelled/off) position, otherwise the switch may be damaged as the wheel is refitted.

b) Feed the wiring harnesses through the steering wheel, and clip the connector into position as the wheel is refitted.

c) Align the marks made on the wheel and the steering column shaft before removal, and align the steering wheel with the guide pins on the air bag contact assembly.

d) Tighten the steering wheel securing nut to the specified torque.

e) Secure the air bag unit to the steering wheel using new Torx bolts, and tighten the bolts to the specified torque.

f) If necessary, the position of the steering wheel on the column shaft splines can be altered in order to centralise it (ensure that the front roadwheels are pointing in the straight-ahead position).

10 Steering column - removal, inspection and refitting

Warning: Later models are equipped with an air bag system. The air bag is mounted in the steering wheel centre pad, and the control module is mounted under the steering column. Make sure that the safety recommendations given in Chapter 12 are followed, to prevent personal injury.

Removal

1 Disconnect the battery negative lead.

2 Remove the steering wheel as described in Section 9.

3 Remove the steering column stalk switches with reference to Chapter 12.

4 Retain the air bag slip ring in its central position using adhesive tape, then unscrew the mounting screws and withdraw it from the top of the column. Note the alignment pointers on the slip ring **(see illustrations)**.

5 Remove the steering column upper shroud, then prise out the ignition lock insert and unscrew the screws securing the lower shroud to the column. Withdraw the lower shroud **(see illustrations)**.

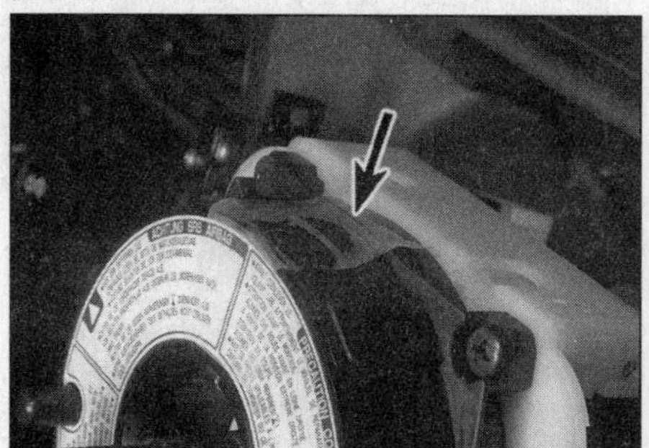
10.4a Use adhesive tape to retain the air bag slip ring in its central position

10.4b Alignment pointers on the air bag slip ring

10.5a Removing the steering column upper shroud

10.5b Prise out the ignition lock insert . . .

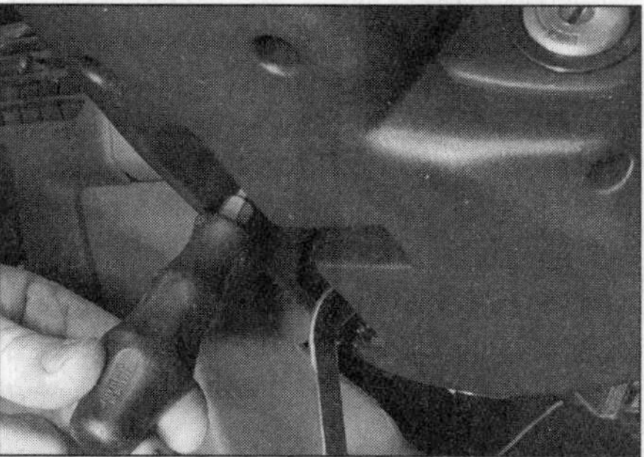
10.5c . . . then unscrew lower shroud screws

10.6 Disconnecting the ignition switch wiring plug

10.8a Release the rubber boot from the steering gear

10.8b Unscrew the nuts and remove the mounting plates . . .

10.8c . . . then pull back the rubber boot to reveal the universal joint

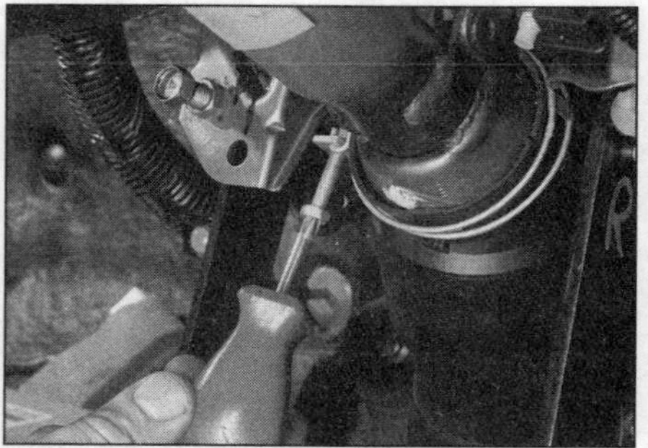
10.10a Loosening the clip on the bottom of the steering column

10.10b Boot cover and mounting nuts on the bulkhead

10.11a Unscrew the lower mounting nuts . . .

10.11b . . . and upper mounting bolts . . .

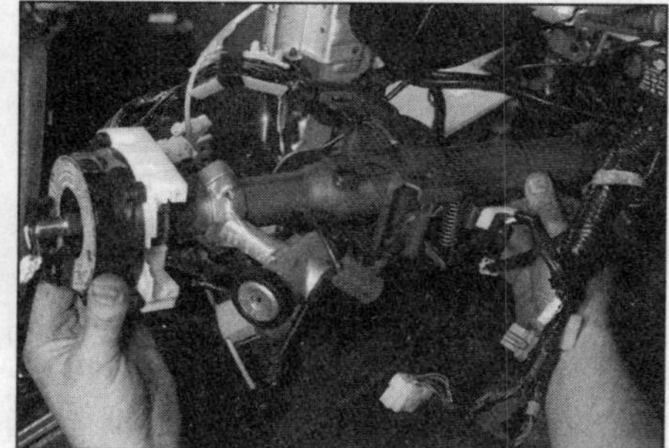
10.11c . . . and withdraw the steering column

6 Disconnect the wiring plug from the ignition switch **(see illustration)**.

7 Remove the screws and withdraw the small shelf from under the steering column. Where necessary disconnect the wiring from the audible warning unit.

8 In the engine compartment, release the clip and unscrew the nuts, then remove the mounting plates and pull back the rubber boot from the lower end of the steering column to reveal the universal joint. If necessary for improved access, raise the front of the vehicle and support on axle stands (see "*Jacking and vehicle support*") **(see illustrations)**.

9 Unscrew and remove the universal joint clamp bolt securing the universal joint to the steering gear pinion shaft. If necessary, temporarily refit the steering wheel and turn the inner column to position the clamp bolt uppermost.

10 Working in the passenger compartment, release the clip then unscrew the nuts and detach the boot cover from the bulkhead **(see illustrations)**.

11 Unscrew the steering column mounting bolts and nuts and withdraw the steering column from inside the vehicle. Slide the boot cover from the bottom of the column **(see illustrations)**.

Inspection

12 The steering column incorporates a telescopic safety feature. In the event of a front-end crash, the shaft collapses and prevents the steering wheel injuring the driver. Before refitting the steering column, examine the column and mountings for signs of damage and deformation, and renew as necessary.

13 Check the steering shaft for signs of free play in the column bushes, and check the universal joints for signs of damage or roughness in the joint bearings. If any damage or wear is found in the steering column universal joints or shaft bushes, the column must be renewed as an assembly.

14 Measure the length of the steering column from the centre of the universal joint pin to the top of the column shaft. If the measurement is outside the specified limits, this is probably due to accident damage, and the complete column assembly should be renewed.

Refitting

15 Commence refitting by sliding the boot cover onto the bottom of the column.

16 Offer the steering column into position, and engage the lower end of the column shaft with the universal joint. Note that there is a master spline, so that the column shaft can only be fitted in one position.

17 Refit the steering column mounting nuts

and bolts and tighten them to the specified torque.
18 Refit and tighten the universal joint clamp bolt.
19 Refit the boot cover to the bulkhead and tighten the nuts.
20 In the engine compartment refit the rubber boot and mounting plates over the universal joint and tighten the nuts. Make sure the plates locate correctly over each other.
21 Reconnect the wiring to the ignition switch.
22 Refit the airbag slip ring and tighten the mounting screws.
23 Refit the steering column stalk switches with reference to Chapter 12.
24 Refit the steering wheel with reference to Section 9 of this Chapter.
25 Reconnect the battery negative lead.

11 Ignition switch/ steering column lock - removal and refitting

Removal

Note: *New shear-screws must be used when refitting the lock assembly.*
1 Remove the steering column as described in Section 10.
2 Remove the grub screw from the rear of the lock and withdraw the switch.
3 To remove the lock assembly, drill out and remove the two shear-screws, then withdraw the two sections of the lock casting from the steering column **(see illustration)**. Note that the lock assembly cannot be removed from the casting.

Refitting

4 Refitting is a reversal of removal, but use new shear-screws and tighten the screws until the heads break off.

12 Steering gear assembly - removal, overhaul and refitting

Warning: Later models are equipped with an air bag system. The air bag is mounted in the steering wheel centre pad, and the control module is mounted under the steering column. Make sure that the safety recommendations given in Chapter 12 are followed, to prevent personal injury.

Note: *A balljoint separator tool will be required for this operation.*

Manual steering gear

Removal

1 Apply the handbrake, then jack up the front of the vehicle and support securely on axle stands (see *"Jacking and vehicle support"*).
2 Move the steering wheel so that the front wheels are pointing in the straight-ahead position, then remove both front roadwheels. On models fitted with an air bag, lock the steering wheel in the straight-ahead position otherwise the air bag slip ring may be damaged on refitting.

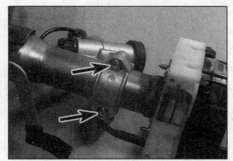

11.3 Shear-screws securing the ignition switch/steering column lock to the steering column

3 Remove the exhaust front pipe as described in Chapter 4A.
4 Working on one side of the vehicle, remove the split pin, then partially unscrew the castellated nut securing the track-rod end to the steering arm. Using a balljoint separator tool, separate the track-rod end from the steering arm. Remove the nut. Discard the split pin - a new one must be used on refitting.
5 Repeat the procedure to disconnect the track-rod end on the other side of the vehicle.
6 Working in the driver's footwell, unscrew the nuts and remove the plates securing the plastic cover to the bulkhead then pull back the cover for access to the lower universal joint. Some models may have a rubber gaiter fitted which allows better access to the joint, however where the plastic type is fitted, better access to the universal joint can be made by loosening the clip and unbolting the rubber gaiter from the engine compartment side of the bulkhead.
7 Temporarily refit the steering wheel, and turn the steering column as necessary for access to the universal joint clamp bolt. Mark the joint and pinion shaft in relation to each other with a dab of paint. Unscrew and remove the clamp bolt securing the joint to the steering gear pinion shaft. **Do not** prise the joint clamp apart with a screwdriver.
8 Using a trolley jack and block of wood, support the weight of the transmission, then unbolt and remove the centre member from the underbody and engine mountings and withdraw it from under the engine compartment.
9 On manual transmission models disconnect the gear linkage control rod and support rod from the transmission with reference to Chapter 7A.
10 On automatic transmission models disconnect the selector cable and remove the mounting bracket from the transmission with reference to Chapter 7B.
11 If the rubber gaiter was not removed in paragraph 5, leave the gaiter attached to the bulkhead but loosen the clip to release it from the steering gear.
12 Unscrew the bolts securing the steering gear mounting brackets to the bulkhead. Support the steering gear, then withdraw the brackets.
13 Rotate the steering gear, and move it out through the left-hand wheel arch sufficiently until it can be lowered from the engine compartment. Note that on left-hand-drive models, it will be necessary to move it through the right-hand wheel arch then lowered from the engine compartment.

Overhaul

14 Examine the assembly for obvious signs of wear or damage.
15 Check the rack for smooth operation through its full stroke of movement, and check that there is no binding or free play.
16 Check the track-rods for deformation and cracks.
17 Check the condition of the steering gear rubber gaiters, and renew if necessary with reference to Section 13.
18 Examine the track-rod ends for wear or damage, and renew if necessary with reference to Section 16.
19 No overhaul of the manual steering gear is possible, and if worn or damaged, the complete assembly (including track-rods) must be renewed.

Refitting

20 Ensure that the steering gear pinion is centralised as follows:

a) Turn the pinion to rotate the steering from lock-to-lock, and count the number of turns of the pinion.
b) With the steering on full lock, turn the pinion back through half the number of turns noted for lock-to-lock, to achieve the centralised position.

21 Manoeuvre the steering gear into position through the wheel arch and engage with the universal joint splines on the bottom of the steering column, then refit the mounting brackets and refit and tighten the securing bolts. The lower bolts should be hand-tightened first, then the upper bolts fully tightened, and the lower bolts fully tightened last. Make sure the pinion is engaged correctly with the column universal joint as previously marked - the joint upper slit should be aligned over the cut-out and the lower slit should be aligned with the plastic guide plate.
22 Insert the clamp bolt in the universal joint and tighten to the specified torque.
23 On manual transmission models, refit the gear linkage control rod and support rod with reference to Chapter 7A.
24 On automatic transmission models, refit the mounting bracket and reconnect the selector cable with reference to Chapter 7B.
25 Refit the centre member and tighten the nuts and bolts. Remove the trolley jack.
26 Refit the rubber gaiter and plastic cover to the bottom of the column and tighten the nuts

onto the bulkhead. Make sure the metal plates are correctly located.

27 Working on one side of the vehicle, reconnect the track-rod end to the steering arm, then refit the castellated nut, and tighten to the specified torque.

28 If necessary, tighten the nut further (ensure that the maximum torque for the nut is not exceeded) until the nearest grooves in the nut are aligned with the split pin hole in the track-rod end, then fit a new split pin.

29 Repeat the procedure to reconnect the track-rod end on the other side of the vehicle.

30 Refit the exhaust front pipe with reference to Chapter 4A.

31 Refit the roadwheels, and lower the vehicle to the ground.

Power steering gear

Removal

32 Apply the handbrake, then jack up the front of the vehicle and support securely on axle stands (see *"Jacking and vehicle support"*).

33 Move the steering wheel so that the front wheels are pointing in the straight-ahead position, then remove both front roadwheels. On models fitted with an air bag, lock the steering wheel in the straight-ahead position otherwise the air bag slip ring may be damaged on refitting.

34 Remove the exhaust front pipe as described in Chapter 4A.

35 On left-hand drive models only, remove the evaporative emission carbon canister and bracket with reference to Chapter 4B. This will allow access to the steering column universal joint.

36 Position a suitable container beneath the fluid feed pipe union on the steering gear, then unscrew the union nut, and disconnect the pipe from the steering gear. Similarly, disconnect the fluid return hose from the steering gear. Drain the fluid into the container, then plug or cover the open ends of the pipe/hose and steering gear to reduce further fluid loss, and to prevent dirt ingress.

37 Working on one side of the vehicle, remove the split pin, then partially unscrew the castellated nut securing the track-rod end to the steering arm. Using a balljoint separator tool, separate the track-rod end from the steering arm. Remove the nut. Discard the split pin - a new one must be used on refitting.

38 Repeat the procedure to disconnect the track-rod end on the other side of the vehicle.

39 Working in the driver's footwell, unscrew the nuts and remove the plates securing the plastic cover to the bulkhead then pull back the cover for access to the lower universal joint. Some models may have a rubber gaiter fitted which allows better access to the joint, however where the plastic type is fitted, better access to the universal joint can be made by loosening the clip and unbolting the rubber gaiter from the engine compartment side of the bulkhead.

40 Temporarily refit the steering wheel, and turn the steering column as necessary for access to the universal joint clamp bolt. Mark the joint and pinion shaft in relation to each other with a dab of paint. Unscrew and remove the clamp bolt securing the joint to the steering gear pinion shaft. **Do not** prise the joint clamp apart with a screwdriver.

41 Using a trolley jack and block of wood, support the weight of the transmission, then unbolt and remove the centre member from the underbody and engine mountings and withdraw it from under the engine compartment.

42 On manual transmission models disconnect the gear linkage control rod and support rod from the transmission with reference to Chapter 7A.

43 On automatic transmission models disconnect the selector cable and remove the mounting bracket from the transmission with reference to Chapter 7B.

44 If the rubber gaiter was not removed in paragraph 5, leave the gaiter attached to the bulkhead but loosen the clip to release it from the steering gear.

45 Unscrew the bolts securing the steering gear mounting brackets to the bulkhead **(see illustration)**. Support the steering gear, then withdraw the brackets.

46 Rotate the steering gear, and move it out through the left-hand wheel arch sufficiently until it can be lowered from the engine compartment. Note that on left-hand-drive models, it will be necessary to move it through the right-hand wheel arch then lowered from the engine compartment.

Overhaul

47 Examine the assembly for obvious signs of wear or damage.

48 Check the rack for smooth operation through its full stroke of movement, and check that there is no binding or free play.

49 Check the track-rods for deformation and cracks.

50 Check the condition of the steering gear rubber gaiters, and renew if necessary with reference to Section 13.

51 Examine the track-rod ends for wear or damage, and renew if necessary with reference to Section 16.

12.45 Power steering gear left-hand side mounting bolt

52 No overhaul of the power steering gear is possible, and if worn or damaged, the complete assembly (including track-rods) must be renewed.

Refitting

53 Ensure that the steering gear pinion is centralised as follows:

a) *Turn the pinion to rotate the steering from lock-to-lock, and count the number of turns of the pinion.*

b) *With the steering on full lock, turn the pinion back through half the number of turns noted for lock-to-lock, to achieve the centralised position.*

54 Manoeuvre the steering gear into position through the wheel arch and engage with the universal joint splines on the bottom of the steering column, then refit the mounting brackets and refit and tighten the securing bolts making sure that the hydraulic fluid pipes are not trapped behind the steering gear. The lower bolts should be hand-tightened first, then the upper bolts fully tightened, and the lower bolts fully tightened last. Make sure the pinion is engaged correctly with the column universal joint as previously marked - the joint upper slit should be aligned over the cut-out and the lower slit should be aligned with the plastic guide plate.

55 Insert the clamp bolt in the universal joint and tighten to the specified torque.

56 Reconnect the fluid feed pipe and the return hose to the steering gear. Tighten the feed pipe union nut to the specified torque. When refitting the return hose make sure the hose is pushed right up to the flare nut before tightening the retaining clip.

57 On manual transmission models, refit the gear linkage control rod and support rod with reference to Chapter 7A.

58 On automatic transmission models, refit the mounting bracket and reconnect the selector cable with reference to Chapter 7B.

59 Refit the centre member and tighten the nuts and bolts. Remove the trolley jack.

60 Refit the rubber gaiter and plastic cover to the bottom of the column and tighten the nuts onto the bulkhead. Make sure the metal plates are correctly located.

61 Working on one side of the vehicle, reconnect the track-rod end to the steering arm, then refit the castellated nut, and tighten to the specified torque.

62 If necessary, tighten the nut further (ensure that the maximum torque for the nut is not exceeded) until the nearest grooves in the nut are aligned with the split pin hole in the track-rod end, then fit a new split pin.

63 Repeat the procedure to reconnect the track-rod end on the other side of the vehicle.

64 Refit the exhaust front pipe with reference to Chapter 4A.

65 Refit the roadwheels, then bleed the power steering hydraulic system as described in Section 14.

66 Finally, lower the vehicle to the ground.

13 Steering gear rubber gaiters - renewal

Note: *New gaiter retaining clips should be used on refitting.*

1 Remove the relevant track-rod end as described in Section 16.

2 If not already done, unscrew the track-rod end locknut from the end of the track-rod.

3 Note the fitted position of the gaiter on the track-rod, then release the gaiter securing clips. Slide the gaiter from the steering gear, and off the end of the track-rod.

4 Thoroughly clean the track-rod and the steering gear housing, then scrape off all the grease from the old gaiter, and apply it to the track rod inner balljoint. If grease has been lost, apply new grease to the balljoint. Smear a little grease onto the gaiter contact surfaces on the steering gear and track rod.

5 Slide the new gaiter onto the track-rod, and locate it on the steering gear housing. Locate the outer end of the gaiter in the special indentation on the track rod. Secure the gaiter in position with new retaining clips.

6 Screw the track-rod end locknut onto the track-rod.

7 Refit the track rod end with reference to Section 16.

14 Power steering hydraulic system - bleeding

General

1 The following symptoms indicate that there is air present in the power steering hydraulic system:

a) *Generation of air bubbles in fluid reservoir.*
b) *"Clicking" noises from power steering pump.*
c) *Excessive "buzzing" from power steering pump.*

2 Before bleeding the hydraulic system check that there are no fluid leaks from the pressure and return hoses. Also check the cooling tube located at the front of the radiator and the interconnecting hoses for possible leaks.

3 Note that when the vehicle is stationary, or while moving the steering wheel slowly, a "hissing" noise may be produced in the steering gear or the fluid pump. This noise is inherent in the system, and does not indicate any cause for concern.

Bleeding

4 Apply the handbrake then jack up the front of the vehicle so that the front wheels are just clear of the ground, and support securely on axle stands (see *"Jacking and vehicle support"*).

5 Check the fluid level in the power steering fluid reservoir located on the right-hand side of the engine compartment, and if necessary top-up to the relevant level mark.

6 Have an assistant turn the steering quickly from lock to lock with the engine switched off, and observe the fluid level. If the fluid level drops, add more fluid, and repeat the operation until the fluid level no longer drops.

7 Start the engine and allow it to run at idle speed, then repeat the procedure described in the previous paragraph.

8 Once the fluid level has stabilised and all air has been bled from the system, switch off the engine and lower the vehicle to the ground.

15 Power steering pump - removal and refitting

Removal

Note: *New copper washers must be fitted when reconnecting the high-pressure fluid hose union to the pump.*

1 For improved access, apply the handbrake then jack up the front of the vehicle and support on axle stands (see *"Jacking and vehicle support"*).

2 Remove the pump drivebelt as described in Chapter 1.

3 Place a suitable container beneath the power steering pump, then loosen the clip and disconnect the fluid return hose. Drain the escaping fluid into the container. Plug or cover the open end of the hose and pump, to reduce further fluid loss and to prevent dirt ingress.

4 Unscrew the banjo bolt from the high-pressure fluid hose union, and disconnect the hose from the pump. Recover the copper washers and discard them - new ones must be used on refitting.

5 Unscrew the mounting bolts and withdraw the power steering pump upwards from the engine compartment. Take care not to spill hydraulic fluid on the vehicle paintwork **(see illustrations)**.

Refitting

6 Refitting is a reversal of removal but use new copper washers when reconnecting the high-pressure fluid hose union, tighten the union bolt to the specified torque, tension the drivebelt as described in Chapter 1, and bleed the hydraulic system as described in Section 14 of this Chapter.

16 Track-rod end - removal and refitting

Note: *A balljoint separator tool will be required for this operation.*

Removal

1 Apply the handbrake, then jack up the front of the vehicle and support on axle stands (see *"Jacking and vehicle support"*). Remove the relevant front roadwheel.

2 Remove the split pin, then partially unscrew the castellated nut securing the track-rod end to the steering arm. Using a balljoint separator tool, separate the track-rod end from the steering arm. Remove the nut. Discard the split pin - a new one must be used on refitting **(see illustrations)**.

3 Counterhold the track-rod end using the flats provided, then loosen the track-rod end locknut **(see illustration)**.

4 Counting the exact number of turns required to do so, unscrew the track-rod end from the track-rod.

Refitting

5 Carefully clean the track-rod end and the track-rod threads.

15.5a Power steering pump upper mounting bolt

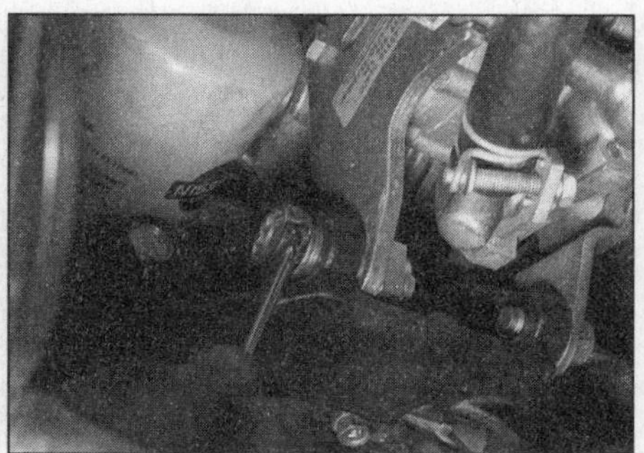

15.5b Loosening the power steering pump lower mounting bolts

15.5c Power steering pump removed from the engine

16.2a Extracting the split pin from the track-rod end

16.2b Using a separator tool to release the track-rod end balljoint

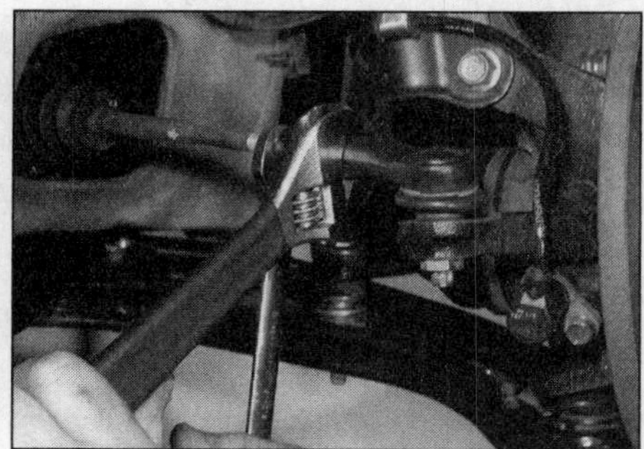
16.3 Loosening the track-rod end locknut

6 Renew the track-rod end if the rubber dust cover is cracked, split or perished, or if the movement of the balljoint is either sloppy or too stiff. Also check for other signs of damage such as worn threads.

7 Screw the track-rod end onto the track-rod by the number of turns noted before removal, then tighten the track-rod end locknut.

8 Ensure that the balljoint taper is clean, then engage the taper with the steering arm on the hub carrier.

9 Refit the castellated nut, and tighten to the specified torque.

10 If necessary, tighten the nut further (ensure that the maximum torque for the nut is not exceeded) until the nearest grooves in the nut are aligned with the split pin hole in the track-rod end, then fit a new split pin.

11 Refit the roadwheel, and lower the vehicle to the ground.

12 Check the front wheel alignment as described in Chapter 1, and adjust if necessary.

Chapter 11
Bodywork and fittings

Contents

Degrees of difficulty

Easy, suitable for novice with little experience 	**Fairly easy,** suitable for beginner with some experience 	**Fairly difficult,** suitable for competent DIY mechanic 	**Difficult,** suitable for experienced DIY mechanic 	**Very difficult,** suitable for expert DIY or professional

Specifications

Torque wrench settings	Nm	lbf ft
Bonnet lock	24	18
Bumper mounting nuts	15	11
Door hinge bolts	24	18
Door lock striker bolts	15	11
Front seat securing bolts	49	36
Rear seat to body bolts	15	11
Rear seat to bracket bolts	6	4
Seat belt mounting bolts	50	37
Tailgate hinge	24	18
Tailgate lock	15	11
Tailgate strut bracket	6	4

1 General information

The bodyshell is made of pressed-steel sections, and is available in three-door or five-door Hatchback versions. Most components are welded together, but some use is made of structural adhesives; the front wings are bolted on.

The bonnet, door, and some other vulnerable panels, are made of zinc-coated metal, and are further protected by being coated with an anti-chip primer, prior to being sprayed. Side impact bars are fitted to the doors and the front and rear body sections incorporate crumple zones.

All models from August 1995 are equipped with a supplementary restraint system (SRS), incorporating a driver's air bag (optional on Shape models) and front seat belt pre-tensioners. The pre-tensioners are integral with the seat belt inertia reels. Models from November 1998 onwards are available with side air bags, which are built into the sides of the front seats - refer to Chapter 12 for the precautions to be observed..

Extensive use is made of plastic materials, mainly in the interior, but also in exterior components. The outer sections of the front and rear bumpers are injection-moulded from a synthetic material which is very strong, and yet light. Plastic components such as wheel arch liners are fitted to the underside of the vehicle, to improve the body's resistance to corrosion.

2 Maintenance - bodywork and underframe

The general condition of a vehicle's bodywork is the one thing that significantly affects its value. Maintenance is easy, but needs to be regular. Neglect, particularly after minor damage, can lead quickly to further deterioration and costly repair bills. It is important also to keep watch on those parts of the vehicle not immediately visible, for instance the underside, inside all the wheel arches, and the lower part of the engine compartment.

The basic maintenance routine for the bodywork is washing - preferably with a lot of water, from a hose. This will remove all the loose solids which may have stuck to the vehicle. It is important to flush these off in such a way as to prevent grit from scratching the finish. The wheel arches and underframe need washing in the same way, to remove any accumulated mud, which will retain moisture and tend to encourage rust. Oddly enough, the best time to clean the underframe and wheel arches is in wet weather, when the mud is thoroughly wet and soft. In very wet weather, the underframe is usually cleaned of large accumulations automatically, and this is a good time for inspection.

Periodically, except on vehicles with a wax-based underbody protective coating, it is a good idea to have the whole of the underframe of the vehicle steam-cleaned, engine compartment included, so that a thorough inspection can be carried out to see what minor repairs and renovations are necessary. Steam-cleaning is available at many garages, and is necessary for the removal of the accumulation of oily grime, which sometimes is allowed to become thick in certain areas. If steam-cleaning facilities are not available, there are some excellent grease solvents available which can be brush-applied; the dirt can then be simply hosed off. Note that these methods should not be used on vehicles with wax-based underbody protective coating, or the coating will be removed. Such vehicles should be inspected annually, preferably just prior to Winter, when the underbody should be washed down, and any damage to the wax coating repaired. Ideally, a completely fresh coat should be applied. It would also be worth considering the use of such wax-based protection for injection into door panels, sills, box sections, etc, as an additional safeguard against rust damage, where such protection is not provided by the vehicle manufacturer.

After washing paintwork, wipe off with a chamois leather to give an unspotted clear finish. A coat of clear protective wax polish will give added protection against chemical pollutants in the air. If the paintwork sheen has dulled or oxidised, use a cleaner/polisher combination to restore the brilliance of the shine. This requires a little effort, but such dulling is usually caused because regular washing has been neglected. Care needs to be taken with metallic paintwork, as special non-abrasive cleaner/polisher is required to avoid damage to the finish. Always check that the door and ventilator opening drain holes and pipes are completely clear, so that water can be drained out. Brightwork should be treated in the same way as paintwork. Windscreens and windows can be kept clear of the smeary film which often appears, by the use of proprietary glass cleaner. Never use any form of wax or other body or chromium polish on glass.

3 Maintenance - upholstery and carpets

Mats and carpets should be brushed or vacuum-cleaned regularly, to keep them free of grit. If they are badly stained, remove them from the vehicle for scrubbing or sponging, and make quite sure they are dry before refitting. Seats and interior trim panels can be kept clean by wiping with a damp cloth. If they do become stained (which can be more apparent on light-coloured upholstery), use a little liquid detergent and a soft nail brush to scour the grime out of the grain of the material. Do not forget to keep the headlining clean in the same way as the upholstery. When using liquid cleaners inside the vehicle, do not over-wet the surfaces being cleaned. Excessive damp could get into the seams and padded interior, causing stains, offensive odours or even rot. If the inside of the vehicle gets wet accidentally, it is worthwhile taking some trouble to dry it out properly, particularly where carpets are involved.

Warning: Do not leave oil or electric heaters inside the vehicle.

4 Minor body damage - repair

Repairs of minor scratches in bodywork

If the scratch is very superficial, and does not penetrate to the metal of the bodywork, repair is very simple. Lightly rub the area of the scratch with a paintwork renovator, or a very fine cutting paste, to remove loose paint from the scratch, and to clear the surrounding bodywork of wax polish. Rinse the area with clean water.

Apply touch-up paint to the scratch using a fine paint brush; continue to apply fine layers of paint until the surface of the paint in the scratch is level with the surrounding paintwork. Allow the new paint at least two weeks to harden, then blend it into the surrounding paintwork by rubbing the scratch area with a paintwork renovator or a very fine cutting paste. Finally, apply wax polish.

Where the scratch has penetrated right through to the metal of the bodywork, causing the metal to rust, a different repair technique is required. Remove any loose rust from the bottom of the scratch with a penknife, then apply rust-inhibiting paint to prevent the formation of rust in the future. Using a rubber or nylon applicator, fill the scratch with bodystopper paste. If required, this paste can be mixed with cellulose thinners to provide a very thin paste which is ideal for filling narrow scratches. Before the stopper-paste in the scratch hardens, wrap a piece of smooth cotton rag around the top of a finger. Dip the finger in cellulose thinners, and quickly sweep it across the surface of the stopper-paste in the scratch; this will ensure that the surface of the stopper-paste is slightly hollowed. The scratch can now be painted over as described earlier in this Section.

Repairs of dents in bodywork

When deep denting of the vehicle's bodywork has taken place, the first task is to pull the dent out, until the affected bodywork almost attains its original shape. There is little point in trying to restore the original shape completely, as the metal in the damaged area will have stretched on impact, and cannot be reshaped fully to its original contour. It is better to bring the level of the dent up to a point which is about 3 mm below the level of the surrounding bodywork. In cases where the dent is very shallow anyway, it is not worth trying to pull it out at all. If the underside of the dent is accessible, it can be hammered out gently from behind, using a mallet with a wooden or plastic head. Whilst doing this, hold a suitable block of wood firmly against the outside of the panel, to absorb the impact from the hammer blows and thus prevent a large area of the bodywork from being "belled-out".

Should the dent be in a section of the bodywork which has a double skin, or some other factor making it inaccessible from behind, a different technique is called for. Drill several small holes through the metal inside the area - particularly in the deeper section. Then screw long self-tapping screws into the holes, just sufficiently for them to gain a good purchase in the metal. Now the dent can be pulled out by pulling on the protruding heads of the screws with a pair of pliers.

The next stage of the repair is the removal of the paint from the damaged area, and from an inch or so of the surrounding "sound" bodywork. This is accomplished most easily by using a wire brush or abrasive pad on a power drill, although it can be done just as effectively by hand, using sheets of abrasive paper. To complete the preparation for filling, score the surface of the bare metal with a screwdriver or the tang of a file, or alternatively, drill small holes in the affected area. This will provide a really good "key" for the filler paste.

To complete the repair, see the Section on filling and respraying.

Repairs of rust holes or gashes in bodywork

Remove all paint from the affected area, and from an inch or so of the surrounding "sound" bodywork, using an abrasive pad or a wire brush on a power drill. If these are not available, a few sheets of abrasive paper will do the job most effectively. With the paint removed, you will be able to judge the severity of the corrosion, and therefore decide whether to renew the whole panel (if this is possible) or to repair the affected area. New body panels are not as expensive as most people think, and it is often quicker and more satisfactory to fit a new panel than to attempt to repair large areas of corrosion.

Remove all fittings from the affected area, except those which will act as a guide to the original shape of the damaged bodywork (eg headlight shells etc). Then, using tin snips or a hacksaw blade, remove all loose metal and any other metal badly affected by corrosion. Hammer the edges of the hole inwards, in order to create a slight depression for the filler paste.

Wire-brush the affected area to remove the powdery rust from the surface of the remaining metal. Paint the affected area with rust-inhibiting paint, if the back of the rusted area is accessible, treat this also.

Before filling can take place, it will be necessary to block the hole in some way. This can be achieved by the use of aluminium or plastic mesh, or aluminium tape.

Aluminium or plastic mesh, or glass-fibre matting, is probably the best material to use for a large hole. Cut a piece to the approximate size and shape of the hole to be filled, then position it in the hole so that its edges are below the level of the surrounding bodywork. It can be retained in position by several blobs of filler paste around its periphery.

Aluminium tape should be used for small or very narrow holes. Pull a piece off the roll, trim it to the approximate size and shape required, then pull off the backing paper (if used) and stick the tape over the hole; it can be overlapped if the thickness of one piece is insufficient. Burnish down the edges of the tape with the handle of a screwdriver or similar, to ensure that the tape is securely attached to the metal underneath.

Bodywork repairs - filling and respraying

Before using this Section, see the Sections on dent, deep scratch, rust holes and gash repairs.

Many types of bodyfiller are available, but generally speaking, those proprietary kits which contain a tin of filler paste and a tube of resin hardener are best for this type of repair. A wide, flexible plastic or nylon applicator will be found invaluable for imparting a smooth and well-contoured finish to the surface of the filler.

Mix up a little filler on a clean piece of card or board - measure the hardener carefully (follow the maker's instructions on the pack), otherwise the filler will set too rapidly or too slowly. Using the applicator, apply the filler paste to the prepared area; draw the applicator across the surface of the filler to achieve the correct contour and to level the surface. As soon as a contour that approximates to the correct one is achieved, stop working the paste - if you carry on too long, the paste will become sticky and begin to "pick-up" on the applicator. Continue to add thin layers of filler paste at 20-minute intervals, until the level of the filler is just proud of the surrounding bodywork.

Once the filler has hardened, the excess can be removed using a metal plane or file. From then on, progressively-finer grades of abrasive paper should be used, starting with a 40-grade production paper, and finishing with a 400-grade wet-and-dry paper. Always wrap the abrasive paper around a flat rubber, cork, or wooden block - otherwise the surface of the filler will not be completely flat. During the smoothing of the filler surface, the wet-and-dry paper should be periodically rinsed in water. This will ensure that a very smooth finish is imparted to the filler at the final stage.

At this stage, the "dent" should be surrounded by a ring of bare metal, which in turn should be encircled by the finely "feathered" edge of the good paintwork. Rinse the repair area with clean water, until all of the dust produced by the rubbing-down operation has gone.

Spray the whole area with a light coat of primer - this will show up any imperfections in the surface of the filler. Repair these imperfections with fresh filler paste or bodystopper, and once more smooth the surface with abrasive paper. Repeat this spray-and-repair procedure until you are satisfied that the surface of the filler, and the feathered edge of the paintwork, are perfect. Clean the repair area with clean water, and allow to dry fully.

If bodystopper is used, it can be mixed with cellulose thinners to form a really thin paste which is ideal for filling small holes.

The repair area is now ready for final spraying. Paint spraying must be carried out in a warm, dry, windless and dust-free atmosphere. This condition can be created artificially if you have access to a large indoor working area, but if you are forced to work in the open, you will have to pick your day very carefully. If you are working indoors, dousing the floor in the work area with water will help to settle the dust which would otherwise be in the atmosphere. If the repair area is confined to one body panel, mask off the surrounding panels; this will help to minimise the effects of a slight mis-match in paint colours. Bodywork fittings (eg chrome strips, door handles etc) will also need to be masked off. Use genuine masking tape, and several thicknesses of newspaper, for the masking operations.

Before commencing to spray, agitate the aerosol can thoroughly, then spray a test area (an old tin, or similar) until the technique is mastered. Cover the repair area with a thick coat of primer; the thickness should be built up using several thin layers of paint, rather than one thick one. Using 400-grade wet-and-dry paper, rub down the surface of the primer until it is really smooth. While doing this, the work area should be thoroughly doused with water, and the wet-and-dry paper periodically rinsed in water. Allow to dry before spraying on more paint.

Spray on the top coat, again building up the thickness by using several thin layers of paint. Start spraying at one edge of the repair area, and then, using a side-to-side motion, work until the whole repair area and about 2 inches of the surrounding original paintwork is covered. Remove all masking material 10 to 15 minutes after spraying on the final coat of paint.

Allow the new paint at least two weeks to harden, then, using a paintwork renovator, or a very fine cutting paste, blend the edges of the paint into the existing paintwork. Finally, apply wax polish.

Plastic components

With the use of more and more plastic body components by the vehicle manufacturers (eg bumpers. spoilers, and in some cases major body panels), rectification of more serious damage to such items has become a matter of either entrusting repair work to a specialist in this field, or renewing complete components. Repair of such damage by the DIY owner is not really feasible, owing to the cost of the equipment and materials required for effecting such repairs. The basic technique involves making a groove along the line of the crack in the plastic, using a rotary burr in a power drill. The damaged part is then welded back together, using a hot-air gun to heat up and fuse a plastic filler rod into the groove. Any excess plastic is then removed, and the area rubbed down to a smooth finish. It is important that a filler rod of the correct plastic is used, as body components can be made of a variety of different types (eg polycarbonate, ABS, polypropylene).

Damage of a less serious nature (abrasions, minor cracks etc) can be repaired by the DIY owner using a two-part epoxy filler repair material. Once mixed in equal proportions, this is used in similar fashion to the bodywork filler used on metal panels. The filler is usually cured in twenty to thirty minutes, ready for sanding and painting.

If the owner is renewing a complete component himself, or if he has repaired it with epoxy filler, he will be left with the problem of finding a suitable paint for finishing which is compatible with the type of plastic used. At one time, the use of a universal paint was not possible, owing to the complex range of plastics encountered in body component applications. Standard paints, generally speaking, will not bond to plastic or rubber satisfactorily. However, it is now possible to obtain a plastic body parts finishing kit which consists of a pre-primer treatment, a primer and coloured top coat. Full instructions are normally supplied with a kit, but basically, the method of use is to first apply the pre-primer to the component concerned, and allow it to dry for up to 30 minutes. Then the primer is applied, and left to dry for about an hour before finally applying the special-coloured top coat. The result is a correctly-coloured component, where the paint will flex with the plastic or rubber, a property that standard paint does not normally possess.

6.5 Removing the wheel arch liner retaining screws

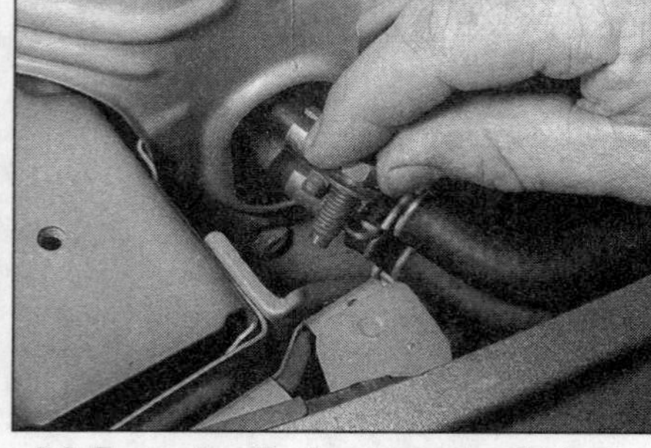
6.8 Removing the front bumper-to-body mounting bolts

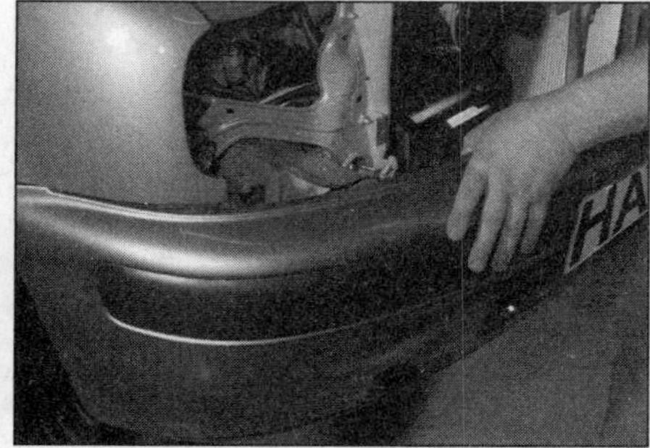
6.9a Withdrawing the front bumper from the vehicle

5 Major body damage - repair

Where serious damage has occurred, or large areas need renewal due to neglect, it means that complete new panels will need welding-in, and this is best left to professionals. If the damage is due to impact, it will also be necessary to check completely the alignment of the bodyshell, and this can only be carried out accurately by a Nissan dealer using special jigs. If the body is left misaligned, it is primarily dangerous, as the car will not handle properly, and secondly, uneven stresses will be imposed on the steering, suspension and possibly transmission, causing abnormal wear, or complete failure, particularly to such items as the tyres.

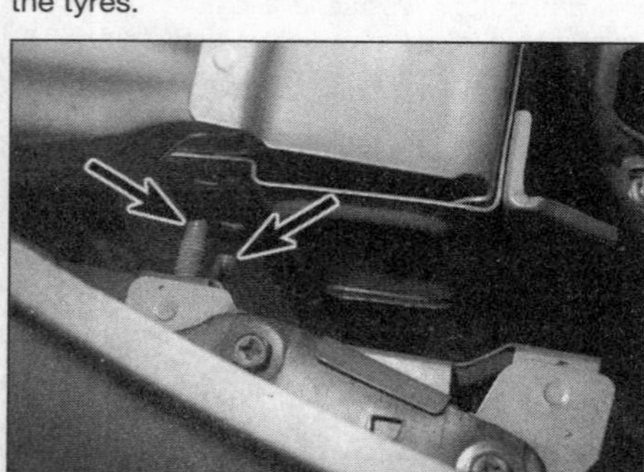
6.9b Mounting studs on the front bumper

6 Bumpers - removal and refitting

Front bumper

Removal

1 To improve access apply the handbrake, then jack up the front of the vehicle, and support on axle stands (see *"Jacking and vehicle support "*). Remove both front wheels.
2 Where fitted, remove the front foglights with reference to Chapter 12. Alternatively, disconnect the wiring.
3 On models up to March 1998, remove the radiator grille as described in Section 20.
4 Unscrew the screws from the bottom edge of the front bumper.
5 Remove the screws securing the wheel arch liners to the front bumper on both sides. Also remove the liner inner screws to allow the liners to be prised away for access to the bumper outer securing bolts **(see illustration)**.
6 Using a socket and extension bar, unscrew the outer securing bolts securing the ends of the bumper to the front valance.
7 On models fitted with a tailgate wiper, remove the right-hand headlight unit as described in Chapter 12.
8 Unscrew the nuts and bolts securing the bumper to the front of the two main underbody members **(see illustration)**.
9 With the aid of an assistant, withdraw the front bumper forwards from the vehicle **(see illustrations)**.
10 If desired, unbolt the brackets from the bumper

Refitting

11 Refitting is a reversal of removal.

Rear bumper

Removal

12 To improve access chock the front wheels, then jack up the rear of the vehicle and support on axle stands (see *"Jacking and vehicle support "*).
13 Where necessary, unbolt and remove both rear mudflaps from the rear bumper.
14 Unscrew both bottom bolts securing the outer ends of the bumper to the wheel arch **(see illustration)**.
15 Working beneath the rear of the vehicle, unscrew the lower nuts securing the bottom of the bumper to the rear valance **(see illustration)**.
16 In the rear luggage area, pull back the carpet then unscrew the upper nuts securing the top of the bumper to the rear valance **(see illustration)**.
17 With the aid of an assistant, withdraw the rear bumper rearwards from the vehicle.
18 If desired, remove the screws retaining the reinforcement bar to the bumper.

Refitting

19 Refitting is a reversal of removal.

6.14 Removing the rear bumper-to-wheel arch mounting bolts

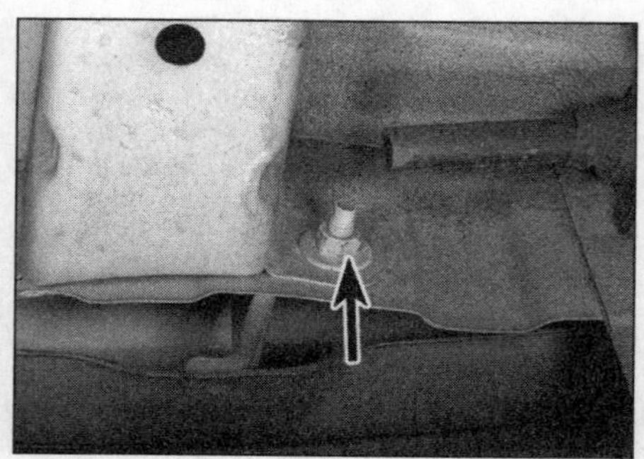
6.15 Rear bumper lower mounting nuts on the rear valance

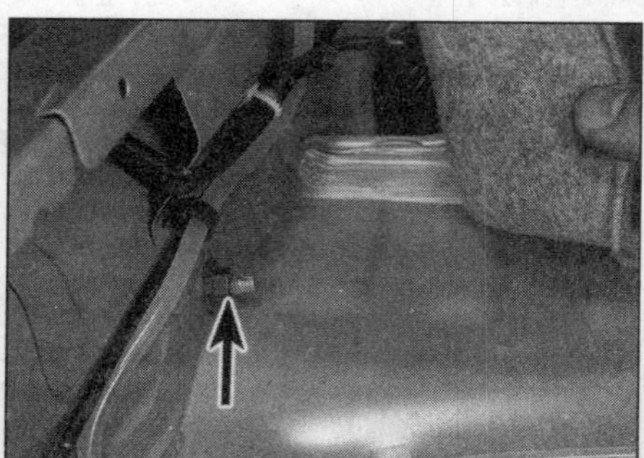
6.16 Rear bumper upper mounting nuts in the rear luggage area

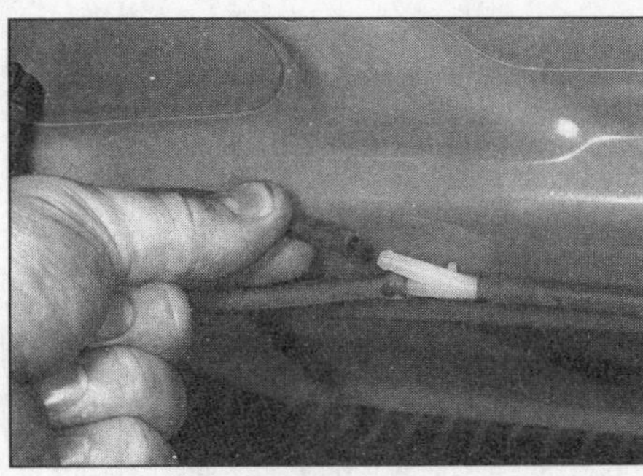

7.2 Disconnecting the windscreen washer fluid supply hose on the bonnet

7 Bonnet - removal, refitting and adjustment

Removal

1 Open the bonnet and have an assistant support it. Using a pencil or felt tip pen, mark the outline of each bonnet hinge relative to the bonnet, to use as a guide on refitting.
2 Disconnect the windscreen washer fluid supply hose from the connector under the bonnet, then release the hose from the clips under the bonnet **(see illustration)**.
3 Unscrew the bolts securing the bonnet to the hinges **(see illustration)** and, with the help of an assistant, carefully lift the bonnet clear. Store the bonnet out of the way in a safe place.
4 Inspect the bonnet hinges for signs of wear and free play at the pivots, and if necessary renew. Each hinge is secured to the body by two bolts.

Refitting

5 With the aid of an assistant, offer up the bonnet, and loosely fit the retaining bolts. Align the hinges with the marks made on removal, then tighten the retaining bolts securely.
6 Reconnect the windscreen washer fluid supply hose, and clip it into position under the bonnet.
7 Adjust the alignment of the bonnet as follows.

Adjustment

8 Close the bonnet, and check for alignment with the adjacent panels. If necessary, slacken the hinge bolts and re-align the bonnet to suit. Once the bonnet is correctly aligned, tighten the relevant hinge bolts securely.
9 Once the bonnet is correctly aligned, check that the bonnet fastens and releases in a satisfactory manner. If adjustment is necessary, slacken the bonnet lock retaining bolts, and adjust the position of the lock to suit. Once the lock is operating correctly, securely tighten its retaining bolts. Make sure that the bonnet striker enters the lock centrally.
10 If necessary, align the front edge of the bonnet with the wing panels by turning the rubbers screwed into the body front panel, to raise or lower the front edge as required.

8 Bonnet release cable - removal and refitting

Removal

1 Open the bonnet. For improved access remove the radiator grille, where applicable.
2 Unscrew the three securing bolts, and remove the lock assembly from the body panel.
3 Pull the return spring to one side, then unhook the end of the bonnet release cable from the lock lever. Withdraw the lock assembly from the vehicle.
4 Where applicable, unscrew the cable securing clip from the front body panel.
5 Working in the passenger's footwell, remove the side trim panel. Release the plastic securing clip, then pull the weatherstrip from the edge of the panel. Pull the panel from the footwell to release the remaining securing clips.
6 Unscrew the securing bolts, and withdraw the bonnet release lever. Unhook the cable end from the lever.
7 Note the routing of the cable, and release it from any clips in the engine compartment, then feed the cable through the bulkhead grommet into the engine compartment. On some models, it may be necessary to move certain components in the engine compartment to one side, to gain access to the cable clips. It is advisable to tie a length of string to the release lever end of the cable before removal, to aid refitting. Pull the cable through into the engine compartment, then untie the string and leave it place until the cable is to be refitted.

Refitting

8 Refitting is a reversal of removal, but use the string to pull the cable into position, and ensure that the bulkhead grommet is securely located. Make sure that the cable is routed as noted before removal, and reposition the cable in its securing clips in the engine compartment. Check the bonnet release mechanism for correct operation on completion.

9.2 Bonnet lock and mounting bolts

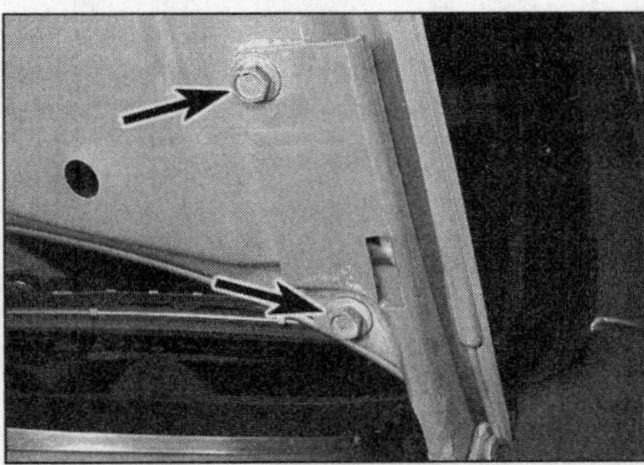

7.3 Hinge mounting bolts on the bonnet

9 Bonnet lock - removal and refitting

Removal

1 Open the bonnet. For improved access, remove the radiator grille.
2 Unscrew the three securing bolts, and remove the lock assembly from the body panel **(see illustration)**.
3 Pull the return spring to one side, then unhook the end of the bonnet release cable from the lock lever, and withdraw the assembly from the vehicle.

Refitting

4 Refitting is a reversal of removal. If necessary, adjust the position of the lock, as described in Section 7.

10 Door - removal, refitting and adjustment

Removal

Note: *A new door check strap roll-pin will be required on refitting.*
1 Remove the door inner trim panel, as described in Section 11.
2 Disconnect all relevant wiring from the components inside the door, and unclip the wiring harnesses from inside the door. Note the way the wire is routed, to aid refitting.
3 Feed the wiring through the aperture in the front edge of the door (pull out the grommet if necessary).
4 Using a suitable punch, drive out the roll-pin securing the door check strap to the body bracket.
5 Mark the positions of the hinges on the door, to aid alignment of the door on refitting.
6 Have an assistant support the door, then

10.6 Door hinge

10.11 Door lock striker on the centre pillar

unscrew the bolts securing the door hinges to the door, and lift the door from the vehicle **(see illustration)**.

7 Examine the hinges for wear and damage. If necessary, the hinges can be unbolted from the body and renewed.

Refitting

8 Refitting is a reversal of removal, but align the hinges with the marks made on the body before removal, and before finally tightening the hinge securing bolts, check the door adjustment as described in the following paragraphs. Use a new roll-pin to secure the door check strap to the body bracket. Lightly oil the hinges and check strap.

Adjustment

9 Close the door (carefully, in case the alignment is incorrect, which may cause scratching on the door or the body as the door is closed), and check the fit of the door with the surrounding panels.

10 If adjustment is required, loosen the hinge securing bolts (the hinge-to-door and the hinge-to-body bolt holes are elongated), and move the hinges as required to achieve satisfactory alignment. Tighten the securing bolts to the specified torque when the alignment is satisfactory.

11 Check the operation of the door lock. If necessary, slacken the securing bolts, and adjust the position of the lock striker on the body pillar to achieve satisfactory alignment. Tighten the bolts to the specified torque on completion **(see illustration)**.

11.3 Removing the front door interior door handle surround . . .

11 Door inner trim panel - removal and refitting

Front door trim panel

Removal

1 Disconnect the battery negative lead.

2 On models with manual windows note the fully closed position of the regulator handle, then use a thin screwdriver to depress the end of the spring clip retaining the handle. Insert the screwdriver along the length of the handle and keep the clip depressed while pulling the handle off the splines. Recover the plastic trim plate.

3 Carefully pull the interior door handle surround from the door panel **(see illustration)**.

4 Where applicable, prise out the screw covers. Remove the screws securing the lower and upper halves of the armrest **(see illustration)**.

5 On models with electric windows or central locking, disconnect the wiring from the switch(es) as the armrest is removed **(see illustration)**.

6 Using a suitable forked tool, release the trim panel securing clips, then lift the trim panel upwards to release the upper edge. If work is to be carried out on the door internal components, it will be necessary to remove the plastic sealing sheet from the inside of the door, as follows.

7 Remove the loudspeaker from the door, with reference to Chapter 12 if necessary.

8 Carefully pull the plastic sealing sheet from the door. Try to keep the sealant intact as far as possible, to ease refitting.

Refitting

9 Refitting is a reversal of removal. On models with manual windows, make sure that the regulator handle is pointing upwards 45° from the vertical with the window fully closed.

Rear door trim panel

Removal

10 Disconnect the battery negative lead.

11 Note the fully closed position of the regulator handle, then use a thin screwdriver to depress the end of the spring clip retaining the handle. Insert the screwdriver along the length of the handle and keep the clip depressed while pulling the handle off the splines. Recover the plastic trim plate **(see illustration)**.

12 Carefully pull the interior door handle surround from the door panel **(see illustration)**.

13 Where applicable, prise out the screw covers. Remove the screws and take off the armrest **(see illustration)**.

14 Using a suitable forked tool, release the trim panel securing clips, then lift the trim panel upwards to release the upper edge **(see illustration)**.

15 If work is to be carried out on the door internal components, it will be necessary to remove the plastic sealing sheet from the

11.4 . . . and armrest retaining screws

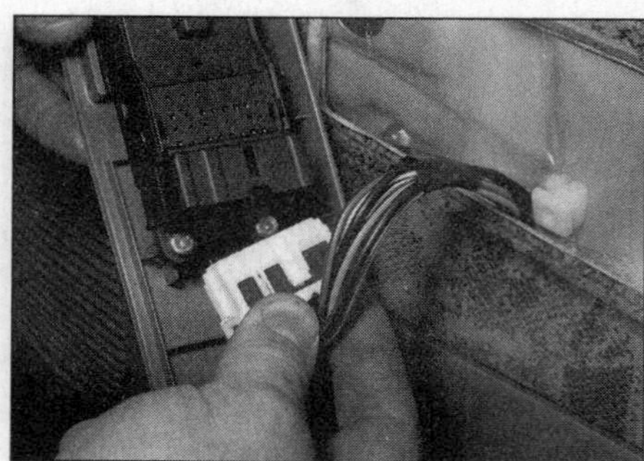
11.5 Disconnecting the wiring from the door switches

11.11 Showing the method of releasing the spring clip in order to remove the window regulator

inside of the door. Carefully pull the sheet from the door, but try to keep the mastic sealant intact as far as possible, to aid refitting **(see illustration)**.

Refitting

16 Refitting is a reversal of removal, but make sure that the regulator handle is pointing upwards 45° from the vertical with the window fully closed.

12 Door handle and lock components - removal and refitting

Interior door handle

Removal

1 Remove the door inner trim panel and the plastic sealing sheet, (Section 11).
2 Release the plastic clip securing the lock operating rods to the door panel.
3 Remove the screw securing the interior handle to the door, then slide the handle towards the front of the door to release the rear securing lug **(see illustration)**.
4 Withdraw the handle assembly from the door, then release the securing clips, and disconnect the lock operating rods, noting their routing. On the front door, it will be necessary to unbolt the intermediate bellcrank bracket before removing the rods.

Refitting

5 Refitting is a reversal of removal.

12.3 Removing the interior door handle securing screw

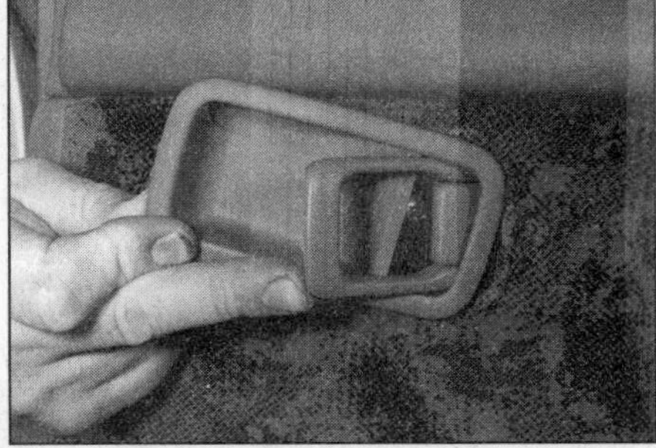

11.12 Removing the interior door handle surround

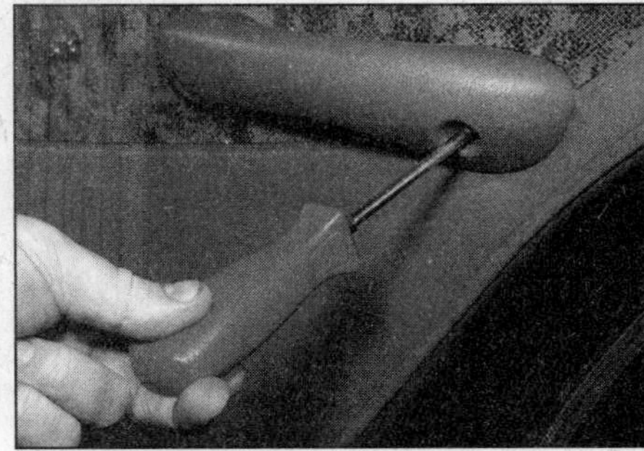

11.13 Removing the armrest

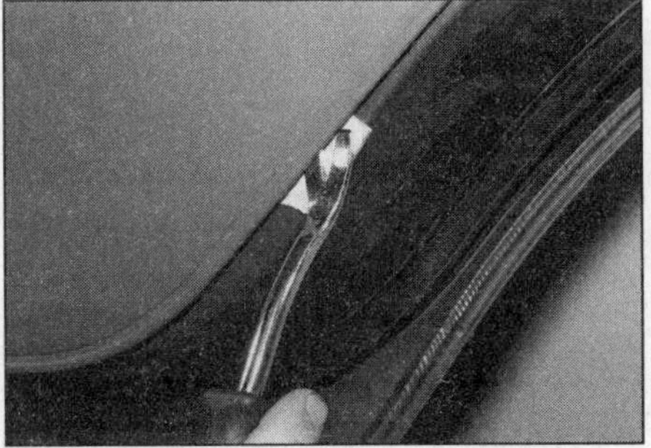

11.14 Using a forked tool to release the trim panel securing clips

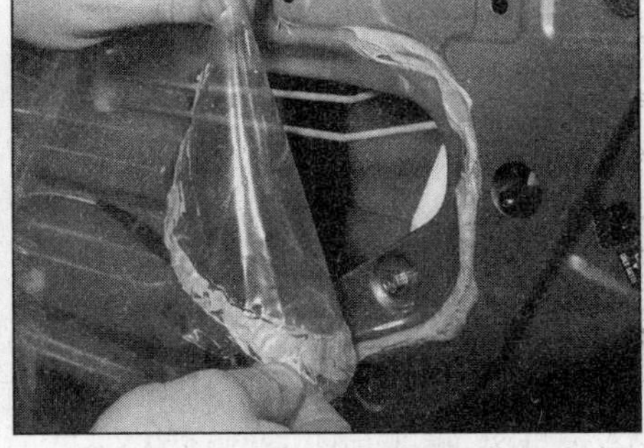

11.15 Removing the plastic sealing sheet from the inside of the door

Front door lock

Removal

6 Remove the interior door handle as described in paragraphs 1 to 4. If desired, the operating rods can remain attached to the lock.
7 Unbolt and remove the security plates **(see illustrations)**.
8 Remove the bolt securing the window rear guide channel to the rear edge of the door. Move the channel clear of the lock.
9 Reach in through the door aperture, and disconnect the operating rods from the lock, noting their locations and routing.
10 Working at the rear edge of the door, unscrew the three screws, then lift the lock out through the door **(see illustration)**. On models with central locking, disconnect the wiring plug from the lock assembly.

Refitting

11 Refitting is a reversal of removal, but check the operation of the lock before refitting the door inner trim panel.

Rear door lock

Removal

12 Remove the interior door handle as described in paragraphs 1 to 4. If desired, the operating rods can remain attached to the lock.
13 Remove the bolts securing the window glass rear guide channel to the door, then pull the guide channel clear of the lock.
14 On models with central locking, remove the screw securing the lock motor to the door panel, and disconnect the wiring plug from the motor **(see illustration)**.
15 Working at the rear edge of the door,

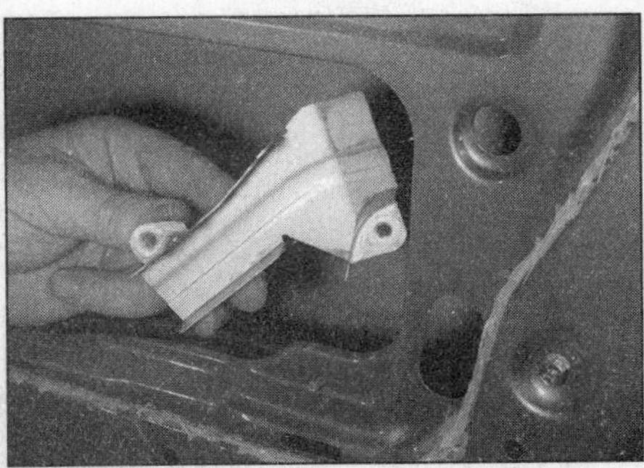

12.7a Front door lock upper security plate . . .

12.7b . . . and lower security plate

12.10 Removing the front door lock complete with operating rods and interior door handle

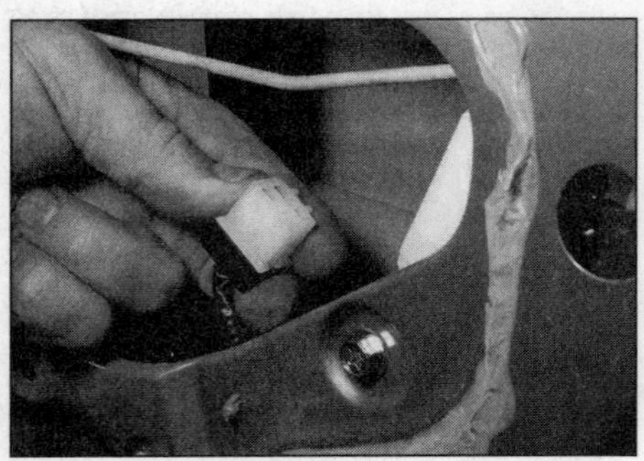
12.14 Disconnecting the wiring from the central locking motor

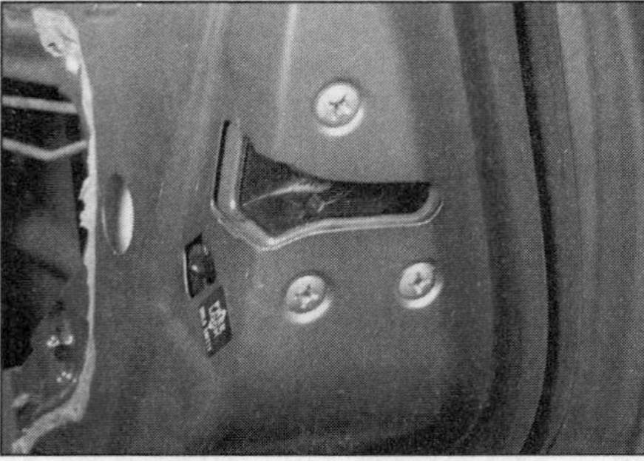
12.15a Rear door lock securing screws

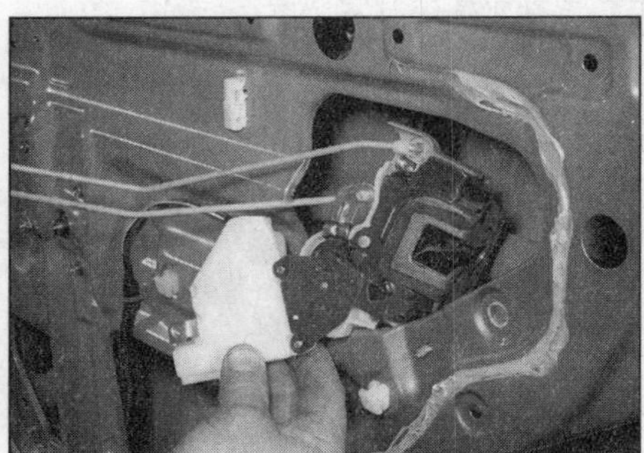
12.15b Removing the rear door lock through the aperture in the door

unscrew the three lock securing screws, then manipulate the lock assembly, complete with operating rods, out through the door aperture **(see illustrations)**.

Refitting

16 Refitting is a reversal of removal, but check the operation of the lock before refitting the door inner trim panel.

Exterior door handle

Removal

17 Remove the interior handle and the door lock assembly, as described previously in this Section.

18 Working through the door aperture, remove the two securing nuts, then withdraw the exterior handle assembly from the outside of the door **(see illustration)**.

Refitting

19 Refitting is a reversal of removal, but check the operation of the handle and lock before refitting the door inner trim panel.

Front door lock cylinder

Removal

20 Remove the interior door handle as described in paragraphs 1 to 4.

21 Disconnect the operating rod from the lock cylinder.

22 Using pliers, pull out the retaining plate, then withdraw the lock cylinder from the outside of the door **(see illustration)**.

Refitting

23 Refitting is a reversal of removal, but check the operation of the lock before refitting the door inner trim panel.

13 Door window glass and regulator - removal and refitting

Front door window glass

Removal

1 Remove the door inner trim panel and the plastic sealing sheet, (Section 11).

2 Temporarily reconnect the electric window switch, and the battery negative lead, or refit the window regulator handle, as applicable. Fully lower the window.

3 Support the glass, then remove the two nuts securing the window glass to the regulator mechanism channel **(see illustration)**.

4 Tilt and lift the glass out through the top of the door, manipulating the glass past the outer weatherstrip as it is withdrawn **(see illustration)**.

Refitting

5 Refitting is a reversal of removal, but check the operation of the window before refitting the door inner trim panel.

Front door window regulator

Removal

6 Remove the door inner trim panel and the plastic sealing sheet, (Section 11).

7 Temporarily reconnect the electric window switch, and the battery negative lead, or refit the window regulator handle, as applicable. Fully lower the window.

8 Support the glass, then remove the two bolts securing the window glass to the regulator mechanism channel. Fully raise the window and support in the raised position using strong adhesive tape. Ensure that the glass cannot drop into the door. Alternatively, lift the glass panel out through the top of the door.

9 On models with power windows, disconnect the wiring **(see illustration)**.

10 Mark the position of the regulator sub-channel mounting nuts using a marker pen **(see illustration)**.

11 Unscrew the mounting bolts and nuts, then manipulate the complete motor/regulator assembly out through the aperture in the door **(see illustration)**.

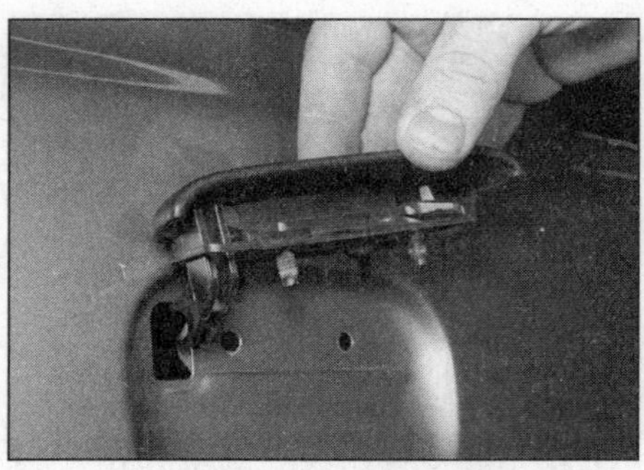
12.18 Removing the exterior door handle from the door

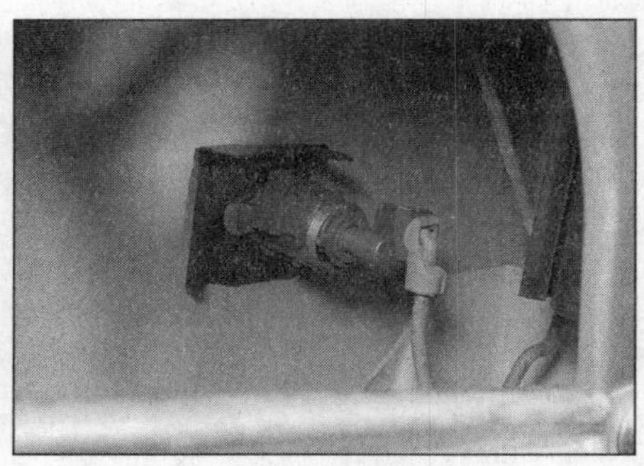
12.22 Front door lock cylinder and retaining clip viewed from inside the door

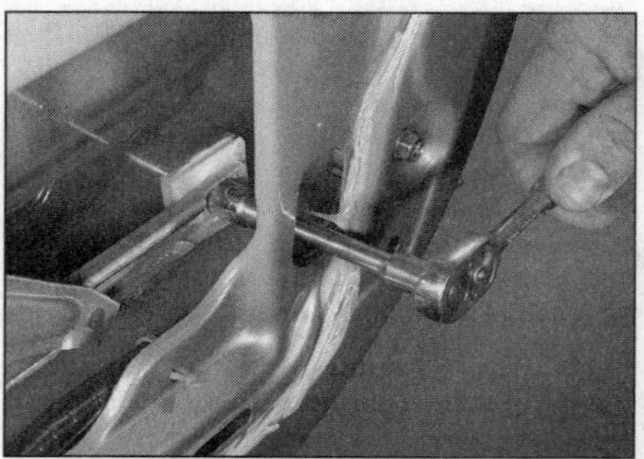
13.3 Unscrew the two nuts securing the window glass to the regulator mechanism channel

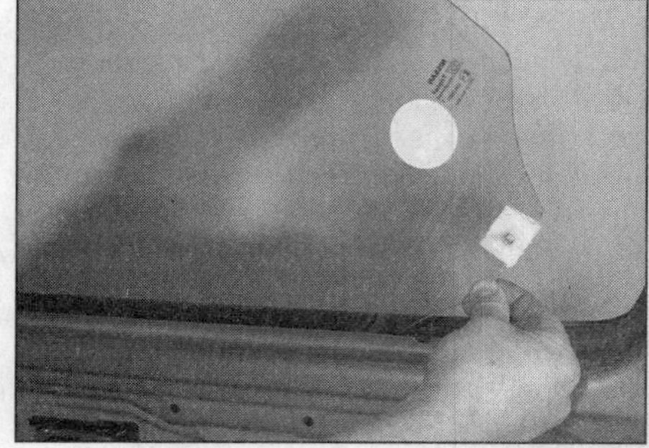
13.4 Tilt the front door window glass to remove it from the door

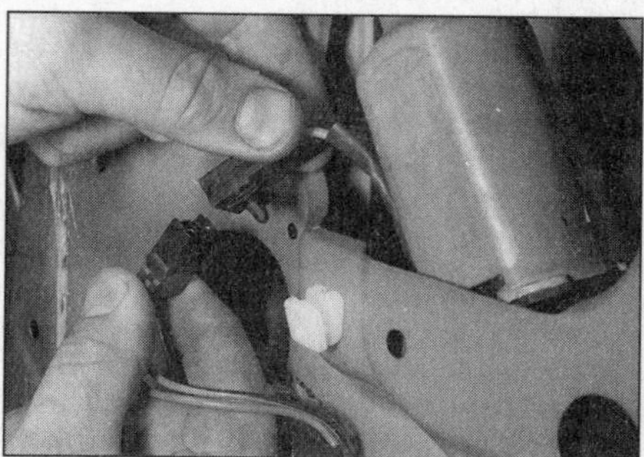

13.9 Disconnecting the wiring from the electric window motor

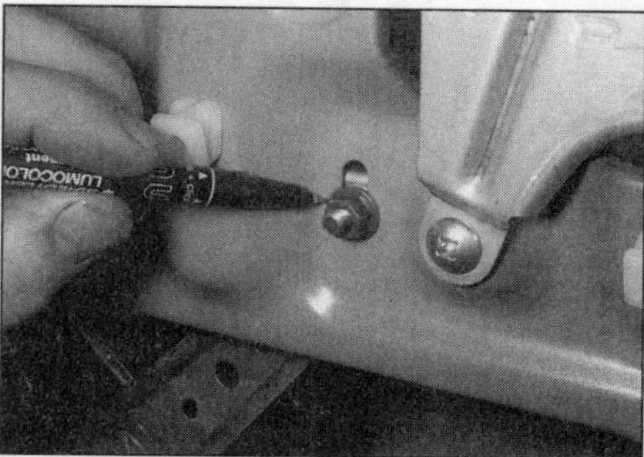

13.10 Mark the position of the regulator sub-channel nuts before removal

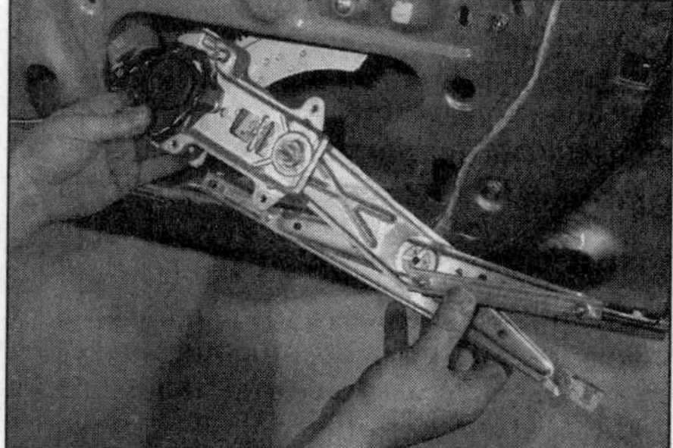

13.11 Removing the window regulator assembly from the door

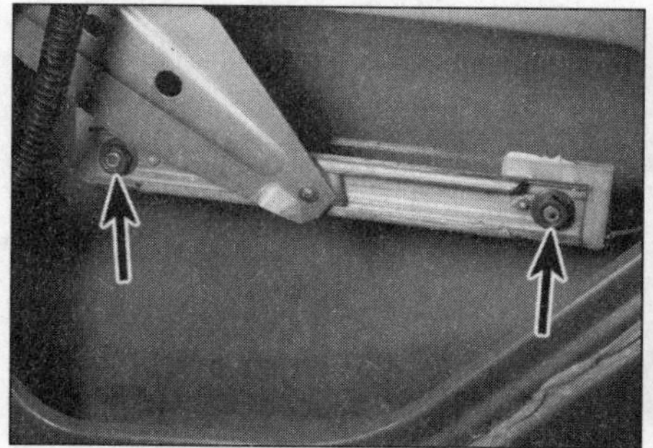

13.15 Rear door window glass-to-regulator channel securing nuts

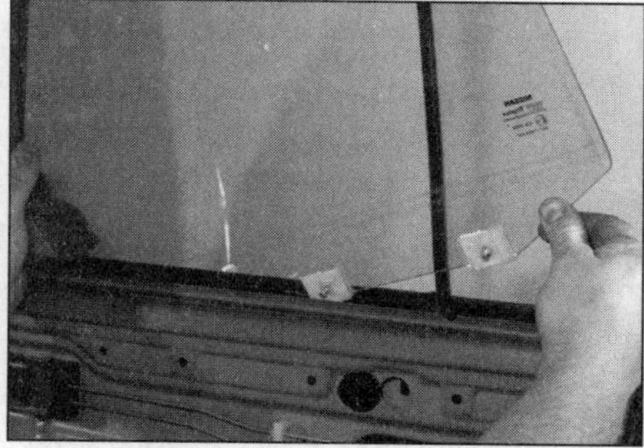

13.16 Tilt the rear door window glass to remove it

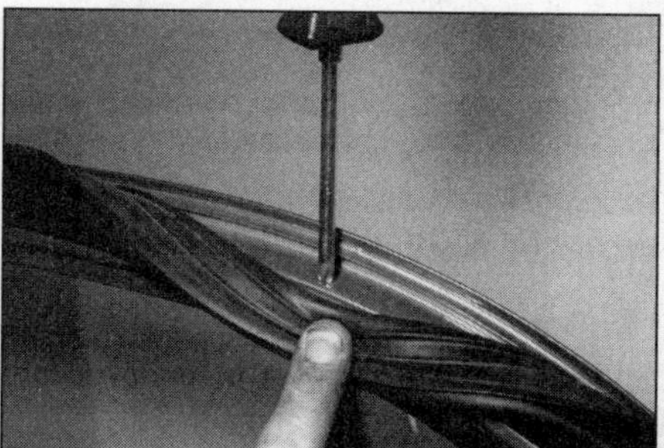

13.20 Rear door rear window channel upper mounting screw removal

Refitting

12 Refitting is a reversal of removal, but before refitting the door inner trim panel align the sub-channel mounting nuts with the previously made marks before tightening them. Check that the top edge of the window aligns correctly with the weatherstrip. If necessary, adjust the sub-channel position to correct the alignment.

Rear door sliding window glass

Removal

13 Remove the door inner trim panel and the plastic sealing sheet, (Section 11).

14 Temporarily refit the window regulator handle and fully lower the window.

15 Support the glass, then remove the two nuts securing the window glass to the regulator mechanism channel **(see illustration).**

16 Tilt and lift the glass out through the top of the door, manipulating the glass past the outer weatherstrip as it is withdrawn **(see illustration).**

Refitting

17 Refitting is a reversal of removal, but check the operation of the window before refitting the door inner trim panel.

Rear door fixed window glass

Removal

18 Remove the rear door sliding window glass, as described in paragraphs 13 to 16.

19 Carefully pull away the sliding window weatherstrip from the top of the door and from the fixed window glass.

20 Unscrew the upper screw and lower bolts and remove the sliding window rear guide channel. Pull the door weatherstrip to one side for access to the upper screw **(see illustration).**

21 Pull the fixed window glass forwards from the door.

Refitting

22 Refitting is a reversal of removal, but check the operation of the sliding window before refitting the door inner trim panel.

Rear door window regulator

Removal

23 Remove the door inner trim panel and the plastic sealing sheet, (Section 11).

24 Temporarily refit the window regulator handle and fully lower the window.

25 Support the glass, then remove the two nuts securing the window glass to the regulator mechanism channel. Fully raise the window and support in the raised position using strong adhesive tape. Ensure that the glass cannot drop into the door. Alternatively, lift the glass panel out through the top of the door.

26 Unscrew the mounting bolts, however it is not necessary to completely remove the upper bolt near the panel cut-out. Lift the regulator assembly to disengage the remaining upper bolt, then manipulate the assembly out through the aperture in the door **(see illustrations).**

Refitting

27 Refitting is a reversal of removal, but before refitting the door inner trim panel check that the upper edge of the window aligns correctly with the weatherstrip. If necessary, loosen the mounting bolts and re-position the regulator to correct the alignment.

13.26a It is not necessary to completely remove this bolt as it can be removed through the cut-out hole

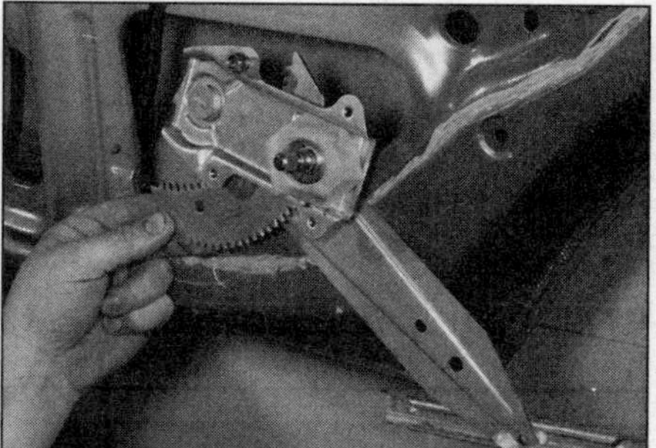

13.26b Removing the rear door window regulator

14.9 Tailgate hinge

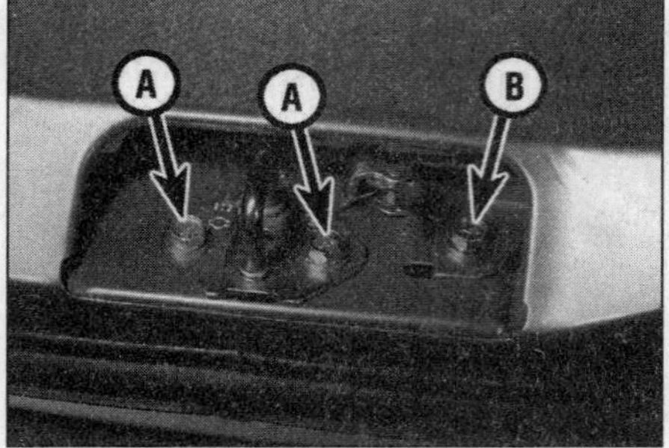

14.12 Mounting bolts for the tailgate striker (A) and tailgate lock release cable bracket (B)

14.15 Prise the spring clip from the support strut balljoint end

14 Tailgate and support struts - removal, refitting and adjustment

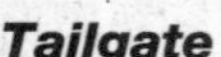

Tailgate

Removal

1 Disconnect the battery negative lead.

2 Open the tailgate then undo the screws securing the metal insert panel. Where applicable, remove the single screw and take out the plastic grip from the insert panel. Withdraw the panel.

3 Working inside the tailgate, disconnect the wiring plugs from the luggage compartment light switch (integral with the tailgate lock), the tailgate wiper motor, the heated rear window element, and the rear number plate lights. Also unbolt the earth lead(s). Check for any other wiring connectors which must be disconnected to facilitate tailgate removal.

4 Tie a length of string to the wiring harness, then prise the grommet from the front corner of the tailgate and feed the wiring through the aperture. Untie the string leaving the string in place in the tailgate to aid refitting.

5 Where fitted, remove the tailgate washer nozzle as described in Chapter 12, then tie a length of string to the fluid hose, and repeat the procedure carried out on the wiring harness.

6 Using a pencil or marker pen, mark the outline of each hinge relative to the tailgate, to use as a guide on refitting.

7 Have an assistant support the tailgate in the open position.

8 Either separate the upper ends of the struts from the balljoint as described later in this Section, or alternatively unbolt the upper brackets from the tailgate.

9 Unscrew the bolts securing the hinges to the tailgate **(see illustration)**, then lift the tailgate from the vehicle.

Refitting

10 Refitting is a reversal of removal, but do not fully tighten the hinge bolts until the tailgate adjustment has been checked, as described in the following paragraphs.

Adjustment

11 Close the tailgate (carefully, in case the alignment is incorrect, which may cause scratching on the tailgate or the body as the tailgate is closed), and check for alignment with the adjacent panels. If necessary, slacken the hinge bolts and re-align the tailgate to suit. Once the tailgate is correctly aligned, tighten the hinge bolts to the specified torque.

12 Once the tailgate is correctly aligned, check that the tailgate fastens and releases in a satisfactory manner. If adjustment is necessary, slacken the tailgate striker retaining bolts and adjust the position to suit **(see illustration)**. Tighten the bolts on completion.

Support strut

Removal

13 Open the tailgate and support it using suitable wooden props.

14 Note which way round the strut is fitted - the piston rod end is located on the rear body pillar.

15 Use a screwdriver to prise the spring clips from the balljoint ends, then withdraw the strut from the mounting brackets **(see illustration)**. Alternatively, unbolt the mounting brackets from the body and tailgate.

Refitting

16 Refitting is a reversal of removal.

15 Tailgate lock components - removal and refitting

Tailgate lock

Removal

1 Open the tailgate then undo the screws securing the metal insert panel. Where applicable, remove the single screw and take out the plastic grip from the insert panel. Withdraw the panel **(see illustration)**.

2 Unscrew the two lock securing bolts **(see illustration)**.

3 Disconnect the lock operating rod from the lock cylinder. Also disconnect the rear luggage area light switch wiring.

4 Manipulate the lock through the aperture in the tailgate.

Refitting

5 Refitting is a reversal of removal.

Tailgate lock cylinder

Removal

6 Open the tailgate then undo the screws securing the metal insert panel. Where applicable, remove the single screw and take out the plastic grip from the insert panel. Withdraw the panel.

7 Pull up the plastic clip and disconnect the operating rod from the lock cylinder.

8 With a pair of pliers, pull out the retaining plate then withdraw the lock cylinder from the outside of the tailgate **(see illustrations)**.

Refitting

9 Refitting is a reversal of removal, but check the operation of the lock cylinder before refitting the insert panel.

15.1 Removing the tailgate insert panel screws

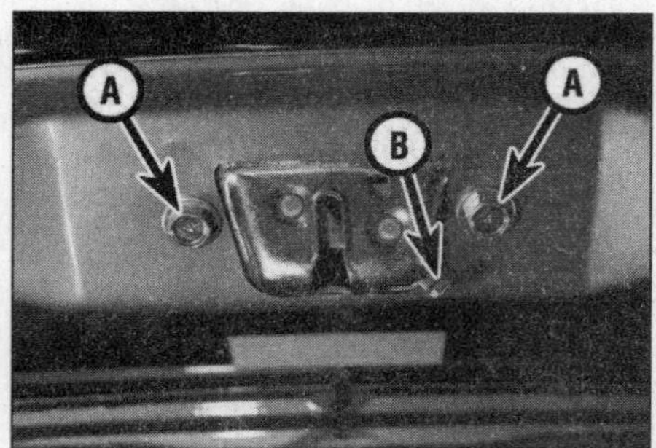

15.2 Tailgate lock securing bolts (A) and lever for lock release with the cable (B)

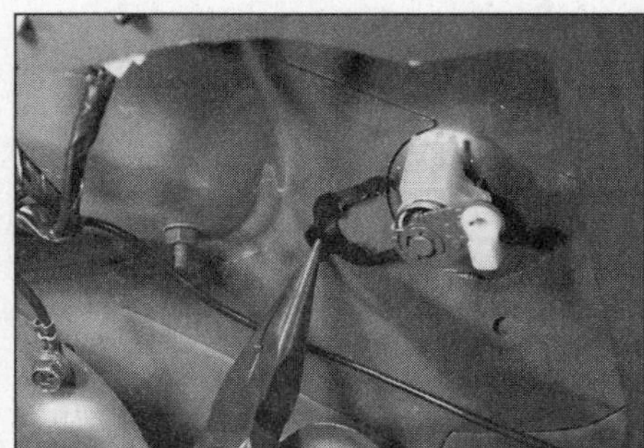
15.8a Pull out the retaining plate . . .

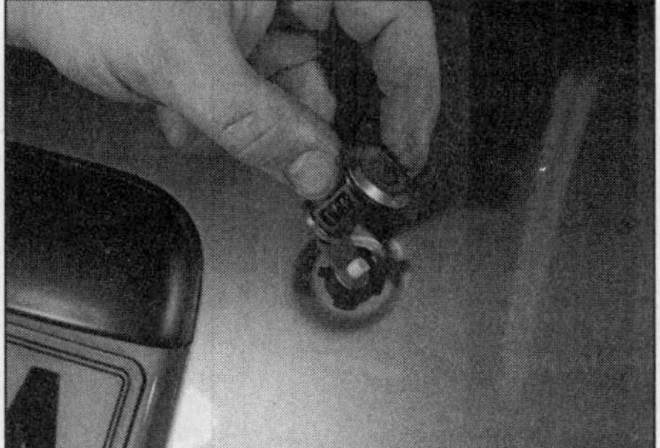
15.8b . . . and withdraw the lock cylinder from the tailgate

Tailgate lock striker

Removal

10 In the rear luggage area remove the vehicle jack, then remove the carpet from the rear valance.

11 Unscrew the two securing bolts, then withdraw the lock striker assembly and disconnect the tailgate release cable from the lever.

Refitting

12 Refitting is a reversal of removal, but check the operation of the tailgate release mechanism before refitting the carpet and vehicle jack.

16 Tailgate and fuel filler flap release cables - removal and refitting

Note: *Not all models are fitted with a fuel filler flap release cable.*

Removal

1 For removal of the tailgate release cable, disconnect the rear end of the cable from the tailgate lock striker, (Section 15).

2 For removal of the fuel filler flap release cable, remove the rear seat cushion as described in Section 21.

3 Remove the rear luggage area interior trim panels as necessary with reference to Section 23.

4 Working on the driver's side of the vehicle for access to the tailgate/fuel filler flap release lever, remove the sill trim panel from the sill, then pull back the carpet panel to expose the lever securing bolts.

5 Unscrew the two securing bolts, then manipulate the lever assembly out through the aperture in the carpet, and disconnect the cable from the lever.

6 Release the rear end of the cable, then unclip and withdraw it. Note the cable routing to aid refitting.

Refitting

7 Refitting is a reversal of removal, but ensure that the cable is routed as noted before removal, and check the operation of the release mechanism before refitting the carpet and trim panels.

17 Exterior mirror and glass - removal and refitting

Mirror assembly

Removal

1 Remove the door inner trim panel, as described in Section 11.

2 Carefully prise the triangular trim from the front corner of the door to reveal the mirror mounting screws.

3 Reach through the aperture in the door, and disconnect the mirror wiring connector. Unclip the mirror wiring from the door, noting its routing.

4 Unscrew the mounting bolts, and withdraw the mirror from the outside of the door **(see illustration).**

Refitting

5 Refitting is a reversal of removal.

Mirror glass

Removal

6 Insert a thin screwdriver between the mirror glass and the mirror body, and lever out the glass to release it from the securing clips. To prevent damage to the mirror body, locate the screwdriver on a cloth pad. If the clips are very tight it may be easier to remove the mirror first then remove the glass on the bench **(see illustrations).**

7 Where applicable, disconnect the heating wiring from the rear of the glass.

Refitting

To aid refitting, lightly grease the securing clips on the rear of the mirror glass.

8 Where applicable, reconnect the wires to the rear of the mirror glass, then push the glass into position to engage the securing clips.

18 Windscreen, tailgate and side opening windows - removal and refitting

Windscreen

1 The windscreen and tailgate window are bonded in position with special adhesive. In addition, the tailgate window is retained in a rubber moulding. Renewal of these windows is a difficult, messy and time-consuming task, which is beyond the scope of the home mechanic. It is difficult, unless one has plenty of practice, to obtain a secure, waterproof fit. Furthermore, the task carries a high risk of breakage. In view of this, owners are strongly advised to have this work carried out by one of the many specialist windscreen fitters.

Rear side opening window

Removal

2 The rear side opening window fitted to

17.4 Exterior mirror mounting bolts

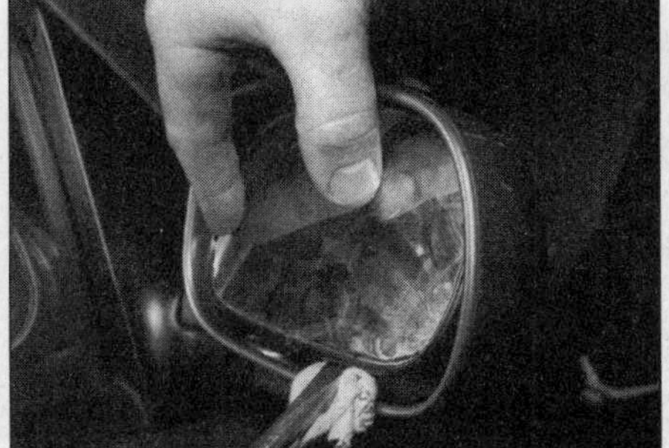
17.6a Prising out the glass from the exterior mirror

17.6b Showing the rear of the mirror glass and the mounting clips

three-door models, can be removed as follows. Have an assistant support the window from the outside, then working inside the vehicle unscrew the mounting screws from the front of the window. Recover the outer cap and inner spacer.

3 Unscrew the single rear mounting screw and recover the outer cap. The window can now be withdrawn from the vehicle.

4 If necessary, remove the screws securing the latch to the body.

Refitting

5 Refitting is a reversal of removal.

19 Sunroof components - removal and refitting

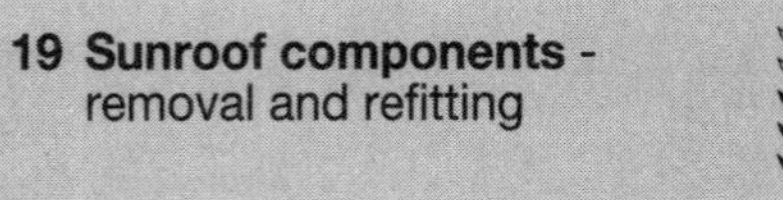

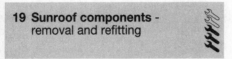

Sunroof rail and cables

1 Removal of the sunroof rail assembly and cables should be referred to a Nissan dealer, who will have the necessary tooling and expertise to carry out the work and make the adjustments.

Sunroof lid

Removal

2 Slide the shade fully to the rear, then make sure that the lid is fully closed.

3 Remove the side trim clips, then unscrew the nuts securing the lid to the cable end fittings.

4 Withdraw the sunroof lid from the outside.

19.10 Prise out the button . . .

Refitting

5 Refitting is a reversal of removal.

Shade assembly

Removal

6 Remove the sunroof lid as described in paragraphs 2 to 4.

7 Undo the screws retaining the rear drains to the roof, then remove the rear drain rail.

8 Withdraw the shade assembly upwards from the outside.

Refitting

9 Refitting is a reversal of removal.

Regulator handle

Removal

10 With the lid fully closed, use a small screwdriver to prise the button from the handle **(see illustration)**.

11 Unscrew the retaining screw and remove the handle from the splines on the regulator **(see illustrations)**.

12 If desired, remove the screws and withdraw the surround from the roof **(see illustration)**.

Refitting

13 Refitting is a reversal of removal.

20 Body exterior fittings - removal and refitting

Radiator grille

Models up to March 1998

1 Open the bonnet, then release the two mounting clips each side by twisting them through 45°, and pressing them out from behind **(see illustration)**.

2 Release the central clip by pressing it down with a screwdriver, then withdraw the grille from the vehicle **(see illustration)**.

3 Refitting is a reversal of removal.

March 1998 and later models

4 The chrome grille sections can be removed from the bonnet if required by removing the plastic nuts behind each section. Refitting is a reversal of removal.

Wheel arch liners

5 The wheel arch liners are secured by a combination of self-tapping screws and plastic clips, and the removal/refitting procedure is self-evident.

Body trim strips and badges

6 The various body trim strips and badges are held in position with a special adhesive tape. Removal requires the trim/badge to be heated, to soften the adhesive, and then cut away from the surface. Due to the high risk of damage to the vehicle paintwork during this operation, it is recommended that this task should be entrusted to a Nissan dealer.

19.11a . . . remove the screw . . .

19.11b . . . and withdraw the handle from the splines

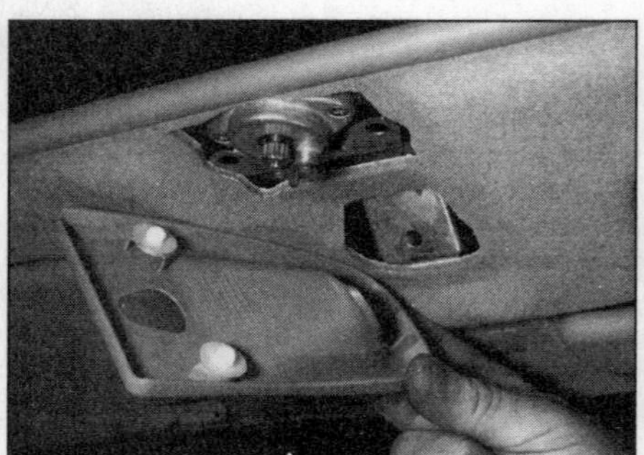

19.12 Removing the surround from the roof

20.1 Turn the mounting clips through 45° to release them

20.2 Removing the radiator grille

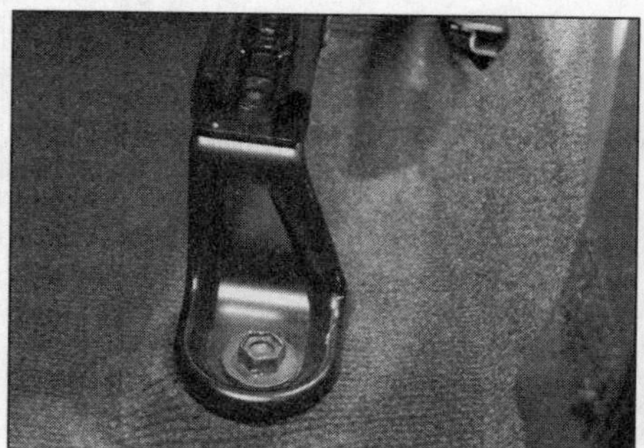

21.3 Front seat outer rail mounting bolt

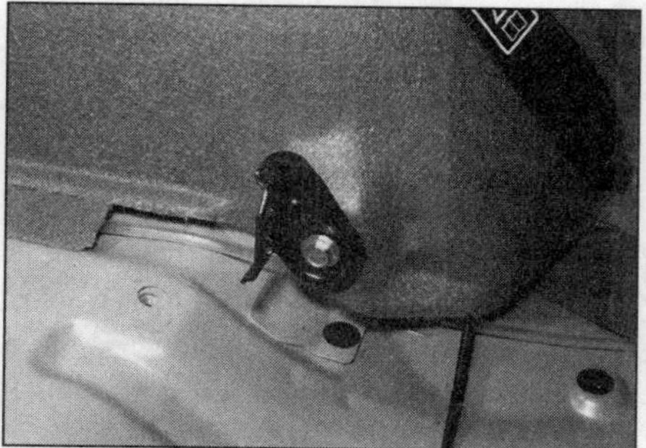

21.8 Rear seat back mounting bracket (with seat back removed)

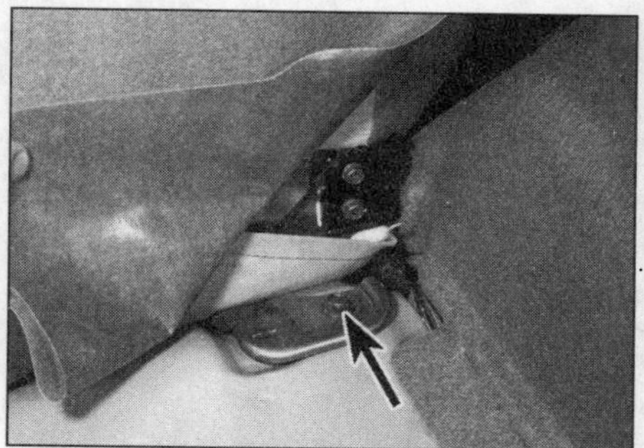

21.12 Rear seat (bench type) cushion mounting bolt

21 Seats - removal and refitting

Front seat

Removal

Warning: On models fitted with side air bags, disconnect the battery negative lead, and wait 10 minutes before proceeding. Failure to observe this precaution may result in the accidental firing of the side air bag unit.

1 Move the seat fully forwards.

2 Unclip the trim cover from the rear of the seat inner rail, and unscrew the mounting bolt.

3 Unscrew the mounting bolt from the rear of the seat outer rail **(see illustration)**.

4 Slide the seat fully rearwards, then remove the caps and unscrew the seat rail front mounting bolts.

5 On models with heated seats or side air bags, disconnect the wiring plugs from the seat.

6 Lift the seat, complete with the rails, from the vehicle.

Refitting

7 Refitting is a reversal of removal, but tighten the mounting bolts to the specified torque.

Rear seat back

Removal

8 Fold the relevant rear seat forwards (split type or bench type), then unbolt the seat from the mounting brackets **(see illustration)**. If necessary the brackets can be unbolted from the floor.

9 Withdraw the seat back from the vehicle.

Refitting

10 Refitting is a reversal of removal, but tighten the mounting bolts to the specified torque.

Rear seat cushion

Removal

11 On the split type rear seat, prise the covers from the mounting bolts located below the front edge of the seat cushion. Unscrew the mounting bolts and withdraw the seat cushion from the vehicle.

12 On the bench type rear seat first remove the rear seat back, then release the front edge of the seat and unbolt the rear mounting bolts **(see illustration)**. Withdraw the seat cushion from the vehicle.

Refitting

13 Refitting is a reversal of removal, but tighten the mounting bolts to the specified torque.

22 Seat belt components - removal and refitting

Front seat belt

Warning: On models equipped with front seat belt pre-tensioners, the mechanism is designed to instantaneously take up any slack in the seat belt, in the event of a sudden frontal impact, therefore reducing the possibility of injury to the front seat occupants. Do not attempt to remove the seat belt inertia reel on models equipped with pre-tensioners - consult a Nissan dealer for advice (see Chapter 12, Section 23). The following procedure is for models without pre-tensioners.

Removal

1 Remove the lower trim from the centre pillar with reference to Section 23.

2 Prise off the trim cap, and unscrew the seat belt lower anchor bolt.

3 Prise off the cover and unscrew the seat belt upper anchor bolt from the centre pillar **(see illustration)**.

4 Unbolt the inertia reel from the centre pillar, and remove the seat belt. Note the location of the spacer.

5 If necessary, prise the weatherstrips from the edge of the centre pillar upper trim panel, then pull the panel from the pillar to release the securing clips. Unbolt the height adjuster from the centre pillar **(see illustration)**.

Refitting

6 Refitting is a reversal of removal, but tighten the anchor bolts to the specified torque.

Front seat belt stalk

Removal

7 The front seat belt stalk is located in the inner edge of the seat. Move the seat fully rearwards.

8 Unscrew the bolt and withdraw the stalk assembly.

Refitting

9 Refitting is a reversal of removal, but tighten the stalk anchor bolt to the specified torque.

Rear seat belt

Removal

10 Remove the rear seat cushion as described in Section 21, and unbolt the seat belt lower anchor.

11 Unbolt and remove the rear parcel shelf side support **(see illustration)**.

12 Unbolt and remove the rear seat belt inertia reel **(see illustration)**.

13 Prise off the trim cap, then unscrew the upper anchor bolt and withdraw the seat belt assembly **(see illustration)**.

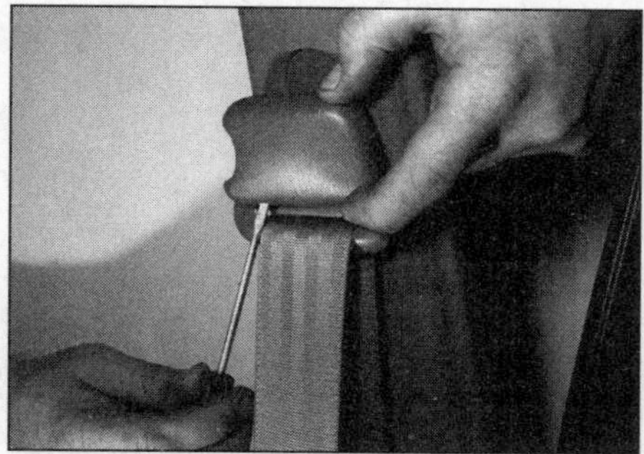

22.3 Prise off the seat belt upper anchor bolt cover

22.5 Seat belt height adjuster and mounting bolt

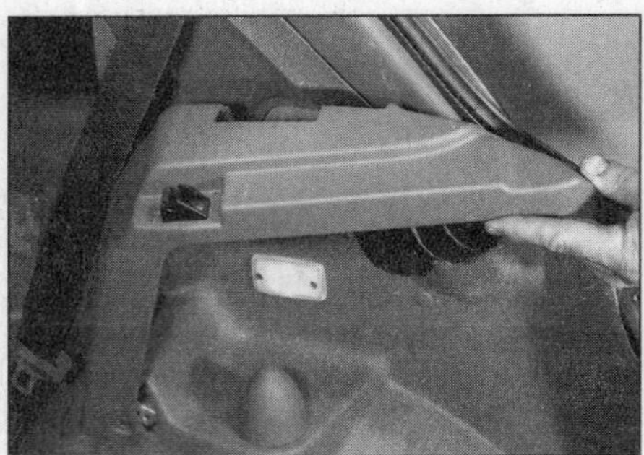

22.11 Removing the rear parcel shelf side support

Refitting

14 Refitting is a reversal of removal, but tighten the seat belt anchor bolts to the specified torque.

Rear centre seat belt and buckle

Removal

15 Remove the rear seat cushion as described in Section 21.

16 Unscrew the anchor bolt and withdraw the seat belt and buckle **(see illustration)**.

Refitting

17 Refitting is a reversal of removal, but tighten the anchor bolt to the specified torque.

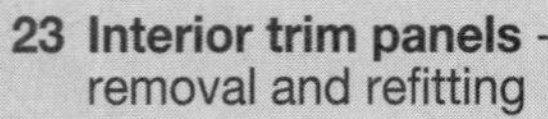

23 Interior trim panels - removal and refitting

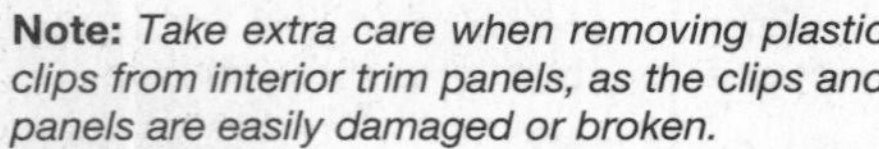

Note: *Take extra care when removing plastic clips from interior trim panels, as the clips and panels are easily damaged or broken.*

General

1 The interior trim panels are secured by a combination of metal and plastic clips and screws. When releasing certain types of securing clips, a suitable forked tool will prove invaluable to avoid damage to the panel and clips. Note that to remove the plastic clips with a centre pin, the pin must be pushed right through the clip, then on refitting the clip is secured by inserting the centre pin flush with the outer surface. In some cases, it may be necessary to remove surrounding panels before a particular panel can be released.

Rear luggage area side panel

2 Prise out the panel clips with a screwdriver, then withdraw the panel.

3 Refitting is a reversal of removal.

Rear luggage area rear panel

4 Remove the screws from the clips and withdraw the panel from the rear valance.

5 Refitting is a reversal of removal.

Rear parcel shelf side support

6 Unscrew the retaining screws, then withdraw the support.

7 Refitting is a reversal of removal.

22.12 Rear seat belt inertia reel and mounting bolt

Rear seat belt pillar trim

8 Unscrew the single retaining screw, then prise the clips free using a wide-blade screwdriver or suitable forked tool.

9 Refitting is a reversal of removal.

Rear seat side panel (3-door models)

10 Remove the screw from the tray, then prise out the top of the tray and lift up from the panel.

11 Prise the panel away from the body by inserting a suitable tool beneath the retaining clips.

12 The upper edge of the panel is secured with metal clips. Pull the panel down to release the clips.

13 Refitting is a reversal of removal.

Centre pillar upper trim

14 Pull off the side beading then insert a suitable tool, and prise the trim away from the centre pillar.

15 Refitting is a reversal of removal.

Centre pillar lower trim

16 Remove the retaining screw, then pull off the side beading and withdraw the trim.

17 Refitting is a reversal of removal.

Front pillar trim

18 Prise out the top and middle of the trim to release it from the metal clips, then lift it from the facia panel.

19 Refitting is a reversal of removal.

Front footwell side panel

20 Remove the screw and nut and withdraw the panel **(see illustrations)**.

21 Refitting is a reversal of removal.

23.20a Remove the screw . . .

22.13 Rear seat belt upper anchor bolt

22.16 Rear centre seat belts and buckles

Door inner trim panels

22 Refer to Section 11.

Tailgate inner metal insert panel

23 Remove the screw and withdraw the plastic grip from the inside of the tailgate.

24 Unscrew the retaining screws and withdraw the panel from the tailgate.

25 Refitting is a reversal of removal.

24 Centre and rear consoles - removal and refitting

Centre console (gear lever surround)

Removal

1 On manual transmission models, prise the

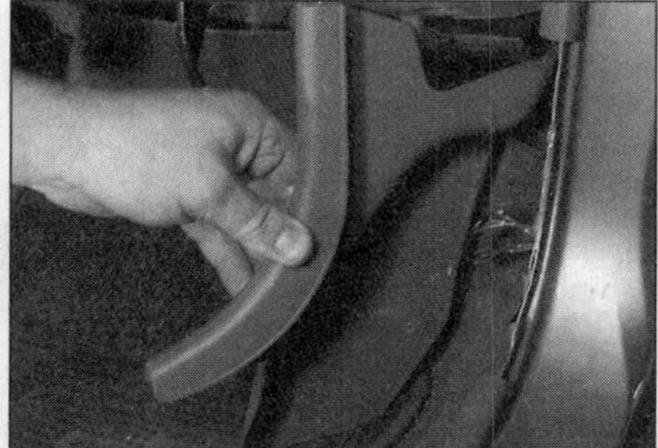

23.20b . . . and withdraw the front footwell side panel

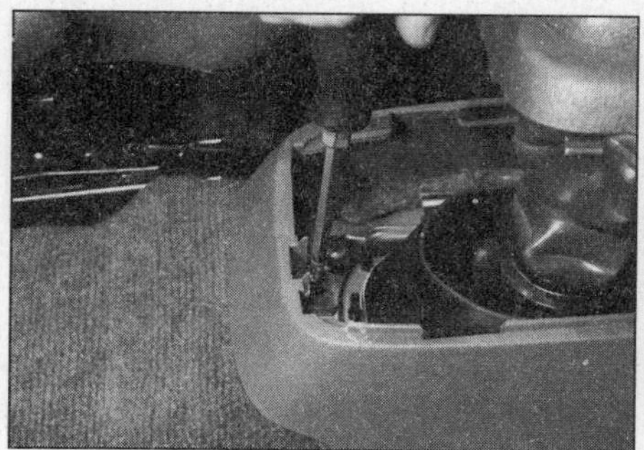
24.3a Unscrew the rear mounting screw . . .

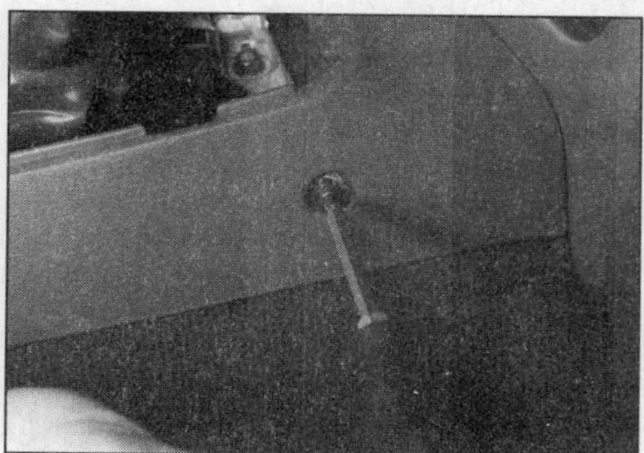
24.3b . . . and side mounting screws . . .

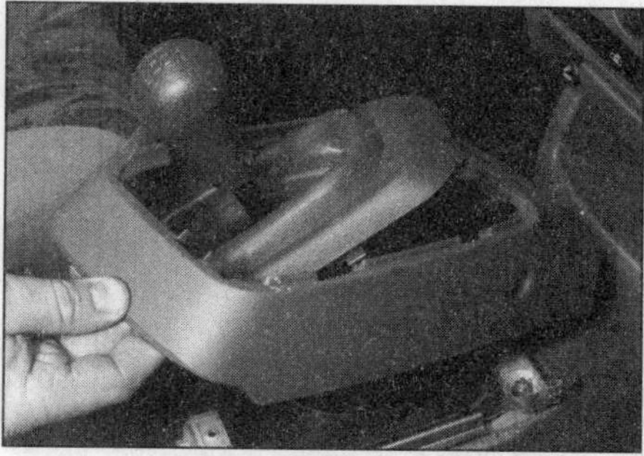
24.4 . . . then lift the centre console over the gear lever

gear lever gaiter surround from the centre console.

2 On automatic transmission models remove the top of the selector lever, then lift the rear of the lever surround and withdraw rearwards.

3 Unscrew the mounting screws both inside the rear of the centre console and on the front outside **(see illustrations)**.

4 Lift the centre console over the gear lever and withdraw. Where applicable, disconnect the wiring from the heated seat switches **(see illustration)**.

Refitting

5 Refitting is a reversal of removal.

Rear console (handbrake lever surround)

Removal

6 Remove the side screws and lift the plastic cover from the top of the handbrake lever.

7 Use a screwdriver to prise the cover from the rear of the console.

8 Unscrew the mounting screws and lift the console over the handbrake lever.

Refitting

9 Refitting is a reversal of removal.

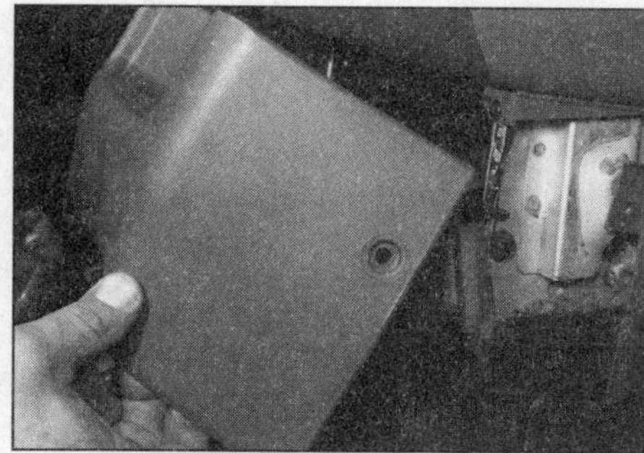
25.4 Removing the facia base unit

25 Facia panel and glovebox - removal and refitting

Warning: Most models from August 1995-on are equipped with an air bag system. Make sure that the safety recommendations given in Chapter 12 are followed, to prevent personal injury. Refer to Chapter 10 when removing the steering wheel and air bag module.

Facia panel

Removal

1 Remove the steering wheel as described in Chapter 10.

2 Remove the steering column shrouds and combination switches as described in Chapter 12.

3 Remove the centre console as described in Section 24 of this Chapter.

4 Remove the side screws and withdraw the facia base unit from under the facia **(see illustration)**.

5 Remove the screws and withdraw the centre trim panels from each side of the heater unit **(see illustration)**.

6 Remove the heater control panel as described in Chapter 3.

7 Remove the radio as described in Chapter 12.

8 Remove the instrument panel as described in Chapter 12.

9 Remove the screws and withdraw the small shelf from under the steering column. Disconnect the wiring from the audio warning unit where fitted.

10 Using a small screwdriver, prise out the plastic covers from the upper front edge of the facia below the windscreen. Undo the facia upper mounting screws **(see illustrations)**.

11 Remove the footwell outer side panels and front pillar trims as described in Section 23.

12 Undo the remaining mounting screws located on the outer edges, the lower centre section and inside the instrument panel aperture **(see illustration)**.

13 Carefully withdraw the facia panel from the bulkhead while disconnecting the heater air ducts, and withdraw it from inside the vehicle. Depending on the model, disconnect the wiring from components mounted on the rear of the facia.

Refitting

14 Refitting is a reversal of removal, but make sure that all electrical wiring is correctly reconnected to the relevant components and tighten the facia mounting screws securely.

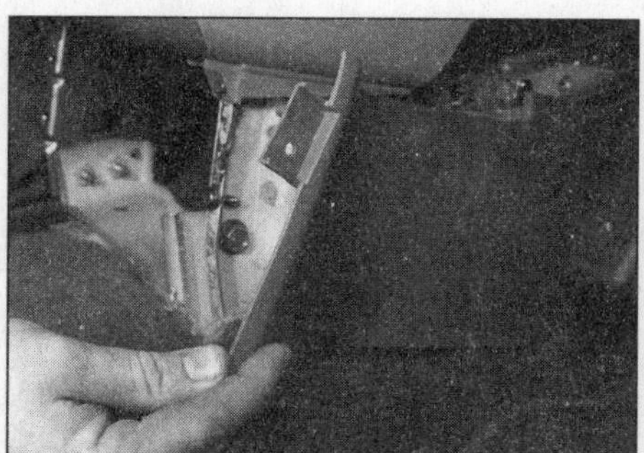
25.5 Removing the centre trim panels

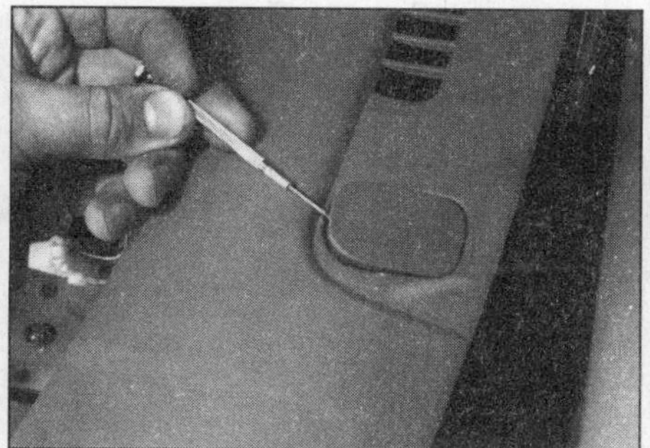
25.10a Prise out the plastic cover . . .

25.10b . . . and unscrew the facia upper mounting screws

25.12 Removing the facia mounting screws

Glovebox

Removal

15 Working under the glovebox extract the two glovebox pivot pins **(see illustration)**.

16 Open the glovebox, then slide it out and withdraw from the facia.

Refitting

17 Refitting is a reversal of removal.

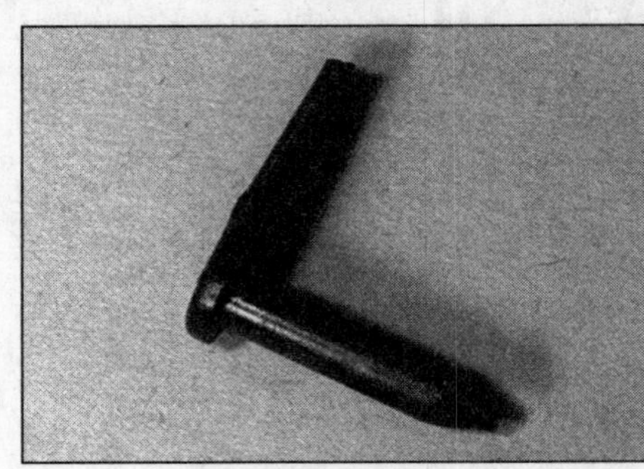

25.15 Glovebox pivot pin - two retain the glovebox in the facia

Chapter 12
Body electrical systems

Contents

Degrees of difficulty

Easy, suitable for novice with little experience 

Fairly easy, suitable for beginner with some experience 

Fairly difficult, suitable for competent DIY mechanic 

Difficult, suitable for experienced DIY mechanic 

Very difficult, suitable for expert DIY or professional

Specifications

Bulb ratings

	Watts
Boot light	5
Front direction indicator light (yellow bulb)	21
Front direction indicator repeater light	5
Front driving light	55
Front foglight	55
Front sidelight	5
Headlights	60/55
High-level stop-light	21
Interior/courtesy light	10
Rear direction indicator light	21
Rear foglight	21
Rear number plate light	5
Reversing light	21
Stop/tail light	21/5

Torque wrench settings

	Nm	lbf ft
Windscreen wiper motor mounting bolts	5	4
Windscreen wiper linkage spindle unit nuts	5	4

1 General information and precautions

Warning: Before carrying out any work on the electrical system, read through the precautions given in "Safety first!" at the beginning of this manual, and in Chapter 5. Most models from August 1995-on are equipped with an air bag system. When working on the electrical system, refer to the precautions given in Section 23, to avoid the possibility of personal injury.

The electrical system is of 12-volt negative earth type. Power for the lights and all electrical accessories is supplied by a lead/acid type battery, which is charged by the alternator.

This Chapter covers repair and service procedures for the various electrical components not associated with the engine. Information on the battery, alternator and starter motor can be found in Chapter 5.

It should be noted that, prior to working on any component in the electrical system, the battery negative terminal should first be disconnected, to prevent the possibility of electrical short-circuits and/or fires.

Caution: If the radio/cassette player fitted to the vehicle is one with an anti-theft security code, as the standard unit is, refer to the information given in the Reference Section at the rear of this manual before disconnecting the battery.

2 Electrical fault-finding - general information

Note: *Refer to the precautions given in "Safety first!" and in Section 1 of this Chapter before starting work. The following tests relate to testing of the main electrical circuits, and should not be used to test delicate electronic circuits (such as anti-lock braking systems), particularly where an electronic control module is used.*

General

1 A typical electrical circuit consists of an electrical component, any switches, relays, motors, fuses, fusible links or circuit breakers related to that component, and the wiring and connectors which link the component to both the battery and the chassis. To help pinpoint a problem in an electrical circuit, wiring diagrams are included at the end of this manual.

2 Before attempting to diagnose an electrical fault, first study the appropriate wiring diagram, to obtain a more complete understanding of the components included in the particular circuit concerned. The possible sources of a fault can be narrowed down by noting whether other components related to the circuit are operating properly. If several components or circuits fail at one time, the problem is likely to be related to a shared fuse or earth connection.

3 Electrical problems usually stem from simple causes, such as loose or corroded connections, a faulty earth connection, a blown fuse, a melted fusible link, or a faulty relay (refer to Section 3 for details of testing relays). Visually inspect the condition of all fuses, wires and connections in a problem circuit before testing the components. Use the wiring diagrams to determine which terminal connections will need to be checked, in order to pinpoint the trouble-spot.

4 The basic tools required for electrical fault-finding include a circuit tester or voltmeter (a 12-volt bulb with a set of test leads can also be used for certain tests); a self-powered test light (sometimes known as a continuity tester); an ohmmeter (to measure resistance); a battery and set of test leads; and a jumper wire, preferably with a circuit breaker or fuse incorporated, which can be used to bypass suspect wires or electrical components. Before attempting to locate a problem with test instruments, use the wiring diagram to determine where to make the connections.

5 To find the source of an intermittent wiring fault (usually due to a poor or dirty connection, or damaged wiring insulation), a "wiggle" test can be performed on the wiring. This involves wiggling the wiring by hand, to see if the fault occurs as the wiring is moved. It should be possible to narrow down the source of the fault to a particular section of wiring. This method of testing can be used in conjunction with any of the tests described in the following sub-Sections.

6 Apart from problems due to poor connections, two basic types of fault can occur in an electrical circuit - open-circuit, or short-circuit.

7 Open-circuit faults are caused by a break somewhere in the circuit, which prevents current from flowing. An open-circuit fault will prevent a component from working, but will not cause the relevant circuit fuse to blow.

8 Short-circuit faults are caused by a "short" somewhere in the circuit, which allows the current flowing in the circuit to "escape" along an alternative route, usually to earth. Short-circuit faults are normally caused by a breakdown in wiring insulation, which allows a feed wire to touch either another wire, or an earthed component such as the bodyshell. A short-circuit fault will normally cause the relevant circuit fuse to blow.

Finding an open-circuit

9 To check for an open-circuit, connect one lead of a circuit tester or voltmeter to either the negative battery terminal or a known good earth.

10 Connect the other lead to a connector in the circuit being tested, preferably nearest to the battery or fuse.

11 Switch on the circuit, bearing in mind that some circuits are live only when the ignition switch is moved to a particular position.

12 If voltage is present (indicated either by the tester bulb lighting or a voltmeter reading, as applicable), this means that the section of the circuit between the relevant connector and the battery is problem-free.

13 Continue to check the remainder of the circuit in the same fashion.

14 When a point is reached at which no voltage is present, the problem must lie between that point and the previous test point with voltage. Most problems can be traced to a broken, corroded or loose connection.

Finding a short-circuit

15 To check for a short-circuit, first disconnect the load(s) from the circuit (loads are the components which draw current from a circuit, such as bulbs, motors, heating elements, etc).

16 Remove the relevant fuse from the circuit, and connect a circuit tester or voltmeter to the fuse connections.

17 Switch on the circuit, bearing in mind that some circuits are live only when the ignition switch is moved to a particular position.

18 If voltage is present (indicated either by the tester bulb lighting or a voltmeter reading, as applicable), this means that there is a short-circuit.

19 If no voltage is present, but the fuse still blows with the load(s) connected, this indicates an internal fault in the load(s).

Finding an earth fault

20 The battery negative terminal is connected to "earth" - the metal of the engine/transmission and the car body - and most systems are wired so that they only receive a positive feed, the current returning via the metal of the car body. This means that the component mounting and the body form part of that circuit. Loose or corroded mountings can therefore cause a range of electrical faults, ranging from total failure of a circuit, to a puzzling partial fault. In particular, lights may shine dimly (especially when another circuit sharing the same earth point is in operation), motors (eg wiper motors or the radiator cooling fan motor) may run slowly, and the operation of one circuit may have an apparently-unrelated effect on another. Note that on many vehicles, earth straps are used between certain components, such as the engine/transmission and the body, usually where there is no metal-to-metal contact between components, due to flexible rubber mountings, etc.

21 To check whether a component is properly earthed, disconnect the battery, and connect one lead of an ohmmeter to a known good earth point. Connect the other lead to the wire or earth connection being tested. The resistance reading should be zero; if not, check the connection as follows.

22 If an earth connection is thought to be faulty, dismantle the connection, and clean back to bare metal both the bodyshell and the wire terminal or the component earth connection mating surface. Be careful to remove all traces of dirt and corrosion, then use a knife to trim away any paint, so that a clean metal-to-metal joint is made. On reassembly, tighten the joint fasteners securely; if a wire terminal is being refitted, use serrated washers between the terminal and the bodyshell, to ensure a clean and secure connection. When the connection is remade, prevent the onset of corrosion in the future by applying a coat of petroleum jelly or silicone-based grease, or by spraying on (at regular intervals) a proprietary ignition sealer.

3 Fuses and relays - general information

Fuses

1 Fuses are designed to break a circuit when a predetermined current is reached, in order to protect the components and wiring which could be damaged by excessive current flow. Any excessive current flow will be due to a fault in the circuit, usually a short-circuit (see Section 2).

2 The main fuses are located in the fusebox on the driver's side of the facia.

3 For access to the main fuses, remove the cover by pulling out the top first.

4 Additional fuses and circuit-breakers are located in an auxiliary fusebox in the engine compartment, attached to a bracket on the left-hand body panel next to the battery. Fusible links are located in a further fusebox in front of the battery.

5 A blown fuse can be recognised from its melted or broken wire **(see illustration)**.

6 To remove a fuse, first ensure that the relevant circuit is switched off.

7 Using the plastic tool clipped to the main fusebox lid, pull the fuse from its location.

8 Spare fuses are provided in the main fusebox.

9 Before renewing a blown fuse, trace and rectify the cause, and always use a fuse of the correct rating (fuse ratings are specified on the inside of the fusebox cover). Never substitute a fuse of a higher rating, or make temporary repairs using wire or metal foil; more serious damage, or even fire, could result.

10 Note that the fuses are colour-coded as follows. Refer to the wiring diagrams for details of the fuse ratings used and the circuits protected.

Colour	Rating
Orange	*5A*
Red	*10A*
Blue	*15A*
Yellow	*20A*
Clear or White	*25A*
Green	*30A*

11 The radio/cassette player fuse is located in the rear of the unit, and can be accessed after removing the radio/cassette player.

Relays

12 A relay is an electrically-operated switch, which is used for the following reasons:

a) A relay can switch a heavy current remotely from the circuit in which the current is flowing, therefore allowing the use of lighter-gauge wiring and switch contacts.

b) A relay can receive more than one control input, unlike a mechanical switch.

c) A relay can have a timer function - for example, the intermittent wiper relay.

13 Various relays are located behind the facia, next to the fusebox, and, depending on model, on the right-hand side of the engine compartment. Most of the engine-related relays are located next to the fusebox.

14 The direction indicator/hazard warning flasher unit is located on a bracket behind the facia, to the left of the steering column.

15 The "headlights on" warning buzzer is screwed to the rear of the facia.

16 If a circuit or system controlled by a relay develops a fault, and the relay is suspect, operate the system. If the relay is functioning, it should be possible to hear it "click" as it is energised. If this is the case, the fault lies with the components or wiring of the system. If the relay is not being energised, then either the relay is not receiving a main supply or a switching voltage, or the relay itself is faulty. Testing is by the substitution of a known good unit, but be careful - while some relays are identical in appearance and in operation, others look similar but perform different functions.

17 To remove a relay, first ensure that the relevant circuit is switched off. The relay can then simply be pulled out from the socket, and pushed back into position.

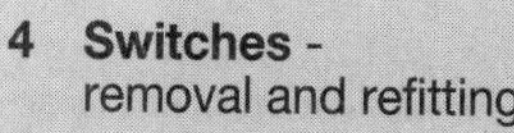

4 Switches - removal and refitting

Note: *Disconnect the battery negative lead before removing any switch, and reconnect the lead after refitting the switch. Refer to the caution in Section 1 if a security-coded radio/cassette player is fitted.*

Ignition switch/steering column lock

1 Refer to Chapter 10.

Steering column combination switches

Removal

2 Remove the mounting screws and withdraw the steering column lower then upper shrouds **(see illustration)**.

3 Disconnect the wiring for the relevant switch, then unscrew the side mounting screws and withdraw the switch **(see illustration)**. On early models, compress the top and bottom fixing wings, then pull the switch from the base.

4 To remove the combination switch base, first remove the steering wheel and where applicable the air bag slip ring as described in Chapter 10. Loosen the clamp bolt, then press the switch downwards while turning it clockwise. Withdraw the base from the top of the column.

Refitting

5 Refitting is a reversal of removal.

Centre facia-mounted pushbutton switches

Removal

6 Remove the facia centre surround panel (described in Chapter 3 for the heater control panel removal), then depress the clips and press the switch out from the rear of the panel, or from the facia, as applicable.

7 Disconnect the wiring from the rear of the switch.

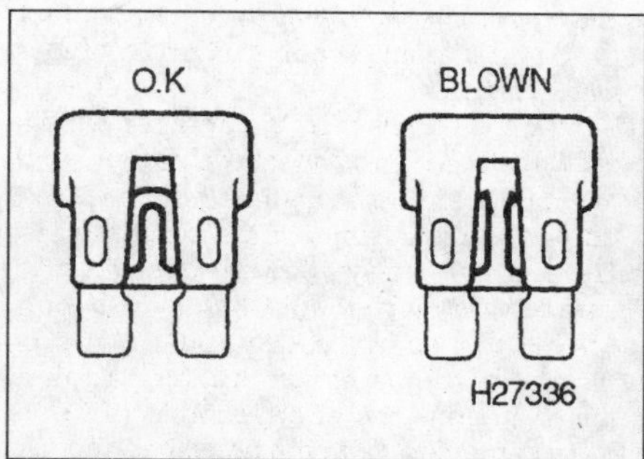

3.5 Checking the condition of a fuse

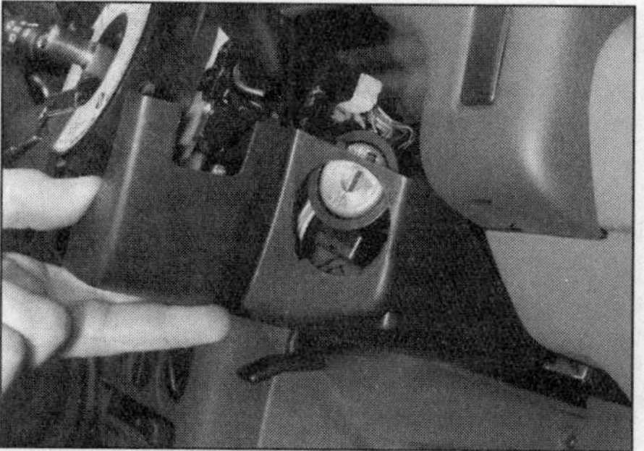

4.2 Removing the steering column lower shroud

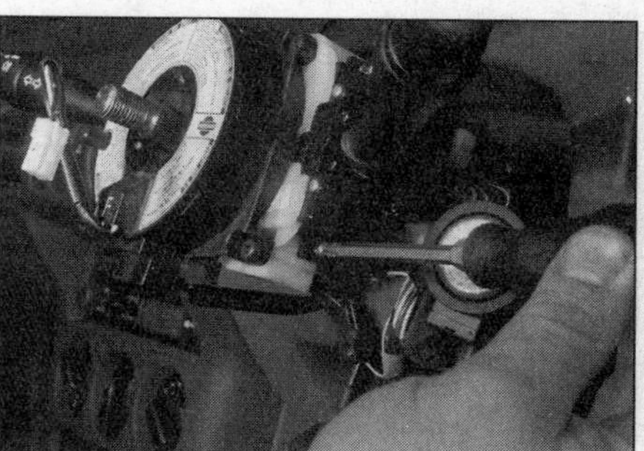

4.3 Unscrew the side mounting screws to remove the combination switches

Refitting

8 Refitting is a reversal of removal.

Heater blower motor switch

Removal

9 Remove the heater/ventilation control panel as described in Chapter 3, however leave the control cables connected.

10 Carefully pull off the control knobs and remove the cover. If using pliers, wrap a suitable piece of cloth or card around each knob to protect it.

11 Release the securing clips using a screwdriver, then pull the blower motor switch from the rear of the control panel.

Refitting

12 Refitting is a reversal of removal.

Centre console-mounted switches

Removal

13 Remove the centre console, as described in Chapter 11.

14 Release the securing clips, then push the switch out through the top of the centre console.

Refitting

15 Refitting is a reversal of removal.

Electric window switch

Removal

16 Remove the armrest from the front door with reference to Chapter 11, Section 11.

17 Undo the mounting screws and withdraw the switch.

Refitting

18 Refitting is a reversal of removal.

Courtesy light/ door ajar warning switch

Removal

19 Open the door to expose the switch in the door pillar.

20 Remove the securing screw, then withdraw the switch from the door pillar and remove the rubber gaiter. Disconnect the wiring connector as it becomes accessible.

Tape the wiring to the door pillar, or tie a length of string to the wiring, to retrieve it if it falls back into the door pillar

Refitting

21 Refitting is a reversal of removal.

Boot light switch

22 The switch is integral with the tailgate lock. Removal and refitting details for the tailgate lock are provided in Chapter 11.

Headlight beam adjuster switch

Removal

23 Remove the heater control panel as described in Chapter 3, Section 9, leaving the control cables connected.

24 Disconnect the wiring plug, then release the switch securing clips and press the switch out of the panel.

Refitting

25 Refitting is a reversal of removal.

5 Bulbs (exterior lights) - renewal

General

1 Whenever a bulb is renewed, note the following points:

a) Make sure the circuit is switched off.

b) Remember that, if the light has just been in use, the bulb may be extremely hot.

c) Always check the bulb contacts and holder, ensuring that there is clean metal-to-metal contact between the bulb and its live contact(s) and earth. Clean off any corrosion or dirt before fitting a new bulb.

d) Wherever bayonet-type bulbs are fitted, ensure that the live contact(s) bear firmly against the bulb contact.

e) Always ensure that the new bulb is of the correct rating (see Specifications), and that it is completely clean before fitting.

Headlight

2 Open the bonnet.

3 Squeeze the securing lugs, and disconnect the wiring plug from the rear of the bulb **(see illustration)**.

4 Pull the rubber boot from the rear of the headlight **(see illustration)**.

5 Squeeze the retaining spring-clip lugs, and release the clip from the rear of the bulb.

6 Withdraw the bulb **(see illustration)**.

7 When handling the new bulb, use a tissue or clean cloth, to avoid touching the glass with the fingers; moisture and grease from the skin can cause blackening and rapid failure of this type of bulb. If the glass is accidentally touched, wipe it clean using methylated spirit.

8 Install the new bulb, ensuring that its locating tabs are correctly located in the light unit cut-outs. Secure the bulb in position with the retaining clip, then refit the rubber boot and reconnect the wiring plug. Note the "TOP" mark on the rubber boot which should be uppermost.

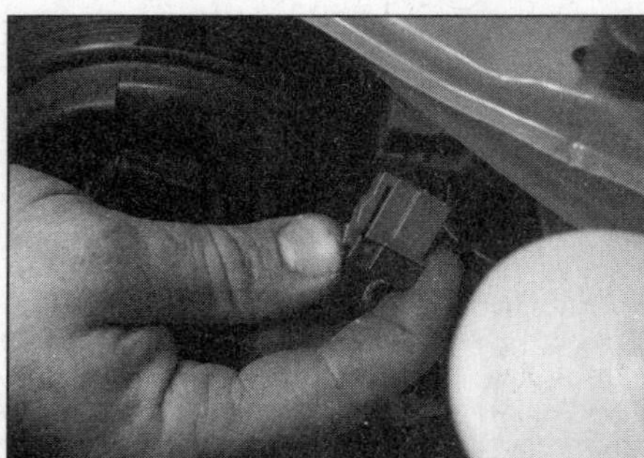

5.3 Disconnecting the wiring plug from the rear of the headlight

5.4 Headlight rear rubber boot removal

5.6 Removing the headlight bulb

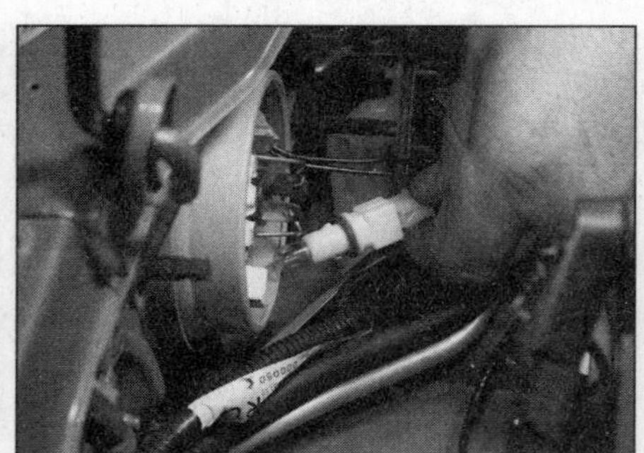

5.12 Remove the front sidelight bulbholder from the headlight . . .

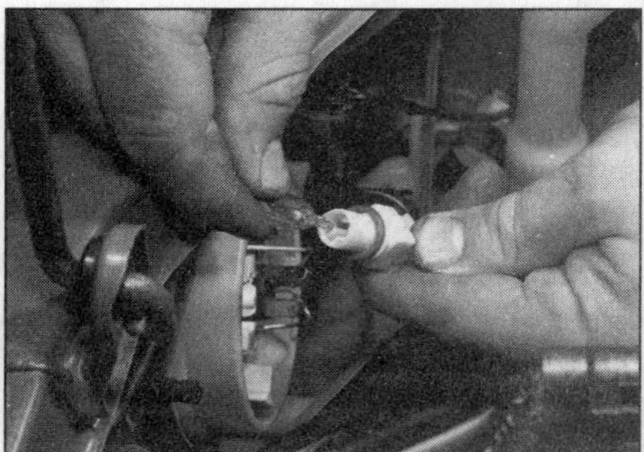

5.13 . . . and pull out the push-fit bulb

5.17 Removing a front direction indicator bulb from its bulbholder

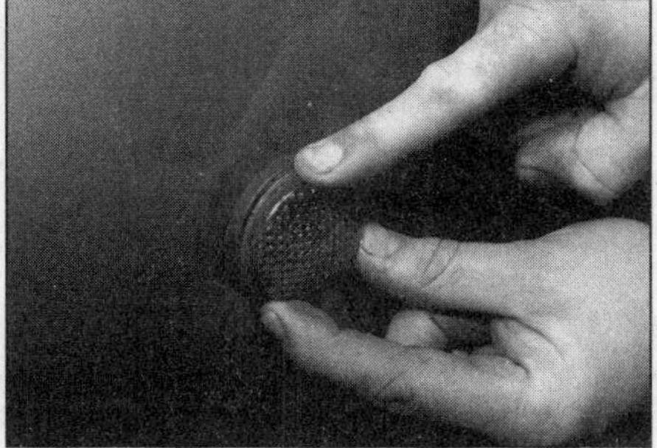
5.19a Push down the side repeater light unit . . .

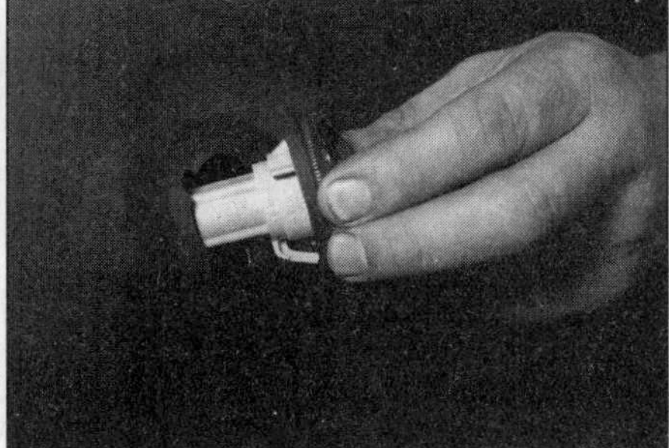
5.19b . . . and withdraw it from the wing . . .

Front sidelight

9 Open the bonnet.

10 Squeeze the securing lugs, and disconnect the wiring plug from the rear of the headlight bulb.

11 Pull the rubber boot from the rear of the headlight.

12 Pull the bulbholder from the rear of the light unit **(see illustration)**.

13 The bulb is a push fit in the bulbholder **(see illustration)**.

14 Fit the new bulb using a reversal of the removal procedure.

Front direction indicator

15 Open the bonnet.

16 Reach into the relevant front corner of the engine compartment, twist the indicator bulbholder anticlockwise, then remove it from the rear of the light unit.

17 Depress and twist the bulb to remove it from the bulbholder **(see illustration)**.

18 Fit the new (yellow) bulb using a reversal of the removal procedure.

Front direction indicator side repeater

19 On models up to 2000, push the light unit downwards and ease the top out from the wing. On models from 2000, push the light unit to the rear and ease the front out from the wing. Lift the light and withdraw **(see illustrations)**.

20 Twist the bulbholder anti-clockwise to release it from the light unit **(see illustration)**.

21 The bulb is a push fit in the bulbholder **(see illustration)**.

5.19c Carefully push the light unit towards the rear of the car . . .

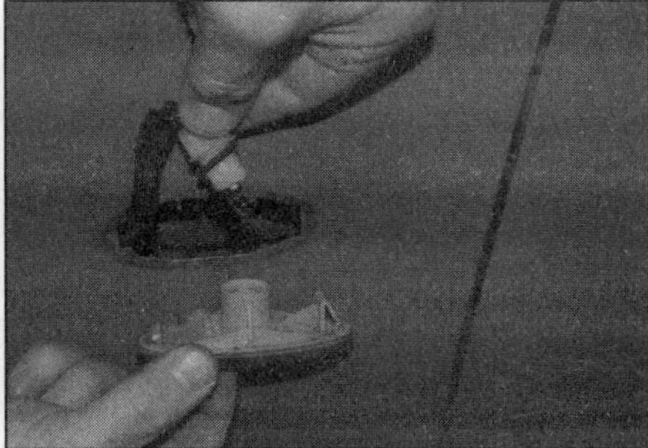
5.19d . . . and withdraw it from the wing

22 Fit the new bulb using a reversal of the removal procedure.

Front driving light/foglight

23 Where fitted, the front driving light is located in the front bumper.

24 On models up to March 1998, unscrew the retaining plate screw, and remove the plate; on models from March 1998 onwards, prise out the light unit surround trim, then remove the two screws beneath.

25 Turn the light unit to release it from the bumper, and withdraw it for access to the rear wiring.

26 According to type, remove the rear cover by either twisting anticlockwise or removing the retaining screws.

27 Disconnect the bulb wiring, then release the spring clip and withdraw the bulb.

28 When handling the new bulb, use a tissue or clean cloth, to avoid touching the glass with the fingers; moisture and grease from the skin can cause blackening and rapid failure of this type of bulb. If the glass is accidentally touched, wipe it clean using methylated spirit.

29 Fit the new bulb using a reversal of the removal procedure, but if necessary adjust the aim before refitting the retaining plate. Use the upper screw to adjust the vertical aim, and both the upper and lower screws to adjust the horizontal aim.

Rear light cluster

30 Open the tailgate.

31 Working in the luggage compartment, pull back the side covering for access to the rear light cluster **(see illustration)**.

32 Squeeze the securing clips to release the bulbholder from the rear of the light unit **(see illustration)**.

33 Depress and twist the bulb to remove it.

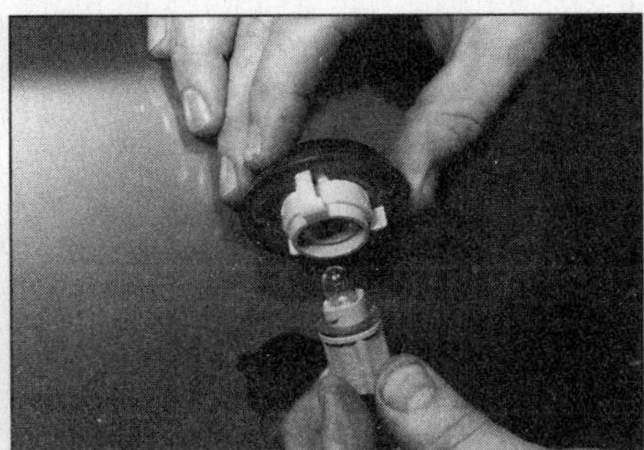
5.20 . . . then release the bulbholder . . .

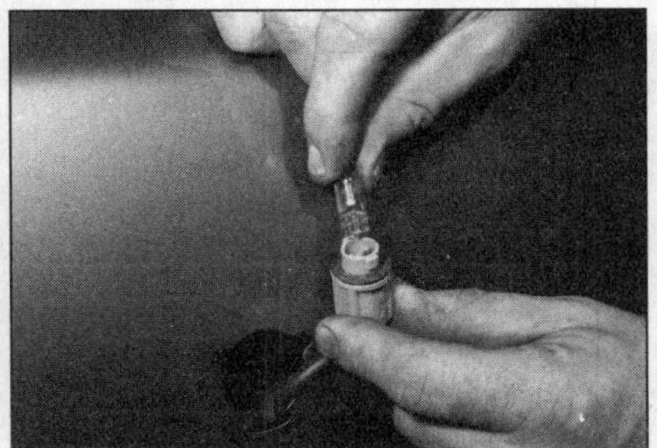
5.21 . . . and pull out the push-fit bulb

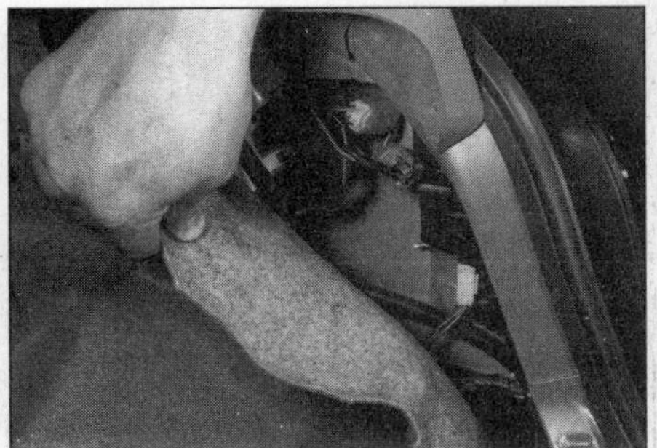
5.31 Pull back the side covering for access to the rear light cluster

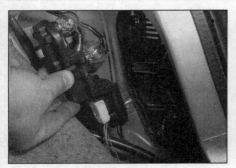

5.32 **Squeeze the securing clips to release the bulbholder**

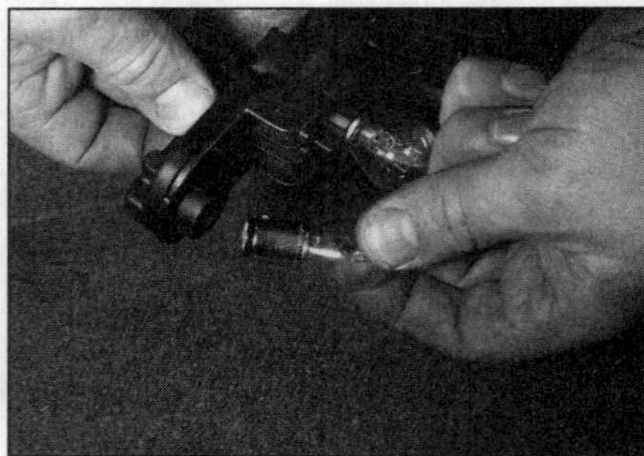

5.33 **Removing the stop/tail bulb from the rear light cluster**

5.36a **Remove the two screws . . .**

5.36b **. . . withdraw the rear number plate light unit lens . . .**

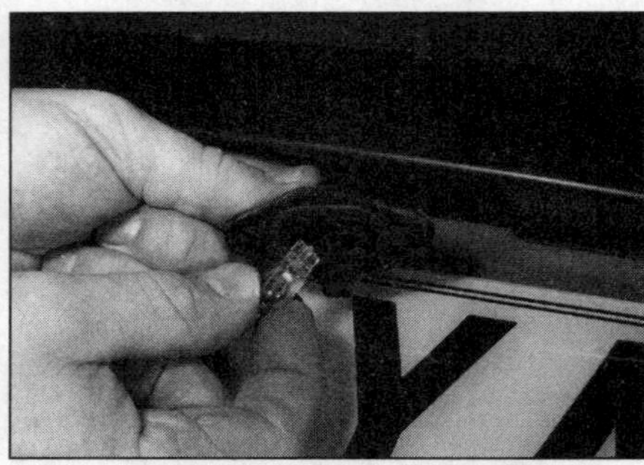

5.37 **. . . and remove the push-fit bulb**

5.40a **Remove the screws . . .**

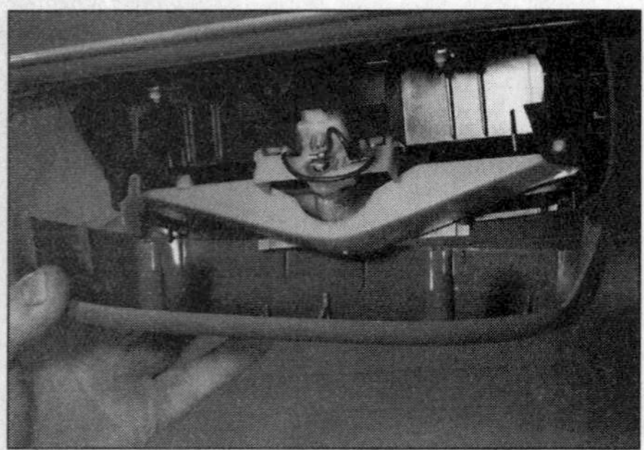

5.40b **. . . and withdraw the high-mounted stop light cover**

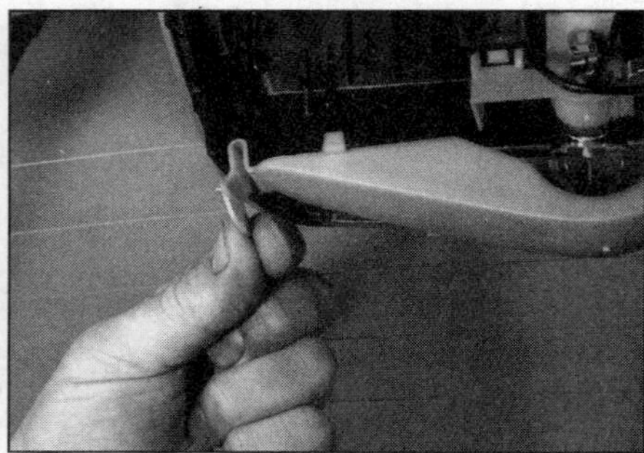

5.41 **Release the clip . . .**

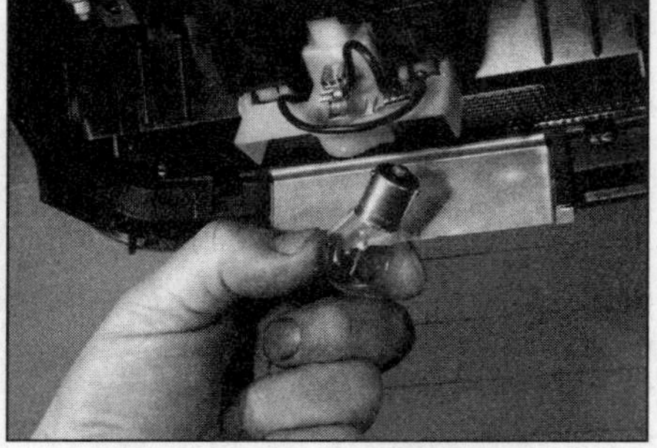

5.42 **. . . and remove the bulb**

The stop/tail bulb is at the top, the direction indicator bulb in the middle, and either the reverse (left-hand side) or fog light (right-hand side) bulb at the bottom **(see illustration)**.

34 Fit the new bulb using a reversal of the removal procedure. Note that the stop/tail light bulb has offset pins, to ensure correct installation.

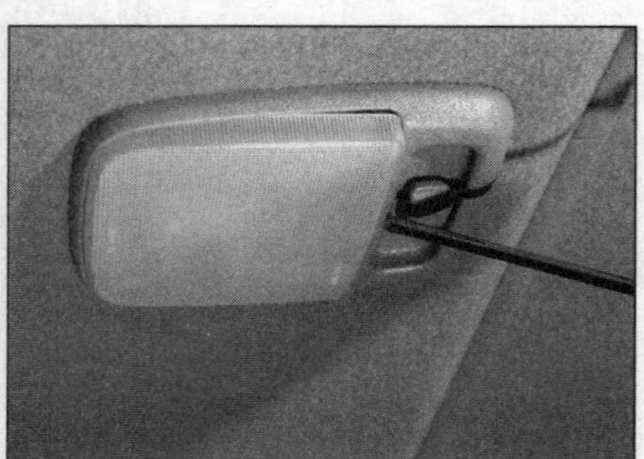

6.2 **Prise the lens from the interior light unit . . .**

Rear number plate light

35 Half raise the tailgate for access to the number plate light.

36 Remove the two screws, and withdraw the light unit lens from the tailgate grip **(see illustrations)**.

37 Pull the push-fit bulb from the bulbholder **(see illustration)**.

38 Fit the new bulb using a reversal of the removal procedure.

High-mounted stop light

39 Open the tailgate.

40 Remove the screws and withdraw the cover from the light **(see illustrations)**.

41 Release the clip, and swivel the reflector away from the bulb **(see illustration)**.

42 Depress and twist the bulb to remove it **(see illustration)**.

6 Bulbs (interior lights) - renewal

General

1 Refer to Section 5, paragraph 1.

Interior/courtesy light

2 Using a small screwdriver, prise the lens from the light unit **(see illustration)**.

3 Remove the festoon-type bulb from the light contacts **(see illustration)**.

4 Fit the new bulb using a reversal of the removal procedure, but make sure the bulb is held firmly between the contacts. Bend the contacts if necessary.

6.3 . . . then remove the festoon-type bulb

6.6 Remove the screws and withdraw the boot light lens . . .

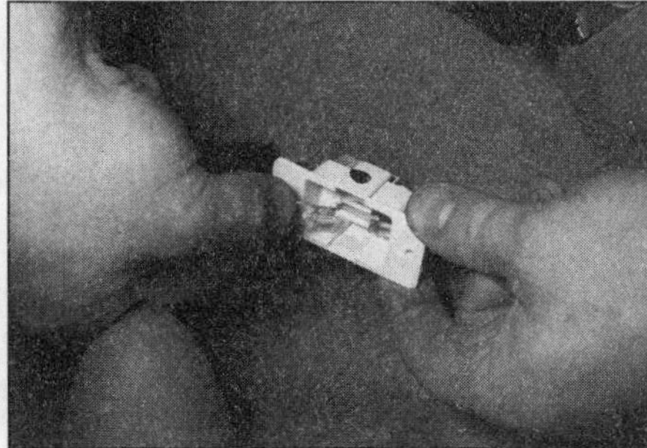
6.7 . . . then remove the push-fit type bulb

Boot light

5 Open the tailgate.
6 Remove the two screws and withdraw the lens **(see illustration)**.
7 The bulb is a push fit in the light assembly **(see illustration)**.
8 Fit the new bulb using a reversal of the removal procedure.

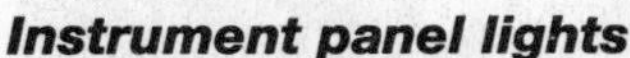

Instrument panel lights

9 Remove the instrument panel (Section 8).
10 Twist the relevant bulbholder anti-clockwise to remove it from the rear of the instrument panel **(see illustration)**.
11 The 3-watt battery charge and low fuel warning bulbs are a push-fit in the bulbholders, however the 1-watt and 2-watt smaller bulbs are integral with the bulbholders **(see illustration)**.
12 Fit the new bulb, and twist it clockwise to lock it into position.
13 Refit the instrument panel as described in Section 8.

Heater control panel illumination bulbs

14 Remove the heater/ventilation control panel as described in Chapter 3, however leave the control cables connected.
15 Carefully pull off the control knobs and remove the cover. If using pliers, wrap a suitable piece of cloth or card around each knob to protect it.
16 Twist the relevant bulbholder anti-clockwise, using a screwdriver if necessary, and withdraw the bulbholder. The bulbs are integral with the bulbholders.
17 Fit the new bulb using a reversal of the removal procedure.

Switch illumination bulb

18 Remove the switch (see Section 4).
19 Twist the bulbholder anticlockwise to remove it from the switch. The bulb is integral with the bulbholder.
20 Fit the new bulb using a reversal of the removal procedure.

Cigarette lighter illumination bulb

21 It is not possible to renew the cigarette lighter illumination bulb separately.

6.10 Removing an instrument panel light bulbholder

6.11 The 3-watt bulbs are a push-fit in the bulbholders

Automatic transmission selector illumination bulb

22 Prise up the selector lever surround from the base unit.
23 Twist the bulbholder anticlockwise and withdraw from the surround.
24 The bulb is a push-fit in the bulbholder.
25 Fit the new bulb using a reversal of the removal procedure.

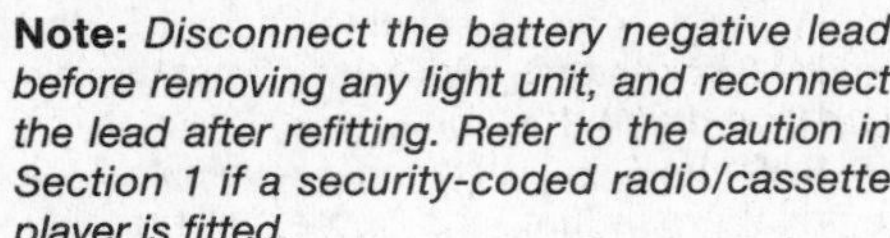

7 Exterior light units - removal and refitting

Note: *Disconnect the battery negative lead before removing any light unit, and reconnect the lead after refitting. Refer to the caution in Section 1 if a security-coded radio/cassette player is fitted.*

Headlight/front direction indicator light

Removal

1 On models up to March 1998, remove the radiator grille as described in Chapter 11, Section 20. With the grille removed, unscrew the headlight lower mounting screw **(see illustrations)**.
2 On models from March 1998 onwards, remove the headlight lower mounting screw from the rear outer corner of the unit.
3 On models equipped with a headlight beam adjuster control, disconnect the actuator wiring plug from the rear of the headlight.
4 Working inside the engine compartment, unscrew the upper and lower mounting nuts **(see illustration)**.
5 Unscrew and remove the upper mounting bolt **(see illustration)**.

7.1a Removing the radiator grille from the headlight

7.1b Headlight lower mounting screw

7.4 Unscrewing the headlight rear mounting nuts

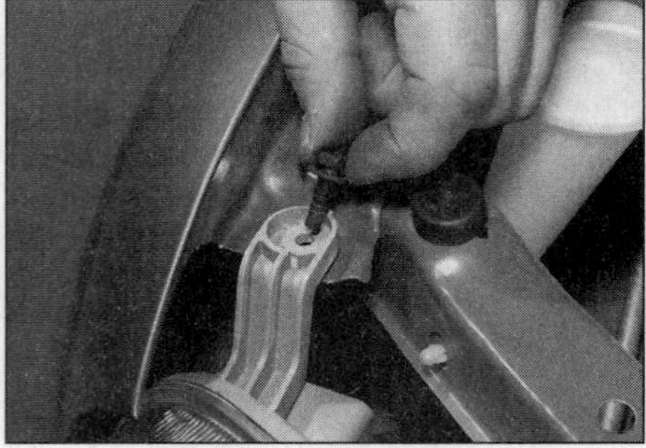

7.5 Removing the headlight upper mounting bolt

7.7a Removing the headlight/front direction indicator light

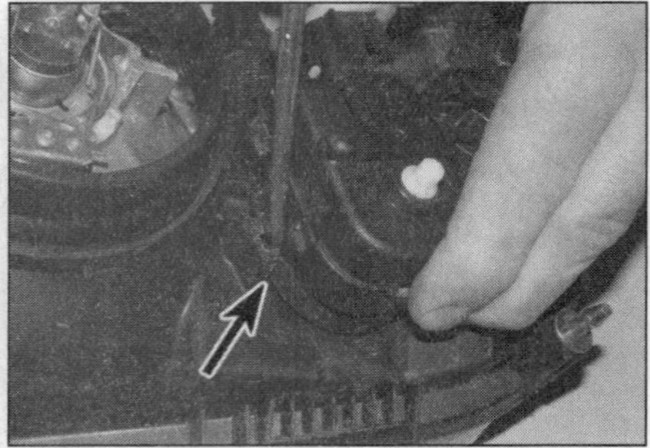

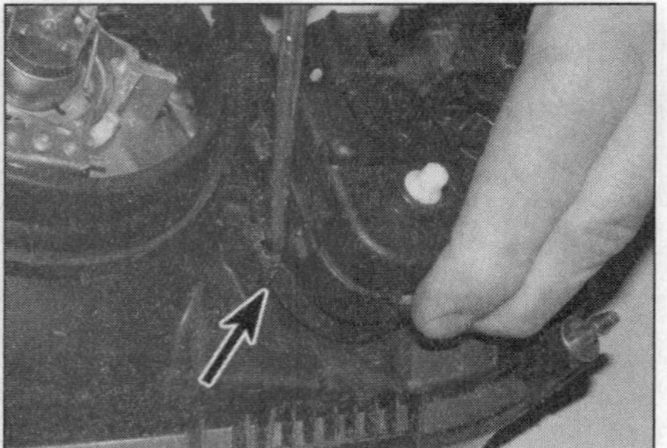

7.7b Carefully release the retaining clip (arrowed) . . .

7.7c . . . and unclip the adjuster from the light unit

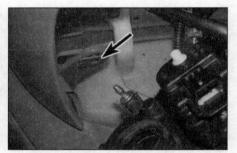

7.8 Make sure the peg on headlight unit locates in the hole (arrowed) in the inner wing panel

6 Disconnect the wiring from the rear of the headlight/direction indicator light.

7 Withdraw the headlight/direction indicator light from the vehicle noting the location of the rubber grommet **(see illustration)**. Where necessary, use a screwdriver to release the retaining clip then twist the headlight adjuster and unclip it from the rear of the light unit **(see illustrations)**.

Refitting

8 Refitting is a reversal of removal, but make sure that the rubber grommet is correctly fitted. On later models make sure the locating peg **(see illustration)** is located correctly when refitting the headlamp. If necessary adjust the headlight beam alignment as described in Chapter 1.

Front direction indicator side repeater light

Removal and refitting

9 The procedure is described as part of the bulb renewal procedure in Section 5.

Front driving light/foglight

Removal and refitting

10 The procedure is described as part of the bulb renewal procedure in Section 5.

Rear light cluster

Note: *Suitable sealant (preferably hot Butyl) will be required on refitting, together with a hot air gun.*

Removal

11 Remove the bulbholder assembly, as described for bulb renewal in Section 5.

12 Unscrew the three mounting nuts and withdraw the light cluster from the body panel **(see illustration)**. If the original unit is being removed, it will be necessary to heat the mastic from inside the rear luggage area using a hot air gun, until the mastic is pliable. If different sealant has been used, it may be necessary to cut the light cluster free.

Refitting

13 Before refitting the light unit, clean all traces of sealant from the light unit and the wing panel.

14 Apply a bead of suitable sealant to the rear of the light unit, making sure that the join is at the bottom.

15 Refit the light unit using a reversal of the removal procedure, and tightening the nuts progressively.

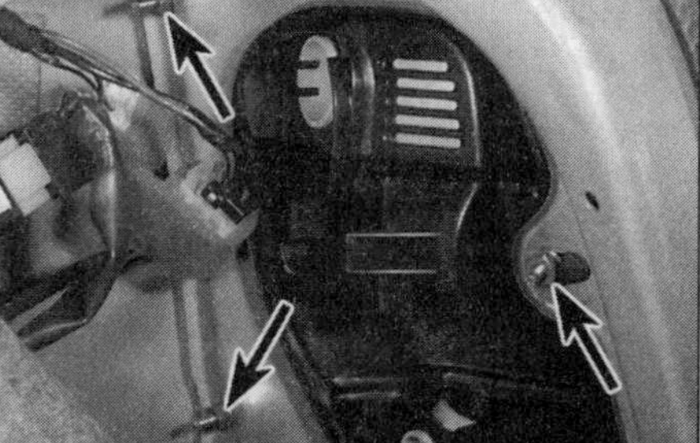

7.12 Rear light cluster mounting nuts

Rear number plate light

Removal and refitting

16 The procedure is described as part of the bulb renewal procedure in Section 5, however it will be necessary to remove the tailgate inner metal insert panel and disconnect the wiring. The wiring from both rear number plate lights is incorporated in the one connector.

High-mounted stop light

Removal

17 Open the tailgate.

18 Remove the screws and withdraw the cover from the light

19 Unscrew the mounting nuts and withdraw the light unit from the tailgate, then disconnect the wiring.

Refitting

20 Refit the light unit using a reversal of the removal procedure.

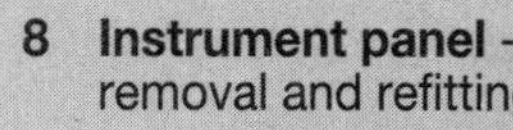

8 Instrument panel - removal and refitting

Removal

1 Disconnect the battery negative lead.

2 Where an adjustable steering column is fitted, adjust it to its lowest position. For improved access, remove the steering wheel completely as described in Chapter 10.

3 Unscrew the mounting screws from the

8.3a Removing the instrument panel cowl upper mounting screws

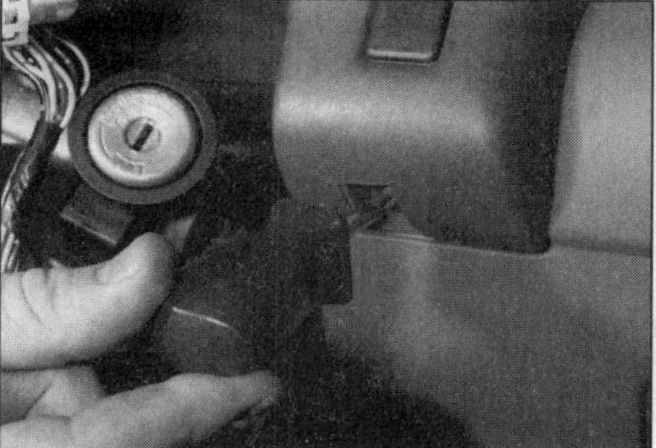

8.3b Removing the instrument panel cowl lower mounting screw

8.3c Removing the instrument panel cowl

8.4 Instrument panel showing mounting screws

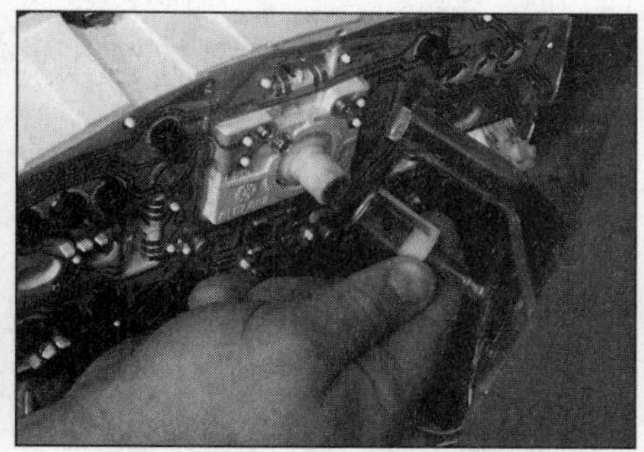

8.5 Disconnecting the speedometer cable from the rear of the instrument panel

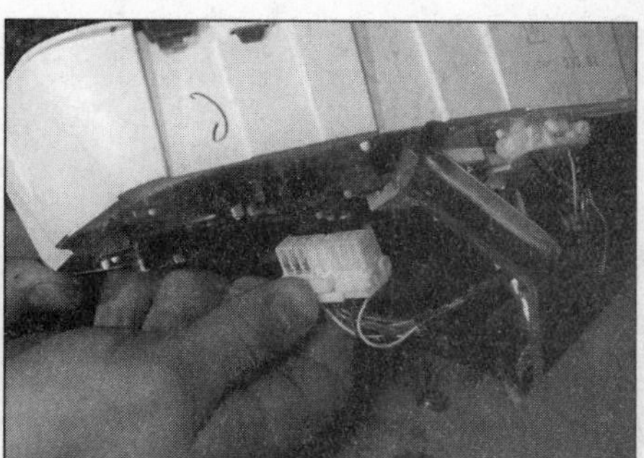

8.6 Disconnecting the wiring plugs from the instrument panel

cowl, then pull the cowl forwards to release the rear clips and withdraw it. Where applicable, disconnect the wiring from the instrument illumination rheostat **(see illustrations)**.

4 Unscrew the three instrument panel mounting screws **(see illustration)**.

5 Withdraw the instrument panel from the facia sufficiently to gain rear access. On models up to March 1998, disconnect the speedometer cable from the rear of the panel by compressing the plastic clip **(see illustration)**.

6 Carefully disconnect the three wiring plugs, noting their locations to aid refitting **(see illustration)**.

7 Withdraw the instrument panel from the facia.

Refitting

8 Refitting is a reversal of removal. Make sure that the wiring connectors (and where applicable, the speedometer cable) are securely reconnected.

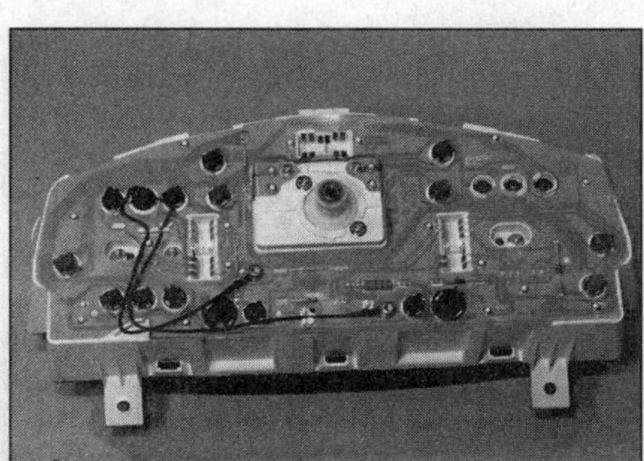

9.4 Rear view of the instrument panel

9 Instrument panel components - removal and refitting

Caution: The instrument panel components are delicate and should be treated with care. Do not place gauges face down, as the needles may be bent and/or damaged resulting in them being inaccurate. Work in a clean environment to prevent dust and dirt entering the instrument panel.

Removal

Note: *On models from March 1998 onwards, it appears that the instrument panel cannot be dismantled; the only parts available separately are the bulbs (see Section 6).*

1 Remove the instrument panel as described in Section 8.

2 Unclip and remove the front cover.

3 Remove the screws and withdraw the upper housing.

4 Unscrew the nuts from the rear of the instrument panel to remove the tachometer and fuel/temperature gauges **(see illustration)**. On some models a digital clock is incorporated in the tachometer or temperature gauge.

5 Remove the screws from the raised area on the rear of the instrument panel to remove the speedometer.

6 To renew any of the illumination bulbs, refer to Section 6.

7 To remove the printed circuit board, remove all bulbs with reference to Section 6, then unscrew the two mounting screws.

Refitting

8 Refitting is a reversal of removal.

10 "Lights on" warning system - general information

On all models, a "lights-on" warning buzzer is fitted. The buzzer will sound if the driver's door is opened when the headlights or sidelights are switched on.

The buzzer unit is located on the rear of the small shelf below the steering column. After removal of the shelf, the unit can be removed by unscrewing the retaining screw and disconnecting the wiring.

11 Cigarette lighter - removal and refitting

Removal

1 Remove the facia centre surround panel (described in Chapter 3 for the heater control panel removal), but leave the control cables connected.

2 Disconnect the wiring, then push out the cigarette lighter from the surround panel, or from the lower facia, and recover the retaining ring **(see illustration)**.

3 The knob and main body of the cigarette lighter may be renewed separately, but the illumination bulb is not replaceable.

11.2 The cigarette lighter is mounted on the facia centre surround panel - models up to 1998

Refitting

4 Refitting is a reversal of removal.

12 Horn - removal and refitting

Removal

1 Disconnect the battery negative lead.

2 Open the bonnet, then disconnect the wiring from the horn.

3 Unscrew the securing bolt, and withdraw the horn complete with its mounting bracket **(see illustration)**.

Refitting

4 Refitting is a reversal of removal. On models with two horns, make sure the correct horn is fitted. The pitch can be adjusted if necessary by turning the bolt on the rear of the horn.

12.3 Horns and mounting bolts

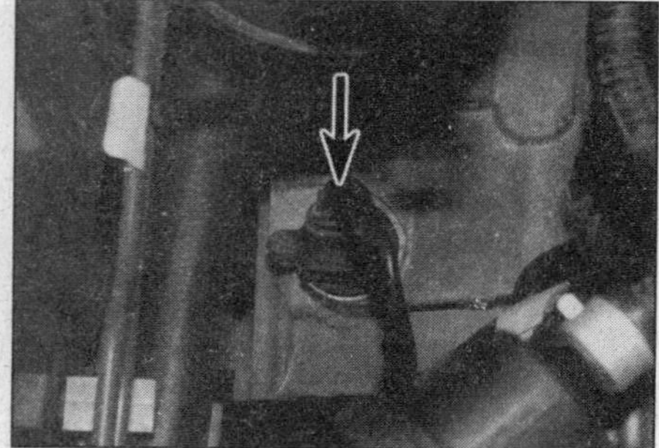

13.0 Sensor (arrowed) in the transmission housing on models from March 1998

13.3 Speedometer cable support bracket in the engine compartment

13 Speedometer drive cable - removal and refitting

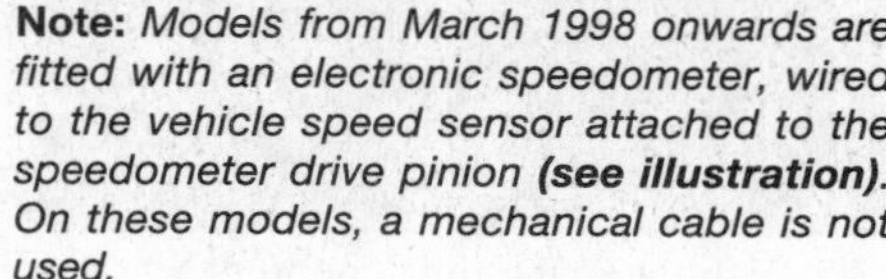

Note: *Models from March 1998 onwards are fitted with an electronic speedometer, wired to the vehicle speed sensor attached to the speedometer drive pinion **(see illustration)**. On these models, a mechanical cable is not used.*

Removal

1 Remove the instrument panel as described in Section 8 for access to the front of the cable **(see illustration)**.

2 Working in the engine compartment, unscrew the sleeve securing the cable end to the transmission, then pull the cable from the transmission. Access to the rear of the transmission can be improved if the air cleaner inlet duct is removed first.

3 Where applicable, release the cable from the bracket on the engine compartment bulkhead, then pull the cable through into the engine compartment **(see illustration)**. If necessary, pull the cable grommet from the bulkhead. On some models the speedometer cable is in two sections.

Refitting

4 Refitting is a reversal of removal.

13.1 Speedometer cable front end fitting

14.3a Lift the cover for access to the windscreen wiper arm spindle nut

14 Wiper arm - removal and refitting

Removal

1 Operate the wiper motor, then switch it off so that the wiper arm returns to the "parked" position.

2 Stick a piece of tape along the edge of the wiper blade, to use as an alignment aid on refitting.

3 Where applicable, lift up the wiper arm spindle nut cover, then unscrew and remove the spindle nut **(see illustrations)**. Lift the blade off the glass, and pull the wiper arm off its spindle. If necessary, the arm can be levered off the spindle using a suitable flat-bladed screwdriver. If both windscreen wiper arms are removed, note their locations, as different arms are fitted to the driver's and passenger's sides.

Refitting

4 Ensure that the wiper arm and spindle splines are clean and dry.

5 When refitting a windscreen or tailgate wiper arm, refit the arm to the spindle, aligning the wiper blade with the tape fitted before removal. If both windscreen wiper arms have been removed, ensure that the arms are refitted to their correct positions as noted before removal.

6 When refitting a headlight wiper arm, hold the arm below the stops at the bottom of the headlight unit, until the spindle nut has been refitted and tightened.

7 Refit the spindle nut, tighten it securely, and where applicable, clip the nut cover back into

14.3b Tailgate wiper arm spindle nut

15.3 Prise out the weatherstrip from the cowl

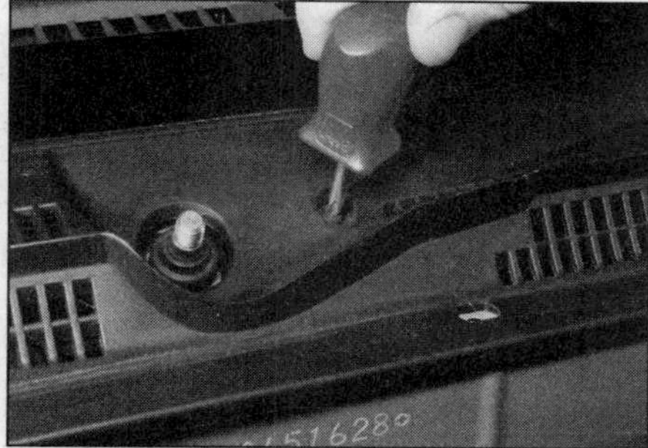

15.4a Removing the cowl panel screws . . .

15.4b . . . and clip

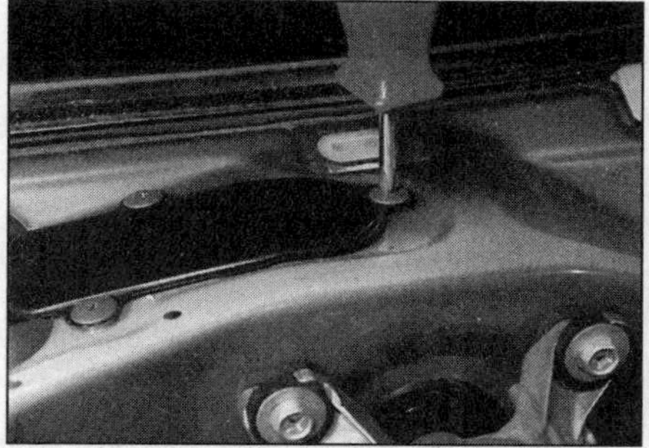

15.5 Removing the wiper linkage access cover

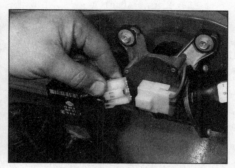

15.7 Disconnecting the wiper motor wiring plug

position. If refitting a headlight wiper arm, once the spindle nut has been tightened, position the wiper blade against the upper surfaces of the stops on the headlight.

15 Windscreen wiper motor and linkage - removal and refitting

Motor

Removal

1 Remove the wiper arms (see Section 14).

2 Open the bonnet then disconnect the battery negative lead.

3 Prise out the clips and withdraw the weatherstrip from the front edge of the bulkhead cowl panel **(see illustration)**.

4 Remove the securing screws and plastic clip, and withdraw the cowl panel **(see illustrations)**.

5 Remove the screws and withdraw the access cover located over the rear of the wiper motor **(see illustration)**.

6 Using a screwdriver through the access aperture, prise the linkage from the crank arm balljoint.

7 Disconnect the motor wiring plug **(see illustration)**.

8 Unscrew the four motor securing bolts, and withdraw the motor **(see illustrations)**.

Refitting

9 Refitting is a reversal of removal, but apply a little grease to the crank arm ball before reconnecting the linkage.

Linkage

Removal

10 Proceed as described in paragraphs 1 to 6 inclusive.

11 Unscrew the spindle unit mounting nuts, and withdraw the linkage from the cowl **(see illustrations)**.

12 If necessary, prise the linkage from the spindle arms.

Refitting

13 Refitting is a reversal of removal, but apply a little grease to the balljoints before reconnecting the linkage.

16 Tailgate wiper motor - removal and refitting

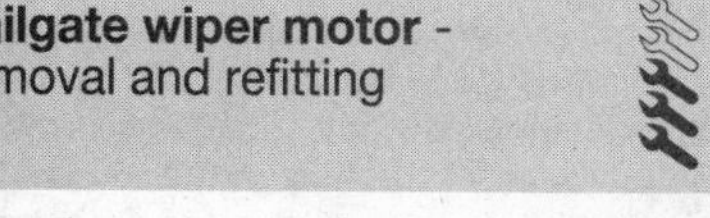

Removal

1 Disconnect the battery negative lead.

2 Open the tailgate then undo the screws securing the metal insert panel. Where applicable, remove the single screw and take

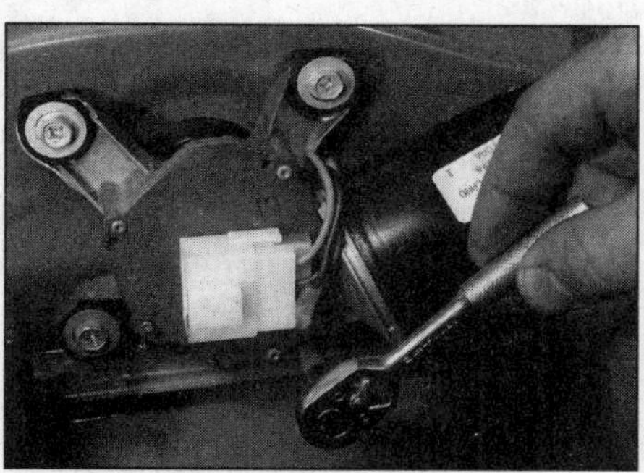

15.8a Unscrew the mounting bolts . . .

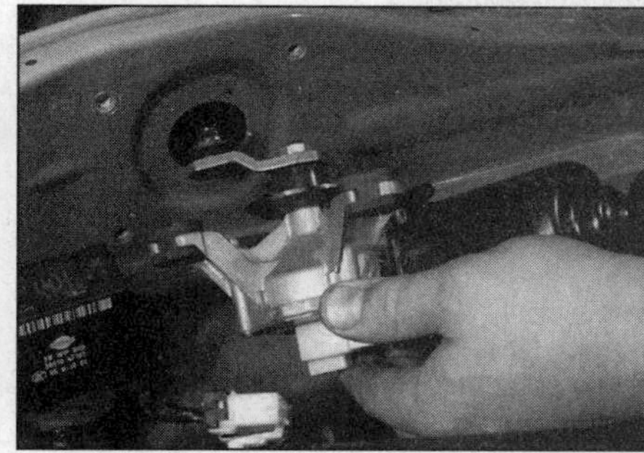

15.8b . . . and withdraw the wiper motor

15.11a Unscrew the spindle unit mounting nuts . . .

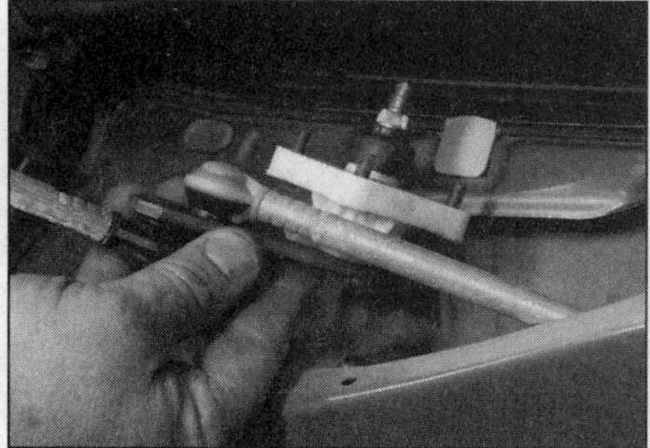

15.11b . . . and withdraw the linkage from the cowl

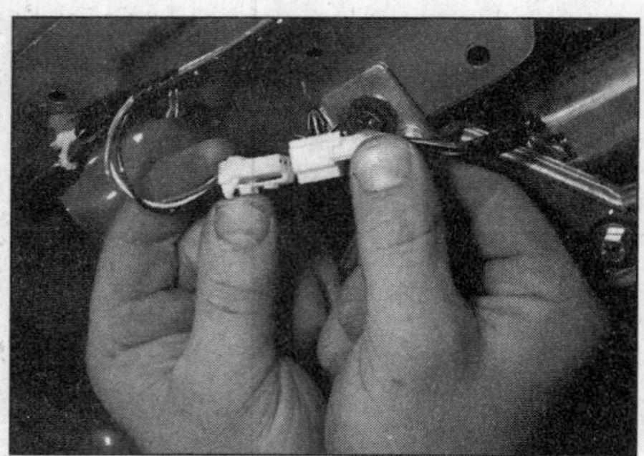
16.4 Disconnecting the tailgate wiper motor wiring

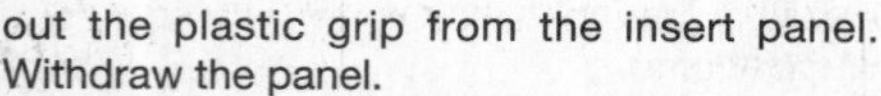

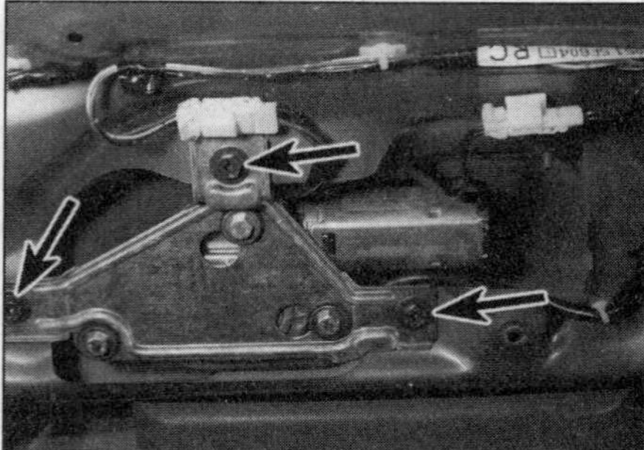
16.5 Unscrew the mounting bolts . . .

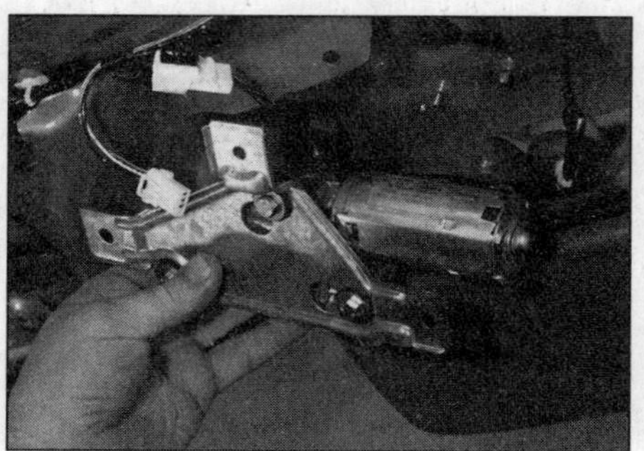
16.6 . . . and withdraw the tailgate wiper motor assembly

out the plastic grip from the insert panel. Withdraw the panel.

3 Remove the wiper arm with reference to Section 14.

4 Disconnect the tailgate wiper motor wiring plug **(see illustration)**.

5 Unscrew the three bolts securing the motor mounting bracket to the tailgate **(see illustration)**.

6 Withdraw the motor assembly from the tailgate **(see illustration)**.

7 The motor is secured to the mounting bracket by three bolts.

8 If desired, the motor spindle grommet can be pulled from the hole in the tailgate.

Refitting

9 Refitting is a reversal of removal, but ensure that the grommet is correctly located in the tailgate, and refit the wiper arm (Section 14).

17 Windscreen/tailgate washer system components - removal and refitting

Washer fluid reservoir

Removal

1 Working in the engine compartment, twist the reservoir filler neck clockwise, then pull it from the top of the reservoir.

2 Apply the handbrake then jack up the front of the vehicle and support securely on axle stands (see *"Jacking and vehicle support"*). Remove the right-hand front roadwheel.

3 Remove the wheel arch liner. If desired for improved access, remove the front bumper (Chapter 11) and the right-hand headlight (Section 7).

4 Disconnect the wiring plug(s) from the washer pump(s).

5 Disconnect the fluid hose(s) from the washer pump(s) - if the reservoir still contains fluid, be prepared for fluid spillage.

6 Unscrew the mounting bolts, then lower the reservoir from under the wheel arch **(see illustration)**.

Refitting

7 Refitting is a reversal of removal.

Washer pump(s)

Removal

8 Proceed as described in paragraphs 2 to 3.

9 Disconnect the wiring plug and the fluid hose from the relevant washer pump **(see illustration)**.

10 Pull the washer pump from the reservoir, and recover the grommet. If the reservoir still contains fluid, be prepared for fluid spillage.

Refitting

11 Refitting is a reversal of removal.

Windscreen washer nozzle

Removal

12 Open the bonnet.

13 Working under the bonnet, release the securing tabs using long-nosed pliers, then push the nozzle from the bonnet. Disconnect the fluid hose, and withdraw the nozzle.

Refitting

14 Refitting is a reversal of removal.

Tailgate washer nozzle

Removal

15 Open the tailgate, and working at the inside top edge, pull the fluid hose from the washer nozzle **(see illustration)**.

16 Unscrew the securing nut, then withdraw the nozzle from the outside of the tailgate.

Refitting

17 Refitting is a reversal of removal.

18 Radio/cassette player - removal and refitting

Caution: If the radio/cassette player fitted to the vehicle is one with an anti-theft security code, as the standard unit is, refer to the information given in the Reference Section at the rear of this manual before disconnecting the battery.

Removal

1 Disconnect the battery negative lead.

2 Remove the facia centre surround panel as described in Chapter 3 for the heater control panel removal.

3 Remove the four radio/cassette player securing screws **(see illustration)**.

4 Pull the unit forwards from the facia, then

17.6 Washer fluid reservoir upper mounting bolt

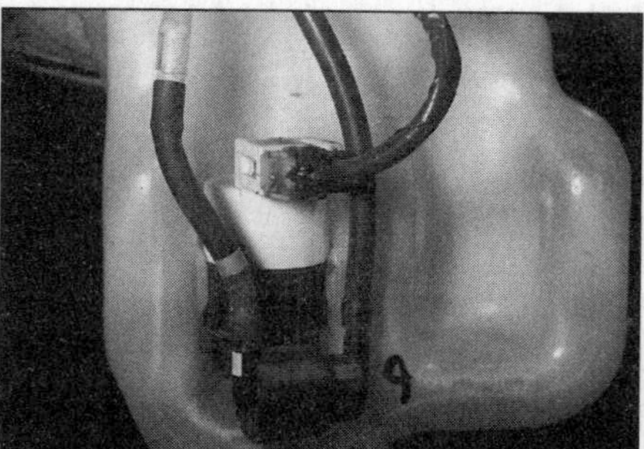
17.9 The windscreen washer pump is mounted on the fluid reservoir

17.15 Pull the fluid hose from the tailgate washer nozzle

disconnect the wiring plugs and the aerial lead from the rear of the unit **(see illustration)**.

Refitting

5 Refitting is a reversal of removal.

19 Loudspeakers - removal and refitting

Front door-mounted loudspeakers

Removal

1 Remove the door inner trim panel as described in Chapter 11.

2 Remove the four securing screws, and withdraw the loudspeaker from the door, then disconnect the wiring plug **(see illustrations)**.

Refitting

3 Refitting is a reversal of removal.

Front body pillar-mounted loudspeakers

Removal

4 Open the relevant front door, and pull the weatherstrip from the edge of the body pillar trim panel.

5 Carefully pull the trim panel from the pillar to release the securing clips.

6 Remove the screw securing the loudspeaker to the pillar, then withdraw the loudspeaker and disconnect the wiring (where necessary, pull the insulating foam from the connector) **(see illustration)**.

Refitting

7 Refitting is a reversal of removal.

Rear loudspeakers

Removal

8 Remove the parcel shelf from the rear luggage compartment, and disconnect the loudspeaker wiring.

9 Prise off the cover, then remove the screws and withdraw the loudspeaker. Unclip and remove the wiring.

10 If necessary, unscrew the loudspeaker mounting plate securing screws and withdraw the plate **(see illustration)**.

Refitting

11 Refitting is a reversal of removal.

20 Radio aerial - removal and refitting

Removal

1 On models with a rear roof-mounted aerial, the aerial mast can be unscrewed from the base if required.

2 Remove the radio (see Section 18), and disconnect the aerial lead from the rear of the unit.

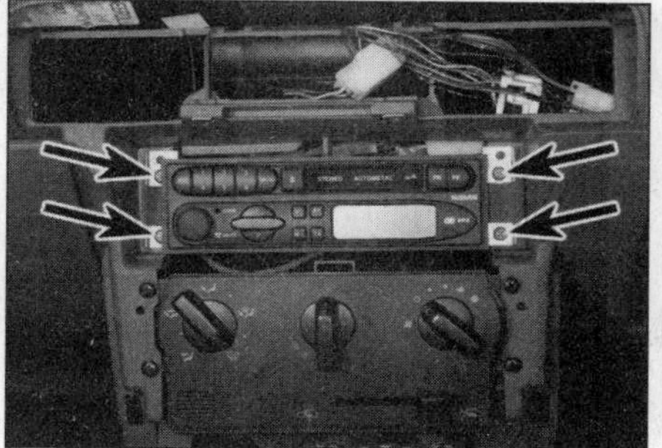

18.3 Radio/cassette player securing screws

18.4 Removing the radio/cassette player

3 Remove the driver's side front pillar trim as described in Chapter 11, Section 23. On models with an aerial mounted at the rear of the roof, carefully loosen and lower the headlining trim in the area below the aerial.

4 On models with the pillar-mounted aerial, remove the securing screw(s) and release the mounting bracket from the roof.

5 On models with a rear roof-mounted aerial, disconnect the aerial lead from below the base of the aerial. Remove the securing screw and detach the aerial base from the roof.

6 Tie a length of string to the end of the aerial lead inside the vehicle, then withdraw the aerial from the roof while feeding the lead down through the front pillar.

7 Untie the string and leave in place to aid refitting.

Refitting

8 Refitting is a reversal of removal, but tighten the mounting screws securely to prevent water entry.

21 Anti-theft immobiliser - general information

Note: *This information is applicable only to standard or optional equipment fitted by Nissan.*

All models in the range are fitted with a Nissan Anti-Theft System (NATS) engine immobiliser, with an alarm offered as an option on later models.

The immobiliser is a sophisticated transponder system. A microchip embedded in the ignition key sends a signal to a reader coil next to the ignition lock barrel - only if the correct code is received will the immobiliser be deactivated, allowing the engine to be started. On models from March 1998 onwards, the

19.2a Remove the securing screws . . .

19.2b . . . and disconnect the wiring from the front door-mounted loudspeakers

19.6 Front body pillar-mounted loudspeaker

19.10 Rear loudspeaker mounting plate securing screws on the rear parcel shelf

system is upgraded to feature a 'rolling code', meaning that a different code is required at each engine start, making it more difficult for the required code to be 'grabbed' electronically by thieves. Additionally, the standard Nissan radio/cassette unit is linked into the immobiliser circuit, meaning that if the unit is removed by thieves, it will not function again until it is connected back into the circuit.

When the ignition is switched off, an LED security indicator blinks to warn outsiders that the vehicle has an anti-theft system installed. If a fault occurs in the system, the Malfunction Indicator Lamp (MIL) will blink. Any suspected faults with the system should be referred to a Nissan dealer.

If any additional keys are required, bear in mind that any keys not supplied by a Nissan dealer will only operate the locks, and will not contain the transponder chip required to deactivate the immobiliser.

22 Heated front seat components - general information

Certain models are fitted with heated front seats. The seats are heated by electrical elements built into the seat cushions. For access to the heating elements, the seats must be dismantled, and this work should be entrusted to a Nissan dealer.

Removal and refitting details for the heated seat switches are given in Section 4.

23 Air bag and supplementary restraint system - general information and precautions

General information

Most models from April 1995-on are fitted with a driver's air bag system (also known as a Supplementary Restraint System - SRS), which is designed to prevent serious chest and head injuries during an accident. The air bag module is fitted in the steering wheel centre pad, with the control module in front of the centre console, under the facia.

The system is armed when the ignition key is in the 'ON' or 'START' positions, and is activated by a 'g' sensor (deceleration sensor). When a frontal impact of sufficient force is detected by the 'g' sensor, a small pyrotechnic (explosive) device is triggered, which inflates the air bag and forces the bag out from its location in the steering wheel; this operation takes less than half a second.

From August 1995-on, the front seat belts incorporate pre-tensioners. In the event of an impact sufficient to trigger the air bag, the pre-tensioners activate and retract the seat belts into the reels, taking up any slack in the belt to ensure maximum restraint effect. On models up to March 1998, the pre-tensioners fitted may be of a spring-operated mechanical type, while later models have a pyrotechnic type triggered directly from the air bag circuit. Similarly, a mechanical system is employed on the rear seat belts, which, combined with the special child seat mounting points, offers extra protection for rear child seat passengers.

Models from March 1998 onwards can be specified with a front passenger air bag, located in the top of the facia panel. The passenger air bag works in the same way as that provided for the driver, and will be triggered together with the driver's air bag in the event of a severe enough front impact.

From November 1998 onwards, side air bags are available. These are incorporated into the sides of the front seats, and are triggered by a separate side impact sensor, so that they can in theory operate independently of the front air bags and pre-tensioners.

Every time the ignition is switched on, the air bag control unit performs a self-test. The self-test takes approximately 7 seconds, and during this time the airbag warning light on the facia is illuminated. After the self-test has been completed, the warning light should go out. If the warning light fails to come on, remains illuminated after the initial 7-second period, flashes, or comes on at any time when the vehicle is being driven, there is a fault in the air bag system. The vehicle should then be taken to a Nissan dealer for examination at the earliest possible opportunity.

Removal and refitting procedures for the driver's air bag are included in the steering wheel and column removal procedures in Chapter 10.

The passenger air bag can be removed from the facia panel after removing the glovebox as described in Chapter 11, Section 25 for access to the special securing bolts and nuts. Be sure to observe the precautions listed at the end of this Section.

As stated in Chapter 11, it is recommended that any work involving the seat belt pre-tensioners is left to a Nissan dealer. Models up to March 1998 may have a mechanical type of pre-tensioner fitted, which must be made safe before it is removed; the later pyrotechnic type can be disconnected at the wiring plug, observing the same precautions as for the air bag system.

The side air bag units are built into the front seats, and their removal requires that the seat fabric be removed. This is not considered to be a DIY operation, and should be referred to a Nissan dealer.

Precautions

Warning: The following precautions must be observed when working on vehicles with an air bag system, to prevent the possibility of personal injury.

a) Do not attempt to test any of the air bag system circuits using test meters or any other test equipment.

b) Before working on the air bag and SRS-related components (steering wheel and column), switch off the ignition, and disconnect the battery negative lead, then wait for at least 10 MINUTES before carrying out any further work.

c) Do not attempt to remove the system electronic control unit (located under the steering column), or the sensor (located under the centre console).

d) Do not attempt to turn the steering wheel or column with the steering gear removed.

e) If the air bag warning light comes on, or any fault in the system is suspected, consult a Nissan dealer without delay. Do not attempt to carry out fault diagnosis, or any dismantling of the components.

Key to symbols

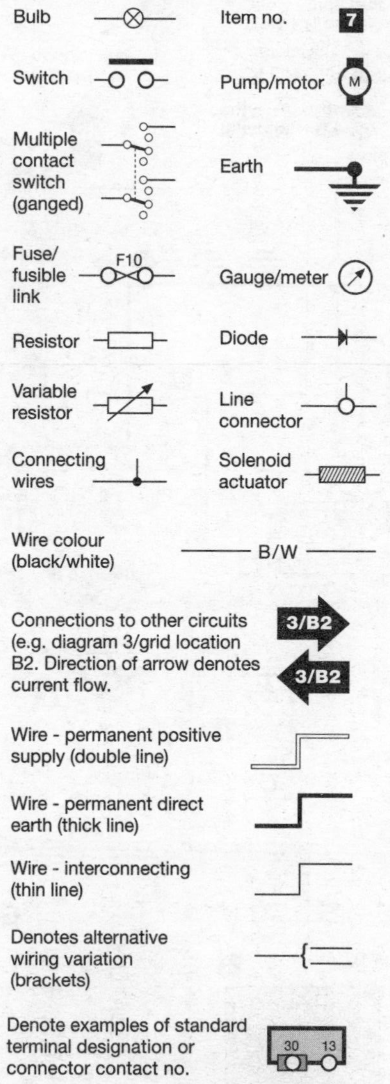

Bulb		Item no.	7
Switch		Pump/motor	M
Multiple contact switch (ganged)		Earth	
Fuse/fusible link	F10	Gauge/meter	
Resistor		Diode	
Variable resistor		Line connector	
Connecting wires		Solenoid actuator	

Wire colour (black/white) —— B/W ——

Connections to other circuits (e.g. diagram 3/grid location B2. Direction of arrow denotes current flow. 3/B2 3/B2

Wire - permanent positive supply (double line)

Wire - permanent direct earth (thick line)

Wire - interconnecting (thin line)

Denotes alternative wiring variation (brackets)

Denote examples of standard terminal designation or connector contact no. 30 13

Main fusebox - typical

Fuse	Rating	Circuit protected
F1	-	Unused
F2	-	Unused
F3	10A	Engine control unit, starter inhibitor relay
F4	10A	Interior lighting, audio, luggage compartment lighting
F5	10A	Stop lights
F6	10A	Rear fog light
F7	10A	Horn
F8	15A	Driving lights
F9	10A	Hazard warning lights
F10	10A	Side lights, number plate lights, illumination
F11	10A	Hazard and direction indicator lights
F12	10A	Instruments, dim/dip control unit, reversing lights, ABS idle-up relay, electric windows, central locking, lights-on warning buzzer
F13	10A	Idle-up relay
F14	-	Unused
F15	-	Unused
F16	10A	Engine control unit, ABS, exhaust gas sensor
F17	15A	Fuel pump
F18	10A	Air bag
F19	10A	ABS (idle-up relay) or blower motor
F20	-	Unused
F21	15A	Blower motor
F22	10A	Audio, clock
F23	10A	Rear wash/wipe
F24	20A	Front wash/wipe
F25	15A	Cigar lighter
F26	15A	Heated rear window

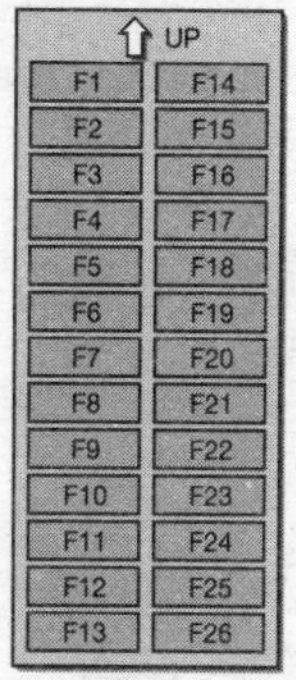

Earth locations

E1	Behind RH kick panel/dashboard
E2	On engine
E3	Near RH front strut tower
E4	Behind RH kick panel/dashboard
E5	Inner wing behind LH headlight
E6	Below battery tray
E7	Behind dashboard LH
E8	Behind LH kick panel/dashboard
E9	Behind LH kick panel/dashboard
E10	On tailgate
E11	At heated rear window
E12	Behind dashboard LH top
E13	Below battery tray
E14	Near RH engine mounting
E15	Near RH front strut tower
E16	Near RH rear light cluster

Main fusebox

UP

F1	F14
F2	F15
F3	F16
F4	F17
F5	F18
F6	F19
F7	F20
F8	F21
F9	F22
F10	F23
F11	F24
F12	F25
F13	F26

Fusible link box

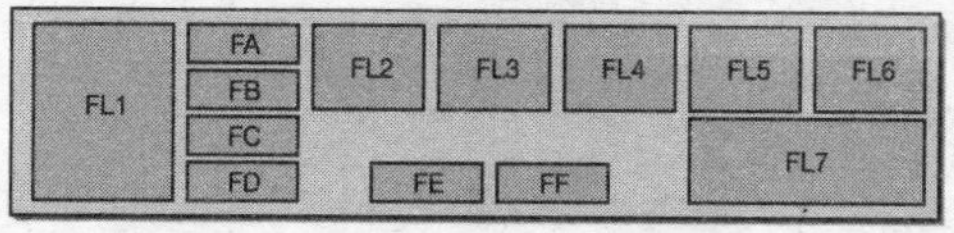

FL1 FA FB FC FD FL2 FL3 FL4 FL5 FL6 FE FF FL7

Fuse	Rating	Circuit protected
FA	10A	Injection system
FB	10A	Charging system
FC	15A	RH headlight
FD	15A	LH headlight
FE	10A	Automatic transmission
FF	15A	Air conditioning

Link	Rating	Circuit protected
FL1	30A	ABS
FL2	25A	Electric windows
FL3	25A	Engine cooling fan
FL4	30A	ABS
FL5	30A	Ignition system
FL6	25A	Injection
FL7	65A	Battery

H29340
T.M.Marke

Diagram 1 : Information for wiring diagrams (1993-99)

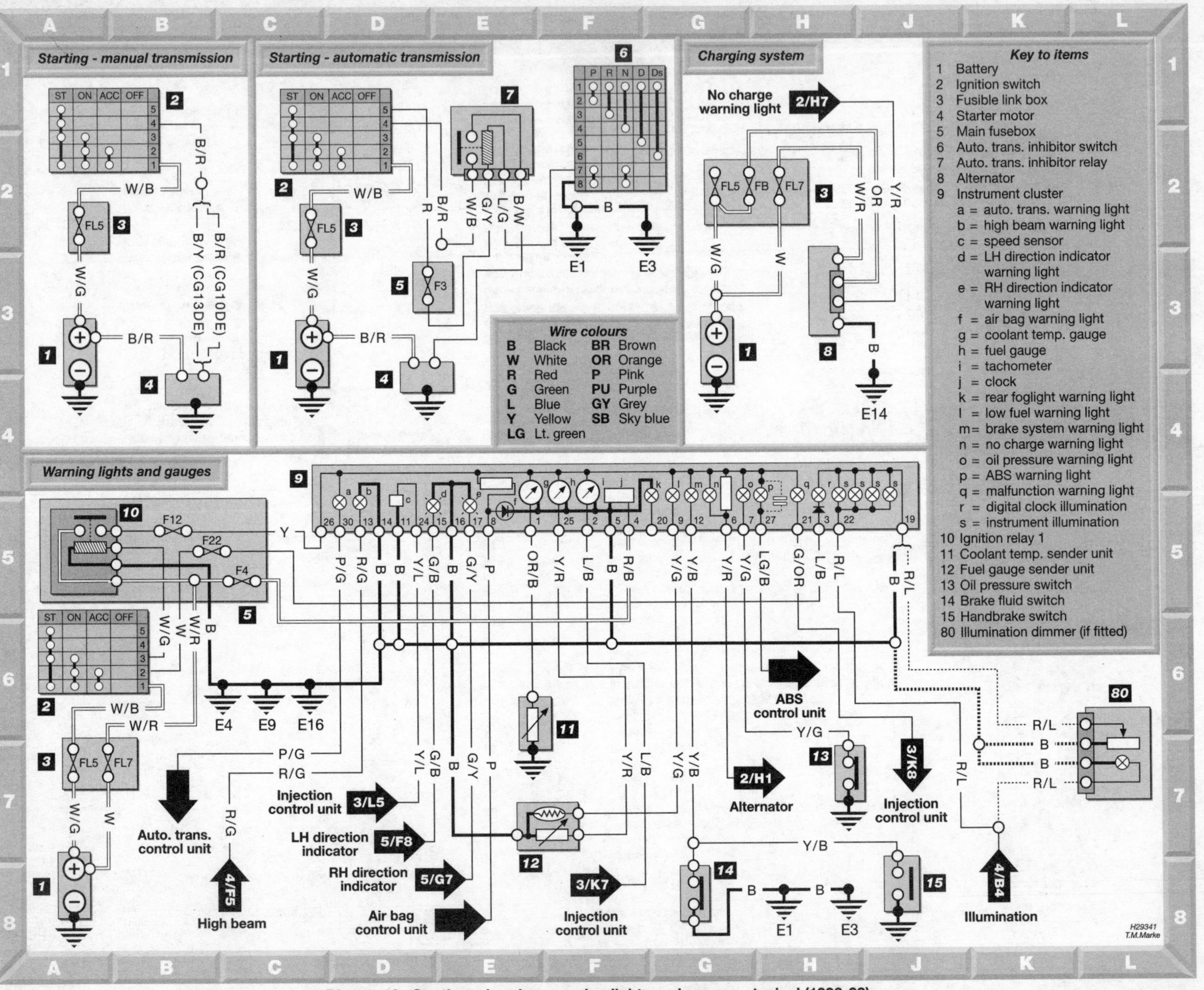
Starting - manual transmission
Starting - automatic transmission
Charging system
No charge warning light
Wire colours
B Black
W White
R Red
G Green
L Blue
Y Yellow
LG Lt. green
BR Brown
OR Orange
P Pink
PU Purple
GY Grey
SB Sky blue
Key to items
1 Battery
2 Ignition switch
3 Fusible link box
4 Starter motor
5 Main fusebox
6 Auto. trans. inhibitor switch
7 Auto. trans. inhibitor relay
8 Alternator
9 Instrument cluster
a = auto. trans. warning light
b = high beam warning light
c = speed sensor
d = LH direction indicator warning light
e = RH direction indicator warning light
f = air bag warning light
g = coolant temp. gauge
h = fuel gauge
i = tachometer
j = clock
k = rear foglight warning light
l = low fuel warning light
m= brake system warning light
n = no charge warning light
o = oil pressure warning light
p = ABS warning light
q = malfunction warning light
r = digital clock illumination
s = instrument illumination
10 Ignition relay 1
11 Coolant temp. sender unit
12 Fuel gauge sender unit
13 Oil pressure switch
14 Brake fluid switch
15 Handbrake switch
80 Illumination dimmer (if fitted)
Warning lights and gauges
B/R (CG10DE)
B/Y (CG13DE)
Auto. trans. control unit
High beam
Injection control unit
LH direction indicator
RH direction indicator
Air bag control unit
ABS control unit
Alternator
Illumination
H29341
T.M.Marke

Diagram 2 : Starting, charging, warning lights and gauges - typical (1993-99)

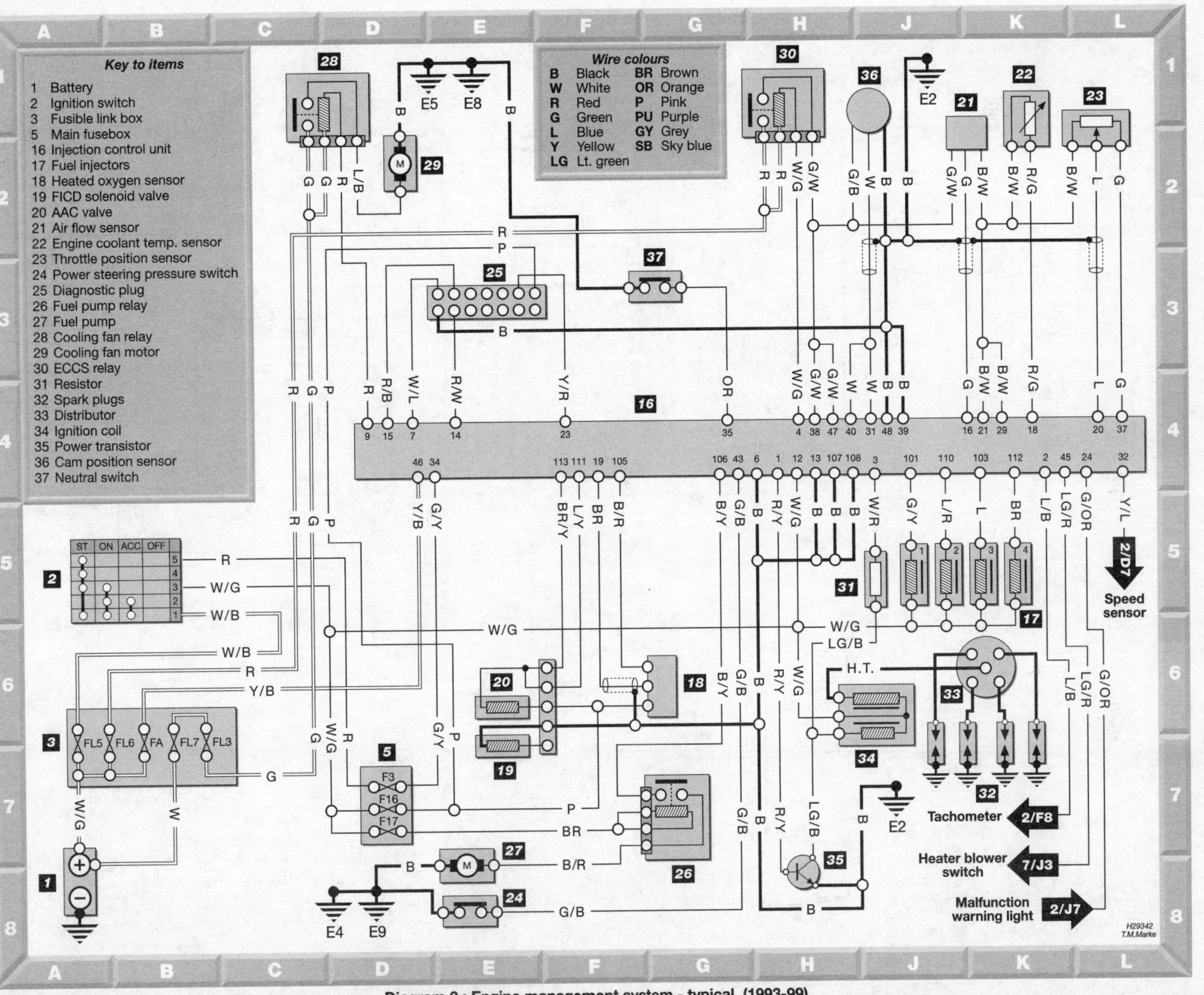

Key to items
1 Battery
2 Ignition switch
3 Fusible link box
5 Main fusebox
16 Injection control unit
17 Fuel injectors
18 Heated oxygen sensor
19 FICD solenoid valve
20 AAC valve
21 Air flow sensor
22 Engine coolant temp. sensor
23 Throttle position sensor
24 Power steering pressure switch
25 Diagnostic plug
26 Fuel pump relay
27 Fuel pump
28 Cooling fan relay
29 Cooling fan motor
30 ECCS relay
31 Resistor
32 Spark plugs
33 Distributor
34 Ignition coil
35 Power transistor
36 Cam position sensor
37 Neutral switch
Wire colours
B Black
W White
R Red
G Green
L Blue
Y Yellow
LG Lt. green
BR Brown
OR Orange
P Pink
PU Purple
GY Grey
SB Sky blue
2/D7 Speed sensor
Tachometer 2/F8
Heater blower switch 7/J3
Malfunction warning light 2/J7
H29342
T.M.Marke

Diagram 3 : Engine management system - typical (1993-99)

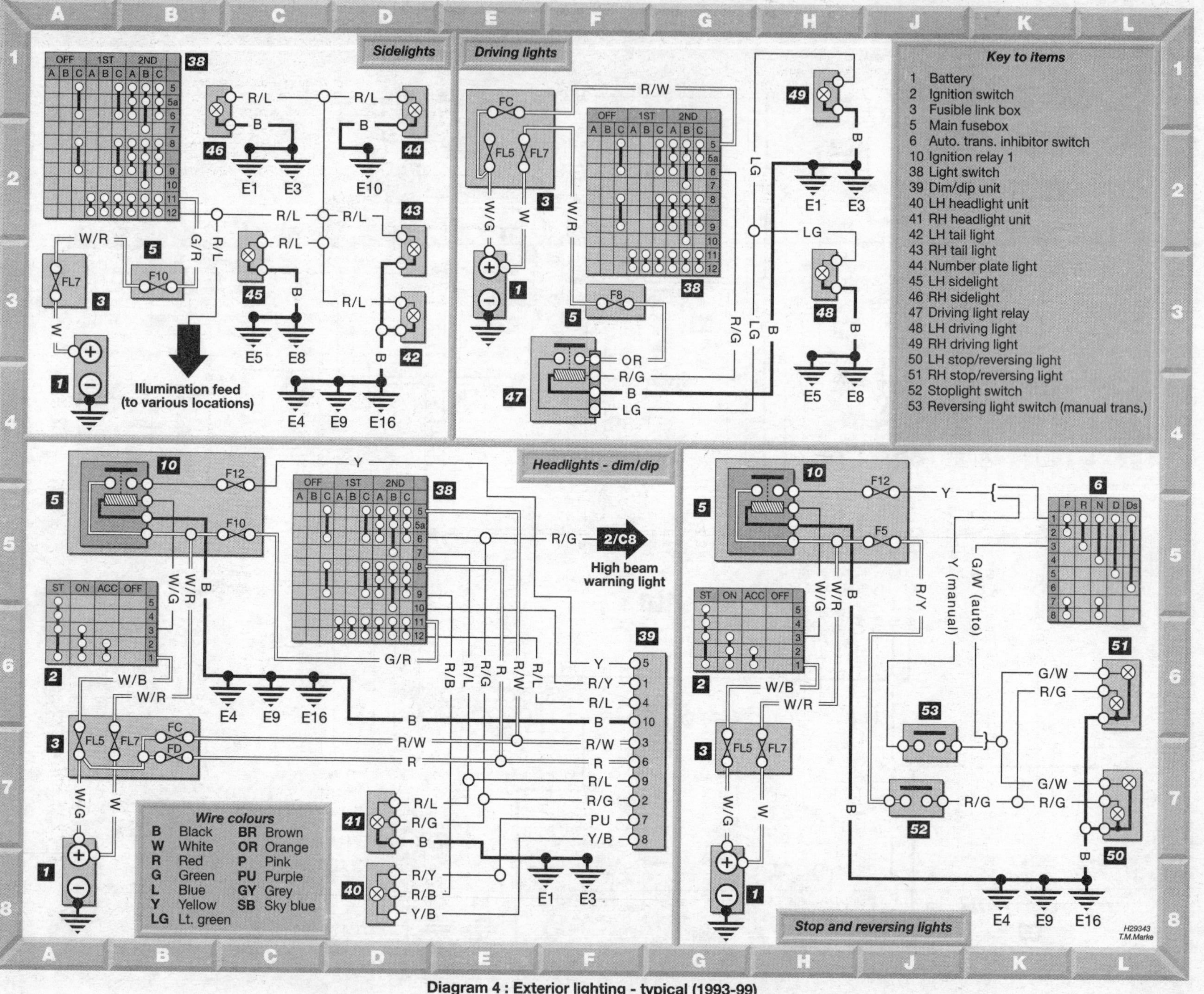
Sidelights
Driving lights
Key to items
1 Battery
2 Ignition switch
3 Fusible link box
5 Main fusebox
6 Auto. trans. inhibitor switch
10 Ignition relay 1
38 Light switch
39 Dim/dip unit
40 LH headlight unit
41 RH headlight unit
42 LH tail light
43 RH tail light
44 Number plate light
45 LH sidelight
46 RH sidelight
47 Driving light relay
48 LH driving light
49 RH driving light
50 LH stop/reversing light
51 RH stop/reversing light
52 Stoplight switch
53 Reversing light switch (manual trans.)
Illumination feed (to various locations)
Headlights - dim/dip
High beam warning light
Stop and reversing lights
Y (manual)
G/W (auto)
Wire colours
B Black
W White
R Red
G Green
L Blue
Y Yellow
LG Lt. green
BR Brown
OR Orange
P Pink
PU Purple
GY Grey
SB Sky blue
H29343
T.M.Marke
Diagram 4 : Exterior lighting - typical (1993-99)

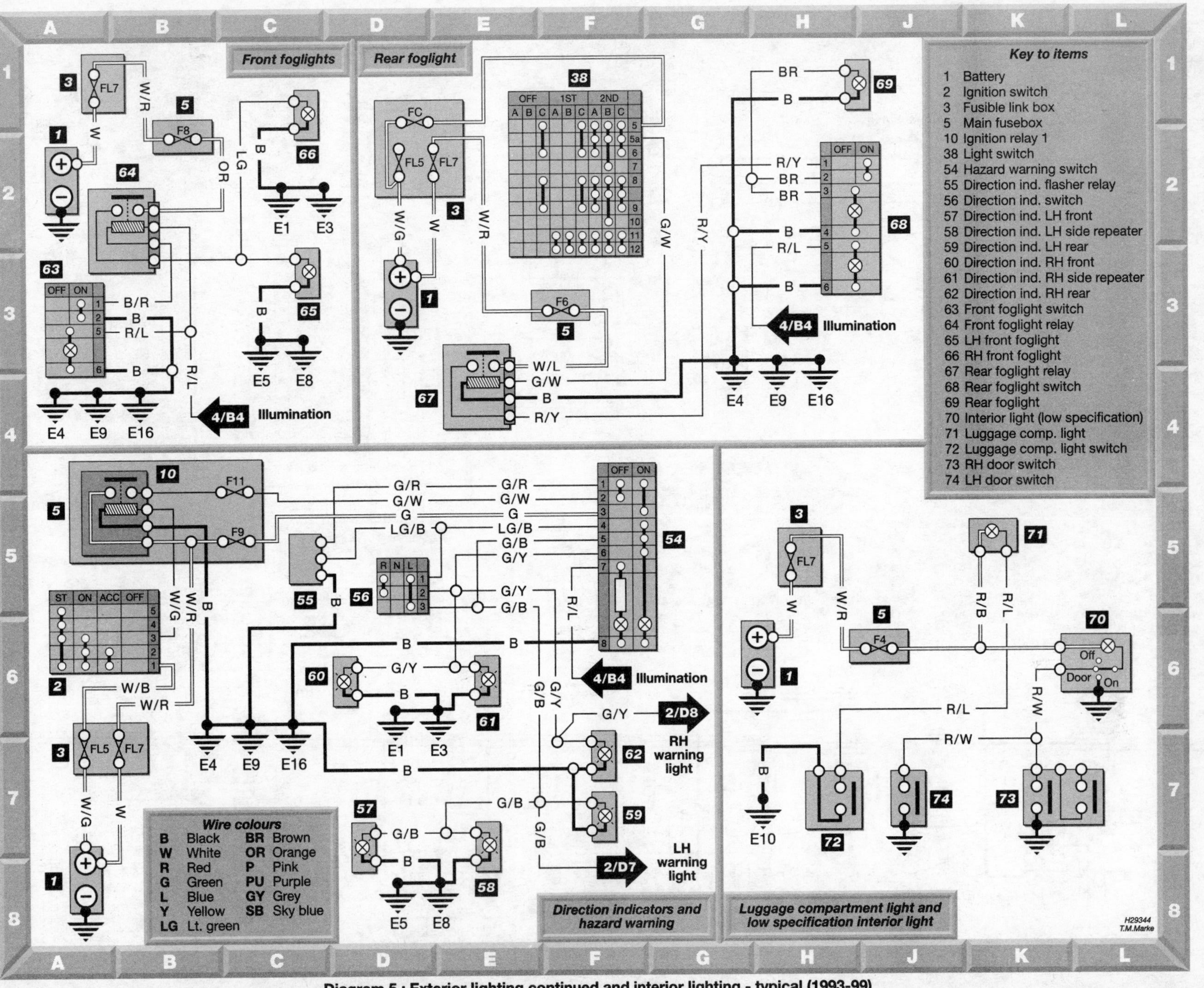

Key to items
1 Battery
2 Ignition switch
3 Fusible link box
5 Main fusebox
10 Ignition relay 1
38 Light switch
54 Hazard warning switch
55 Direction ind. flasher relay
56 Direction ind. switch
57 Direction ind. LH front
58 Direction ind. LH side repeater
59 Direction ind. LH rear
60 Direction ind. RH front
61 Direction ind. RH side repeater
62 Direction ind. RH rear
63 Front foglight switch
64 Front foglight relay
65 LH front foglight
66 RH front foglight
67 Rear foglight relay
68 Rear foglight switch
69 Rear foglight
70 Interior light (low specification)
71 Luggage comp. light
72 Luggage comp. light switch
73 RH door switch
74 LH door switch
Wire colours
B Black
W White
R Red
G Green
L Blue
Y Yellow
LG Lt. green
BR Brown
OR Orange
P Pink
PU Purple
GY Grey
SB Sky blue
Front foglights
Rear foglight
Direction indicators and hazard warning
Luggage compartment light and low specification interior light
Illumination
RH warning light
LH warning light
H28344
T.M.Marks

Diagram 5 : Exterior lighting continued and interior lighting - typical (1993-99)

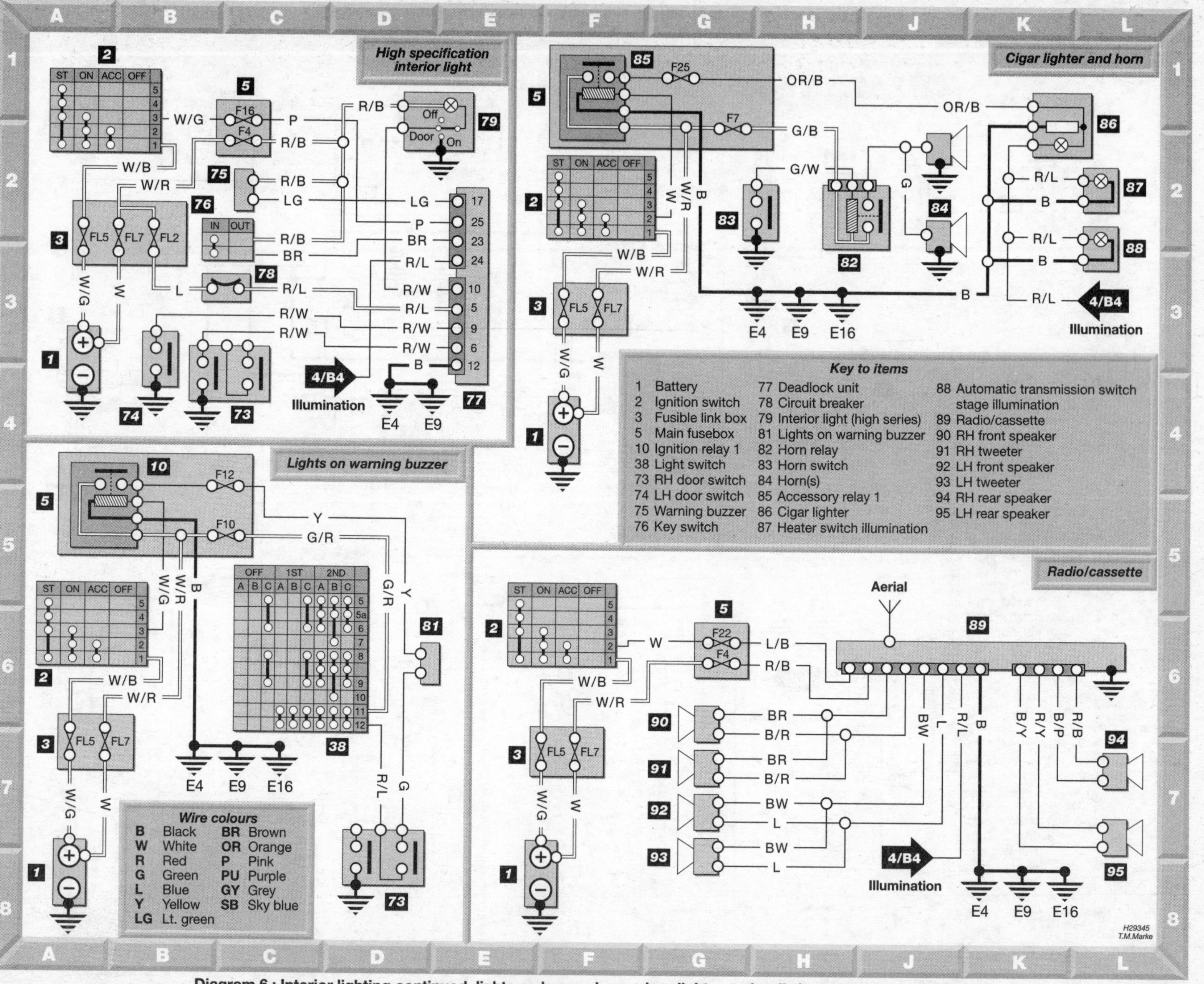

High specification interior light
Cigar lighter and horn
Lights on warning buzzer
Radio/cassette
Key to items
1 Battery
2 Ignition switch
3 Fusible link box
5 Main fusebox
10 Ignition relay 1
38 Light switch
73 RH door switch
74 LH door switch
75 Warning buzzer
76 Key switch
77 Deadlock unit
78 Circuit breaker
79 Interior light (high series)
81 Lights on warning buzzer
82 Horn relay
83 Horn switch
84 Horn(s)
85 Accessory relay 1
86 Cigar lighter
87 Heater switch illumination
88 Automatic transmission switch stage illumination
89 Radio/cassette
90 RH front speaker
91 RH tweeter
92 LH front speaker
93 LH tweeter
94 RH rear speaker
95 LH rear speaker
Wire colours
B Black
W White
R Red
G Green
L Blue
Y Yellow
LG Lt. green
BR Brown
OR Orange
P Pink
PU Purple
GY Grey
SB Sky blue
Illumination
Aerial
H29345 T.M.Marke

Diagram 6 : Interior lighting continued, lights on buzzer, horn, cigar lighter and radio/cassette - typical (1993-99)

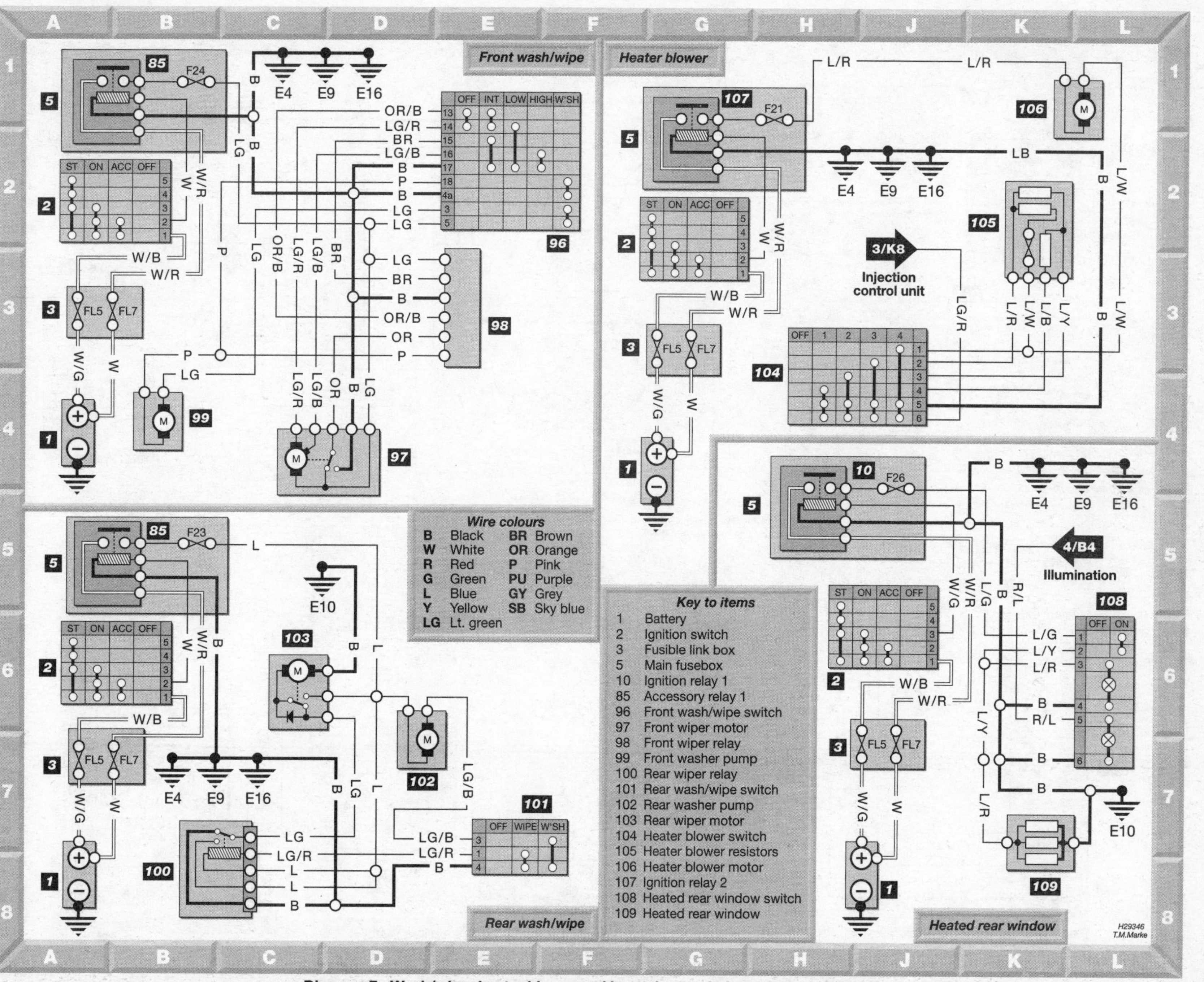
Front wash/wipe
Heater blower
Rear wash/wipe
Heated rear window
Injection control unit
3/K8
Illumination
4/B4
Wire colours
B Black
W White
R Red
G Green
L Blue
Y Yellow
LG Lt. green
BR Brown
OR Orange
P Pink
PU Purple
GY Grey
SB Sky blue
Key to items
1 Battery
2 Ignition switch
3 Fusible link box
5 Main fusebox
10 Ignition relay 1
85 Accessory relay 1
96 Front wash/wipe switch
97 Front wiper motor
98 Front wiper relay
99 Front washer pump
100 Rear wiper relay
101 Rear wash/wipe switch
102 Rear washer pump
103 Rear wiper motor
104 Heater blower switch
105 Heater blower resistors
106 Heater blower motor
107 Ignition relay 2
108 Heated rear window switch
109 Heated rear window
H29346
T.M.Marke

Diagram 7 : Wash/wipe, heater blower and heated rear window - typical (1993-99)

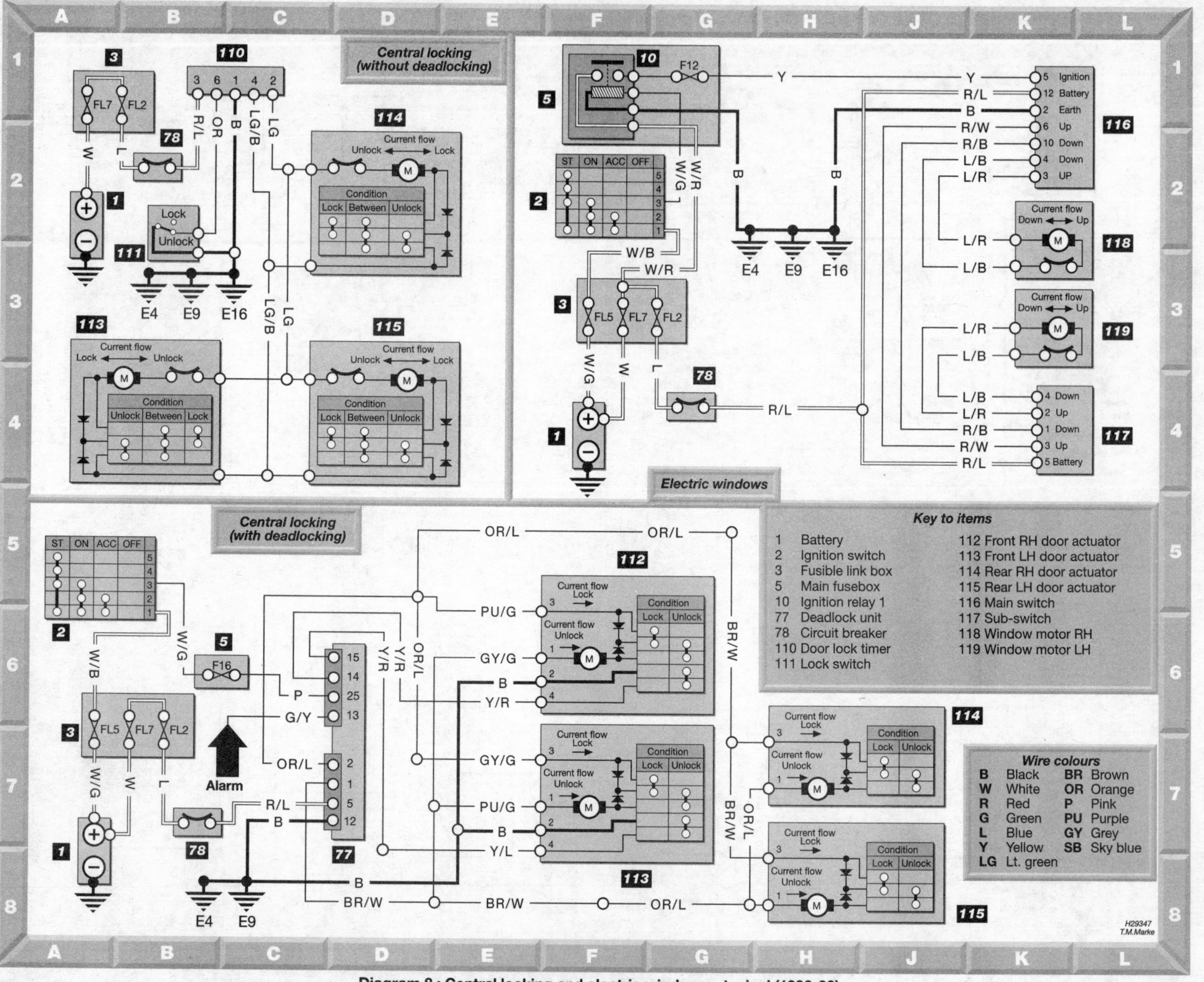

Central locking (without deadlocking)
Electric windows
Central locking (with deadlocking)
Key to items
1 Battery
2 Ignition switch
3 Fusible link box
5 Main fusebox
10 Ignition relay 1
77 Deadlock unit
78 Circuit breaker
110 Door lock timer
111 Lock switch
112 Front RH door actuator
113 Front LH door actuator
114 Rear RH door actuator
115 Rear LH door actuator
116 Main switch
117 Sub-switch
118 Window motor RH
119 Window motor LH
Wire colours
B Black
W White
R Red
G Green
L Blue
Y Yellow
LG Lt. green
BR Brown
OR Orange
P Pink
PU Purple
GY Grey
SB Sky blue
Alarm
H29347
T.M.Marke

Diagram 8 : Central locking and electric windows - typical (1993-99)

Nissan Micra 2000 to 2003

Diagram 1

Fuse table

Battery fuse holder

Fuses	*Rating*	*Circuit protected*
F1	15A	Air conditioning
F2	15A	RH headlights
F3	15A	LH headlights
F4	10A	Fog lights
F5	10A	Alternator
F6	-	Not used
F7	-	Not used
F8	-	Not used
F9	-	Not used
F10	-	Not used
F11	80A	Passenger fuse box
F12	40A	ABS
F13	30A	Ignition switch
F14	40A	ABS
F15	60A	Glow plugs
F16	-	Not used
F17	30A	Central locking
F18	30A	Electric windows
F19	30A	Engine cooling fans

Passenger fuse box

Fuses	*Rating*	*Circuit protected*
F1	20A	Air conditioning
F2	-	Not used
F3	20A	Heated rear window
F4	10A	Horn
F5	15A	Fog lights
F6	10A	Air conditioning
F7	10A	Central locking
F8	10A	Electric windows, reversing lights, instrument panel
F9	15A	ABS, rear wiper
F10	15A	Radio
F11	10A	Direction indicators
F12	10A	ABS
F13	15A	Cigarette lighter
F14	10A	ABS, brake lights
F15	10A	Direction indicators
F16	10A	Automatic transmission
F17	15A	Fuel pump
F18	10A	Heated seats
F19	20A	Front wiper relay
F20	10A	Alarm, engine control unit
F21	10A	Engine control unit
F22	10A	Airbag
F23	10A	Wash/wipe
F24	10A	Radio, central locking
F25	10A	Alarm, engine control unit
F26	10A	Engine control unit
F27	-	Not used
F28	-	Not used
F29	15A	Headlight washer

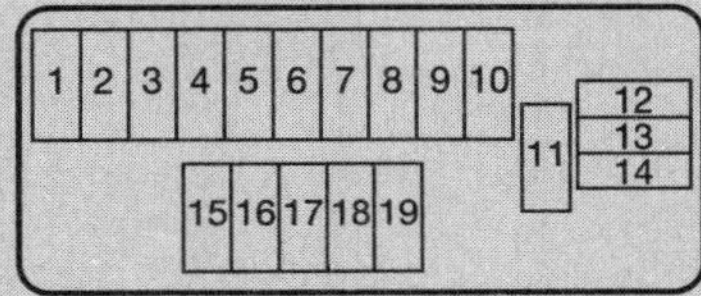

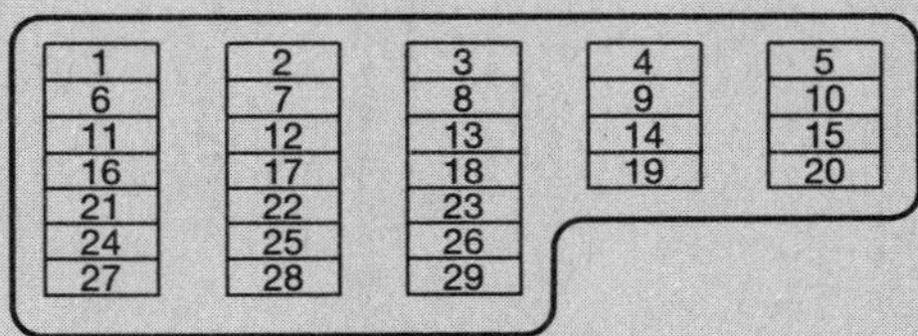

Key to circuits

Diagram 1	Information for wiring diagrams
Diagram 2	Starting and charging, airbag, heated rear window, horns and radio
Diagram 3	Cigarette lighter, ABS and central locking
Diagram 4	Electric windows, wash/wipe and air conditioning
Diagram 5	Heater blower, front fog lights, reverse lights, direction indicators, headlights, tail lights and licence plate lights
Diagram 6	Stop lights, rear fog light, interior lights, engine cooling and headlight levelling
Diagram 7	Instrument panel

Earth points

E1	Battery earth
E2	LH dashboard
E3	RH dashboard
E4	RH wing
E5	Tailgate
E6	ABS earth
E7	Battery fuse box
E8	Passenger fuse box
E9	RH tail light
E10	Center of the tailgate
E11	RH ABS sensor
E12	RH headlight

Key to symbols

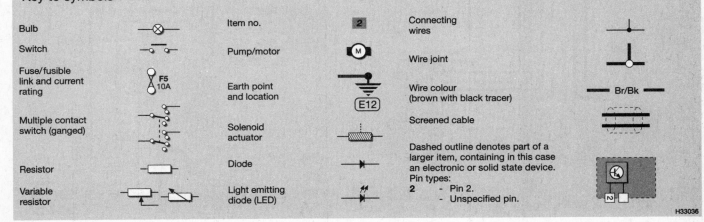

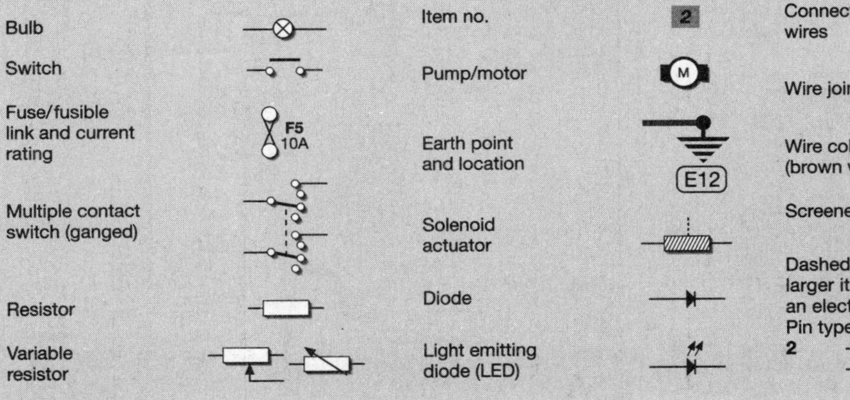

Connecting wires

Wire joint

Wire colour (brown with black tracer)

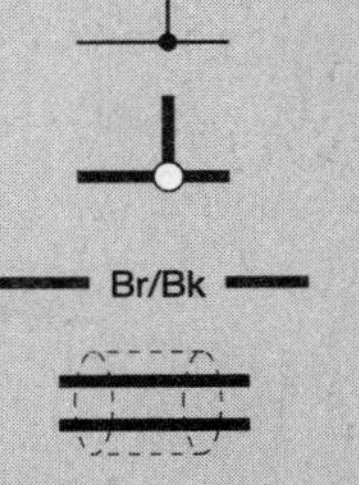

Screened cable

Dashed outline denotes part of a larger item, containing in this case an electronic or solid state device.
Pin types:
2 - Pin 2.
- Unspecified pin.

H33036

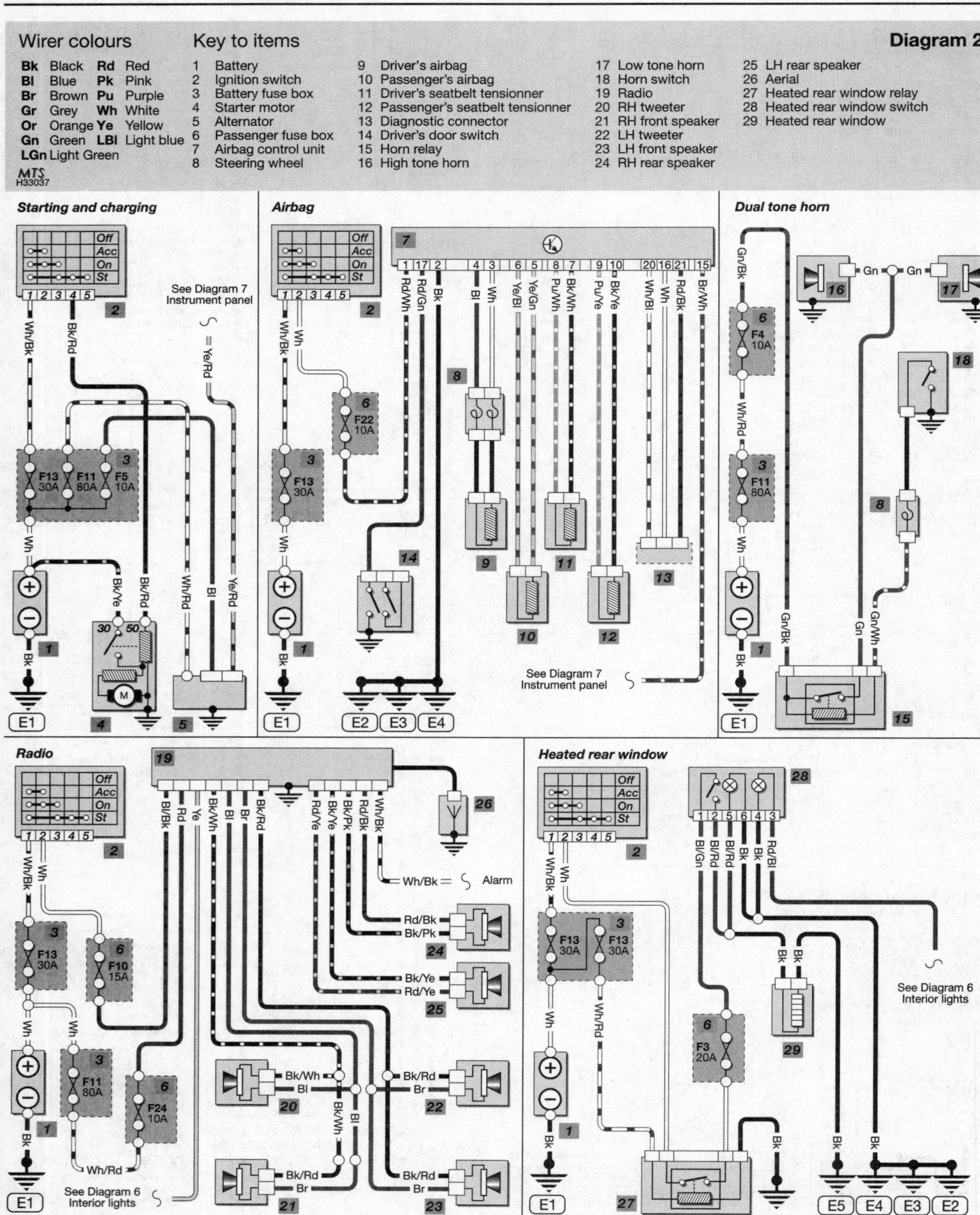
Wire colours
Bk Black
Bl Blue
Br Brown
Gr Grey
Or Orange
Gn Green
LGn Light Green
Rd Red
Pk Pink
Pu Purple
Wh White
Ye Yellow
LBl Light blue
MTS H33037
Key to items
1 Battery
2 Ignition switch
3 Battery fuse box
4 Starter motor
5 Alternator
6 Passenger fuse box
7 Airbag control unit
8 Steering wheel
9 Driver's airbag
10 Passenger's airbag
11 Driver's seatbelt tensionner
12 Passenger's seatbelt tensionner
13 Diagnostic connector
14 Driver's door switch
15 Horn relay
16 High tone horn
17 Low tone horn
18 Horn switch
19 Radio
20 RH tweeter
21 RH front speaker
22 LH tweeter
23 LH front speaker
24 RH rear speaker
25 LH rear speaker
26 Aerial
27 Heated rear window relay
28 Heated rear window switch
29 Heated rear window
Diagram 2
Starting and charging
Airbag
Dual tone horn
Radio
Heated rear window
Off
Acc
On
St
See Diagram 7 Instrument panel
See Diagram 6 Interior lights
Alarm
F13 30A
F11 80A
F5 10A
F22 10A
F4 10A
F10 15A
F24 10A
F3 20A
E1
E2
E3
E4
E5

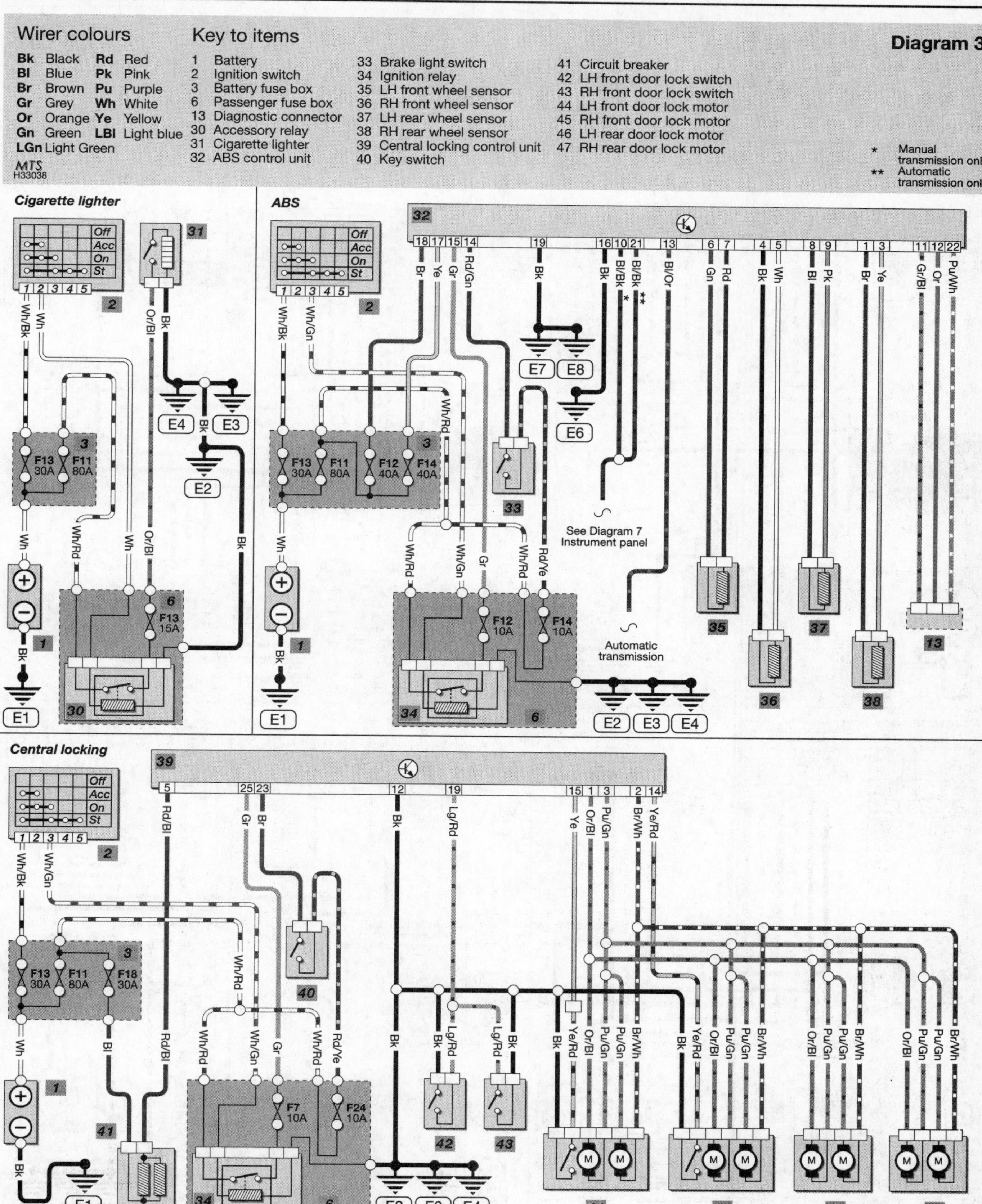
Wirer colours
Bk Black
Bl Blue
Br Brown
Gr Grey
Or Orange
Gn Green
LGn Light Green
Rd Red
Pk Pink
Pu Purple
Wh White
Ye Yellow
LBl Light blue
MTS
H33038
Key to items
1 Battery
2 Ignition switch
3 Battery fuse box
6 Passenger fuse box
13 Diagnostic connector
30 Accessory relay
31 Cigarette lighter
32 ABS control unit
33 Brake light switch
34 Ignition relay
35 LH front wheel sensor
36 RH front wheel sensor
37 LH rear wheel sensor
38 RH rear wheel sensor
39 Central locking control unit
40 Key switch
41 Circuit breaker
42 LH front door lock switch
43 RH front door lock switch
44 LH front door lock motor
45 RH front door lock motor
46 LH rear door lock motor
47 RH rear door lock motor
Diagram 3
* Manual transmission only
** Automatic transmission only
Cigarette lighter
ABS
Central locking
Off
Acc
On
St
F13 30A
F11 80A
F12 40A
F14 40A
F18 30A
F13 15A
F12 10A
F14 10A
F7 10A
F24 10A
E1
E2
E3
E4
E6
E7
E8
See Diagram 7 Instrument panel
Automatic transmission

Diagram 4

Wirer colours

Bk	Black	Rd	Red
Bl	Blue	Pk	Pink
Br	Brown	Pu	Purple
Gr	Grey	Wh	White
Or	Orange	Ye	Yellow
Gn	Green	LBl	Light blue
LGn	Light Green		

MTS
H33039

Key to items

1 Battery
2 Ignition switch
3 Battery fuse box
6 Passenger fuse box
30 Accessory relay
34 Ignition relay
48 RH electric window switch
49 RH electric window motor
50 LH electric window switch
51 LH electric window motor
52 Front wash/wipe switch
53 Wiper amplifier
54 Front washer motor
55 Front wiper motor
56 Front wiper relay
57 Rear wiper switch
58 Rear washer motor
59 Rear wiper motor
60 Rear wiper relay
61 Blower relay
62 Air conditioning relay
63 Blower motor
64 Air conditioning switch
65 Dual pressure switch
66 Fan switch
67 Resistor pack
68 Air conditioning compressor
69 Cooling fan motor

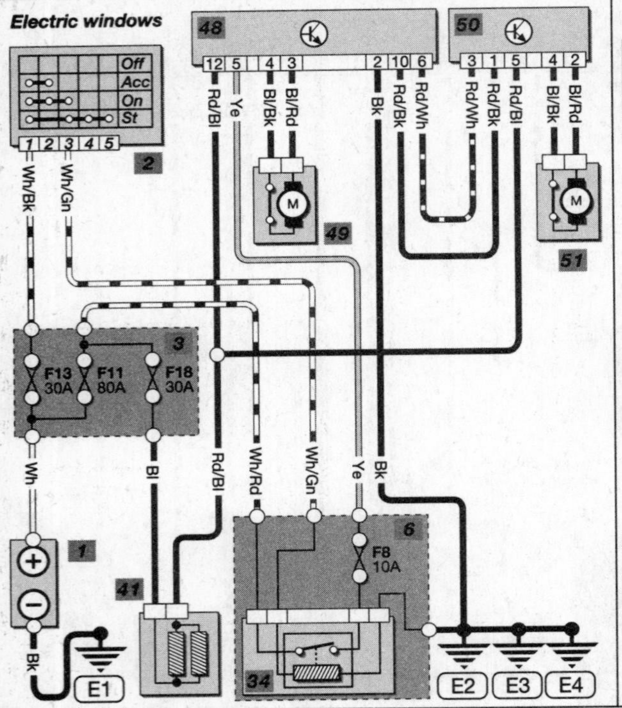

Electric windows

F13 30A
F11 80A
F18 30A
F8 10A
E1 E2 E3 E4

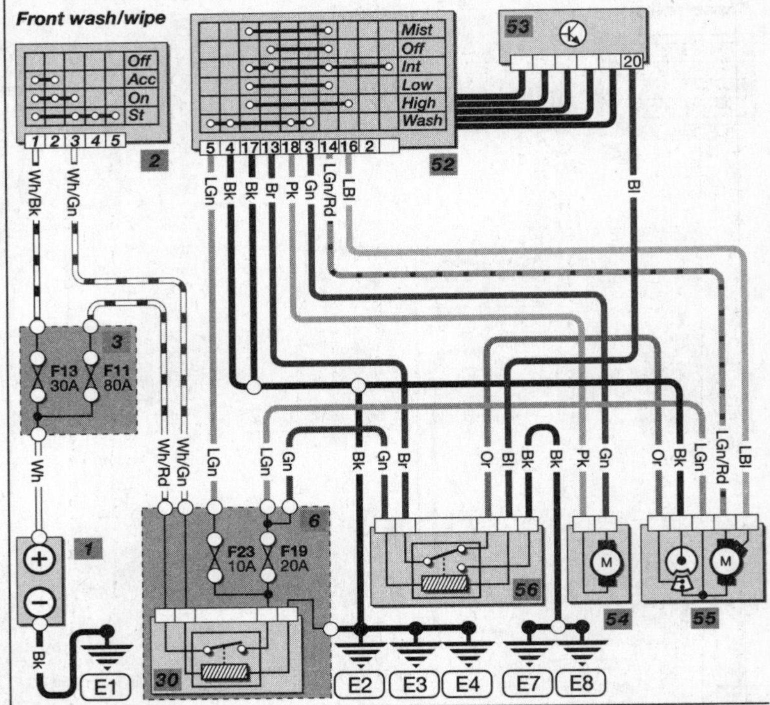

Front wash/wipe

Mist Off Int Low High Wash
F13 30A
F11 80A
F23 10A
F19 20A
E1 E2 E3 E4 E7 E8

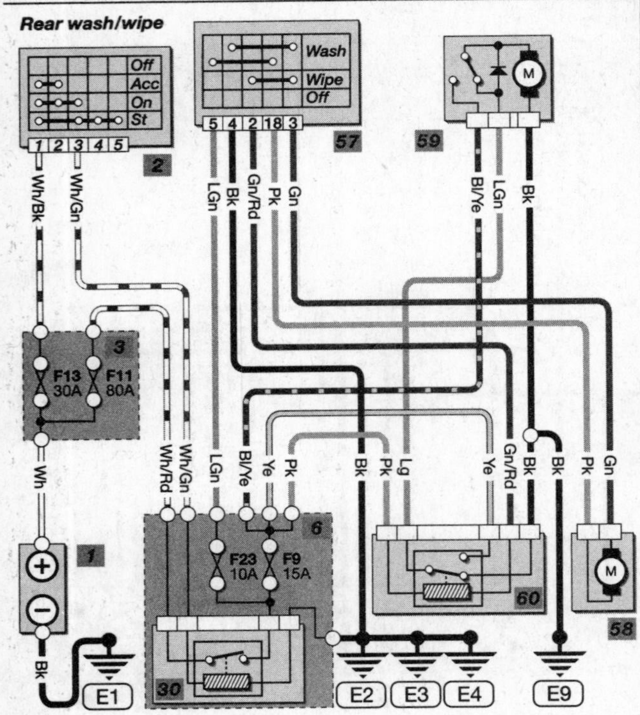

Rear wash/wipe

Wash Wipe Off
F13 30A
F11 80A
F23 10A
F9 15A
E1 E2 E3 E4 E9

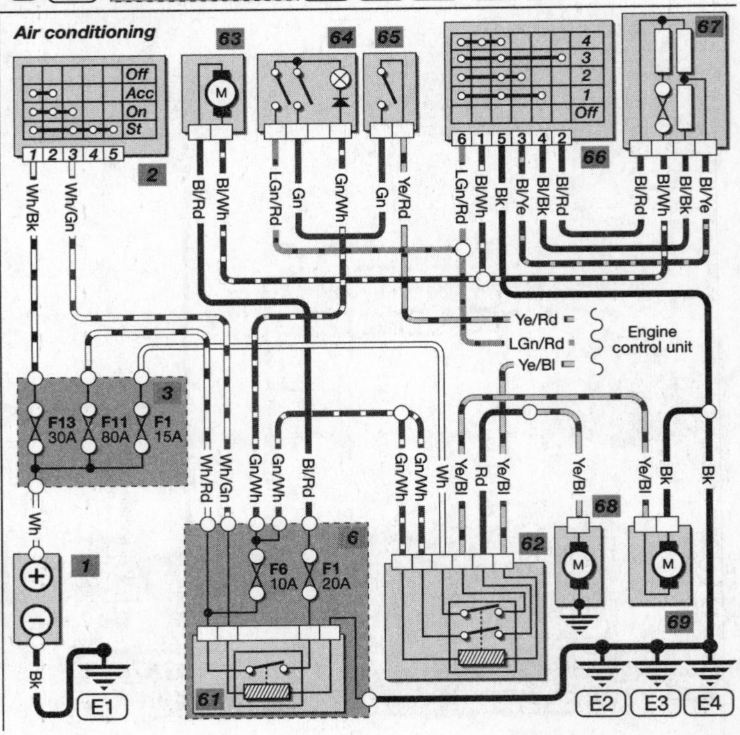

Air conditioning

F13 30A
F11 80A
F1 15A
F6 10A
F1 20A
Ye/Rd
LGn/Rd
Ye/Bl
Engine control unit
E1 E2 E3 E4

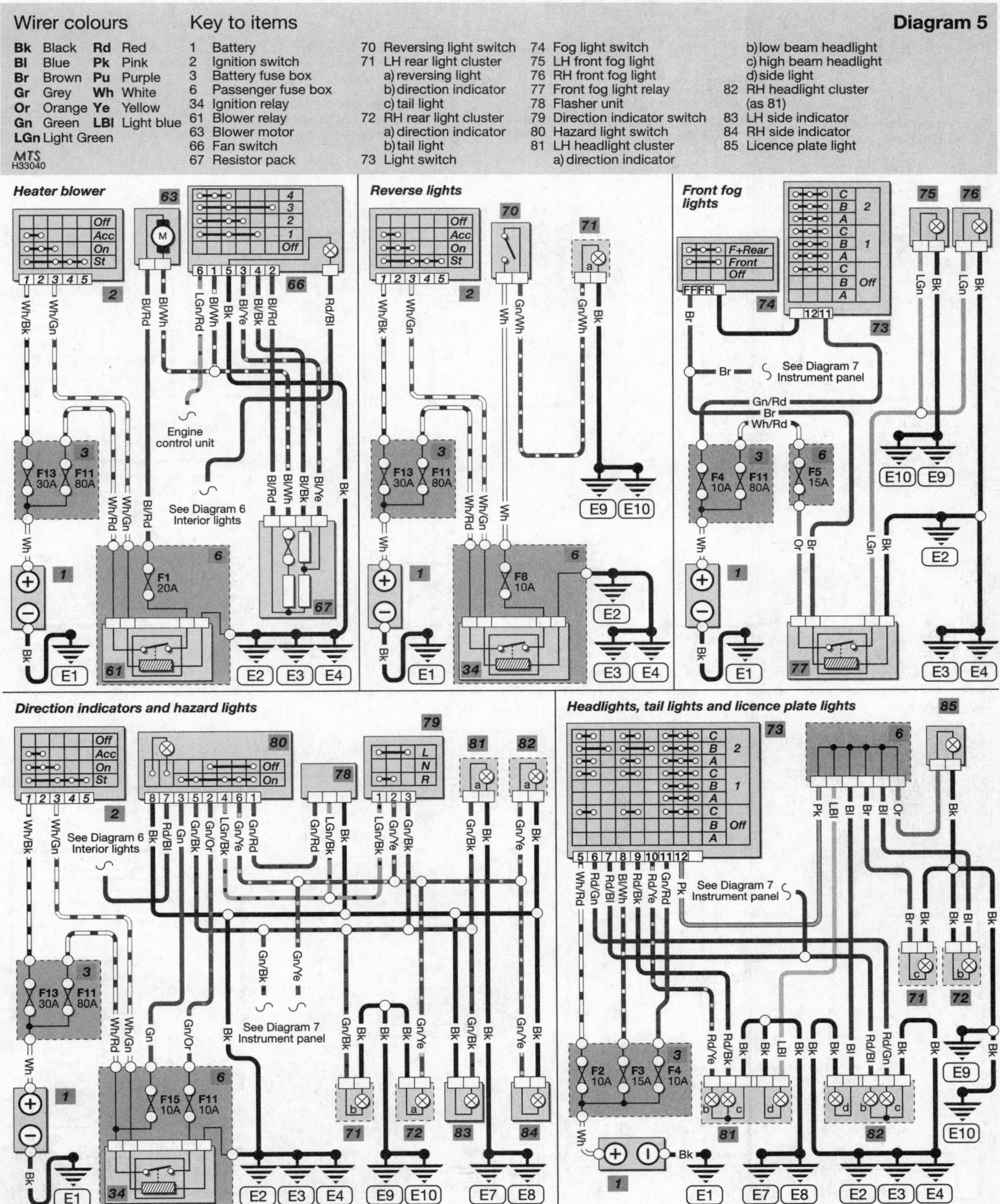

Wirer colours
Bk Black
Bl Blue
Br Brown
Gr Grey
Or Orange
Gn Green
LGn Light Green
Rd Red
Pk Pink
Pu Purple
Wh White
Ye Yellow
LBl Light blue
MTS H33040
Key to items
1 Battery
2 Ignition switch
3 Battery fuse box
6 Passenger fuse box
34 Ignition relay
61 Blower relay
63 Blower motor
66 Fan switch
67 Resistor pack
70 Reversing light switch
71 LH rear light cluster
a) reversing light
b) direction indicator
c) tail light
72 RH rear light cluster
a) direction indicator
b) tail light
73 Light switch
74 Fog light switch
75 LH front fog light
76 RH front fog light
77 Front fog light relay
78 Flasher unit
79 Direction indicator switch
80 Hazard light switch
81 LH headlight cluster
a) direction indicator
b) low beam headlight
c) high beam headlight
d) side light
82 RH headlight cluster (as 81)
83 LH side indicator
84 RH side indicator
85 Licence plate light
Diagram 5
Heater blower
Engine control unit
See Diagram 6 Interior lights
Reverse lights
Front fog lights
See Diagram 7 Instrument panel
Direction indicators and hazard lights
See Diagram 6 Interior lights
See Diagram 7 Instrument panel
Headlights, tail lights and licence plate lights
See Diagram 7 Instrument panel

Diagram 6

Wirer colours

Bk	Black	**Rd**	Red
Bl	Blue	**Pk**	Pink
Br	Brown	**Pu**	Purple
Gr	Grey	**Wh**	White
Or	Orange	**Ye**	Yellow
Gn	Green	**LBl**	Light blue
LGn	Light Green		

Key to items

1 Battery
2 Ignition switch
3 Battery fuse box
6 Passenger fuse box
14 Driver's door switch
33 Brake light switch
34 Ignition relay
71 LH rear light cluster
d) stop light
72 RH rear light cluster
c) stop light
d) fog light
73 Light switch
74 Fog light switch
86 High level brake light
87 LH headlight levelling motor
88 RH headlight levelling motor
89 Headlight level switch
90 Luggage light
91 Luggage light switch
92 Interior light
93 Passenger's door switch
94 Diode
95 Engine fan relay 1
96 Engine fan relay 2
97 Engine fan
98 Temperature switch
99 Engine fan resistor

MTS
H33041

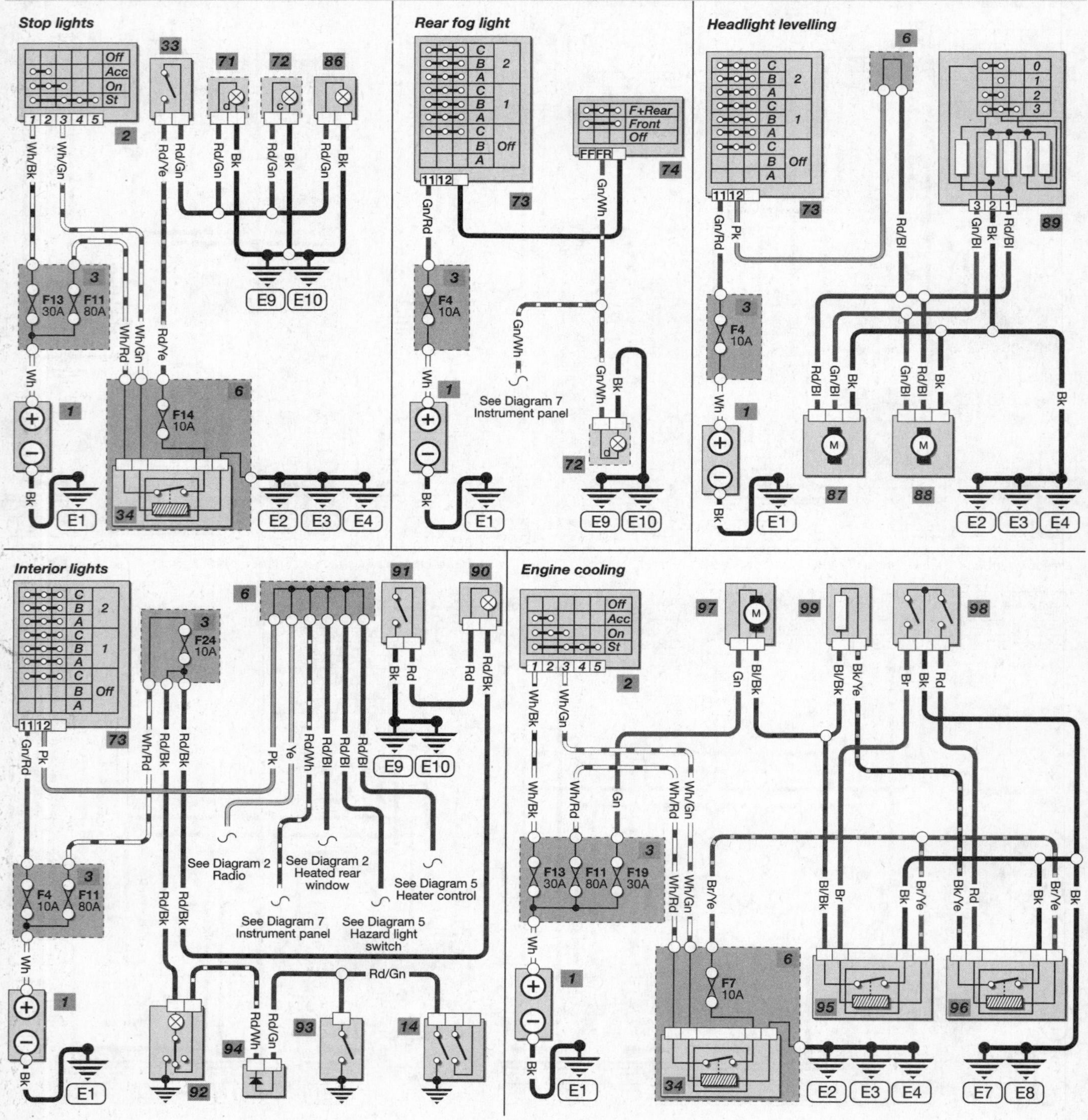

Stop lights

Rear fog light

See Diagram 7 Instrument panel

Headlight levelling

Interior lights

See Diagram 2 Radio

See Diagram 2 Heated rear window

See Diagram 5 Heater control

See Diagram 7 Instrument panel

See Diagram 5 Hazard light switch

Engine cooling

Diagram 7

Wirer colours

Bk	Black	**Rd**	Red
Bl	Blue	**Pk**	Pink
Br	Brown	**Pu**	Purple
Gr	Grey	**Wh**	White
Or	Orange	**Ye**	Yellow
Gn	Green		
LGn	Light Green		
LBl	Light blue		

MTS
H33042

Key to items

1 Battery
2 Ignition switch
3 Battery fuse box
6 Passenger fuse box
14 Driver's door switch
34 Ignition relay
100 Instrument panel
- a) rear fog light warning light
- b) LH indicator warning light
- c) RH indicator warning light
- d) high beam warning light
- e) front foglight relay light
- f) instrument illumination
- g) combination meter - speedometer, fuel guage, tachometer, water temperature guage
- h) low fuel warning light
- i) brake warning light
- j) engine warning light
- k) charge warning light
- l) low oil warning light
- m) ABS warning light

101 Water temperature sensor
102 Fuel level sensor
103 Handbrake switch
104 Brake fluid level switch
105 Oil level switch
106 Vehicle speed sensor

Instrument panel

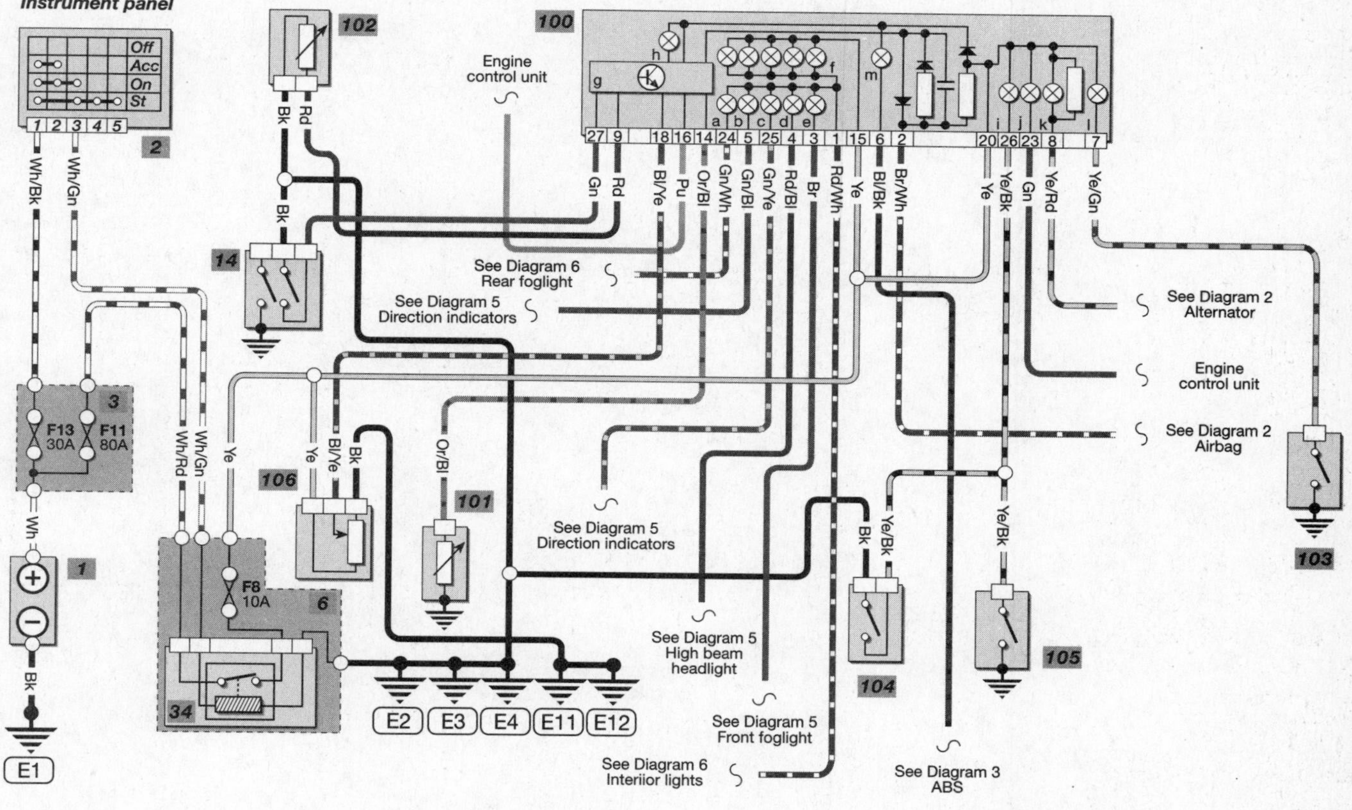

Dimensions and weights

Note: *All figures are approximate, and may vary according to model. Refer to manufacturer's data for exact figures.*

Dimensions

Overall length:
- Models up to 1998 . . . . 3695 mm
- 1998 to 2000 . . . . 3720 mm
- 2000 on . . . . 3746 mm

Overall width:
- Models up to 2000 . . . . 1585 mm
- 2000 on . . . . 1595 mm

Overall height (unladen):
- Models up to 2000 . . . . 1430 mm
- 2000 on . . . . 1440 mm

Track:
- Front . . . . 1360 mm
- Rear . . . . 1325 mm

Wheelbase . . . . 2360 mm

Weights

Kerb weight . . . . 775 to 870 kg*

Towing weight:
- 1.0 litre models (with brake):
  - Manual transmission models . . . . 600 kg
  - Automatic transmission models . . . . 450 kg
- 1.3 and 1.4 litre models:
  - Manual transmission models . . . . 750 kg
  - Automatic transmission models . . . . 650 kg

Maximum roof rack load . . . . 75 kg

* *Depending on model and specification*

Conversion factors

Length (distance)

Inches (in)	x 25.4	= Millimetres (mm)	x 0.0394	= Inches (in)
Feet (ft)	x 0.305	= Metres (m)	x 3.281	= Feet (ft)
Miles	x 1.609	= Kilometres (km)	x 0.621	= Miles

Volume (capacity)

Cubic inches (cu in; in^3)	x 16.387	= Cubic centimetres (cc; cm^3)	x 0.061	= Cubic inches (cu in; in^3)
Imperial pints (Imp pt)	x 0.568	= Litres (l)	x 1.76	= Imperial pints (Imp pt)
Imperial quarts (Imp qt)	x 1.137	= Litres (l)	x 0.88	= Imperial quarts (Imp qt)
Imperial quarts (Imp qt)	x 1.201	= US quarts (US qt)	x 0.833	= Imperial quarts (Imp qt)
US quarts (US qt)	x 0.946	= Litres (l)	x 1.057	= US quarts (US qt)
Imperial gallons (Imp gal)	x 4.546	= Litres (l)	x 0.22	= Imperial gallons (Imp gal)
Imperial gallons (Imp gal)	x 1.201	= US gallons (US gal)	x 0.833	= Imperial gallons (Imp gal)
US gallons (US gal)	x 3.785	= Litres (l)	x 0.264	= US gallons (US gal)

Mass (weight)

Ounces (oz)	x 28.35	= Grams (g)	x 0.035	= Ounces (oz)
Pounds (lb)	x 0.454	= Kilograms (kg)	x 2.205	= Pounds (lb)

Force

Ounces-force (ozf; oz)	x 0.278	= Newtons (N)	x 3.6	= Ounces-force (ozf; oz)
Pounds-force (lbf; lb)	x 4.448	= Newtons (N)	x 0.225	= Pounds-force (lbf; lb)
Newtons (N)	x 0.1	= Kilograms-force (kgf; kg)	x 9.81	= Newtons (N)

Pressure

Pounds-force per square inch (psi; lbf/in^2; lb/in^2)	x 0.070	= Kilograms-force per square centimetre (kgf/cm^2; kg/cm^2)	x 14.223	= Pounds-force per square inch (psi; lbf/in^2; lb/in^2)
Pounds-force per square inch (psi; lbf/in^2; lb/in^2)	x 0.068	= Atmospheres (atm)	x 14.696	= Pounds-force per square inch (psi; lbf/in^2; lb/in^2)
Pounds-force per square inch (psi; lbf/in^2; lb/in^2)	x 0.069	= Bars	x 14.5	= Pounds-force per square inch (psi; lbf/in^2; lb/in^2)
Pounds-force per square inch (psi; lbf/in^2; lb/in^2)	x 6.895	= Kilopascals (kPa)	x 0.145	= Pounds-force per square inch (psi; lbf/in^2; lb/in^2)
Kilopascals (kPa)	x 0.01	= Kilograms-force per square centimetre (kgf/cm^2; kg/cm^2)	x 98.1	= Kilopascals (kPa)
Millibar (mbar)	x 100	= Pascals (Pa)	x 0.01	= Millibar (mbar)
Millibar (mbar)	x 0.0145	= Pounds-force per square inch (psi; lbf/in^2; lb/in^2)	x 68.947	= Millibar (mbar)
Millibar (mbar)	x 0.75	= Millimetres of mercury (mmHg)	x 1.333	= Millibar (mbar)
Millibar (mbar)	x 0.401	= Inches of water (inH$_2$O)	x 2.491	= Millibar (mbar)
Millimetres of mercury (mmHg)	x 0.535	= Inches of water (inH$_2$O)	x 1.868	= Millimetres of mercury (mmHg)
Inches of water (inH$_2$O)	x 0.036	= Pounds-force per square inch (psi; lbf/in^2; lb/in^2)	x 27.68	= Inches of water (inH$_2$O)

Torque (moment of force)

Pounds-force inches (lbf in; lb in)	x 1.152	= Kilograms-force centimetre (kgf cm; kg cm)	x 0.868	= Pounds-force inches (lbf in; lb in)
Pounds-force inches (lbf in; lb in)	x 0.113	= Newton metres (Nm)	x 8.85	= Pounds-force inches (lbf in; lb in)
Pounds-force inches (lbf in; lb in)	x 0.083	= Pounds-force feet (lbf ft; lb ft)	x 12	= Pounds-force inches (lbf in; lb in)
Pounds-force feet (lbf ft; lb ft)	x 0.138	= Kilograms-force metres (kgf m; kg m)	x 7.233	= Pounds-force feet (lbf ft; lb ft)
Pounds-force feet (lbf ft; lb ft)	x 1.356	= Newton metres (Nm)	x 0.738	= Pounds-force feet (lbf ft; lb ft)
Newton metres (Nm)	x 0.102	= Kilograms-force metres (kgf m; kg m)	x 9.804	= Newton metres (Nm)

Power

Horsepower (hp)	x 745.7	= Watts (W)	x 0.0013	= Horsepower (hp)

Velocity (speed)

Miles per hour (miles/hr; mph)	x 1.609	= Kilometres per hour (km/hr; kph)	x 0.621	= Miles per hour (miles/hr; mph)

Fuel consumption*

Miles per gallon (mpg)	x 0.354	= Kilometres per litre (km/l)	x 2.825	= Miles per gallon (mpg)

Temperature

Degrees Fahrenheit = (°C x 1.8) + 32

Degrees Celsius (Degrees Centigrade; °C) = (°F - 32) x 0.56

** It is common practice to convert from miles per gallon (mpg) to litres/100 kilometres (l/100km), where mpg x l/100 km = 282*

Spare parts are available from many sources, including maker's appointed garages, accessory shops, and motor factors. To be sure of obtaining the correct parts, it may sometimes be necessary to quote the vehicle identification number. If possible, it can also be useful to take the old parts along for positive identification. Items such as starter motors and alternators may be available under a service exchange scheme - any parts returned should always be clean.

Our advice regarding spare part sources is as follows.

Officially-appointed garages

This is the best source of parts which are peculiar to your car, and are not otherwise generally available (eg badges, interior trim, certain body panels, etc). It is also the only place at which you should buy parts if the vehicle is still under warranty.

Accessory shops

These are very good places to buy materials and components needed for the maintenance of your car (oil, air and fuel filters, spark plugs, light bulbs, drivebelts, oils and greases, brake pads, touch-up paint, etc). Parts like this sold by a reputable shop are of the same standard as those used by the car manufacturer.

Motor factors

Good factors will stock all the more important components which wear out comparatively quickly and can sometimes supply individual components needed for the overhaul of a larger assembly. They may also handle work such as cylinder block reboring, crankshaft regrinding and balancing, etc.

Tyre and exhaust specialists

These outlets may be independent or members of a local or national chain. They frequently offer competitive prices when compared with a main dealer or local garage, but it will pay to obtain several quotes before making a decision. Also ask what 'extras' may be added to the quote - for instance, fitting a new valve and balancing the wheel are both often charged on top of the price of a new tyre.

Other sources

Beware of parts or materials obtained from market stalls, car boot sales or similar outlets. Such items are not invariably sub-standard, but there is little chance of compensation if they do prove unsatisfactory. In the case of safety-critical components such as brake pads there is the risk not only of financial loss but also of an accident causing injury or death.

Second-hand components or assemblies obtained from a car breaker can be a good buy in some circumstances, but this sort of purchase is best made by the experienced DIY mechanic.

Vehicle identification

Modifications are a continuing and unpublicised process in vehicle manufacture, quite apart from major model changes. Spare parts lists are compiled upon a numerical basis, the individual vehicle identification numbers being essential to correct identification of the component concerned.

When ordering spare parts, always give as much information as possible. Quote the car model, year of manufacture, body and engine numbers, as appropriate.

The Vehicle Identification Number (VIN) plate is riveted to the right-hand side of the engine compartment bulkhead, and can be viewed once the bonnet is open. The plate carries the VIN, vehicle weight information, and paint and trim colour codes. The vehicle identification number is also stamped into the bulkhead by the side of the plate **(see illustrations)**.

The *Engine number* is stamped on a machined surface on the front side of the cylinder block, at the flywheel end. The first part of the engine number gives the engine code - eg "CG10" **(see illustration)**.

The *Transmission number* is located on top of the bellhousing.

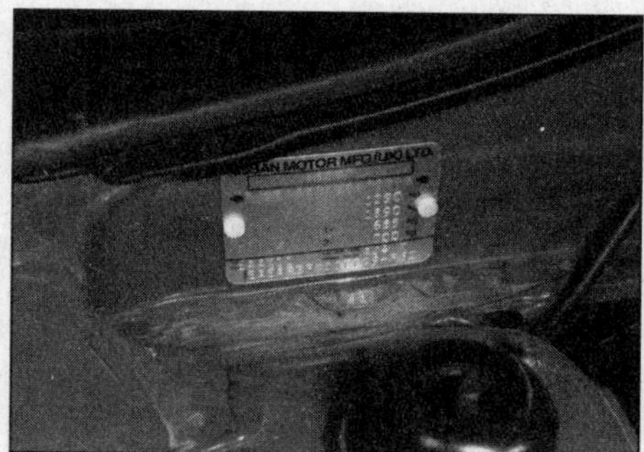

The vehicle identification (VIN) plate is riveted to the right-hand side of the engine compartment bulkhead

The VIN number is also stamped into the bulkhead

The engine number is stamped on the front of the cylinder block

Whenever servicing, repair or overhaul work is carried out on the car or its components, observe the following procedures and instructions. This will assist in carrying out the operation efficiently and to a professional standard of workmanship.

Joint mating faces and gaskets

When separating components at their mating faces, never insert screwdrivers or similar implements into the joint between the faces in order to prise them apart. This can cause severe damage which results in oil leaks, coolant leaks, etc upon reassembly. Separation is usually achieved by tapping along the joint with a soft-faced hammer in order to break the seal. However, note that this method may not be suitable where dowels are used for component location.

Where a gasket is used between the mating faces of two components, a new one must be fitted on reassembly; fit it dry unless otherwise stated in the repair procedure. Make sure that the mating faces are clean and dry, with all traces of old gasket removed. When cleaning a joint face, use a tool which is unlikely to score or damage the face, and remove any burrs or nicks with an oilstone or fine file.

Make sure that tapped holes are cleaned with a pipe cleaner, and keep them free of jointing compound, if this is being used, unless specifically instructed otherwise.

Ensure that all orifices, channels or pipes are clear, and blow through them, preferably using compressed air.

Oil seals

Oil seals can be removed by levering them out with a wide flat-bladed screwdriver or similar implement. Alternatively, a number of self-tapping screws may be screwed into the seal, and these used as a purchase for pliers or some similar device in order to pull the seal free.

Whenever an oil seal is removed from its working location, either individually or as part of an assembly, it should be renewed.

The very fine sealing lip of the seal is easily damaged, and will not seal if the surface it contacts is not completely clean and free from scratches, nicks or grooves. If the original sealing surface of the component cannot be restored, and the manufacturer has not made provision for slight relocation of the seal relative to the sealing surface, the component should be renewed.

Protect the lips of the seal from any surface which may damage them in the course of fitting. Use tape or a conical sleeve where possible. Lubricate the seal lips with oil before fitting and, on dual-lipped seals, fill the space between the lips with grease.

Unless otherwise stated, oil seals must be fitted with their sealing lips toward the lubricant to be sealed.

Use a tubular drift or block of wood of the appropriate size to install the seal and, if the seal housing is shouldered, drive the seal down to the shoulder. If the seal housing is unshouldered, the seal should be fitted with its face flush with the housing top face (unless otherwise instructed).

Screw threads and fastenings

Seized nuts, bolts and screws are quite a common occurrence where corrosion has set in, and the use of penetrating oil or releasing fluid will often overcome this problem if the offending item is soaked for a while before attempting to release it. The use of an impact driver may also provide a means of releasing such stubborn fastening devices, when used in conjunction with the appropriate screwdriver bit or socket. If none of these methods works, it may be necessary to resort to the careful application of heat, or the use of a hacksaw or nut splitter device.

Studs are usually removed by locking two nuts together on the threaded part, and then using a spanner on the lower nut to unscrew the stud. Studs or bolts which have broken off below the surface of the component in which they are mounted can sometimes be removed using a stud extractor. Always ensure that a blind tapped hole is completely free from oil, grease, water or other fluid before installing the bolt or stud. Failure to do this could cause the housing to crack due to the hydraulic action of the bolt or stud as it is screwed in.

When tightening a castellated nut to accept a split pin, tighten the nut to the specified torque, where applicable, and then tighten further to the next split pin hole. Never slacken the nut to align the split pin hole, unless stated in the repair procedure.

When checking or retightening a nut or bolt to a specified torque setting, slacken the nut or bolt by a quarter of a turn, and then retighten to the specified setting. However, this should not be attempted where angular tightening has been used.

For some screw fastenings, notably cylinder head bolts or nuts, torque wrench settings are no longer specified for the latter stages of tightening, "angle-tightening" being called up instead. Typically, a fairly low torque wrench setting will be applied to the bolts/nuts in the correct sequence, followed by one or more stages of tightening through specified angles.

Locknuts, locktabs and washers

Any fastening which will rotate against a component or housing during tightening should always have a washer between it and the relevant component or housing.

Spring or split washers should always be renewed when they are used to lock a critical component such as a big-end bearing retaining bolt or nut. Locktabs which are folded over to retain a nut or bolt should always be renewed.

Self-locking nuts can be re-used in non-critical areas, providing resistance can be felt when the locking portion passes over the bolt or stud thread. However, it should be noted that self-locking stiffnuts tend to lose their effectiveness after long periods of use, and should then be renewed as a matter of course.

Split pins must always be replaced with new ones of the correct size for the hole.

When thread-locking compound is found on the threads of a fastener which is to be re-used, it should be cleaned off with a wire brush and solvent, and fresh compound applied on reassembly.

Special tools

Some repair procedures in this manual entail the use of special tools such as a press, two or three-legged pullers, spring compressors, etc. Wherever possible, suitable readily-available alternatives to the manufacturer's special tools are described, and are shown in use. In some instances, where no alternative is possible, it has been necessary to resort to the use of a manufacturer's tool, and this has been done for reasons of safety as well as the efficient completion of the repair operation. Unless you are highly-skilled and have a thorough understanding of the procedures described, never attempt to bypass the use of any special tool when the procedure described specifies its use. Not only is there a very great risk of personal injury, but expensive damage could be caused to the components involved.

Environmental considerations

When disposing of used engine oil, brake fluid, antifreeze, etc, give due consideration to any detrimental environmental effects. Do not, for instance, pour any of the above liquids down drains into the general sewage system, or onto the ground to soak away. Many local council refuse tips provide a facility for waste oil disposal, as do some garages. If none of these facilities are available, consult your local Environmental Health Department, or the National Rivers Authority, for further advice.

With the universal tightening-up of legislation regarding the emission of environmentally-harmful substances from motor vehicles, most vehicles have tamperproof devices fitted to the main adjustment points of the fuel system. These devices are primarily designed to prevent unqualified persons from adjusting the fuel/air mixture, with the chance of a consequent increase in toxic emissions. If such devices are found during servicing or overhaul, they should, wherever possible, be renewed or refitted in accordance with the manufacturer's requirements or current legislation.

Note: It is antisocial and illegal to dump oil down the drain. To find the location of your local oil recycling bank, call this number free.

Jacking and vehicle support

The jack supplied with the vehicle tool kit should only be used for changing the roadwheels - see *"Wheel changing"* at the front of this manual. When carrying out any other kind of work, raise the vehicle using a hydraulic (or "trolley") jack, and always supplement the jack with axle stands positioned under the vehicle jacking points **(see illustration)**.

When using a hydraulic jack or axle stands, always position the jack head or axle stand head under one of the relevant jacking points (note that the jacking points for use with the vehicle jack are different from those for a hydraulic trolley jack). NISSAN recommend the use of adapters when supporting the vehicle with axle stands - the adapters are grooved, and fit over the sill edge to prevent the vehicle weight damaging the sill **(see illustration)**. **Do not** jack the vehicle under the sump or any of the steering or suspension components other than those indicated.

Never work under, around, or near a raised vehicle, unless it is adequately supported on stands.

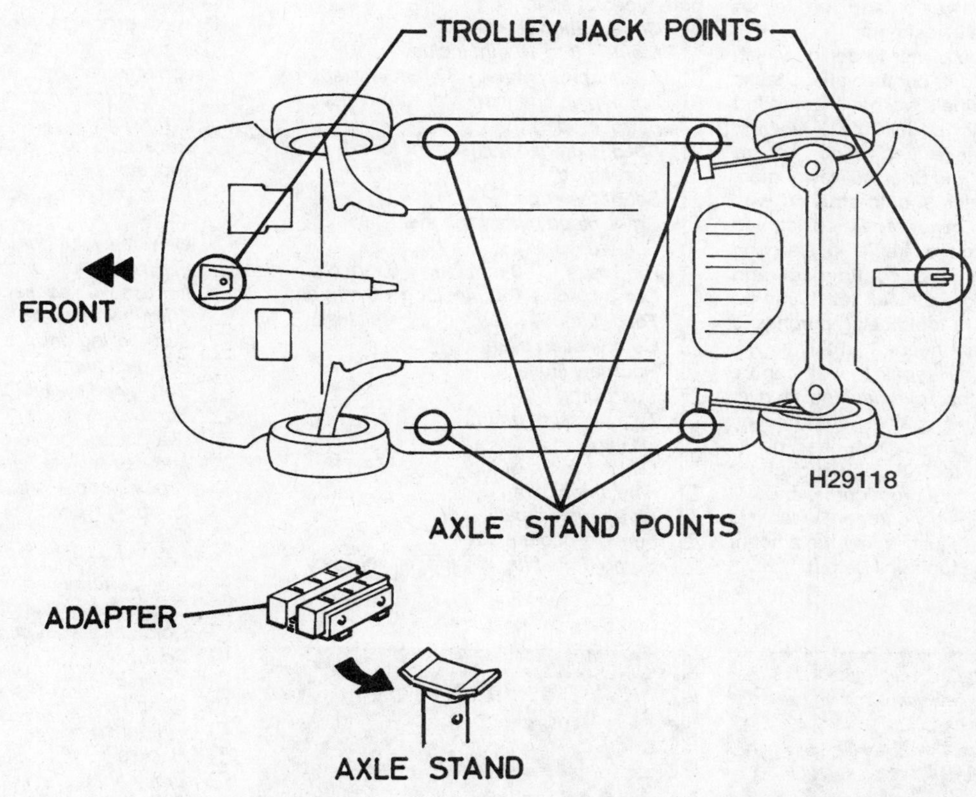

Jacking and vehicle support points on the underbody

Radio/cassette unit anti-theft system - precaution

The radio/cassette unit fitted as standard equipment by NISSAN is equipped with a built-in security code, to deter thieves. If the power source to the unit is cut, the anti-theft system will activate. Even if the power source is immediately reconnected, the radio/cassette unit will not function until the correct security code has been entered. Therefore if you do not know the correct security code for the unit, **do not** disconnect the battery negative lead, or remove the radio/cassette unit from the car.

A number of different types of radio/cassette player may be fitted, with different methods of entering the security code.

If the incorrect code is entered a number of times, the unit will lock.

If the security code is lost or forgotten, seek the advice of your NISSAN dealer. On presentation of proof of ownership, a NISSAN dealer will be able to provide you with a new security code.

On models from March 1998 onwards, the radio/cassette unit is wired into the immobiliser system. This means that the unit can only be used in its original vehicle - if removed, the unit will not function when disconnected from the immobiliser circuit.

Introduction

A selection of good tools is a fundamental requirement for anyone contemplating the maintenance and repair of a motor vehicle. For the owner who does not possess any, their purchase will prove a considerable expense, offsetting some of the savings made by doing-it-yourself. However, provided that the tools purchased meet the relevant national safety standards and are of good quality, they will last for many years and prove an extremely worthwhile investment.

To help the average owner to decide which tools are needed to carry out the various tasks detailed in this manual, we have compiled three lists of tools under the following headings: *Maintenance and minor repair, Repair and overhaul*, and *Special*. Newcomers to practical mechanics should start off with the *Maintenance and minor repair* tool kit, and confine themselves to the simpler jobs around the vehicle. Then, as confidence and experience grow, more difficult tasks can be undertaken, with extra tools being purchased as, and when, they are needed. In this way, a *Maintenance and minor repair* tool kit can be built up into a *Repair and overhaul* tool kit over a considerable period of time, without any major cash outlays. The experienced do-it-yourselfer will have a tool kit good enough for most repair and overhaul procedures, and will add tools from the *Special* category when it is felt that the expense is justified by the amount of use to which these tools will be put.

Maintenance and minor repair tool kit

The tools given in this list should be considered as a minimum requirement if routine maintenance, servicing and minor repair operations are to be undertaken. We recommend the purchase of combination spanners (ring one end, open-ended the other); although more expensive than open-ended ones, they do give the advantages of both types of spanner.

- ☐ *Combination spanners:*
  Metric - 8 to 19 mm inclusive
- ☐ *Adjustable spanner - 35 mm jaw (approx.)*
- ☐ *Spark plug spanner (with rubber insert) - petrol models*
- ☐ *Spark plug gap adjustment tool - petrol models*
- ☐ *Set of feeler gauges*
- ☐ *Brake bleed nipple spanner*
- ☐ *Screwdrivers:*
  Flat blade - 100 mm long x 6 mm dia
  Cross blade - 100 mm long x 6 mm dia
  Torx - various sizes (not all vehicles)
- ☐ *Combination pliers*
- ☐ *Hacksaw (junior)*
- ☐ *Tyre pump*
- ☐ *Tyre pressure gauge*
- ☐ *Oil can*
- ☐ *Oil filter removal tool*
- ☐ *Fine emery cloth*
- ☐ *Wire brush (small)*
- ☐ *Funnel (medium size)*
- ☐ *Sump drain plug key (not all vehicles)*

Repair and overhaul tool kit

These tools are virtually essential for anyone undertaking any major repairs to a motor vehicle, and are additional to those given in the *Maintenance and minor repair* list. Included in this list is a comprehensive set of sockets. Although these are expensive, they will be found invaluable as they are so versatile - particularly if various drives are included in the set. We recommend the half-inch square-drive type, as this can be used with most proprietary torque wrenches.

The tools in this list will sometimes need to be supplemented by tools from the *Special* list:

- ☐ *Sockets (or box spanners) to cover range in previous list (including Torx sockets)*
- ☐ *Reversible ratchet drive (for use with sockets)*
- ☐ *Extension piece, 250 mm (for use with sockets)*
- ☐ *Universal joint (for use with sockets)*
- ☐ *Flexible handle or sliding T "breaker bar" (for use with sockets)*
- ☐ *Torque wrench (for use with sockets)*
- ☐ *Self-locking grips*
- ☐ *Ball pein hammer*
- ☐ *Soft-faced mallet (plastic or rubber)*
- ☐ *Screwdrivers:*
  Flat blade - long & sturdy, short (chubby), and narrow (electrician's) types
  Cross blade – long & sturdy, and short (chubby) types
- ☐ *Pliers:*
  Long-nosed
  Side cutters (electrician's)
  Circlip (internal and external)
- ☐ *Cold chisel - 25 mm*
- ☐ *Scriber*
- ☐ *Scraper*
- ☐ *Centre-punch*
- ☐ *Pin punch*
- ☐ *Hacksaw*
- ☐ *Brake hose clamp*
- ☐ *Brake/clutch bleeding kit*
- ☐ *Selection of twist drills*
- ☐ *Steel rule/straight-edge*
- ☐ *Allen keys (inc. splined/Torx type)*
- ☐ *Selection of files*
- ☐ *Wire brush*
- ☐ *Axle stands*
- ☐ *Jack (strong trolley or hydraulic type)*
- ☐ *Light with extension lead*
- ☐ *Universal electrical multi-meter*

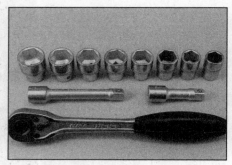

Sockets and reversible ratchet drive

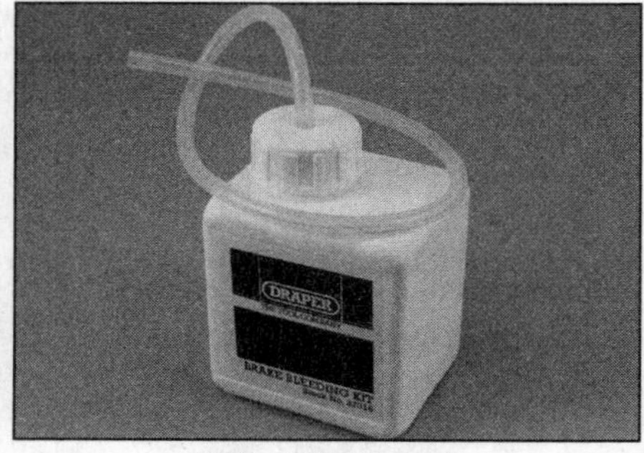

Brake bleeding kit

Torx key, socket and bit

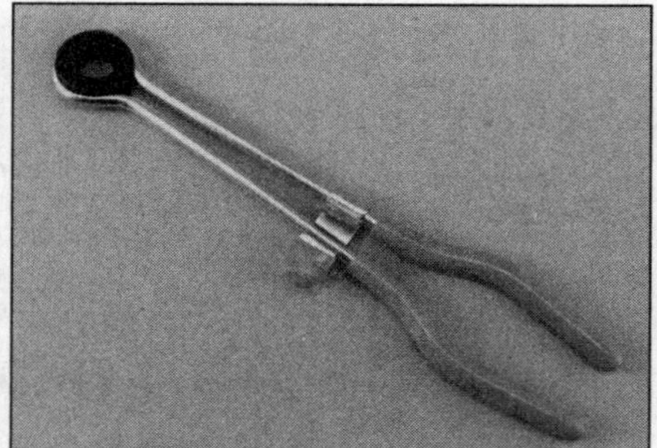
Hose clamp

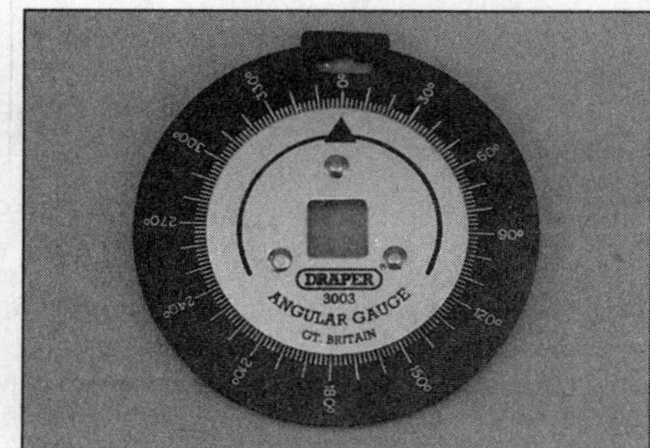

Angular-tightening gauge

Special tools

The tools in this list are those which are not used regularly, are expensive to buy, or which need to be used in accordance with their manufacturers' instructions. Unless relatively difficult mechanical jobs are undertaken frequently, it will not be economic to buy many of these tools. Where this is the case, you could consider clubbing together with friends (or joining a motorists' club) to make a joint purchase, or borrowing the tools against a deposit from a local garage or tool hire specialist. It is worth noting that many of the larger DIY superstores now carry a large range of special tools for hire at modest rates.

The following list contains only those tools and instruments freely available to the public, and not those special tools produced by the vehicle manufacturer specifically for its dealer network. You will find occasional references to these manufacturers' special tools in the text of this manual. Generally, an alternative method of doing the job without the vehicle manufacturers' special tool is given. However, sometimes there is no alternative to using them. Where this is the case and the relevant tool cannot be bought or borrowed, you will have to entrust the work to a dealer.

- ☐ *Angular-tightening gauge*
- ☐ *Valve spring compressor*
- ☐ *Valve grinding tool*
- ☐ *Piston ring compressor*
- ☐ *Piston ring removal/installation tool*
- ☐ *Cylinder bore hone*
- ☐ *Balljoint separator*
- ☐ *Coil spring compressors (where applicable)*
- ☐ *Two/three-legged hub and bearing puller*
- ☐ *Impact screwdriver*
- ☐ *Micrometer and/or vernier calipers*
- ☐ *Dial gauge*
- ☐ *Stroboscopic timing light*
- ☐ *Dwell angle meter/tachometer*
- ☐ *Fault code reader*
- ☐ *Cylinder compression gauge*
- ☐ *Hand-operated vacuum pump and gauge*
- ☐ *Clutch plate alignment set*
- ☐ *Brake shoe steady spring cup removal tool*
- ☐ *Bush and bearing removal/installation set*
- ☐ *Stud extractors*
- ☐ *Tap and die set*
- ☐ *Lifting tackle*
- ☐ *Trolley jack*

Buying tools

Reputable motor accessory shops and superstores often offer excellent quality tools at discount prices, so it pays to shop around.

Remember, you don't have to buy the most expensive items on the shelf, but it is always advisable to steer clear of the very cheap tools. Beware of 'bargains' offered on market stalls or at car boot sales. There are plenty of good tools around at reasonable prices, but always aim to purchase items which meet the relevant national safety standards. If in doubt, ask the proprietor or manager of the shop for advice before making a purchase.

Care and maintenance of tools

Having purchased a reasonable tool kit, it is necessary to keep the tools in a clean and serviceable condition. After use, always wipe off any dirt, grease and metal particles using a clean, dry cloth, before putting the tools away. Never leave them lying around after they have been used. A simple tool rack on the garage or workshop wall for items such as screwdrivers and pliers is a good idea. Store all normal spanners and sockets in a metal box. Any measuring instruments, gauges, meters, etc, must be carefully stored where they cannot be damaged or become rusty.

Take a little care when tools are used. Hammer heads inevitably become marked, and screwdrivers lose the keen edge on their blades from time to time. A little timely attention with emery cloth or a file will soon restore items like this to a good finish.

Working facilities

Not to be forgotten when discussing tools is the workshop itself. If anything more than routine maintenance is to be carried out, a suitable working area becomes essential.

It is appreciated that many an owner-mechanic is forced by circumstances to remove an engine or similar item without the benefit of a garage or workshop. Having done this, any repairs should always be done under the cover of a roof.

Wherever possible, any dismantling should be done on a clean, flat workbench or table at a suitable working height.

Any workbench needs a vice; one with a jaw opening of 100 mm is suitable for most jobs. As mentioned previously, some clean dry storage space is also required for tools, as well as for any lubricants, cleaning fluids, touch-up paints etc, which become necessary.

Another item which may be required, and which has a much more general usage, is an electric drill with a chuck capacity of at least 8 mm. This, together with a good range of twist drills, is virtually essential for fitting accessories.

Last, but not least, always keep a supply of old newspapers and clean, lint-free rags available, and try to keep any working area as clean as possible.

Micrometers

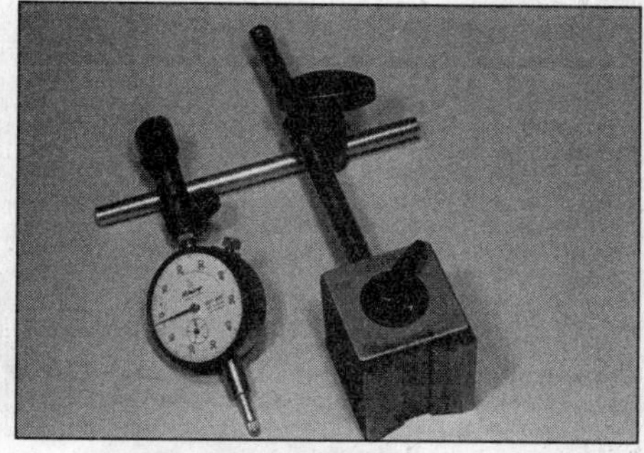

Dial test indicator ("dial gauge")

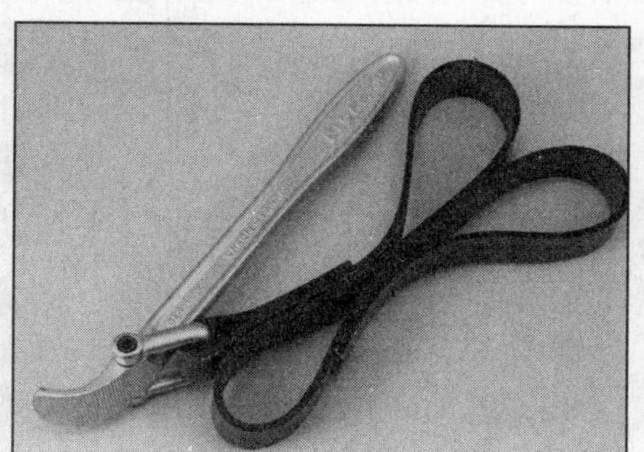

Strap wrench

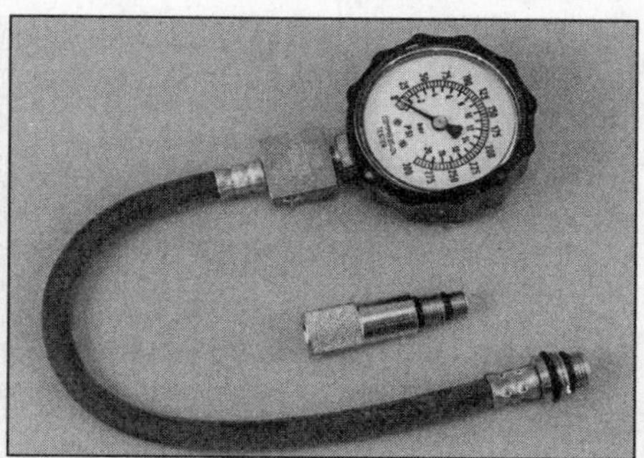

Compression tester

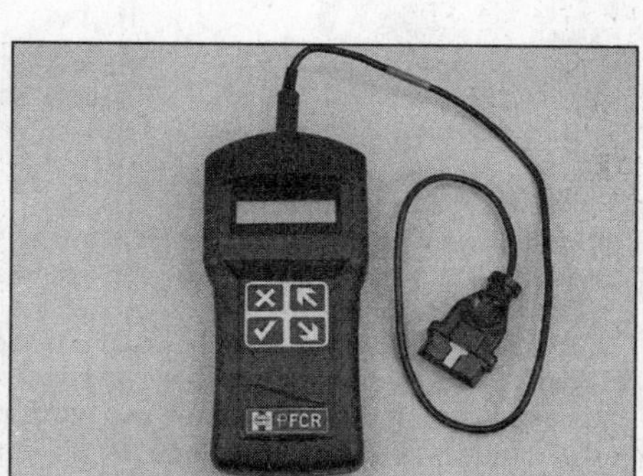

Fault code reader

MOT test checks

This is a guide to getting your vehicle through the MOT test. Obviously it will not be possible to examine the vehicle to the same standard as the professional MOT tester. However, working through the following checks will enable you to identify any problem areas before submitting the vehicle for the test.

Where a testable component is in borderline condition, the tester has discretion in deciding whether to pass or fail it. The basis of such discretion is whether the tester would be happy for a close relative or friend to use the vehicle with the component in that condition. If the vehicle presented is clean and evidently well cared for, the tester may be more inclined to pass a borderline component than if the vehicle is scruffy and apparently neglected.

It has only been possible to summarise the test requirements here, based on the regulations in force at the time of printing. Test standards are becoming increasingly stringent, although there are some exemptions for older vehicles.

An assistant will be needed to help carry out some of these checks.

The checks have been sub-divided into four categories, as follows:

1 Checks carried out **FROM THE DRIVER'S SEAT**

2 Checks carried out **WITH THE VEHICLE ON THE GROUND**

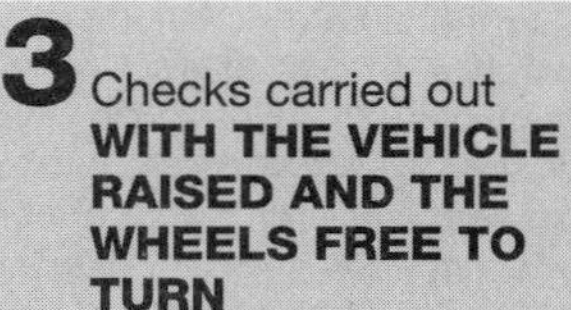

3 Checks carried out **WITH THE VEHICLE RAISED AND THE WHEELS FREE TO TURN**

4 Checks carried out on **YOUR VEHICLE'S EXHAUST EMISSION SYSTEM**

1 Checks carried out FROM THE DRIVER'S SEAT

Handbrake

☐ Test the operation of the handbrake. Excessive travel (too many clicks) indicates incorrect brake or cable adjustment.

☐ Check that the handbrake cannot be released by tapping the lever sideways. Check the security of the lever mountings.

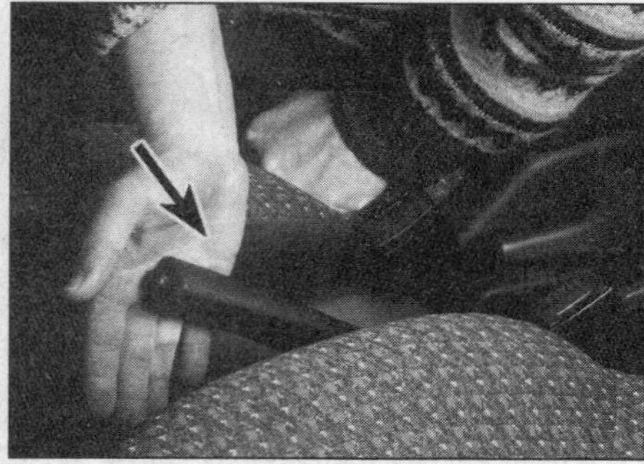

Footbrake

☐ Depress the brake pedal and check that it does not creep down to the floor, indicating a master cylinder fault. Release the pedal, wait a few seconds, then depress it again. If the pedal travels nearly to the floor before firm resistance is felt, brake adjustment or repair is necessary. If the pedal feels spongy, there is air in the hydraulic system which must be removed by bleeding.

☐ Check that the brake pedal is secure and in good condition. Check also for signs of fluid leaks on the pedal, floor or carpets, which would indicate failed seals in the brake master cylinder.

☐ Check the servo unit (when applicable) by operating the brake pedal several times, then keeping the pedal depressed and starting the engine. As the engine starts, the pedal will move down slightly. If not, the vacuum hose or the servo itself may be faulty.

Steering wheel and column

☐ Examine the steering wheel for fractures or looseness of the hub, spokes or rim.

☐ Move the steering wheel from side to side and then up and down. Check that the steering wheel is not loose on the column, indicating wear or a loose retaining nut. Continue moving the steering wheel as before, but also turn it slightly from left to right.

☐ Check that the steering wheel is not loose on the column, and that there is no abnormal

movement of the steering wheel, indicating wear in the column support bearings or couplings.

Windscreen, mirrors and sunvisor

☐ The windscreen must be free of cracks or other significant damage within the driver's field of view. (Small stone chips are acceptable.) Rear view mirrors must be secure, intact, and capable of being adjusted.

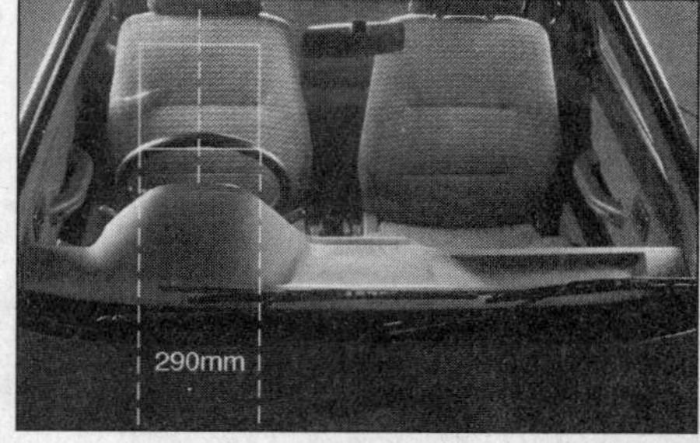

☐ The driver's sunvisor must be capable of being stored in the "up" position.

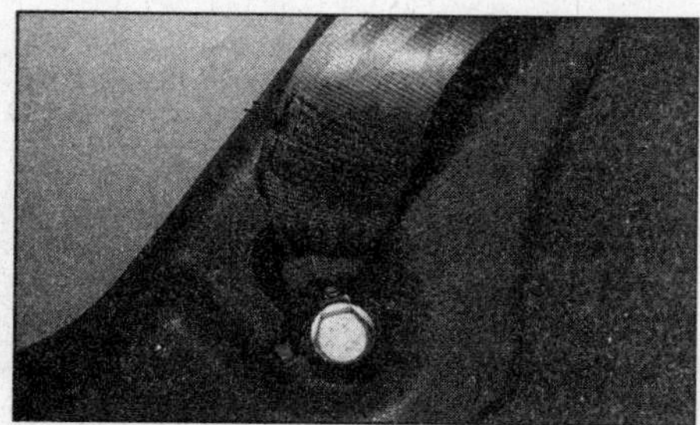

Seat belts and seats

Note: *The following checks are applicable to all seat belts, front and rear.*

□ Examine the webbing of all the belts (including rear belts if fitted) for cuts, serious fraying or deterioration. Fasten and unfasten each belt to check the buckles. If applicable, check the retracting mechanism. Check the security of all seat belt mountings accessible from inside the vehicle.

□ Seat belts with pre-tensioners, once activated, have a "flag" or similar showing on the seat belt stalk. This, in itself, is not a reason for test failure.

□ The front seats themselves must be securely attached and the backrests must lock in the upright position.

Doors

□ Both front doors must be able to be opened and closed from outside and inside, and must latch securely when closed.

2 Checks carried out **WITH THE VEHICLE ON THE GROUND**

Vehicle identification

□ Number plates must be in good condition, secure and legible, with letters and numbers correctly spaced – spacing at (A) should be at least twice that at (B).

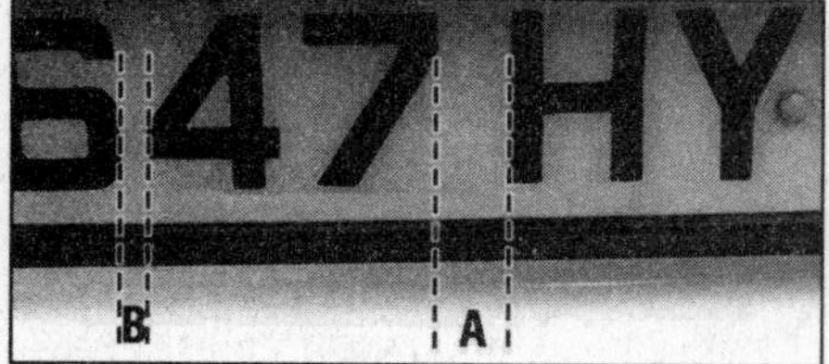

□ The VIN plate and/or homologation plate must be legible.

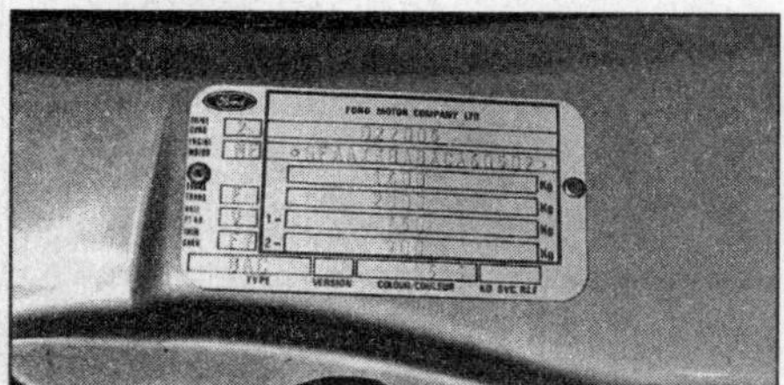

Electrical equipment

□ Switch on the ignition and check the operation of the horn.

□ Check the windscreen washers and wipers, examining the wiper blades; renew damaged or perished blades. Also check the operation of the stop-lights.

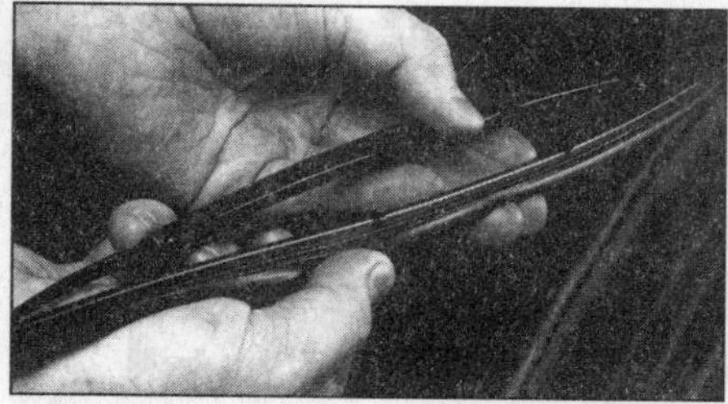

□ Check the operation of the sidelights and number plate lights. The lenses and reflectors must be secure, clean and undamaged.

□ Check the operation and alignment of the headlights. The headlight reflectors must not be tarnished and the lenses must be undamaged.

□ Switch on the ignition and check the operation of the direction indicators (including the instrument panel tell-tale) and the hazard warning lights. Operation of the sidelights and stop-lights must not affect the indicators - if it does, the cause is usually a bad earth at the rear light cluster.

□ Check the operation of the rear foglight(s), including the warning light on the instrument panel or in the switch.

□ The ABS warning light must illuminate in accordance with the manufacturers' design. For most vehicles, the ABS warning light should illuminate when the ignition is switched on, and (if the system is operating properly) extinguish after a few seconds. Refer to the owner's handbook.

Footbrake

□ Examine the master cylinder, brake pipes and servo unit for leaks, loose mountings, corrosion or other damage.

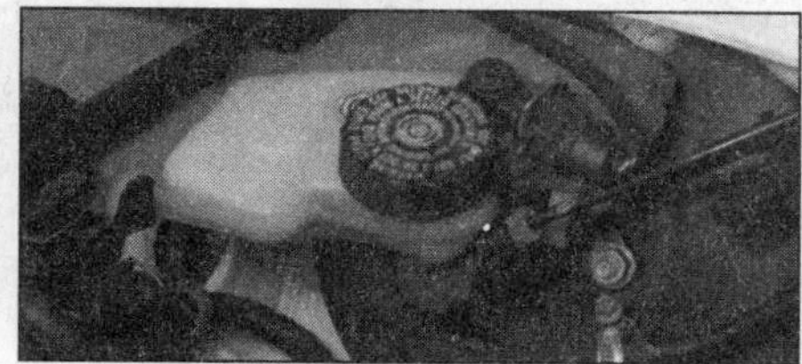

□ The fluid reservoir must be secure and the fluid level must be between the upper (**A**) and lower (**B**) markings.

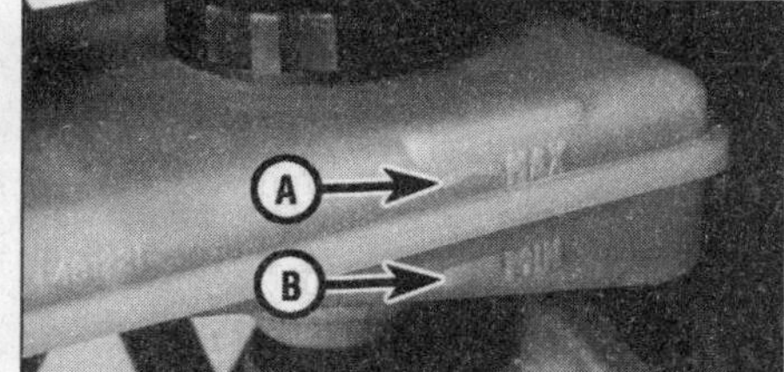

□ Inspect both front brake flexible hoses for cracks or deterioration of the rubber. Turn the steering from lock to lock, and ensure that the hoses do not contact the wheel, tyre, or any part of the steering or suspension mechanism. With the brake pedal firmly depressed, check the hoses for bulges or leaks under pressure.

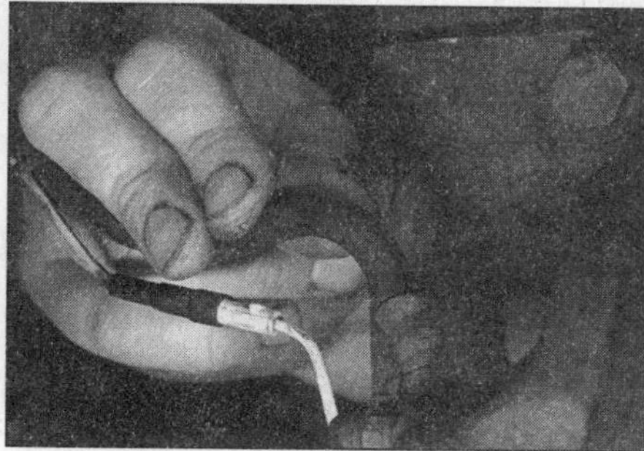

Steering and suspension

□ Have your assistant turn the steering wheel from side to side slightly, up to the point where the steering gear just begins to transmit this movement to the roadwheels. Check for excessive free play between the steering wheel and the steering gear, indicating wear or insecurity of the steering column joints, the column-to-steering gear coupling, or the steering gear itself.

□ Have your assistant turn the steering wheel more vigorously in each direction, so that the roadwheels just begin to turn. As this is done, examine all the steering joints, linkages, fittings and attachments. Renew any component that shows signs of wear or damage. On vehicles with power steering, check the security and condition of the steering pump, drivebelt and hoses.

□ Check that the vehicle is standing level, and at approximately the correct ride height.

Shock absorbers

□ Depress each corner of the vehicle in turn, then release it. The vehicle should rise and then settle in its normal position. If the vehicle continues to rise and fall, the shock absorber is defective. A shock absorber which has seized will also cause the vehicle to fail.

Exhaust system

☐ Start the engine. With your assistant holding a rag over the tailpipe, check the entire system for leaks. Repair or renew leaking sections.

3 Checks carried out
WITH THE VEHICLE RAISED AND THE WHEELS FREE TO TURN

Jack up the front and rear of the vehicle, and securely support it on axle stands. Position the stands clear of the suspension assemblies. Ensure that the wheels are clear of the ground and that the steering can be turned from lock to lock.

Steering mechanism

☐ Have your assistant turn the steering from lock to lock. Check that the steering turns smoothly, and that no part of the steering mechanism, including a wheel or tyre, fouls any brake hose or pipe or any part of the body structure.
☐ Examine the steering rack rubber gaiters for damage or insecurity of the retaining clips. If power steering is fitted, check for signs of damage or leakage of the fluid hoses, pipes or connections. Also check for excessive stiffness or binding of the steering, a missing split pin or locking device, or severe corrosion of the body structure within 30 cm of any steering component attachment point.

Front and rear suspension and wheel bearings

☐ Starting at the front right-hand side, grasp the roadwheel at the 3 o'clock and 9 o'clock positions and rock gently but firmly. Check for free play or insecurity at the wheel bearings, suspension balljoints, or suspension mountings, pivots and attachments.
☐ Now grasp the wheel at the 12 o'clock and 6 o'clock positions and repeat the previous inspection. Spin the wheel, and check for roughness or tightness of the front wheel bearing.

☐ If excess free play is suspected at a component pivot point, this can be confirmed by using a large screwdriver or similar tool and levering between the mounting and the component attachment. This will confirm whether the wear is in the pivot bush, its retaining bolt, or in the mounting itself (the bolt holes can often become elongated).

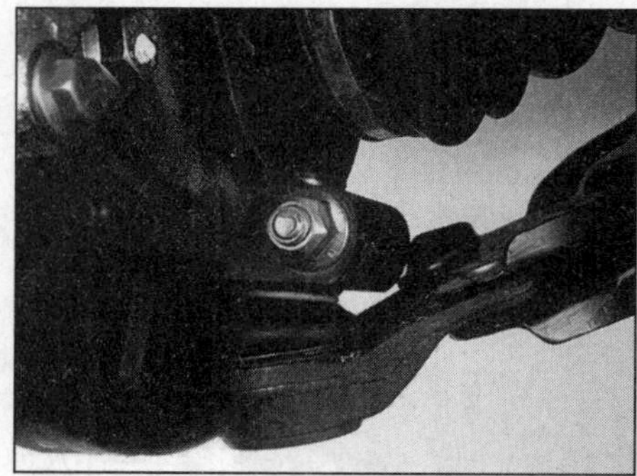

☐ Carry out all the above checks at the other front wheel, and then at both rear wheels.

Springs and shock absorbers

☐ Examine the suspension struts (when applicable) for serious fluid leakage, corrosion, or damage to the casing. Also check the security of the mounting points.
☐ If coil springs are fitted, check that the spring ends locate in their seats, and that the spring is not corroded, cracked or broken.
☐ If leaf springs are fitted, check that all leaves are intact, that the axle is securely attached to each spring, and that there is no deterioration of the spring eye mountings, bushes, and shackles.
☐ The same general checks apply to vehicles fitted with other suspension types, such as torsion bars, hydraulic displacer units, etc. Ensure that all mountings and attachments are secure, that there are no signs of excessive wear, corrosion or damage, and (on hydraulic types) that there are no fluid leaks or damaged pipes.
☐ Inspect the shock absorbers for signs of serious fluid leakage. Check for wear of the mounting bushes or attachments, or damage to the body of the unit.

Driveshafts (fwd vehicles only)

☐ Rotate each front wheel in turn and inspect the constant velocity joint gaiters for splits or damage. Also check that each driveshaft is straight and undamaged.

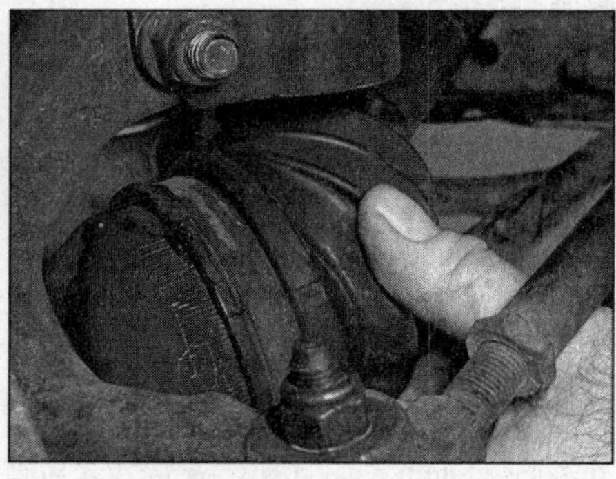

Braking system

☐ If possible without dismantling, check brake pad wear and disc condition. Ensure that the friction lining material has not worn excessively, (A) and that the discs are not fractured, pitted, scored or badly worn (B).

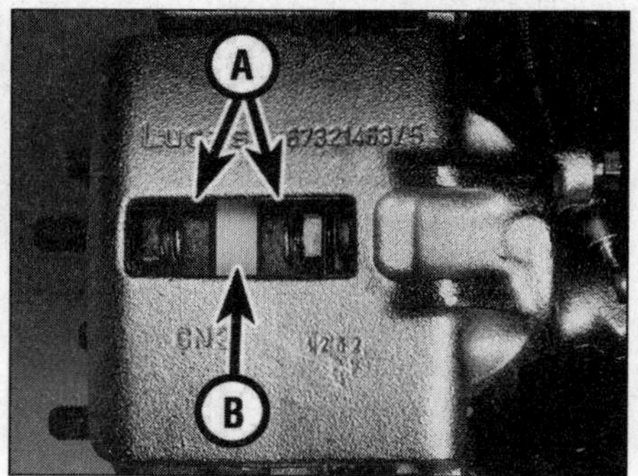

☐ Examine all the rigid brake pipes underneath the vehicle, and the flexible hose(s) at the rear. Look for corrosion, chafing or insecurity of the pipes, and for signs of bulging under pressure, chafing, splits or deterioration of the flexible hoses.
☐ Look for signs of fluid leaks at the brake calipers or on the brake backplates. Repair or renew leaking components.
☐ Slowly spin each wheel, while your assistant depresses and releases the footbrake. Ensure that each brake is operating and does not bind when the pedal is released.

☐ Examine the handbrake mechanism, checking for frayed or broken cables, excessive corrosion, or wear or insecurity of the linkage. Check that the mechanism works on each relevant wheel, and releases fully, without binding.

☐ It is not possible to test brake efficiency without special equipment, but a road test can be carried out later to check that the vehicle pulls up in a straight line.

Fuel and exhaust systems

☐ Inspect the fuel tank (including the filler cap), fuel pipes, hoses and unions. All components must be secure and free from leaks.

☐ Examine the exhaust system over its entire length, checking for any damaged, broken or missing mountings, security of the retaining clamps and rust or corrosion.

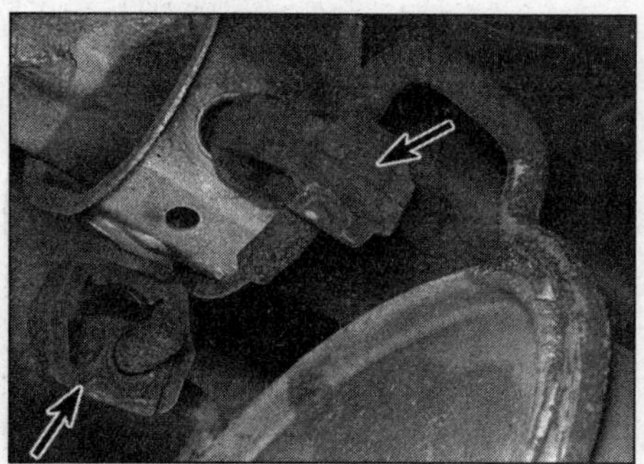

Wheels and tyres

☐ Examine the sidewalls and tread area of each tyre in turn. Check for cuts, tears, lumps, bulges, separation of the tread, and exposure of the ply or cord due to wear or damage. Check that the tyre bead is correctly seated on the wheel rim, that the valve is sound and properly seated, and that the wheel is not distorted or damaged.

☐ Check that the tyres are of the correct size for the vehicle, that they are of the same size and type on each axle, and that the pressures are correct.

☐ Check the tyre tread depth. The legal minimum at the time of writing is 1.6 mm over at least three-quarters of the tread width. Abnormal tread wear may indicate incorrect front wheel alignment.

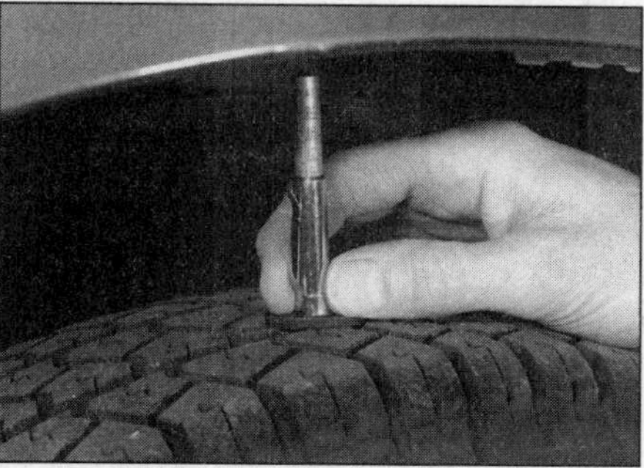

Body corrosion

☐ Check the condition of the entire vehicle structure for signs of corrosion in load-bearing areas. (These include chassis box sections, side sills, cross-members, pillars, and all suspension, steering, braking system and seat belt mountings and anchorages.) Any corrosion which has seriously reduced the thickness of a load-bearing area is likely to cause the vehicle to fail. In this case professional repairs are likely to be needed.

☐ Damage or corrosion which causes sharp or otherwise dangerous edges to be exposed will also cause the vehicle to fail.

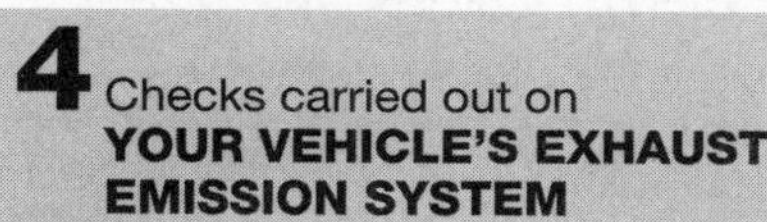

4 Checks carried out on **YOUR VEHICLE'S EXHAUST EMISSION SYSTEM**

Petrol models

☐ Have the engine at normal operating temperature, and make sure that it is in good tune (ignition system in good order, air filter element clean, etc).

☐ Before any measurements are carried out, raise the engine speed to around 2500 rpm, and hold it at this speed for 20 seconds. Allow the engine speed to return to idle, and watch for smoke emissions from the exhaust tailpipe. If the idle speed is obviously much too high, or if dense blue or clearly-visible black smoke comes from the tailpipe for more than 5 seconds, the vehicle will fail. As a rule of thumb, blue smoke signifies oil being burnt (engine wear) while black smoke signifies unburnt fuel (dirty air cleaner element, or other carburettor or fuel system fault).

☐ An exhaust gas analyser capable of measuring carbon monoxide (CO) and hydrocarbons (HC) is now needed. If such an instrument cannot be hired or borrowed, a local garage may agree to perform the check for a small fee.

CO emissions (mixture)

☐ At the time of writing, for vehicles first used between 1st August 1975 and 31st July 1986 (P to C registration), the CO level must not exceed 4.5% by volume. For vehicles first used between 1st August 1986 and 31st July 1992 (D to J registration), the CO level must not exceed 3.5% by volume. Vehicles first used after 1st August 1992 (K registration) must conform to the manufacturer's specification. The MOT tester has access to a DOT database or emissions handbook, which lists the CO and HC limits for each make and model of vehicle. The CO level is measured with the engine at idle speed, and at "fast idle". The following limits are given as a general guide:

At idle speed -
CO level no more than 0.5%
At "fast idle" (2500 to 3000 rpm) -
CO level no more than 0.3%
(Minimum oil temperature 60°C)

☐ If the CO level cannot be reduced far enough to pass the test (and the fuel and ignition systems are otherwise in good condition) then the carburettor is badly worn, or there is some problem in the fuel injection system or catalytic converter (as applicable).

HC emissions

☐ With the CO within limits, HC emissions for vehicles first used between 1st August 1975 and 31st July 1992 (P to J registration) must not exceed 1200 ppm. Vehicles first used after 1st August 1992 (K registration) must conform to the manufacturer's specification. The MOT tester has access to a DOT database or emissions handbook, which lists the CO and HC limits for each make and model of vehicle. The HC level is measured with the engine at "fast idle". The following is given as a general guide:

At "fast idle" (2500 to 3000 rpm) -
HC level no more than 200 ppm
(Minimum oil temperature 60°C)

☐ Excessive HC emissions are caused by incomplete combustion, the causes of which can include oil being burnt, mechanical wear and ignition/fuel system malfunction.

Diesel models

☐ The only emission test applicable to Diesel engines is the measuring of exhaust smoke density. The test involves accelerating the engine several times to its maximum unloaded speed.

Note: *It is of the utmost importance that the engine timing belt is in good condition before the test is carried out.*

☐ The limits for Diesel engine exhaust smoke, introduced in September 1995 are:

Vehicles first used before 1st August 1979:
Exempt from metered smoke testing, but must not emit "dense blue or clearly visible black smoke for a period of more than 5 seconds at idle" or "dense blue or clearly visible black smoke during acceleration which would obscure the view of other road users".

Non-turbocharged vehicles first used after 1st August 1979: 2.5m^{-1}

Turbocharged vehicles first used after 1st August 1979: 3.0m^{-1}

☐ Excessive smoke can be caused by a dirty air cleaner element. Otherwise, professional advice may be needed to find the cause.

Introduction

The vehicle owner who does his or her own maintenance according to the recommended service schedules should not have to use this section of the manual very often. Modern component reliability is such that, provided those items subject to wear or deterioration are inspected or renewed at the specified intervals, sudden failure is comparatively rare. Faults do not usually just happen as a result of sudden failure, but develop over a period of time. Major mechanical failures in particular are usually preceded by characteristic symptoms over hundreds or even thousands of miles. Those components which do occasionally fail without warning are often small and easily carried in the vehicle.

With any fault-finding, the first step is to decide where to begin investigations. Sometimes this is obvious, but on other occasions, a little detective work will be necessary. The owner who makes half a dozen haphazard adjustments or replacements may be successful in curing a fault (or its symptoms), but will be none the wiser if the fault recurs, and ultimately may have spent more time and money than was necessary. A calm and logical approach will be found to be more satisfactory in the long run. Always take into account any warning signs or abnormalities that may have been noticed in the period preceding the fault - power loss, high or low gauge readings, unusual smells, etc - and remember that failure of components such as fuses or spark plugs may only be pointers to some underlying fault.

The pages which follow provide an easy-reference guide to the more common problems which may occur during the operation of the vehicle. These problems and their possible causes are grouped under headings denoting various components or systems, such as Engine, Cooling system, etc. The Chapter and/or Section which deals with the problem is also shown in brackets. Whatever the fault, certain basic principles apply. These are as follows:

Verify the fault. This is simply a matter of being sure that you know what the symptoms are before starting work. This is particularly important if you are investigating a fault for someone else, who may not have described it very accurately.

Don't overlook the obvious. For example, if the vehicle won't start, is there fuel in the tank? (Don't take anyone else's word on this particular point, and don't trust the fuel gauge either!) If an electrical fault is indicated, look for loose or broken wires before digging out the test gear.

Cure the disease, not the symptom. Substituting a flat battery with a fully-charged one will get you off the hard shoulder, but if the underlying cause is not attended to, the new battery will go the same way. Similarly, changing oil-fouled spark plugs for a new set will get you moving again, but remember that the reason for the fouling (if it wasn't simply an incorrect grade of plug) will have to be established and corrected.

Don't take anything for granted. Particularly, don't forget that a "new" component may itself be defective (especially if it's been rattling around in the boot for months), and don't leave components out of a fault diagnosis sequence just because they are new or recently-fitted. When you do finally diagnose a difficult fault, you'll probably realise that all the evidence was there from the start.

1 Engine

Engine fails to rotate when attempting to start

- ☐ Battery terminal connections loose or corroded (*"Weekly checks"*).
- ☐ Battery discharged or faulty (Chapter 5A).
- ☐ Broken, loose or disconnected wiring in the starting circuit (Chapter 5A).
- ☐ Defective starter solenoid or switch (Chapter 5A).
- ☐ Defective starter motor (Chapter 5A).
- ☐ Starter pinion or flywheel/driveplate ring gear teeth loose or broken (Chapter 2A or 5A).
- ☐ Engine earth strap broken or disconnected (Chapter 2A).
- ☐ Automatic transmission not in Park/Neutral position or starter inhibitor switch faulty (Chapter 7B).

Engine rotates, but will not start

- ☐ Fuel tank empty.
- ☐ Battery discharged (engine rotates slowly) (Chapter 5A).
- ☐ Battery terminal connections loose or corroded (*"Weekly checks"*).
- ☐ Ignition components damp or damaged (Chapter 1 and 5B).
- ☐ Broken, loose or disconnected wiring in the ignition circuit (Chapters 1 and 5B).
- ☐ Anti-theft immobiliser fault (Chapter 12).
- ☐ Worn, faulty or incorrectly-gapped spark plugs (Chapter 1).
- ☐ Fuel injection system fault (Chapter 4A).
- ☐ Major mechanical failure (eg timing chain) (Chapter 2B).

Engine difficult to start when cold

- ☐ Battery discharged (Chapter 5A).
- ☐ Battery terminal connections loose or corroded (*"Weekly checks"*).
- ☐ Worn, faulty or incorrectly-gapped spark plugs (Chapter 1).
- ☐ Fuel injection system fault (Chapter 4B).
- ☐ Other ignition system fault (Chapters 1 and 5B).
- ☐ Low cylinder compressions (Chapter 2A).

Engine difficult to start when hot

- ☐ Air filter element dirty or clogged (Chapter 1).
- ☐ Fuel injection system fault (Chapter 4A).
- ☐ Ignition system fault (Chapters 1 and 5B).
- ☐ Low cylinder compressions (Chapter 2A).

Starter motor noisy or excessively-rough in engagement

- ☐ Starter pinion or flywheel/driveplate ring gear teeth loose or broken (Chapter 2A or 5A).
- ☐ Starter motor mounting bolts loose or missing (Chapter 5A).
- ☐ Starter motor internal components worn or damaged (Chapter 5A).

Engine starts, but stops immediately

- ☐ Loose or faulty electrical connections in the ignition circuit (Chapters 1 and 5B).
- ☐ Vacuum leak at the throttle body or inlet manifold (Chapter 4A).
- ☐ Fuel injection system fault (Chapter 4A).

Engine idles erratically

- ☐ Air filter element clogged (Chapter 1).
- ☐ Vacuum leak at the throttle body, inlet manifold or associated hoses (Chapter 4A).
- ☐ Worn, faulty or incorrectly-gapped spark plugs (Chapter 1).
- ☐ Uneven or low cylinder compressions (Chapter 2A).
- ☐ Camshaft lobes worn (Chapter 2A).
- ☐ Timing chain(s) incorrectly fitted (Chapter 2A).
- ☐ Fuel injection system fault (Chapter 4A).

Engine misfires at idle speed

- ☐ Worn, faulty or incorrectly-gapped spark plugs (Chapter 1).
- ☐ Faulty spark plug HT leads (Chapter 1).
- ☐ Vacuum leak at the throttle body, inlet manifold or associated hoses (Chapter 4A).
- ☐ Fuel injection system fault (Chapter 4A).
- ☐ Distributor cap cracked or tracking internally (Chapter 1).
- ☐ Uneven or low cylinder compressions (Chapter 2A).
- ☐ Disconnected, leaking, or perished crankcase ventilation hoses (Chapter 4B).

Engine misfires throughout the driving speed range

- ☐ Fuel filter choked (Chapter 1).
- ☐ Fuel pump faulty, or delivery pressure low (Chapter 4A).
- ☐ Fuel tank vent blocked, or fuel pipes restricted (Chapter 4A).
- ☐ Vacuum leak at the throttle body, inlet manifold or associated hoses (Chapter 4A).
- ☐ Worn, faulty or incorrectly-gapped spark plugs (Chapter 1).
- ☐ Faulty spark plug HT leads (Chapter 1).
- ☐ Distributor cap cracked or tracking internally (Chapter 1).
- ☐ Faulty ignition coil (Chapter 5B).
- ☐ Uneven or low cylinder compressions (Chapter 2A).
- ☐ Fuel injection system fault (Chapter 4A).

Engine hesitates on acceleration

- ☐ Worn, faulty or incorrectly-gapped spark plugs (Chapter 1).
- ☐ Vacuum leak at the throttle body, inlet manifold or associated hoses (Chapter 4A).
- ☐ Fuel injection system fault (Chapter 4A).

Engine stalls

- ☐ Vacuum leak at the throttle body, inlet manifold or associated hoses (Chapter 4A).
- ☐ Fuel filter choked (Chapter 1).
- ☐ Fuel pump faulty, or delivery pressure low (Chapter 4A).
- ☐ Fuel tank vent blocked, or fuel pipes restricted (Chapter 4A).
- ☐ Fuel injection system fault (Chapter 4A).

1 Engine (continued)

Engine lacks power

- ☐ Fuel filter choked (Chapter 1).
- ☐ Fuel pump faulty, or delivery pressure low (Chapter 4A).
- ☐ Uneven or low cylinder compressions (Chapter 2A).
- ☐ Worn, faulty or incorrectly-gapped spark plugs (Chapter 1).
- ☐ Vacuum leak at the throttle body, inlet manifold or associated hoses (Chapter 4A).
- ☐ Fuel injection system fault (Chapter 4A).
- ☐ Brakes binding (Chapters 1 and 9).
- ☐ Clutch slipping - manual transmission models (Chapter 6).

Engine backfires

- ☐ Vacuum leak at the throttle body, inlet manifold or associated hoses (Chapter 4A).
- ☐ Fuel injection system fault (Chapter 4A).

Oil pressure warning light illuminated with engine running

- ☐ Low oil level, or incorrect oil grade ("*Weekly Checks*").
- ☐ Faulty oil pressure sensor (Chapter 2A).
- ☐ Worn engine bearings and/or oil pump (Chapter 2A or 2B).
- ☐ Excessively high engine operating temperature (Chapter 3).
- ☐ Oil pressure relief valve defective (Chapter 2A).
- ☐ Oil pick-up strainer clogged (Chapter 2A).

Engine runs-on after switching off

- ☐ Excessive carbon build-up in engine (Chapter 2A or 2B).
- ☐ High engine operating temperature (Chapter 3).
- ☐ Faulty fuel injection system fault (Chapter 4A).

Engine noises

Pre-ignition (pinking) or knocking during acceleration or under load

- ☐ Ignition timing incorrect/ignition system fault (Chapters 1 and 5B).
- ☐ Incorrect grade of spark plug (Chapter 1).
- ☐ Incorrect grade of fuel (Chapter 4A).
- ☐ Vacuum leak at throttle body, inlet manifold or associated hoses (Chapter 4A).
- ☐ Excessive carbon build-up in engine (Chapter 2A or 2B).
- ☐ Fuel injection system fault (Chapter 4A).

Whistling or wheezing noises

- ☐ Leaking inlet manifold or throttle body gasket (Chapter 4A).
- ☐ Leaking exhaust manifold gasket or pipe-to-manifold joint (Chapter 4A).
- ☐ Leaking vacuum hose (Chapters 4A, 4B, 5B and 9).
- ☐ Blowing cylinder head gasket (Chapter 2A).

Tapping or rattling noises

- ☐ Worn valve gear, timing chain or camshaft (Chapter 2A).
- ☐ Incorrect valve clearances (Chapter 2A)
- ☐ Ancillary component fault (water pump, alternator, etc) (Chapters 3, 5A, etc).

Knocking or thumping noises

- ☐ Worn big-end bearings (regular heavy knocking, perhaps less under load) (Chapter 2B).
- ☐ Worn main bearings (rumbling and knocking, perhaps worsening under load) (Chapter 2B).
- ☐ Piston slap (most noticeable when cold) (Chapter 2B).
- ☐ Ancillary component fault (water pump, alternator, etc) (Chapters 3, 5A, etc).

2 Cooling system

Overheating

- ☐ Auxiliary drivebelt broken - or incorrectly adjusted (Chapter 1).
- ☐ Insufficient coolant in system ("*Weekly Checks*").
- ☐ Thermostat faulty (Chapter 3).
- ☐ Radiator core blocked, or grille restricted (Chapter 3).
- ☐ Electric cooling fan or thermostatic switch faulty (Chapter 3).
- ☐ Pressure cap faulty (Chapter 3).
- ☐ Ignition timing incorrect, or ignition system fault (Chapters 1 and 5B).
- ☐ Inaccurate temperature gauge sender unit (Chapter 3).
- ☐ Airlock in cooling system (Chapter 1).

Overcooling

- ☐ Thermostat faulty (Chapter 3).
- ☐ Inaccurate temperature gauge sender unit (Chapter 3).

External coolant leakage

- ☐ Deteriorated or damaged hoses or hose clips (Chapter 1).
- ☐ Radiator core or heater matrix leaking (Chapter 3).
- ☐ Pressure cap faulty (Chapter 3).
- ☐ Water pump internal seal leaking (Chapter 3).
- ☐ Boiling due to overheating (Chapter 3).
- ☐ Core plug leaking (Chapter 2B).

Internal coolant leakage

- ☐ Leaking cylinder head gasket (Chapter 2A).
- ☐ Cracked cylinder head or cylinder block (Chapter 2A or 2B).

Corrosion

- ☐ Infrequent draining and flushing (Chapter 1).
- ☐ Incorrect coolant mixture or inappropriate coolant type ("*Weekly Checks*").

3 Fuel and exhaust systems

Excessive fuel consumption

- ☐ Air filter element dirty or clogged (Chapter 1).
- ☐ Fuel injection system fault (Chapter 4A).
- ☐ Ignition timing incorrect or ignition system fault (Chapters 1 and 5B).
- ☐ Tyres under-inflated ("*Weekly checks*").

Fuel leakage and/or fuel odour

- ☐ Damaged fuel tank, pipes or connections (Chapters 1 and 4A).

Excessive noise or fumes from exhaust system

- ☐ Leaking exhaust system or manifold joints (Chapters 1 or 4A).
- ☐ Leaking, corroded or damaged silencers or pipe (Chapters 1 or 4A).
- ☐ Broken mountings causing body or suspension contact (Chapter 4A).

4 Clutch

Pedal travels to floor - no pressure or resistance

- ☐ Broken clutch cable (Chapter 6).
- ☐ Incorrect clutch cable adjustment (Chapter 6).
- ☐ Broken clutch release bearing or fork (Chapter 6).
- ☐ Broken diaphragm spring in clutch pressure plate (Chapter 6).

Clutch fails to disengage (unable to select gears)

- ☐ Incorrect clutch cable adjustment (Chapter 6).
- ☐ Clutch disc sticking on splines (Chapter 6).
- ☐ Clutch disc sticking to flywheel or pressure plate (Chapter 6).
- ☐ Faulty pressure plate assembly (Chapter 6).
- ☐ Clutch release mechanism worn or poorly assembled (Chapter 6).

Clutch slips (engine speed increases, with no increase in vehicle speed)

- ☐ Incorrect clutch cable adjustment (Chapter 6).
- ☐ Clutch disc linings excessively worn (Chapter 6).
- ☐ Clutch disc linings contaminated with oil or grease (Chapter 6).
- ☐ Faulty pressure plate or weak diaphragm spring (Chapter 6).

Judder as clutch is engaged

- ☐ Clutch disc linings contaminated with oil or grease (Chapter 6).
- ☐ Clutch disc linings excessively worn (Chapter 6).
- ☐ Clutch cable sticking or frayed (Chapter 6).
- ☐ Faulty or distorted pressure plate or diaphragm spring (Chapter 6).
- ☐ Worn or loose engine or transmission mountings (Chapter 2A).
- ☐ Clutch disc hub or shaft splines worn (Chapter 6).

Noise when depressing or releasing clutch pedal

- ☐ Worn clutch release bearing (Chapter 6).
- ☐ Worn or dry clutch pedal bushes (Chapter 6).
- ☐ Faulty pressure plate assembly (Chapter 6).
- ☐ Pressure plate diaphragm spring broken (Chapter 6).
- ☐ Broken clutch disc cushioning springs (Chapter 6).

5 Manual transmission

Noisy in neutral with engine running

- ☐ Input shaft bearings worn (noise apparent with clutch pedal released, but not when depressed) (Chapter 7A).*
- ☐ Clutch release bearing worn (noise apparent with clutch pedal depressed, possibly less when released) (Chapter 6).

Noisy in one particular gear

- ☐ Worn, damaged or chipped gear teeth (Chapter 7A).*

Difficulty engaging gears

- ☐ Clutch fault (Chapter 6).
- ☐ Oil level low (Chapter 1).
- ☐ Worn or damaged gear linkage (Chapter 7A).
- ☐ Worn synchroniser units (Chapter 7A).*

Jumps out of gear

- ☐ Worn or damaged gear linkage (Chapter 7A).
- ☐ Worn synchroniser units (Chapter 7A).*
- ☐ Worn selector forks (Chapter 7A).*

Vibration

- ☐ Lack of oil (Chapter 1).
- ☐ Worn bearings (Chapter 7A).*

Lubricant leaks

- ☐ Leaking oil seal (Chapter 7A).
- ☐ Leaking housing joint (Chapter 7A).*
- ☐ Leaking input shaft oil seal (Chapter 7A).*

**Although the corrective action necessary to remedy the symptoms described is beyond the scope of the home mechanic, the above information should be helpful in isolating the cause of the condition, so that the owner can communicate clearly with a professional mechanic.*

6 Automatic transmission

Note: *Due to the complexity of the automatic transmission, it is difficult for the home mechanic to properly diagnose and service this unit. For problems other than the following, the vehicle should be taken to a dealer service department or automatic transmission specialist.*

Fluid leakage

- ☐ Automatic transmission fluid is usually deep red in colour. Fluid leaks should not be confused with engine oil, which can easily be blown onto the transmission by air flow.
- ☐ To determine the source of a leak, first remove all built-up dirt and grime from the transmission housing and surrounding areas, using a degreasing agent or by steam-cleaning. Drive the vehicle at low speed, so that air flow will not blow the leak far from its source. Raise and support the vehicle, and determine where the leak is coming from. The following are common areas of leakage.

a) Oil pan (Chapter 7B).
b) Dipstick tube (Chapter 7B).
c) Transmission-to-fluid cooler fluid pipes/unions (Chapter 7B).

General gear selection problems

- ☐ The most likely cause of gear selection problems is a faulty or poorly-adjusted gear selector mechanism. The following are common problems associated with a faulty selector mechanism.

a) Engine starting in gears other than Park or Neutral.
b) Indicator on selector lever pointing to the wrong gear.
c) Vehicle moves when in Park or Neutral.
d) Poor gear shift quality, or erratic gear changes.

- ☐ Refer any problems to a NISSAN dealer, or an automatic transmission specialist.

Transmission will not downshift (kickdown) with accelerator pedal fully depressed

- ☐ Low transmission fluid level (Chapter 1).
- ☐ Incorrect selector cable adjustment (Chapter 7B).
- ☐ Incorrect kickdown cable adjustment (Chapter 7B).

Engine will not start in any gear, or starts in gears other than Park or Neutral

- ☐ Incorrect starter inhibitor switch adjustment (Chapter 7B).
- ☐ Incorrect selector cable adjustment (Chapter 7B).

Transmission slips, shifts roughly, is noisy, or has no drive in forward or reverse gears

- ☐ There are many probable causes for the above problems, but the home mechanic should be concerned with only one possibility - fluid level. Before taking the vehicle to a dealer or transmission specialist, check the fluid level and condition of the fluid as described in Chapter 1. Correct the fluid level as necessary, or change the fluid if needed. If the problem persists, professional help will be necessary.

7 Driveshafts

Clicking or knocking noise on turns (at slow speed on full-lock)

- ☐ Lack of constant velocity joint lubricant, possibly due to damaged gaiter (Chapter 8).
- ☐ Worn outer constant velocity joint (Chapter 8).

Vibration when accelerating or decelerating

- ☐ Worn inner constant velocity joint (Chapter 8).
- ☐ Bent or distorted driveshaft (Chapter 8).

8 Braking system

Note: *Before assuming that a brake problem exists, make sure that the tyres are in good condition and correctly inflated, that the front wheel alignment is correct, and that the vehicle is not loaded with weight in an unequal manner.*

Vehicle pulls to one side under braking

- ☐ Worn, defective, damaged or contaminated front or rear brake pads/shoes on one side (Chapters 1 and 9).
- ☐ Seized or partially-seized front or rear brake caliper/wheel cylinder piston (Chapter 9).
- ☐ A mixture of brake pad/shoe lining materials fitted between sides (Chapter 9).
- ☐ Brake caliper mounting bolts loose (Chapter 9).
- ☐ Worn or damaged steering or suspension components (Chapters 1 and 10).

Noise (grinding or high-pitched squeal) when brakes applied

- ☐ Brake pad or shoe friction lining material worn down to metal backing (Chapters 1 and 9).
- ☐ Excessive corrosion of brake disc/drum - may be apparent after the vehicle has been standing for some time (Chapters 1 and 9).

Excessive brake pedal travel

- ☐ Inoperative rear brake self-adjust mechanism - rear drum brake models (Chapters 1 and 9).
- ☐ Faulty master cylinder (Chapter 9).
- ☐ Air in hydraulic system (Chapter 9).
- ☐ Faulty vacuum servo unit (Chapter 9).

Brake pedal feels spongy when depressed

- ☐ Air in hydraulic system (Chapter 9).
- ☐ Deteriorated flexible rubber brake hoses (Chapters 1 and 9).
- ☐ Master cylinder mountings loose (Chapter 9).
- ☐ Faulty master cylinder (Chapter 9).

Excessive brake pedal effort required to stop vehicle

- ☐ Faulty vacuum servo unit (Chapter 9).
- ☐ Disconnected, damaged or insecure brake servo vacuum hose (Chapters 1 and 9).
- ☐ Primary or secondary hydraulic circuit failure (Chapter 9).
- ☐ Seized brake caliper/wheel cylinder piston(s) (Chapter 9).
- ☐ Brake pads/shoes incorrectly fitted (Chapter 9).
- ☐ Incorrect grade of brake pads/shoes fitted (Chapter 9).
- ☐ Brake pads/shoes contaminated (Chapter 9).

Judder felt through brake pedal or steering wheel when braking

- ☐ Brake pad/shoe linings worn (Chapters 1 and 9).
- ☐ Brake caliper/rear brake backplate mounting bolts loose (Chapter 9).
- ☐ Excessive run-out or distortion of brake disc/drum (Chapter 9).
- ☐ Wear in suspension or steering components or mountings (Chapters 1 and 10).

Brakes binding

- ☐ Seized brake caliper/wheel cylinder piston(s) (Chapter 9).
- ☐ Incorrectly-adjusted handbrake mechanism (Chapter 9).
- ☐ Faulty master cylinder (Chapter 9).

Rear wheels locking under normal braking

- ☐ Rear brake shoe linings contaminated (Chapters 1 and 9).
- ☐ Faulty brake pressure regulator (Chapter 9).

9 Suspension and steering

Note: *Before diagnosing suspension or steering faults, be sure that the trouble is not due to incorrect tyre pressures, mixtures of tyre types, or binding brakes.*

Vehicle pulls to one side

- ☐ Defective tyre (*"Weekly checks"*).
- ☐ Excessive wear in suspension or steering components (Chapters 1 and 10).
- ☐ Incorrect front wheel alignment (Chapter 1).
- ☐ Accident damage to steering or suspension components (Chapters 1 and 10).

Wheel wobble and vibration

- ☐ Front roadwheels out of balance (vibration felt mainly through the steering wheel) (Chapter 1 and *"Weekly Checks"*).
- ☐ Rear roadwheels out of balance (vibration felt throughout the vehicle) (Chapter 1 and *"Weekly Checks"*).
- ☐ Roadwheels damaged or distorted (Chapter 10).
- ☐ Faulty or damaged tyre (*"Weekly checks"*).
- ☐ Worn steering or suspension joints, bushes or components (Chapters 1 and 10).
- ☐ Wheel nuts loose.

Excessive pitching and/or rolling around corners, or during braking

- ☐ Defective shock absorbers (Chapters 1 and 10).
- ☐ Broken or weak coil spring and/or suspension component (Chapters 1 and 10).
- ☐ Worn or damaged anti-roll bar or mountings (Chapter 10).

Wandering or general instability

- ☐ Incorrect front wheel alignment (Chapter 1).
- ☐ Worn steering or suspension joints, bushes or components (Chapters 1 and 10).
- ☐ Roadwheels out of balance (Chapter 1 and *"Weekly Checks"*).
- ☐ Faulty or damaged tyre (*"Weekly checks"*).
- ☐ Wheel nuts loose.
- ☐ Defective shock absorbers (Chapters 1 and 10).

Excessively-stiff steering

- ☐ Lack of steering gear lubricant (Chapter 10).
- ☐ Seized track rod end balljoint or suspension balljoint (Chapters 1 and 10).
- ☐ Broken or incorrectly adjusted auxiliary drivebelt on power steering models (Chapter 1).
- ☐ Incorrect front wheel alignment (Chapter 1).
- ☐ Steering rack or column bent or damaged (Chapter 10).

Excessive play in steering

- ☐ Worn steering column universal joint(s) (Chapter 10).
- ☐ Worn steering track rod end balljoints (Chapters 1 and 10).
- ☐ Worn rack-and-pinion steering gear (Chapter 10).
- ☐ Worn steering or suspension joints, bushes or components (Chapters 1 and 10).

Lack of power assistance

- ☐ Broken or incorrectly-adjusted auxiliary drivebelt - water pump also inoperative (Chapter 1).
- ☐ Incorrect power steering fluid level (*"Weekly Checks"*).
- ☐ Restriction in power steering fluid hoses (Chapter 1).
- ☐ Faulty power steering pump (Chapter 10).
- ☐ Faulty rack-and-pinion steering gear (Chapter 10).

Tyre wear excessive

Tyres worn on inside or outside edges

- ☐ Tyres under-inflated (wear on both edges) (*"Weekly checks"*).
- ☐ Incorrect camber or castor angles (wear on one edge only) (Chapter 1).
- ☐ Worn steering or suspension joints, bushes or components (Chapters 1 and 10).
- ☐ Excessively-hard cornering.
- ☐ Accident damage.

Tyre treads exhibit feathered edges

- ☐ Incorrect toe setting (Chapter 1).

Tyres worn in centre of tread

- ☐ Tyres over-inflated (*"Weekly checks"*).

Tyres worn on inside and outside edges

- ☐ Tyres under-inflated (*"Weekly checks"*).
- ☐ Worn shock absorbers (Chapters 1 and 10).

Tyres worn unevenly

- ☐ Tyres out of balance (Chapter 1).
- ☐ Excessive wheel or tyre run-out (Chapter 1).
- ☐ Worn shock absorbers (Chapters 1 and 10).
- ☐ Faulty tyre (*"Weekly checks"*).

10 Electrical system

Note: *For problems associated with the starting system, refer to the faults listed under "Engine" earlier.*

Battery will not hold a charge for more than a few days

- ☐ Battery defective internally (Chapter 5A).
- ☐ Battery electrolyte level low - where applicable (Chapter 5A).
- ☐ Battery terminal connections loose or corroded (*"Weekly checks"*).
- ☐ Auxiliary drivebelt worn - or incorrectly adjusted (Chapter 1).
- ☐ Alternator not charging at correct output (Chapter 5A).
- ☐ Alternator or voltage regulator faulty (Chapter 5A).
- ☐ Short-circuit causing continual battery drain (Chapters 5A and 12).

Ignition/no-charge warning light remains illuminated with engine running

- ☐ Auxiliary drivebelt broken, worn, or incorrectly adjusted (Chapter 1).
- ☐ Alternator brushes worn, sticking, or dirty (Chapter 5A).
- ☐ Alternator brush springs weak or broken (Chapter 5A).
- ☐ Internal fault in alternator or voltage regulator (Chapter 5A).
- ☐ Broken, disconnected, or loose wiring in charging circuit (Chapter 5A).

Ignition/no-charge warning light fails to come on

- ☐ Warning light bulb blown (Chapter 12).
- ☐ Broken, disconnected, or loose wiring in warning light circuit (Chapter 12).
- ☐ Alternator faulty (Chapter 5A).

Lights inoperative

- ☐ Bulb blown (Chapter 12).
- ☐ Corrosion of bulb or bulbholder contacts (Chapter 12).
- ☐ Blown fuse (Chapter 12).
- ☐ Faulty relay (Chapter 12).
- ☐ Broken, loose, or disconnected wiring (Chapter 12).
- ☐ Faulty switch (Chapter 12).

Instrument readings inaccurate or erratic

Instrument readings increase with engine speed

- ☐ Faulty voltage regulator (Chapter 12).

Fuel or temperature gauges give no reading

- ☐ Faulty gauge sender unit (Chapters 3 and 4A).
- ☐ Wiring open-circuit (Chapter 12).
- ☐ Faulty gauge (Chapter 12).

Fuel or temperature gauges give continuous maximum reading

- ☐ Faulty gauge sender unit (Chapters 3 and 4A).
- ☐ Wiring short-circuit (Chapter 12).
- ☐ Faulty gauge (Chapter 12).

Horn inoperative, or unsatisfactory in operation

Horn operates all the time

- ☐ Horn contacts permanently bridged or horn push stuck down (Chapter 12).

Horn fails to operate

- ☐ Blown fuse (Chapter 12).
- ☐ Wiring or wiring connections loose, broken or disconnected (Chapter 12).
- ☐ Faulty horn (Chapter 12).

Horn emits intermittent or unsatisfactory sound

- ☐ Wiring connections loose (Chapter 12).
- ☐ Horn mountings loose (Chapter 12).
- ☐ Faulty horn (Chapter 12).

Windscreen/tailgate wipers inoperative, or unsatisfactory in operation

Wipers fail to operate, or operate very slowly

- ☐ Wiper blades stuck to screen, or linkage seized or binding (Chapter 12).
- ☐ Blown fuse (Chapter 12).
- ☐ Wiring or wiring connections loose, broken or disconnected (Chapter 12).
- ☐ Faulty relay (Chapter 12).
- ☐ Faulty wiper motor (Chapter 12).

Wiper blades sweep over too large or too small an area of the glass

- ☐ Wiper arms incorrectly positioned on spindles (Chapter 12).
- ☐ Excessive wear of wiper linkage (Chapter 12).
- ☐ Wiper motor or linkage mountings loose or insecure (Chapter 12).

Wiper blades fail to clean the glass effectively

- ☐ Wiper blade rubbers worn or perished (Weekly Checks).
- ☐ Wiper arm tension springs broken, or arm pivots seized (Chapter 12).
- ☐ Insufficient windscreen washer additive to adequately remove road film ("*Weekly Checks*").

Windscreen/tailgate washers inoperative, or unsatisfactory in operation

One or more washer jets inoperative

- ☐ Blocked washer jet (Chapter 1).
- ☐ Disconnected, kinked or restricted fluid hose (Chapter 12).
- ☐ Insufficient fluid in washer reservoir ("*Weekly Checks*").

Washer pump fails to operate

- ☐ Broken or disconnected wiring or connections (Chapter 12).
- ☐ Blown fuse (Chapter 12).
- ☐ Faulty washer switch (Chapter 12).
- ☐ Faulty washer pump (Chapter 12).

Washer pump runs for some time before fluid is emitted from jets

- ☐ Faulty one-way valve in fluid supply hose (Chapter 12).

Electric windows inoperative, or unsatisfactory in operation

Window glass will only move in one direction

- ☐ Faulty switch (Chapter 12).

Window glass slow to move

- ☐ Regulator seized or damaged, or in need of lubrication (Chapter 11).
- ☐ Door internal components or trim fouling regulator (Chapter 11).
- ☐ Faulty motor (Chapter 11).

Window glass fails to move

- ☐ Blown fuse (Chapter 12).
- ☐ Faulty relay (Chapter 12).
- ☐ Broken or disconnected wiring or connections (Chapter 12).
- ☐ Faulty motor (Chapter 11).

A

ABS (Anti-lock brake system) A system, usually electronically controlled, that senses incipient wheel lockup during braking and relieves hydraulic pressure at wheels that are about to skid.

Air bag An inflatable bag hidden in the steering wheel (driver's side) or the dash or glovebox (passenger side). In a head-on collision, the bags inflate, preventing the driver and front passenger from being thrown forward into the steering wheel or windscreen.

Air cleaner A metal or plastic housing, containing a filter element, which removes dust and dirt from the air being drawn into the engine.

Air filter element The actual filter in an air cleaner system, usually manufactured from pleated paper and requiring renewal at regular intervals.

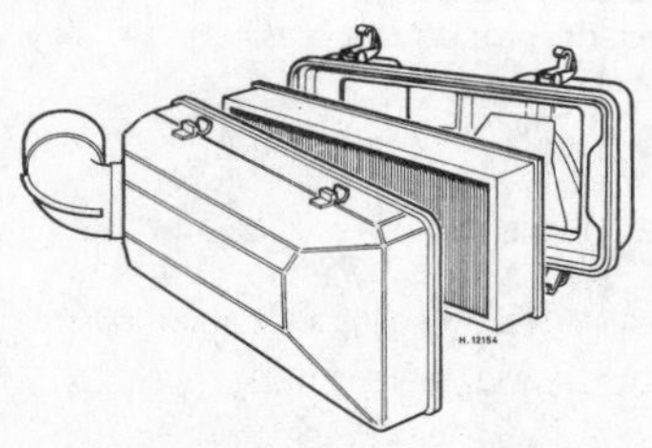

Air filter

Allen key A hexagonal wrench which fits into a recessed hexagonal hole.

Alligator clip A long-nosed spring-loaded metal clip with meshing teeth. Used to make temporary electrical connections.

Alternator A component in the electrical system which converts mechanical energy from a drivebelt into electrical energy to charge the battery and to operate the starting system, ignition system and electrical accessories.

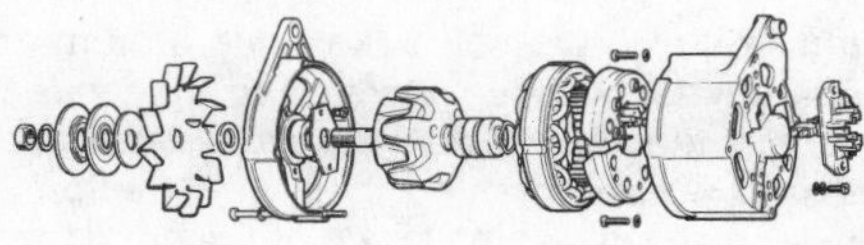

Alternator (exploded view)

Ampere (amp) A unit of measurement for the flow of electric current. One amp is the amount of current produced by one volt acting through a resistance of one ohm.

Anaerobic sealer A substance used to prevent bolts and screws from loosening. Anaerobic means that it does not require oxygen for activation. The Loctite brand is widely used.

Antifreeze A substance (usually ethylene glycol) mixed with water, and added to a vehicle's cooling system, to prevent freezing of the coolant in winter. Antifreeze also contains chemicals to inhibit corrosion and the formation of rust and other deposits that would tend to clog the radiator and coolant passages and reduce cooling efficiency.

Anti-seize compound A coating that reduces the risk of seizing on fasteners that are subjected to high temperatures, such as exhaust manifold bolts and nuts.

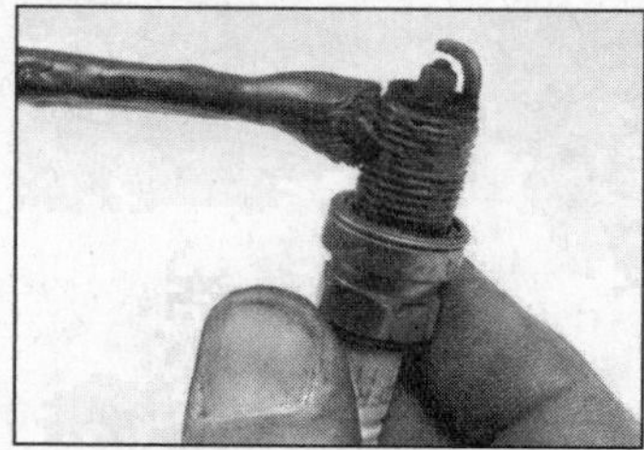

Anti-seize compound

Asbestos A natural fibrous mineral with great heat resistance, commonly used in the composition of brake friction materials. Asbestos is a health hazard and the dust created by brake systems should never be inhaled or ingested.

Axle A shaft on which a wheel revolves, or which revolves with a wheel. Also, a solid beam that connects the two wheels at one end of the vehicle. An axle which also transmits power to the wheels is known as a live axle.

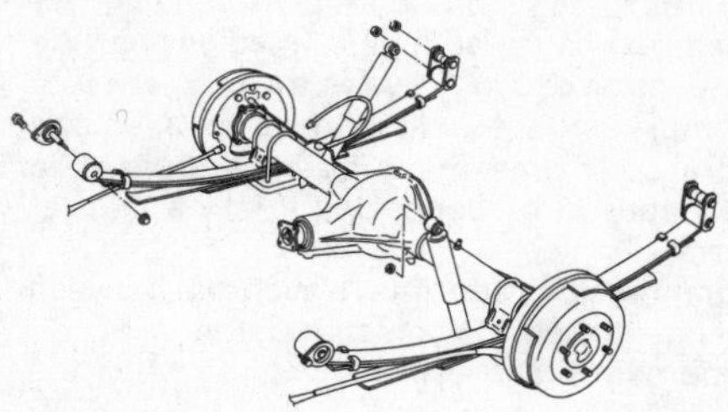

Axle assembly

Axleshaft A single rotating shaft, on either side of the differential, which delivers power from the final drive assembly to the drive wheels. Also called a driveshaft or a halfshaft.

B

Ball bearing An anti-friction bearing consisting of a hardened inner and outer race with hardened steel balls between two races.

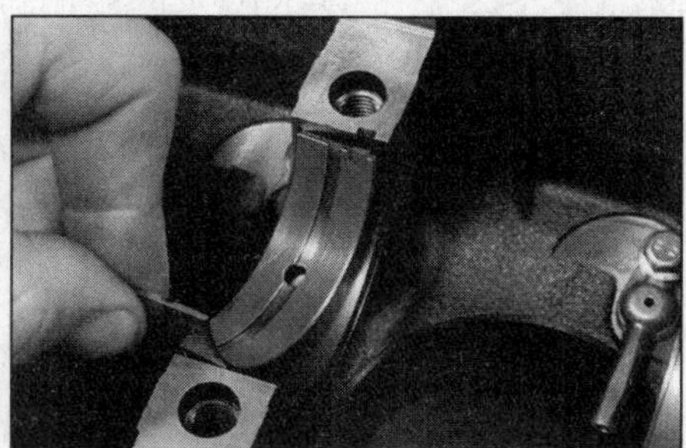

Bearing

Bearing The curved surface on a shaft or in a bore, or the part assembled into either, that permits relative motion between them with minimum wear and friction.

Big-end bearing The bearing in the end of the connecting rod that's attached to the crankshaft.

Bleed nipple A valve on a brake wheel cylinder, caliper or other hydraulic component that is opened to purge the hydraulic system of air. Also called a bleed screw.

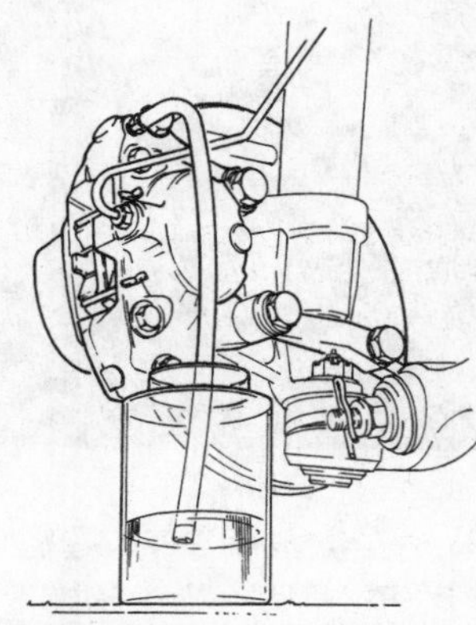

Brake bleeding

Brake bleeding Procedure for removing air from lines of a hydraulic brake system.

Brake disc The component of a disc brake that rotates with the wheels.

Brake drum The component of a drum brake that rotates with the wheels.

Brake linings The friction material which contacts the brake disc or drum to retard the vehicle's speed. The linings are bonded or riveted to the brake pads or shoes.

Brake pads The replaceable friction pads that pinch the brake disc when the brakes are applied. Brake pads consist of a friction material bonded or riveted to a rigid backing plate.

Brake shoe The crescent-shaped carrier to which the brake linings are mounted and which forces the lining against the rotating drum during braking.

Braking systems For more information on braking systems, consult the *Haynes Automotive Brake Manual*.

Breaker bar A long socket wrench handle providing greater leverage.

Bulkhead The insulated partition between the engine and the passenger compartment.

C

Caliper The non-rotating part of a disc-brake assembly that straddles the disc and carries the brake pads. The caliper also contains the hydraulic components that cause the pads to pinch the disc when the brakes are applied. A caliper is also a measuring tool that can be set to measure inside or outside dimensions of an object.

Camshaft A rotating shaft on which a series of cam lobes operate the valve mechanisms. The camshaft may be driven by gears, by sprockets and chain or by sprockets and a belt.

Canister A container in an evaporative emission control system; contains activated charcoal granules to trap vapours from the fuel system.

Canister

Carburettor A device which mixes fuel with air in the proper proportions to provide a desired power output from a spark ignition internal combustion engine.

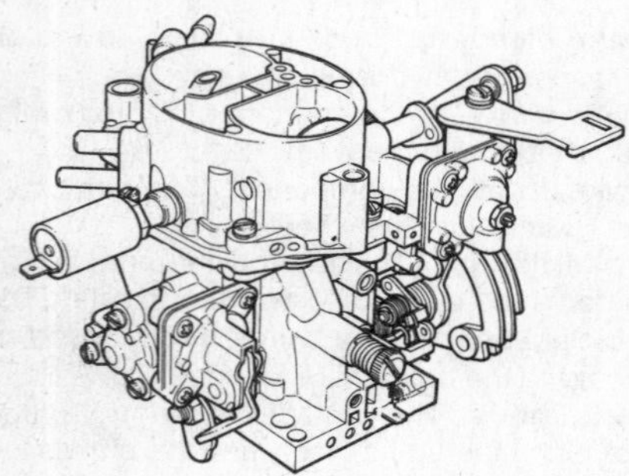

Carburettor

Castellated Resembling the parapets along the top of a castle wall. For example, a castellated balljoint stud nut.

Castellated nut

Castor In wheel alignment, the backward or forward tilt of the steering axis. Castor is positive when the steering axis is inclined rearward at the top.

Catalytic converter A silencer-like device in the exhaust system which converts certain pollutants in the exhaust gases into less harmful substances.

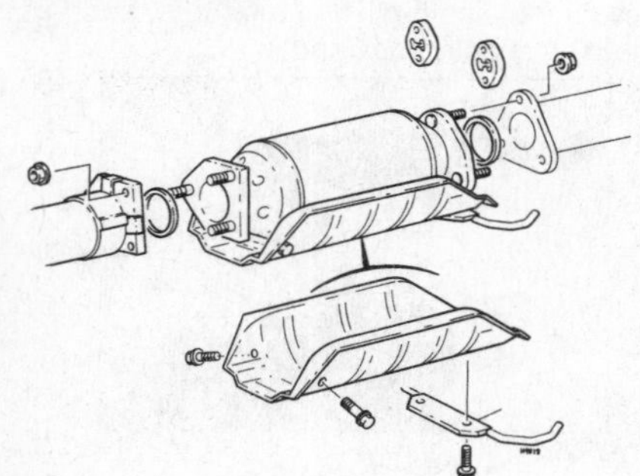

Catalytic converter

Circlip A ring-shaped clip used to prevent endwise movement of cylindrical parts and shafts. An internal circlip is installed in a groove in a housing; an external circlip fits into a groove on the outside of a cylindrical piece such as a shaft.

Clearance The amount of space between two parts. For example, between a piston and a cylinder, between a bearing and a journal, etc.

Coil spring A spiral of elastic steel found in various sizes throughout a vehicle, for example as a springing medium in the suspension and in the valve train.

Compression Reduction in volume, and increase in pressure and temperature, of a gas, caused by squeezing it into a smaller space.

Compression ratio The relationship between cylinder volume when the piston is at top dead centre and cylinder volume when the piston is at bottom dead centre.

Constant velocity (CV) joint A type of universal joint that cancels out vibrations caused by driving power being transmitted through an angle.

Core plug A disc or cup-shaped metal device inserted in a hole in a casting through which core was removed when the casting was formed. Also known as a freeze plug or expansion plug.

Crankcase The lower part of the engine block in which the crankshaft rotates.

Crankshaft The main rotating member, or shaft, running the length of the crankcase, with offset "throws" to which the connecting rods are attached.

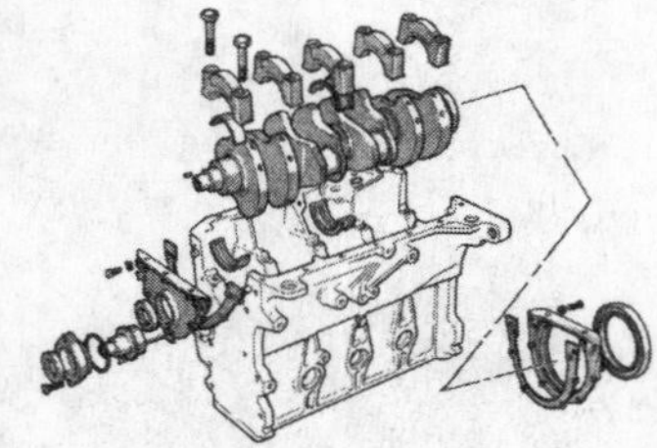

Crankshaft assembly

Crocodile clip See Alligator clip

D

Diagnostic code Code numbers obtained by accessing the diagnostic mode of an engine management computer. This code can be used to determine the area in the system where a malfunction may be located.

Disc brake A brake design incorporating a rotating disc onto which brake pads are squeezed. The resulting friction converts the energy of a moving vehicle into heat.

Double-overhead cam (DOHC) An engine that uses two overhead camshafts, usually one for the intake valves and one for the exhaust valves.

Drivebelt(s) The belt(s) used to drive accessories such as the alternator, water pump, power steering pump, air conditioning compressor, etc. off the crankshaft pulley.

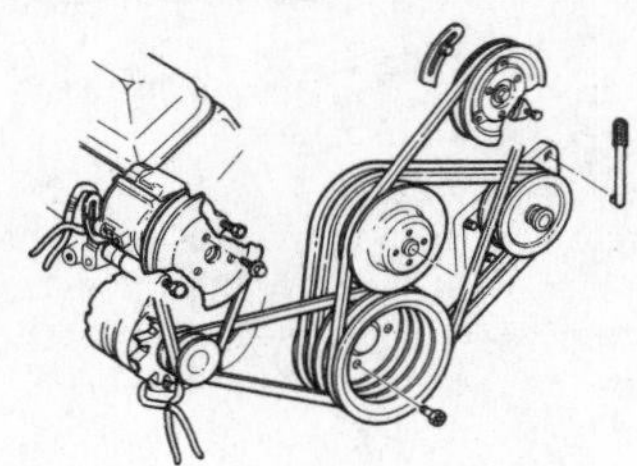

Accessory drivebelts

Driveshaft Any shaft used to transmit motion. Commonly used when referring to the axleshafts on a front wheel drive vehicle.

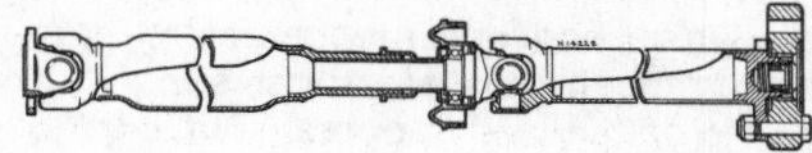

Driveshaft

Drum brake A type of brake using a drum-shaped metal cylinder attached to the inner surface of the wheel. When the brake pedal is pressed, curved brake shoes with friction linings press against the inside of the drum to slow or stop the vehicle.

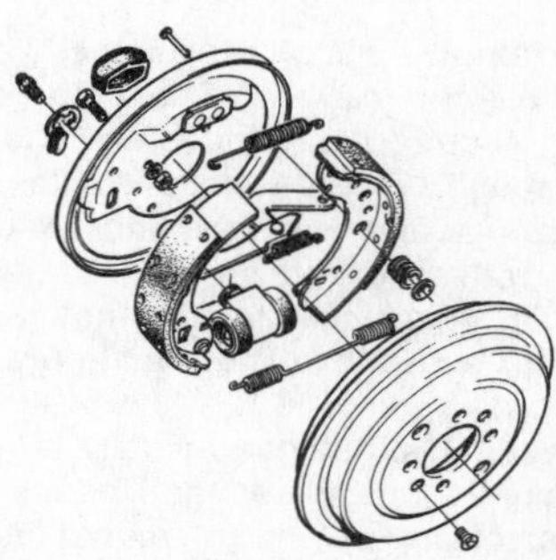

Drum brake assembly

E

EGR valve A valve used to introduce exhaust gases into the intake air stream.

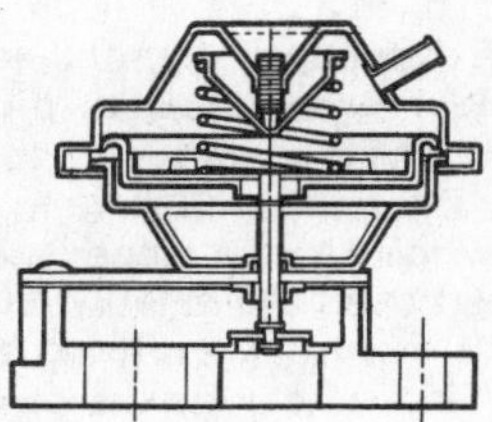
EGR valve

Electronic control unit (ECU) A computer which controls (for instance) ignition and fuel injection systems, or an anti-lock braking system. For more information refer to the *Haynes Automotive Electrical and Electronic Systems Manual.*

Electronic Fuel Injection (EFI) A computer controlled fuel system that distributes fuel through an injector located in each intake port of the engine.

Emergency brake A braking system, independent of the main hydraulic system, that can be used to slow or stop the vehicle if the primary brakes fail, or to hold the vehicle stationary even though the brake pedal isn't depressed. It usually consists of a hand lever that actuates either front or rear brakes mechanically through a series of cables and linkages. Also known as a handbrake or parking brake.

Endfloat The amount of lengthwise movement between two parts. As applied to a crankshaft, the distance that the crankshaft can move forward and back in the cylinder block.

Engine management system (EMS) A computer controlled system which manages the fuel injection and the ignition systems in an integrated fashion.

Exhaust manifold A part with several passages through which exhaust gases leave the engine combustion chambers and enter the exhaust pipe.

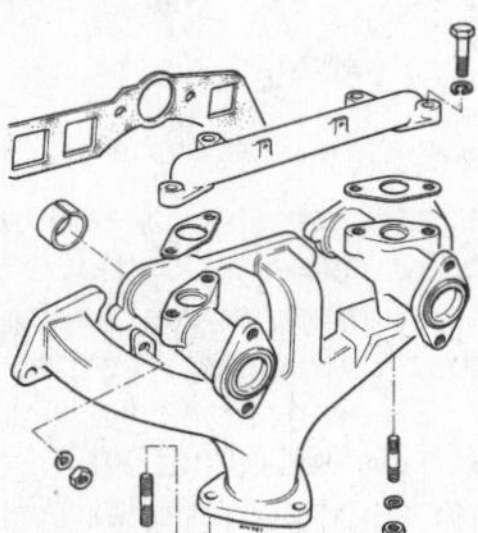
Exhaust manifold

F

Fan clutch A viscous (fluid) drive coupling device which permits variable engine fan speeds in relation to engine speeds.

Feeler blade A thin strip or blade of hardened steel, ground to an exact thickness, used to check or measure clearances between parts.

Feeler blade

Firing order The order in which the engine cylinders fire, or deliver their power strokes, beginning with the number one cylinder.

Flywheel A heavy spinning wheel in which energy is absorbed and stored by means of momentum. On cars, the flywheel is attached to the crankshaft to smooth out firing impulses.

Free play The amount of travel before any action takes place. The "looseness" in a linkage, or an assembly of parts, between the initial application of force and actual movement. For example, the distance the brake pedal moves before the pistons in the master cylinder are actuated.

Fuse An electrical device which protects a circuit against accidental overload. The typical fuse contains a soft piece of metal which is calibrated to melt at a predetermined current flow (expressed as amps) and break the circuit.

Fusible link A circuit protection device consisting of a conductor surrounded by heat-resistant insulation. The conductor is smaller than the wire it protects, so it acts as the weakest link in the circuit. Unlike a blown fuse, a failed fusible link must frequently be cut from the wire for replacement.

G

Gap The distance the spark must travel in jumping from the centre electrode to the side electrode in a spark plug. Also refers to the spacing between the points in a contact breaker assembly in a conventional points-type ignition, or to the distance between the reluctor or rotor and the pickup coil in an electronic ignition.

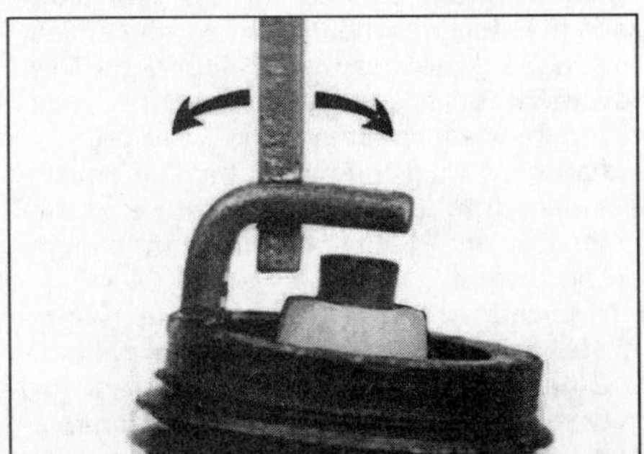
Adjusting spark plug gap

Gasket Any thin, soft material - usually cork, cardboard, asbestos or soft metal - installed between two metal surfaces to ensure a good seal. For instance, the cylinder head gasket seals the joint between the block and the cylinder head.

Gasket

Gauge An instrument panel display used to monitor engine conditions. A gauge with a movable pointer on a dial or a fixed scale is an analogue gauge. A gauge with a numerical readout is called a digital gauge.

H

Halfshaft A rotating shaft that transmits power from the final drive unit to a drive wheel, usually when referring to a live rear axle.

Harmonic balancer A device designed to reduce torsion or twisting vibration in the crankshaft. May be incorporated in the crankshaft pulley. Also known as a vibration damper.

Hone An abrasive tool for correcting small irregularities or differences in diameter in an engine cylinder, brake cylinder, etc.

Hydraulic tappet A tappet that utilises hydraulic pressure from the engine's lubrication system to maintain zero clearance (constant contact with both camshaft and valve stem). Automatically adjusts to variation in valve stem length. Hydraulic tappets also reduce valve noise.

I

Ignition timing The moment at which the spark plug fires, usually expressed in the number of crankshaft degrees before the piston reaches the top of its stroke.

Inlet manifold A tube or housing with passages through which flows the air-fuel mixture (carburettor vehicles and vehicles with throttle body injection) or air only (port fuel-injected vehicles) to the port openings in the cylinder head.

J

Jump start Starting the engine of a vehicle with a discharged or weak battery by attaching jump leads from the weak battery to a charged or helper battery.

L

Load Sensing Proportioning Valve (LSPV) A brake hydraulic system control valve that works like a proportioning valve, but also takes into consideration the amount of weight carried by the rear axle.

Locknut A nut used to lock an adjustment nut, or other threaded component, in place. For example, a locknut is employed to keep the adjusting nut on the rocker arm in position.

Lockwasher A form of washer designed to prevent an attaching nut from working loose.

M

MacPherson strut A type of front suspension system devised by Earle MacPherson at Ford of England. In its original form, a simple lateral link with the anti-roll bar creates the lower control arm. A long strut - an integral coil spring and shock absorber - is mounted between the body and the steering knuckle. Many modern so-called MacPherson strut systems use a conventional lower A-arm and don't rely on the anti-roll bar for location.

Multimeter An electrical test instrument with the capability to measure voltage, current and resistance.

N

NOx Oxides of Nitrogen. A common toxic pollutant emitted by petrol and diesel engines at higher temperatures.

O

Ohm The unit of electrical resistance. One volt applied to a resistance of one ohm will produce a current of one amp.

Ohmmeter An instrument for measuring electrical resistance.

O-ring A type of sealing ring made of a special rubber-like material; in use, the O-ring is compressed into a groove to provide the sealing action.

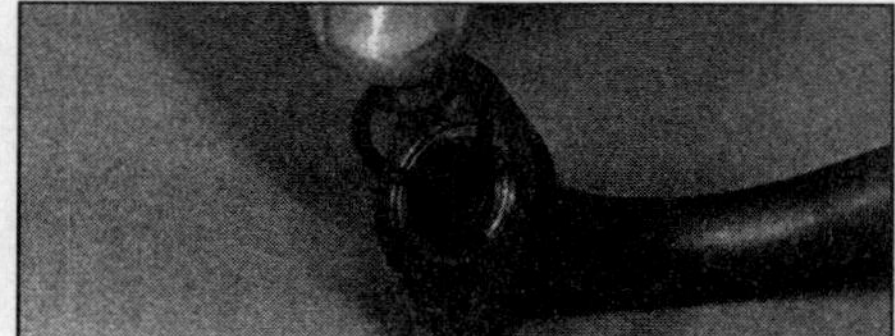

O-ring

Overhead cam (ohc) engine An engine with the camshaft(s) located on top of the cylinder head(s).

Overhead valve (ohv) engine An engine with the valves located in the cylinder head, but with the camshaft located in the engine block.

Oxygen sensor A device installed in the engine exhaust manifold, which senses the oxygen content in the exhaust and converts this information into an electric current. Also called a Lambda sensor.

P

Phillips screw A type of screw head having a cross instead of a slot for a corresponding type of screwdriver.

Plastigage A thin strip of plastic thread, available in different sizes, used for measuring clearances. For example, a strip of Plastigage is laid across a bearing journal. The parts are assembled and dismantled; the width of the crushed strip indicates the clearance between journal and bearing.

Plastigage

Propeller shaft The long hollow tube with universal joints at both ends that carries power from the transmission to the differential on front-engined rear wheel drive vehicles.

Proportioning valve A hydraulic control valve which limits the amount of pressure to the rear brakes during panic stops to prevent wheel lock-up.

R

Rack-and-pinion steering A steering system with a pinion gear on the end of the steering shaft that mates with a rack (think of a geared wheel opened up and laid flat). When the steering wheel is turned, the pinion turns, moving the rack to the left or right. This movement is transmitted through the track rods to the steering arms at the wheels.

Radiator A liquid-to-air heat transfer device designed to reduce the temperature of the coolant in an internal combustion engine cooling system.

Refrigerant Any substance used as a heat transfer agent in an air-conditioning system. R-12 has been the principle refrigerant for many years; recently, however, manufacturers have begun using R-134a, a non-CFC substance that is considered less harmful to the ozone in the upper atmosphere.

Rocker arm A lever arm that rocks on a shaft or pivots on a stud. In an overhead valve engine, the rocker arm converts the upward movement of the pushrod into a downward movement to open a valve.

Rotor In a distributor, the rotating device inside the cap that connects the centre electrode and the outer terminals as it turns, distributing the high voltage from the coil secondary winding to the proper spark plug. Also, that part of an alternator which rotates inside the stator. Also, the rotating assembly of a turbocharger, including the compressor wheel, shaft and turbine wheel.

Runout The amount of wobble (in-and-out movement) of a gear or wheel as it's rotated. The amount a shaft rotates "out-of-true." The out-of-round condition of a rotating part.

S

Sealant A liquid or paste used to prevent leakage at a joint. Sometimes used in conjunction with a gasket.

Sealed beam lamp An older headlight design which integrates the reflector, lens and filaments into a hermetically-sealed one-piece unit. When a filament burns out or the lens cracks, the entire unit is simply replaced.

Serpentine drivebelt A single, long, wide accessory drivebelt that's used on some newer vehicles to drive all the accessories, instead of a series of smaller, shorter belts. Serpentine drivebelts are usually tensioned by an automatic tensioner.

Serpentine drivebelt

Shim Thin spacer, commonly used to adjust the clearance or relative positions between two parts. For example, shims inserted into or under bucket tappets control valve clearances. Clearance is adjusted by changing the thickness of the shim.

Slide hammer A special puller that screws into or hooks onto a component such as a shaft or bearing; a heavy sliding handle on the shaft bottoms against the end of the shaft to knock the component free.

Sprocket A tooth or projection on the periphery of a wheel, shaped to engage with a chain or drivebelt. Commonly used to refer to the sprocket wheel itself.

Starter inhibitor switch On vehicles with an automatic transmission, a switch that prevents starting if the vehicle is not in Neutral or Park.

Strut See MacPherson strut.

T

Tappet A cylindrical component which transmits motion from the cam to the valve stem, either directly or via a pushrod and rocker arm. Also called a cam follower.

Thermostat A heat-controlled valve that regulates the flow of coolant between the cylinder block and the radiator, so maintaining optimum engine operating temperature. A thermostat is also used in some air cleaners in which the temperature is regulated.

Thrust bearing The bearing in the clutch assembly that is moved in to the release levers by clutch pedal action to disengage the clutch. Also referred to as a release bearing.

Timing belt A toothed belt which drives the camshaft. Serious engine damage may result if it breaks in service.

Timing chain A chain which drives the camshaft.

Toe-in The amount the front wheels are closer together at the front than at the rear. On rear wheel drive vehicles, a slight amount of toe-in is usually specified to keep the front wheels running parallel on the road by offsetting other forces that tend to spread the wheels apart.

Toe-out The amount the front wheels are closer together at the rear than at the front. On front wheel drive vehicles, a slight amount of toe-out is usually specified.

Tools For full information on choosing and using tools, refer to the *Haynes Automotive Tools Manual.*

Tracer A stripe of a second colour applied to a wire insulator to distinguish that wire from another one with the same colour insulator.

Tune-up A process of accurate and careful adjustments and parts replacement to obtain the best possible engine performance.

Turbocharger A centrifugal device, driven by exhaust gases, that pressurises the intake air. Normally used to increase the power output from a given engine displacement, but can also be used primarily to reduce exhaust emissions (as on VW's "Umwelt" Diesel engine).

U

Universal joint or U-joint A double-pivoted connection for transmitting power from a driving to a driven shaft through an angle. A U-joint consists of two Y-shaped yokes and a cross-shaped member called the spider.

V

Valve A device through which the flow of liquid, gas, vacuum, or loose material in bulk may be started, stopped, or regulated by a movable part that opens, shuts, or partially obstructs one or more ports or passageways. A valve is also the movable part of such a device.

Valve clearance The clearance between the valve tip (the end of the valve stem) and the rocker arm or tappet. The valve clearance is measured when the valve is closed.

Vernier caliper A precision measuring instrument that measures inside and outside dimensions. Not quite as accurate as a micrometer, but more convenient.

Viscosity The thickness of a liquid or its resistance to flow.

Volt A unit for expressing electrical "pressure" in a circuit. One volt that will produce a current of one ampere through a resistance of one ohm.

W

Welding Various processes used to join metal items by heating the areas to be joined to a molten state and fusing them together. For more information refer to the *Haynes Automotive Welding Manual.*

Wiring diagram A drawing portraying the components and wires in a vehicle's electrical system, using standardised symbols. For more information refer to the *Haynes Automotive Electrical and Electronic Systems Manual.*

Note: *References throughout this index are in the form - "Chapter number" • "page number"*

D

E

F

O

P

R

S

Haynes Manuals – The Complete **UK Car** List

Title	Book No.
ALFA ROMEO Alfasud/Sprint (74 - 88) up to F *	0292
Alfa Romeo Alfetta (73 – 87) up to E *	0531
AUDI 80, 90 & Coupe Petrol (79 – Nov 88) up to F	0605
Audi 80, 90 & Coupe Petrol (Oct 86 – 90) D to H	1491
Audi 100 & A6 Petrol & Diesel (May 91 – May 97) H to P	3504
Audi A3 Petrol & Diesel (96 – May 03) P to 03	4253
Audi A3 Petrol & Diesel (June 03 – Mar 08) 03 to 08	4884
Audi A4 Petrol & Diesel (95 – 00) M to X	3575
Audi A4 Petrol & Diesel (01 – 04) X to 54	4609
Audi A4 Petrol & Diesel (Jan 05 – Feb 08) 54 to 57	4885
AUSTIN A35 & A40 (56 – 67) up to F *	0118
Mini (59 – 69) up to H *	0527
Mini (69 – 01) up to X	0646
Austin Healey 100/6 & 3000 (56 – 68) up to G *	0049
BEDFORD/Vauxhall Rascal & Suzuki Supercarry (86 – Oct 94) C to M	3015
BMW 1-Series 4-cyl Petrol & Diesel (04 – Aug 11) 54 to 11	4918
BMW 316, 320 & 320i (4-cyl)(75 – Feb 83) up to Y *	0276
BMW 3- & 5- Series Petrol (81 – 91) up to J	1948
BMW 3-Series Petrol (Apr 91 – 99) H to V	3210
BMW 3-Series Petrol (Sept 98 – 06) S to 56	4067
BMW 3-Series Petrol & Diesel (05 – Sept 08) 54 to 58	4782
BMW 5-Series 6-cyl Petrol (April 96 – Aug 03) N to 03	4151
BMW 5-Series Diesel (Sept 03 – 10) 53 to 10	4901
BMW 1500, 1502, 1600, 1602, 2000 & 2002 (59 – 77) up to S *	0240
CHRYSLER PT Cruiser Petrol (00-09) W to 09	4058
CITROEN 2CV, Ami & Dyane (67 – 90) up to H	0196
Citroen AX Petrol & Diesel (87- 97) D to P	3014
Citroen Berlingo & Peugeot Partner Petrol & Diesel (96 – 10) P to 60	4281
Citroen C1 Petrol (05 – 11) 05 to 11	4922
Citroen C3 Petrol & Diesel (02 – 09) 51 to 59	4890
Citroen C4 Petrol & Diesel (04 – 10) 54 to 60	5576
Citroen C5 Petrol & Diesel (01 – 08) Y to 08	4745
Citroen C15 Van Petrol & Diesel (89 – Oct 98) F to S	3509
Citroen CX Petrol (75 – 88) up to F	0528
Citroen Saxo Petrol & Diesel (96 – 04) N to 54	3506
Citroen Visa Petrol (79 – 88) up to F	0620
Citroen Xantia Petrol & Diesel (93 – 01) K to Y	3082
Citroen XM Petrol & Diesel (89 – 00) G to X	3451
Citroen Xsara Petrol & Diesel (97 – Sept 00) R to W	3751
Citroen Xsara Picasso Petrol & Diesel (00 – 02) W to 52	3944
Citroen Xsara Picasso (Mar 04 – 08) 04 to 58	4784
Citroen ZX Diesel (91 – 98) J to S	1922
Citroen ZX Petrol (91 – 98) H to S	1881
FIAT 126 (73 – 87) up to E *	0305
Fiat 500 (57 – 73) up to M *	0090
Fiat 500 & Panda (04 – 12) 53 to 61	5558
Fiat Bravo & Brava Petrol (95 – 00) N to W	3572
Fiat Cinquecento (93 – 98) K to R	3501
Fiat Panda (81 – 95) up to M	0793
Fiat Punto Petrol & Diesel (94 – Oct 99) L to V	3251
Fiat Punto Petrol (Oct 99 – July 03) V to 03	4066
Fiat Punto Petrol (03 – 07) 03 to 07	4746

Title	Book No.
Fiat Punto Petrol (Oct 99 – 07) V to 07	5634
Fiat X1/9 (74 – 89) up to G *	0273
FORD Anglia (59 – 68) up to G *	0001
Ford Capri II (& III) 1.6 & 2.0 (74 – 87) up to E *	0283
Ford Capri II (& III) 2.8 & 3.0 V6 (74 – 87) up to E	1309
Ford C-Max Petrol & Diesel (03 – 10) 53 to 60	4900
Ford Escort Mk I 1100 & 1300 (68 – 74) up to N *	0171
Ford Escort Mk I Mexico, RS 1600 & RS 2000 (70 – 74) up to N *	0139
Ford Escort Mk II Mexico, RS 1800 & RS 2000 (75 – 80) up to W *	0735
Ford Escort (75 – Aug 80) up to V *	0280
Ford Escort Petrol (Sept 80 – Sept 90) up to H	0686
Ford Escort & Orion Petrol (Sept 90 – 00) H to X	1737
Ford Escort & Orion Diesel (Sept 90 – 00) H to X	4081
Ford Fiesta Petrol (Feb 89 – Oct 95) F to N	1595
Ford Fiesta Petrol & Diesel (Oct 95 – Mar 02) N to 02	3397
Ford Fiesta Petrol & Diesel (Apr 02 – 08) 02 to 58	4170
Ford Fiesta Petrol & Diesel (08 – 11) 58 to 11	4907
Ford Focus Petrol & Diesel (98 – 01) S to Y	3759
Ford Focus Petrol & Diesel (Oct 01 – 05) 51 to 05	4167
Ford Focus Petrol (05 – 09) 54 to 09	4785
Ford Focus Diesel (05 – 09) 54 to 09	4807
Ford Fusion Petrol & Diesel (02 – 11) 02 to 61	5566
Ford Galaxy Petrol & Diesel (95 – Aug 00) M to W	3984
Ford Galaxy Petrol & Diesel (00 – 06) X to 06	5556
Ford Granada Petrol (Sept 77 – Feb 85) up to B *	0481
Ford Ka (96 – 08) P to 58	5567
Ford Mondeo Petrol (93 – Sept 00) K to X	1923
Ford Mondeo Petrol & Diesel (Oct 00 – Jul 03) X to 03	3990
Ford Mondeo Petrol & Diesel (July 03 – 07) 03 to 56	4619
Ford Mondeo Petrol & Diesel (Apr 07 – 12) 07 to 61	5548
Ford Mondeo Diesel (93 – Sept 00) L to X	3465
Ford Sierra V6 Petrol (82 – 91) up to J	0904
Ford Transit Connect Diesel (02 – 11) 02 to 11	4903
Ford Transit Diesel (Feb 86 – 99) C to T	3019
Ford Transit Diesel (00 – Oct 06) X to 56	4775
Ford 1.6 & 1.8 litre Diesel Engine (84 – 96) A to N	1172
HILLMAN Imp (63 – 76) up to R *	0022
HONDA Civic (Feb 84 – Oct 87) A to E	1226
Honda Civic (Nov 91 – 96) J to N	3199
Honda Civic Petrol (Mar 95 – 00) M to X	4050
Honda Civic Petrol & Diesel (01 – 05) X to 55	4611
Honda CR-V Petrol & Diesel (02 – 06) 51 to 56	4747
Honda Jazz (02 to 08) 51 to 58	4735
JAGUAR E-Type (61 – 72) up to L *	0140
Jaguar Mk I & II, 240 & 340 (55 – 69) up to H *	0098
Jaguar XJ6, XJ & Sovereign, Daimler Sovereign (68 – Oct 86) up to D	0242
Jaguar XJ6 & Sovereign (Oct 86 – Sept 94) D to M	3261
Jaguar XJ12, XJS & Sovereign, Daimler Double Six (72 – 88) up to F	0478
JEEP Cherokee Petrol (93 – 96) K to N	1943
LAND ROVER 90, 110 & Defender Diesel (83 – 07) up to 56	3017
Land Rover Discovery Petrol & Diesel (89 – 98) G to S	3016

Title	Book No.
Land Rover Discovery Diesel (Nov 98 – Jul 04) S to 04	4606
Land Rover Discovery Diesel (Aug 04 – Apr 09) 04 to 09	5562
Land Rover Freelander Petrol & Diesel (97 – Sept 03) R to 53	3929
Land Rover Freelander (97 – Oct 06) R to 56	5571
Land Rover Series II, IIA & III 4-cyl Petrol (58 – 85) up to C	0314
Land Rover Series II, IIA & III Petrol & Diesel (58 – 85) up to C	5568
MAZDA 323 (Mar 81 – Oct 89) up to G	1608
Mazda 323 (Oct 89 – 98) G to R	3455
Mazda B1600, B1800 & B2000 Pick-up Petrol (72 – 88) up to F	0267
Mazda MX-5 (89 – 05) G to 05	5565
Mazda RX-7 (79 – 85) up to C *	0460
MERCEDES-BENZ 190, 190E & 190D Petrol & Diesel (83 – 93) A to L	3450
Mercedes-Benz 200D, 240D, 240TD, 300D & 300TD 123 Series Diesel (Oct 76 – 85) up to C	1114
Mercedes-Benz 250 & 280 (68 – 72) up to L *	0346
Mercedes-Benz 250 & 280 123 Series Petrol (Oct 76 – 84) up to B *	0677
Mercedes-Benz 124 Series Petrol & Diesel (85 – Aug 93) C to K	3253
Mercedes-Benz A-Class Petrol & Diesel (98 – 04) S to 54	4748
Mercedes-Benz C-Class Petrol & Diesel (93 – Aug 00) L to W	3511
Mercedes-Benz C-Class (00 – 07) X to 07	4780
Mercedes-Benz Sprinter Diesel (95 – Apr 06) M to 06	4902
MGA (55 – 62)	0475
MGB (62 – 80) up to W	0111
MGB 1962 to 1980 (special edition) *	4894
MG Midget & Austin-Healey Sprite (58 – 80) up to W *	0265
MINI Petrol (July 01 – 06) Y to 56	4273
MINI Petrol & Diesel (Nov 06 – 13) 56 to 13	4904
MITSUBISHI Shogun & L200 Pick-ups Petrol (83 – 94) up to M	1944
MORRIS Minor 1000 (56 – 71) up to K	0024
NISSAN Almera Petrol (95 – Feb 00) N to V	4053
Nissan Almera & Tino Petrol (Feb 00 – 07) V to 56	4612
Nissan Micra (83 – Jan 93) up to K	0931
Nissan Micra (93 – 02) K to 52	3254
Nissan Micra Petrol (03 – Oct 10) 52 to 60	4734
Nissan Primera Petrol (90 - Aug 99) H to T	1851
Nissan Qashqai Petrol & Diesel (07 – 12) 56 to 62	5610
OPEL Ascona & Manta (B-Series) (Sept 75 – 88) up to F *	0316
Opel Ascona Petrol (81 – 88)	3215
Opel Ascona Petrol (Oct 91 – Feb 98)	3156
Opel Corsa Petrol (83 – Mar 93)	3160
Opel Corsa Petrol (Mar 93 – 97)	3159
Opel Kadett Petrol (Oct 84 – Oct 91)	3196
Opel Omega & Senator Petrol (Nov 86 – 94)	3157
Opel Vectra Petrol (Oct 88 – Oct 95)	3158
PEUGEOT 106 Petrol & Diesel (91 – 04) J to 53)	1882
Peugeot 107 Petrol (05 – 11) 05 to 11)	4923
Peugeot 205 Petrol (83 – 97) A to P	0932
Peugeot 206 Petrol & Diesel (98 – 01) S to X	3757

* Classic reprint